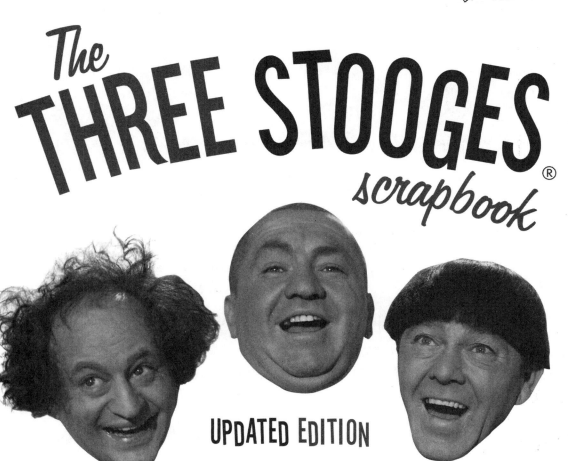

# The THREE STOOGES® scrapbook

## UPDATED EDITION

JEFF LENBURG * JOAN HOWARD MAURER * GREG LENBURG

CHICAGO
REVIEW
PRESS

An A Cappella Book

This updated edition is published by arrangement with the authors. First edition originally published by Citadel Press, a division of Lyle Stuart, Inc.

Published by Chicago Review Press, Incorporated
814 North Franklin Street
Chicago, Illinois 60610

ISBN 978-1-61374-074-3

*The Three Stooges*® *is a registered trademark of C3 Entertainment, Inc.*

**Library of Congress Cataloging-in-Publication Data**
Lenburg, Jeff.
    The Three Stooges scrapbook / Jeff Lenburg, Joan Howard Maurer, and Greg Lenburg.
— Updated ed.
        p. cm.
    Originally published: Secaucus, N.J. : Citadel Press, 1982.
    Includes filmography.
    ISBN 978-1-61374-074-3
    1. Three Stooges films—Miscellanea.  I. Maurer, Joan Howard.  II. Lenburg, Greg.
III. Title.

PN1995.9.T5L4 2012
791.4302'80922—dc23

2011046838

Cover design: Andrew Brozyna, AJB Design, Inc.
Cover photographs: (front center) © Columbia Pictures, courtesy of Jeff Lenburg
    Collection; (front bottom, left to right) © Columbia Pictures, courtesy of Moe
    Howard Collection; © Normandy Productions, courtesy of Moe Howard Collection;
    courtesy of WGN Television; photo by Norman Maurer, courtesy of Moe Howard
    Collection; (back, top to bottom) courtesy of Moe Howard Collection; courtesy of
    Norman Maurer Collection; courtesy of Moe Howard Collection
Interior design: Scott Rattray

Printed in the United States of America
5  4  3  2  1

To the Six Stooges:
*Moe Howard*
*Larry Fine*
*Jerome "Curly" Howard*
*Shemp Howard*
*Joe Besser*
*and Joe DeRita*

Three cheers to you *all* for providing us and the world with over 50 years of memorable antics

# Contents

# Foreword

The highest honor any comedian can be paid is either to win an Academy Award or to have a book written about him.

Well, I have neither won any awards nor had a book written about me. But I am happy to report that three nice people have not only taken the time to get my association with The Three Stooges straightened out but have documented all the wonderful aspects of their careers as well, putting it all down in this book.

I always get mail from fans asking when I first met the Stooges. Well, here is the answer. I recall my first encounter with the Stooges when I was playing in a Broadway show for J. J. Shubert called *The Passing Show of 1932*. Ted Healy's Stooges during this period were Moe, Larry, and Shemp, and I never dreamed, at the time of our meeting, that our paths would ever cross again.

When Healy got into an argument with Shubert and left, taking Moe and Larry with him, Shemp stayed on with the show. Needing a Stooge replacement, Moe sent for his kid brother Curly to take Shemp's place in the act. Although I never got to know him personally, I felt that Curly was the greatest comedian in show business and a truly wonderful man.

Later, when we were both working at Columbia, Shemp and I became good friends, and my wife Ernie and I would often visit him and his wife Gertrude. It was ironic that when Shemp died, in 1955, I would replace him.

I played my own character in the Stooges comedies and hope to this day that fans appreciated what I did. I always tried to do the best job possible. I never tried to imitate Curly, nor did Shemp. We knew that Curly was a comedian in his own right, and we thought we would carry out the third Stooge role the best way we knew how. My only regret is not having been with the Stooges longer, since it was a lot of fun. But fate stepped in when my wife Ernie became ill and Moe and Larry hired Joe DeRita to take my place.

To me, The Three Stooges are a team that deserves as much recognition as Abbott and Costello and Laurel and Hardy. I swell with pride every time I tell people that I was a member of the Stooges. And adults and children continue to recognize me to this day, in such places as supermarkets and restaurants, even though I am now just voicing Saturday-morning cartoons. I know that if it weren't for my brief association with The Three Stooges, maybe I would not be recognized today.

Therefore, I am grateful that three beautiful people—Jeff and Greg Lenburg and Joan Maurer—have written this book. It finally gives the Stooges the recognition they have long deserved. I also know that Jeff, Greg, and Joan made sure that every fan's request for information was heard by covering such interesting sections of the Stooges' careers as comic books, television, merchandise, and record albums. They even compiled a comically hilarious section on Three Stooges impersonators and sniffed out all the technical credits and summaries of every Three Stooges film and television appearance, and even solo film appearances by Ted Healy, Shemp Howard, Moe Howard, Curly Howard, Joe DeRita, and yours truly.

I know that Jeff and Greg have been collecting information about the Stooges for more than ten years out of the sixteen years I have known them. I consider them family and know that they have made a conscientious effort to give the fans everything they want.

Of course, Moe's daughter, Joan, has my blessings on anything she may want to do. I had great respect for her father, Moe, and know that she is as thoughtful and professional as he was.

So three cheers for those three musketeers of comedy—for without The Three Stooges, the word *slapstick* would be without a complete definition.

Joe Besser
1988

# Preface

The *Three Stooges Scrapbook* is the first official, authorized book on the history of The Three Stooges comedy team and on all aspects of their career. Meticulously researched and written, this updated edition has been thoroughly corrected and incorporates new information, along with more than four hundred illustrations, providing the most complete and accurate account ever published.

No amount of time has been spared to separate fact from fiction regarding the Stooges' history and to correct the many erroneous accounts that have appeared in other publications. Most of the data contained herein originally took over ten years to research and compile. Contracts, scripts, films, letters, scrapbooks, tape recordings, and other rare materials culled from personal family collections have been extensively reviewed to help paint an accurate picture of The Three Stooges' monumental career.

In addition, exclusive interviews were previously conducted over a period of years with Moe Howard, Larry Fine, Joe Besser, and Joe DeRita—and with such coworkers as Edward Bernds, Jules White, Elwood Ullman, Norman Maurer, Charles Lamont, Lou Breslow, Emil Sitka, and many others.

And, for the insatiable Stooges fan, *The Three Stooges Scrapbook* features the most comprehensive filmography ever compiled, which includes the Stooges' appearances as a team as well as its members' solo film appearances. Detailed summaries, production sidelights, and production footnotes highlight each Stooge film listed; technical credits and complete cast listings of supporting actors and the characters they played are also included.

*The Three Stooges Scrapbook* also provides the first and only history extensively documenting Stooges merchandise, Three Stooges comic books, the team's countless television appearances, and their record album career. And this book would not be complete without giving each of the Stooges his own intimate biographical sketch.

For fun and laughter, *The Three Stooges Scrapbook* also takes a close look at Three Stooges impersonators. Even the comical antics of Stooges fans are recounted in a chapter on the growing cult of Stooges enthusiasts and their attempts to glorify their comic heroes.

It's a review of Three Stooges trivia, history, illustrations, and comedy n'yuk-n'yuks at their best.

# Acknowledgments

The authors wish to acknowledge the following people who offered us their invaluable assistance in order to make this book an accurate history.

First, we recognize the Stooges themselves, their families, and their many friends: Moe and Helen Howard, Larry Fine, Joe and Ernie Besser, Joe and Jean DeRita, Joe Baker, Charles and Julie Barton, Harold Bell, Edward Bernds, Joey Bishop, Lou Breslow, Dick Brown, Elaine Diamond, Mike Douglas, Morris Feinberg, Jim Hawthorne, Marie Howard, Paul Howard, Joe Kubert, Charles Lamont, Irma Leveton, Michael Maurer, Norman Maurer, Ken Murray, Leon Robb, MD, Dolly Sallin, Jeffrey Scott, Clarice and Harry Seiden, Emil and Edith Sitka, Elwood Ullman, and Jules White.

Likewise, the authors extend a special tip of the hat to the many dedicated individuals, corporations, and facilities that gave us their unselfish cooperation and support: Dorothy Allard, Shirley Fain, Roger Mayer, and Herbert S. Nusbaum of Metro-Goldwyn-Mayer; Sal Amico, Martin E. Appel, and Ed Foote of WPIX-TV in New York; Dennis Aubrey of Meadowlane Productions; Sarah Baisley, William Hanna, and John Michaeli of Hanna-Barbera Productions; Theodore J. Bass of the Department of the Treasury (US Savings Bond Division); Ira Steven Behr; Tom Bertino; Ann Best of Don Fedderson Productions; Eddie Brandt and Mike Hawks of Eddie Brandt's Saturday Matinee; Larry D. Bullion of The Three Stooges Deli; Ken Carberry and Patricia Gray of KPWR-TV in Bakersfield; John Cawley Jr.; Charles Christ; Sal Cincotta; David Collins; Jill Coplan of National Telefilm Associates; Gordon Cordoza; Mary Corliss of the Museum of Modern Art Film/Still Archives; Chris Costello; Cottage Hospital and its staff; Steve Cox; Charles M. Crane of Williamson-Dickie Mfg. Co.; Carol Cullen and Sam Gill of the Academy of Motion Picture Arts and Sciences and Margaret Herrick Library; Gary Deeb; Linda S. Downey of *The World of Yesterday*; Glenn Dyckoff of Columbia Pictures' merchandising division; Ruth Engelhardt and Susan Shay of the William Morris Agency; Nisan Eventoff and Milt Larsen of the Variety Arts Center; John Ewaniuk; Maxine Fleckner of the Wisconsin Center for Film and Theater Research; Ira Friedman of The Official Three Stooges Fan Club; and Ralph Schiller, Gary Lassin, Bill Cappello, Richard Finegan, Frank Reighter, Brent Seguine, and Ed Shifres of The Three Stooges Fan Club Inc. and publishers of *The Three Stooges Journal*.

Our heartfelt gratitude as well to: Bob Frischman; Tom Hatten; David Hayes; Link Hullar; Rick Ingersol of ICPR; Larry Jensen; George Karamidas of ABC-TV; Bernard Klotz of Carry-Case Manufacturing Co.; Barry Kluger; Kenneth A. Knox; Dave and Joe Koenig; Cleve Landesberg of 20th Century Fox Television; Mike, Nanci, and Bobby Lefebvre; Catherine and John L. Lenburg; Debby Lenburg, Edna Lenburg, Jake Lenburg, and John Lenburg; Mark Lipschutz; Los Angeles Hall of Records and its staff; Teresa Yoder, Special Collections, the Chicago Public Library; Scott M. Forsythe, The National Archives at Chicago; Sylvia Wang, The Shubert Archive; Mark Lyons; Ron Maloney; Leonard Maltin (*The Great Movie Shorts*); Marilyn Miller; Helen Molletta, Motion Picture and Television Hospital, Country Home and Lodge; New York Hall of Records and its staff; Maria Peters of United Artists; Robert Precht; Ron Holder and Marty Silverstein of Sullivan Productions; Lee Prusinski; Julie Radin of NBC-TV Program Research; Zvi Shoubin of WPHL-TV in Philadelphia; Charlotte Shurman; Randy Skretvedt; Spencer and Zelda Skretvedt; Glenn Sonnenberg; Ray Strait; Frank Thompson; Omer Tomlinson; Brian Tracy; Brent Walker; Joe Wallison; Thomas J. Watson of CBS-TV; Jerry Weisfeldt of TV Cinema Sales Corp.; Greg Wilkin; and Jordan Young for excerpts from his Paul "Mousie" Garner interview.

And, saving the best for last, a very special thank you to our editor Yuval Taylor and our publisher, Chicago Review Press, for making this new edition a reality.

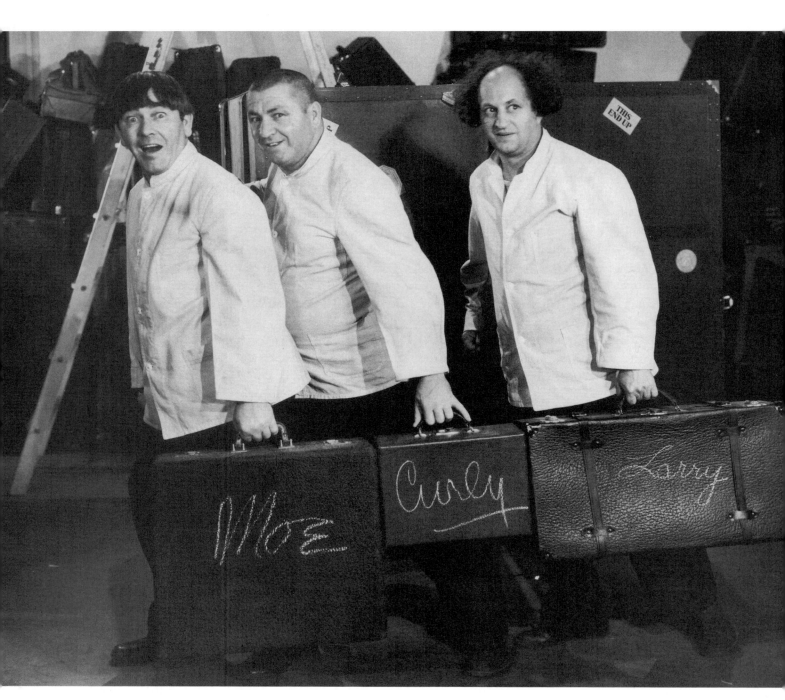

Moe, Curly, and Larry shuffle off with suitcases bearing their signatures in a publicity photo for the Stooges comedy *Idle Roomers* (1944).

*© Columbia Pictures, courtesy of Moe Howard Collection*

# The THREE STOOGES scrapbook

# TED HEALY

*Courtesy of Jeff Lenburg Collection*

2

*T*ed Healy, the Stooges' original straight man, was born Charles Earnest Lee Nash on October 1, 1896, in Kaufman, Texas, to Charles McKinney Nash, an outlaw also known as "Black Charlie" Nash, and the former Mary Eugenia McGinty. Of Scotch Irish descent, he was educated at Holy Innocents School in nearby Houston and completed his high school education at De LaSalle Institute in New York, where his family had moved in 1908.

Healy's childhood friend growing up was Moe Howard. They saw each other every summer vacation from 1909 until 1914, when Moe joined a showboat performing troupe. Of Healy's career aspirations, Howard said, "He never intended to be in show business. He was going to be a businessman in Texas." It took Ted over ten years to realize that he wasn't cut out for business life, and he finally tried the theater.

The brown-haired, brown-eyed Healy worked hard at polishing his skills as a comedian, coming up with an act, as a single in blackface, that was comprised of imitations and burlesque jokes. The act was entirely impromptu, because Ted was unable to memorize his lines. His graphic impersonations of such film luminaries as Ed Wynn, Eddie Cantor, and Al Jolson, which he performed at local amateur shows, sparked considerable audience interest, but though the audiences appreciated his talent, he made little headway toward a stable career. He finally abandoned his amateur act and decided to become a full-fledged professional performer. It was then that he changed his name to Ted Healy. His first work behind the footlights as a professional comedian came in 1917, in the burlesque show *Cuddle Up*. Thereafter, he became a familiar figure in American vaudeville houses.

Healy's comically crushed hat, an integral part of his wardrobe, received as many good reviews, as his act. A critic for a Baltimore newspaper wrote, "Healy is remembered for the dilapidated hat he always wears, and about which there is much speculation as to whether it is always the same one. Many, as a matter of fact, hang on the wall of his dressing room. Healy's one of the most informal of comedians. His naturalness makes for his success."

Healy became a Broadway star and continued with his solo act on the vaudeville circuit through the pre–World War I years and beyond. In 1920, billing himself as "the one-man jazz," he received high praise for his Thanksgiving week performance in the musical comedy vaudeville revue *Girls Will Be Girls*, at the Fays Theatre in Providence, Rhode Island. A local critic called him "an amusing monologist."

Then, in 1922, he teamed up with the vaudeville dancer-singer who would sometimes be known as his "girl stooge": Elizabeth "Betty" Braun (a.k.a. Brown). Betty lived in Queens, New York, and had been one-half of the dancing act The Braun Sisters. Ted met her backstage in Indianapolis, Indiana, and they were married in Indianapolis on June 5, 1922. Onstage, the couple billed themselves as "Ted and Betty Healy: The Flapper and the Philosopher." Ted wrote all the comedy sketches for the act, which also featured a performing German shepherd named Pete. Their first performance at a Keith Theatre in Jersey City was a smash success, and they were signed to a forty-six-week contract by the Keith Circuit. During a subsequent engagement at the Temple Theatre in Rochester, New York, a critic noted that "the best of the three [acts] are that of Ted and Betty Healy."

Ted with his first wife, the former Betty Braun.
*Courtesy of Moe Howard Collection*

Healy's slick talk and quick wit made him the highest-paid vaudevillian of his day; he earned as much as $8,500 a week. But he found that it took a particular brand of slapstick physical comedy for him to induce audience laughter, and he realized he would need true stooges to take the brunt of his comedy shtick.

In late winter 1922, when Moe Howard paid him a visit one afternoon at Brooklyn's Prospect Theatre, Healy brought his boyhood pal into his act. As the two performed, Moe heard his brother Shemp laughing in the audience. He had Healy call him up onstage, and what resulted was a completely ad-libbed, wild slapstick performance that had the theater vibrating with laughter.

Moe and Shemp remained in the act from that day forward. Healy recruited a third Stooge, Kenneth Lackey, in 1923.

Theater ads dubbed Healy "The King of Stooges," and once, in a newspaper interview, he explained the purpose in having stooges: "They're handy guys to have around. If a star's too busy to give an interview, he can send his stooge. And a stooge is a swell alibi. If a star's wife or girl friend says she saw him in Sardi's [a swank Hollywood restaurant] with another doll, he can always say, 'It must've been my stooge.'

Happy Ted Healy in a scene from a Stooges home movie.
*Courtesy of Moe Howard Collection*

"And then a stooge always comes in handy when you feel like throwing something at somebody. Whenever I'm in doubt or feel mixed up, I always hit the nearest stooge. Makes me feel better. Nothing like it. Hollywood's tired of 'yes-men.' That's why the stooge is coming into his own. A stooge is a 'guess-man.' You can never guess what he's going to do next."

On occasion, Healy and his wife, Betty, still performed without Moe and Shemp in the act. In September 1924, they took the stage in a vaudeville revue at the Princess Theatre in Montreal, Canada, that once again won over critics, with one stating, "Ted and Betty Healy won the audience in an act which is just one laugh after another. Ted Healy is a born comedian, and everything he does or says produces its quota of merriment." In July 1925, both were featured in Broadway's *Earl Carroll's Vanities* at New York's Earl Carroll Theatre. In 1926, Ted was signed by the Shubert brothers for one year to headline *The Passing Show of 1926*. His success in that show caused them to sign him for two more years. Also in 1926, Hal Roach signed the Healys to star in a series of silent comedy short subjects. However, only one was made, without Betty: *Wise Guys Prefer Brunettes*, directed by Stan Laurel, one-half of the comedy team Laurel and Hardy.

Otherwise, Healy and his Stooges, Moe and Shemp (Lackey had left the act in the summer of 1925), continued to fracture audiences on the vaudeville circuit. In late 1926, Moe left the act to pursue a career in real estate. The following year, Healy and Shemp appeared in the Shuberts' Broadway show *A Night in Spain*. When Shemp decided he wanted to leave Healy's act as well in April 1928, Healy added a replacement: a young violinist named Larry Fine, who thus started on his own long and successful career as a Stooge.

In 1929, with Moe and Shemp back in the fold along with Larry, Healy starred with them in a new Shubert Broadway musical revue, *A Night in Venice*. Afterward, "Ted Healy and His Racketeers" (Moe, Larry, Shemp, and newcomer Fred Sanborn), as they were billed, made their first screen appearance in the classic 1930s comedy feature *Soup to Nuts* for Fox Studios. This film was followed by a series of five headlining short-subject comedies and several feature films as Ted Healy and His Stooges for Metro-Goldwyn-Mayer (MGM).

(1934), *The Band Plays On* (1934), *The Casino Murder Case* (1935), *Speed* (1936), *San Francisco* (1936) opposite Clark Gable, and *The Longest Night* (1936), and light comedies, musicals, and comedy dramas, such as *The Winning Ticket* (1935), *Reckless* (1935), *Murder in the Fleet* (1935), *Here Comes the Band* (1935), *Mad Holiday* (1936), and others. Likewise, MGM featured him as an American newspaper photographer in the cult horror film *Mad Love* (1935), starring Peter Lorre, and as Jack Benny's sidekick "Clip" McGurk in the comedy short *It's in the Air* (1935). He also teamed with actor Nat Pendleton, later a supporting player in Abbott and Costello features. In 1936, he appeared in his first feature for Fox since *Soup to Nuts*, the musical *Sing Baby Sing*. After signing a lucrative contract with

Ted with his childhood pal Moe Howard, enjoying happier moments during a Wisconsin hunting trip in 1929. *Courtesy of Moe Howard Collection*

By the early 1930s, Healy remained the highest-paid comic in the country, making an eye-popping $30,000 a week. In 1932, with their ten-year marriage having produced no children, Ted and Betty were divorced. Later, she would come out of retirement to play Stan Laurel's wife, Bubbles, in the 1936 Laurel and Hardy feature *Our Relations*.

After Larry, Moe, and Curly (who had replaced his brother Shemp in the act in 1932) left Healy's act in 1934, Healy appeared in a succession of films for Fox, Warner Bros., and MGM. At MGM, he continued to receive good roles and was featured prominently in both dramas, including *Death on the Diamond*

Theater handbill featuring a top-billed Ted Healy as "The King of Stooges."
*Courtesy of Moe Howard Collection*

Warner Bros. in 1936, he received costarring roles in two major Busby Berkeley musicals: *Varsity Show* (1937) and *Hollywood Hotel* (1938). He did three more films for MGM, *Man of the People* (1937), *Good Old Souk* (1937), and the comedy romance *Love Is a Headache*, released after his death in 1938.

On May 15, 1936, Healy eloped to marry his second wife, twenty-one-year-old blonde UCLA coed Alma Elizabeth "Betty" Hickman, the daughter of a socially prominent family from Pasadena, California. Healy and his bride-to-be took a chartered plane at midnight from Union Air Terminal in Los Angeles to Yuma, Arizona, where they were wedded by Superior Judge Kelly. Healy's manager Jack Marcus was on hand for the ceremony. The couple lived

Ted Healy with real-life and MGM-film girlfriend Bonnie Bonnell.
*Courtesy of Moe Howard Collection*

Newlyweds Ted Healy and his second wife, Betty Hickman, a UCLA alumna, in a May 16, 1936, photo.
*Courtesy of Jeff Lenburg Collection*

in Beverly Hills thereafter. They separated on August 28, 1936, after only a few months of marriage, and on September 22, Betty filed for divorce, charging him with using objectionable language in her presence and being rude to her releatives and friends. On October 8, Los Angeles Superior Judge Charles Bogue granted her a decree of divorce, with Betty signing a property settlement and waiving alimony, attorney's fees, and court costs.

Ted relaxes on the set at MGM. *Courtesy of Jeff Lenburg Collection*

Curly, Larry, and Moe welcome Ted's sister, Marcia Healy, to the set of *The Sitter Downers* (1937).
© *Columbia Pictures, courtesy of Moe Howard Collection*

Ted's only sibling, his sister Marcia, worked briefly as an actress. Her only credit was an appearance in the Three Stooges Columbia short with Moe, Larry, and Curly, *The Sitter Downers* (1937).

Healy was forty-one and under contract to MGM at the time of his death on December 21, 1937. His untimely passing occurred the day after preview audiences acclaimed his work in *Hollywood Hotel*. (He was reportedly scheduled to costar in another MGM feature, *Of Human Hearts*, but the film was completed without him.)

A cloud of mystery still hangs over the cause of Healy's demise. Conflicting newspaper accounts stated that he sustained serious head injuries in a nightclub brawl while celebrating the birth of his first child, a son, or that he died of a heart attack at his Los Angeles home. Apparently his family physician, Dr. Wyant La Mont, refused to confirm a heart seizure as the cause and would not sign the death certificate.

Days before his death, Healy had visited Moe's wife, Helen, at their Hollywood apartment with the news that his wife Betty, with whom he had reconciled before their divorce became final, was expecting. Excited at the prospect of his first child, Healy told Moe's wife, "I'll make him the richest kid in the world." Moe later related in an interview that Ted had always wanted children. "He was nuts about kids. He used to visit our homes and envied the fact we were all married and had children. Healy always loved kids and often gave Christmas parties for underprivileged youngsters and spent hundreds of dollars on toys."

At the time of Ted's death, the Stooges—Moe, Larry, and Curly—were at Grand Central Station in New York preparing to leave for a personal appearance in Boston. Before their departure, Moe called Rube Jackter, head of Columbia Pictures' sales department, to confirm their benefit performance at Boston's Children's Hospital. During the conversation, Jackter told Howard that the night editor of *The New York Times* wanted to talk to him.

Moe phoned the *Times*. The editor, without even a greeting, queried curtly, "Is this Moe?" Howard replied, "Yes." Then the editor asked, "Would you like to make a statement on the death of Ted Healy?" Moe was stunned. He dropped the phone. Then, folding his arms over his head, he started to sob. Curly and Larry rushed into the phone booth to warn Moe that their train was about to leave and saw him crumpled over, crying. Since Moe never showed his emotions, Larry cracked to Curly, "Your brother's

Ted Healy with Mabel Todd in his next-to-last film appearance, *Hollywood Hotel* (1938).
© *Warner Bros., courtesy of Jeff Lenburg Collection*

alone. His stops included the Seven Seas, the Trocadero on the Sunset Strip, Clara Bow's "It" Cafe, where he borrowed fifty dollars to continue his late-night celebration, and finally the Hollywood Brown Derby. At the Trocadero, Healy became so intoxicated that H. W. Hoffman, the club manager, issued orders not to sell him any more whiskey. In the early-morning hours on Monday, an argument broke out between Ted and three other Trocadero patrons whom preliminary reports would call "college fellows." Actually, Healy got into a heated confrontation with famed gangster Pat DiCicco and fellow MGM actor Wallace Beery. Also present was DiCicco's cousin, a Long Island–born twentysomething named Albert Broccoli, who would go on to fame as the film producer behind the legendary James Bond series.

A police investigation afterward reported that fisticuffs broke out between Healy and Broccoli during the height of Healy's wild celebration; Broccoli claimed that Healy staggered toward him, struck him in the nose and the chin, and "almost floored me." He said that he pushed Healy but denied hitting him. Many years later, however, the aging filmmaker admitted greater involvement in an altercation outside the Trocadero: Under the influence, Ted picked a fight, asking the three men to step out into the club's parking lot. There, according to Broccoli, they savagely beat Healy. The police report never named DiCicco and Beery; reportedly, Louis B. Mayer, MGM's powerful studio chieftain with his own mob ties, covered up the incident.

Furthermore, Healy was involved in another brawl that night at the Trocadero, with two unidentified men and their dates whom attendants led out of the club. Once outside, the men engaged in fisticuffs with Healy, punching him in the head and stomach. Someone called Healy a cab and he left the scene dazed and bleeding.

Later in front of the Brown Derby, three of Healy's friends, comedian Joe Frisco and actors Joseph E. "Doc" Stone and Jack Antler, found Healy delirious and bleeding on the sidewalk. They took him by cab

nuts. He is actually crying." Moe didn't explain the reason for his sudden emotional breakdown until he got aboard the train.

It was when Howard arrived back in Hollywood that he learned the details leading up to Healy's death from a writer friend, Henry Taylor. On Friday, December 17, 1937, Betty had given birth to an eleven-pound son, John Jacob, at University Hospital in Culver City, California, delivered by Dr. La Mont. The following Sunday, Ted went to the hospital to see Betty and his newborn son for what turned out to be the last time. He was ecstatic over the glowing reviews he had received for his performance in *Hollywood Hotel* and shared the news with her. As he departed, he complained to hospital attendants that he was having pain around his heart but left the hospital untreated.

That night, Ted went nightclubbing to celebrate. He was usually accompanied by his bodyguard, Hymie Marx, but on this occasion Healy went out to the Hollywood Plaza Hotel, where famed behemoth wrestler Man Mountain Dean was curbside as Healy staggered out of the cab bleeding from a cut over one eye. At 2:15 that morning, Frisco called Healy's sister, Marcia, who persuaded her incoherent brother to summon Dr. Sydney L. Weinberg of Hollywood to treat his injuries, including the deep gash over his left eye. Man Mountain Dean accompanied Healy to Weinberg's office for treatment. Healy then proceeded to a Beverly Hills hotel, and from there Frisco took him to his home at 10749 Weyburn Avenue in West Los Angeles. This sequence of events was later corroborated by police detectives who investigated the incident.

Healy spent that Monday in bed, where he was frequently stricken by seizures while moaning deliriously about the fight from the night before. Reportedly, he was stricken with a heart attack at three o'clock Tuesday morning and went into a coma at dawn. Dr. La Mont was called to the scene when Healy's condition became grave. La Mont had oxygen and glucose administered to Healy and brought in a heart specialist, Dr. John Ruddock, for consultation. But by then it was too late.

At 11:30 AM, Healy was pronounced dead. His sister was among those present when he passed away. Six days after his death, although a coroner's examination revealed external injuries, including a red streak across his left temple and deep red bruises above the left eyelid, the county autopsy surgeon ruled that Healy's death was due to acute toxic nephritis, the result of acute chronic alcoholism—not the blows he'd incurred in the nightclub brawl.

Despite his sizeable salary, Healy died penniless. In fact, MGM staff members got together a fund to pay for his burial. Moe later mentioned that comedian Brian Foy of the Eddie Foy family footed a great part of the bill for Healy's funeral. On December 24, 1937, a funeral Mass was held at St. Augustine's Church, across from the MGM studios in Culver City. Healy's body was laid to rest beside his mother at Calvary Cemetery in East Los Angeles. (A week later, his son, John Jacob, was baptized at St. Augustine's. As an adult, he legally changed his name to Theodore John Healy to honor his late father. Healy Jr. died in July 2011.)

According to Moe, even in the heyday of his stage career Ted had refused to put any money away; he spent every dime of his salary as fast as he received it. He enjoyed hunting and fishing and loved the horses; his favorite reading material was racetrack charts.

Ted was also a heavy drinker. Liquor had killed his father and uncle and ruined the life of his sister, Marcia, so Ted had made a pledge when he was very young never to touch liquor. But the strain of show business life got him started and he was never able to stop. Although Ted was the essence of refinement when sober, Moe often said that his drinking led to outbreaks of violence, such as the incident that led to his tragic, untimely death.

As a salute to Healy and his many contributions to the world of show business as a comedian, Helen Howard, Moe's wife, wrote the following poem to Healy on one of his birthdays:

The poet, the scholar, the painter
Each in their own art reign
But we don't chant much of the actor
Who has slowly risen to fame.
Of the man who uses his talent
To make us laugh as he'll joke
While deep in his heart there's an aching
And 'round his neck is a yoke.
We lounge in our chair at the theatre
And laugh at his merriment
Then when it is o'er we go to our homes
Feeling light-hearted and content.
But when the curtain drops
And we leave the man who clowns
The greasepaint of smiles is rubbed away
And naught is left but the frowns.
So let's drink a toast to a "comedian"
Who has reached the heights to which not
   many soar
Health, happiness and long life, Ted Healy—
Could we wish you anything more?

The legendary success of Ted Healy can best be explained in a remark the comedian made to actor Jimmy Stewart. "Never treat an audience as customers—always treat them as partners."

# MOE HOWARD

*M*oe Howard, the irascible one with the world-famous bangs, was born on June 19, 1897, in Bensonhurst, New York, a small Jewish community on the outskirts of Brooklyn. His real name was Moses Horwitz (only later did he adopt the name Harry), and he was the son of real estate entrepreneur Jennie Horwitz and clothing cutter Solomon Horwitz. Moe was the second youngest of the five Howard brothers; all but two, Jack and Irving, entered show business.

Throughout Moe's career, columnists the world over tried to find words to describe his unusual haircut; Buster Brown, spittoon, Sugar Bowl, Rose Bowl, and Beatle were but a few. The five-feet-four-inches-tall Stooge boss's hair color changed with the years from black in his youth to reddish-brown (when he dyed it), to silver-white (its final natural color) during the 1970s. He had a marvelous mop of hair until the day he died, but during grammar school days it was the bane of his existence. He was constantly taunted by his classmates over his head of shoulder-length curls—which his mother adored, having always wanted a girl. One day, tired of fighting with his school chums, Moe grabbed a pair of shears and hacked off the curls that encircled his freckled face; the resulting hairstyle was a raggedy version of the one that became his trademark.

Moe was an extremely bright child and at a very young age displayed an ability to quickly memorize anything. This ability would carry over into later life, making him a quick study during his acting career. Brother Jack reminisced about his love for books in his youth: "I had many Horatio Alger books, and it was Moe's greatest pleasure to read them. They started his imaginative mind working and gave him ideas by the dozen. I think they were instrumental in putting thoughts into his head—to become a person of good character and to become successful."

Moe carried his penchant for learning and a love of the theater right with him to school, where he acted in a play he also dramatized and directed, *The Story of Nathan Hale*. He was fascinated with acting and played hooky to catch the shows at the melodrama theaters during the week. Years later, recalling his lost school days, Moe said, "I used to stand outside the theater knowing the truant officer was looking for me. I would stand there 'til someone came along and then ask them to buy my ticket. It was necessary for an adult to accompany a juvenile into the theater.

When I succeeded I'd give him my ten cents—that's all it cost—and I'd go up to the top of the balcony where I'd put my chin on the rail and watch, spellbound, from the first act to the last. I would usually select the actor I liked the most and follow his performance throughout the play."

As his interest in the theater grew, Moe's excellent marks in school began to suffer. In spite of his truancy, he graduated from P.S. 163 in Brooklyn, but he attended Erasmus High School for only two months, never completing his high school education. This greatly disturbed his parents, who were not in favor of his show business aspirations and urged him to go into a profession or some kind of trade. Moe tried to please them and did take a class in electric shop at the Baron DeHirsch Trade School in New York. His interest was short lived, however, and within a few months he gave up all thought of school to pursue the career that was closest to his heart: show business.

In 1909, Moe embarked on a film career at the Vitagraph Studios in Brooklyn, where he earned his entrée into filmmaking by running errands, "for no tips," for performers such as Maurice Costello. As a result of his persistence, Moe soon appeared as a child actor in films with such silent stars as John Bunny, Flora Finch, Earle William, Herbert Rawlinson, and Walter Johnson, including two known short subjects, *We Must Do Our Best* (1909) and *Fish Hookey* (1910), making between fifty cents and one dollar a day.

That same year, Moe met Ted Healy for the first time. They became close friends, and in the summer of 1912 the two joined Annette Kellerman's aquatic act as diving "girls." This job lasted through the summer.

Then in 1913, Moe and his brother Shemp tried their hand at singing, using the family room at Sullivan's Saloon to gain their much-needed experience in front of an audience. The Howards sang along in a quartet with the talented bass singer of that time, Babe Tuttle, and an Irish tenor, Willie O'Connor. Moe sang baritone, while Shemp sang lead. Together, the foursome harmonized such popular old songs as "Dear Old Girl," "Oh, You Beautiful Doll," "By the Light of the Silvery Moon," "Heart of My Heart," and "I've Been Through the Mill, Bill." Moe and Shemp continued to sing every night until nine or ten o'clock, until their father found out what they were doing and soon put a stop to it.

The following year, as he turned seventeen, Moe felt a bit of Huck Finn in his blood, so he wangled himself a job with a performing troupe on Captain Billy Bryant's showboat *Sunflower*. For two summers he acted with the company in the same melodramas he had seen as a kid, performing his favorite roles in *St. Elmo*, *Ten Nights in a Barroom*, and *Bertha, the Sewing Machine Girl*. Starting in 1917, Moe worked a successful blackface act with Shemp in vaudeville; he toured the country for the next five years, including performing together with the Marguerite Bryant Players, a stock company, beginning in 1919. Besides stage work, Moe also appeared in twelve two-reel shorts with baseball great Hans Wagner. The first was shot in 1919 in an open field in Bakerstown, Pennsylvania, while Moe was working in the same stock company in Oakford Park.

Late in 1922, Moe renewed his acquaintance with Ted Healy after seeing him at the Prospect Theatre in Brooklyn. Together with Shemp, he answered Healy's call to become a Stooge. They formed a partnership that, except for a few short breaks, would last for almost ten years.

In 1922 and 1923, Moe also worked in amateur theater, directing three plays—*Too Many Husbands, Brewster's Millions,* and *Potash & Perlmutter* (the last opening on May 27, 1923)—for the Dramatic Society of the Young Folks League of the Congregation Sons of Israel in Bensonhurst. In addition, he codirected (with Seymour Solomon) his first serious production, a one-act play about the French Revolution, for the national "Little Theatre Contest" at the Belasco Theatre, a legitimate Broadway theater in New York City.

In the summer of 1922, Moe had met his future bride, the delightful, intelligent, and darling Helen Schonberger, a cousin of the late Harry Houdini. On June 7, 1925, they were married. In 1926, Helen urged Moe to leave the stage and Ted Healy in order to spend more

Moe in his twenties—a real Dapper Dan—on tour with Healy in Alabama in 1923. *Courtesy of Moe Howard Collection*

Moe lifeguarding in the early twenties, flanked by Helen and her sister Clarice.
*Courtesy of Moe Howard Collection*

Moe and six-month-old daughter Joan in 1927.
*Courtesy of Moe Howard Collection*

time with her, as she was expecting a child. Daughter Joan, born in 1927, would be the first of their two children. A son, Paul, would be born eight years later.

Getting his real estate license in October 1926, Moe left show business to work in real estate with his mother. In 1927, he made $40,000 buying and selling land; a year later, he lost it all building homes. When that didn't work out, in late 1928, he opened a small retail store and attempted to sell distressed merchandise; this turned into a hysterical fiasco. During 1927, Moe also worked intermittently at the Jewish Community House in Bensonhurst, producing and directing musical-comedy stage productions. In March of that year, one of his early efforts, which he cowrote with Dr. Sam Cohen, *Stepping Along*, was reviewed by a critic at *The New York Times*, who wrote, "A Musical Dream in Three Episodes was probably as good a description as anything else and it was a dream from which none wanted to awaken." That June, he directed his second production, *Still Stepping*.

Larry Fine's impression of Moe in a pencil sketch.
*Courtesy of Moe Howard Collection*

Sorely missing the old gang and unable to make a living in the workaday world, Moe rejoined Healy in 1929 to appear with Larry and Shemp in the Shubert brothers' original two-act musical extravaganza that opened on Broadway that May, *A Night in Venice*. Afterward they headlined additional vaudeville engagements. They also starred in movies—features and short-subject comedies—for Fox and MGM between 1930 and 1934. When Healy decided to star in features at MGM and the Stooges left to star in their two-reel comedies at Columbia, Moe became the permanent leader of the group—a leadership that would last through the Stooges' twenty-four years with Columbia, the longest single contract ever held by a comedy team.

Moe was the businessman of the team; he ran the group and made most of its decisions. Curly and Larry were carefree individuals who never prided themselves on punctuality and had absolutely no regard for money. Moe did the worrying for all of them. Director Edward Bernds, who knew him for forty years, felt the businesslike side of Moe certainly helped on the set. "Moe was all business, but he was interested in making the film as good as he could. He

Moe reminds daughter Joan it's never safe to steal the silverware.
*Courtesy of Moe Howard Collection*

didn't take anything away from the director, but he did see to it that the boys shaped up. He liked making suggestions and was very creative."

In many ways, Moe's offscreen persona was far removed from the character he played on-screen. In the theater or before the cameras, Moe would open up and let his nervous energies flow, but at home he was a very different man. While Larry was gregarious, Moe was introverted, very serious, and very nervous, a man who found it very hard to relax. He also had difficulty expressing his true feelings and emotions. Moe felt his inability to demonstrate his emotions stemmed from his family upbringing. As he once wrote, "I recall that my father rarely kissed my mother and that I rarely kissed them. Expressing our love for one another was difficult."

As a means of expressing his love, Moe often bought gifts for family and friends. Although he was cautious about saving money in certain respects, he would go crazy in other directions. His son-in-law, writer-producer-director Norman Maurer, nicknamed him "Wholesale Charlie," since his fondest pleasure was buying clothes for all the members of his family. He'd buy everything by the dozen (it seemed that all his boyhood friends had wound up in the wholesale garment business). Norman felt that he wasted

Moe, Curly, and an innocent spectator get all wrapped up while hooking a rug. *Courtesy of Moe Howard Collection*

a good deal of money on these spending sprees, but Moe got untold enjoyment out of them. Despite his inability to relax and enjoy life to its fullest like Curly and Larry, Moe's goal in life was to give his family their every wish, and this he did. He and his wife Helen traveled to just about every city in the world, where they were treated like royalty by their fans.

Norman Maurer explains it this way: "If he liked you, he would do anything for you." Like his mother, he worked for charity organizations and loved to watch people's faces when they opened their gifts. On one occasion during the Hanukkah/Christmas season, Moe went grocery shopping for Emil Sitka and his family of seven and delivered the groceries himself. Howard made the gesture without being asked. Sitka, a character actor who had played in many of the Stooges' comedies, was surprised to come home and find the cupboards and refrigerator packed with

Moe and Curly prepare to use Joan to fuel their fire engine on the set of their 1936 comedy *False Alarms.*

*Courtesy of Moe Howard Collection*

Moe mugging with son Paul. *Courtesy of Moe Howard Collection*

Despite his tough demeanor on-screen, at home Moe was quite softhearted. His wife Helen remembered with nostalgia the different ways Moe liked to mark their wedding anniversary each year. As she recalled, "He was a very sentimental man and wrote me hundreds of love poems when we were first married. On our tenth anniversary, the phone rang and a strange voice on the other end asked me if I would take Moe Horwitz for my lawful wedded husband. The voice then proceeded to perform the entire wedding ceremony with me on one end and Moe, the mystery voice, on the other. He was also a singer at the end of the ceremony; in a beautiful baritone voice, he sang 'Oh Promise Me,' the song sung at our wedding."

Helen eyeing Moe in drag on the set of *Self Made Maids* (1950). *Courtesy of Moe Howard Collection*

groceries. Emil expressed his gratitude to the comedian in a letter he wrote: "The oil burns for eight days during Hanukkah—but my torch burns in gratitude for you forever."

Moe's desire to give a helping hand to the needy continued throughout his life—as a member and three-time president of the Spastic Children's Guild starting in 1944, playing Santa Claus for the Guild's palsied children, rounding up their gifts, and committing himself and the other two Stooges to hundreds of benefit performances whenever and wherever he was asked.

Moe and Helen on their twenty-fifth wedding anniversary. *Courtesy of Moe Howard Collection*

Moe gets it on the set of *The Three Stooges Meet Hercules* (1962). *Photo by Norman Maurer, courtesy of Moe Howard Collection*

Moe feeding Carnation milk to a real, live contented buffalo.
*Courtesy of Moe Howard Collection*

Most of Moe's friends, as strange as it seems, were judges, lawyers, and doctors, and any people his wife befriended. Unlike his brother Shemp, he rarely mingled with a show business crowd. Although he loved his profession, Moe's first thoughts were for his family, and he dreaded the separation caused by hectic shooting schedules and personal appearance tours.

Moe had a wide range of interests over the years that included traveling, gardening, ceramics, and cooking. He could whip up a mean cioppino and a marvelous lasagna—neither of which he ate; he cooked them

Moe enjoying another hobby, fishing, with son-in-law Norman Maurer and friend Bud Basolo in 1963. *Courtesy of Moe Howard Collection*

because his wife loved them. For exercise he liked to golf and took a brisk two-mile walk every morning.

In his younger days, Moe enjoyed going to the fights, football games, and midget auto racing and had hobbies that included hooking rugs and stamp and coin collecting. Moe even tried the art of wine making. His daughter, Joan, about ten at the time, later recalled vaguely what happened: "It seems that my father decided to make wine. Never one for reading directions carefully, he made a radical mistake somewhere down the line. Something to do with not removing the bung from the wine barrel at the right time . . . or maybe not removing it at all. When the day arrived for my father to taste his wine, he pulled out the bung and all hell broke loose. The entire contents of the barrel—wine, skins, and seeds—exploded out like they were shot out of a cannon. The room,

Moe enjoying one of his favorite hobbies, ceramics, in 1970.
*Courtesy of Moe Howard Collection*

which had white walls, was splashed with vivid red, but the strangest sight of all was my father. He was wine red from head to toe and peppered with grape seeds. They were stuck to him everywhere: his ears, his nostrils, his hair. Even the walls of the room were plastered with seeds. My dad was able to take a bath after and clean himself up, but that house must still have telltale signs of what went on that fateful day."

Moe's favorite music was quite diverse. It included anything sung by a barbershop quartet, the music of Andre Segovia, and his favorite song, "How Deep Is the Ocean." His favorite Stooges comedies were *You Nazty Spy!* (1940) and *I'll Never Heil Again* (1941). He considered the Stooges' best short with Curly to be *Micro-Phonies* (1945), and his favorite comedy with Shemp was *Out West* (1947).

After the loss of his brothers Curly and Shemp, Moe once remarked that he had mixed feelings about watching them in television reruns of their Stooges comedies. As he said, "How strange it is that people can laugh at comedians who are dead and never give it a second thought. At the same time, it's good to think that Shemp and my kid brother, Curly, are still remembered."

In the early 1970s, Moe kept active, playing golf occasionally, taking long walks in the morning, and going to a ceramics class twice a week. Then, in between his moments of leisure, he appeared on such television programs as *The Mike Douglas Show*, on which he made five appearances, and toured colleges with his own special one-man Three Stooges show. Moe screened several classic Stooges comedies for the

The last photograph taken of Larry and Moe together, in the summer of 1974. © *Jeff and Greg Lenburg, all rights reserved, courtesy of Jeff and Greg Lenburg*

Moe in one of his last professional portraits—still stooging.
*Courtesy of Moe Howard Collection*

audience, and answered their questions afterward. He played to standing-room-only audiences everywhere he went. His last campus appearance was at the University of Buffalo on September 24, 1974.

In 1975, years after first announcing in 1958 that he was writing his autobiography, originally titled *I Stooged to Conquer*, Moe fulfilled his dream, completing most of the manuscript—writing it all in longhand. On May 4, 1975, he died, a month and a half shy of his seventy-eighth birthday. Funeral services were held at Culver City's Hillside Memorial Park Cemetery, where he was entombed. Five months later, Helen, his wife of nearly fifty years, died of breast cancer.

With the aid of his daughter, Joan, who did the final work on the manuscript, Moe's profusely illustrated memoir, retitled *Moe Howard and the 3 Stooges*, was published in 1977 by Citadel Press. It would become the biggest-selling Stooge book of all time.

When once asked how long the Stooges would remain in show business, Howard replied, "Forever is a long time, but with a little luck, we just might make it."

# LARRY FINE

The team's middleman, Larry Fine, was born Louis Feinberg on October 5, 1902, on the south side of Philadelphia, Pennsylvania. His father, Joseph Feinberg, and mother, Fanny Lieberman, owned a watch repair and jewelry shop. Larry was the first of four children; he had two brothers, Morris and Philip (Philip, the younger of the two, died early), and a sister, Lyla, who became a school teacher.

Larry wasn't even a year old when his parents and friends started treating him like a celebrity. He stole the show as an entertainer while still in diapers. One time, when Larry was just two years of age, his father propped him up on top of a jewelry showcase to show relatives how well he could dance. Larry managed to do a few dance steps before losing his balance and falling backward through the glass top of the display case. Luckily, he emerged unharmed.

Morris Feinberg recalled that Larry had another close call in his youth. "Larry wasn't so fortunate the next time he got into trouble. It happened when Dad was testing metals to see which were gold. He used a powerful acid that when applied to base metals would turn them green or burn a hole in them. Gold, however, was not affected by the acid. One day Dad had removed the stopper from the acid bottle, leaving it uncovered. A thirsty Larry stood unnoticed at his side. As he reached for the bottle of acid to raise it to his mouth and drink, Dad saw him out of the corner of his eye and smacked the bottle from his hand, splashing acid on his left arm and burning it badly."

Larry required immediate medical attention, and a skin graft was done on his arm. After the surgery, doctors recommended that he be given violin lessons as a form of therapy. It was believed that the action of drawing the bow over the strings would strengthen his damaged arm muscles. Little did Larry realize that the violin would become an important tool in his career.

At age ten, as a student at Southwalk Grammar School, he soloed at a children's concert at the Roseland Dance Hall in Philadelphia. Backed by Howard Lanin's orchestra, he played "Humoresque" on his violin. Morris remembered that Larry eventually became a versatile musician. "He was a natural-born performer and could play any instrument he got his hands on—piano, clarinet, saxophone, and brass. He even constructed a violin out of a cigar box and a broom handle. He played its single string like a cello, holding it between his knees."

In his teens, Larry had aspirations of becoming a comedian—even a star. He enjoyed putting on shows for anyone who would watch him. As a result, he gained valuable experience.

Larry's skill as a violinist became so impressive that he was asked to play professionally. Music now in his blood, he played on the bill of local theater amateur nights, taking top prizes in most of these contests. This didn't surprise his peers, since he was certainly good at his craft. He interspersed his musical achievements with pugilistic accomplishments, earning money as a lightweight boxer, fighting over forty bouts. In 1917, at age fifteen, he landed his first professional job singing along with movie slides at Philadelphia theaters—the Keystone, Alhambra, Broadway, Nixon's Grand, and the Allegheny—where he received two dollars for each performance. All of this was accomplished while he was still a student at Central High School. In later years, he would go on to develop an act in which he would do a Russian dance while playing the violin.

Larry joined his father's jewelry business. But after three months, his father gave him a hundred-dollar bonus and two weeks' salary to quit, because little work got done since he kept everyone laughing so much on the job. In 1921, he landed a job in Gus Edwards's Newsboy Sextette, playing the violin, dancing, and telling jokes in a Jewish dialect. On the bill with him was Mabel Haney, who would later become his bride, on June 22, 1926. Mabel, with her sister, Loretta, joined Larry in an act called The Haney Sisters and Fine. Starting in 1922, the trio worked together in vaudeville, playing the RKO, Orpheum, and the Keith Circuit throughout the Northeast and Midwest and the Delmar Circuit through the South until 1926. That year, Larry accepted an offer to go solo to play the Canadian circuit, from Toronto to Vancouver, where he became a smash hit, while the Haney Sisters toured the vaudeville circuit without him in the United States.

During the Canadian tour, however, not everyone was a fan of Larry's violin playing. While Larry was rehearsing for his show at the historic Uptown Theatre in Toronto, producer Jack Arthur walked up to him with a pained look and asked politely, "Are you going to play that way in the show?"

"Yes," Larry said, "that's the only way I know."

Arthur didn't say another word. Instead, without Larry's knowledge, he arranged to have someone grease Larry's four-stringed instrument and bow with soap and stationed the show's concertmaster, Grant Milligan (who took over the same position that year with the Toronto Symphony Orchestra), in the wings during Larry's performance. Larry started to play, but the violin produced no sound. Instead, as Larry kept going through the motions, the audience heard Milligan's beautiful acoustic tones from off stage. Following the performance, Larry confronted Arthur; he was mad over his little trick, but he got over it.

Larry gave up the tour to be with Mabel; he rejoined her on Christmas Day, 1926, and never left. The couple would go on to have two children, Phyllis and Johnny.

In 1927, Larry performed additional vaudeville dates with Mabel and Loretta, including the Palace Theatre in Stamford, Connecticut, in January and Keith-Albee Theatre in Youngstown, Ohio, in May (incorrectly billed as "Lew" Fine at the latter). During their Ohio engagement, a critic for the *Youngstown Vindicator* called their hodgepodge of songs and dances "a real treat."

Larry then became permanent emcee of the Rainbo Room at Fred Mann's famed Chicago nightclub the Rainbo Gardens, after impressing him as a last-minute replacement—Mann reportedly signed him to a seven-year deal. Located at 4812–36 North Clark Street, the club lured patrons with its eclectic mix of traditional vaudeville acts, trendy jazz bands, top-flight entertainers, and easygoing dance and liquor policies. Although previous accounts have indicated Larry joined Ted Healy's act three years earlier (others have erroneously reported 1926 and 1930 as the years of his joining), it was at the Rainbo Room, in 1928, that Larry was first asked to become a Stooge. Healy and Shemp Howard took in Larry's performance one evening. As Larry told authors Jeff and Greg Lenburg in an interview, "Ted Healy was playing Chicago, and he had Shemp with him. Shemp wanted to quit. He wanted to do another act, and they came to see me."

Shemp told Healy he was quitting to start a new act with comedian Jack Waldron, a Shubert company leftover. (Moe was not part of the act then; he had left it to go into

business for himself before the birth of his daughter, Joan, in 1927.) Shemp suggested Larry to Healy as a suitable replacement: "What about this Fine guy?" Healy liked the idea, and at the conclusion of the show they went backstage to meet with Fine. Ted made Larry an offer: $90 a week to become a Stooge and an extra $10 a week if he'd throw away his fiddle.

Though his joining would mark the beginning of what would eventually be The Three Stooges, Larry did not accept Healy's offer right away. But fate intervened on his behalf: after a raid by Prohibition agents resulted in the Rainbo Gardens closing for violating Prohibition laws, Larry reconsidered Healy's offer.

In April 1928, Larry performed with both Healy and Shemp for the first time in the Shuberts' musical revue *A Night in Spain*, shortly before it ended its twenty-week run on April 7 at the Four Cohans Theatre in Chicago. Then, on April 16, 1928, he officially replaced Shemp when the show opened for one week at The Alvin Theatre in Pittsburgh. Fine toured with the show for thirty-five weeks altogether. As critic Richard S. Davis noted in his May 14, 1928, review after the show opened at the Hartman Theatre in Columbus, Ohio, "A little fellow, whose name presumably is Larry Fine, is the funniest of the second flight humorists."

Larry and his wife, Mabel, in 1933. *Courtesy of Moe Howard Collection*

After Shemp's stint with Waldron did not pan out, he returned to Healy's act. Moe rejoined them as well. In 1929, Moe, Larry, and Shemp worked as a trio with Healy for the first time—billed as Ted Healy and His Three Southern Gentlemen—in the on- and off-Broadway production *A Night in Venice*. The engagement lasted through 1930, and then the group starred in their first feature film comedy for Fox, *Soup to Nuts* (1930).

The rest of Larry's career would parallel Moe's. Larry, Moe, and Shemp left Healy briefly in 1930 after doing *Soup to Nuts* to start their own act, known as "Howard, Fine, and Howard," before billing themselves in late December 1931 as Three Lost Souls. In 1932 they rejoined Healy to star in the Shuberts' Broadway revue *The Passing Show of 1932*. Then, in 1933, they signed with MGM to star in comedy shorts and features. When the team left MGM (and Ted Healy again) in 1934, the Stooges consisted of Moe, Larry, and Curly. They went on to star in two-reel comedies for Columbia Pictures, where the team remained for twenty-four years.

Offstage, Larry was a social butterfly. He liked a good time and surrounded himself with friends. Larry and his wife, Mabel, loved having parties, and every Christmas they threw lavish midnight suppers. Larry was what some friends have called a "yes man," since he was always so agreeable no matter what the circumstances. As film director Charles Lamont recalled after directing Fine in two Stooges comedies, "Larry was a nut. He was the kind of guy who always said anything. He was a yapper."

Larry's devil-may-care personality carried over to the world of finance. He was a terrible business-man who spent his money as soon as he earned it. He would gamble it away either at the track or at high-stakes gin rummy games. In an interview, Fine even admitted that he often gave money to actors and friends who needed help, and he never asked to be reimbursed. Joe Besser and director Edward Bernds remember that because of his free spending, Larry was almost forced into bankruptcy when Columbia terminated the Three Stooges comedies in 1958.

Norman Maurer recalled that Larry was surrounded by friends, some of whom were ready and waiting to take his money. "Larry would wait around at the end of a booking during personal appearance tours. Then, the minute Moe would go to the theater manager to get their money, Larry would take his cut and ten minutes later it was gone. It would be spent on life's luxuries: diamond rings, fur coats, and on the horses. Or if one of his friends would say, 'Larry, I've got a deal—this nonsinkable bathing suit . . . all we need is $15,000'—Larry was had!"

On another occasion, Larry convinced Moe to finance a fast-food restaurant in Glendale, California, called Mi Patio. Larry's two friends, who conceived the idea, planned to sell Stoogeburgers, which would be served in little plastic baskets with the Stooges' faces printed on the sides. After several months of so-so business, the partners skipped town with everything they could get their hands on, including the burgers. As a result, Moe and Larry were left holding the bag.

Because of his prodigal ways and his wife's dislike for housekeeping, Larry and his family lived in hotels—first in the President Hotel in Atlantic City,

Larry with daughter Phyllis, circa 1935.
*Courtesy of Moe Howard Collection*

where his daughter, Phyllis, was raised, and then the Knickerbocker Hotel in Hollywood. Not until 1944 did Larry buy a home—a splendid old Mediterranean structure in the Los Feliz area of Los Angeles.

Larry's screen personality was as laid back as his real-life one, and thus his character was never forced. Prior to the filming of a scene, he'd come up with a gag idea that he'd toss at the director; he would always shrug it off when his ideas were ignored. He was said to be a bit of a whiner, though, sometimes complaining about the smallest things. If he stubbed his toe on a chair during a scene, he'd carry on until the prop man cushioned the chair leg with a sponge pad to protect him from injuring the toe again. In the early days, Larry would put on an act in public, trying to appear aloof, to make people believe he was a serious intellectual—the complete opposite of his screen persona. But this false front disappeared as he matured.

Fine was also known for his tardiness, which even the cast's call-sheets bear out. He rarely got to the set, or to any other engagement, on time. Several times during his career, Moe had to cover for him until he showed up. In fact, one time while the Stooges were performing in Atlantic City, a newspaper photographer had arranged a photo session with them in advance of their engagement. When Larry forgot the appointment, Moe had to ask the theater manager to take his place.

Edward Bernds, who directed Larry in numerous Stooges films, recalled that he wasn't as dedicated to his career as the other Stooges. "He tended to be a

Theater manager Charles Funk fills in for Larry during a publicity photo session in Buffalo, New York, in August 1959 with Moe and Curly-Joe as a result of Fine's tardiness.
*Courtesy of Moe Howard Collection*

bit of a goof-off," Bernds said. "But not a real goldbricker; he just wasn't as dedicated as Moe was."

But Norman Maurer believes that Larry's talents as an actor and comedian were commonly overlooked in Stooges comedies. As he put it, "I think Larry was

Larry, in a later undated photo, having a little fun at Moe's expense as Shemp looks on.
*Courtesy of Moe Howard Collection*

At Moe's son Paul's wedding: (clockwise) Larry, Mabel, Joe DeRita, Phyllis Lamond (Larry's daughter), Don Lamond (Larry's son-in-law), Jeffrey and Michael Maurer (Moe's grandsons), Claretta White, Sam White (Jules White's brother), Norman Maurer, Joan Howard Maurer, and Bill Dyer.
*Courtesy of Moe Howard Collection*

Larry takes it like a man.

*Photo by Norman Maurer, courtesy of Moe Howard Collection*

the best actor of the three. I used to argue with Moe about giving him more lines because Larry was good, but Moe was against it."

Fine's favorite hobbies included teaching serious music, preferably jazz, the kind André Previn, Percy Faith, Morton Gould, and Andre Kostelanetz popularized. Larry's favorite sport was baseball, the Los Angeles Dodgers his favorite team. He also enjoyed going to the boxing matches. Larry's favorite actors were Spencer Tracy, Clark Gable, and Peter Falk, while Milton Berle, Jack Benny, and Redd Foxx were his choices for favorite comedians.

Larry's favorite Stooge was Curly. As he once commented, "Personally, I thought Curly was the greatest because he was a natural comedian who had no formal training. Whatever he did he made up on the spur of the moment." His favorite Stooges films were *Scrambled Brains* (1951) and *The Three Stooges Meet Hercules* (1962). Runner-up favorites included *You Nazty Spy!* (1940) and *I'll Never Heil Again* (1941).

On November 17, 1961, Larry's son, Johnny, died in a tragic automobile accident at age twenty-four.

Six years later, on May 30, 1967, his wife, Mabel, died of a sudden heart attack. Then, in January 1970, Larry himself suffered a debilitating stroke.

The stroke left Larry partially paralyzed on his left side. He lived out his final years in reasonable comfort at the Motion Picture Country House and Hospital in Woodland Hills, California, in a room smaller than a studio apartment. Confined to a wheelchair, he regularly received physical therapy with the hope of walking again. As he once told authors Jeff and Greg Lenburg, "Nobody's going to beat me, kid. I'm going to get out of here."

Larry remained quite active despite his disability and became the life of the party at the Motion Picture Country House and Hospital. Fellow residents included former screen stars Mary Astor, Donald Crisp, Jean Hagen, and Allyn Joslyn. Fine's favorite event was the annual Wheelchair Parade, in which patients decorated their chairs in accordance with each year's theme. In fact, he participated in the event every year and garnered most of the awards.

Larry remembers to duck during the sketch "The Maharaja" in *The Three Stooges Go Around the World in a Daze* (1963). © *Columbia Pictures, courtesy of Moe Howard Collection*

One year, with "Favorite Movie Titles" as the theme, forty patients entered the parade, including Larry. He dressed up as a baby to represent the movie title *What Ever Happened to Baby Jane?* Seated in his wheelchair, Fine was decked out in diapers and held an empty whiskey bottle topped with the nipple from a baby's bottle. Instead of winning the "Most Humorous" category as he did each year, Larry took first place for having the "Most Original" costume.

Larry wasn't surprised that he was often judged the winner. He once said, "Hell, I *can't* lose. All of my friends are judges on the panel. There's Jerry Colonna, Chill Wills, Harry Ackerman and Walter Pidgeon. If you ask me, I think it's *fixed!*" But Larry also said

that the awards were given to the wrong people and that the decorator of his wheelchair (and his escort for three years), Peg Hart, deserved the awards that he had won. Each year Hart spent over two hours helping Larry with his wheelchair in preparation for the parade.

Besides wheelchair parades, Larry was active in stage productions as one of the Ding-A-Lings, a choir composed of patients from the hospital. Twice yearly the choir staged a variety show composed of skits and songs that was held at the Louis B. Mayer Theatre and was open to the public. Famous celebrities were invited to guest star in the shows and participate in skits and songs with the choir.

Larry waiting to participate in the annual wheelchair parade at the Motion Picture Country House and Hospital in 1973.

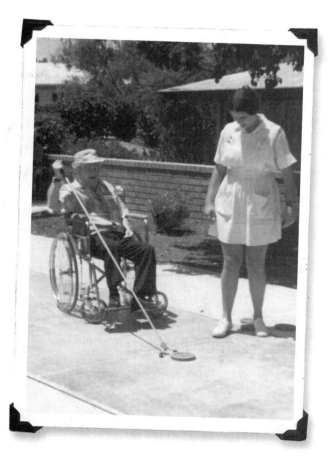

Larry prepares to push a weighted puck down the court in a shuffleboard match.

Larry with Ed Asner at a shuffleboard match at the Motion Picture Country House and Hospital in July 1973.

Every year Larry invited Moe to come and perform a routine with him onstage. One year, Moe couldn't make it, which really put Larry on the spot. He had been accustomed to performing with Moe for over forty years, and it had been an eternity since he went onstage as a single. But he did, delighting the audience by comically reciting a nursery rhyme: "Mary had a little lamb. Its fleece was black as soot. And everywhere that lambie went, his sooty foot he put." (The Stooges had used the rhyme for years in their stage act with Curly-Joe DeRita.) He was, of course, the hit of the show. As Larry said afterward, "I was never so scared in all my life. I felt lost without Moe at my side." A year earlier, Moe and Larry had fractured audiences with their version of "Take Me Out to the Ball Game."

Although Larry was able to speak after his stroke, his voice was thick and his pronunciation was somewhat garbled. Later, Moe admitted that when he

Program cover for Larry's last high school concert appearance to raise funds for stage equipment for Loara High School in Anaheim, California. © *Jeff and Greg Lenburg, all rights reserved, courtesy of Jeff and Greg Lenburg*

Larry relates a funny story during his final concert appearance at Loara High School on March 2, 1974. © *Jeff and Greg Lenburg, all rights reserved, courtesy of Jeff and Greg Lenburg*

went to see Larry, tears would well up in his eyes, and it became more and more trying each time, but he went as often as possible. One time, when Moe was over forty minutes late, Larry quipped, "Who knows where Moe's been? Knowing him, he could get lost in a paper bag!"

Despite his handicap, Larry also brought delight to high school and college audiences with his own Three Stooges show. He appeared at several colleges in the San Fernando Valley area and on many occasions took with him actress Babe London, who also resided at the Motion Picture Country House and had costarred in the Stooges comedy *Scrambled Brains* (1951). At his final concert appearance on March 2, 1974, at Loara High School in Anaheim, California, at the invitation of his close friends Jeff and Greg Lenburg to help raise funds for the school's

stage equipment, Larry assured the fans that he would walk again, and during several performances he stood up in his wheelchair for the crowds. As Fine once said, "It only takes five minutes to have a stroke, but it takes five years to recover."

Larry also appeared on several talk shows in the Los Angeles area and wrote a book in 1973 called *Stroke of Luck* (Siena Publishing Co.), which covers his life from childhood to his years as a resident at the Motion Picture Country House. *Stroke of Luck* was published privately by James Carone, who helped Larry compile the book. Fine pulled it from distribution when Carone failed to pay him his share of the profits. The book, which was rife with errors, is no longer available.

As Larry approached his seventy-second birthday, his health had improved markedly. But on Octo-

At his final concert appearance, accompanied by master of ceremonies Jeff Lenburg, Larry assures his fans he'll walk again by standing for them.

Larry's last public appearance, along with a chimp friend, on August 24, 1974, at California's Lion Country Safari. *Courtesy of Jeff Lenburg Collection*

ber 4, 1974, one day before his birthday, Fine suffered another stroke and was rushed to the J Ward of the hospital, which treats the critically ill. Two weeks later, he was alert and talking again, but his speech was more garbled and slurred than before. Then, on the same day that Jack Benny died, Larry suffered a massive stroke that put him into a coma. Two weeks later, Larry suffered no more; he died on January 24, 1975. Funeral services were held at Forest Lawn Memorial Park in Glendale, California, with his remains entombed in the Freedom Mausoleum, Sanctuary of Liberation. He was survived by his daughter, Phyllis, who would die of cancer, at age sixty, on April 3, 1989.

In the end, Larry was remembered for what he loved best. For more than fifty years, he brought joy and laughter into the hearts of millions of fans around the world. Nothing made him prouder than to enrich the lives of so many as the frizzy-haired Stooge in the middle.

# CURLY HOWARD

© Columbia Pictures, courtesy of Moe Howard Collection

*C*urly Howard, the one with the shaven head that Moe referred to as "looking like a dirty tennis ball," was the most popular member of The Three Stooges and the most inventive of the six. His hilarious improvisations and his classic catchphrases "N'yuk-n'yuk-n'yuk!" and "Wooo-wooo-wooo!" have established him as a great American cult hero.

His real name was Jerome Lester Horwitz, and he was born to Jennie and Solomon Horwitz on October 22, 1903, in Bath Beach, a summer resort in a section of Brooklyn. He was the fifth and youngest of the Horwitz sons and weighed eight and a half pounds at birth. He was delivered by Dr. Duffy, the brother of Moe Howard's sixth-grade schoolteacher. Curly-Jerome, to complicate matters, was nicknamed "Babe" by his brother Moe.

Curly was a quiet child who gave his parents very little trouble. Moe and Shemp made up for him in spades. Moe recalled one mischievous incident when Curly was an infant: "We took his brand-new baby carriage, removed the wheels, made a pair of axles from two-by-fours and built our own version of a 'soap box racer.' We put Curly in it and dragged him all over town. It was a lucky thing we didn't kill him. When our parents found out, we had the devil to pay."

When Curly was about four, Moe and Shemp started to instill in their brother the idea of becoming a comedian. Quite frequently they would stage small theater productions in the basement of their friends' homes; the cast would usually consist of Shemp, Moe, and Curly. They charged two cents for admission, but the ventures could not have been very lucrative, as the boys had to split the take three ways. It is believed that during these performances Curly got his first taste of comedy.

Moe also recalled that Curly was only a fair student in school. A boyhood friend, Lester Friedman, remembered that he was a fine athlete, though, making a name for himself on the elementary school basketball team. Although Curly never graduated from school, he kept himself busy doing odd jobs, following Moe and Shemp wherever they went.

As a young man, Curly loved to dance and listen to music, and he became an accomplished ballroom dancer. He would go regularly to the Triangle Ballroom in Brooklyn, where on several occasions he met actor George Raft, who in the early days of his career was a fine ballroom dancer. Curly also tried his hand

Curly Howard (top left), at about age fifteen, with his school's basketball team. At his feet, friend Lester Friedman.
*Courtesy of Moe Howard Collection*

at the ukulele, singing along as he strummed. As Moe once said, "He was not a good student but he was in demand socially, what with his beautiful singing voice." Moe continued to influence his kid brother's theatrical education, taking Curly along with him to vaudeville shows and the melodrama theaters, but Curly's first loves were musicals and comedy.

In 1928, Curly landed a job as a guest comedy musical conductor for the Orville Knapp Band, which, to that date, was his only stage experience. Moe recalled that his brother's performances visually overshadowed those of the band. "He was billed as the guest conductor and would come out and lead the band in a breakaway tuxedo. The sections of the suit would fall away, piece by piece, while he stood there swinging his baton."

Young Curly's interest in show business continued to grow as he watched his brothers, Shemp and Moe, perform as Stooges in Ted Healy's act. Joe Besser, who worked with them in *The Passing Show of 1932*, recalled that Curly liked to hang around backstage. "He was there all the time and would get sandwiches for all of us in the show, including Ted Healy and his Stooges. He never participated in any of the routines but liked to watch us perform." During this period Curly remained in the shadow of his brothers and watched as their careers began to skyrocket them to stardom along with Healy.

It was in 1932, during the Shuberts' *Passing Show*, that Healy had an argument with J. J. Shubert over his contract and walked off the show, taking Larry and Moe along with him. Shemp, disenchanted with Healy's drunken bouts and practical jokes, decided to remain in the Shubert show.

Later that afternoon, Moe suggested to Healy that his kid brother was available and would make an excellent replacement for Shemp, since he was familiar with the act. Ted agreed, with one condition. In an interview, Curly recalled Healy's terms: "I had beautiful wavy hair and a waxed moustache. When I went to see Ted Healy about a job as one of the Stooges, he said, 'What can you do?' I said, 'I don't know.' He said, 'I know what you can do. You can shave off your hair to start with.' Then later on I had to shave off my poor mustache. I had to shave it off right down to the skin."

Curly's wacky style of comedy started to emerge, first onstage and then on-screen, when Healy and his Stooges starred in numerous features and comedy shorts for MGM. Later, in 1934, Curly played an integral part in the team's rise to fame as The Three Stooges at Columbia Pictures, where he would star as a Stooge in ninety-seven two-reel comedies.

But success virtually destroyed Curly. He started to drink heavily, feeling that his shaved head robbed him of his sex appeal. Larry Fine once remarked that Curly wore a hat in public to confirm an image of masculinity, since he felt like a little kid with his hair shaved off. Curly was also unable to save a cent. When he received his check he'd rush out to spend it on life's pleasures: wine, women, an automobile, a new house, or a new dog—Curly was mad about dogs. Since Curly was certainly no businessman, Moe usually handled all of his affairs, helped him manage his money, and even made out his income tax returns.

Curly's homes were San Fernando Valley showplaces, and most of them were either purchased from or sold to a select group of Hollywood personalities. One house Curly purchased, on Cahuenga Boulevard and Sarah Street in North Hollywood, was purchased from child star Sabu. Later Curly sold the property to

Autographed fan photo of Curly, Moe, and Larry from *Uncivil Warriors* (1935).
*Courtesy of Moe Howard Collection*

Curly's bride-to-be Elaine Ackerman shows off her engagement ring to a delighted Curly and Curly's parents, Jennie and Solomon Horwitz.
*Courtesy of Moe Howard Collection*

a promising young actress of the 1940s, Joan Leslie. Curly also bought a lot next door to Moe Howard's palatial home in Toluca Lake, expecting to build on it, but he never did. It was eventually sold to film director Raoul Walsh.

As for Curly's personality, he was basically an introvert, barely speaking on the set between takes, the complete antithesis of his insanely hilarious screen character. Charles Lamont, who directed

Curly and his new bride, Elaine, watch helplessly as Moe and Larry clown around after moving into Curly's new home in 1937.
*Courtesy of Moe Howard Collection*

Curly did clown around, but only if Moe, Shemp, and Larry were with him. Or if his immediate group of friends or family were there. But the minute there were strangers, he retreated."

But Curly's main weakness was women; to paraphrase an old adage, Curly couldn't live with women—or live without them. Mrs. Leveton remembered that women were his favorite pastime for a number of reasons. As she said, "He just liked a good time and that was it. And women . . . he loved women. I don't have to tell you . . . not always the nicest women. You

Curly in two Stooges comedies, related in an interview that "Curly was pretty dull. This may not be a very nice thing to say, but I don't think he had all of his marbles. He was always on Cloud Nine whenever you talked to him."

Clarice Seiden, the sister of Moe Howard's wife, Helen, remembered Curly differently. She saw him offscreen whenever there was a party at his home, and recalled, "Although he wasn't 'on' all the time, I wouldn't call him a quiet person. . . . He was a lot of fun. He was quiet at times, but when he had a few drinks—and he drank quite a bit—he was more gregarious."

Curly's niece, Dolly Sallin, agreed with Mrs. Seiden that Curly liked people, but shared Lamont's viewpoint that he could be quiet at times. "I can remember his wanting to be with people. He wasn't a recluse, and I wouldn't call him dull. He wasn't an intellect, nor did he go in for discussions. But when I think of someone as dull, I'd think of them as being under par intelligence-wise, and Curly wasn't that."

Friends remember that Curly refrained from any crazy antics in private life, reserving them for his performances in the comedies. However, when he got together with his brothers, Moe and Shemp, it was a totally different story. As Irma Grenner Leveton, a friend of Moe and Helen Howard, recalled, "Yes,

Larry, Curly, and Moe mugging. Their straight man is brother Jack Howard.
*Courtesy of Moe Howard Collection*

Moe and Curly touring the British Isles in 1939.
*Courtesy of Moe Howard Collection*

Curly and Moe share a laugh with brother Shemp on the Columbia lot.
© *Columbia Pictures, courtesy of Moe Howard Collection*

Curly, Larry, and Moe with the "Mysterious Wrestler."
*Courtesy of Moe Howard Collection*

know why, because he was so shy. Curly didn't know how to speak to a woman, so he would wind up conversing with anyone that approached him."

Dolly Sallin viewed his love for women in a similar manner: "I can remember his wanting to be around people, and that included the current woman in his life. That was the most important thing—if she was good, bad, or whatever. If he decided she was interesting, that was that! As long as there was a woman around the house, he would stay home instead of running around. He seemed restless to me."

Director-producer Norman Maurer first met Curly in 1945 and remembered that he "was a push-over for women. If a pretty girl went up to him and gave him a spiel, Curly would marry her. Then she would take his money and run off. It was the same when a real estate agent would come up and say, 'I have a house for you,' Curly would sell his current home and buy another one. It seemed as though every two weeks he would have a new girl, a new car, a new house, and a new dog."

But as much as Curly loved women, they were his downfall. He was married four times. On August 5, 1930, in New York, at age twenty-six, he married one Julia Rosenthal. Born on November 26, 1900, to Julius Rosenthal and Besse Lipins, she was a Bangor,

Maine, native. Rabbi Jacob Schacter officiated the ceremony, held at 5415 Fourteenth Avenue in Brooklyn. Little is known about their relationship or when or why it ended.

On June 7, 1937, less than two months after meeting her early that spring, Curly married Elaine Ackerman. The wedding took place shortly before the Stooges were to depart on their annual personal appearance tour to theaters across the country; the trip became a combination honeymoon and business trip for Curly and his new bride. In 1938 Elaine gave birth to Curly's first child, a daughter, Marilyn. Due to the addition to their family, Curly and Elaine moved to a home in the 400 block of Highland Avenue in Hollywood, near where Moe lived at the time. But slowly the marriage began to crumble, and Elaine filed for divorce on July 11, 1940, after only three years of marriage.

During the next five years, Curly ate, drank, and made merry. He gained a tremendous amount of weight and his blood pressure soared. On January 23, 1945, he entered the Cottage Hospital in Santa Barbara, where he was diagnosed with extreme hypertension, a retinal hemorrhage, and obesity. He remained at the hospital for tests and treatment and was discharged on February 9, 1945.

Eight months later, while on a personal appearance in New York, Moe introduced Curly to an attractive petite blonde, Marion Marvin Buchsman, the daughter of a theater owner, with a ten-year-old son from a previous marriage. Curly instantly fell in love with her, and he married her in New York City on October 17, 1945, after knowing her for only two weeks.

Irma Leveton remembered that Moe talked Curly into the marriage with Marion, since Moe did not like the kind of wild life his brother was leading. He wanted Curly to settle down and take care of his health. As Leveton remarked, "Moe fixed them up—Marion and Curly. He wanted Curly to get married and pushed him into it. He wanted Curly to quit the life he was leading, as he was getting sick. Curly had very high blood pressure."

But, Leveton added, "that marriage to Marion didn't help. It was very aggravating for Curly and a very unhappy time for all concerned." It was felt

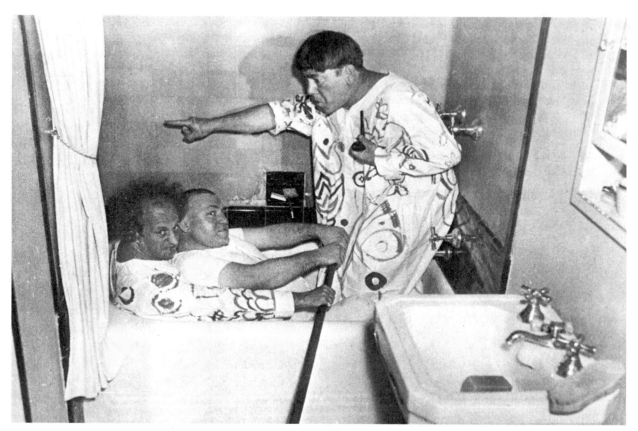

A happy moment at home taking their Saturday-night bath.

*Courtesy of Moe Howard Collection*

that Marion used Curly to her advantage. He spent a fortune on her—buying everything from fur coats to expensive jewelry. Curly even bought her a new home on Ledge Avenue in Toluca Lake (a corner house only two blocks from Moe's house on Kling Street). As Marie Howard, Jack Howard's wife, recalled: "She was just after his money."

It didn't take long for Curly to realize that Marion wasn't for him. After a miserable three months of arguments and accusations, Marilyn came home from work one day and found Curly sitting out in front of their house in his car, which was packed with all his luggage. He told her then that he was leaving. Marion and Curly separated on January 14, 1946, and Curly sued for divorce.

Curly in his own world on the set of *Phony Express* (1943).
© *Columbia Pictures, courtesy of Moe Howard Collection*

Curly's divorce was quite scandalous; notices were carried in all the local papers. Dolly Sallin recalled, "It was horrible. She tried to get everything she could from him and even accused Curly of never bathing, which was totally untrue. Curly was fat but he was always immaculate. That marriage nearly ruined him."

Marion was awarded the decree on July 22, 1946, less than nine months after they were married. Curly sold their home and moved into the house on Cahuenga Boulevard, where he lived by himself.

With his third marriage a disaster, the question surfaced: why had Curly's marriages failed? Irma Leveton believed that it was a combination of Curly's immaturity and a succession of mismatched partners. "He couldn't contribute anything to a marriage. Most likely his wives married him because he was a [film] personality. But he had nothing to back it up. There was no substance of any kind. He always seemed to be in a trance . . . kinda dopey. Once in awhile he would come out with something very funny. And I can't even imagine him saying 'I love you' to any woman."

But Dolly Sallin had another point of view. "I don't think Curly ever grew up. He couldn't make it in a one-to-one relationship. He was sweet and loving but not really mature. He was very restless. He seemed to need women to soothe his restless quality, not just for sex. I would guess that he was restless and that nothing seemed to help."

It was soon after his separation from Marion that Curly's health started its rapid decline. Then, on May 6, 1946, he suffered a stroke during the filming of his ninety-seventh Three Stooges comedy, *Half-Wits Holiday* (1947). Curly had to leave the team to recuperate from his illness, and his condition began to improve.

A year later, still not fully recovered from his stroke, Curly met a thrice-married widow of thirty-two who really seemed to care for him: Valerie Newman, whom he married on July 31, 1947. As Marilyn Ellman, Curly's first daughter, once related, "Out of the clear sky Curly came home one day. He wasn't even dressed to get married. He and Valerie went to the courthouse."

Curly and his fourth wife rented a home on 12555 Riverside Drive in North Hollywood. Valerie was a very caring woman who nursed him through those last, awful years. Although his health worsened after the marriage, Valerie gave birth to a daughter, Curly's second child, Janie. As Irma Leveton recalled, "Valerie was the only decent thing that happened to Curly and the only one that really cared about him. I remember she nursed him twenty-four hours a day."

Finally, in 1949, Curly's health took a severe turn for the worse when he suffered a second stroke and was rushed to Cedars of Lebanon Hospital in Holly-

Curly after his first stroke, at his niece Joan's wedding in 1947. *Courtesy of Moe Howard Collection*

wood. Doctors contemplated doing spinal surgery on him, since the stroke had left him partially paralyzed. But the final decision was not to operate.

Curly was confined to a wheelchair, and doctors put him on a diet of boiled rice and apples. It was hoped that this would bring down his weight and his high blood pressure. As a result of his illness, Curly's weight dropped dramatically. As Norman Maurer recalled, "I'll never forget him at this point in his life. His hand would constantly fall off the arm of the wheelchair, either from weakness or the paralysis, and he couldn't get it back on without help." When Curly's condition failed to improve, Valerie admitted him into the Motion Picture Country House and Hospital in Woodland Hills on August 29, 1950. He was released after several months of treatment and medical tests, on November 15, 1950, though he would return periodically to the hospital up until 1952.

Back at home, Curly was confined to his bed, where Valerie nursed him. When his health worsened in February 1951, she made a request for a male nurse to help her. Later that same month, Curly was placed in a nursing home, the Colonial House, located in Los Angeles. In March, he suffered another stroke, and Moe had to move him out of the facility, due to the fact that the nursing home did not meet state fire codes.

In April 1951 Curly was moved to North Hollywood Hospital and Sanitarium. In December, the hospital supervisor advised the family that Curly was becoming a problem to the nursing staff due to mental deterioration and that they could no longer care for him. It was suggested that he be placed in a mental hospital, but Moe would not hear of it. On January 7, 1952, Moe was called from the filming of a Stooges comedy, *He Cooked His Goose* (1952), to help move Curly again, this time to the Baldy View Sanitarium in San Gabriel. Eleven days later, on January 18, 1952, Curly died of a massive cerebral hemorrhage. He was forty-eight years old. He was subsequently laid to rest at Home of Peace Cemetery in East Los Angeles.

Curly Howard was gone before his time, and one can only wonder what it would have been like if he had lived and worked with the Stooges through the 1960s. Imagine Curly starring in full-length features in black-and-white and in color. Stooges cartoons could have been voiced with the original Curly n'yuk-n'yuk-ing and wooo-wooo-ing. Television audiences could have realized the true genius of Curly Howard on talk and variety shows. When the Stooges' popularity suddenly burgeoned in 1959, Curly could have been around to take the bows with Moe and Larry.

Hopefully, if there is a Stooges' heaven, Curly is there watching, seeing his talent, his art of comedy, and his contributions as a Stooge still being enjoyed by millions throughout the world.

# SHEMP HOWARD

*Courtesy of Moe Howard Collection*

36

Shemp Howard, his hair slicked down over loving-cup ears, became one of the most famous comedy stooges in the history of stage and screen. The third-eldest brother of team leader Moe, and the tallest of the famed Howard brothers at five feet six inches tall, Shemp was born Samuel Horwitz in Brooklyn, New York, on March 17, 1895 (not 1900 as listed in studio biographies).

Moe once recalled how his brother acquired the name Shemp. "Shemp was given the Hebrew name Schmool, after his mother's grandfather. Schmool was Anglicized to Samuel and then shortened to Sam. When his mother, with her broad European accent, would call him, the name 'Sam' came out 'Sams,' and if you weren't listening carefully it could sound like Shemp . . . which it did! So from the time he was seven that's what his family called him. It was Shemp in school and in the world of the theater. In later years, no one knew it was anything else."

Shemp was a very mischievous child, and Moe recalled his favorite pastime was stuffing everything from woolen stockings to sweaters down the hallway toilet. "I remember one time when Shemp tore the pages out of our brother Irving's history book and jammed them into the toilet in our home in Bensonhurst," Moe recalled with a chuckle. "Because of this he had to run the family gauntlet: a smack from Mother, a belt across the head from Dad, a shove from Irving, and a kick in the fanny from me."

Shemp attended P.S. 163 in Brooklyn, the same grammar school as his brother Moe. Moe recalled that in their school days, Shemp was not athletically inclined and as a student he was nil. He tried to pay attention in class but seemed unable to concentrate. Jack and Irving tried to help him with his schoolwork, but Shemp was already playing the comedian. He'd laugh everything off with a cute remark, draw funny drawings, or make faces at the other students to make them laugh and get them in trouble along with him. Shemp craved attention.

When Shemp reached the age of thirteen, he was a completely different person; he had outgrown most of his mischief making. Moe remembered that friends of the family had always predicted that Shemp was going to be an actor or a great comedian. But Shemp thought otherwise and never seriously entertained the idea of entering show business. Moe, on the other hand, worked like a demon at it, planned

his future, and eventually made it to the footlights before his brother.

Shemp graduated from P.S. 163 and got as far as starting New Utrecht High School. Like Moe, he failed to finish his secondary education. Their parents, Jennie and Solomon Horwitz, urged them both to go to a trade school. Late in 1911, Moe and Shemp enrolled at the Baron DeHirsch Trade School in New York, where Moe studied to be an electrician and Shemp took up plumbing. While Moe learned the definition of an ampere, an ohm, and a volt, Shemp learned the basics of threading and cutting pipe. Neither of the boys ever finished these courses; instead they put their lessons into practice in a rare act of mischief.

Moe remembered that while learning the tricks of their trade they got the tricks down pat: "Neither Shemp nor I ever finished the course, but we did find a use for lesson number one: the push-button door latch. We wired it into our apartment so that by pushing a concealed button we could open the front-door latch when we got home late at night without our parents being the wiser. I'd just reach under the doorstep, press the button, wait for the click of the latch, and open the door from the outside. This worked well until Dad found out. One night we came home very late and reached for the button, but the button wasn't there. That particular evening Shemp and I had borrowed Jack and Irving's new long-pants suits to go to a party. We came home about three in the morning, and there was no way to get in without waking our parents. Then I got the bright idea of going to the back of the house. The bathroom window was open and I climbed through the darkened opening, head down, arms outstretched and probing, right into a half-filled tub that either Irving or Jack had left from that night's bath. I landed face down in the water. I rolled over and sat up laughing hysterically. I had forgotten all about Shemp and letting him in. A moment later he climbed in and found himself in the same boat. There we were when my father entered, the two of us sopping wet with our brothers' good clothes on. Somehow our father's smacks on our wet faces sounded much louder and were more painful than on a dry face."

Moe also said that Shemp was industrious for his age. The two brothers worked together at many different neighborhood jobs. First, they tried the plumbing business, but when Shemp burned his hand on hot solder he quit. The brothers next tried setting up pins in a local bowling alley, then delivering newspapers for the *Brooklyn Eagle*. This continued until, finally, Shemp realized there was nothing left for them but the theater.

In the hope of acquiring some stage experience, Shemp agreed to do an act with Moe at dance halls and theater amateur nights in the area. At the time, comedy was neither Moe nor Shemp's forte. Moe had been directing his energies toward dramatic theater while Shemp, except for fooling around at parties, had practically no theatrical experience. The two boys wrote a short skit, rehearsed it, and went onstage at an amateur night at the Bath Beach Theatre. Three minutes into their performance, they were thrown bodily out of the theater. Needless to say, Shemp was terribly discouraged, but Moe felt it was a step in the right direction—Shemp had finally performed on a stage.

Charlotte Shurman, an old Bensonhurst friend of the Howards when they were in their twenties, watched many of their performances around the neighborhood. She recalled, "They were just starting out in dance halls, and everyone got a big kick out of them and the shows they put on. Shemp and Moe worked together, and I followed them around wherever they went . . . because I was so proud. I remember Shemp. He was a riot . . . simply a riot. And it came so naturally."

Sometime during the course of World War I, Moe and Shemp formed a blackface vaudeville act, which disbanded for a brief period when Shemp was drafted into the army. He was discharged after only a few months (he was discovered to be a bed wetter) and

Moe and Shemp in blackface in stock with the Marguerite Bryant Players in the summer of 1919. *Courtesy of Moe Howard Collection*

rejoined Moe in vaudeville. In 1917 Shemp and Moe took their comedy act back to the boards and played on both the Loews and RKO circuits, managing to work for the rival outfits through a ruse: they played a blackface routine for RKO and a whiteface one for Loews. They successfully continued with their stage appearances through 1922. Starting in 1919, they also appeared in blackface in the Marguerite Bryant Players stock company. Shemp jokingly recalled the darkest moment of his life as the time he was working blackface in a minstrel show and the manager skipped with the payroll and the cold cream. Despite his show business desires, Shemp once said, "My parents wanted me to grow up to be a gentleman."

Then, one afternoon in late 1922, Shemp got his biggest show business break. A former schoolmate

Shemp in his teens, onstage with a fellow vaudevillian.
*Courtesy of Moe Howard Collection*

and vaudeville comedian, Ted Healy, was playing at the Prospect Theatre in Brooklyn. Moe had already agreed to help out Healy, filling in for an acrobat in his act, and Shemp happened to be in the audience during their performance. At Moe's urging, Healy prevailed upon Shemp to come up out of the audience and perform in the show. Shemp went onstage with Moe and Ted and fractured the audience with an entirely ad-libbed routine. Healy's act with Moe and Shemp as his Stooges kept up its frantic pace from that night on.

But a short-lived problem arose at the beginning of the brothers' careers. Their mother, Jennie Horwitz, was totally against the idea of her sons joining Ted Healy. Jack Howard later remembered what Ted Healy said to persuade her to change her mind. "It seems my mother did not want Shemp or Moe to be actors. She thought it would be much better if they became professionals. Ted Healy came to the house one day to plead with my mother to let Moe and Shemp join the act. He was getting nowhere. Suddenly, Ted said to my mother, 'Jennie, I'll give you one hundred dollars for your synagogue building fund if you let the boys come with me.' She thought about the good that the money would do and agreed, reluctantly."

Following his debut as a Stooge, Shemp's association with Healy continued to prosper. He was prominently billed in such Shubert brothers musicals as *A Night in Spain* (1927) and *A Night in Venice* (1929). In September 1925, Shemp, then thirty years old, married a fellow New Yorker, twenty-eight-year-old beauty Gertrude "Babe" Frank. She gave birth to a son, Morton, in 1927. A year after Mort's birth, Shemp left Healy, only to later return.

Shemp proudly displays his first paycheck from Fox Studios in 1930. *Courtesy of Moe Howard Collection*

Shemp with his wife, Gertrude, in 1930. *Courtesy of Moe Howard Collection*

Shemp in costume from *A Night in Venice*, 1929, from home movie footage. *Courtesy of Moe Howard Collection*

A frame blowup from a 1930s home movie featuring Shemp with Gertrude and their son, Mort. *Courtesy of Moe Howard Collection*

Then, in 1930, it was off to Hollywood to costar in Rube Goldberg's critical sensation *Soup to Nuts*. A short time later Larry, Moe, and Shemp left Healy to form an act of their own, simply called "Howard, Fine, and Howard" before being renamed "Three Lost Souls" in late December 1931. But a year later they returned to Healy to star in *The Passing Show of 1932*, a Shubert Broadway revue. Healy left the show over a contract dispute, taking Moe and Larry with him. Shemp decided to stay behind. Shemp's leaving the act also gave his kid brother Curly the opportunity of a lifetime—to become the world's favorite Stooge.

Leaving the team gave Shemp a chance to use his wide-ranging talents in various film productions produced on the East Coast, including features and featurettes. He accepted an offer from Warner Bros. and went on to star in at least thirty-five two-reel sound comedies for its Brooklyn-based Vitaphone studios, including bit speaking roles in numerous Jack Haley, Fatty Arbuckle, Ben Blue, and George Givot shorts, beginning with 1933's *Salt Water Daffy*. He also costarred in his own series of comedy shorts with Harry Gribbon, Daphne Pollard, and Roscoe Ates, among them *Corn on the Cop* (1934), *Art Trouble* (1934) (which, coincidentally, featured a young James Stewart in his first film role), *Mummy's Arms* (1934), *Smoked Hams* (1934), *So You Won't T-T-T-Talk* (1934), *A Peach of a Pair* (1934), and many others. He appeared as a nearsighted pitcher in the premier short of Vitaphone's Dizzy and Daffy Dean series starring the dazzling St. Louis Cardinals pitching duo, *Dizzy and Daffy* (1934). Afterward Shemp was featured in his own starring comedies, starting with 1935's *Serves You Right*, costarring Johnnie Berkes and Lee Weber as his foils.

In 1934, Shemp also starred in three known comedy shorts for Van Beuren released by RKO Radio: *Henry the Ache*, a Bert Lahr short, and two others in which he unsuccessfully tried to lead his own "stooges" (billed as Shemp Howard and His Stooges): *The Knife of the Party* and *Everybody Likes Music*. From 1936 to 1937, he then played the role of boxing manager Knobby Walsh in seven installments of Vitaphone's short-subject series Joe Palooka, based on the popular comic strip of the same name, beginning with *For the Love of Pete*.

In 1937, after his work in Van Beuren comedies panned out, Shemp moved to the West Coast. On Thursday, October 20, 1938, he opened a combination restaurant and cocktail bar on Wilshire Boulevard in Hollywood with actor/partner Wally Vernon. The establishment, Stage One Café (which later became Andre's restaurant), regularly featured live stage acts in which Shemp and Vernon often performed and tried out new material. In 1939, syndicated newspaper columnist Mitchell Woodbury said of Howard's roughhouse comedy act that he "heads a funny show." The club also became a favorite hangout for many of Shemp's friends, including Phil Silvers, Harry James, and Huntz Hall. Shemp also took his act on the road, appearing in vaudeville shows.

Shortly after the club opened, Shemp picked up supporting roles in films and enjoyed a very successful solo career. That year, he signed a contract to costar in a string of Andy Clyde and The Glove Slingers short subjects at Columbia, directed by Stooges directors Del Lord and Jules White. Starting in 1944, he was given his own starring series. For the next three years, he starred in eight Shemp Howard two-reel comedies for Columbia, including *Open Season for Saps* (1944), *Off Again, On Again* (1945), *Where the Pests Begin* (1945), *A Hit with a Miss* (1945), *Mr. Noisy* (1946), *Jiggers, My Wife* (1946), *Society Mugs* (1946), and *Bride and Gloom* (1947). The films featured the same supporting cast as Columbia's Three Stooges comedies and were directed by White and longtime Stooges helmsman Edward Bernds.

Between 1935 and 1949, Shemp appeared as a supporting actor in forty-nine feature films, mostly for Columbia Pictures and Universal Studios but also for 20th Century-Fox, Hal Roach Studios, Monogram, Republic Pictures, and others. Under the direction of Luther Reed, his first feature film role, filmed at the Photocolor studio beginning in July 1934, was as the character Dan Higgins in First Division's *Convention Girl* (1935).

In 1940, for his outstanding performances in movies like *The Leatherpushers*, *The Bank Dick*, and *Give Us Wings*, Universal Pictures awarded Shemp a contract. He was featured prominently in many Universal film comedies and dramas thereafter, including *Buck Privates* (1941), *In the Navy* (1941), *Hold That Ghost* (1941), *Hellzapoppin'* (1941), *Tight Shoes* (1941), and *Pittsburgh* (1942), starring opposite Abbott and Costello, Olsen and Johnson, Broderick Crawford, and John Wayne. He also provided comic relief in

Charlie Chan and The Thin Man murder mysteries and several Universal B musicals, such as *Strictly in the Groove*, *How's About It?*, *Moonlight and Cactus*, and *San Antonio Rose* (paired in the latter with Lon Chaney Jr. as a "fake" Abbott and Costello). He then briefly teamed with comedian Billy Gilbert and boxer-turned-actor Maxie Rosenbloom for three B-comedy features for Monogram in 1944 and 1945, including *Three of a Kind*, *Crazy Knights*, and *Trouble Chasers*.

When times were good, Shemp and his wife Gertrude's greatest pleasure was entertaining actor friends in the movie community. The Howards' parties at their North Hollywood homes at 4604 Placidia Avenue and 10522 Riverside Drive (their last residence) included such guests as Morey Amsterdam, Phil Silvers, Harry Silvers (Phil Silvers's brother and manager), Huntz Hall, Gabe Dell, Martha Raye, and Murray Alper. On rare occasions, brothers Moe and Curly would drop by with their wives, but when things went sour work-wise, some of Shemp's friends were known to abandon ship. Clarice Seiden, Moe Howard's sister-in-law,

One of Moe's favorite photos of the Stooges with Shemp.
© *Columbia Pictures, courtesy of Moe Howard Collection*

recalled, "I remember when Shemp's contract was not renewed with Universal—the partygoers that were always at his house disappeared. When his contract was renewed everyone would come back."

Whatever the situation, no matter how unnerving, Shemp was always a warm, caring, understanding man, though a bit of an introvert at times. Once he was at ease with people, Shemp opened up and the jokes and humorous anecdotes poured forth. Shemp loved to tell stories, some of them pretty earthy. "His manner of telling them was funny," director Edward Bernds remembered. "They were not jokes, but experiences . . . stage stories."

Norman Maurer, who first met Shemp in 1945, remembered the comedian as always being jovial and never without a kind word. Maurer recalled, "Shemp was a delightful man. He was the funniest of the three brothers . . . he was a riot. He would just open his mouth and he was funny."

Dolly Sallin, daughter of Jack Howard, remembered Shemp as informal and casual. She said, "Shemp was really a quiet family man who had evening get-togethers where friends would drop in. He was quite devoted to his wife and son. Moe was the one who kept up on world affairs and kept his mind active, while Shemp simply didn't care. He wanted things to be easy and uncomplicated." Friends also revealed that Shemp was not a businessman and spent most of his time sitting at home listening to his favorite radio show or, in his later years, watching television.

Shemp also shared many intimate moments with his son, Mort, who was an only child and bore more resemblance to his mother than to Shemp. Irma Leveton, a friend of Moe's wife, Helen, remembered that Shemp liked to go fishing with Mort. Dolly Sallin added that Shemp and Mort used to produce their own tape-recorded music on a reel-to-reel recorder Shemp owned.

Shemp also had his share of phobias that he was never able to outgrow—a fear of heights, a fear of driving or being driven in a car, and a fear of water. Moe told of the time that Shemp insisted he was getting seasick . . . just standing on the dock fishing. Because of Shemp's fears, the Stooges always traveled by train whenever they went across country on personal appearance tours; it was impossible to get him on an airplane. Irma Leveton recalled that Shemp also had a fear of dogs, even though he had a dog of his own, a collie named Wags. As Leveton said, "He used to walk

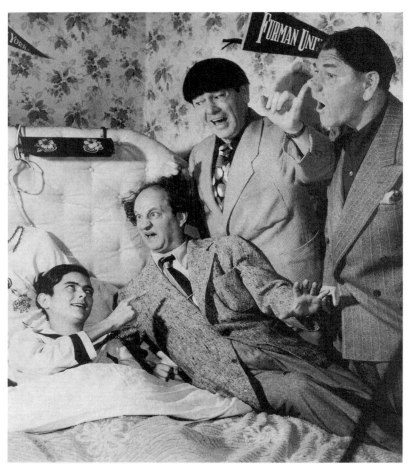

Moe, Larry, and Shemp cheer up a hospital patient the only way they know how.
*Courtesy of Moe Howard Collection*

down the street with a stick in his hand to protect himself. If a dog ever came near him, he would have fainted. There was no way he would ever hit a dog. He couldn't kill a fly. It's hard to imagine that a man with a face like that—he looked like a killer—was really a gentle man." Norman Maurer also remembered Shemp's gentleness, calling him "the world's greatest environmentalist. He couldn't step on an ant."

Emil Sitka, who worked with Shemp in many comedies, remembered his fear on the set of *Hold That Lion!* (1947). "We had a lion in this film who was so sickly he would fall asleep in the middle of a take. When Shemp heard that there was a lion on the set, he was really panicked. I thought he was kidding, but he wasn't. When he finally shot the scene, the technicians had to put a glass plate between the lion and Shemp . . . he was that scared."

Another anecdote concerning Shemp's phobias comes from the filming of *Africa Screams*, a 1949 romp for Nassour Studios featuring Shemp and star-

ring Abbott and Costello. In it was Joe Besser, Shemp's good personal friend who later replaced him as the third Stooge. Charles Barton directed the epic and remembered that Shemp's fear of heights and water seemed funny to everyone but Shemp: "I remember when we did *Africa Screams* together, there were some funny scenes between Joe Besser and Shemp Howard where they were sitting on a raft floating down a river, and Shemp was beside himself with fear and refused to get on the raft, even though the water wasn't up to his knees. I had to literally carry him onto the raft. When it started moving, he was so afraid of falling off, he kept clutching at Joe Besser's shirt. This brought on a lot of teasing from the cast and crew. After the scene, they left him sitting on the raft as a gag. And he kept yelling, 'Will someone get me down from here? How much longer do I have to stay here? I'm getting seasick!' Everybody just laughed."

Besser recalled another incident during production on *Africa Screams* that illustrated the comedian's inborn fear: "Every night Shemp would wait outside the studio for a cab. One time I stopped to give him a lift. He seemed nervous and didn't want to go with me. Finally, I convinced him to get in the car, but he couldn't relax. In desperation, I took his hands and made him hold them as if he was holding an imaginary steering wheel, hoping that would help. He seemed more at ease, but when I took off down the street, he started madly turning his hands back and forth as if he were actually driving the car!"

Shemp loved spectator sports, the more aggressive the better. It was probably a form of release for his fear and tension. He also filled his leisure time with fishing, attending the fights in addition to watching them on television, listening to Cole Porter's music, and playing cards with his inner circle of friends at his Toluca Lake home. As close friend and famed Dead End Kid and Bowery Boys member Huntz Hall remembered, "Shemp was a sweetheart until you got him into a serious card game. Then he was all

Shemp readies himself to jump over the candlestick in *Fiddlers Three* (1948).
© *Columbia Pictures, courtesy of Moe Howard Collection*

Winston, and Silverberg to his North Hollywood home. He was laughing and telling jokes as he lit up a Havana cigar. Then, suddenly, he slumped over into Winston's lap, burning Al with the stogie. They rushed him to St. Joseph's Hospital in Burbank, but he was dead on arrival. On November 24, 1955, he was buried at Home of Peace Cemetery in East Los Angeles, the same cemetery where his brother Curly was laid to rest.

Shemp and Gertrude's only son, Mort, died of cancer on January 13, 1972, at the age of forty-four. Gertrude, who was married to Shemp for thirty years, outlived them both. She died in May 1982 at age seventy-seven.

Shemp's mother had always wished her son to be a gentleman . . . and according to everyone who knew him, he certainly was a *gentle* man!

business. If Shemp didn't like your play at pinochle, he'd kick you under the table—hard! He was ruthless that way; it didn't matter if you were a friend or not. But he also had this manner about him, like no other actor. Shemp was naturally funny. I remember one morning, we were changing into our wardrobe and I noticed a huge, ugly carbuncle on Shemp's leg. I said, 'Shemp! You should see a doctor and have that thing removed.' He just shrugged and said, 'Nah, it holds up my socks.'"

Richard Arlen, Andy Devine, and Horace Mac-Mahon were Shemp's favorite actors; Patsy Kelly was his favorite actress and Fred Allen, his choice for radio comedian. His favorite Three Stooges comedy was the first one he made with the group, *Fright Night* (1947)—which, coincidentally, dealt with boxing.

On the evening of November 22, 1955, Shemp was out with friends Al Winston and Bobby Silverberg to attend his favorite sporting event: boxing at the Hollywood Legion Stadium. He had reason to celebrate; that day, Columbia had officially announced that they had signed the Stooges to a new one-year contract to star in eight new two-reelers. After the fights were over, Shemp hailed a taxicab to take him,

Larry and Moe in one of the last photographs with Shemp, taken in front of the Edgewater Gulf Motel in Edgewater Park, Mississippi, during a stop on a personal appearance tour.
*Courtesy of Jeff Lenburg Collection*

AUGUST 12, 1907–MARCH 1, 1988

# JOE BESSER

*Courtesy of Joe Besser*

*J*oe Besser, who replaced Shemp Howard as the third Stooge in 1956, caught the attention of theatergoers with his impish grin and childlike demeanor. He was certainly a comedian in his own right.

Joe's stooging began when he was a youngster growing up in St. Louis, Missouri, where he was born on August 12, 1907, to Fanny and Morris Besser. His parents were orthodox Jews from Poland. They were married in England, where Morris worked as a baker, before immigrating to the United States in 1895. Joe became the ninth child (two of his siblings died before his birth) in a family consisting of seven daughters—Rose, Esther, Molly, Lilly, Gertrude, Florence, and Henrietta—and an older brother, Manny, who entered show business as a comedian whose speciality was using a Jewish dialect as part of his act.

Joe became enthralled with magic and show business at an early age, and his parents encouraged him. They might have thought twice had they known their son would spend more time watching vaudeville matinees than attending Glascoe Elementary School. Besser once remarked, "I learned more in the theater than I did in school."

Joe Besser at age five. *Courtesy of Joe Besser*

Joe was a very independent and enterprising young man. He worked as a Western Union delivery boy, a song-plugger for a sheet music store called Waterson, Berlin & Snyder, and a distributor of handbills for the Fox Theatre Circuit in St. Louis. By age thirteen Joe had decided to become a professional magician. His favorite magician, Thurston Howard, appeared in St. Louis annually. Whenever Thurston was in town, Joe eagerly went backstage to ask the world-renowned magician if he could join his act. Each time Thurston replied, "When you get a little bit older, we'll talk about it." Thurston gave Besser the same answer for five years!

Finally, in 1920, the night Thurston's act closed in St. Louis, Joe watched avidly as the stagehands loaded all the scenery and trunks into a nearby freight train. Besser remembered, "I was so anxious to join his act that I stowed away that night on the train with Thurston's act on board, heading for Michigan. The following morning as the train pulled into Detroit, Thurston and his manager found me fast asleep on top of the lion's cage. They wired my folks to tell them where I was, and from that day on I was part of the act." Onstage, Joe would comically foil Thurston's feats of legerdemain. He would tiptoe in from the audience and reach into Thurston's coat pocket, yanking out trick flowers and other magic-shop props.

In 1923, once Besser discovered that comedy was his forte, he decided to leave Thurston and went on to serve as magician's assistant to Madame Herrmann; six months later he became prop assistant to Queenie DeNeenen, a circus tightrope performer. Eventually, Joe teamed with several vaudeville acts, including the popular comedy team Alexandria and Olsen, which costarred John Olsen, the brother of Chic from the comedy team of Olsen and Johnson.

Joe's career was quickly finding a direction; his current pursuit, in 1928, was that of a solo comedian. While on tour, he was introduced to an Allan K. Foster dancer, Erna Dora Kretschmer, who shortened her name to Erna Kay and then was nicknamed Ernie. They courted for four years and were married on November 18, 1932. During their courtship, Ernie served as a choreographer on the 1929 Paramount film *The Cocoanuts*, featuring the Marx Brothers.

In 1930, Joe toured the Keith Circuit with a new act containing two hilarious skits, "Wild Cat

Joe after leaving the popular comedy team Alexandria and Olsen in 1928.
*Courtesy of Joe Besser*

Joe toured England as a solo act. Accompanied by Royce, he played many of the same locations the Stooges later would and for two weeks was booked at London's Palladium Theatre, where he was enthusiastically received and held over for three more weeks. Then, two years later, Besser took Columbia Pictures contractee Jimmy Little on tour as his straight man. These acts were billed not jointly but as "Joe Besser with An Added Attraction." Soon Besser became a headliner on the Orpheum, RKO, Paramount, and Loews theater circuits. He also appeared on the Broadway stage in two Shubert brothers revues, *The Passing Show of 1932* and *The Greenwich Village Follies*. (In 1946, Besser returned to Broadway in *If the Shoe Fits*, a Cinderella story.)

Joe displaying two favorite props from his act with his straight man Sam Critcherson in the 1930s.
*Courtesy of Joe Besser*

Duggan" and "Spanish Omelet." Sam Critcherson (known onstage as Dick Dana) signed as Joe's first professional straight man. By 1938, however, Besser broke in a new act with nightclub singer Lee Royce, who sang a baritone rendition of "Ol' Man River." That same year, a full year before the Stooges' (Moe, Larry, and Curly's) famous tour of the British Isles,

Joe's portrayal of an exasperated, whining child earned him a spot in Olsen and Johnson's long-running Broadway show *Sons of Fun* and a chance to spring his act on audiences everywhere. In times of mass confusion, his retort was a simple wave of his hand and a sputtering assault of such catchphrases as "Not so fast!" and "You crazy you!" He was occasionally booked to bolster Fatty Arbuckle's personal appearance tours (Arbuckle, before his untimely death, entertained thoughts of starring Besser as his younger brother in a series of comedy shorts), but *Sons of Fun* was the biggest break of Joe's career.

It was Columbia producer Irving Briskin and director Charles Barton who, upon seeing Besser during *Sons of Fun*, urged the studio to sign him. Barton recalled his initial reaction to Besser's antics: "I had never seen anything so wild in my whole life. Irving's and my reactions were 'Get the little guy . . . get him . . .' because he was so cute."

Columbia Pictures signed Besser to an exclusive contract and cast him in features and comedy two-reelers. He made his screen debut in a 1938 All-Star Comedy short for Columbia, *Cuckoorancho*. His credits at Columbia included three starring features, *Hey, Rookie* (1944) with Ann Miller and Larry Parks, and *Eadie Was a Lady* (1945) and *Talk About a Lady* (1946) with Jinx Falkenburg.

Slowly Besser made his climb to stardom. Soon radio comedians like Jack Benny, Fred Allen, Eddie Cantor, and Milton Berle were all clamoring to have him on their shows. Besser made frequent appear-

ances on *The Jack Benny Show*, *The Fred Allen Show*, *The Eddie Cantor Show*, *Tonight on Broadway* (a summer replacement show in 1946), and *The Vaughan Monroe Show*. From 1945 to 1949 he appeared as the delirious character Mr. Know It All on *Let Yourself Go*, starring Milton Berle.

Besser's television debut came on the Standard Brands variety series *Hour Glass*, the first live, hour-long entertainment series of any kind produced for network television. It premiered on NBC on May 9, 1946. Besser stole the opening of the broadcast with his hilarious military sketch "The Rookie."

In 1949, Joe starred in his second short for Columbia Pictures' All-Star Comedy series, *Waiting in the Lurch*. A year later, the studio cast him in his own series of two-reel comedies, which proved popular with theater exhibitors and lasted through 1955. The first film in the series was *Dizzy Yardbird* (1950), followed in succession by *Fraidy Cat* (1951), *Aim, Fire, Scoot* (1952), *Caught on the Bounce* (1952), *Spies and Guys* (1953), *The Fire Chaser* (1954), *G.I. Dood It* (1955), *Hook a Crook* (1955), and *Army Daze* (1956). Each was directed by Jules White, who helmed most of Columbia's Three Stooges comedy-short series, and they were written by Stooges screenwriters Elwood Ullman, Felix Adler, and Jack White (Jules White's brother).

Besser's series straight man was an outrageously funny thirty-one-year-old bespectacled radio disc jockey and comic actor, Jim Hawthorne, who came to fame in 1947 on Pasadena, California, radio station KXLA (now KRLA). He went on to produce and narrate a set of television blackouts (a series of short gags and comedy bits) called *Jim Hawthorne's Funnyworld* and remained a popular fixture on radio in Los Angeles and Denver. Hawthorne, who died in 2007, had nothing but high praise when speaking of Besser. He credited Joe with helping him develop into a comedian: "I believe Joe gave of his talents what others would jealously guard. I felt the relationship was short-lived, but a fascinating one for me, with fond memories. I think Joe and I might have developed into a good comedy team which could have replaced the Stooges. The comedies were really fun to make, and he was so good in them."

Jules White also believed Besser and Hawthorne were a natural combination. "Joe was the little boy with the temper who clenches his fist, threatens, backs

Joe with straight man Jimmy Little as they appeared in Joe's second starring feature for Columbia Pictures, *Eadie Was a Lady*, in 1945.

away, runs, and never really wants to fight you. That was Joe's character," White explained. "This fellow Hawthorne was a good foil for Joe. He was a comic straight man. They were two dummies, each telling the other how dumb they are and neither believing each other. This was a good combination."

Behind the scenes, Joe got along with everybody on the set. Such directors as Jules White and Charles Barton have said that Besser didn't make demands as to how his character should be played. "Joe was a real gentleman," Jules White said in an interview. "He had good ideas for his character. But if I asked him to do something that wasn't quite right, although he wasn't happy at first, he'd never let

Joe Besser pictured with his offscreen friend Lou Costello on the set of *Little Giant* (1946). © *Universal Pictures, courtesy of Joe Besser*

me down once we talked things out." Contrary to White's interpretation of events, Joe had the highest respect for White and viewed it as all part of the creative process in being true to his character and style of comedy.

Joe didn't do much socializing after or during working hours. He got strictly down to business when it came to performing. Seldom did Besser take the initiative in starting up new friendships. He just went to the studio, did his job, and returned home to the quiet life.

From the late 1940s through the early 1950s, television producers also clamored for Besser, casting him in a series of programs. They included Jim Backus's *Hollywood House* (NBC, 1949); four episodes of *The Ken Murray Show* (CBS, 1950); *The Private Eyes* (1950), an unaired pilot teaming Joe with Sheldon Leonard; *The Colgate Comedy Hour* (NBC, 1951); *The Alan Young Show* (CBS, 1951); *Front Page Detective* (DuMont Network, 1951); and *Gang Busters* (NBC, 1952).

In 1952 Joe made famous his malevolent, bratty character Stinky (whose full name was Stinky Davis). After Joe originated the character a year earlier on *The Alan Young Show*, Stinky became as a series regular on *The Abbott and Costello Show*. He appeared in twelve episodes altogether, including "The Drugstore,"

"The Birthday Party," "The Vacuum Cleaner Salesman," "The Army Story," "The Charity Bazaar," "The Haunted Castle," and "Peace and Quiet."

Thereafter, Joe continued to wow audiences on such television programs as *I Married Joan* (NBC, 1953, two episodes); *Meet Mr. McNutley*, retitled *The Ray Milland Show* (CBS, 1953–54), produced by his old friend, director Charles Barton; the syndicated detective series *The Lone Wolf* (1954); *The Spike Jones Show* (NBC, 1954); *Mr. District Attorney* (ABC, 1954); *Private Secretary* (CBS, 1954); and Alan Young's *Saturday Night Revue* (NBC, 1954). In May 1954, Joe also made the first of eight appearances—three alone that year—on *The Jack Benny Show* (CBS). He would guest star again in two episodes in 1956, one in 1958, and two others in 1961, including his most memorable episode, "Tennessee Ernie Ford Show."

In the mid-1950s, Joe was called upon to guest star in numerous other programs, including *My Favorite Story* (as a small-town mayor in "No Tears"); *The Millionaire* (CBS, 1955), in the episode "Harvey Blake," directed by Stooges director Edward Bernds; the Desilu sitcom *Wily* (CBS, 1955); *My Little Margie* (CBS, 1955) in "Vern's Butterflies"; *The Damon Runyon Theatre* (CBS, 1955), in "The Mink Doll"; *The Gene Autry Show* (CBS, 1955), as a railroad conductor in "The

Million Dollar Fiddle"; *December Bride* (CBS, 1955); *The Martha Raye Show* (NBC, 1955); and episodes of *The Eddie Cantor Comedy Theatre* (first-run syndication, 1955–56). In early 1955, Joe also appeared as a club manager in an unsold color television pilot for a half-hour musical sitcom starring singer Mel Tormé, *Everything Happens to Mel.*

Throughout the 1950s, Joe's unique talents were utilized in both dramatic and comedy features, including *Joe Palooka Meets Humphrey* (1950); *Outside the Wall* (1950); *The Desert Hawk* (1950), in which he was teamed with Jackie Gleason; *I, the Jury* (1953); *Sins of Jezebel* (1953); *Abbott and Costello Meet the Keystone Kops* (1955); *Headline Hunters* (1955); *Mad at the World* (1955); *Two-Gun Lady* (1956); and *The Helen Morgan Story* (1957). In 1953, he also narrated the 3-D featurette *A Day in the Country* for Lippert Pictures.

Joe continued making his own comedy shorts for Columbia until joining The Three Stooges in 1956. While he didn't see partners Moe and Larry offscreen, Joe had nothing but fond memories of his association with them. Besser recalled, "Moe and Larry were great. We had a lot of fun and I had no problems with them. I knew them when they were with Ted Healy. So we all went back some years together. After the Healy days, I continued to follow their careers. I'm glad I did join the Stooges and I have never regretted it."

Besser left the Stooges in 1958 when his wife became ill. He went on to star in feature films for 20th Century-Fox, such as *Say One for Me* (1959) with Bing Crosby; *The Rookie*, starring the short-lived comedy team Noonan and Marshall; *The Story of Page One* (1959); *Let's Make Love* (1960) with Marilyn Monroe; and *Hand of Death* (1962). He also worked with comedian Jerry Lewis on two comedies during this period, as a gag writer on *Cinderfella* (1960) and in a cameo appearance in *The Errand Boy* (1961), both for Paramount.

Meanwhile, Joe served up laughs on many other prime-time television favorites of the early 1960s. His appearances included Spike Jones's *Club Oasis* (NBC, 1958), as a singing telegram boy in the episode "Forgetfulness"; Don Fedderson Productions' *The Betty White Show* (ABC, 1958); *The Kraft Music Hall* (NBC, 1959), twice with Milton Berle; *The TV Guide Awards Show* (NBC, 1960) with Fred MacMurray and Nanette Fabray; *Angel* (CBS, 1960); and *The Shirley Temple Theatre* (NBC, 1960), where he joined comics Carl Ballantine and Jerry Colonna in a rendition of the children's classic "Babes in Toyland." Likewise he delivered memorable performances as a mailman in "Kathy Delivers the Mail" on *The Danny Thomas Show* (CBS, 1960); on *My Sister Eileen* (CBS, 1960), a sitcom adaptation of the famed Broadway play and 1942 film; *Here's Hollywood* (NBC, 1961); as Samuel "Chubby" Stone on *Peter Gunn* (NBC, 1961); as Charles Bronson's fight manager in "Memory in White," costarring Sammy Davis Jr., on *General Electric Theater* (CBS, 1961), hosted by Ronald Reagan; and as the voice of the fire-breathing dragon on *The Alvin Show* (CBS, 1962). Joe also appeared in an unsold pilot for the syndicated instructional series *Better Bowling* (1960).

Joe's popularity, however, soared to new heights after he became a regular on the revamped sitcom *The Joey Bishop Show* for three seasons (fifty-four episodes from 1962 to 1965), as the ever-cheerful apartment superintendent Mr. Jillson.

After Besser's memorable association with the Bishop show ended, he was continually called upon to grace the small screen in cameo roles: on *Batman* (ABC, 1966), in "His Honor the Penguin"; *The Hollywood Palace* (ABC, 1967–68), twice with Milton Berle; *The Danny Thomas Hour*, in "It's Greek to Me" (NBC, 1967); *The Mothers-in-Law* (NBC, 1968), in "How to Manage a Rock Group," "The First Anniversary Is the Hardest," and "Two on the Aisle"; *That's Life* (ABC, 1968); *That Girl* (ABC, 1968), in "Eleven Angry Men and That Girl"; *The Don Rickles Show* (ABC, 1968); and *The Jerry Lewis Show* (NBC, 1969), on which he appeared three times. In 1965 Joe also provided his voice for the unsold cartoon pilot *The Marx Brothers* for Filmation Studios, in which Groucho Marx was to appear in live action as a narrator and commentator. A year later, he also appeared in a television commercial for Caesar's Palace in Las Vegas. Then, in 1967, he was cast as a regular—one of the "Son-of-a-Gun Players"—on comedian Joey Bishop's late-night talk show (titled, like his sitcom, *The Joey Bishop Show*), which was cohosted by Regis Philbin for ABC.

Joe also evoked laughs in *My World and Welcome to It* (NBC, 1969), in "The Night the House Caught Fire"; *The Good Guys* (CBS, 1969), in two episodes, "Win, Place and Kill" and "No Orchids for the Diner"; *The Bold Ones: The Protectors* (NBC, 1969),

Joe with his first love, children, in scenes from the *Joey Bishop Show* episode "The Baby's First Christmas."
© *NBC, courtesy of Joe Besser*

with Leslie Nielsen; the ABC Sunday Night Movie *The Monk* (ABC, 1969); and the unaired special *Burlesque Is Alive and Living in Burbank* (NBC, 1969). He also turned in funny performances on the special *Bing Crosby's Christmas Show* (NBC, 1970); in four appearances on *Love American Style* (ABC, 1970–71), his funniest being as a toupee salesman in "Love and the Lady Barber" (1971), with his customer Frank Sutton of *Gomer Pyle, U.S.M.C.* fame; in OFF! insect repellent and Scope mouthwash commercials in 1971; and in *Arnie* (CBS, 1972).

Joe's final feature film appearances were in a low-budget horror movie from Congdon Films, *Savage Intruder* (1969), and his third and final film with Jerry Lewis, *Which Way to the Front?* (1970) for Warner Bros.

In the 1970s and 1980s, Joe enjoyed tremendous success while doing cartoon voices as a regular in four series: *The Houndcats* (NBC, 1972–73), as the character, Puttypuss; *Jeannie* (CBS, 1973–75), as the bumbling apprentice genie, Babu; *Scooby's All-Star Laff-a-Lympics* (1977–79), reprising his Babu role as a member of the Scooby Doobies; and his last series, *Yogi's Space Race* (1978–79), as the voice of Scarebear

(spelled as one word in the series' scripts and two words—Scare Bear—in character model sheets) in the segments "Yogi's Space Race" and "The Galaxy Goof-Ups." Joe likewise supplied his voice in one-shot episodes of *Where's Huddles?* (CBS, 1970); *The New Scooby-Doo Movies* (ABC, 1973), as Babu in the episode, "Mystery in Persia"; *The Oddball Couple* (NBC, 1975); *The Pink Panther Laugh and a Half Hour and a Half Show* (NBC, 1976); *Baggy Pants & the Nitwits* (NBC, 1977); *The Thing* (NBC, 1979); and *The Shirt Tales* (NBC, 1982). His last voice role was as Cupid in Hanna-Barbera's highly rated prime-time Valentine's Day special *My Smurfy Valentine* (NBC, 1983).

One of Joe's favorite activities in his spare time was building toys for neighborhood children and gardening with his wife, Ernie. He was also a camera buff. His favorite comedians were Jack Benny and Abbott and Costello, and Ann Miller was his choice for favorite actress. Joe never saw all of his Stooges comedies, but his favorite was *Flying Saucer Daffy* (1958). His fans prefer *Hoofs and Goofs* (1957) and *A Merry Mix-Up* (1957).

The character that Joe's voice made famous: Babu, from Hanna-Barbera's *Jeannie*.
© *Hanna-Barbera Productions, courtesy of Jeff Lenburg Collection*

In 1984 Joe penned his autobiography with Jeff and Greg Lenburg. The volume, titled *Not Just a Stooge* (Excelsior Books), chronicled his prolific sixty-year comedy career in vaudeville, on radio, in motion pictures, on television, and as a third Stooge. The book generated tremendous interest, with the famed comic conducting numerous radio, television, and print interviews. Four years later, the book was updated and republished posthumously under the new title *Once a Stooge, Always a Stooge* (Roundtable Publishing).

On March 1, 1988, Joe Besser's life ended sadly. He was found dead of heart failure in his North Hollywood home. Fourteen months later, his wife, Ernie, succumbed to septic shock on July 1, 1989, at the Motion Picture and Television Hospital in Woodland Hills. She was eighty-nine. Both are buried in the same plot in Glendale's Forest Lawn Memorial Park Cemetery.

Admittedly, the one element that kept Joe going in later years was knowing that fans still loved him. "I love working for kids," he beamed. "They are my best fans, my best audience, and my best friends. My biggest thrill is having kids like me. As long as this happens, I've got it made."

Joe with his wife, Ernie, in 1980.

Joe as he appeared in the 1980s.

Joe stooging around at the December 1984 Beverly Hills book signing for his autobiography, *Not Just a Stooge*.

JULY 12, 1909–JULY 3, 1993

# JOE DeRITA

The youngest member of The Three Stooges, Joseph DeRita—whose real name was Joseph Wardell—was born July 12, 1909, in Philadelphia, Pennsylvania. Of French Canadian and English ancestry, he was the only one of the Stooges who came from a show business family. His mother, Florenz DeRita, was a dancer (known in vaudeville as The Girl in the Moon), and his father, Frank Wardell, was a stage technician.

Joe's mother worked in vaudeville and traveled the country, so Joe just happened to be born in Philadelphia. He once stated he was "not a native of anywhere, I've never been in one spot long enough." From age seven, Joe accompanied his parents on tour, going with them from theater to theater across the country. He made his stage debut with his sister Phillis at a Topeka, Kansas, Red Cross benefit during World War I. Joe remembered this act: "We did an aesthetic dance. I had a wreath around my head and a toga and gave her a rose . . . that kind of stuff. I was quite small in those days. Of course, they called me Junior.

"We had a small-time act; we never played any major circuits. In those days there were the Western Vaudeville Circuit, the Bert Levy Vaudeville Circuit, and the junior Orpheum Circuit which the smaller acts played."

Joe, sister Phillis (left) and mother, Florenz, (right) in the act DeRita Sisters and Junior. *Courtesy of Joe DeRita*

Joe as a dancer at age eight.
*Courtesy of Joe DeRita*

Then, for seven seasons, Joe played the title role in a stage version of *Peck's Bad Boy* with his mother and father. In 1927, at age eighteen, with his mother retired and his sister married, Joe decided to do a comedy single in which he sang and danced. As DeRita recalled, "I originally started out as a dancer because my mother was a dancer. Then I went into burlesque in 1921 because vaudeville was just about gone. At least my type of vaudeville was gone. I never worked too risqué."

Playing in tabloid shows on the Gus Sun Circuit and tent shows in Kansas and Nebraska, Joe worked in burlesque with Bud Abbott when he was straight man before his teaming with Lou Costello, and, in 1928, with the late, great Red Skelton. He would continue to play the New Columbia Burlesque Circuit until 1942. As a young comic, Joe met his first wife, a chorus girl from Reading, Pennsylvania, who went by Bonnie Brooks (her real name was Esther M. Hartenstine). On July 13, 1935, as he was beginning a thirty-week run at the Roxy Theater in Cleveland,

Joe and Bonnie were married by a justice of the peace in Cuyahoga County, Ohio.

In 1942, because of his friendship with Bud Abbott, Joe went to California to appear in a nightly midnight wartime revue that Abbott's brother, Harry, had asked Bud to bankroll; but it didn't work out like Joe had hoped. Instead Joe headlined a show at the Music Box Theatre in Hollywood. Even so, he enjoyed a close friendship with Abbott during Abbott and Costello's gravy years as top film stars for Universal Pictures and beyond. "I used to go to his house every Sunday and sit around, play poker, have lunch. They were making so much money in those days, he just wanted people around him," Joe stated.

After arriving in Hollywood, Joe was cast to play a meek man in the 1943 Warner Bros. musical comedy *Thank Your Lucky Stars*, but his scenes ended up on the cutting room floor. His notices for his Music Box Theatre show were so good, however, that MGM signed him to a contract—but, ironically, he never made a picture for them. His actual film debut was in the Warner Bros. feature *The Dough-girls* (1944) with Ann Sheridan, Jack Carson, Jane Wyman, and others; he played "a fellow looking for a room." In this same period he made four other feature films, *The Sailor Takes a Wife* (1945) for MGM; the Paramount film *People Are Funny* (1946), costarring Rudy Vallee and Ozzie Nelson; and *The French Key* (1946) and *High School Hero* (1946), both Republic films.

During World War II, Joe performed in shows at various service camps for the Hollywood Victory Committee, providing entertainment for soldiers. In 1943, he started working for the USO and toured the South Pacific with a good friend, actor Randolph Scott, as his straight man. They entertained servicemen stationed at Nouméa, Guadalcanal, Munda, and Bougainville. He went on several tours overseas as well, to bring cheer to American servicemen in England and France, this time with Bing Crosby as his straight man.

Between tours, Joe appeared on radio for thirteen weeks on NBC's *The Fred Brady Show*, the summer 1943 replacement for *The Bob Burns Show*. Then he worked on *The Burns and Allen Show*, performing a comedy bit each week. He nearly became a regular on the program, but his character was dropped, for reasons unknown, when the series resumed after the death of President Franklin Roosevelt in April 1945. He also did guest spots on the national radio shows of crooner Andy Russell and Big Band singer/actress Ginny Simms, who costarred in movies in the 1940s with Edgar Bergen and Charlie McCarthy, Abbott and Costello, Fibber McGee and Molly, and others.

After the USO tour with Crosby ended, Joe played the Hollywood Casino in Los Angeles, and made guest appearances with Crosby on two radio programs. The first was on the *Philco Radio Hall of Fame*, for the December 24, 1944, Christmas Eve

Joe as he appeared in his own Columbia short-subject series in the 1940s.
© *Columbia Pictures, courtesy of Joe DeRita*

broadcast of "The Happy Prince," with Orson Welles. The other was a re-creation of Joe's USO tour, "The Road to Berlin," on the February 5, 1945, broadcast of the long-running NBC anthology drama series *Cavalcade of America*.

In 1946, director Jules White hired Joe to star in a series of two-reel comedies for Columbia. His first, *Slappily Married*, was for the studio's All-Star Comedy series. The three others were the Joe DeRita series comedies *The Good Bad Egg* (1947), *Wedlock Deadlock* (1947), and *Jitter Bughouse* (1948).

Regarding his Columbia shorts series, DeRita said, "My comedy in those scripts was limited to getting hit on the head with something, then going over to my screen wife to say, 'Honey, don't leave me!' For this kind of comedy material, you could have gotten a bus boy to do it and it would have been just as funny."

Next, Joe appeared as a bartender in his sixth feature film, the Randolph Scott western *Coroner Creek* (1948), also for Columbia. But when his Bonnie became ill, Joe went back to work in burlesque again. Starting in 1950, he starred in the Minsky burlesque tour, working at the Rialto Theatre in Chicago and at the Dunes Hotel in Las Vegas for the next eight years. He was also featured with other burlesque acts on a risqué LP for Cook Records entitled *Burlesque Uncensored* (1950).

Meanwhile, Joe made guest appearances in episodes of such popular network television programs as Don McNeil's *TV Club* (1951), an ABC prime-time musical/interview/comedy/audience-participation show from Chicago, in the January 24 broadcast with actress Joan Blondell; and *I Married Joan* (1952). He did small roles on three others, all from 1958: *This Is Alice*, the short-lived first-run syndicated sitcom

Joe with Larry and Moe during a lighter moment on the set of *Have Rocket--Will Travel* (1959).
*Courtesy of Moe Howard Collection*

for National Telefilm Associates and Desilu Productions starring child actress Patty Ann Gerrity; CBS's *Westinghouse Desilu Playhouse*, as a man at the bar in Rod Serling's "The Time Element"; and the same network's *Bachelor Father*, as the character Arthur Fletcher in "Bentley's Big Case," with John Forsythe. Before joining the Stooges in late 1958, Joe had a major role as the bearded hangman in director Henry King's widescreen CinemaScope western *The Bravados*, filmed in Mexico for 20th Century-Fox; it starred Gregory Peck and Joan Collins.

Joe with Moe and Larry backstage following a 1960 Philadelphia nightclub appearance. *Courtesy of Joe DeRita*

In 1958, Joe wound up his Minsky tour with one of the most successful burlesque revues of his career, *Minsky's Follies of 1958* on the Las Vegas Strip, in two sketches, "Judge Montfort Rides Again" and "Woman Haters Club." (A live recording of the show was released that year on Rondo Records.) On the same bill was Lou Costello, a year after his split from Abbott, and longtime Abbott and Costello foil Sid Fields as Costello's new straight man; the two performed their classic routines. But it was DeRita's performance in the revue that left a lasting impression on Larry Fine, who took in the show while vacationing with his wife and recommended to Moe that they immediately sign DeRita as the new third Stooge after Joe Besser's departure.

Up to this point, Joe DeRita's name was far from a household word. It would be his twelve-year association with The Three Stooges as Curly-Joe that catapulted him to stardom. As Norman Maurer, who served as the Stooges' manager and wrote, produced, and directed many of their later feature-length films, explained, "He was the best Curly replacement the Stooges ever had. Joe was great on ad-libs. He would give a little extra [in his scenes]. We never used to cut with him. You finished the scene and let the camera roll. He was like Curly in several respects, with his weight and his ballet-like grace despite his weight. Joe could do a little shuffle—not quite like Curly—but just as graceful, and it was hard to believe a guy that big was doing it."

Curly-Joe, Larry, and Moe take time out for their fans during a personal appearance tour for *The Three Stooges in Orbit* (1962).

*Courtesy of Moe Howard Collection*

On the set, however, Joe had his share of bad days. "Every now and then Joe would become temperamental, but it was a passing thing," Maurer recalled. "In most cases, Joe was a good sport and got the job done."

During his years as a Stooge, Joe recalled that he seldom saw Moe and Larry off the set. "We never socialized much, unless it was a film promotion, a premiere, or a business meeting. Moe knew judges, doctors, wealthy people—he had his circle of friends. Larry had his friends. And I knew some people out of Hollywood—friends of mine that I'm fond of, and I enjoy their company. But I don't go out of my way to meet people."

Contrary to popular belief, Curly-Joe and his predecessor, Joe Besser, met more than once. Besser remembered in an interview with authors Jeff and Greg Lenburg shortly before his death that he

Curly-Joe, Moe, and Larry raid a refreshment counter in a New York movie theater to peddle Slow Poke candy bars while on tour for *The Three Stooges Meet Hercules* (1962). *Courtesy of Moe Howard Collection*

Larry and Moe with Curly-Joe and his second wife, Jean, in Moe's home a few months after the couple's marriage in December 1966.
*Courtesy of Joe DeRita*

met DeRita briefly for the first time at Columbia Pictures when they both were starring in their own short-subject series. It wasn't until the late 1970s that they would run into each other again, while shopping at a supermarket in North Hollywood in close proximity to their Toluca Lake and North Hollywood homes. They exchanged pleasantries, complimented each other on their work, and then continued their shopping. Curly-Joe also met Curly and Shemp at various times during their careers and later admitted he enjoyed watching them in the Stooges shorts on late-night television.

During Joe's seventh year as a Stooge, on September 6, 1965, his wife, Bonnie, died. He subsequently met Jean Sullivan, who became his second wife on December 28, 1966. They resided in a modest home on Moorpark Street in North Hollywood that he originally purchased in the early 1960s from Moe, one of the Stooge leader's many real estate holdings at the time. The DeRitas sold the house in 1989 and moved to nearby Burbank.

In retirement, Joe led a rather quiet life. He spent most of his time reading and watching television,

Larry, Curly-Joe, Moe, and dog Moose enjoying a break during the filming of *Kook's Tour* (1970).
*© Norman Maurer Productions, courtesy of Moe Howard Collection*

Curly-Joe as he looked in the 1980s.

but his favorite pastime was listening to classical music. As for Joe's likes and dislikes: He considered Hollywood's three worst actors to be George Raft, Buster Crabbe, and Johnny Weissmuller. His favorite Stooges film was *The Three Stooges Go Around the World in a Daze* (1963).

On July 3, 1993, Joe DeRita died of pneumonia at the Motion Picture & Television Country House and Hospital in Woodland Hills, California, nine days shy of his eighty-fourth birthday. His remains were interred at the Valhalla Memorial Park Cemetery in North Hollywood, where the epitaph on his tombstone reads "The Last Stooge." Surviving him were his second wife, Jean, (until her death on November 22, 2004) and stepsons Earl and Robert Benjamin, now president/CEO and executive vice president/general counsel, respectively, of C3 Entertainment, the owner of all trademarks and rights to The Three Stooges.

Later in life, Curly-Joe called becoming a Stooge the best thing to ever happen to his career. "Moe and Larry were the best," he said proudly. "We worked well together and enjoyed every minute of it."

The roly-poly comic's legacy still burns bright today, leaving behind his special gift . . . the gift of laughter.

# Chapter 1

Caricatures of Ted Healy and His Gang—Shemp, Moe, and Larry.

*Courtesy of Moe Howard Collection*

# Historical Overview

For over seven decades, fans have been roaring with laughter at the wild, two-fisted, knockabout antics of The Three Stooges. Their trademark blend of slaps in the face, bops on the head, and pokes in the eye continue to fracture audiences of all ages, races, and creeds throughout the world. Although success was not easily attained, the Stooges, like wine, have improved with age.

The winning formula that catapulted the Stooges into the limelight was first conceived on a bitter cold and snowy night in late winter 1922, when Ted Healy, booked into the Brooklyn Prospect Theatre in New York as part of an eight-act vaudeville bill, ran into trouble with his German acrobatic act: they walked out before their scheduled performance because of an argument with him. Unaware of his dilemma, Ted's childhood pal Moe Howard decided to go see him at the theater. Moe, by his own account, hadn't seen Healy in ten years. The two reminisced backstage. Then Healy said, "Moe, I'm in a jam. My acrobats quit on me."

Healy asked Moe if he would take the place of one of the acrobats for the rest of the week as part of a famous stunt he did onstage called "Fire and Water"—played for laughs, of course. In this trick, Healy would put a clean-cut acrobat in a box (one of those gimmick prop boxes with an escape hatch underneath), pour water on him, and cover him up. "When I take off the cover," Healy would proclaim, "the man will be gone, and instead you'll see three beautiful dancin' girls!" He'd then fire a prop revolver into the box, there would be a big explosion—and the box would be empty. The gag got big laughs every time as Ted ran offstage.

"Remember those backflips we used to do on the island at Coney?" Healy asked Moe, smiling. "Well, that's all you have to do. A backflip and a toehold." Moe agreed. He performed in the show the next day as a volunteer out of the audience. He jumped onstage, did a bit of slapstick with Healy, then did the backflip and toehold and jumped into the box for "Fire and Water."

During their performance, Moe heard "an unmistakable laugh" emanating from the audience. It was his brother Shemp—who had also decided to come to the theater that afternoon—in another part of the audience, laughing so hard at Moe making a fool of himself. Moe whispered to Healy, "Shemp's out there."

Healy, in typical wisecracking fashion, walked out to center stage and invited Shemp, another old friend, to join them onstage. He said, "I would like to have another young man come up, preferably one from Brooklyn." Munching on a pear, Shemp sauntered up onstage with a pair of rubber overshoes stashed in his pocket, because it had been raining outside. He and Ted engaged in comic patter: Shemp offered him the pear, asking, "Want a bite?" Ted replied, "No, no, I don't want any bite." The bit culminated in Ted smashing the pear into Shemp's face. Moe, standing close by, watched Shemp get pear juice all over the silk shirt he was wearing—which happened to be his brother's! Moe got so mad, he chased after Shemp. The routine stuck and so did Shemp, who agreed to become Healy's second Stooge.

Moe and Shemp performed brilliantly that first week. One night, working with Ted on the trapeze, Moe pulled off his pants by mistake. It got such a big laugh that afterward Healy made it part of the act. After the show closed, the Howard brothers stayed on as Healy's Stooges. (In a 1963 newspaper interview, Moe was quoted as saying he and Shemp actually called themselves The Two Stooges as part of Healy's act, but no evidence has been found to support this claim.) For the next ten weeks, into 1923, the three performed together on the Delmar Circuit in the South and the Interstate Amusement Company Circuit in Texas.

In a 1947 newspaper interview in Charlotte, North Carolina, Moe confirmed that 1923 was the first full year he and Shemp performed in Healy's act: "We were here in 1923. That was the first year we worked together and we've been stuck with each other ever since."

That same year, during a play date in Indiana, Healy advertised for another Stooge to round out his original group to "three" Stooges. He hired a young man who at the time lived in nearby Fort Wayne: Kenneth Lackey. To start, Healy paid the Plymouth, Indiana, native thirty-five dollars a week plus expenses; within six months, he'd upped his salary to seventy-five dollars weekly. (Reports that Healy's original Stooges were comprised of Shemp Howard, Lou Warren, and Dick Hakins are untrue.)

Moe with fellow Stooge Kenneth Lackey in 1923, walking Healy's German shepherds. *Courtesy of Moe Howard Collection*

Healy and his Stooge trio went on to fracture their audiences with their ad-libbed routines. From theater circuit to theater circuit, the crowd's reaction was always the same: instantaneous laughter.

In July and September of 1925, Moe and Shemp wedded their respective wives, Helen and Gertrude. During their courtship, since neither woman liked the idea of them traipsing around the country with Healy, Moe and Shemp had worked out a compromise: Moe traveled for three months, then came home while Shemp played Ted's Stooge for three months. Eventually, they returned to touring together with Healy instead of switching off as Stooges.

Lackey remained in the group until the summer of 1925. From July to December of that year, he performed on Broadway in *Earl Carroll's Vanities* with Ted and his wife, Betty, minus Moe and Shemp. After the show ended, he quit Healy's act. Then, in February 1926, he returned to Plymouth for the first time after a nearly three-year absence, before touring with Carroll's *Vanities* during the latter half of the year. In 1927, Lackey would leave show business altogether and return to Indiana, where he would go on to become a US district court clerk before retiring in 1965.

In 1926, the act, with Moe and Shemp as Healy's remaining Stooges, toured vaudeville houses as "Ted Healy and His Racketeers" and "Ted Healy and His Gang." At the end of 1926, however, Moe left the act to go into business for himself and be closer to his family, as his daughter Joan was due to be born. That left Shemp as Healy's sole Stooge.

On May 3, 1927, Healy, Shemp, and a gang of funsters frolicked without Moe in the Broadway premiere of the Shuberts' musical revue *A Night in Spain*. Also appearing in the production were Betty Healy, Phil Baker, Sid Silvers, and Helen Kane. Following its opening run at New York's Forty-Fourth Street Theatre, the show moved to the Winter Garden Theatre; in all, it ran for 174 performances over six months. After its New York engagement, the Shuberts

took *A Night in Spain* on the road, where it was moderately successful.

On November 28, 1927, *A Night in Spain* opened at Chicago's Four Cohans Theatre, where it played for twenty weeks. On March 11, 1928, famous blackface comedian Al Jolson joined the cast for a four-week engagement, with the Shuberts paying him $12,500 a week for his services.

Around this time, Shemp found an opportunity to form a new act—at a much higher salary—with an old friend and vaudeville comedian, Jack Waldron. But who would replace him in Healy's act? One evening, most likely in March 1928 after Al Jolson was added to the cast, famed Chicago nightclub

Moe and Kenneth Lackey pose with a very tall cowboy during a vaudeville stop in San Antonio, Texas, in January 1924. *Courtesy of Moe Howard Collection*

owner Fred Mann threw a party honoring the revue's cast at his "million-dollar playground after dark," the Rainbo Gardens. Healy and Shemp were there that night, as was Jolson. They caught the performance of a new act on the bill, whom Mann had signed to a seven-year contract: a song-and-dance man named Larry Fine, who played the violin and did a Russian dance to the tune of "My Old Kentucky Home." As Larry later related, "I was doing a single act in Chicago when they found me."

Shemp broke the news to Healy that night, giving him two weeks' notice that he wanted to leave the show and his act. During Fine's performance, Shemp turned to Healy and suggested that Fine might make a perfect Stooge replacement. As Shemp put it, "Take him out of that tuxedo and he'd be a good Stooge. He's got the kisser for it." Ted agreed. After the show was over, they called Larry over to their table. Ted made him the offer to become a Stooge in the Shubert revue.

Larry recalled, "I was hesitant about accepting Healy's offer. I had never done comedy before and was afraid of the outcome." Healy agreed to give Larry some time to think the offer over.

(This is all contrary to the long-standing belief, reported for many years, that Larry joined the act in 1925, which is erroneous. In his autobiography and at times during his career, Moe stated that Larry was recruited that year after he, Healy, and Shemp spotted him at the mob-owned Chicago nightclub Marigold Gardens. Similarly, Larry's older brother Morris Feinberg once related that Moe and Shemp were on hand at the Rainbo Gardens nightclub when Healy asked Larry to join. The story went as follows: Healy and company were playing in Chicago when they learned that baggy-browed comedian Phil Baker was also in town with his stooges, Beetle and Bottle. This supposedly irked Healy, who said, "Nobody is bigger than Healy. If Baker has two stooges, I get three." Afterward, Healy happened to see Larry at the club with them and decided "then and there he wanted him." As Feinberg recalled, "Larry hit it off with Shemp and Moe perfectly. The zonking started from the moment they met." However, Larry was in fact still performing with the Haney Sisters through the spring of 1927, and Moe was out of show business and thus not part of Healy's act when Larry joined up. The chronology of events and evidence, such as Shubert archival records and recently discovered

handwritten notes by Moe for his autobiography, noting that Larry was added in 1928, prove as much.)

Healy invited Larry to the next Wednesday matinee performance of *A Night in Spain*. Afterward, Larry told him flat out that he didn't think he could do the show, because of his contract with Mann. But that very evening, he would change his mind. He returned to the Rainbo Gardens only to find it was closed. At the time, Prohibition was in effect, so serving alcoholic beverages was against the law; since 1927, federal agents had staged after-dark raids of hundreds of clubs. Rainbo Gardens' closure was presumably a consequence of such efforts, and as a result of its closure that night, Mann released Larry from his contract. (By early May 1928, federal authorities would shut down and padlock the Rainbo Gardens for an entire year, and by February 1929, Mann would fall into bankruptcy. Then, in early October 1930, he would commit suicide, shooting himself.)

His contract with Mann voided, Larry decided to accept Healy's offer. One evening, he hailed a taxi to take him to the Four Cohans Theatre, where Healy and Shemp were performing. Backstage, Fine dashed into the wings, where he hoped to catch Healy's attention. Larry explained what happened next: "Ted was quick-witted and sharp. The moment he saw me, he signaled to Al Jolson, who was also in the show, to push me out onstage. To my surprise, there we were, ad-libbing the entire scene together. In the excitement I actually didn't know what Healy was saying. He would talk to me out loud and then whisper in my ear what I should answer. I can't remember what happened but the audience was laughing like hell. After the show, Shemp came up to Healy and said, 'You don't need me anymore. You've got a great replacement in Larry.' And that's how I became a Stooge."

Although records do not confirm it, Larry recounted performing in three shows over three days in Chicago before Shemp left Healy's act. According to Shubert records, Larry officially replaced Shemp when *A Night in Spain* went on tour on April 16, 1928, opening for one week only at the Shubert Alvin Theatre in Pittsburgh. In a quarter-page ad published in *The Pittsburgh Press* on April 14, Shemp was still listed among the cast of performers, but he never appeared in the Pittsburgh show. Instead Healy paired Larry with comedian and song-and-dance man Bobby

Pinkus (also known as Peter James and later part of Spike Jones and His City Slickers) and fellow vaudevillian Sam Braun. Healy's three so-called stooges performed the same routines Shemp had done previously with Pinkus and Braun, including an absurdly funny burlesque singing act. After the Pittsburgh engagement, Larry toured with the show, which opened next at the Shubert Opera House in Detroit on Sunday, April 29. (Advance publicity again erroneously listed Shemp as part of the all-star cast.)

It took Fine several months to become comfortable with his new role as a Stooge and as a comedian. Thereafter, he toured with the show for a total of thirty-five weeks, playing at theaters from coast to coast, including Hartman Theatre in Stamford, Connecticut; the Curran Theatre in San Francisco; the Davidson Theatre in Milwaukee; and many others. On September 2, 1928, the production debuted at Chicago's new Majestic Theatre, marking the grand opening of the venue built by by Karl Hoblitzelle for his Interstate Amusement Company theater chain.

In 1929, Moe (then calling himself Harry Howard) and Shemp rejoined the act, after Healy invited them and Larry to team up with him to star in the Broadway revue *A Night in Venice*. The lavish revue, with twenty-five dazzling sketches, was directed and

choreographed by the legendary Busby Berkeley. Healy and his trio of Stooges—billed as Ted Healy and His Three Southern Gentlemen—won a permanent place on the bill after successful tryout engagements in New Haven, Atlantic City, and Akron. The production opened on May 21, 1929, at the Shubert Theatre in New York but was also staged at the Majestic Theatre on Broadway during its six-month run.

Postcard promoting *A Night in Venice* (1929).
*Courtesy of Moe Howard Collection*

Artist's conception of a scene from *A Night in Venice* (1929), the Shuberts' Broadway musical revue featuring Ted Healy and Shemp, Moe, and Larry. *Courtesy of Moe Howard Collection*

Healy and the Stooges' raucous style of rough-house shenanigans caught on. They played to sell-out crowds even after touring with the show to vaude-ville theaters across the country. *The New York Times* reported that Healy's hilarious trio was "three of the frowziest numbskulls ever assembled," while a *Variety* review called their performance "a riot" and another added that they "make the show." Nevertheless, with the onset of the Depression, *A Night in Venice* closed after 175 performances.

Although it lacked longevity, *A Night in Venice* turned a spotlight on Healy and his troupe, driv-

Artist's conception of a scene from *A Night in Venice* (1929), the Shuberts' Broadway musical revue featuring Ted Healy and Moe (billed as Harry), Larry, and Shemp.
*Courtesy of Moe Howard Collection*

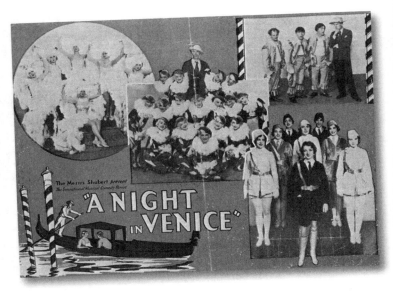

Program for *A Night in Venice*. *Courtesy of Moe Howard Collection*

New York *Daily News* photographic cartoon by Mark Hellinger of Ted Healy with Shemp, Larry, and Moe, from *A Night in Venice*.
*Courtesy of Moe Howard Collection*

ing their careers to new heights and even attracting interest from Hollywood talent scouts, who came en masse when the act was booked at New York's Palace Theatre in 1930. Fox Studios, the forerunner to 20th Century-Fox (spelled with a hyphen from 1935 to 1985), was among the film studios represented.

The Fox scout, impressed with the team's performance, immediately signed them to star in Rube Goldberg's comedy *Soup to Nuts*. Fox also signed another Palace Theatre performer, xylophone player Freddie Sanborn. Moe, Larry, Shemp, and Fred were billed in the film as Healy's "Racketeers." Lou Breslow wrote the film's screenplay from Goldberg's original story, and Benjamin Stoloff directed. (It is interesting to note that several years later, Breslow worked with the Stooges at Columbia, directing the team's second comedy, *Punch Drunks* [1934].) *Soup to Nuts* showcased the Stooges' crazy antics, casting them in several roles: as part-time firemen who aid Healy in crashing a society affair and as soldiers from the Mexican Revolution. Later, in a 1948 newspaper interview, Moe assessed his and his partners' perfor-

mances in the film this way: "The picture was so bad we couldn't even look at soup or nuts, let alone eat them, for at least a year."

While the feature was less than sensational, Fox was tremendously impressed with the Stooges, and studio executives offered Moe, Larry, and Shemp a seven-year contract to star in features. Up until then, they had answered to Healy with respect to all contracts, since their working agreement with Ted was a verbal pact of faith. Under this unusual arrangement, it was Healy and not the studio or vaudeville theater manager who paid the Stooges their weekly salaries. Ted's salary to star in *Soup to Nuts* was a third less than his usual vaudeville salary, but still lucrative enough at $1,250 per week. Out of this, Healy paid each Stooge $150 per week to star in the Fox film. Unbeknownst to them, when Healy learned of the studio's offer of an exclusive contract to the Stooges themselves, he stormed into the office of Fox's studio head, Winnie Sheehan, arguing that the contract was invalid without his approval. In a rage, Ted took the contract from Sheehan's desk and tore it to shreds.

Larry, Moe, Ted Healy, Shemp, and new addition Fred Sanborn in their first feature film for Fox, *Soup to Nuts* (1930).
*© 20th Century Fox, courtesy of Moe Howard Collection*

He then left town for New York. When the Stooges returned to Fox a week later to sign the contract, they were told the deal had been "called off."

As soon as Moe, Larry, and Shemp caught wind of Healy's latest double-dealing, they left his act to form one of their own. Within days, they had signed with Harry Stanley, an agent with the Los Angeles office of the William Morris Agency, to exclusively represent them. Stanley immediately landed them vaudeville bookings. From 1930 through 1931, they performed under the name "Howard, Fine, and Howard" and were paid $900 per engagement, split equally, far more than they had earned with Healy. In the summer of 1930, the trio performed on the West Coast. Their first booking was for two weeks, starting on August 23, 1930, at the Paramount Theatre in Los Angeles as part of a multiact Paramount stage show called *Looney Lunatics*, preceding the premiere of the Marx Brothers classic comedy *Animal Crackers*. Afterward, in September, they played engagements at the Paramount theaters, tied with the on-screen premieres of the latest Hollywood feature films, in Seattle (opposite Walter Huston's *The Bad Man*), San Francisco (with Gary Cooper's *The Spoilers*), and Portland (opposite *Follow Thru*, starring Charles Rogers and Nancy Carroll).

During the Los Angeles Paramount Theatre engagement, they originated their famous eye-poking routine. It all happened when the three of them were playing a few hands of three-handed bridge one afternoon. As Larry remembered, "I said, 'I have all the honors [four honor cards].' I had just taken a trick, the ace of spades. Shemp became mad and said, 'You did, eh?' And whack—right in the eye! He really did it, knuckle deep. I teared all day. Moe got hysterical. He laughed, and he fell over in the chair, and fell right through a French window. And the next day, he remembered it and did it again [in the show]." The routine became a staple of the act thereafter.

Watching Howard, Fine, and Howard climb the ladder of success, Ted Healy realized his act wasn't the same without them. He tried to steal first one and then all three of them back, using a number of underhanded methods, but they refused to return. In desperation, Ted held auditions at New York's Imperial Theatre—with nearly a hundred would-be stooges showing up. Out of them he hired three novice comics as *his* stooges—Paul "Mousie" Garner,

Dick Hakins, and Jack Wolf, who floundered with Healy on the vaudeville circuit in 1930.

Ted also filed legal suit against Moe, Larry, and Shemp for promoting themselves in newspaper ads as "Howard, Fine and Howard—Former associates of Ted Healy in *A Night in Venice*." Healy claimed the use of his name, combined with the Stooges' use of his comedy material in their act, was illegal. The material over which Healy filed suit consisted of skits taken from portions of the Stooge's performance in *A Night in Venice*. However, Moe Howard, always the team's manager, had secured permission from the show's producer, J. J. Shubert, to incorporate certain pieces of material from the show into their new act. The suit went to trial on September 30, 1930, and a US district court ruled in favor of Moe, Larry, and Shemp, claiming that Healy had no rights to the material.

Healy's Irish temper was slow to cool, and in frustration he resorted to constant threats in a vain attempt to stop the team from using any of "his" material. Moe, Larry, and Shemp became concerned for their own well-being and decided to change some of the material, hoping to pacify Ted. Before one engagement, working at fever pitch, they sketched out about a half dozen new routines in one evening. As Larry Fine recalled, "We worked in between the first and second show and did a complete turnabout. We worked out an old bit where we were musicians and faked a riot, breaking instruments over each others' heads and staging a fight. The audience just loved us, and so did the manager, who booked us for eight more weeks."

Even with their act revamped, Shemp continued to fear Healy. He became so concerned over what action the comedian might take next that he expressed his desire to leave the act. To entice him to stay, Moe agreed that he and Larry would raise his salary, paying him more than they themselves were making. According to Moe, Shemp took 36 percent of the team's salary, while he and Larry retained 32 percent apiece. The trio then divided, using this new formula, the lucrative salary of $900 a week.

Shemp must have had a sixth sense about Healy, who, continuing with his threats, warned them to quit using their comedy material or he would actually sabotage one of their engagements with a bomb. Ted was the kind of person who, if he was mad enough, would carry out his threats. But as the comedian's temper began to cool, his threats also waned.

In the meantime, the Stooges continued to fracture audiences young and old, and critics continued to acclaim the team's growing success as vaudeville comedians. Some critics went so far as to say that Moe, Larry, and Shemp "remind us somehow of the Marx Brothers. Their humor is natural and unforced and they have good gags."

In 1931, after returning to the East Coast, Moe, Larry, and Shemp signed with the Blondell-Mack Agency and hired Jack Walsh as their straight man. The act still featured many routines from the Healy days, but an additional bit of nonsense had the Stooges constantly interrupting Walsh's singing of "Shine On, Harvest Moon." Together they wreaked havoc on the stages of the RKO-Keith Theatre Circuit. On the same bill were such prominent vaudeville performers as Adelaide Hall ("The Crooning Blackbird"), magician Fred Keating, and the Hazel Mangean Girls.

The Walsh-Stooges combination was a huge success. Audiences cheered wildly over the Stooges' antics, and critics reported that Walsh complemented the trio's broad, physical style of comedy to perfection. One theater critic raved, "Howard, Fine and Howard have one of the most amusing acts in show business. The way they punch each other (apparently) right in the eyes and slap each other around is nobody's business but we should make it ours if we were on the receiving end. They have a straight man, Jack Walsh, whose handsome presence and easy style make a strong contrast."

Around mid-December 1931, Moe, Larry, and Shemp took out a classified ad promising to pay five dollars to any person who provided a new name for their act. In subsequent bookings that month, they began billing themselves on the vaudeville circuit as "Three Lost Souls—Howard, Fine and Howard."

Meanwhile, Ted Healy and his replacement stooges continued to struggle. In 1931, they appeared in two short-lived Broadway musical revues, *The Gang's All Here* and *Billy Rose's Crazy Quilt*, the latter with Fanny Brice. At a vaudeville show at New York's Palace Theatre, a reviewer opined that Healy's three new knockabout comics were "less menacing than Shemp Howard and his associated malefactors." Later, a Milwaukee newspaper critic characterized

Ad published by the Stooges around mid-December 1931 in a New York newspaper personal column requesting suggestions for a new name for the team. *Courtesy of Moe Howard Collection*

Straight man Jack Walsh seen with Three Lost Souls—Shemp, Moe, and Larry—in 1932. *Courtesy of Moe Howard Collection*

them as "a group of dull looking fellows who were slapped about worse than the Tobey comics of the old days of burlesque," while others reported that the new performers "don't equal the comedian's original Stooges in any professional way." Finally, Ted came to the realization that this new act was not working and begged Moe, Larry, and Shemp to forgive and forget.

By now, Moe Howard had become not only the team's manager but also its driving force. He made the decisions when it came to theater bookings and the team's salaries, so he reviewed the matter of Healy's offer. Shemp was reticent but Larry was willing. So Moe gave Ted an ultimatum: if he wanted a deal, with all three of them returning as his Stooges, he had to stop drinking. Ted vowed never to take another drink, and in the summer of 1932 the Stooges made the deal official. Moe, Larry, and Shemp returned to Healy's act, and the comedian let Mousie Garner, Dick Hakins, and Jack Wolf go.

(Six years later, after Moe, Larry, and Curly spent four years as Columbia's Three Stooges, Garner, Wolf, and Hakins would file a lawsuit against the trio, claiming that they had stolen the name "Three Stooges" from them and kept them from achieving similar success. Their claim was proven bogus. A legal document signed by Moe Howard, Larry Fine, and Curly Howard demonstrated that they were the first to conceive of the name "Three Stooges." Garner also claimed that he, Wolf, and Hakins starred

in Vitaphone comedies as Stooges before The Three Stooges went to Columbia and that he occasionally replaced Shemp Howard as a third Stooge during Shemp's association with Ted Healy, Moe, and Larry. Sammy Wolfe, who in 1934 rounded out a new trio for Healy's act, likewise attested that they had used the name "The Three Stooges" first—that, on Christmas Eve 1934, the marquee for the act at the Palace Theatre was changed to read, "Ted Healy and the Three Stooges." Research has found these claims to be untrue as well.)

As soon as Healy and his original Stooges got together again, as announced in early July 1932, the Shuberts booked them in a new edition of their Broadway show *The Greenwich Village Follies*, which also featured Ethel Merman, Lou Holtz, and Sid Silvers among the cast. On Saturday, July 9, rehearsals got underway in New York, with the show set to open with a tryout tour on August 8 in Atlantic City. The lights went out on the production, however, before it could premiere, when producer Morris Green filed for bankruptcy.

The Shuberts instead cast Healy and his Stooges to headline their forthcoming production *The Passing Show of 1932*. But on August 19, 1932, Healy withdrew himself and the Stooges from the show after an argument between him and the Shuberts over a loophole Healy's personal manager, Paul Dempsey, had noticed in the comedian's contract. As Moe later explained, "We started rehearsing with the show, and rehearsals went past the four-week limit, when Ted Healy found that his contract didn't contain a closing date of the show," thus making it void. Healy broke his contract with the Shuberts to take an offer from the Balaban & Katz Circuit for $6,000 a week (the Shuberts were only paying him $2,800 a week). The Stooges, meanwhile, would go back to their original salaries of only one hundred dollars a week.

Shemp did not want any part of Ted's deviousness and refused to leave the Shubert musical. (Also on the Shubert bill with Shemp was another comedian who later became a Stooge himself, Joe Besser; he'd also been originally featured in the cast of *The Greenwich Village Follies*.) Not long after this, Shemp accepted an offer from Warner Bros. Vitaphone Studios in New York to star in comedy short subjects. In September 1933, he costarred in his first film for the studio, *Salt Walter Daffy*, and three years later established himself in the role of Knobby Walsh in Vitaphone's *Joe Palooka* series.

At the time of his departure, though, Shemp was reluctant to let go. As he told Larry and Moe, "Well, what are you going to do for a third man?" Moe told him not to worry—they'd get their brother Jerry, later nicknamed Curly. "We'll break him in and we'll take him along."

In the meantime, Healy hired xylophonist Freddie Sanborn (who had worked with the Stooges before in *Soup to Nuts*) as a temporary third Stooge for the team's exclusive six-week engagement with Balaban & Katz. Despite Shemp's departure, Ted and his Stooges drew packed houses every night and continued to leave the audiences in stitches. Once the engagement ended, Sanborn left the group and returned to his xylophone playing.

With Sanborn gone, Moe then recruited Jerry to take over the role. Jerry at that time sported long, wavy brown hair and a waxed mustache. Legend has it that when he joined the team, he shaved off both his hair and mustache, but photographs of the early team show that he shaved his head but kept his stubby mustache. He would snip off the mustache later, when the Stooges and Healy landed their contract to star in films at MGM. With Curly aboard, the team's salary structure changed. Curly received $75 a week, while Moe's salary climbed to $140, and Larry took home $155 a week.

Curly's previous theatrical work was limited to a brief stint as musical conductor for the Orville Knapp Band. Moe later recalled that Ted was concerned about Curly's inexperience. "What Curly did for the first three weeks was just run across the stage in a bathing suit, carrying a little pail of water. That's all he did, run back and forth, until we gradually worked him into the act." But Curly's inexperience did not inhibit him from becoming a tremendous asset to the group. In his first stage appearance, Curly's nervousness caused him to speak in a very high-pitched voice. That voice became one of his trademarks—as did the silly grunts and squeals he used to cover up his inability to remember his lines.

In 1932, with Curly in tow, the team was again billed as "Ted Healy and His Gang" and "Ted Healy and His Racketeers," and then, in 1933, "Ted Healy and His Laugh Racketeers." But Healy's ensemble was never called "Ted Healy and the Three Stooges." (Larry Fine erroneously reported in his book *Stroke of Luck* that he, Moe, and Shemp were billed in vaudeville as The Three Stooges, which is completely false.)

Once again, Healy and his Stooges played top vaudeville circuits to sold-out audiences throughout the nation. Critics responded enthusiastically to the new ensemble. Of their stage engagement at Loew's Rochester Theatre, which ran from September 30 to October 6, 1932, reviewer Charles E. Welch enthused, "There's a lot of what might be called 'broad

Moe performs the "Telling Time" routine for Ted Healy as Larry and Curly (in a mustache after replacing Shemp in 1932) look on. *Courtesy of Moe Howard Collection*

comedy' in Healy's contribution to the new combination screen [movie] and vaudeville. The majority know Healy as a good entertainer and he does not disappoint in his present offering. He is particularly fortunate in having such capable comedy assistants. They keep the fun moving, and while it is moving, the audience gets plenty of entertainment."

When the team performed on March 2, 1933, at the New Yorker Café in the basement of Hollywood's old Christie Hotel, a studio scout for Metro-Goldwyn-Mayer was present. MGM producer Harry Rapf invited them to play a charity benefit at the Uplifters Ranch in Hollywood. Afterward, all the major studio chieftains—Jack Warner (Warner Bros.), Louis B. Mayer (MGM), and Harry Cohn (Columbia)—reportedly offered them contracts. Ultimately, MGM won out. The group, as Ted Healy and His Stooges, signed a one-year studio contract. In keeping with their earlier arrangement, Healy signed the contracts for all of them.

Unlike the Stooges' previous journey to Hollywood for Fox's *Soup to Nuts*, this time the team's trip west was for keeps. MGM executives had made plans to star Healy and His Stooges in comedic short-subject series and full-length features. However, as they prepared to star in their first film for MGM, it was revealed that Healy had also accepted an offer to star them in their first short for Columbia. On May 17, 1933, *The Hollywood Reporter* broke word of the production, reporting that Healy, Moe, Larry, and Curly were set to star in a series of Columbia comedies, starting with one entitled *We're in the Money*. Ralph Staub was signed to direct this two-reel effort. If the film had gone into production, it would have changed the entire history of the Stooges at Columbia Pictures. But at the last minute, MGM stepped in and voided the Columbia deal since Healy had not fulfilled his MGM contract. Consequently, the film was never produced. A month later, on June 28, Universal Pictures and its producer Brian Foy also announced plans to make four features starring Healy and the Stooges. Universal would reportedly finance 100 percent of the production costs and get all rights to three pictures, while rights to the fourth would go to Foy and Healy, to be sold independently. But, ultimately, only one feature would result from the deal.

First, Healy and His Stooges would make a joint appearance in a musical short for MGM, *Nerts-ery Rhymes* (1933), costarring Ted's then real-life girlfriend Bonnie Bonnell (billed in their films as "Bonny"). Bonnell had also worked with the group onstage during their vaudeville days. *Nertsery Rhymes* was a novelty in another respect: it was the first in the series filmed in two-strip experimental color. Thereafter, Healy and the boys starred in four additional MGM short subjects: *Beer and Pretzels* (1933); *Hello Pop!* (1933), also filmed in two-strip experimental color; *Plane Nuts* (1933); and *The Big Idea* (1934). Jack Cummings was the series' producer and director. The films were a combination of new comedy sketches starring Healy and the Stooges and stock footage of dance extravaganzas lifted from MGM musicals.

Ted Healy with Moe, Curly, and Larry and costar Bonnie Bonnell in a scene from their first MGM short, *Nertsery Rhymes* (1933).
© *Metro-Goldwyn-Mayer, courtesy of Moe Howard Collection*

ALL POSES BY TED HEALY AND HIS STOOGES, AP-
PEARING IN METRO-GOLDWYN-MAYER COMEDIES.

Artist's concept of the Stooges from the MGM comedy short, *Plane Nuts* (1933). *Courtesy of Moe Howard Collection*

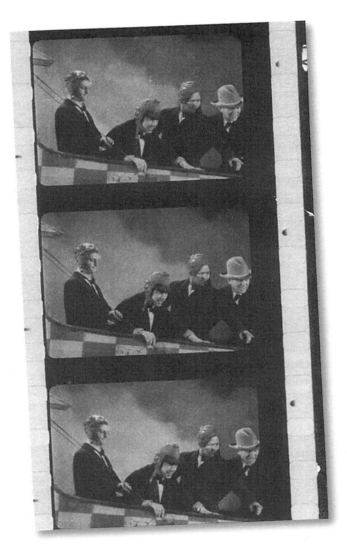

Nitrate film clip of a deleted scene from *Plane Nuts* (1933).
*Courtesy of Moe Howard Collection*

four feature-length films for Universal Pictures' Brian Foy, *Myrt and Marge* (1933). In it, the Stooges play Healy's bumbling stagehands. Al Boasberg, whom the trio worked under at MGM, directed the team in the film. For unknown reasons, however, the Stooges never fulfilled their contractual obligation with Universal by starring in the other three features.

In addition, the team had agreements to star, jointly or separately, in a number of MGM productions that, for reasons unclear, either fell through or were recast: *The Gang's All Here* (a working title for a film based on the popular Broadway show); a film version of Billy Rose's *Crazy Quilt*; *Going Hollywood* (1933) with Bing Crosby and Marion Davies (The

Moe, Larry, and Curly made their MGM feature debut with Lee Tracy and Mae Clarke in *Turn Back the Clock* (1933), in which they appeared without Healy. Their first feature with Healy was *Meet the Baron* (1933), with Jimmy Durante, ZaSu Pitts, and Edna May Oliver. It was followed by roles in *Dancing Lady* (1933), starring Joan Crawford and Clark Gable; also cast in the picture were Franchot Tone, Nelson Eddy, Robert Benchley, and Fred Astaire. MGM next used the Stooges and Healy in *Fugitive Lovers* (1934), with Nat Pendleton, and then spotted them in a comedy feature—their last MGM screen appearance—*Hollywood Party* (1934), along with Jimmy Durante, Mickey Mouse, Polly Moran, and a comedy team in their own right, Laurel and Hardy.

Also in 1933, Ted Healy, Moe, Larry, and Curly starred in what was supposed to be the first of their

A Loew's State Theatre newspaper ad for Ted Healy and His Stooges' first MGM feature, *Meet the Baron* (1933).
*Courtesy of Moe Howard Collection*

The Stooges ham it up during an MGM photo session in 1933.
*© Metro-Goldwyn-Mayer, courtesy of Moe Howard Collection*

Three Radio Rogues, a trio of comical musical imitators, appeared in the film instead); and *Employment Agency for Stooges*, written by Herman Timberg and first planned as a feature film, then as a short. Originally, *Employment Agency* was meant to launch the team's career in features as "filmdom's successors to the Marx Brothers." According to a *Hollywood Reporter* article dated December 29, 1933, "MGM has finally found a vehicle that they consider right to make the debut of the knockabouts." Ten days later, the production was downgraded, with the studio announcing it as another possible Ted Healy and His Stooges two-reeler and retitling it *An Employment for Stooges*. Even this version of the film failed to materialize.

During their time with the studio, the comics also made individual appearances in other MGM films. Healy's solo work included a single short subject with Cliff Edwards that was never released entitled *Stop, Sadie, Stop* (1933). In June 1933, Moe made a previously undocumented appearance in the Metro-Goldwyn-Mayer musical featurette *Give a Man a Job*, starring comedian Jimmy Durante. Made in the style of the Stooges' later Columbia short *Woman Haters*, with all dialogue spoken in rhyme, the two-minute public service film was adapted from the song of the same title by Richard Rodgers and Lorenz Hart, who also wrote songs for the Healy and Stooges 1933 feature *Meet the Baron*. It was produced in part to promote President Franklin Roosevelt's National Recovery Administration (NRA), a product of Roosevelt's New Deal, the purpose of which was to help restore industrial and business activity following the Great Depression. Moe, with his hair slicked back instead of in his famous bowl cut, appears as an audience member in a scene in which Durante is pleading for a job.

Moe and Curly made cameo appearances as two German- or Dutch-accented clowns in makeup, Otto and Fritz, in the MGM feature *Broadway to Hollywood*, released in September 1933. Directed by Willard Mack, the film costarred many other studio contract players, including Frank Morgan, Alice Brady, Madge Evans, Jimmy Durante, Mickey Rooney, and Jackie Cooper. The original full-length film featured some early two-strip Technicolor sequences and several sequences from the uncompleted MGM musical *The March of Time* (1930). Meanwhile, Larry appeared as a music store customer with Healy and actresses Alice Brady and Maureen O'Sullivan in the musical drama *Stage Mother* (1933). Curly would also make a cameo appearance in *Roast-Beef and Movies* (1934), another experimental color short. Larry recalled that MGM tried to reproduce the magic of the Stooges by pairing Curly with two other comedians, George Givot and Bobby Callahan. This attempt didn't pan out, even though the film was a critical success. Curly also appeared, along with Moe, in another MGM comedy, *Jail Birds of Paradise*, which was released in color on March 10, 1934.

During this period of their careers, the boys' on-screen shenanigans carried over offscreen. There was just no way these classic film clowns could refrain from livening up their social affairs. A prime example of their comedic offstage antics occurred when Healy, Moe, Larry, and Curly attended the August 30, 1933, Los Angeles premiere of *Dinner at Eight* (1933), which was being screened at the Chinese Theatre (later renamed Grauman's Chinese Theatre). As limousines arrived carrying filmdom's top celebrities, Healy and his trio could be seen pedaling up to the theater on a bicycle built for four! Ted sat on the first seat, gloriously resplendent in a white top hat with feathers, boots, breeches, and bright-colored tails. Taking up the rear were comrades Moe, Larry, and Curly, garbed in high hats and immaculate evening clothes. They were definitely the hit of the evening.

The riotous antics of the team didn't stop there. Backstage at MGM, as all was quiet on the set, Moe, Larry, and Curly broke new ground with their slapstick brand of tomfoolery. Wearing ghoulish makeup, the Stooges wandered over to another MGM sound stage and ran smack into Greta Garbo. Witnesses reported that it was hard to tell who was the most non-plussed, Garbo or the Stooges. It is also believed that the Stooges' monster makeup scared Garbo, who came out with her then-famous line: "I vant to be alone!"

Photo taken in November 1933 of Ted Healy, Larry, Curly, and Moe during filming of their appearance in their final MGM feature, *Hollywood Party* (1934). © *Metro-Goldwyn-Mayer, courtesy of Moe Howard Collection*

Even Curly got into the act while making a personal appearance in Philadelphia. Ted had just bought a dozen very expensive imported shirts that he was simply mad about. In fact, he loved them so much that he warned the Stooges not to lay a finger on them. One evening, during a performance, Curly grabbed Healy by the shirt and, for comedic effect, literally tore it off Healy's back. Ted, not realizing until the act was over that he was wearing his favorite shirt, never thought to stop Curly.

Although the team continued to ride on a wave of successes at MGM, the Stooges were very unhappy serving strictly as Healy's comic relief. On March 6, 1934,

when Healy's contract came up for renewal, the Stooges decided to break with him. Evidently, Moe, Larry, and Curly did some soul searching to arrive at this decision, but their meager salaries became the deciding factor. As Moe once remarked in an interview, "In the early days, what Ted paid us was laughable. And there were times when Ted didn't get paid, so we didn't get paid. This was later reflected in the period at MGM, where some weeks Ted would give me one hundred, some weeks only fifty dollars. I went along with it since I understood his financial situation was such that he couldn't pay us what he owed us." But as time wore on and Healy's lapses in payment continued, Moe found it an impossible situation, as did Larry and Curly. They all wanted out. In a meeting with Healy and Paul Dempsey (Healy's manager), Moe induced them to draw up a paper releasing him and the Stooges from working with Ted.

It was with sadness that reporters in the trades noted the Healy/Stooges breakup. One columnist wrote, "Sad note. Ted Healy and his completely mad Stooges have unfortunately come to the parting of the ways. The Stooges felt they could make more money and get along better sans their discoverer. Wezel see." Ted did try, on several occasions, to get the Stooges to come back, but they just weren't interested. (While costarring in supporting roles in motion pictures for MGM in 1934,

Bonnie Bonnell and Ted Healy and His Stooges in their last MGM short, *The Big Idea* (1934). © *Metro-Goldwyn-Mayer, courtesy of Moe Howard Collection*

Healy recruited three new stooges: Jimmy Brewster, who was also Healy's writer, John "Red" Pearson, and Sammy Wolfe, whose real name was Sammy Glasser. They proved to be pale imitations when they made their first screen appearance together in MGM's *San Francisco* in 1936.) Moe, Larry, and Curly were finally free, and now they were off to find out whether there was a place for them in the movie industry.

The trio made their historic jump from MGM to Columbia Pictures on March 19, 1934. The trio signed a one-picture contract, with an option for additional comedies to be made if the reception for the first one was favorable. The pact included a sixty-day waiting period that Columbia would use to decide whether to exercise the option, and it stipulated that if Columbia did request further comedies, the team would film eight two-reel comedies in a forty-week period with twelve weeks off (which could be used for any sort of work other than films).

Eight days after the studio approved the team's contract, Columbia cast them in *Woman Haters* (1934) opposite a rising contract starlet, Marjorie White. Besides being the team's first starring film without Ted Healy, *Woman Haters* provided the first screen role for actor Walter Brennan; he played a bit part as a train conductor. In the film, Curly, Larry, and Moe were billed not as The Three Stooges but as Jerry Howard, Larry Fine, and Moe Howard.

Larry, Curly, and Moe with costar Marjorie White on the set of *Woman Haters*, their first comedy short for Columbia Pictures. © *Columbia Pictures, courtesy of Jeff Lenburg Collection*

It was Moe who finally conceived the name "The Three Stooges." As he later stated, "I came up with the name based on the fact we were three and we were stooges and I thought that was appropriate." On June 2, 1934, he made it official, executing an agreement with Larry and Curly that made him the sole owner of the name, while stipulating that all salaries and monies earned by the group would be split evenly three ways. The pact also gave Moe the right to replace "either or both [of the other Stooges] at his discretion" and to sign all contracts on their behalf as the manager of the act.

(Coincidentally, while the team had not ever previously billed themselves as The Three Stooges, to coincide with MGM's release of *Meet the Baron* in October 1933, Moe, Larry, and Curly jointly penned a newspaper article in which they called themselves "Ted Healy's Three Stooges." And while they were making the 1934 MGM film *Fugitive Lovers*, entertainment gossip columnists referred to them as Healy's "three stooges.")

Columbia gave the go-ahead for the boys to film more two-reelers. On their second two-reel comedy for the studio, *Punch Drunks*, the trio clearly showed promise as film comedians, even receiving a story credit. (The eight-page treatment the Stooges wrote was entitled *A Symphony of Punches*, an original copy of which still exists.) *Punch Drunks* was also the first film in which the team was billed on-screen as "The Three Stooges," although Columbia originally announced it as a "Howard, Fine and Howard" comedy.

*Men in Black* (1934), the team's third comedy and the first "official" Three Stooges short, was a spoof of MGM's Clark Gable–Myrna Loy movie *Men in White*, released earlier that year. Opening on September 28, 1934, at the Carthay Circle Theatre in Los Angeles, it became the only film for which the Stooges received an Academy Award nomination for "Best Short Subject—Comedy." Even though the Stooges' film was worthy of the honor, it was another movie, *La Cucaracha*, a

$65,000 three-strip Technicolor musical short for RKO Radio Pictures—in which Moe later claimed the Stooges were to star—that won the Oscar that year.

History has identified *Men in Black* as the turning point in the Stooges' film career. Jules White, the film's producer, stated that the film convinced Columbia to keep the Stooges on, since their Academy Award nomination proved to the studio the comedians' worth to the industry. The Stooges' salary for starring in *Woman Haters* was a paltry $1,000 a

Larry, Moe, and Curly in a classic totem-pole pose. © *Columbia Pictures, courtesy of Jeff Lenburg Collection*

week, split three ways. But as the team's popularity grew, Columbia increased their salary to as much as $7,500 a week for the team, divided equally.

Next, the Stooges starred in a college football comedy, *Three Little Pigskins* (1934), featuring a new contract player, Lucille Ball. Years later, in a *Look* magazine interview, Ball recounted what it was like working with the Stooges: "The only thing I learned from them was how to duck!"

Some of the most enduringly popular Stooges shorts of the 1930s and 1940s were with the original trio of Moe, Larry, and Curly. In their films following *Woman Haters*, these three had begun to convey distinct screen personalities, newly developed at the time but now world famous: Moe was the bullying, self-appointed leader of the trio. Curly was an enigma, happily lost in his own magical world and frustrated when the harsh real world intruded. And Larry was the ultimate middleman, existing only to serve his two stronger-willed partners.

Along with character development, the Stooges' comedies also managed to mirror many social and political themes that are still with us: crises of government, war, unemployment, and crime that made headlines as often then as they do today. And during a time when America was experiencing the aftershocks of the Great Depression, the stories also included the basic story line of the Stooges poking fun at the upper classes. Audiences identified with the working-class Stooges conquering the highest reaches of society—working as plumbers in ritzy mansions, seeking elegant employment, and spoofing US military brass in World War II.

Besides timely satirical and social themes, Moe remarked that it was a combination of slapstick and "the upsetting of dignity" that gave them the basic foundation for their comedy. "We subtly, the three of us, always went into an area of life which we were not supposed to understand. If we were going to go into society, the picture would open with us as garbage collectors. We would take a man with a high hat, a monocle and spats, and smash him in the nose with a pie, thus bringing him down to our level. I think that we appealed to all age brackets and all class brackets. We did stupid things but they were excusable because we didn't know any better."

In addition to their annual output of short comedies, the team appeared as comic relief in five Columbia feature films. But Moe asserted in numerous interviews that the Stooges' firebrand style of humor worked better in short form. In 1935, when Columbia proposed to star them in their own full-length feature, they rebuffed the idea. As Moe said at the time, "It's a hard job inventing, rewriting or stealing gags for our two-reel comedies for Columbia Pictures without having to make a seven-reeler [a feature]. We can make short films out of material needed for a starring feature and then we wouldn't know whether it would be funny enough to click."

Therefore, the Stooges' feature-film appearances were usually limited to five- to ten-minute cameos. In the 1930s and '40s, they appeared in such features as *The Captain Hates the Sea* (1934), *Start Cheering* (1938), *Time Out for Rhythm* (1941), *My Sister Eileen* (1942), and *Rockin' in the Rockies* (1945). Later on, the boys also appeared in an independently produced feature for Monogram Pictures called *Swing Parade of 1946*, which, unlike their features for Columbia, featured the team throughout the entire production.

The team was also set to appear in three more features, Universal's *Gift of Gab* (1934); Columbia's *Chinese Hooey* (1938), with Joe E. Brown; and *Right Guy*, which was retitled *Good Luck, Mr. Yates* (1943). However, studio head Harry Cohn nixed the Stooges' appearance in *Gift of Gab* (1934). Producer Rian James solved his casting dilemma by signing three other actors (Skins Miller, Jack Harling, and Sid Walker), all described as "experienced stooge singles," to step into the Stooges' places. In *Chinese Hooey*, the Stooges were going to perform material written by Moe's wife, Helen Howard, but production was canceled. In the *Mr. Yates* feature, scenes were filmed on April 16, 1943, on Stage 8, of the Stooges performing "Niagara Falls," with Jules White directing *only* the Stooges' routine; Ray Enright was the feature's overall director. Footage of the Stooges, however, was cut from the final release print and shelved until a story could be written based around the scenes. Later this entire sequence became the basis for the Stooges short *Gents Without Cents* (1944).

Between fulfilling their filming commitments, Moe, Larry, and Curly (and later Shemp) also went on tour every year, making countless personal appearances at movie houses across the country. They entertained theatergoers with a special stage show before the screening of whatever Hollywood feature film was on the marquee that week. The first time the name

"The Three Stooges" appeared on a marquee was at the Paramount Theatre on Market Street in San Francisco in 1934. The Stooges hired a photographer to take a picture of it, but as Moe once related, "All he got was a photo of the policeman on a horse standing in front of the theater." Moe took the photo himself another time, when their names appeared in lights during an engagement at the Orpheum Theatre in Los Angeles, which featured as its main attraction the Fox Studios comedy *365 Nights in Hollywood*, starring Alice Faye

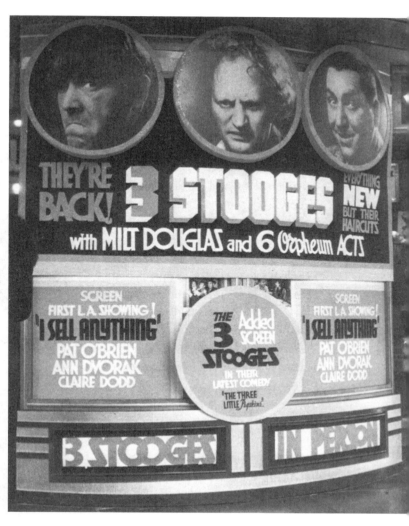

Display for the Stooges' return engagement in late 1934 at the Orpheum Theatre in Los Angeles. *Courtesy of Moe Howard Collection*

The Stooges prepare to board a train for a cross-country tour.

*Courtesy of Moe Howard Collection*

and James Dunn. Capitalizing on their popularity, in 1935 Columbia Pictures also licensed the first official Stooges merchandise: a set of handcrafted Three Stooges hand puppets.

In 1939, during a hiatus from their immensely popular two-reel comedies, the Stooges were signed to tour the British Isles. Their first stop was England, to play a two-week engagement at the London Palladium, which was held over. Their tour continued with further stops in Blackpool, Dublin, and Glasgow. Then it was back to the United States to open as Broadway stars in *George White's Scandals of 1939*, which was tried out in Atlantic City and then opened in New York at the Alvin Theatre on August 28, 1939. The production lasted for 120 performances and marked the Stooges' first Broadway show in over seven years.

The boys performed for the first time a sketch called "The Stand-In," a parody of the Hollywood stand-in that included a very messy pie-throwing battle at its finish. The all-star cast that grabbed laughter and applause in this first-rate entertainment also included Willie and Eugene Howard, Ella Logan, Ben Blue, and a young dancer by the name of Ann Miller. As critic Robert Coleman of the *New York Daily Mirror* wrote, the Stooges "come through with flying colors and faces dripping with gooseberry pies. . . . They lured laughter from the first nighters like a wringer does water from damp shirts."

The Stooges enjoyed phenomenal success in movies but found that audiences were divided roughly into two groups: one made up of persons who laughed at them and the other of those who wondered why. Those who appreciated the Stooges had several reasons. First, the trio's slapstick routines and insane antics were usually improvised, resulting in a balanced blend of ingenuity and creativity. Rival comedy teams, such as Abbott and Costello or Laurel and Hardy, stuck mainly to the script. Moe felt that improvising added to the spontaneity in a given scene—unless the Stooges went overboard, but that usually wasn't the case. Larry and Moe were good studies when it came to knowing their lines. Moe, however, was the only one to memorize every player's lines, not just his own; he did so for the sake of pacing and timing. Curly was the antithesis, terrible at remembering his lines; consequently he improvised the most. As Moe related in an interview, "If he forgot his lines, it was a temporary thing. I could tell, because his eyes would roll around a little bit and he'd fall to the floor and spin around like a top—or do a backward kick, or go on his back and move like a snake." Curly's reliance on ad-libbing usually

accelerated the already frantic pace of the team's comedies and frequently was their savior.

That's because a second vital factor in the Stooges' broad, slapstick comedy was tempo. A brisk pace and split-second timing were crucial—unlike, for instance, in the films starring Laurel and Hardy, who worked at a much slower pace. Laurel and Hardy took several minutes to build up to one laugh-riot

Cover for the June 1939 edition of *Theatre Royal News* touting the Stooges' tour in Dublin. *Courtesy of Jeff Lenburg Collection*

A 1940 newspaper ad for one of The Three Stooges' many stage appearances. *Courtesy of Moe Howard Collection*

The Stooges reprise their acrobatic act from their days with Ted Healy. *Courtesy of Moe Howard Collection*

moment, while the Stooges' wham-bam style elicited ten times the guffaws in a single scene. Moe remarked that the team abided by three rules to keep the tempo moving: "Watch, listen, and plan. We watched the tempo of the act, listened to the other member when one was in the spotlight, and planned our routines. There was a lot more to it than just going up and telling funny stories and smacking each other around. We checked the slapstick carefully in order not to overdo it. If comedy goes on too long, the audience begins to think about it. We aimed not to give anyone time to think."

The Stooges with straight man Eddie Laughton during a stage appearance. *Courtesy of Moe Howard Collection*

Moe reminds Larry that he has just insulted the sovereign state of Texas (clap-clap-clap!) during a stage performance.
*Courtesy of Moe Howard Collection*

Larry also attributed the Stooges' success on-screen to "a matter of timing" and to the execution of their slapstick comedy. Even when Moe slapped and poked their eyes, as he noted in an interview, "if you noticed, neither of us [Larry or Curly] flinched, nor tried to draw back. Moe's timing was perfect; he knew exactly where to place the palm of his hand, and I trained myself to keep perfectly still."

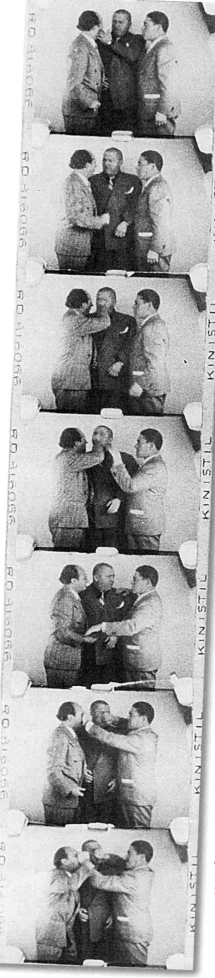

A still photographer captures the Stooges in action.
*Courtesy of Moe Howard Collection*

Another valuable element of The Three Stooges' film magic was their stock company of supporting players. Hollywood usually recognizes the stars of a long-running series but forgets the incidental actors; Moe was one of the film industry's few comedians who not only realized the importance of their contribution but also gave recognition to them in interviews. Columbia's stock company was composed of veteran character actors from silent films (Keystone and Sennett stars) and from the legitimate stage. Bud Jamison and Vernon Dent, who started out in silent comedies, were in many Three Stooges films and made every scene count. Symona Boniface, who launched her career in legitimate theater, invariably wound up as the perfect dowager who got a pie in the face for her efforts. Christine McIntyre, the fans' favorite heroine and villainess, played in dozens of Three Stooges shorts; in the film *Micro-Phonies* (1945), she made her singing debut as she belted out the tune "The Voices of Spring," which unfortunately was never produced as a record single. Dorothy Appleby, Kenneth MacDonald, Gene Roth, Phil Van Zandt, Gino Corrado, Fred Kelsey, Dick Curtis, Emil Sitka, and Harold Brauer were among the many dramatic actors–turned–comics in Stooges films. Even people such as Jock Mahoney, Walter Brennan, Lloyd Bridges, and Lucille Ball used Stooges comedies as stepping-stones in their careers.

A competent staff of writers and directors was also behind the success of each Stooges film. Felix Adler, Clyde Bruckman, and Elwood Ullman were just three of the team's prominent screenwriters. Del Lord, Preston Black (his real name was Jack White), and Ray McCarey were the team's first directors. The Stooges' staff of skilled directors also featured the likes of Charles Lamont and Charley Chase and, later, Edward Bernds and Jules White (Preston Black's brother). Recognition is also due such staffers as prop man Ray Hunt, sound effects editor Joe Henrie, and script girl Dorothy Gumming.

According to Moe and Larry, the violence quota per film depended on which director was making the two-reeler. People like Del Lord and Charley Chase were more interested in slapstick and visual gags than outright violence. Edward Bernds also relied on visual gags but even more on coherent stories. Jules White, who produced many non-Stooge Columbia two-reel comedies as well, earned the distinction of

leaning heavily on unnecessary violence in the films. White enjoyed injecting many grotesque and overly cruel gags into their films, such as using scissors, mallets, and saws on areas of the human anatomy that should be given a little respect.

A greater risk of injury threatened the Stooges themselves, however, in films that contained a higher measure of violence. According to Moe, the Stooges sustained a variety of bumps and bruises and injuries by the dozens: broken noses, fractured ribs, sprained ankles, and cracked teeth. Columbia prop man Stan Dunn was present several times when the Stooges were injured on the set. The first time, Dunn said, was when Moe broke his nose when he missed his timing going through a revolving door. On another occasion, Curly broke his big toe when he delivered a swift kick at Larry and hit a table leg instead.

The Stooges relax on the set of *In the Sweet Pie and Pie* (1941).
© Columbia Pictures, courtesy of Jeff Lenburg Collection

(Dunn also recalled a story concerning Larry Fine's periodic hunger pangs. As Dunn remembered, "Fine was always hungry. He spent his money on wine and women, but not on food." Dunn had set aside a dish of dog food for a trained dog who was to appear in a scene with the Stooges. Larry was famished and gobbled the dog food right out of the dish. When Larry found out what he had eaten, he allegedly turned green, then quipped, "That was great! What brand was it?")

Curly, Larry, and Moe during a tense moment onstage. *Courtesy of Moe Howard Collection*

The Stooges were also concerned with the development of story situations and gags written for them in the scripts. Moe always believed it was of paramount importance to hold story conferences with the writer and director. His reason: "All we asked of the writers was a situation. We would look for certain sequences where we could put in some satire and still make it part of the story. It was very important for us to be part of the story and not just be dragged into it. After all, we were naturally the best judges of what lines and actions were most appropriate for each of us in any given situation."

At these conferences, Moe himself would actively provide creative input, writing new gags and coming up with his own ideas. He was an inveterate doodler and scribbled down many of these ideas on hotel letterheads, matchbooks, and notepaper. Larry and Curly were the least resourceful when it came to brainstorming new ideas. As director Edward Bernds, who started directing the Stooges in 1945, said, "Moe was good at adding ideas but needed help when it came to constructing a good storyline. Larry's sugges-

tions were usually off target, but once in a while he would come up with a gem that would get us started on something. Curly was usually more subdued at these meetings."

Stooges script sessions ran right through preproduction. The Stooges were usually asked to report for a run-through of the script's first draft, and then suggestions were made. Edward Bernds, who wrote as well as directed many Stooges comedies, once explained what transpired at these meetings: "We'd usually have a kind of bull session in which the boys would wander all over the place, ad-libbing routines, reminiscing, and I would make notes. I would borrow from old scripts, too, but mostly I listened. I would stockpile routines, devise some sort of framework for them to hang on. I would then write a rough draft script and call in the Stooges. They would go through the first draft. It gave them other notions, and I would make cuts and additions and somehow hammer out another draft. It was pretty much agreed upon by the time it went into final draft."

Stooges screenwriter Elwood Ullman recalled that ideas for Stooges comedies didn't come easily. "It took me a great deal of time to get used to writing their comedies. I thank Del Lord for providing me with some guidance. But ideas for these scripts weren't easy to conceive. I'd be at my desk perusing *Variety* when the boss, Jules White, might buzz me and say,

A September 30, 1944, ad from the *Motion Picture Herald* for *Gents Without Cents*. *Courtesy of Moe Howard Collection*

'There's an English manor set on Stage 2 that's available to us. Take a stroll through the set and see if you can come up with something for The Three Stooges.' There were many nervous times when I would pace all over until I finally struck on an idea."

By the mid-1940s, however, the Stooges started facing problems. In their films, Curly's physical appearance began showing signs of deterioration. His vitality and mobility had begun to languish. He was unable to do the brilliant physical comedy that had been his forte. No longer could he fall on the floor and spin like a top. His high-pitched squeal of a voice had become a hoarse croak. He couldn't even muster up enough strength to do his ever-popular "wooo-wooo-wooo." The Curly Howard that moviegoers saw in 1946 was, as Larry Fine later remarked, "a shell of a man."

The critical reason for Curly's sudden decline was that he had suffered a series of minor strokes, none great enough to fully disable him, but each contributing to his decline. Doctors suggest that this can happen without the person even knowing it. The fact that Curly drank heavily could have contributed to this; a stroke could have been written off as just a hangover. As Larry Fine once stated, "We think that Curly had many small strokes in 1945 but was afraid to tell us because he was afraid that we would have to break up the act."

Edward Bernds agreed with this theory. In an interview, Bernds recalled the progression of Curly's decline in each of the films in the order in which they were shot. In addition, Bernds said that Curly's physical capabilities changed from day to day; the director was able to pinpoint the changes in the diary he kept sporadically during the period of Curly's decline. He believed the strokes started on about January 31, 1945, and continued thereafter.

In March 1945, while Bernds was filming *Micro-Phonies* (1945)—known around the studio simply as a "Stooge operetta"—he noted that Curly was having

A happier moment, in a promotional photo for *Monkey Businessmen* (1946). © *Columbia Pictures, courtesy of Jeff Lenburg Collection*

some ups and downs. On March 10 (three days after Bernds rewrote the script for the upcoming *A Bird in the Head*, which was running long), producer Hugh McCollum walked into the director's office with the grim news that Curly had again suffered some sort of episode. The next day, they viewed the film rushes of the Stooge's previous day's work, and despite whatever had happened to him on set, they deemed it "not too bad." As Bernds stated, "Whatever it was, he recovered, and his disability didn't show too badly in the film."

On March 12, Bernds visited to watch the Stooges film their scenes, and Curly appeared fine, more up for his performance. "He was suddenly the old Curly," Bernds recalled. "I can't think of a fault; he was himself again." But during a conference with the Stooges four days later, Curly seemed unusually subdued and incoherent. "Apparently, he was not his old self. And I was familiar with the old Curly," noted Bernds, who had worked on many Stooges comedies dating back to his days as a soundman, including their first, *Woman Haters* (1934).

But in April, Bernds became acutely aware of Curly's worsening condition when he directed him in the Stooges' eighty-ninth comedy short, *A Bird in the Head* (1946). In his words, "Curly was slow-moving, slow-reacting, couldn't remember his lines." As Bernds recalled, "I had seen Curly at his greatest, and his work in this film was far from great. The wallpaper scene was agony to direct because of the physical movements required to roll up the wallpaper and to react when it curled up on him. It just didn't work. As a fledgling director, my plans were based on doing everything in one nice neat shot. But when I saw scenes were not playing, I had to improvise and use other angles to make it play. It was the wallpaper scene that we shot first, and during the first two hours of filming, I became aware that we had a problem with Curly."

Bernds didn't remember having any great difficulty with Curly—he wasn't any worse—a month later during filming of *The Three Troubledoers*. But during the making of *Monkey Businessmen*, Curly was at his worst. "Moe coached him the way one would a child, getting him to repeat each line after him. We had to shoot Curly repeating one line at a time," Bernds said.

When Norman Maurer was on leave from the navy in 1945, he paid a visit to the set as the Stooges were filming *Rhythm and Weep* (1946). Maurer, too, remembered that Curly "was having trouble with his coordination. He was supposed to pop pills in his mouth during the scene, but the scene was switched to Moe putting the pills into Curly's mouth because of Curly's physical problems."

Then, on Monday, May 6, 1946, Curly suffered a massive stroke that would impair his health for the rest of his life. It was the final day of filming on the Stooges' ninety-seventh short, *Half-Wits Holiday* (1947). Curly had completed the "Sword of Damocles" scene with actress Symona Boniface, and he was sitting in a canvas chair waiting to do his last scene of the day. As Moe remembered, "His mouth became distorted, and when he got up from the chair he fell to his knees. It seemed that one side of him seemed to be slightly paralyzed."

Curly devours pie in a scene from *Half-Wits Holiday* (1947), minutes before suffering a stroke. © *Columbia Pictures, courtesy of Greg Lenburg Collection*

Character actor Emil Sitka also starred in *Half-Wits Holiday*, as a high-society butler in what was ironically both his first Stooges comedy and Curly's last film as a Stooge. Sitka recalled that word of what had happened to Curly was never revealed to the film's supporting cast. "Nobody was informed. Curly was doing a scene, then all of a sudden we were told there was going to be a big pie fight in the end. Moe and Larry—even Jules [White, the director]—never said a thing. We did the whole scene thinking that Curly was coming in later. He never did. If we had been told, we all would have probably been downcast."

The untimely, tragic loss of Curly from the act came just as Bernds had finished writing the Stooges' planned next comedy, *Pardon My Terror*, the forerunner to Bernds's later Stooges comedy *Who Done It?* (1949). Because of Curly's sudden illness, Bernds rewrote the script and cast Columbia's Gus Schilling and Dick Lane as the leads, two detectives hunting for clues to the mysterious death of millionaire Jonas Morton. Filming commenced four days after Curly's stroke, and the two-reel comedy was released September 12, 1946.

Moe and Larry were hoping that Curly would recover and return to the team. As Norman Maurer remembered, "Moe used to encourage Curly that he was going to get better and rejoin the act. And Curly really felt he was going to get better." Moe stated as much in a handwritten letter to Curly that September: "It might encourage you, and in a way delight you to know that brother Shemp was agreeable to step into your boots, in the act, and finish the comedies that were intended to be made by you, I and Larry, until such time as you are well enough to return to the trio."

Indeed, Moe had suggested to Columbia's executives that Shemp Howard, their older brother, replace Curly on a temporary basis until Curly recovered. (Rubbery-faced comedian Buddy Hackett later stated that director Jules White had asked him to replace Curly after his death but he turned him down. However, based on the team's existing partnership agreement, any final selection and approval of partners was solely Moe's to make.) At the time, Shemp was starring in his own series of Columbia two-reelers. At first, Columbia was opposed to the idea, since Shemp looked too much like Moe. But he was the obvious candidate, because he was so well acquainted with the trio's routines. Shemp, too, was reluctant about rejoining the team. He sought assurances from Moe that he could leave once Curly was able to return. Moe agreed.

First, however, Larry suggested that each of them take fifty dollars out of his weekly salary and send it to Curly. Moe was extremely touched that Larry, although he wasn't a brother, acted like one with this generous idea. The trio agreed to send Curly this $150 a week; it was put toward his medical expenses.

On September 30, 1946, Curly signed a letter of acceptance written by Moe. Then, on September 31,

Shemp returns in late 1946 as the third Stooge, replacing Curly.
*Courtesy of Academy of Motion Picture Arts and Sciences, Margaret Herrick Library Collection*

1946, Moe, Larry, Curly, and Shemp signed a new agreement with Columbia. The agreement made Shemp a party to the Stooges' last studio contract, dated March 30, 1944, employing him in Curly's place for a term commencing May 27, 1946, and continuing for "any picture that has commenced prior to the time Jerry Howard is ready, willing and able to render his services."

Although Shemp was already appearing publically as the new third Stooge a month before the boys signed their new Columbia contract, Columbia Pictures and Moe kept a tight lid on the cause of Curly's departure, in an effort to protect his privacy. One newspaper scribe, touting the Stooges' first Chicago public engagement with Shemp, on August 28, 1946, at the famous Colosimo's café nightclub, wrote, "Curly, the fat lad with the Kraut haircut, isn't with the boys on this excursion from Hollywood, and so it is Shemp who absorbs all the punishment." On March 18, 1947, however, an Associated Press article reported that Shemp had replaced Curly because he had been "ailing since the time he fell down an elevator shaft during the filming of one of the shorts"—of course, patently untrue. In interviews, Moe addressed Curly's absence this way: "He's taking a rest. Brother Curly likes nothing better than a long rest."

Last 2 Days—ROSENBLOOM-BAER "Knockout Revue"

OPENING WEDNESDAY, AUGUST 28th

DIRECT FROM HOLLYWOOD
COURTESY COLUMBIA PICTURES
FIRST CHICAGO CAFE APPEARANCE

The 3 Stooges

WITH THEIR
OWN STAR-STUDDED REVUE

NEW
THEATER RESTAURANT
Colosimo's
2126 SO. WABASH
RESERVATIONS
CALumet 7200

An August 28, 1946, ad promoting the Stooges' first Chicago appearance with Shemp at the famed Colosimo's nightclub, a month before they signed a new contract with Columbia replacing Curly. *Courtesy of Moe Howard Collection*

After Shemp came onboard, studio publicity and newspaper stories played up the new trio as the "original Three Stooges." Furthermore, Shemp received top billing over Larry and Moe—in that order—in the opening titles of their Columbia Pictures comedies and on all posters distributed to theater exhibitors. (It should be noted that around 1940, Columbia had likewise begun giving Curly top billing before Larry and Moe—again in that order—on posters and lobby cards.)

On March 6, 1947, the first Stooges comedy with Shemp was released to theaters. The two-reel short, *Fright Night*, had been filmed before the Stooges

signed their new Columbia contract in September 1946. Interestingly, two months after Shemp's first film, the Parent-Teachers Association (PTA) of Chicago awarded The Three Stooges two-reelers with Moe, Larry, and Shemp their highest recognition, selecting them as "ideal entertainment for children."

In his letter to Curly, Moe wrote, "The first picture in which Shemp operates in your place was very good, but altho [*sic*] Shemp is a great comic in his own right, Larry and I miss you very much and we are hoping and praying to have you back with us soon now." Unfortunately, Curly never regained his old stamina and was unable to return. Thus, Shemp stayed on permanently. It was a thankless task, since the enormously popular Curly was a tough act to follow. But, as Norman Maurer once stated, "Shemp gave the act a little variety. He had a certain personality of his own. He wasn't Curly, but it worked."

Edward Bernds agreed. He felt Shemp was a natural for the job. "Shemp was a trouper, a very willing guy. He was always prepared. It was a delight to work with him. Comparing him to Curly is not fair. He could never be Curly, and never tried to be. Basically, he was a very good actor. I don't think Curly could have been anything but Curly of The Three Stooges. The transition, as far as I was concerned, was all for the good. From then on, I approached the Stooges with anticipation and pleasure."

Shemp, who plastered his hair down with grease so he looked like a small-town slicker, took his work as a

The Stooges use the tricks of their trade on director Jules White between takes of *The Ghost Talks* (1949).

*© Columbia Pictures, courtesy of Moe Howard Collection*

Stooge in stride. As he confessed to a reporter two years after stepping in for Curly, "I look more stupid than the other two and I think I get the most laughs." Although his style did not resemble Curly's, he was able to interject his own special brand of insanity into a scene: exaggerated mugging, hilarious double takes, and his own high-pitched, frightened cry of "Heeep-heeep-heeep!"

Bernds enjoyed letting the cameras roll at the end of Shemp's scenes, since he gave everything he could to his performance. According to Bernds, in fact, Shemp didn't know when to quit. He recalled one incident while shooting *Brideless Groom* (1947) that demonstrated Shemp's method: "In the story, Shemp had a few hours in which to get married if he wanted to inherit his uncle's fortune. He called on Christine McIntyre, who mistook him for her cousin and greeted him with hugs and kisses. Then the real cousin phoned, and she accused Shemp of kissing her, as it were, under false pretenses. At this point, she was supposed to slap Shemp around. Lady that she was, Chris couldn't do it right; she dabbed at him daintily, afraid of hurting him. After a couple of bad takes, Shemp pleaded with her. 'Honey,' he said, 'if you want to do me a favor, cut loose and do it right. A lot of half-hearted slaps hurts more than one good one. Give it to me, Chris, and let's get it over with.' Chris got up her courage and on the next take, let Shemp have it. 'It' wound up as a whole series of slaps—the timing was beautiful; they rang out like pistol shots. Shemp was knocked into a chair, bounced up, met another ringing slap, fell down again, scrambled up, trying to explain, only to get another stinging slap. Then Chris delivered a haymaker—a right that knocked Shemp through the door. When the take was over, Shemp was groggy, really groggy. Chris put her arms around him and apologized tearfully. 'It's all right, honey,' Shemp said painfully. 'I said you should cut loose and you did. You sure as hell did!'"

In 1948, Columbia Pictures awarded Moe, Larry, and Shemp a new two-year contract that called for them to make two-reel comedies and feature-length productions. Veteran Stooge screenwriter Elwood Ullman drafted and finished a feature-length script for a backwoods comedy, entitled *Where There's a Will*, but it was never produced.

Meanwhile, Curly had come back in 1947 to make a cameo appearance with the Stooges in *Hold That Lion!* It marked the only occasion in which all three Howard brothers appeared together in a film. Curly was the train passenger wearing a derby over his face and a clothespin over his nose. Director Jules White later recalled that the bit with Curly came about after he visited the set one day and decided to film it for fun. According to costar Emil Sitka, the whole picture was finished and the set was closed when they filmed Curly's cameo.

Curly makes his first film appearance following his stroke—marking the only time all three Howard brothers appeared on film together—in *Hold That Lion!* (1947). © *Columbia Pictures, courtesy of Moe Howard Collection*

A dramatically thin and mustachioed Curly filmed a second cameo two years later as an irate cook in the 1949 Stooges comedy *Malice in the Palace*, but he was physically unable to perform. So his footage was not used in the final print of the film released to theaters, and the chef role was instead played by Larry. All that remains of the scene is a production still showing Curly waving a hatchet and pulling Larry's hair while Moe and Shemp cower. The still was used on the studio's one-sheet and lobby title card for the film.

That year, even as Shemp starred in new Three Stooges comedies, Curly was featured as the third Stooge in the first of two licensed Three Stooges comic books drawn and created for Jubilee Publications by Moe's son-in-law, then–comic book artist Norman Maurer, and his partner Joe Kubert. Thereafter, the company changed its name to St. John Publishing Company and continued to publish Stooges comics in the 1950s, but with Shemp instead of Curly.

Moe had hoped giving Curly cameo work would build up his morale, but it didn't help. In 1950, he

A dramatically thin Curly making a second cameo appearance, deleted from the final print, in the Stooges comedy *Malice in the Palace* (1949). © *Columbia Pictures, courtesy of Jeff Lenburg Collection*

A 1950 trade ad for a Stooges stage tour with Shemp.
*Courtesy of Moe Howard Collection*

became gravely ill. Two years later, on January 18, 1952, at the age of forty-eight, Curly died of a cerebral hemorrhage resulting from a series of strokes.

Despite Curly's tragic death, the quality of the comedies picked up. Shemp's seasoned performances were instrumental in keeping production going at a rapid pace. From 1936 to 1956, The Three Stooges consistently ranked among film's top ten short-subject moneymakers, alongside cartoon stars Mickey Mouse, Donald Duck, Pluto, Mr. Magoo, and Popeye and live-action screen greats Robert Benchley, Pete Smith, and John Nesbitt, as polled by film buyers for *Motion Picture Exhibitor* magazine's annual Laurel Awards. During Shemp's tenure, they were awarded Exhibitor Laurel Awards for the top two-reel moneymakers for the years 1950, 1951, 1953, 1954, and 1955. Moe was proud of the team for these achievements. As he told a United Press reporter, "Other comedians win academy awards, but we've got five plaques from the theaters. We've never been out of the first ten money makers in the comedy field. That's what counts."

Shemp appeared in seventy-seven Stooges shorts and one feature film—*Gold Raiders* (1951), which they were loaned out to United Artists to make. (Overseas, Monarch Film Corp. would issue the film under the title *The Stooges Go West.*) On November 25, 1950, the boys commenced filming *Gold Raiders* after completing their latest personal appearance tour in New York, Washington, Pittsburgh, and Buffalo. Unlike most of their other feature films, in which

In 1954 the boys show off their *Motion Picture Exhibitor* Laurel Awards, which they won for many years in a row.
© *Columbia Pictures, courtesy of Jeff Lenburg Collection*

they appear only for comic relief, the Stooges display their antics throughout the film. Unfortunately, aside from their salaries, they never saw a dime for their participation in the picture.

After rejoining the team, Shemp made only one feature film with the Stooges, *Gold Raiders* (1951), costarring western film star George O'Brien. *Courtesy of Jeff Lenburg Collection*

On September 26, 1950, *The Los Angeles Times* reported that the Stooges' appearance in *Gold Raiders* was to mark the first of three features planned for them by United Artists. The other two films would supposedly be *Tucson Joe* and *Gasoline Alley*, both starring George O'Brien, who was featured in *Gold Raiders* as well. But according to the film's director, Edward Bernds, Hollywood puffery clouded this article; in fact, no additional United Artists/Stooges features had been scheduled for production.

The Shemp years marked another major milestone: the Stooges' first appearance on television. In 1948, they guest starred on Milton Berle's popular *Texaco Star Theater* and comedian Morey Amsterdam's *The Morey Amsterdam Show*. More importantly, a year later, they starred in a pilot for their own weekly television comedy program, titled *Jerks of All Trades*; unfortunately, it never sold. However, their slapstick brand of humor kept them in great demand. They went on to appear on other popular programs of the day, including *Camel Comedy Caravan* (1950, also known as *The Ed Wynn Show*), *The Kate Smith Hour* (1950), *The Colgate Comedy Hour* (1951), *The Frank Sinatra Show* (1952), and many others.

In 1952, however, the Stooges lost some key personnel responsible for some of their best and brightest on-screen moments when Columbia downsized its short-subject division. Producer Hugh McCollum was let go, and out of loyalty to McCollum, director Edward Bernds resigned. Bernds's departure also stemmed from the fact that there was no love lost between him and Jules White; this left only White to produce and direct the Stooges' film series. Screenwriter Elwood Ullman followed Edward Bernds out the door. As Ullman explained, "I just had to get out of those shorts. No prestige in shorts. I had to get out if I wanted to stay in the business." Ullman and Bernds accepted an offer to write and direct Allied Artists' Bowery Boys features, while McCollum went on to produce several Jack Wrather television series. The absence of Bernds and Ullman was strongly felt in the later Stooges comedies, especially as White took over complete control of Stooges production.

Actual handbill used in *Merry Mavericks* (1951), later reproduced by Moe as one of his favorite giveaway photos for fans. *Courtesy of Moe Howard Collection*

Even though the popularity of the Stooges' films remained relatively constant, Columbia Pictures started looking for new methods to increase the team's appeal. In 1953, after the success of the first-ever 3-D feature, *Bwana Devil* (1952), started the three-dimensional movie boom, producer Jules White decided to star the Stooges in the first 3-D comedy ever produced, *Spooks!* It was followed later that year by a second 3-D Stooges short, *Pardon My Backfire*. Contrary to erroneous reports in other publications, Columbia Pictures did release both films to

The Stooges get "spooked" by a lively skeleton in their first 3-D comedy, *Spooks!* (1953). © *Columbia Pictures, courtesy of Moe Howard Collection*

theaters in 3-D, not just *Spooks!* Columbia even provided movie theaters with exhibitor one-sheets that were displayed during screenings of these films.

Critics were less than enthusiastic about these new Stooges offerings, as was Columbia, and the studio abandoned the idea of producing additional 3-D shorts. But Moe was sure the Stooges would survive Hollywood's 3-D and widescreen movie crazes. As he told a reporter on May 16, 1953, four days before the premiere of *Spooks!*, "We'll make these things [film comedies] till we have to lie down, and then we'll make the last one lying down."

On November 22, 1955, the same day Columbia announced they had signed the Stooges to a new one-

year contract, death again visited the Stooges. That evening, Shemp, at age sixty, died suddenly of a cerebral hemorrhage on his way home from a boxing match.

Shemp's death was another crushing blow to Moe and Larry—first Curly, now Shemp. Moe admitted that he found it difficult to accept the deaths of his brothers and seriously considered breaking up the act. But this was impossible, since the Stooges' Columbia contract called for Moe and Larry to star in the balance of the comedies—with or without Shemp. Larry and Moe honestly considered making the additional shorts without a third Stooge; Larry later revealed that there had been some talk of starring Moe and him in comedies as The Two Stooges but that Columbia had balked at the idea. Fine asserted afterward that Columbia was probably right—"Comedy always comes in threes."

Shemp had already shot material for four of the eight comedies produced for the 1956 season, all remakes combining new footage of the Stooges with stock footage from their old shorts. Shemp's final appearances were in *Husbands Beware*, a remake of *Brideless Groom* (1947); *Creeps*, a new version of *The Ghost Talks* (1949); *For Crimin' Out Loud*, a remake of *Who Done It?* (1949); and *Flagpole Jitters* (1956), incorporating footage from *Hokus Pokus* (1949).

For the four remakes left to produce after Shemp's death, Stooge stand-in Joe Palma was pressed into ser-

Moe's and Larry's screen wives react in horror to the boys' culinary catastrophe in *Husbands Beware* (1956), one of the last films to feature new footage of Shemp. © *Columbia Pictures, courtesy of Moe Howard Collection*

vice. Palma had been around the Columbia lot since the mid-1930s. His most notable appearances in Stooges shorts were in *Three Loan Wolves* (1946) and as Mad Bill Hookup in *Guns A Poppin!* (1957). He had also appeared in guest shots in several of Shemp Howard's and Joe Besser's films. Now, Palma was made up to look like Shemp so he could appear alongside

Moe and Larry in the new footage needed for the remakes. Palma's face was never seen; his back was always to camera. His four appearances as the so-called Fake Shemp were in *Hot Stuff, Rumpus in the Harem, Scheming Schemers,* and *Commotion on the Ocean.*

It has long been asserted that Joe Besser quickly stepped in to replace Shemp in late 1955, but at that point Besser's old studio contract hadn't yet run out. On December 12 of that year, shortly after Shemp's death, Moe amended the original 1934 agreement between himself and Larry, giving him the sole and final say in the selection of "any new partner that might be asked to join us as a 'Third Stooge' in the combination known as 'The 3 Stooges.'" Moe chose Besser for the new third Stooge, and Besser signed an official contract to that effect on January 1, 1956.

Besser's contract was signed separately from the Stooges'—since, he claimed, he made more money that way ($3,500 a film). He also inserted a provision that withheld Moe or Larry from "slapping or causing him bodily harm." Besser's reason for this contract stipulation was that "I wasn't used to doing that wild kind of slapstick—and felt rather uncomfortable about it, since I usually played the kind of character who would hit others back." As a result, Jules White had Larry take all the hits and knocks in the head in

The loss of Shemp forced Moe and Larry to go it alone in four film remakes. A scene from *Hot Stuff* (1956).
*© Columbia Pictures, courtesy of Moe Howard Collection*

Stooge stand-in Joe Palma fills in for Shemp Howard in one of four comedy remakes. A scene from *Rumpus in the Harem* (1956). *© Columbia Pictures, courtesy of Moe Howard Collection*

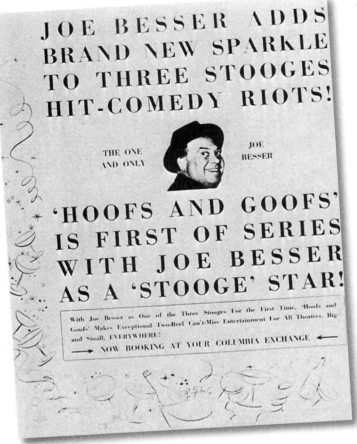

Columbia Pictures announces the signing of comic Joe Besser as the new third Stooge. *Courtesy of Joe Besser*

tion between Moe and Larry that was mandatory in making even the weakest films play for laughs. Joe was also one of the only Stooge replacements to dare to hit Moe in the films—not accidentally but in self-defense when he felt threatened.

Besser introduced another dimension to the team when he suggested that Moe and Larry comb their hair back in the comedies in order to make them appear more like gentlemen. Although Jules White

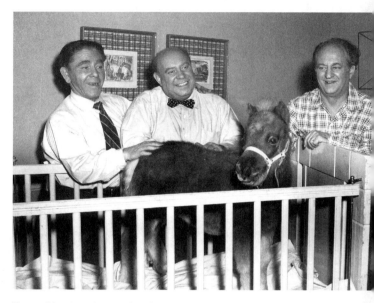

Moe and Larry getting used to their new hairstyles, at the suggestion of Joe Besser, in *Horsing Around* (1957). © *Columbia Pictures, courtesy of Jeff Lenburg Collection*

Besser's place. Larry told Joe, "Don't worry. If you don't want Moe to hit you, I'll take all the belts."

As before, any claims that Columbia's executives or Jules White picked the Stooge successors are totally erroneous. Columbia's only involvement was to approve Moe Howard's selections and make them official.

But Columbia Pictures was wise to approve Moe's selection of Besser as Shemp's replacement, for several reasons. The Stooges series had all but run its course and needed a real boost; Besser's vibrant energy on-screen provided one. And Columbia could ill afford to let Moe pick a lesser-known, less capable, less proven comedian than Shemp and Curly. Besser had the necessary track record, as proven by his successful roles in features and his own two-reel series for Columbia.

Joe was also a real innovator. His feisty-little-kid character was quite different from either of the previous third Stooges, and when he was incorporated into stories that fit this unique personality, he presented the perfect contrast to the other two Stooges. His impish, childlike qualities created the sort of fric-

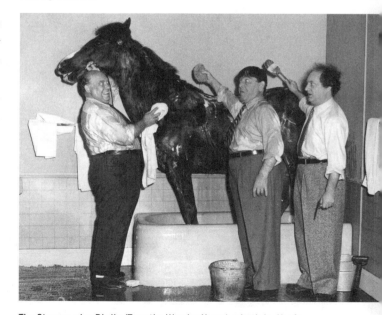

The Stooges give Birdie (Tony the Wonder Horse) a bath in *Hoofs and Goofs* (1957), Joe Besser's first short with the Stooges.
© *Columbia Pictures, courtesy of Moe Howard Collection*

The Stooges rehearse their old vaudeville act in *Fifi Blows Her Top* (1958). *© Columbia Pictures, courtesy of Moe Howard Collection*

A newspaper ad for Joe Besser's only personal appearance with the Stooges, at the Paramount Theatre in Los Angeles. *Courtesy of Joe Besser*

Moe and Larry say good-bye to Joe Besser and director Jules White as they end their twenty-four-year Columbia Pictures short-subject career on December 20, 1957. *© Columbia Pictures, courtesy of Moe Howard Collection*

approved of the idea, he had to use the new hairstyles sparingly if he wanted to be able to match the old stock footage in shorts that were remakes.

On January 31, 1957, Columbia released the first new Stooges comedy with Besser, *Hoofs and Goofs*, to theaters. Joe would go on to star in a total of sixteen shorts. With Besser aboard, the Stooges charted new ground, unknowingly preparing themselves for the future when they would become primarily a kiddie attraction. At Besser's suggestion, the team became more kid friendly, toning down the violence. New shorts were more story driven, with the Stooges' brand of slapstick sprinkled throughout. Remakes or reworkings of earlier Stooges shorts, on the other hand, had more of the traditional Stooges look and feel.

The shorts were churned out at the speed of television situation comedies. Remakes of the old films were usually shot in one or two days, while new stories took the maximum three days. Due to rising costs and declining budgets, the running times were dramatically shorter. The early comedies with Curly, which had comparably higher production values, ran twenty minutes; Besser's were only sixteen minutes in duration.

In 1957, Besser made his first and only personal appearance with Moe and Larry, at the Paramount Theatre in Los Angeles. A couple of Three Stooges comedies were shown, and then the Stooges took the stage to sign autographs and hand out a promotional ballpoint pen that bore the inscription "Stolen From The 3 Stooges: Larry, Moe, Joe." It was the only promotional item distributed during Besser's tenure as one of the Stooges.

On December 20, 1957, The Three Stooges finished filming their last short with Besser—and with Columbia. The studio had come to a decision that since the costs of film production had risen and there was almost no market for the short subject anymore (Columbia was the last studio to have such a department), they would not pick up the option on the Stooges' contract. The boys' careers as they knew them had suddenly come to an end. They were at Columbia one day and gone the next—no thank yous, no farewell party for their twenty-four years of dedication and service and the dollars their comedies had reaped for the studio. Columbia would parse out the release of the remaining Besser Stooges comedies into early June 1959, with their last being *Sappy Bullfighters*.

Joe Besser ends his career as a Stooge on a high note in *Sappy Bullfighters* (1959). © *Columbia Pictures, courtesy of Moe Howard Collection*

Moe Howard recalled that a few weeks after their exit from Columbia, he drove to the studio to say good-bye to several studio executives when he was stopped at the gate by a guard (obviously not a Stooges fan). Since he did not have the current year's studio pass, he was refused entry. For the moment, it was a crushing blow.

During the weeks that followed, Moe and Larry discussed their future plans with Besser. They told him they were considering making personal appearances throughout the country; but Joe's wife had suffered a heart attack and he was unwilling to leave her. Besser's decision was difficult, but he had to quit the team. (Shortly thereafter, Joe signed a five-year pact with Fox to costar in a number of feature films. His first was *Say One for Me* with Bing Crosby.)

Moe and Larry then seriously contemplated retirement. As Larry recalled in an interview, Besser's departure had left them with very few other options. "Moe and I thought of retiring after Columbia let us go. Moe was thinking of quitting show business altogether, since he was pretty well off. I was thinking of managing apartments." Moe had invested his money wisely in real estate and would be able to survive financially. Larry, on the other hand, was on the verge of bankruptcy.

But instead of retiring, Moe and Larry began searching for a new third Stooge. Larry recommended an erstwhile cronie, former Ted Healy stooge Paul "Mousie" Garner. Moe rehearsed with him for three days, later remarking, "He was completely unacceptable." Then, while on vacation in Las Vegas, Larry caught a performance of *Minsky's Follies of 1958* featuring famed burlesque comedian Joe DeRita. Larry informed Moe on his return from Vegas that DeRita might make a good "Curly." Moe contacted DeRita's agent and set up a meeting.

DeRita recalled in an interview that this meeting was the first time Moe asked him to join the Stooges. Throughout the years, distorted reports have surfaced that DeRita was asked several times before—by Moe or Jules White—to become a third Stooge, following Shemp's death in 1955 and even Curly's stroke in 1946. But as DeRita said, "It sounds good. It adds a lot of romance to the story. Around 1958, Moe and Larry wanted to do some personal appearances, and they contacted me for the very *first* time about working with them. We met at an agent's office and I agreed to work with them."

Moe tested DeRita's comic expertise as the new third Stooge in the trio's first public appearance together, entertaining the troops at the Camp Pendleton marine base in Oceanside, California. Next, they were booked for their first professional nightclub engagement, for two weeks starting on October 16, 1958, in Bakersfield, California. Moe recalled that the play date was a disaster and that DeRita wasn't working out. The owner of the club, seeing that the Stooges weren't drawing, tried to suspend their engagement and asked them to take a cut in their $2,500 a week salary. Moe was again having second thoughts about the team's future.

Fortunately, the Stooges stuck it out with DeRita, and the team's fortunes turned around, thanks to an unexpected savior: television. Back in January, Columbia's TV subsidiary Screen Gems had released a package of seventy-eight Three Stooges comedies to television stations. The old comedies racked up respectable television ratings during their first months of release, and by eleven months later, they had become the hottest thing going. Until then, old theatrical Popeye cartoons were the number-one children's TV property; within a period of several months the Stooges knocked Popeye out of the box as king of children's television. In the markets where The Three Stooges were playing, Popeye dropped in the ratings to an average television viewing audience percentage of 13.8. The Stooges comedies, meanwhile, were setting ratings records in city after city—Philadelphia (33.3), Nashville (22.0), Pittsburgh (25.3), Buffalo (27.7), Cleveland (23.3). *Variety* dubbed them "the hit show of this year."

From the release to television of the first package of Stooges shorts alone, Hollywood trade papers reported that Columbia made a $12 million profit. But despite the astronomical revenue Stooges shorts created for Columbia, Moe and Larry didn't receive a dime in residuals. This was because of a Screen Actors Guild ruling that only post-1960 films broadcast on television would earn residuals for actors. (Interestingly, Moe had tried to buy the shorts from Columbia in 1954, but he later recalled that his $1.25 million bid was "laughed out of the office." Failing that, he urged Columbia for years to release the films to television, which they finally did of their own accord.)

Moe, Larry, and Curly-Joe continued to rehearse and did more shows, including a two-show-a-night,

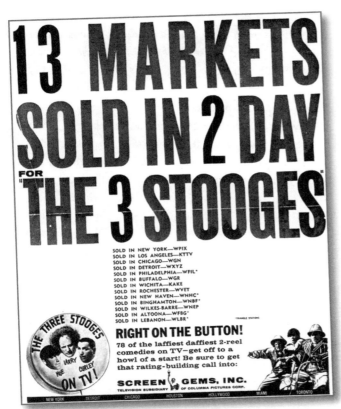

Columbia Pictures' release of Three Stooges shorts to TV in 1958 proved to be a gigantic moneymaker. *Courtesy of Moe Howard Collection*

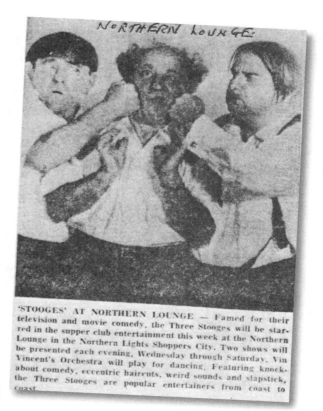

Moe, Larry, and Joe DeRita—with a full head of hair in an early appearance with the Stooges—in a publicity still promoting a 1958 Pennsylvania nightclub appearance.

*Courtesy of Moe Howard Collection*

Wednesday-through-Sunday engagement starting December 17, 1958, at the Northern Lounge in Rochester, Pennsylvania. However, it was the Stooges' next nightclub engagement—the Holiday House in Pittsburgh—that proved the most successful of their career and the turning point in their revival. John Bertera, the club's owner, had considered closing the club Christmas week, traditionally its poorest seven days of business in the year. But after coming home one afternoon to find his kids laughing uncontrollably at old Stooges comedies on television, he booked the Stooges for a single week. Less than six hours after their appearance was announced, the house capacity of seven hundred was sold out—for good reason.

On December 22, 1958, the night the Stooges opened at Holiday House, a major blizzard hit the area, but people carried their kids on their shoulders just to see the trio perform. The Stooges became the first act in the room's history to win a contract extension beyond their original play dates. They played to more than five thousand kids and were held over for three weeks, into January 1959, setting an all-time attendance record of playing to nearly thirty thousand people in twenty days. On the strength of their Pittsburgh engagement, the Stooges were booked to appear on *The Steve Allen Show*, with Bertera releasing them from the final day of their deal, Sunday, January 11, to appear on Allen's program. It was the first of three guest appearances they made on Allen's show that year, and producers clamored to book them on many other major comedy-variety programs thereafter.

In his initial appearances with the team, DeRita wore his hair parted down the middle like Shemp; publicity photographs bear this out. He also went under the name of Joe. Since the old Curly shorts were being rebroadcast daily on television, when kids met him during the trio's first personal appearances, many were expecting to see him with a shaven head like Curly and were naturally confused. As he later reminisced, "The kids would look at me funny and wonder, 'Who is this guy?' I was fat like Curly, but had hair like Shemp."

While they were in New York for an appearance, Joe told Moe at the hotel that he was afraid that kids

The supper club appearance that was responsible for the Stooges' comeback. *Courtesy of Moe Howard Collection*

could not relate to which Stooge he was. He suggested that he shave his head. ("I'll cut my hair—but I'm not going to do an imitation of Curly.") Moe agreed, and the next morning, Joe had the hotel barber give him a crew cut. In addition, Norman Maurer pushed for Joe to add "Curly" to his first name, and Moe concurred. Joe went along with it, and thus he took on the Stooge name "Curly-Joe."

In March 1959, by popular demand, Screen Gems released forty more pre-1948 Stooge comedies to television. By that November, the number of markets in which the films were shown had practically doubled, from 78 to 135; that year as many as 156 television stations would air the comedies nationwide. Similarly, theater bookings of the Stooges' old comedy two-reelers increased 200 percent. To further capitalize on the films' popularity, in September, studio officials

offered ten of the sixteen Stooges shorts with Joe Besser to movie theaters so they could create their own feature program, entitled *Three Stooges Fun-O-Rama* (1959). From September 8, 1959, to June 1968, Columbia would continue to reissue the popular Stooges comedies with Curly, Shemp, and Joe to theaters.

Even though Stooges films were drawing large audiences both in theaters and on television, parental action groups and other concerned organizations wanted TV stations to pull the Stooges comedies from their daily programming. The National Association for Better Radio and TV found the films "objectionable" and claimed that they "degraded the dignity of man." Moe rebutted these claims in interviews, remarking that Stooge comedies were less violent than Popeye cartoons and old westerns. As he said, "We were not as sadistic as westerns, which to my mind are as violent as gangster movies. Kids don't mind seeing somebody get it over the head as long as they know that that person will get right up." Even world-famous anthropologist Margaret Mead agreed with Moe on this point.

Any resulting controversy over the Stooges' humor had no impact whatsoever on their popularity. Requests for the new trio to perform at theaters, auditoriums, and nightclubs skyrocketed. Oftentimes, additional matinees were added to accommodate the overflow of children wanting to see their comedy heroes. Suddenly, they found themselves on the top of the heap, with offers pouring in every day for appearances at fairs, shopping centers, even the Shrine Circus—and at ten to twenty times their previous salary. The Stooges' earnings skyrocketed from $2,500 per week in Bakersfield in 1958 to $25,000 for *one day* to dedicate a new shopping center in Rochester, New York. In 1959, the team's earnings reached an all-time high: a remarkable $750,000 split three ways, according to a *Hollywood Reporter* article, compared to their previous income high reached during their last ten years at Columbia, when they made an average of $70,000 a year, including salaries and personal appearances. Their tsunami-like popularity that year also spawned the first wave of official Three Stooges toys and merchandise, a fan club, and new series of comic books featuring Moe, Larry, and Curly-Joe. By the following year, sponsors would also be clamoring for their services, as they were cast in the first of several television commercials.

Moe simultaneously bonks Curly-Joe and Larry in this 1959 photo.
*Courtesy of Moe Howard Collection*

"When we left Columbia a few years ago after 24 years of service, we couldn't find anybody to say goodbye to," Larry proudly stated at the time. "Now it costs them money to see us."

As Moe added, "The future looks brighter than ever, thanks to the kids."

Larry and Moe drown in fan mail as TV kiddie show host Paul Shannon and Curly-Joe look on. *Courtesy of Moe Howard Collection*

In February 1959, news had broken that the Stooges were negotiating with Screen Gems and several producers to star in a feature-length parody of *The Three Musketeers* and a series of thirty-nine original half-hours produced especially for television, believed to be preliminary discussions for the program later

titled *Three Stooges Scrapbook*. (It would not be the first attempt to star the new trio in a TV series. In late 1958, Norman Maurer proposed utilizing his revolutionary Artiscope process to produce a new half-hour animated series, *Stooge Time*, which never sold.) Instead, Columbia Pictures, the same studio that had booted the Stooges out a year earlier, offered the team a one-picture deal to star in their first feature film, *Have Rocket--Will Travel*. The Stooges were cast as three missile plant handymen who find themselves headed for Venus in a rocket ship.

On March 31, 1959, *The Hollywood Reporter* announced news of the Stooges' forthcoming film (which was spelled *Have Rocket, Will Travel* in all newspaper and trade stories and exhibitor materials for movie theaters but appeared in the film's opening title as *Have Rocket--Will Travel*). Filming was set to begin on May 25, 1959, with David Lowell Rich as director. The producer was Harry Romm, who had also been the Stooges' agent and manager for many years. For their efforts, the Stooges received $30,000 and had to split one-half of Romm's 50 percent of the net profits derived from the film's distribution.

*Have Rocket--Will Travel* opened on August 1, 1959, to mixed reviews but was a box-office success. The film rolled up $127,000 during the first five days of a multiple-theater engagement in the Los Angeles area; the Stooges feature was double-billed with *The Legend of Tom Dooley*, a low-budget Civil War film. *Rocket* was produced on a $380,000 budget and ultimately grossed more than $2.5 million for Columbia.

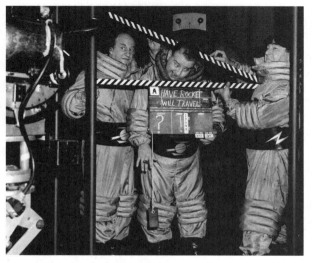

Larry, Curly-Joe, and Moe clowning around on the *Have Rocket* set.
© *Columbia Pictures, courtesy of Moe Howard Collection*

The Stooges onstage with Joe DeRita. *Courtesy of Moe Howard Collection*

Due to the fact that *Have Rocket--Will Travel* was a moneymaker, Columbia sought to star the Stooges in a sequel or follow-up feature they could rush into theaters. Norman Maurer had noted the blockbuster success of producer and distributor Joseph E. Levine's 1959 Italian import *Hercules* and recalled Abbott and Costello's success with their series of "meet" films, so he proposed a story for their next film, eventually titled *The Three Stooges Meet Hercules*. It was a film the Stooges were determined to make, and their agent and manager Harry Romm was eager to make another feature deal. During negotiations with Romm, the trio leveraged their newfound popularity on the big screen, asking for $50,000 and 75 percent of his share of the profits for the film. Romm, wanting his usual 50 percent, refused to improve the terms of their contract. On Norman Maurer's advice, they turned down his offer at their old salary, and the deal hit a stalemate.

But Columbia was desperate to cash in on the Stooges' success. The studio hired Romm to produce, without the trio's knowledge, a new feature pieced together from old footage from existing Stooges comedies. Romm assembled clips from several shorts with Curly Howard, bridging them with newly filmed footage of ventriloquist Paul Winchell and his dummies and The Marquis Chimps (seen in one sequence late in the film) to create some eleven sequences altogether. The film (in which Moe, Larry, and Curly were billed as The Original Three Stooges) was *Stop! Look! and Laugh!* (1960).

During production on *Have Rocket--Will Travel*, a rift had begun to grow between Moe and Romm over decision making. Romm's latest production was the final straw. It culminated in Moe terminating Harry's services as the team's manager and naming Norman Maurer as his replacement. (Later, the Stooges and Maurer would form their own production company, Normandy Productions; under this new arrangement, their compensation per film would be $50,000 salary up front and 50 percent of the net profits.) Incensed, the Stooges, with the help of Maurer, took Romm and Columbia to court, protesting that *Stop! Look! and Laugh!* was illegal, since Columbia had no right to cut up old Stooges comedies and reuse them in a new form without the team's permission.

In January 1960, after engaging in feature-film discussions with 20th Century-Fox, Maurer struck a deal to star the Stooges in a new Fox comedy film—and at a much higher salary of $75,000 collectively—*Snow White and the Three Stooges* (1961). Plans for the send-up of the famous fairytale were officially announced that February. During the time of 20th Century-Fox's interest, Maurer had also shopped the Stooges and their Hercules concept to American International Pictures (AIP), the same studio responsible for distributing Levine's *Hercules* to American theaters. The studio offered to produce the film as long as it was completed in time for an Easter 1961 release. With *Snow White and the Three Stooges* slated for a worldwide release the following June, the Stooges considered it unethical to make *Hercules* ahead of Fox's release. So they turned down AIP's offer.

In March 1960, after reaching an agreement in February, the Stooges began filming another unsold pilot for yet another weekly half-hour television series—both live-action and animated—called *Three Stooges Scrapbook*. That same month, the trio also contemplated offers to star in one of two off-Broadway productions adapted for them, the George Abbot–John Cecil Holm comedy *Three Men on a Horse* or the John Murray–Allen Boretz smash hit *Room Service*, but neither progressed beyond the talking stage.

In June, while Maurer had discussions with Allied Artists over an unknown project for the Stooges, a Los Angeles Superior Court heard evidence of his and the trio's case against Columbia Pictures over *Stop! Look! and Laugh!* The judge ruled in their favor, issuing a temporary restraining order to stop the scheduled release of the film in theaters in the United States. Faced with a huge monetary loss, Columbia ended up settling with the Stooges out of court. Among other things, the studio reimbursed them for all their legal costs and awarded the Stooges both a cash settlement and a contract to make a new feature at their terms: $50,000 and 50 percent of the profits, with Maurer producing and sharing equally in the profits. The matter settled, *Stop! Look! and Laugh!* premiered in select theaters on June 26, 1960, before opening nationally on July 1.

In December 1960, the Stooges began principal filming on 20th Century-Fox's *Snow White and the Three Stooges*, which costarred 1960 Olympic skating champion Carol Heiss as Snow White. As originally announced in the Hollywood trades, Frank Tashlin was set to direct the film at a budget of $750,000, but Fox replaced him with Academy Award–winning director Walter Lang and gave Lang carte blanche. As a result, the budget of *Snow White* skyrocketed to $3.5 million. Twentieth Century-Fox had no way of recovering its costs, because the comedy-fantasy was tailored strictly for children, who paid only fifty cents each for admission. It would have taken an audience of over fifteen million kids for the film just to break even. Another problem that led to the film's box-office failure was that many adults, believing the film was a perfect babysitter, dropped their kids off at the theaters and left them there all day; thus, theaters were often filled to capacity but there was no turnover between screenings. Moe often called this film "a Technicolor mistake."

Afterward, the team returned to Columbia to star in *The Three Stooges Meet Hercules*, under the terms of a final deal reached on October 14, 1960. Columbia had thought the Hercules concept was sensational, and Maurer had commenced to write the story and produce the film, which was originally announced under the working title of *Hercules and the Three Stooges* in December 1960.

Filming of *The Three Stooges Meet Hercules* was completed in late June 1961 on a budget of under $450,000. It opened first in theaters in New York on January 26, 1962 (double billed with Chubby Checker's *Twist Around the Clock*) before being released nationwide in February, and went on to become a blockbuster, outgrossing *Have Rocket--Will Travel*. The release of *Hercules* followed *Snow White and the Three Stooges*, and theater by theater, it outperformed the higher-budget Fox feature.

Fans await the big moment—the arrival of the Stooges for a personal appearance in conjunction with the theatrical opening of *The Three Stooges Meet Hercules* (1962). *Courtesy of Moe Howard Collection*

Columbia immediately signed Maurer and the Stooges to another feature, *The Three Stooges in Orbit* (1962). Plans for the film, originally titled *The Three Stooges Meet the Martians*, were announced in January 1962 as the Stooges prepared to go on tour the following month to promote the opening of *The Three Stooges Meet Hercules*. Their follow-up feature, in which the boys took to warding off Martians Ogg and Zogg, didn't disappoint. Released on July 4, 1962, *The Three Stooges in Orbit* was hailed by *The Hollywood Reporter* as "solid farce entertainment," and it became yet another in a series of box-office hits for the team.

Sandwiched in among the Stooges' released features up to this point were several productions that never got off the ground. In October 1960, Norman Maurer had drafted an eleven-page treatment for *The Three Stooges Meet Pinocchio* (alternately titled *The Three Stooges and Pinocchio* or *Pinnochio and His Three Stooges*), which was to star Jimmy Durante as Geppetto and continue Maurer's plan for a *Three Stooges Meet . . .* series. The film never got past the treatment

The Three Stooges discover the camera between filming scenes for *The Three Stooges in Orbit* (1962). *Photo by Norman Maurer, courtesy of Moe Howard Collection*

The Three Stooges in Artiscope costume and makeup from *The Three Stooges in Orbit* (1962). © *Columbia Pictures, courtesy of Moe Howard Collection*

Moe practices one of his greatest skills—pie throwing—on special effects man Dick Albain between scenes of *The Three Stooges in Orbit* (1962). *Courtesy of Moe Howard Collection*

stage. Other features Maurer planned included *The Three Stooges in King Arthur's Court*, *The Three Stooges Meet Robin Hood*, and *The Three Stooges Meet Captain Bligh*. When it came to rewriting classic tales to fit the Stooges style, Maurer would first write a treatment, and afterward Moe would meet with him to review the treatment for, as the Stooge described it, "certain sequences where we can put in some satire and still

A newspaper ad for *The Three Stooges in Orbit* (1962), boasting the trio's hectic personal appearance schedule. *Courtesy of Moe Howard Collection*

make it part of the story; Moe was uniquely involved in the stories' development. In November 1961, MGM had protested *The Three Stooges Meet Captain Bligh*, because the studio was nearing completion of its remake of *Mutiny on the Bounty*, one of the costliest motion pictures in history at the time, starring Marlon Brando. Maurer subsequently withdrew the project.

While promoting *Orbit* in January 1962, Moe had told a reporter that their next film would have a circus setting. "I think that should afford us the best opportunity for our kind of comedy," he said.

The project never happened. The team's next successful project was a different spoof, a take on Jules Verne originally called *The Three Stooges Go Around the World on 80 Cents* and ultimately titled *The Three Stooges Go Around the World in a Daze* (1963). It was the first film Maurer directed in addition to producing. The Stooges were then signed for guest appearances in two independent productions—in color—Stanley Kramer's United Artists feature *It's a Mad, Mad, Mad, Mad World* (1963), in which they made a brief cameo appearance as firefighters, and the Warner Bros. film *4 for Texas* (1963), starring Frank Sinatra, Dean Martin, Anita Ekberg, and Ursula Andress, in which they play deliverymen entrusted with a painting.

After *The Three Stooges in Orbit*, profits on Columbia's Three Stooges features started to dip. Norman Maurer recalled, "The boys' popularity had reached its peak with *Hercules* and *Orbit,* and then as production costs took an upswing, their popularity took a nose dive. No other studio was making children's films, and with increased production costs it was an uphill battle to recoup negative costs from the kids' twenty-five-cent admissions. Accordingly, Columbia wasn't too anxious to produce another Stooges feature."

Nevertheless, Maurer wrote a new story and convinced Columbia to star the team in one last roundup, *The Outlaws IS Coming!* (1965), for which principal photography started on May 5, 1964. The film featured Adam West (in his pre–*Batman* television series days) and the willowy brunette beauty Nancy Kovack in the romantic leads, and it was the second film both directed and produced by Maurer. Originally titled *The Three Stooges Meet the Gunslingers*, the film used the sixty-six-thousand-acre B-Bar-B Buffalo Ranch in Gillette, Wyoming, as its backdrop. On January 13, 1965, the zany western comedy made its world premiere in San Antonio, Texas. The screening was held for San Antonio–area dignitaries. Nighttime festivities included a downtown parade, and the Stooges and other stars appeared for the opening at the famed Texas Theater. The film began playing in theaters nationwide the following day. It proved to be a fitting swan song, with the famed comedy trio generating plenty of laughs as they expose the schemes of a dastardly gang boss, Rance Roden, and induce the notorious gunslingers of the Old West to mend their ways.

Many fans consider *The Three Stooges Meet Hercules*, directed by Edward Bernds, to be the Stooges' best feature, while others prefer the two that Maurer directed, *The Three Stooges Go Around the World in a Daze* and *The Outlaws IS Coming!*

In the feature films with Joe DeRita, the Stooges went through a noticeable change in their slapstick routines. Moe made the boys tone down the violence and eliminate some of the slapping and hitting, trying to establish the Stooges as family-oriented comedians. Moe even agreed to discontinue his famous two-finger poke in the eyes, since he felt it set a bad example for the kids. Thus, when the Stooges were

The Stooges broke a seventy-six-year attendance record by appearing before a crowd of eighty-five thousand at the Canadian National Exposition on August 19, 1963. *Courtesy of Moe Howard Collection*

Director Norman Maurer has a gentlemanly disagreement with the Stooges on the set of their last released feature film, *The Outlaws IS Coming!* (1965). *Courtesy of Moe Howard Collection*

making features, there was very little deliberate violence in their routines.

In considering what point of view the Stooges' comedy took, Joe DeRita explained in an interview that he didn't think the Stooges had one. As he recalled, "I don't think the Stooges were funny. I'm not putting you on, I'm telling the truth—they were physical, but they just didn't have any humor about them. Take, for instance, Laurel and Hardy. I can watch their films and I still laugh at them, and maybe I've seen them four or five times before. But when I see that pie or seltzer bottle, I know that it's not just lying around for no reason. It's going to be used for something. I was with the Stooges for twelve years, and it was a very pleasant association, but I just don't think they were funny."

But Larry Fine disagreed. He believed that the mystique of the Stooges' comedy was centered around one question: what's going to happen next? Larry remarked in an interview that the Stooges were not method actors, but they did what came to mind, not what they had been trained to do. He saw the Stooges' comedy as a comedy of anticipation: "Everyone in the audience anticipates that when you reach that door the tray of dishes you were balancing will

The Three Stooges take a trolley car ride down Main Street at Disneyland. *Courtesy of Moe Howard Collection*

topple and crash to the floor. So give the audiences what they expect. The door swings open, the tray tips over and the plates fly in all directions and everyone gets a laugh. That was our comic foundation—we gave people what they expected."

The Stooges leave in style after visiting the Movieland Wax Museum in Buena Park, California.
*Courtesy of Moe Howard Collection*

In the fall of 1965, following *The Outlaws IS Coming!*, the Stooges returned to television to star in their own live-action/animated color series for Cambria Studios, *The New 3 Stooges*, which was syndicated nationally. Over the next four years, they made occasional guest appearances on prime-time television shows and served as pitchmen in new commercials while Maurer considered other vehicles in which to star them.

On May 30, 1967, over the Memorial Day weekend, tragedy again struck the team when Larry Fine's wife, Mabel, died of a sudden heart attack. At the time, the Stooges were on a four-city tour to Boston, Providence, St. Louis, and Awagam, Massachusetts. Larry immediately left the show when he learned the news. In true show business tradition, Moe and Curly-Joe, as The Two Stooges, carried on the team's tour for five days without him.

Earlier that year, Maurer had commenced ongoing discussions with Dick Brown (producer of *The*

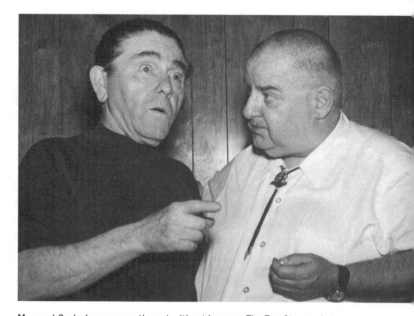

Moe and Curly-Joe carry on the act without Larry as The Two Stooges between their Sunday performances, on June 4, 1967, at Riverside Amusement Park in Agawam, Massachusetts, following the sudden death of Fine's wife Mabel.
*Courtesy of Moe Howard Collection*

*New 3 Stooges)* to produce a brand-new color live-action feature starring the Stooges, originally called *Bush Pilots*. In March of that year, Maurer met with Brown and shook hands on a deal to make the film, by then known as *The Flying Hutch*, from a script by Brown and animator Dave Detiege. The script was based on a previous story treatment, written by Edward Bernds, titled *The Three Stooges Meet the Killers*. On April 3, 1968, they settled on the final title, *The Three Stooges Meet the Gang*. Estimated to cost under $300,000 to make, filming was projected to start on or around July 1, 1968, in Vancouver, Canada. Brown intended to shoot the film using the more "mod" filming techniques popularized in movies starring The Beatles.

Basically, the story cast the Stooges as laborers working in a Los Angeles junkyard. A telegram informs Curly-Joe that a long-lost uncle in Canada has died, leaving him the sole owner of UCA Airways. Curly-Joe later learns that UCA stands for Uncle Curly's Airways (called UCIA or United Curly International Airways in Bernds' original treatment). Naturally, the Stooges believe they'll become tycoons and so burn all their bridges. But the airline turns out to be less prestigious than the Stooges first think: a broken-down single-engine bush-pilot's Flivver turns out to be the sole aircraft of UCA. From here on out, the Stooges turn the film into a sweeping romp, constantly struggling at odd jobs to make a few bucks and keep their single-engine wreck airborne.

Edward Bernds rewrote the Brown-Detiege script, which consisted mainly of "cartoon-type gags," and Bernds was also set to direct the picture. But production and other problems arose. First, Bernds was never paid the $7,500 that Brown had promised to deliver for his services. Then, Brown met with United Artists and Columbia Pictures about distributing the film, but they passed. At the time, studios were more interested in producing huge-budget, elaborate James Bond–type productions or sophisticated films like *Georgy Girl* than children's movies. Trans-Lux, a motion picture distributor and television syndicator, showed considerable interest, however, and in September 1967, Brown appeared to have locked up financing. But he was unable to obtain sufficient financial backing, and the film was scrapped in late summer 1968.

The Stooges made their first film appearance after *The Outlaws IS Coming!* in a twenty-minute US Treasury Department sales film called *Star Spangled Salesman* (1968). Norman Maurer produced and directed the film. The film featured an all-star cast of such favorites as Carol Burnett, Milton Berle, Howard Morris, John Banner and Werner Klemperer (both of TV's *Hogan's Heroes*), Rafer Johnson, Tim Conway, Harry Morgan, and Jack Webb; Carl Reiner served as emcee. The services of the producer, director, and all the actors were donated free to the government. In this, the team's fourth color film appearance with DeRita, Howard Morris convinces the Stooges to join the government's payroll savings plan.

In the late 1960s, Maurer considered other film and television offers for the Stooges, most of which fell through. In March 1968, the Knox-Reeves Agency in Minneapolis inquired about starring the trio in three thirty-second commercials for General Mills. The spots would be test marketed for one year; if successful, they would then air nationally. In addition, Maurer and producer Bud Cole discussed doing a live and taped television series that never manifested.

In July 1968, Maurer lunched with former Bowery Boys producer Ben Schwalb, director Edward

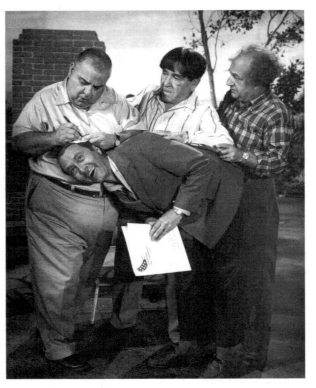

The Stooges and Howard Morris kidding around during the filming of *Star Spangled Salesman* (1968), a color twenty-minute sales film for the US Treasury Department.
*Courtesy of Moe Howard Collection*

Bernds, and writer Elwood Ullman to propose a new *Three Stooges Meet . . .* movie, based on an idea he had developed called *The Three Stooges Meet the Mobsters*. This unique project would pit Moe, Larry, and Curly-Joe against famous and notorious underworld criminals of the twentieth century such as Bonnie and Clyde, John Dillinger, Al Capone, and Baby Face Nelson, all of whose stories at one time had been adapted into successful motion pictures in their own right. Again, no deal could be made since the market for children's films had vanished.

That same month, Gerald Fine of Gerald Fine Productions offered the Stooges $160,000 to star in four features—$40,000 per picture. That September, Maurer and the Stooges accepted Fine's offer, by then reduced to $120,000 for four films ($30,000 per picture) for their services. But the deal turned out to be typical Hollywood talk, and no films resulted.

The following April, Moe, Larry, and Curly-Joe signed a letter of agreement with John Holiday of Cal-Al Productions to star in a new full-color feature based on the screenplay *War Party*. As Maurer wrote, "We have read the screenplay and feel that it is well written, easily adaptable to THE THREE STOOGES and capable of making an exciting, funny film that will not only appeal to today's young adult audience, but is also refreshingly different material for the Stooges." Like previous attempts, the project, unfortunately, never got off the ground.

Throughout this period, Moe, Larry, and Curly-Joe made personal appearances entertaining adults and children with their family-friendly humor. On July 23, 1969, they performed in Tucson, Arizona, at what would be their last public engagement. The event, which benefited the Pima County Association for Mental Health, was held at Hi Corbett Field,

Moe, Larry, and Curly-Joe pose with airline stewardess Stephanie Beare of Houston after arriving in Tucson in July 1969 to perform at the Pima County Association for Mental Health benefit, their last public appearance as a team. *Courtesy of Moe Howard Collection*

then the spring training site for the Cleveland Indians. Curly-Joe made the trip and performed at the benefit that night despite having had a 102-degree fever earlier in the day.

After a short hiatus, in September 1969 the Stooges started filming a TV movie called *Kook's Tour*, in color. In this comedy-travelogue, Moe suggests they retire and see the rest of the world, since they've been stars for fifty years and have never seen the outside of their dressing rooms. This film is really about what not to do when going camping and fishing— and with the Stooges there are a lot of what-nots!

On Sunday, September 7, Maurer and the Stooges departed from Los Angeles for Pocatello, Idaho, and began principal photography the next day; filming lasted four weeks. Afterward, the Stooges shot additional interior and exterior footage at Moe's palatial home in the Hollywood Hills area. A month later, the boys taped their final television appearance, on Bob Barker's popular game show *Truth or Consequences*; the episode began airing the following January.

Before *Kook's Tour* could be finished, on January 9, 1970, Larry Fine suffered a severe stroke at his apartment that left him paralyzed on the left side of his body. He was admitted to the Motion Picture Country House and Hospital in Woodland Hills, California, for care and treatment. As a result, *Kook's Tour* was completed without him in 1970 as a one-hour TV special, but it was never aired. (Maurer would license the release of the film on home video and on Super 8 later in the 1970s.)

Even though Larry's illness had incapacitated him and crippled the team, Moe was not about to abandon the Three Stooges act. In September 1970, Norman Maurer's son Jeff, who would later be known by the pen name Jeffrey Scott, finished writing an original treatment for a new Three Stooges feature for Premiere Productions, *Make Love, Not War* (later retitled *Make Mine Manila*), in which the Stooges are trapped in a World War II prison camp even though

Larry with a set of mechanical Stooge puppets originally used in the opening of KTTV Channel 11 Los Angeles's daytime kiddie show *Billy Barty and the 3 Stooges. Courtesy of Jeff and Greg Lenburg Collection*

the war is over. Moe asked veteran Stooges foil Emil Sitka to join the project as Larry's replacement.

Moe and Norman Maurer held serious negotiations with producer Alan J. Factor of Bedford Productions (with an office on the 20th Century-Fox lot) and the Philippine government, which was going to finance the film. On April 8, 1971, Factor signed off on Scott's script. With Sitka signed on as a Stooge, Factor set up a meeting at the Friars Club in Beverly Hills with Moe, Emil, Joe DeRita, and the film's potential backers to review the production plans. But, Maurer recalled, Sitka's actions at the lunch meeting may have contributed to Factor's decision to back out of the production: "Alan Factor brought in his finance people to join us at lunch. Moe, Joe, and I were shocked at the way Emil acted at the meeting. Suddenly, it was star time. While executives announced what days we would be filming in Manila, Emil said, 'Well, I don't know if I'm available,' and 'I'll need a limousine.' Moe and I were slack jawed. Joe was shocked." Maurer never heard another word on the Philippine film after that meeting.

A short time later, Moe abandoned the idea of continuing as part of a Stooges team and concentrated his energies on pursuing dramatic roles. He made a solo cameo appearance in the Cinerama science-fiction release *Doctor Death: Seeker of Souls* (1973). Even though Moe had very little to do in the film, he was excited at the idea of working again. That same year he was booked to make the first of five appearances on *The Mike Douglas Show*, in addition to speaking engagements at colleges and universities.

In November 1974, Columbia Pictures paid tribute to The Three Stooges by releasing a program of unedited Stooges comedies to theaters. Called *The 3 Stooges Follies*, it consisted of three of the Stooges' comedies with Curly and non-Stooge shorts from the 1930s and 1940s, including several with Buster Keaton and Vera Vague, an original *Batman* movie serial chapter, and a Kate Smith musical.

On January 24, 1975, Moe's longtime friend and partner Larry Fine died of a massive stroke. Moe sobbed when he heard the news of Larry's death, but despite the loss of his former partner, Howard tried to remain active. About a month later, it was announced that Moe, Curly-Joe, and Emil Sitka (playing the role of Larry's brother, Harry) were set to star in an R-rated comedy, *The Jet Set*. (The film was later recast and released under the new title *Blazing Stewardesses*.) Moe was to play a hairdresser, Curly-Joe a masseur, and Emil a manicurist. The Stooges rehearsed their roles and met with the film's producer at the Sheraton-Universal Hotel in Hollywood. At the meeting, Moe appeared rundown, thin, and sickly. His voice was barely above a whisper. But despite his failing health, Moe never let on that he was ill. His mind was as sharp as ever as he spouted out dozens of gags and routines that the Stooges could perform. The producer was pleased, and filming was to begin in Palm Springs a week later.

But Moe was now seriously ill. He continued to call DeRita and Sitka each week telling them that filming had been postponed. Sitka recalled, "The next call I got was from Moe's son. He told me the sad news . . . that Moe was dead."

Moe Howard died of lung cancer on May 4, 1975, at the age of seventy-eight. As Norman Maurer told reporters when interviewed after his father-in-law's death, "When Moe died, the act died with him." Joe Besser and Joe DeRita were the sole survivors of the Three Stooges comedy team.

Recognition of the slapstick trio only heightened after the deaths of Moe Howard and Larry Fine. On May 28, 1975, the same month as Moe's death, The Three Stooges (Moe Howard, Shemp Howard, Larry Fine, and Jerry "Curly" Howard) were installed in The Motion Picture Hall of Fame, part of Doug Wright's Old Movie Theatre in Anaheim, California, which Wright founded in 1971. A special film program, called "The Three Stooges Plus One," featuring Curly and Shemp shorts, highlighted the evening. An awards ceremony followed, with Norman and Joan Maurer;

Moe, sans his famous bowl cut, is interviewed by Jeff and Greg Lenburg at his palatial Hollywood Hills home in 1972. © *Jeff and Greg Lenburg, all rights reserved, courtesy of Jeff and Greg Lenburg*

The *new* new Three Stooges who never saw the light: Curly-Joe, Moe, and longtime Stooges foil Emil Sitka filling in for Larry.
*Courtesy of Moe Howard Collection*

Moe's widow, Helen; and Shemp's widow, Gertrude "Babe" Howard, on hand to accept the honors.

Although The Three Stooges received worldwide public acclaim and years of uninterrupted success, the Hollywood Chamber of Commerce long avoided recognizing them with a star on its Walk of Fame. The Walk consists of bronze stars embedded in the sidewalks of Hollywood Boulevard, each inscribed in honor of a radio, television, recording, or motion picture personality.

The omission of the Stooges brought about cries of discrimination throughout the years. The Stooges themselves had once tried to rectify the situation with their usual zaniness. In 1964, Moe, Larry, and Curly-Joe came up with the clever idea of painting a huge gold star, at midnight, in the center of the intersection of Hollywood and Vine. The boys planned to dress up in painter's overalls, block off the street, and paint their names inside a gigantic mock-up of a Walk of Fame star. Moe abandoned the plan for the midnight escapade at the last minute, evidently fearing the police might arrest them.

It was not until the early 1980s, following a six-month letter-writing campaign drive headed by radio/TV personality Gary Owens, with the assistance of Jeff and Greg Lenburg, founders of the A Star for The Three Stooges Committee, that the Stooges finally received a star.

On August 20, 1983, Joe Besser, representing the trio, joined Joan Maurer and Phyllis Fine Lamond in carrying out the honors of unveiling it. Hordes of media turned out to cover the event—newspapers, magazines, and television news crews—plus nearly three thousand fans, then considered the largest turnout for a Hollywood Walk of Fame event. (The star, the 1,767th handed out by the Walk of Fame, is near the famous corner of Hollywood and Vine).

During the ceremonies, Besser thanked the fans for turning out and for supporting the drive to get the Stooges their very own star. Pointing to three clouds in an otherwise sunny, cloudless Southern California sky, he remarked, "You know who's looking down at you from heaven? The boys. My years with them were the highlight of my career. All I can say is thanks a million. We love you as much as you love us."

Milton Berle, who'd worked with Moe, Larry, and Shemp on his 1950s television series, summed up the ceremony best when he said, "What these men gave to the world is timeless. These great gentlemen, who brought laughter to millions and millions of people, will never be forgotten."

The surviving Stooges, Besser and DeRita, died five years apart—in 1988 and 1993, respectively. Despite the loss of the original trio and their successors, however, the memory of The Three Stooges' comedy does indeed linger on. Their countless films continue to fracture audiences young and old on television stations around the world. In terms of laughs, the Stooges remain the kings of comedy. These mechanics of mirth held no secret to success, other than that the Stooges were funny and not out to win any popularity contests. Maybe that's why they are more appreciated today than any other comedy team in history.

Joe Besser leads the cheers following the unveiling of the Three Stooges star on the Hollywood Walk of Fame in August 1983. © Jeff and Greg Lenburg, all rights reserved, courtesy of Jeff and Greg Lenburg

Even though the Stooges never won an Oscar for their achievements, they have, at least, won the hearts of millions of filmgoers everywhere, and will continue to do so as long as society has a need for that one basic thing: laughter.

# Chapter 2

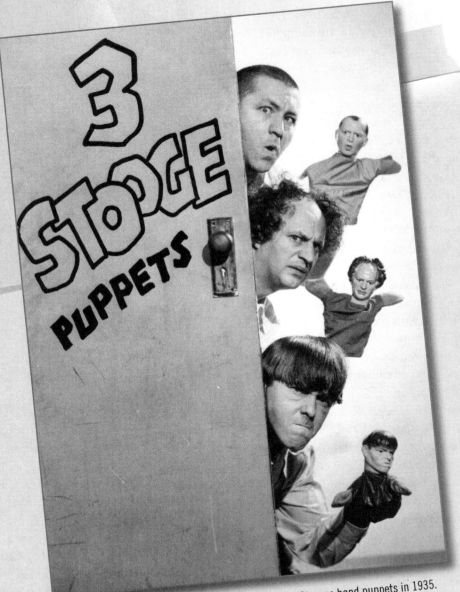

Curly, Larry, and Moe pose with the first licensed Three Stooges hand puppets in 1935.

*Courtesy of Moe Howard Collection*

# *Three Stooges Merchandise*

For over seven decades, manufacturers have created a potpourri of Three Stooges merchandise—with many items becoming brisk sellers. By purchasing these many merchandising novelties, Stooge fans have been able to experience another dimension of the team's worldwide appeal.

In 1935, after the popularity of The Three Stooges became apparent, Columbia Pictures licensed the first official merchandise item: a set of beautifully crafted hand puppets bearing their comical likenesses, designed by a well-known Italian artist. When the puppets were first made available to stores, Columbia's publicity department took a series of promotional stills of the Stooges holding their puppet lookalikes, and additional stills of the studio's feature film stars playing with the Stooges puppets as well. Larry Fine once recalled that the puppets were a losing venture for the toy company that made them, since the production costs were outrageously high.

Moe, Larry, and Curly mug with their hand puppet look-alikes. © *Columbia Pictures, courtesy of Moe Howard Collection*

Two years later, the Stooges' names and likenesses were featured prominently when the Pillsbury Mills Flour Co. (later known as the Pillsbury Co.) launched a nationwide promotion to help stimulate sales of its Farina cereal. The Minneapolis-based company sponsored the construction of The 3 Stooges Moving Picture Machine, a three-dimensional cardboard projector featuring Moe, Larry, and Curly, and distributed it at movie-theater matinees across the country. The machine, which was made out of heavy, die-cut cardboard, included a double set of Three Stooges "movies"—actually frame blowups from Stooges comedies printed on squares of cardboard, which moved in full action when cranked through the camera-shaped machine. Each set contained fifty-six pictures, and eight sets altogether were offered, based on the following films (in this order): *Uncivil Warriors*; *Grips, Grunts and Groans*; *Restless Knights*; *Pop Goes the Easel*; *False Alarms*; *Three Little Pigskins*; *Movie Maniacs*; and *Half Shot Shooters*. At weekly matinees, theaters involved in the promotion provided filmgoers with the opportunity to win one of several of these clever gadgets, while everyone else in attendance received consolation prizes: five-by-seven autographed photographs of the Stooges, signed by Moe, Larry, and Curly.

Stooges ham it up with child star Edith Fellows promoting Pillsbury's 3 Stooges Moving Picture Machine in 1937.
© *Columbia Pictures, courtesy of Moe Howard Collection*

Theater managers also received a handsome campaign packet with which to advertise the Pillsbury promotion. The kit was composed of a deluxe sound trailer (featuring the Stooges demonstrating the item), a lobby poster, the autographed photographs of The Three Stooges for the audience, follow-up circulars, and short film trailers for subsequent matinees. Pillsbury also promoted the campaign through colorful displays in grocery stores across the country, through its radio program *Today's Children* (which was broadcast daily over thirty-five NBC stations and affiliates), and through newspaper advertising and Sunday comics supplements that reached over ten million homes. Despite the rarity of the Pillsbury-Stooges picture machine, reports continue to surface periodically that many of them have been found and sold at collectors' auctions around the nation.

Ten years later, in 1947, under licensing arrangements with Columbia, Excel Corp. of Chicago sold and manufactured a red toy projector called Jolly Theatre that played fifty- and one-hundred-foot 16 mm versions of The Three Stooges, Andy Clyde, and Our Gang comedies and Barney Google, Krazy Kat, and Scrappy cartoons. (Some films were also released in 150- and 200-foot versions.) The films had to be cranked by hand to project them; the top of the Jolly Theatre box, which was white on the inside, doubled as a movie screen. Stooge films included in the collection were all retitled. For example, *Half Shot Shooters* (1936) was issued as two films under two different titles, *Heavy Gunners* and *The Three Stooges Join the Army*. Others in the series included: *Out of Business, Bear Hunting, Fake Medicine Show, Prize Boarders, Accidentally Scalped, Hungry Three, Rough Stuff, Join the Army, Three Fakers, Milk and Money, Plane Crazy, Crazy Pilots, Some Trappers, Pain in the Pullman, Smashed Tomatoes, Grin and Bear It*, and *Dangerous Buckaroos*. (Interestingly enough, many years later Excel also released a few 8 mm versions of the Stooges films for home use, including a derivative of the retitled *Plane Crazy* and of *Whoops, I'm an Indian!*)

Theatrical poster promoting Pillsbury's Three Stooges toy projector.
*Courtesy of Moe Howard Collection*

Curly, Moe, and Larry display the autographed giveaway photos of themselves included with every Pillsbury toy projector in 1937.
*© Columbia Pictures, courtesy of Moe Howard Collection*

Original box for a Three Stooges 16 mm short, part of a series of condensed and retitled versions of the Stooges Columbia comedies sold by Excel Movie Products for home use beginning in 1947.
*Courtesy of Jeff Lenburg Collection*

Although very little merchandise came out on the original film trio, almost no official merchandise was manufactured featuring Shemp, who had replaced Curly in 1946. Columbia received no firm offers from toy and game manufacturers. But in 1948, outside the realm of wholly licensed Three Stooges merchandise, BC Cinemas in England produced a ten-card set of trading cards to be given out to their patrons. These ABC Film Stars cards were issued in two different sizes—smaller versions measuring 1⅜ inches by 2½ inches and the larger versions measuring 1⁷⁄₁₆ inches by 2¹¹⁄₁₆ inches—and they featured cinema stars like Roy Rogers, Johnny Weissmuller, Shirley Temple, Laurel and Hardy, Gene Autry, and Abbott and Costello. They also included the earliest known cards of The Three Stooges and the East Side Kids. Shemp was featured as the third Stooge—though his name was misspelled as "Shep." Then, in the late 1940s, when the first Three Stooges Toy Watch was produced, it bore the faces of Moe, Larry . . . and Curly.

In 1949, the Stooges again broke new ground in the field of merchandise when Jubilee Publications published two issues of the first-ever Three Stooges comic book series—again starring Curly. Finally, in 1953, Shemp was included in another Three Stooges comic book series, published under Jubilee Publications' new name, St. John Publishing Company.

In the early 1950s Moe Howard ordered fancy decks of Three Stooges playing cards, printed by a Chicago firm, for himself and the other Stooges. Though they could not be considered true merchandise, they featured the faces of Moe, Larry, and Shemp on the back. Although Moe originally conceived them as a Christmas gift, he mailed many of them to politicians, lawyers, and doctors for publicity

purposes. The cards are rare, since Moe ordered very few sets and they were never distributed to stores.

When Joe Besser replaced Shemp Howard in 1956, Columbia again had no offers from game and novelty manufacturers to produce additional Stooges merchandise. However, in a wise promotional move, Columbia Pictures did manufacture hundreds of fountain pens that were inscribed with the words "Stolen From The 3 Stooges: Larry, Moe, Joe." The Stooges handed these out at a personal appearance in Los Angeles in 1957. Like the playing cards, the pens received no national distribution to gift shops or novelty stores.

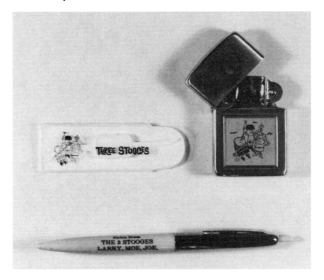

Three rare Stooges collectibles: plastic toothpick and case, cigarette lighter, and pen. *Courtesy of Moe Howard Collection*

In 1958, Three Stooges merchandise exploded onto the scene when the Stooges shorts became a hit on TV and Joe DeRita, who resembled Curly Howard, joined the team and took the nickname "Curly-Joe." Because of the trio's sudden rebirth in popularity with children and adults, Norman Maurer Productions licensed Henry Saperstein of Television Personalities Inc. to merchandise The Three Stooges' names and likenesses. Saperstein's firm did an excellent job, securing many merchandising deals for advances of $1,000 and more, plus 5 percent of gross sales, often for products featuring the original trio of Moe, Larry, and Curly. The year 1959 was a record sales period for Three Stooge merchandise. Under the expert guidance of Saperstein and Norman Maurer, over thirty-six different toys and games were distributed and sold worldwide.

Sampling of Three Stooges playing cards, circa 1950.
*Courtesy of Jeff Lenburg Collection*

Curly-Joe, Moe, and Larry caught up in the jungle of Three Stooges merchandise that flooded the marketplace in 1959.
*Courtesy of Moe Howard Collection*

Norman Maurer recalled that the most popular and most successful piece of merchandise was Three Stooges Bubble Gum Cards, produced by the Frank H. Fleer Company in May 1959. Each full-color, four-inch-by-three-inch trading card featured a still from a Stooges action scene and a caption by Stooges screenwriter Elwood Ullman. Packets sold in stores for five cents a piece; the Stooges' share of the profits alone was over $20,000.

A very popular collectible was the Frank H. Fleer Company's first set of Three Stooges Bubble Gum Cards, originally manufactured in May 1959. *Courtesy of Moe Howard Collection*

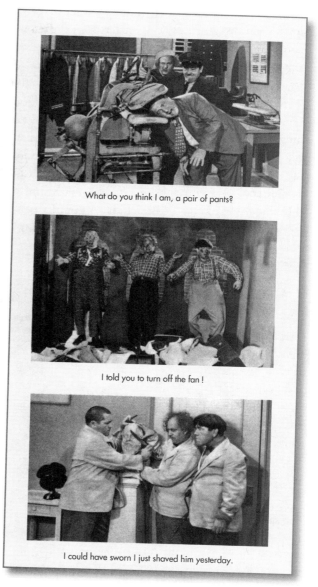

What do you think I am, a pair of pants?

I told you to turn off the fan !

I could have sworn I just shaved him yesterday.

Sample strip of cards from Fleer's successful Three Stooges gum-card series. *Courtesy of Jeff Lenburg Collection*

Another supersuccessful merchandising venture was the first Three Stooges Fan Club, which Norman marketed out of his own home in Los Angeles. Henry Saperstein, who was a genius when it came to making merchandise deals, turned down Maurer's initial proposal for the Stooges Fan Club, since his company had lost money when it marketed the unsuccessful Elvis Presley Fan Club. Confident that the Stooge club would make a profit, Maurer spearheaded the operation on his own and advertised the club on the back cover of Dell's Three Stooges comic books. Fifty cents entitled applicants to an official Three Stooges Fan Club card, a special engraved club certificate, two large photographs of the Stooges, a set of Three Stooges stamps, and a personal letter from the team.

Maurer recalled that the initial fan reaction was tremendous. Thousands of pieces of mail flooded the Hollywood post office. In an interview, Maurer remembered the comical situations this flood presented: "On one occasion the response from an announcement on Sally Starr's TV show in Philadelphia was so great that I almost collapsed from dragging a bag of mail down the post office steps. You can imagine the size and weight of a mailbag with almost $3,000 in assorted coins. Often kids sent in fifty pennies, and we had to pay heavy postage-due penalties."

Original Three Stooges Fan Club kit, circa 1959.
*Courtesy of Moe Howard Collection*

On another occasion, Maurer experienced difficulty at a local bank when he asked the head teller to count the coins received from the fan club applications in the bank's automatic coin counter. Evidently fans took extreme care when enclosing the coins with their club applications. "Sometimes the kids sewed their coins to cardboard and more often glued them into the envelope," Maurer recalled. They used everything from Scotch tape to Wilhold glue. These sticky substances had never been completely removed from the money, and they jammed the coin machine. The bank's president was dismayed when he heard the news. He called Norman into his office, returned the bag of coins, and ordered him never again to darken the bank's doors with his definitely filthy lucre.

While Saperstein remained skeptical over the club's chances to turn a profit, Maurer proved his merchandise representative wrong. The Three Stooges

Fan Club netted an astronomical $22,000 during the first year of operation, and the earnings continued to increase as more fans learned of its existence.

One of the first collectibles produced and licensed under Norman Maurer Productions Inc. in 1959 was The Three Stooges Flying Cane, made by Empire Plastic Corp. of Pelham Manor, New York. The two-piece plastic cane sold for a suggested retail price of forty-nine cents. A rubber band was attached to the inside of the cane so that when it bounced on the ground, it would spring back up into the air and "fly."

That same year, many other merchandise novelties were produced and distributed to retail stores. Candy items originally retailed for five cents or more; coloring books and toys, twenty-nine cents and up; and games, one dollar or more. From January through July 1959, they included the following (with contracted release dates and manufacturers listed where available): Three Stooges Magic Re-Color Book (January 26, Fun-Bilt Toys Inc.); Three Stooges Vinyl Inflatable Toys and Three Stooges Hand Puppets (February 1, Ideal Toy Corp.); Three Stooges Hats (March 1, Clinton Toy Corp.); 3 Stooges Punching Balloons (March 5, Van Dam Rubber Co.); Three Stooges Candy Taffy Kisses (May 1, Phoenix Candy Co.); Three Stooges Bowling Set; Three Stooges Knock 'Em Set, with plastic milk-type bottles and balls; Three Stooges Spin Toy (May 1, Empire Plastic Corp.), which promised, "It Spins . . . It Whistles . . . It Dances . . . It Sings"; and The Three Stooges T-shirts (Allison Mfg. Co.).

Fun-Bilt's The Three Stooges Magic Re-Color Book, January 1959.
*Courtesy of Moe Howard Collection*

Ideal Toy Corp.'s Three Stooges hand puppets—Moe, Larry, and Curly—first sold in retail stores in February 1959.
*Courtesy of Moe Howard Collection*

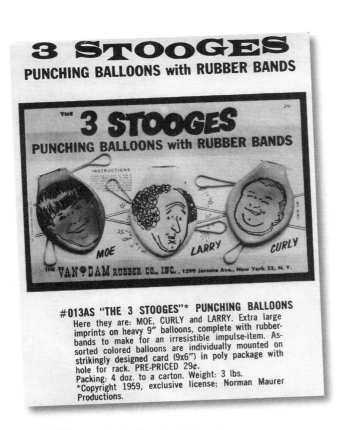

A 1959 product ad for Van Dam Rubber Co.'s 3 Stooges Punching Balloons with Rubber Bands.
*Courtesy of Moe Howard Collection*

Curly-Joe, Moe, and Larry mugging with a mock set of Three Stooges balloons produced in 1959.
*Courtesy of Moe Howard Collection*

Other novelties that followed included: Three Stooges Finger Puppets; Three Stooges Kazoo, featuring dancing figures, and Three Stooges Walking Spring Toy (May 1, Wilkening Manufacturing Co.); Three Stooges Masks, in the images of Moe, Larry, and Curly made out of plastic and buckram; The Three Stooges Funny Coloring Book (June 1, Samuel Lowe Inc.); Three Stooges Halloween Costumes (June 1, Dessart Bros. Inc.); The Three Stooges Fun House Game and Boxed Board Games (July 1, Lowell Toy Manufacturing Co.); and Three Stooges Nutty Putty (July 1, Nadel and Sons Corp.).

In 1959, a real treat for moppet members of the Stooges fan club was the official Three Stooges Beanie.
*Courtesy of Moe Howard Collection*

Original sketch by Norman Maurer for a Three Stooges hat, circa 1959. *Courtesy of Norman Maurer Collection*

Wilkening Manufacturing Co.'s Three Stooges Finger Puppets manufactured in May 1959. *Courtesy of Moe Howard Collection*

From August through October of that year, additional licensed games and toys sold and marketed were: the first Three Stooges Jigsaw Puzzle (August 1, Colorforms); Three Stooges Silly Riddle Game (August 1959, Colorforms), featuring a board with dials that when turned gave answers to riddles; two Three Stooges Slap-Stick-On Colorforms sets (August 1959, Colorforms); Three Stooges Color by Pencil Sets and Three Stooges Rubber Stamp Sets (August 1, Colorforms). Other fully licensed items included a Three Stooges Plastic Gum Dispenser and Three Stooges Pin-On Action Pictures (September 23, L. M. Becker and Co.); Three Stooges Flicker-Action Rings and Three Stooges Ring Ding (October 15, L. M. Becker and Co.), featuring rings and sugar stick candy; Three Stooges Stuffed Dolls (Juro Novelty Company Inc.); Three Stooges Inflatable Vinyl Punches (Hampshire Manufacturing Inc.); Three Stooges Magnetic Toy (Smethport Specialty Co.); Three Stooges Musical Toys (Spec-Toy-Culars Inc.); and Three Stooges Buttons (Green Duck Metal Stamping Co.).

Three Stooges Plastic Gum Dispenser from September 1959.
*Courtesy of Moe Howard Collection*

L. M. Becker and Co.'s Three Stooges Flicker-Action Rings, first produced in October 1959. *Courtesy of Moe Howard Collection*

Newspaper ad of Curly-Joe, Moe, and Larry promoting the Stooges Colorforms set. *Courtesy of Moe Howard Collection*

Comic book ad for the Three Stooges Magic Foto Club, featuring artwork created in September 1960. *Courtesy of Norman Maurer Collection*

Carry-Case Manufacturing's Three Stooges School Bag for child and teenage fans. *Courtesy of Moe Howard Collection*

In 1960, a smaller but fun-packed batch of official Three Stooges merchandise also spilled into the toy and game marketplace. Items included: Three Stooges Halloween Costumes and Masks (June 1, Ben Cooper Inc.); Kenner's Easy Show Projector 8mm Film Strips and Give-a-Show Projector, for 35 mm color filmstrips of the Stooges (July 1, Kenner Products Inc., a division of Bromo-Mint Co.); Three Stooges Paper Mache Figurines; Three Stooges Bobbing Head Figurines; ceramic Three Stooges Drinking Mugs and three-sided Three Stooges Bank of Moe, Larry, and Curly (July 1, Mahana Importing Co.); Three Stooges Pencil Coloring Set (Colorforms); Three Stooges School Bag and Loose-Leaf Ring Binders (Carry-Case Manufacturing Co.); and Vinyl Inflatable Toys and Hand Puppets (Ideal Toy Corp.).

Also in 1960, Kenosha, Wisconsin–based Samuel Lowe published a second ninety-six-page Three Stooges Funny Coloring Book, and in 1961 a third and fourth book in the series. That same year, using similar artwork to the Lowe editions, Bonnie Books issued its own Three Stooges Coloring Book featuring Moe, Larry, and Curly. It is unknown whether this was part of a second series of books starring the original trio. (In June 1960, a forthcoming children's book, *The Three Little Stooges and See How They Grow*, was announced. Details of the project are sketchy, and it appears the book was never published.)

In 1961, another unique item was also marketed: The Three Stooges Movie Viewer, with film strips of "complete '3 Stooges' stories," followed a year later by

Giveaway photo for *The Three Stooges Meet Hercules* (1962), one of many such items given to fans during the Stooges' personal appearance film tours. *Courtesy of Moe Howard Collection*

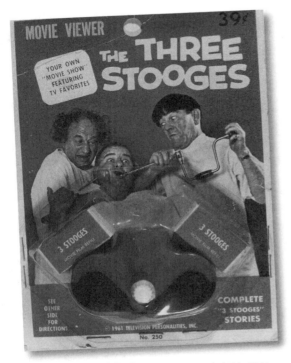

Playable film clips of the Stooges accompanied this 1961 Three Stooges Movie Viewer. *Courtesy of Moe Howard Collection*

The 3 Stooges Color TV Set (Acme Toy Corp.), complete with five rolls of film of the Stooges in action.

In 1962, Golden Press of New York, an imprint of Western Printing, published the first Three Stooges Punch-Out Book. This was followed a year later by Kenner's Sparkle, Presto, and Presto-Sparkle Paint Sets, featuring The Three Stooges, Mr. Magoo, and Rocky and Bullwinkle, and, in 1964, Kenner's The Three Stooges Presto-Sparkle Coloring and Glitter Paint Set and the first Kenner's See-A-Show viewer, a compact and affordable plastic stereo viewer (available in red or blue) with 55 mm slides of the Stooges and other popular characters.

In 1964, Whitman Publishing Co. of Racine, Wisconsin, took advantage of the Stooges' popular-

The Three Stooges Punch-Out Book, complete with cutout figures of the Stooges, from 1962. *Courtesy of Moe Howard Collection*

ity with children and produced The Three Stooges Coloring Book. Originally sold for twenty-nine cents, this authorized 128-page edition featured a full-color cover of Moe and Larry in sombreros and Mexican garb atop a donkey, with Curly-Joe pushing them from behind; inset above the color images was a black-and-white photo of the trio from their Columbia Pictures feature *The Three Stooges Go Around the World in a Daze* (1963). Whitman also manufactured a fine array of additional Stooges merchandise such as: The Three Stooges Punch-Out Book, The Three Stooges Cut-Out Book, The Three Stooges Stamp Book, and The Three Stooges Sticker Fun Book. Then, in 1965, the Frank H. Fleer Company produced a second series of Three Stooges Bubble Gum Cards with scenes from Columbia Pictures' and Normandy Productions' Stooges features on each card. When assembled, the backs of the entire collection of cards made a poster-size color photograph of the Stooges from the movie *The Outlaws IS Coming!* (1965). Also that year, Yankee manufactured The Famous 3 Stooges Photo Printing Set ("Print your own 3 Stooges Photos directly from Famous TV and Movie Negatives"; "Make your own Comedy Gallery"; "HOURS OF SAFE HILARIOUS FUN!"). It

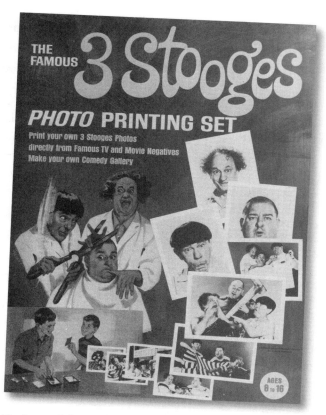

The Famous 3 Stooges Photo Printing Set, which enabled young fans to make photos from real negatives of the famed comedy trio. *Courtesy of Jeff Lenburg Collection*

The second set of Fleer Three Stooges Bubble Gum Cards, 1965. *Courtesy of Jeff Lenburg Collection*

featured ten negatives of Larry, Moe, and Curly-Joe, including portraits of the trio and pictures of them in classic poses, twenty-five sheets of print paper, contact paper, two developing trays, photo developer and fixer, and fold-out instructions. Two years later, M.

Shimmel Sons of Brooklyn, New York, manufactured The Three Stooges Cartoonist Stamp Set, which featured a nontoxic stamp pad and six rubber stamps—two each of Moe, Larry, and Curly-Joe.

Around 1965, *Snow White and the Three Stooges*, a non-Columbia Stooges feature, appeared on the home movie market, released in a 200-foot, 8 mm digest version under the Americom banner. Americom was a producer of 8 mm silent films with an accompanying record that could be played along with the film to provide the movie's dialogue and music track in sync with the picture. The company had obtained permission from 20th Century-Fox, which produced *Snow White*, to release a ten-minute version of the feature in color and black-and-white. The abridged black-and-white versions sold for $9.95, while the ones in color were $15.95. In 1966, Americom reissued the film in Super 8 mm sound. By 1973, however, Americom would go bankrupt and the company's entire library of films would be liquidated.

By the late 1960s, the flow of Three Stooges merchandise had diminished. But despite the fact that the team's popularity had begun to wane, Columbia Pictures' 8 mm division marketed its own 8 mm versions of Three Stooges comedies with Curly and Shemp for home movie viewing. These silent, abridged Stooges films, available in 50-foot and 200-foot versions, were stocked by discount houses and camera stores, which carried other Columbia 8 mm offerings as well. Titles included *Ants in the Pantry*, *Cash and Carry*, *Goofs and Saddles*, *Malice in the Palace*, *A Pain in the Pullman*, *Studio Stoops*, and *Whoops, I'm an Indian!* Television distributor Associated Artists Productions (a.a.p.) also issued silent Stooge comedies: two 8 mm

*Gold Raiders*, the Stooges' only feature with Shemp, saw additional distribution in both 8 mm and Super 8 home movie versions. This full-length Super 8 sound version, released in England by Walton Films under the title *Stooges Go West*, is a rare collector's find.
*Courtesy of Jeff Lenburg Collection*

Two examples of Three Stooges unedited 400-foot Super 8 sound home movies marketed by Columbia Pictures' 8 mm division starting in 1974. *Courtesy of Jeff and Greg Lenburg Collection*

Columbia Pictures' 8 mm division packaged and sold this 3-D home-movie version of *Spooks!* (1953), retitled *Tails of Horror*. *Courtesy of Moe Howard Collection*

abridgements of the Stooges' only feature film with Shemp, *Gold Raiders*, one of them called *Eye Doctors*. Then, in 1974, as part of its Comedy Classics line, Columbia expanded the Stooges film series to also include unedited 400-foot Super 8 sound versions of Three Stooges comedies featuring Curly and Shemp. These sound films retailed for $39.95, as compared to the original retail price of $12.95 for Columbia's earlier silent formats.

The 1970s and 1980s were more promising than the late 1960s for Three Stooges–related merchandise. In 1973, Samuel Gelfman, president of the Cartrivision Corporation, a videotape company, acquired the rights to market a videocassette version of the Stooges' previously unreleased comedy travelogue *Kook's Tour*. For a short period of time the cassette was distributed by the Sears, Roebuck stores. In 1975, the film went into a minor form of distribution: Niles Film Products, a home movie distributor, signed an agreement with Normandy Productions to market *Kook's Tour* in Super 8 color and sound for a price tag of about $200. But in 1981, Niles went bankrupt. (In 1999, Anchor Bay would release a VHS home video edition of the Niles Super 8 version.)

In 1977, General Foods offered six different eleven-inch-by-fourteen-inch posters of the Stooges

Flyer promoting Niles Film Products' licensed Super 8 sound version of *Kook's Tour*, the Stooges' last film. *Courtesy of Jeff Lenburg Collection*

free in boxes of Post Super Sugar Crisps. One year later, Norman Maurer Productions and Hanna-Barbera Productions licensed the use of Maurer's animated TV characters from the cartoon titled *The Robonic Stooges*, to be published in a Skatebirds Coloring Book. Then, in 1980, Columbia Pictures released a collection of its full-length features, cartoons, and comedies on videocassette. Among the impressive list of Columbia favorites were three volumes of Three Stooges comedies on tape for $59.95. That same year, Esco Products also produced a set of well-detailed, seventeen-inch-tall Three Stooges Statues of Larry, Moe, and Curly in classic "see no evil, hear no evil, speak no evil" poses.

By 1981, Three Stooges merchandise had entered a new phase of production under the direction of Columbia Pictures' merchandising department. In January 1981, Norman Maurer Productions, which had managed all rights to The Three Stooges' names and likenesses since the late 1950s, signed an exclusive five-year merchandising contract with Columbia, entitling

the New York–based company to merchandise Three Stooges products. According to Columbia's merchandising director at the time, Glenn Dyckoff, more than five thousand wholesalers, nationwide and abroad, were actively selling Three Stooges merchandise.

During Columbia's first, trial-run year as the Stooges' merchandise representatives, the company licensed such items as Three Stooges Statues (Moe, Larry, and Curly, each thirty-seven inches high), Three Stooges Stick-Ons, a Three Stooges Wrist Watch (which told time backward), Three Stooges Posters, and Three Stooges Greeting Cards. Columbia Pictures and Norman Maurer Productions also approved the first jointly licensed Official Three Stooges Fan Club, which offered new Three Stooges merchandise to fans and provided information about the Stooges through a bimonthly journal. Also in 1981, Horsman, makers of licensed ventriloquist's dolls, manufactured the first ventriloquist's dummy of Moe (as part of its Ventriloquist Pal series for boys and girls); it was a great likeness, including the head Stooge's trademark bangs and scowl.

One of the most unusual items of the 1980s was a set of machine-washable and machine-dryable, soft, squishy, and cuddly Three Stooges dolls (Collins Co.) manufactured for children in 1982. Other popular items included a 1984 limited-edition Three Stooges collector's plate (Bradford Exchange), featuring

Columbia Pictures and Norman Maurer Production licensed Three Stooges Statues in 1980. *Courtesy of Moe Howard Collection*

A set of official Three Stooges 3-D stickers, 1981. *Courtesy of Moe Howard Collection*

lished two editions of The Three Stooges Coloring & Activity Book. Norman Maurer was credited as an artist on the series, as was Stan Goldberg. Stories were adapted from Maurer's Hanna-Barbera cartoon series *The Robonic Stooges*, including the first story in the first edition, "Curly of the Apes," also the title of a 1977 cartoon episode. Also in 1985, Fantasy Trading Card Co. released a new set of Three Stooges trading cards (they would release a second set four years later), and Expressive Designs Inc. issued its first line of Three Stooges collectibles as part of its The Great Entertainer Series: a Three Stooges Plate and a set of fourteen-inch Three Stooges Statues, beautifully hand-painted in "Movie Black & White" colors. Expressive Designs would produce a second set of statues in 1988.

Between 1982 and 1985, RCA/Columbia Pictures Home Video released a total of thirteen Three Stooges volumes on Beta, VHS, and Laserdisc. Each release contained three comedy shorts. From 1988 to 1990, Columbia would release eighteen additional video volumes, including, for the first time, comedies with Shemp.

Columbia Pictures' line of Three Stooges videocassettes featuring Curly. *Courtesy of Moe Howard Collection*

In February of 1986, Hallmark published its first in a line of licensed Three Stooges greeting cards, featuring black-and-white poses of Moe, Larry, and Curly wishing birthday thoughts, get-well wishes, and greetings for Valentine's Day, Mother's Day, Father's Day, and Christmas. That spring, Pressman Toy Corporation released its newest addition to its popular lineup of VCR games, *The Three Stooges: The VCR Game*. Designed for players aged eight years to

an image drawn by artist Bill Markowski; only ten thousand plates were issued. That same year, Mylstar Electronics produced the first Three Stooges arcade game, *The Three Stooges in Brides Is Brides*, which tasked the famed comedy trio with finding three kidnapped brides. In 1985, Playmore Inc. Publishers and Waldman Publishing Corp. of New York pub-

adult, the game included a sixty-minute videocassette featuring scenes of the Stooges favorite slapstick routines, among them "Niagara Falls," "Census Takers," and many more, along with Stooge action cards, penalty cards, six stand-up Stooge figure cards, and a scoring pad.

Pressman Toy Corporation's first-ever Three Stooges VCR game (1986), which includes a sixty-minute videocassette featuring scenes of the Stooges' favorite slapstick routines.
*Courtesy of Norman Maurer Collection*

In 1987, Lyle Stuart, the publisher of Citadel Press, published the first twelve-month Three Stooges calendar, which would continue publication through 1989. (The following year, Landmark Calendars would take over as the publisher of the Stooges' official yearly calendar.) Other new Stooges merchandise included a Three Stooges Wall Clock, resembling a giant watch, from the same maker of new Three Stooges wristwatches (Bradley Time); a rubber stamp set (Uptown Rubber Stamp); metal buttons (Button Up Co.); Three Stooges shorts and shirts (Life's A Beach Inc.); a line of Stooges bookmarks (Antioch Publishing); and many other products.

Later in 1987, game developers Cinemaware Corporation of Westlake Village, California, the company behind the smash bestselling game *Defender of the Crown*, released the first interactive Three Stooges computer game. The original 1987 releases were for Amiga and Commodore 64 game systems; Atari ST, PC, and Apple IIGS home computer editions were issued in April and May 1988. This computer comedy classic featured voices, sound effects, and scenes digitized from the Stooges' Columbia Pictures two-reel comedies—everything from pie-throwing to their famous routine "Calling Dr. Howard, Dr. Fine, Dr. Howard" from their Oscar-nominated short *Men in Black* (1934)—plus a Stooges trivia quiz and many other surprises. The original game was so successful that it would be reissued for Game Boy Advance in 2002 and PlayStation in 2004.

Cinemaware's *The Three Stooges* computer game (1987) was the first interactive game to feature voices, sound effects, and scenes digitized from Columbia Pictures' Three Stooges two-reel comedies and more. *Courtesy of Norman Maurer Collection*

Also in the late 1980s, Tapco Enterprises produced a set of three-dimensional, color, 8½- to 9½-inch-high masks of Moe, Larry, and Curly. In January 1989, Activision Video Games debuted a Three Stooges video game, a redo of the Cinemaware computer game, for the 8-bit Nintendo Entertainment System at the annual Consumer Electronics Show. This version, too, featured scenes from Stooge shorts; as a company representative said, "You can actually hear your favorite Stooges wisecrack and experience the pie-throwing mania that only the Stooges can provide." It was released to the public that October.

Also unleashed that spring was a new sixty-card Three Stooges trading card set, consisting of 2½-inch-by-3½-inch cards with portraits of Moe, Larry, and Curly and scenes from their films. The backs of the cards served as pieces of two different puzzles: the pink-toned cards could be assembled to form a football scene from *Three Little Pigskins*, while the blue-toned cards formed a "gorilla" scene from *Three Missing Links*.

The 1990s witnessed a continued onslaught of Stooge-licensed collectibles and merchandise. In 1990, items unleashed onto the marketplace included Three Stooges bookmarks, doorknob hangers, textbook covers, wipe-off memo boards, and children's storybooks with stickers (Antioch Publishing Co.); postcards (Ludlow Sales Corp.); posters (Class Publications Inc.); twelve-inch polyvinyl chloride figures, bop bags, and puffy vinyl stickers (Imperial Toy Corp.); notepads and magnets (The Beverly Hills Mint Inc.); rubber stamps and stamp pads (Uptown Rubber Stamp); vinyl and cloth dolls, including talking dolls (Hamilton Gift Ltd.); boys' and girls' sleepwear (The Wormser Co.); a set of Christmas ornaments (Presents); and much more.

In early 1991, Changes Inc. produced a series of six new T-shirts featuring Moe in take-offs of the popular Nike ads featuring Bo Jackson ("Bo knows . . ."); sayings emblazoned on the front proclaimed that "Moe knows eye-poking," "Moe knows face-slapping," and so on. Changes also released three other T-shirts that featured Andy Warhol–inspired

Set of Three Stooges dolls by Presents, a division of Hamilton Gifts, made in 1988.
*Courtesy of Norman Maurer Collection*

depictions of Moe, Larry, and Curly, respectively. Other newly released shirts included a black T-shirt, depicting Moe eye-poking Iraqi dictator Saddam Hussein, that read "Get Outta There, Ya Wise Guy." That year Hamilton Gifts also distributed a Three Stooges Music Box that played "Three Blind Mice" when opened. In 1992, Changes also made a new T-shirt that featured the Stooges as if they were presidential candidates, along with the caption "Leadership for the '90s."

Another widely popular item, first released in early 1991 by Class Publications, was a poster (measuring twenty-two inches by twenty-eight inches) of Moe, Larry, and Curly in golfing attire, along with the slogan "Golf With Your Friends."

In 1992, American Royal Arts released hand-painted cels of the Stooges, and Dart Mart Inc. of New York issued four different dart flights (accessories made to guide game darts more efficiently), one each of Moe, Larry, and Curly, and a fourth featuring all three. Lunar Models manufactured one-eighth-scale model kits of the Stooges, and Ralph Martin & Co. produced two Stooges neckties, followed a year later by Stooge-themed boxer shorts, suspenders, silk ties, and a golf necktie. Meanwhile, Stand-ups Centric Corp. of Hollywood, California, issued seventeen-inch-tall cardboard stand-ups of Moe, Larry, and Curly dressed in fireman's clothes. In 1993, the Franklin Mint offered a limited-edition eight-inch color collector's plate of the Stooges from their wartime comedy *You Nazty Spy!* (1940). Each plate was hand numbered and bordered in twenty-four-karat gold. Clark Oil and Refining Co., a midwestern gas station chain with 850 stores in a twelve-state region at the time, also released a series of three mugs featuring Moe, Larry, and Curly—twelve-ounce Larry, twenty-ounce Moe, and thirty-four-ounce Curly—during a special promotion that fall and early winter.

Between 1993 and 1996, Sony Pictures Entertainment, the successor to RCA/Columbia Pictures Home Video, reissued previous video sets of Three Stooges shorts on VHS and unveiled fourteen new volumes. In 1995, six Columbia Stooges features were also released on home video: *Have Rocket-- Will Travel* (1959), *Stop! Look! and Laugh!* (1960), *The Three Stooges in Orbit* (1962), *The Three Stooges Meet Hercules* (1962), *The Three Stooges Go Around the World in a Daze* (1963), and *The Outlaws IS Com-*

*ing!* (1965). (They would reissue the same volumes on DVD between 2000 and 2004.)

From 1994 to 1995, the Stooges continued to shine as licensed characters on a myriad of other official merchandise. Changes released three new white T-shirts featuring photographic images of Moe, Larry, or Curly. Ralph Martin & Co. manufactured new black polyester Stooge neckties, while Rainbow Connection produced cotton suspenders with artwork of the boys from film frames. Following these was a new limited-edition set of Three Stooges Bobbin' Head Dolls (The S.A.M. Co.), with an original retail price of $135; the first Stooge long-distance calling card (Amerivox), with a scene of the Stooges from *Dizzy Doctors*; Franklin Mint's third and fourth in a series of Three Stooges Collector Plates from its Lifetime of Laughter collection; a set of Russian-made wooden nesting dolls of Moe, Larry, Curly, and the whole trio; a Stooges desk clock (Centric Corp.); and four additional Three Stooges T-shirts (Changes Inc.) featuring all new designs.

Three Stooges "Cooking Lesson" plate from Franklin Mint's Lifetime of Laughter collection, 1994. *Courtesy of Jeff Lenburg Collection*

Existing lines of Stooge merchandise were expanded during this period, and new ones were introduced. Items included a second "Golf With Your Friends" poster (Western Graphics); a die-cut Stooges paper gift bag (Triangle Enterprises); and another batch of Stooges T-shirts (Sony Signatures).

Since 1995, under the direction of C3 Entertainment, holder of The Three Stooges' licensing rights, the Stooges have continued their phenomenal success as licensed characters. The following year, 1996, marked the release of a second series of Three Stooges collector plates (Franklin Mint); a seventy-six-inch life-size stand-up of Moe, Larry, and Curly-Joe in tuxedos and top hats from the movie *Have Rocket--Will Travel* (Advanced Graphics); a CD-ROM screensaver for Windows 95 (Quester Video); the first computer-generated Three Stooges card (American Greetings), available through kiosks nationwide; five-inch-tall Three Stooges magnets (Polar Magnetics); T-shirts that read "Friends," "Curly for President," "De-Moe-crat," and "You Can Pick Your Friends" (Sony Signatures); and golf balls and an apron featuring Curly (Salamander). Items released in 1996 also included a Stooge-style hat with the words "Nyuk, nyuk, nyuk" (American Needle), a three-headed Three Stooges Halloween mask (Forum Novelties); two styles of musical collector watches (Valdawn); a series of four Stooge "throws" (Rug Barn); a line of forty Stooge magnets (Omnitech Designs); seven Stooge clocks/watches/alarms (Dallas Sales Co.); four metal-constructed Stooge nostalgia signs (Dugan Specialties); and much more.

Among the merchandise for 1997 were computer mouse pads (American Covers Inc.); a dozen cotton T-shirts (new designs from Balzout Inc.); Three Stooges Collector lighters (Zippo); new limited edition dolls (Exclusive Toy Co.); a new Stooges lithograph (Bradford Salamon); a Three Stooges Whoopie Cushion (Gordy International); a line of gold-plated keychains, magnets, and lapel pins (Gift Creations); talking Three Stooges golf-club head covers (Rainbow Companies); a new set of Three Stooges "Duo-cards" trading cards (Comic Images); Three Stooges light-switch plates (Desperate Enterprises); and shot glasses (Kalan Inc.). Many more items followed that same year, including Three Stooges playing cards and hair tonic (Boston America); Three Stooges ceramics, namely, a cookie jar, salt and pepper shakers, a three-dimensional oversized mug, and a coin bank (Clay Art Inc.); a set of wall plaques with plaster heads of Moe, Larry, and Curly (Esco Products); Three Stooges Trivia Toilet Paper (On a Roll Inc.); Three Stooges "Golf With Your Friends" coasters (Polar Magnetics); Three Stooges Teddy Bears (Cooperstown Bears);

and eight-inch bendable magnets and Mix 'n Match Adventure Playset of the Stooges (Atta Boy Magnet Co.). Creator of *The Ren and Stimpy Show* John Kricfalusi also designed and produced a wildly exaggerated looking set of licensed Three Stooges dolls (Spumco), released to stores that Christmas.

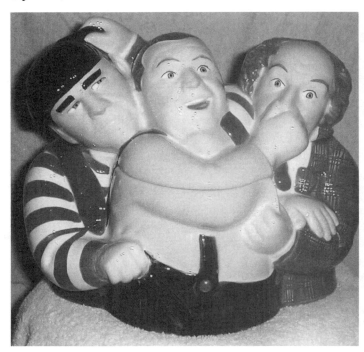

Clay Art Inc.'s Three Stooges Ceramic Cookie Jar, 1997. *Courtesy of Jeff Lenburg Collection*

Rounding out the decade were numerous items such as: Three Stooges String Confetti (Rite-Off); a Three Stooges pendulum clock (Atta Boy Co.); a new series of computer mouse pads (Salamander); a set of limited edition resin figurines (David Grossman Creations); two styles of boxed jigsaw puzzles (Sunsout Inc.); a Three Stooges card game (Archangel Entertainment); a pocket watch/desk clock (Valdawn); Stooge auto accessories, including holographic decals, an etched decal, a novelty license plate, and a static-cling windshield screen (Chromographics Corp.); and a set of Three Stooges fountain pens (Writek Corp.). Additional products included four hand-painted ceramic tiles of Moe, Larry, and Curly individually and all together (Nostalgic Notions); Three Stooges nostalgia tins (Crystal Art Gallery); greeting card puzzles (Puzzling Pieces); a new baseball cap (Rainbow Connection); Lucite mugs, keyrings, rulers, and other items featuring "film frames" of the

Stooges (Lights, Camera, Action Co.); Three Stooges Beer (Panther Brewing Co.); a Three Stooges lunch box (American Specialties Co.); and talking plush doll heads (Great American Fun Co).

The sheer volume of licensed Stooges merchandise remained remarkably high even into the new millennium. In May 2000, Shuffle Master developed a Three Stooges–themed video game for Native American casinos in the state of Washington, to be used on Sierra Design Group (SDG) gaming machines and systems. Then, in July of that year, Shuffle Master produced the first video slot machines based on The Three Stooges and two well-known television shows, *Let's Make a Deal* and *The Honeymooners*. A quarter-slot version of the Stooges game was issued first, followed by a nickel-slot version in 2001.

Sparked by the team's seventy-fifth anniversary in 2003, many new items flooded the marketplace. They included a Three Stooges Camp Shirt; an anniversary trading card set; plastic Three Stooges model kits of Moe, Larry, and Curly; Three Stooges Crackle Lounge Pants for men; Three Stooges Football Head Knocker of Larry, Moe, and Curly with footballs; and many others. In 2005, Breygent Marketing released a colorized seventy-two-card set of Three Stooges trading cards, featuring all six Stooges and Ted Healy and spanning the Stooges' entire film careers, from 1930 to 1969.

In 2007, Sony Pictures Entertainment began remastering and releasing all 190 of the Stooges comedy shorts on DVD for the first time. The shorts were released in chronological order, beginning that October with the first two-disc set, entitled *The Three Stooges Collection, Volume One: 1934–1936*. Eight volumes in all were produced, with the final volume released on June 1, 2010.

In light of the team's impressive marketing history and enduring commercial appeal, it would appear that The Three Stooges' niche in the field of merchandising will be safe and secure for some time to come.

From 2000, Shuffle Master's 3 Stooges Nickel Slot Machine, the first of two video slot machines featuring the comedy trio. *Courtesy of Jeff Lenburg Collection*

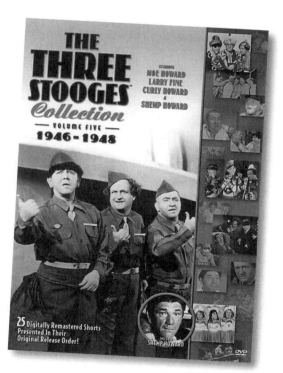

*The Three Stooges Collection, Volume Five* (2009) was one of eight DVD volumes featuring completely remastered versions of all 190 Stooge comedies released in chronological order. *Courtesy of Jeff Lenburg Collection*

# Chapter 3

A young Norman Maurer puts the finishing touches on a Three Stooges comic book panel.

*Courtesy of Norman Maurer Collection*

# Comic Book Stooges

Generations of comic book buffs like to remember the time they purchased their first comic book. But how many comics enthusiasts of old recall a series, made in 1949, that featured The Three Stooges?

The idea of using the Stooges in comic books was conceived in May 1947. Norman Maurer, who later managed The Three Stooges and wrote, produced, and directed their feature-length films, was at that time a well-established comic book illustrator, working on *Daredevil*, *Boy*, and other comic book series. His boyhood pal Joe Kubert had a deal with Archer St. John, owner of Jubilee Publications, to produce and edit a number of comics. Joe called Norman, asked him to be a partner, and suggested they create a Three Stooges comic book series.

Norman started negotiations with the Stooges to license the rights to publish Three Stooges comics featuring Larry, Moe, and Curly. (Even though Curly had left the team in 1946, Columbia continued to distribute the shorts in which he appeared.) On May 28, 1947, the Stooges granted permission, under an agreement with Norman Maurer and Jubilee Publications that entitled Maurer and the Stooges to 5 percent of the net profits from the comic book sales, while Columbia got 20 percent. (Six days earlier, the Jewish weekly *The Sentinel* had announced that the Stooges had signed a contract with Coast to Coast Publishing Co. of New York, then publishers of *Everywoman's* magazine, to have their antics appear as "a comic cartoon book." However, no evidence has been found to support this claim, and no such series is known to have been published.)

Maurer wrote, illustrated, and edited the Stooges comics, which were produced at Jubilee's principal offices on 220 West Forty-Second Street in New York. The stories were adapted from actual Three Stooges shorts—and even shared the same titles.

The premiere issue of the Three Stooges comic book series was published in February 1949. For a mere ten cents, comic book enthusiasts got two Three Stooges stories, plus a special adventure featuring detective Mark Montage in "The Eyes of Kali," illustrated by Joe Kubert. Each Stooge story held the readers' interest and definitely captured the trio's madcap humor.

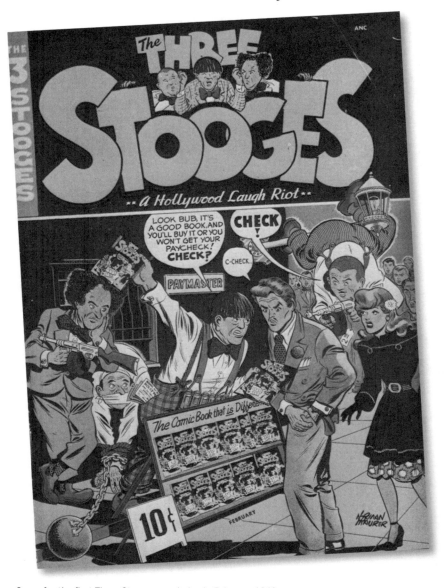

Cover for the first Three Stooges comic book, February 1949. *Courtesy of Norman Maurer Collection*

"Uncivil Warriors," the first adaptation in issue #1, was based on a 1935 short. In this version, the boys are three nutty Union spies—Lieutenant Al Mond, Captain Ches Nutt, and Major Phil Bert—assigned to infiltrate General Cornligger's headquarters at a Confederate army camp and liberate Operator 13, who turns out to be a luscious blonde named Miss Draindrop Ansby. Curly's initial reaction to Ansby's shapely figure is—what else?—"Wooo-wooo-wooo!"

When Confederate informants learn that the Stooges are Union spies, they dispatch a message to headquarters to notify General Cornligger (played by Bud Jamison in the film version). Curly takes the top-secret message from the messenger and starts reading it to himself. He instantly realizes that their cover has been blown and tries hiding the confidential note despite constant demands from General Cornligger for him to surrender it. In order to appease the gen-

Sampling of the Stooges' humor in comic strip form, from *The Three Stooges* issue #1. *Courtesy of Norman Maurer Collection*

eral, Curly follows orders and starts to read the message over a burning candle, turning it to ashes.

Through some clever maneuvering, the Stooges free Miss Draindrop Ansby and dash off, with the Confederates in pursuit. They comically shake off their pursuers by hiding inside a hollow tree trunk. They're sure they'll be safe when the Union starts its attack. Instantly, rebel soldiers dash to the hollow log and pull it away, revealing that it was being used to camouflage a huge cannon. *Kabloom!* They blast our heroes back to the friendly confines of Union headquarters.

The issue's second adaptation, "Hoi Polloi," also sticks relatively close to the storyline of its film predecessor. The boys are garbage collectors who dump rubbish on two upper-class citizens, Professor Duzz and Professor Kool (named Professors Richmond and Nichols in the two-reeler). Professor Kool bets Professor Duzz $10,000 that he can turn persons of the lowest strata into social lions. Duzz believes Kool is talking about the impossible. That's definitely the case when he chooses The Three Stooges as guinea pigs for his experiment!

The Stooges are given a series of lessons meant to transform them into gentlemen. Miss Fox Trotter teaches them how to dance, with disastrous results. During the lesson, a fly crawls down her back, making her wriggle uncontrollably; the Stooges comically imitate every step. Further lessons are provided in reading, eating, and walking. Finally, after days of tutoring, Professor Kool, confident of success, unleashes the Stooges on a swank high-society party. Slapstick bedlam reigns and a pie melee breaks out with the trio caught in the middle as usual. Duzz not only wins his bet with Kool but gets something he wasn't expecting—a pie in the face.

The second issue of *The Three Stooges*, published in May 1949, has as many laughs as the first issue, if not more. Unlike in the first book, the Stooges headline only one story, "Three Missing Links." This issue also contains another cliffhanger featuring detective Mark Montage.

"Three Missing Links" resembles the film version more than the previous adaptations do. Every facet of the strip is identical, except for the names of the characters and the studio that serves as the setting. The boys work in Hollywood as janitors for Carnation Pictures (for contented actors) and aspire to become actors. Marlena Marlena, the studio's famed leading lady, is being cast opposite a gorilla in a new epic, *The Gorilla Girl*. But studio president B. O. Botsfiddle finds himself in a pickle over whom to cast as the male lead.

The Stooges, meanwhile, have trouble impressing Botsfiddle, who fires them for not drying off a hall floor he slipped on. As the Stooges plead for a second chance, Botsfiddle notices that Curly has all the right physical features necessary to play the gorilla and signs him to a contract. Moe and Larry are rehired as Curly's costars.

With everything set, they head for Africa and begin filming. Before production gets under way, the Stooges visit a cannibal medicine man who casts hungry eyes on Curly, envisioning him on a platter surrounded by garnishes. Moe swiftly inquires about the medicine man's ancient pottery. The cannibal informs him that their contents vary: poison in one and love candy in another. Curly, who must feed his constant craving for food, pilfers some candy before leaving the witch doctor's straw hut.

The crew is about to start shooting when the zipper on Curly's gorilla suit gets stuck. Meanwhile, as Curly struggles with the zipper, Kongo, a *real* gorilla, ambles onto the set and starts to play Curly's big scene. Moe and Larry think the real gorilla is Curly. When Curly comes on the set dressed as a gorilla, he tries making friends with Kongo, feeding him love candy. Instantly, the candy's potent formula overpowers Kongo, who falls in love with Curly and starts chasing him through the wilds of Africa. Moe and Larry have to rescue him, and after a series of comical scenes, the Stooges ward off Kongo's affection and win out in the end.

Although this issue and its predecessor both achieved reasonable success, publication of the series was suspended when Jubilee cut back its publication schedule. Later, in 1953, Archer St. John changed the company name from Jubilee to St. John Publishing Company and hired Joe and Norman to do a new series of comics. Norman went back to the drawing board and took a new crack at Three Stooges comic books—for the first time featuring Shemp instead of Curly.

The new series debuted under the St. John banner in September 1953. Despite the long gap between issues, fans were not disappointed. The price was still a dime, and readers were treated to three hilarious yarns featuring the three makers of fun. In fact, the

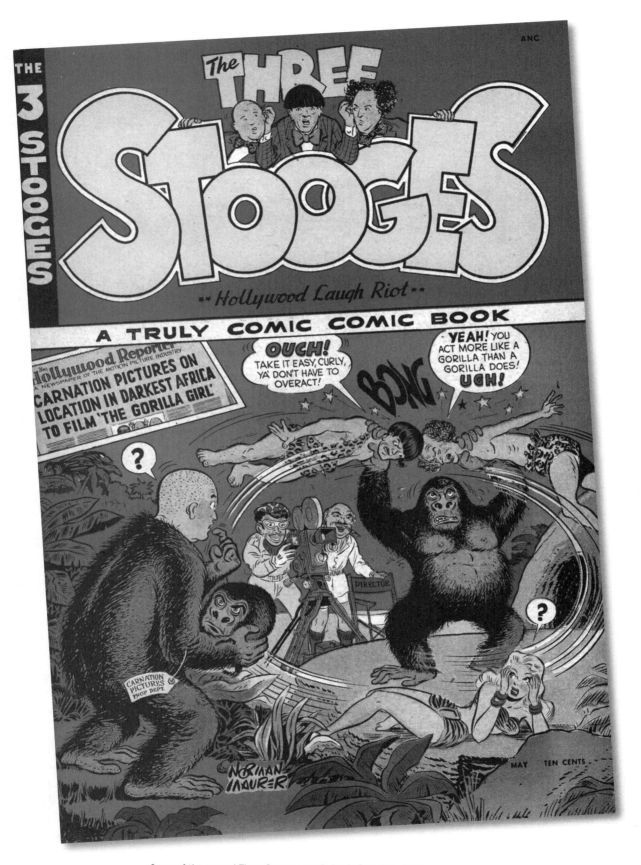

Cover of the second Three Stooges comic book, from May 1949. *Courtesy of Norman Maurer Collection*

Series of comic strip panels showing a remake of a Stooges comedy. *Courtesy of Norman Maurer Collection*

Shemp comics were far superior to the earlier issues in terms of both design and story. Although Norman had seen many Three Stooges comedies, it took working with their characters in comic book form to get a complete feel for their unique personalities and humor. Thus, over a period of time, Maurer developed many fresh and clever ideas—unseen in the Stooges films—and incorporated popular Stooges sketches as well.

Colors were rich and bright, and the artwork was lavishly detailed. The Stooges' adventures were no longer just direct adaptations of Stooges shorts; they often featured new, especially creative stories. Whereas the Curly comics had relied more on coherent plotlines and less on slapstick, the new series also featured intelligent and carefully orchestrated gags and a greater number of comedy routines. The new tales even featured a perfect foil for Moe, Larry, and Shemp: one Benedict Bogus, a shiftless con man constantly out to swindle the Stooges.

Furthermore, the first Shemp comic book has a more personal touch than preceding issues. On the inside flap, Norman and Joe introduce themselves to readers in cartoon form, inviting fans to send in suggestions on how to improve their work. The front cover shows a nervous cartoonist (Norman) fidgeting with his pen as the Stooges complain about being depicted as "idiots" and "a bunch of knuckleheads" when, in fact, "We're morons and we don't wanna be drawn as anything but morons!"

Cover for first Stooges comic book with Shemp, from September 1953. *Courtesy of Norman Maurer Collection*

Inside flap showing cartoonists Norman Maurer and Joe Kubert in cartoon form. *Courtesy of Norman Maurer Collection*

The first story in the new issue #1, "Bogus Takes a Beating," casts our trio as proprietors of the Flop 'n Sop Cafe. Inside, the café is deserted save for The Three Stooges dressed in soiled waiter's uniforms. Thoroughly depressed, they stand behind a counter laden with huge stacks of unpaid bills for food and supplies.

Suddenly, the boys are startled by an outside sound. They turn to see a crowd of well-dressed businessmen hastily heading toward the front door. Elated, Larry shouts, "Moe! Look outside . . . customers!" Moe remarks that he knew all the time that if they stuck it out, they'd make a success of the business.

The Stooges take on a new character in the Shemp comics, Benedict Bogus, in "Bogus Takes a Beating." *Courtesy of Norman Maurer Collection*

Page from the first Stooges comic with Shemp. *Courtesy of Norman Maurer Collection*

As the door swings open, an angry mob of creditors pours in, making violent threats, demanding that their bills be paid immediately. Outside, Benedict Bogus peers in through the café window. He reasons that if these stupid characters could operate a café with all these richly dressed customers, it surely has to be a gold mine. Thus, he approaches the Stooges and swaps them ownership of the café for a bogus deed to the National Firecracker Factory (a recently abandoned property).

Moe, Larry, and Shemp then turn in their dirty chefs linens and run down to view their new property. Meanwhile, word breaks out that two crooks—Trigger Mortise (a character also used years later in the 1965 Stooges feature *The Outlaws IS Coming!*, where his name would be spelled "Mortis") and Stiletto—have pulled a million-dollar gold heist and are using the fireworks factory as a hideout to grind the stolen gold bricks into gold dust and stuff it into firecrackers. The Stooges, of all people, walk right into trouble and believe the criminals' alibi—that they are making fireworks with shiny explosive powder.

Later, while Shemp is snooping around, a bag of gold powder falls on his head, knocking him unconscious. Moe revives him, but the glowing powder refuses to come out of Shemp's hair, which is now golden blond.

Suspicious, the Stooges mail a gold-filled firecracker to Police Lieutenant Holmes of the 14th Precinct. Obviously, the Stooges have done business with him before! Holmes receives the package and discovers a firecracker that busts wide open, exposing a mound of gold powder. The lab checks the powder and discovers it is from the heist, leading Holmes to crack the gigantic gold caper. The Stooges get a $50,000 reward for their efforts, and Bogus ends up with all the bill collectors he thought were customers.

The issue concludes with two additional Stooges episodes. "Big Brush Off" has them as house painters who mix up a street address and ruin a millionaire's mansion with paint remover. And in "Bell Bent for Treasure," a $1,000 reward is offered to anyone capable of recovering the Lost Bell of Adonomo. The Stooges accidentally find the bell, win the money, and help a financially crippled widow send her son to a hospital for a leg operation. The subplot was adapted from the Stooges comedy *Cash and Carry* (1937).

Issues #2 and #3, published in October and November 1953, were even more illustrious, since they employed a new process to bring three-dimensional images to comics. By 1953, 3-D films were a huge success, and comics were the next logical art form in which to experiment. Joe Kubert, Norman Maurer, and Norman's brother Leonard were directly responsible for developing the method for producing 3-D comics, a revolutionary process that opened new avenues for comic books.

Moe Howard with Norman Maurer and Maurer's brother Leonard, cocreator of the 3-D comic book process. *Courtesy of Norman Maurer Collection*

*3-D Illustereo*, as it was called, operated under the same principle as 3-D film: the viewer sees a slightly different image with each eye, and his or her brain combines them into a single three-dimensional image. In films, a polarized projector and polarized glasses are used to filter out the two images, but this method doesn't work on the printed page. Instead, the comic book pages would be printed in red and green ink, and red-and-green-tinted glasses would be used to separate the images. In the midst of refining their new concept, Norman, Joe, and Leonard developed a makeshift pair of glasses out of cardboard, with red and green cellophane for lenses, in order to test their new process. Norman remembered what it took for them to find the cellophane. "We had worked all night, and I'll never forget how we waited on the street for the Woolworth's store in midtown Manhattan to open because we figured we could get red and green cellophane from lollipop wrappers. We bought two packages and made a funny pair of glasses which, believe it or not, worked perfectly."

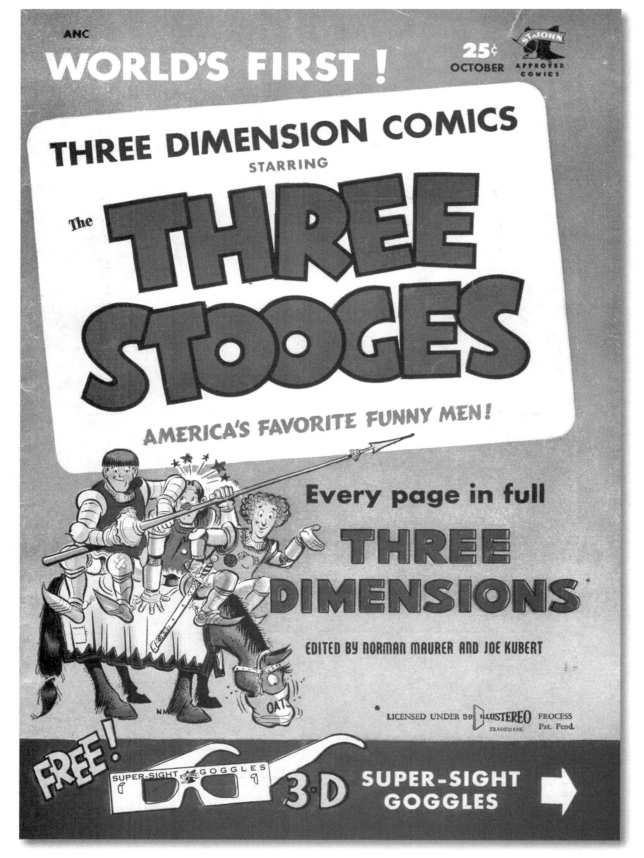

Cover for the first 3-D Stooges comic book, from October 1953. *Courtesy of Norman Maurer Collection*

Cover for the second 3-D Stooges comic, from November 1953. *Courtesy of Norman Maurer Collection*

From there, Norman and Joe rushed over to show the 3-D concept to Archer St. John, who was pessimistic about the idea; in fact, he thought what they were proposing was impossible. Confident, Joe and Norman handed him the 3-D sketches and makeshift glasses. Maurer later recalled that St. John leaned back in his chair for more light with which to view the art—and almost fell out the window when he saw drawings that literally popped out from the paper!

Now keenly aware of the technique's potential, St. John bought the idea. His company first used the process in a 1953 *Mighty Mouse* comic book, produced and drawn by Norman and Joe. (Later, it was recognized in *Encyclopaedia Britannica* as "the world's first 3-D comic book.") It sold millions at twenty-five cents a copy, which inspired Maurer and Kubert to follow suit with the Three Stooges series in 3-D using their process.

Around this time, Joe and Norman also increased production on the number of comics they produced and created for St. John. They had four series being drawn at once: *The Three Stooges, Meet Miss Pepper, Whack,* and *Tor: 1 Million B.C.* Maurer estimated that each book took as long as one month to produce. Due to increased production costs, the 3-D Stooges comics were trimmed down to thirty-two pages from their original sixty-four. Production stages included writing the story, doing the artwork, and lettering and coloring the silverprints. Each series was bimonthly.

As successful as 3-D comics and films were, Joe and Norman begged St. John not to overproduce, since they felt the 3-D craze was just a fad that would soon fizzle out. Archer St. John disagreed. He saw 3-D as a huge moneymaking device that would last for years. Profits were apparently so tremendous on Mighty Mouse and the Stooges (actual figures are not available) that St. John wanted to put out thirty-five additional books in 3-D. He believed that flooding the market would generate millions for his company and for him personally. To maintain his increased production schedule, St. John expanded his New York offices from one to two floors and rented hotel rooms for additional working space.

Maurer recalled how St. John's superexpansion turned into an unforgettable fiasco. "Joe and I warned him this was a temporary fad. He wouldn't listen. He put fifty girls to work inking and painting artwork.

He dumped in every penny he had and borrowed to put a mess of 3-D books out. The demand stopped, and he was stuck with the books and lost a fortune, which eventually caused him to go bankrupt."

But the demise of St. John Publishing Company would not come right away. Before it did, four more regular 2-D issues of Three Stooges comics would hit the newsstands.

Issue #4 was published in March 1954. It evoked the same zaniness that permeated the other editions. The Stooges brought their romps up to date in two new capers while Norman created another new feature, "The New Adventures of Li'l Stooge," written by Michael Brand. (It was retitled "The Adventures of Li'l Stooge" in subsequent installments.) The lead character was a prankish, small-fry version of Moe.

The issue opens with "Up an' Atom," in which Benedict Bogus cons the Stooges into overpaying for a broken-down jalopy that he claims is a super race-car. The Stooges drive off to compete in the big race in Reno, Nevada, and get stranded in the middle of a desert sandstorm. While looking for a gas station, Shemp discovers a sign that reads "Atom Bomb Testing Grounds. No Admittance Beyond This Point!" Squinting through the sand, Shemp shouts back that there is a town called "No Admittance" just beyond this point. The boys drive on, and their car conks out right next to a miniaturized atom bomb that is about to be detonated in a test.

In a frenzy of slapstick action, Shemp removes a mountain of assorted parts from the engine, which end up strewn all over the desert sand. In putting everything back together, Shemp mistakes the miniaturized atom bomb, which is shaped like a carburetor, for the real thing and attaches it to the car's engine. Meanwhile, the real carburetor lies harmless and unnoticed on the sand.

Consequently, when Moe turns the starter key, a terrifying ear-splitting atomic blast bursts from the car's exhaust pipe. The smoke clears to reveal the car and the Stooges charred black as they zoom over the horizon at incredible speed with a mushroom cloud spewing from their tailpipe. (Years later, Norman used this original gag of mixing up an atom bomb for a carburetor in a Stooges feature film he produced for Columbia, *The Three Stooges in Orbit*, for which he also wrote the story.)

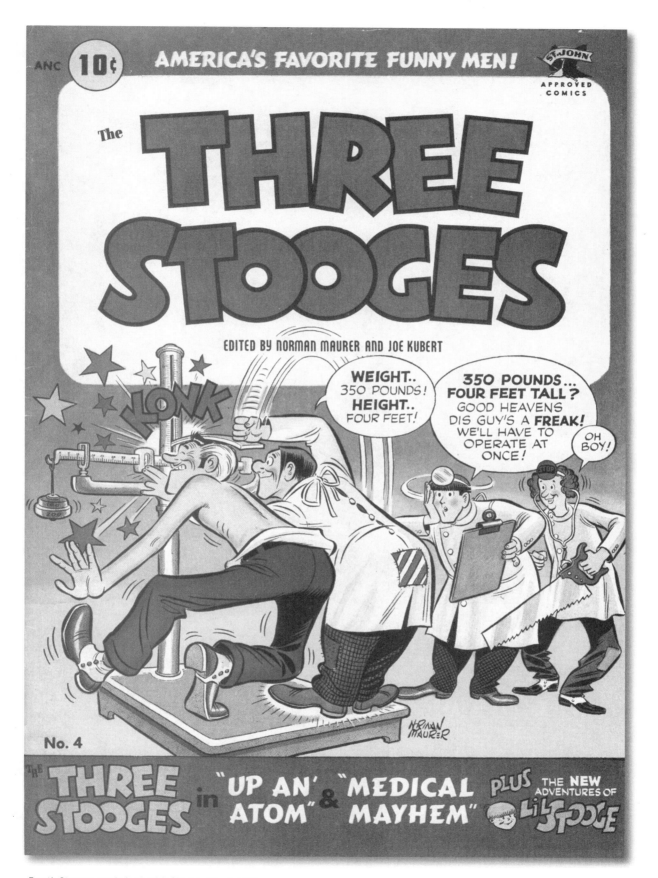

Fourth Stooges comic book with Shemp, March 1954. *Courtesy of Norman Maurer Collection*

The Stooges mistake an atom bomb for a carburetor in "Up an' Atom." *Courtesy of Norman Maurer Collection*

Later, the Stooges enter the big race in Reno. Their souped-up atomic hot rod overpowers all competition to set a new racetrack record, and they win hands down. A team of foreign spies learns that the new minibomb is in the Stooges' car, and the villains are ordered to steal it. They succeed when Moe sells them the car for ten times what the Stooges paid for it. When the spies bring the bomb to their leader, he is furious—since the bomb looks like a harmless carburetor. He becomes so livid that he throws the bomb to the floor. The end result is an explosion unmatched since Hiroshima!

In the second feature, "Medical Mayhem," the boys are psychiatrists out to cure Benedict Bogus of a rare disease: klepto-swindliac-skeetzo-frinnic. This is a disease that only habitual swindlers and shoplifters like Bogus can contract. Moe, Larry, and Shemp put Bogus through a series of tests and operations that are totally successful: Bogus is born anew as a super-honest man. No temptation seems to crack him. But, as always, Bogus loses in the end. At the windup of this episode, he gets arrested at the scene of a bank robbery when he attempts to return a hundred-dollar bill the real crooks accidentally dropped.

The Stooges continue to thwart Bogus in the June 1954 issue, another solid comic book effort. In "Alotta the Bull," our trio lose their jobs at S.O. Seedy Florists, when Shemp ruins $3,000 worth of orchids by eating garlic and breathing on them. A process server chases the Stooges, who think the man has been sent by their former boss and that he is going to sue them for damages. In a panic, they head for Benedict Bogus's place for help. For a price, Bogus provides them with his usual bogus passports and plane tickets to Mexico.

The Stooges' wild attempts to elude the process server fail as he chases them all the way to Mexico City, where Moe, Larry, and Shemp duck through a wooden door. They slam it behind them and bolt it from the inside. Instead of winding up safely away from the process server, they panic as they realize they're inside the unsafe confines of a bull ring, with a snorting bull thundering toward them.

Moe and Larry scram as the bull approaches with a full head of steam. Nibbling on his garlic, Shemp stands his ground, smiles, and remarks, "Imagine bein' scared of a li'l old black cow?" Just as the bull is about to slam into him, it sniffs Shemp's power-ful garlic breath, snorts, grimaces, coughs, squints, vibrates, screeches to a stop with a gasp, and keels over. The audience cheers wildly and "El Shempador" becomes an instant hero. Within weeks, El Shempador becomes the most famous matador in all Mexico. Pablo Diablo, the jealous former world-famous bullfighter, grows suspicious and discovers Shemp's garlic secret, and he sets out to find a bull immune to the smell of garlic. He discovers Alotta the Bull and pits her against Shemp.

Back in America, before the big fight with Alotta, Bogus learns of Shemp's huge success and income and decides to become Shemp's manager. He hops the first plane to Mexico and convinces Shemp's agent to sell him a half interest in El Shempador. It costs Bogus $5,000, but, to his mind, the sum is a mere pittance considering the profits he'll make. His plans to cash in, however, turn sour in the fight between Alotta and Shemp as the bull, immune to Shemp's garlic breath, plasters him all over the ring.

With disappointed fans chasing after them, the Stooges and Bogus are fortunate to get out of Mexico alive. With our heroes back home, the process server (who isn't a process server at all) finally catches up with them and informs them that their ex-boss wants to give them a $500 bonus. It appears the smell of Shemp's garlic breath only temporarily affected the orchids. After their apparent demise, they grew to five times their normal size!

A second yarn, "99⁴⁴/₁₀₀% Puritan," transports Bogus and the Stooges back to London in the year 1681. This is the first of a new series in which Bogus daydreams himself into various times in history, an idea reminiscent of James Thurber's popular story "The Secret Life of Walter Mitty." In this adventure, Bogus imagines himself as a real estate tycoon, pioneering the New World and buying an island—Manhattan—from the Indians.

The Stooges, leading jewelry merchants in the New World, team up with Bogus for an expedition to buy a different island on the West Coast. Moe also operates Moehawk Real Estate ("If You Got Beads, We Got Deeds"). While the Stooges are guiding Bogus to his dream island, they accidentally stumble into Indian territory and break up an important craps game. The Indian chief becomes upset and orders the foursome burned at the stake.

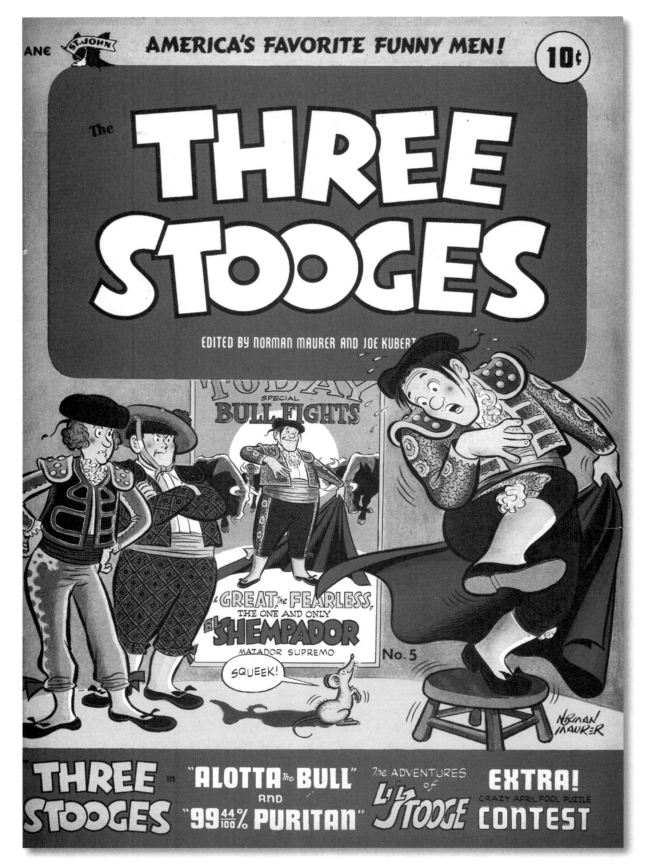

Fifth Stooges comic book with Shemp, from June 1954. *Courtesy of Norman Maurer Collection*

The fifth Stooges comic book with Shemp includes "The Adventures of Li'l Stooge," with a character designed after Moe Howard.

*Courtesy of Norman Maurer Collection*

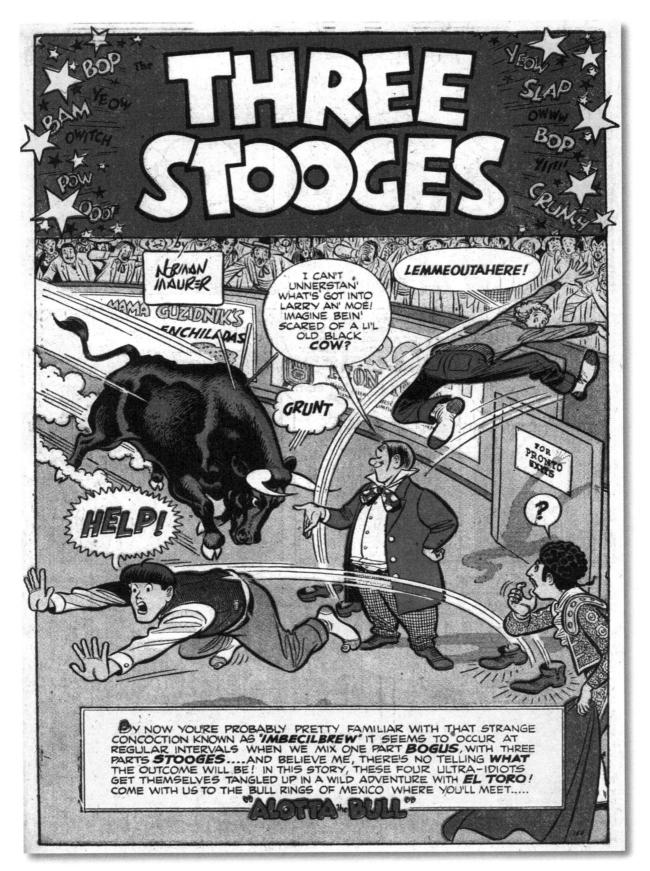

Shemp turns bullfighter in "Alotta the Bull." *Courtesy of Norman Maurer Collection*

They will be spared, however, if they will marry three old squaws and the chief's sixteen-year-old daughter. The Stooges convince Bogus that marriage is better than death. Thus, a parade of women emerges from a tepee to meet their future husbands. Moe, Larry, and Shemp whistle deliriously and gawk lasciviously as their brides turn out to be curvaceous brunettes. Bogus gasps in horror as he gets stuck with the chief's rotund, plain-Jane daughter who has all the markings of a rump roast. With marriage looking like much less of a bargain, Bogus and the Stooges are tied to stakes and flames lick at their feet. Shemp pours gunpowder into the flames, and they blast away, stakes and all, like four antique rockets. In the windup, Bogus buys his island, which turns out to be Alcatraz, and the prison is built right around him.

For the Stooges, nothing was more fitting for their style of comedy than the age-old problems of ghosts and goblins and of wealth and matrimony. In issue #6, published August 1954, they poked fun at both. "Fluke Spook" has Moe, Larry, and Shemp helping Bogus run a Kentucky plantation that was willed to him. There they meet some frightening characters who are out to steal the deed. And in "Bogus Takes a Bride," Benedict joins the Matri-Moe Lonely Hearts Club, hoping to snatch a wealthy bride. He finds one, all right: a stuffy old dowager who's as broke as Bogus.

This edition also features the first of a special satirical series that would continue in future issues. Norman and Joe began spoofing time-honored comic strips and films. Their first attempt was "Bringing Up Mama," satirizing George McManus's strip *Bringing Up Father*. Norman even credits himself as George McMaurer.

The final Stooges strip in this issue is a miniversion of the 1934 Curly short *Punch Drunks*, with some minor alterations. Shemp enters the world of boxing and draws his power in the ring from hearing the popular ballad "Dixieland" (in the original film it was "Pop Goes the Weasel"). Another change from the original has a jukebox in place of Larry's broken violin as the means by which they play the fight-inspiring song. The jukebox fails and Shemp loses the fight, while in the Columbia two-reeler, Curly wins.

Issue #7 was published in October 1954 and brought the second series of Three Stooges comics to an abrupt close, despite plans for an eighth issue. The final issue dealt out some wild stuff, with the Stooges as "Nautical Nitwits" vacationing on a gambling ship, the SS *Betchalife*. The boys go from rags to riches, of course, while Bogus gets a no-way ticket to the poor farm. The Stooges continue their penchant for messing up situations as publisher's assistants in "The Memoirs of Benedict Bogus." The final story is a tantalizing special feature titled "The Crisco Kid," which spoofs the Cisco Kid movies.

St. John's entire line of comics died on the vine, so to speak, with the death of owner and publisher Archer St. John. A short time later, Maurer left the comic book field to pursue a career in motion pictures. Kubert, his longtime partner, continued to illustrate comic books and several years later started an art school in New Jersey.

Comic book buffs were not treated to another Three Stooges series until 1959. Then, as the team's popularity skyrocketed and Norman Maurer Productions launched a full-scale merchandising push, Western Publishing was granted a licensing agreement to publish a quarterly series of Stooges comics. These books were published by Western but distributed by Dell Publishing, which had the ability to get comic books onto the newsstand and into the markets. (The Dell name would appear in capital letters on the cover.) Once the series proved itself, Western bumped it up to bimonthly publication. The first such issue was published for October–November 1959, and nine four-color Dell comics were published altogether from October 1959 to June 1962. Twelve cents won comic enthusiasts two freshly written stories featuring Moe, Larry, and Curly-Joe. The issues also featured, in alternating installments, "Professor Putter" and "The Little Monsters." The team also answered fan questions in a bimonthly column labeled Dear Stooges, and in another special feature the boys offered safety tips.

The Western/Dell books were quite inferior to the St. John series in many ways. Perhaps their best asset was the fact that the cover of every issue featured a full-color photograph of the Stooges. Some fans consider the covers priceless, more vauable than the strips inside, which just didn't have the same charisma as the earlier series. Stories were nonsensical, and the team's customary slapstick, quite prevalent in the St. John books, was made less prominent, in an effort to appease parents by toning down the Stooges' violence. The few gags that were included were abysmal; instead, the tales relied heavily on wordplay in dialogue.

Sixth Stooges comic book with Shemp, from August 1954. *Courtesy of Norman Maurer Collection*

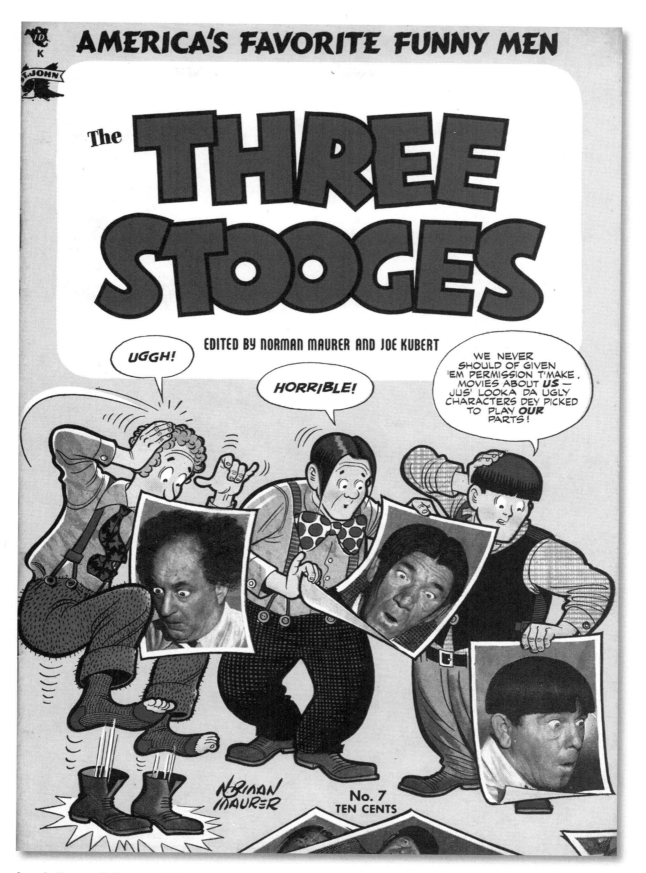

Cover for the seventh Stooges comic book with Shemp, released in October 1954. *Courtesy of Norman Maurer Collection*

Cover of the first Dell Three Stooges comic, from October 1959. *Courtesy of Norman Maurer Collection*

Dell cartoonists introduced the Stooges to readers with a page featuring them in cartoon form. *Courtesy of Norman Maurer Collection*

Panel from the first Dell Three Stooges comic with Curly-Joe. *Courtesy of Norman Maurer Collection*

Back-page advertisement from the first Dell Stooges comic, promoting the team's film *Have Rocket--Will Travel* and the first Three Stooges fan club. *Courtesy of Norman Maurer Collection*

Western employed their own artists and writers to produce the strips—and it definitely showed! Character drawings of the Stooges were inconsistent, ranging from fair to mediocre. Curly-Joe was as appealing as the Pillsbury Doughboy, while Larry looked like a different character—his frizzy hair was less rumpled and his nose had lost its prominence. Moe actually came the closest to looking like himself. Had Maurer been supervising the series, he could have ensured that the artists did a much more credible job.

In 1962, Western/Dell published a Three Stooges Comic Album, the last in Dell's Comic Album series, and a movie comic edi-

Fifth issue of the Dell Three Stooges comic book series, from June–August 1961, which sold for a retail price of fifteen cents. *Courtesy of Norman Maurer Collection*

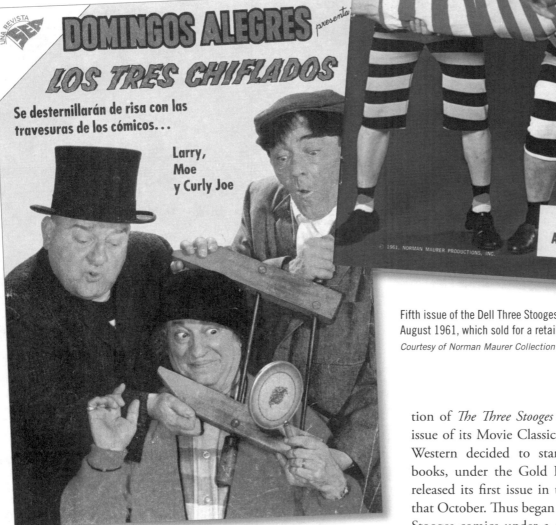

First Dell Stooges comic book, republished in Spanish on April 23, 1961. *Courtesy of Norman Maurer Collection*

tion of *The Three Stooges Meet Hercules*, the final issue of its Movie Classics series. That same year, Western decided to start distributing its own books, under the Gold Key imprint. Gold Key released its first issue in the Three Stooges series that October. Thus began the longest run of Three Stooges comics under a single publisher; during the next ten years, Western/Gold Key would publish forty-six comics bearing the *Three Stooges* title.

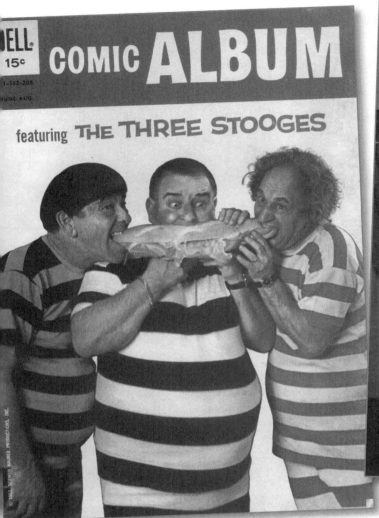

Special comic book edition of the film *The Three Stooges Meet Hercules*, from July 1962. *Courtesy of Norman Maurer Collection*

Moe, Curly-Joe, and Larry mugging over a sandwich on the cover of The Three Stooges' Comic Album, June–August 1962.
*Courtesy of Norman Maurer Collection*

Gold Key continued Dell's movie comics series, publishing an adaptation of the Stooges latest feature, *The Three Stooges in Orbit*, in 1962, followed by special issues of two others: *The Three Stooges Go Around the World in a Daze* and *The Outlaws IS Coming!* The comic adaptation of *The Three Stooges in Orbit* was an unusual oddity since it incorporated actual frame blow-ups from the film to tell the story.

Dell artwork for the *Three Stooges Meet Hercules* comic book.
*Courtesy of Norman Maurer Collection*

The Stooges wreak havoc on the cover of the *Three Stooges in Orbit* comic published in November 1962.
*Courtesy of Norman Maurer Collection*

Zogg suddenly puts the machine into a steep climb, causing Joe to lose his balance and jam his head into the mouth of the cannon.

With Larry working to free Joe, Moe stops Ogg from using the cannon by pouring a bag of water down the periscope into his face.

A last desperate tug pulls Joe's head out of the cannon's mouth. "Quick," yells Moe. "They're getting ready to shoot this thing again. Help me turn it." The three boys use their combined strength to swivel the deadly weapon upwards, away from the city.

The film comic book of *The Three Stooges in Orbit* features panels of frames from the film to tell the story.

*© Normandy Productions, courtesy of Norman Maurer Collection*

Comic book cover for the January 1964 issue of *The Three Stooges Go Around the World in a Daze*. © Normandy
*Productions, courtesy of Norman Maurer Collection*

In 1962, after K.K. Publications joined forces with Western and Gold Key, they also published a series of half-sized comics, called *March of Comics*, nine issues of which featured The Three Stooges.

They would be distributed to retailers up until 1972. In 1967, the Stooges were also featured in two issues of another series, *Top Comics*, by K.K. Publications and Gold Key.

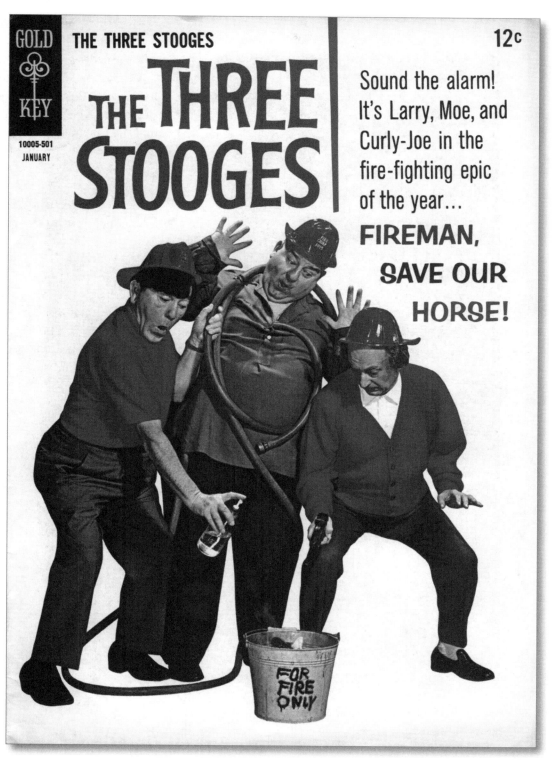

The Stooges help fuel a fire on the cover of a Gold Key comic book from January 1964.

*Courtesy of Norman Maurer Collection*

Gold Key's March 1965 comic book based on the Stooges' last feature film, *The Outlaws IS Coming!* © *Normandy Productions, courtesy of Norman Maurer Collection*

Western published from 450,000 to 700,000 books per issue. Stooge comics ranked second to Walt Disney comics in circulation (Disney printed almost one million copies every month). Even so, copies of the special movie editions, such as *The Three Stooges Meet Hercules* and *The Three Stooges in Orbit*, have become collectors' items; they sell for as much as seventy-five and eighty-five dollars in near-mint condition, respectively. By contrast, Jubilee editions with Curly go for as high as $850 in similar condition, while selling prices for the St. John 3-D Stooge editions with Shemp range from $42 to $340 based on their condition.

When Western dropped the Stooges comics in 1972, Norman Maurer proposed a new series starring the teenage sons of Moe, Larry, and Curly-Joe, who prove to be just as clumsy and nitwitted as their famous fathers. Western liked the idea, and the first edition of *The Little Stooges* was published under the Gold Key imprint in September 1972. In many respects, the new series was more entertaining than Western's *The Three Stooges* run, mainly because Maurer was once again writing the stories and doing the artwork. The stories were fresh and clever; even Norman's son Jeff Maurer (who later took the pen name Jeffrey Scott), wrote several. Others were updates of the best titles from the earlier series featuring Shemp, including such favorites as "99⁴⁴/₁₀₀% Puritan," "Alotta the Bull" (changed to "The Bull-Dozers"), and "The Fluke Spook."

Norman began each story with the young Stooges—under the watchful eyes of their fathers—picking up where the elder Stooges left off. In each tale, trouble ensues wherever they go, but they usually emerge from their misfortunes victorious. In order to satisfy the ardent Stooges fan's appetite for traditional slapstick gags, a bit more slapping and hitting prevails where necessary. (For instance, in "Prisoner in a Candy Factory" from issue #4, all six Stooges gather to celebrate Curly-Joe Jr.'s birthday at a swank restaurant, where the stage is set for the kind of slap-happy Stooges antics fans remember.) The main characters also deal with adolescent trials and tribulations: how to survive the teen years. As for character design, teenage Moe, Larry, and Curly-Joe's charming, hip look reflects the fashion of the early 1970s: mod hairstyles, beads, and freaky clothes.

Also introduced in issue #1 was Moose, The Little Stooges' canine retriever. Moose was actually based

March of Comics — The THREE STOOGES

on Maurer's own Labrador retriever, who made his live-action screen debut in the Stooges' final film, *Kook's Tour* (1970). Maurer revived another stock character, his personal favorite, Benedict Bogus, in the form of his son, Benedict Jr. Young Bogus was just as devilish, in fact more scheming, than Benedict Sr. But in the traditional fashion of his father, Bogus Jr. was unsuccessful in conning The Little Stooges; he always got it in the end. The young Stooges also had girlfriends: Moon, a typical girl next door; Pixie, the richest girl in town; and Lovey, a cute, chubby gal who shares Curly's weakness for chocolate sodas.

An issue of *March of Comics*, special half-sized Three Stooges comics published from 1962 to 1967. *Courtesy of Norman Maurer Collection*

Norman Maurer's original 1971 caricature drawings of the cast of his Gold Key comic book series *The Little Stooges*.
*Courtesy of Norman Maurer Collection*

Norman Maurer introduced The Little Stooges in a series of Gold Key comics. The cover shown is for the first edition, from September 1972.
*Courtesy of Norman Maurer Collection*

A young trio of Stooges go ape in the second Gold Key *Little Stooges* comic book, from December 1972. *Courtesy of Norman Maurer Collection*

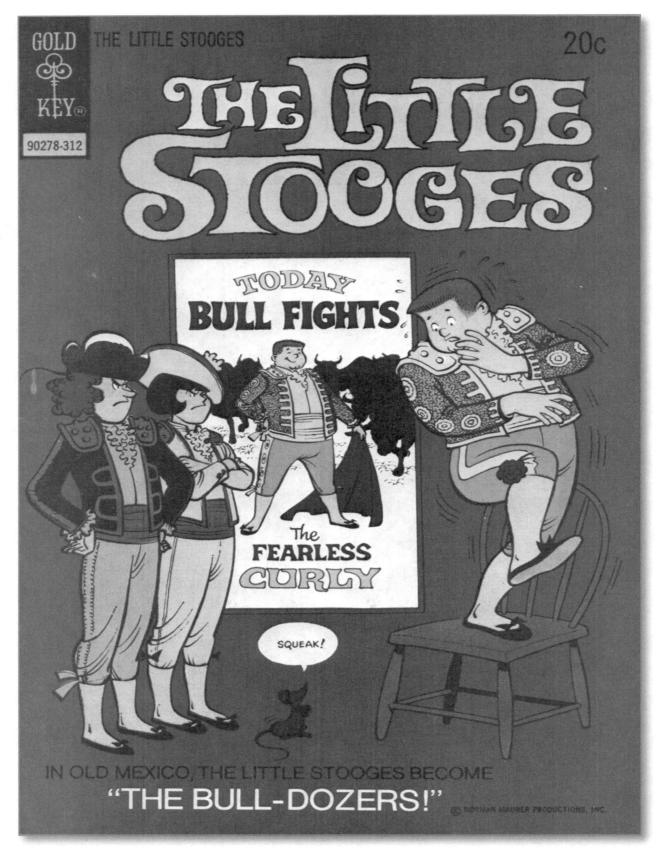

The Little Stooges in "The Bull-Dozers," a remake of a Shemp comic book story, in the December 1973 issue, the second to the last in the series.
*Courtesy of Norman Maurer Collection*

Despite the success of the *Little Stooges* series, it had a formidable obstacle in the changing economy. Comic book companies had fallen on bad times, and sales throughout the industry were down. Their struggle to survive was mirrored in comic book prices: an inflationary twenty cents! And that was for just one story per issue! Nonetheless, *The Little Stooges* did well enough to warrant seven issues, equaling the output of issues from the St. John series. The last edition was published in March 1974, thus ending the Stooges' fifteen-year association with Western Publishing, quite a successful run for a comic book series.

In 1982, Norman Maurer made one last attempt to revive the trio in a new newspaper comic strip called *Larry, Moe and Curly*, by The Three Maurers. The Three Maurers were none other than Norman, who did the artwork, and sons Jeffrey and Michael, who wrote the gags. Unfortunately, despite the strip's topical humor, it never sold.

Norman Maurer's interpretation of the Stooges for his proposed but unpublished 1982 comic strip *Larry, Moe and Curly*, cowritten with his sons, Jeffrey and Michael, as The Three Maurers.
*Courtesy of Norman Maurer Collection*

First issue of Eclipse Comics' *The Three Stooges* 3-D comic books from 1986.
*Courtesy of Jeff Lenburg Collection*

Ultimately, twelve years would pass between the demise of *The Little Stooges* and the appearance of the next new Three Stooges comic book. In 1986, Eclipse Comics produced a series of three 3-D Stooges comics, which were essentially remakes of the St. John 3-D comics from the early 1950s, with one exception: Curly is featured as the third Stooge instead of Shemp. In the summer of 1987, Brooklyn-based Solson Comics announced plans to release a new series of black-and-white Stooges comics, which, unlike the Eclipse series, were to feature entirely new stories, but the deal between Solson and Columbia Pictures fell through.

The Eclipse comics were followed, in 1989, by Malibu Graphics Inc.'s first in a series of Three Stooges comics, *The Knuckleheads Return*. Two more installments were copublished with Eternity Com-

ics in 1991: *The Three Stooges in 3-D* and *The Three Stooges in Full Color*. Malibu's volumes reprinted panels from previous St. John's and Gold Key comics. Then, in 1992, Fox Comics, an Australian publisher, published *The Six 3-Stooges*, a comic book biography of the Stooges that spans from their early years with Ted Healy through their feature film career with Curly-Joe DeRita.

As the years have passed, The Three Stooges' success in the world of comic books has not diminished one iota. They have been tops in whatever field of endeavor they have been associated with, and as with their classic film comedies, their comics have without a doubt helped catapult these three crazy comedians into the world of legend.

# Chapter 4

A slapstick publicity still of the Stooges doing the popular "Hospital Operation" sketch, which they first performed on *The Steve Allen Show* in 1959. *Courtesy of Moe Howard Collection*

# The Three Stooges on Television

In 1946, it was the growing popularity of television, which some critics dubbed "the one-eyed monster," that helped give longevity to some comedians' careers and cut short others. The Three Stooges came to television with a special purpose—they wanted to explore another horizon in the realm of comedy.

The Stooges—Moe, Larry, and Shemp—first appeared before the tube-watching public on Milton Berle's *Texaco Star Theater*, broadcast by NBC on October 19, 1948. Neither a kinescope recording of the show nor a script is available for review, so, unfortunately, the material they performed in their television debut will remain unknown. However, according to Larry Fine, the show was well received, and fans wanted to see more of their antics on the small screen. Two months later, the boys returned to TV to guest star on

CBS's two-hour New Year's Eve special, an expanded episode of comedian Morey Amsterdam's half-hour variety-comedy series *The Morey Amsterdam Show*.

Larry once remarked, however, that television's lack of rehearsal time hampered the Stooges' style. In a 1950 radio interview, he explained the team's feelings about television. "It's new—hard to get used to—but we like it. The difficulty is, it doesn't give us time to prepare our act and to put on the kind of show we're used to doing and that people expect from us. I imagine TV would be pretty tough to do every week."

Although vaudeville had fallen out of public favor in the early 1940s, television seemed to revive it for a time, as a mighty legion of comedians brought their tried-and-true vaudeville and burlesque routines to the small screen. The Stooges were no exception; they came to television with routines that had been lifted from both their films and their vaudeville appearances. The trio hardly ever had fresh, newly written material to work with, at least during the primitive stages of this new entertainment medium.

Moe, Larry, and Shemp first performed new material on television when they starred in a pilot for a weekly television series titled *Jerks of All Trades*. The pilot was shot at ABC on October 12, 1949 (it took only one day to film). It was produced by Phil Berle, Milton Berle's brother. Henry Taylor had been hired to script it, and George McCahan took the helm as director.

The story revolved around the Stooges and their inability to hold a job (a similar device was later employed in a weekly TV series featuring Abbott and Costello). Emil Sitka and Symona Boniface were hired in supporting roles as a high-society couple, and Joseph Kearns (Mr. Wilson from the *Dennis the Menace* TV series) performed a memorable cameo as a pressure-cooker salesman from Punxsutawney, Pennsylvania.

In the show's opening, the announcer speaks in a high, bubbling pitch as he introduces the Stooges individually. Interspersed with the announcer's remarks, we hear the boys introducing themselves to the audience. The announcer continues to gush: "Yes, ladies and gentlemen, it's The Three Stooges! For mirth and madness—" The camera cuts to Moe grinning as he intones, "I'm Moe." The announcer then interjects, "Simple and screwy!" Turning to the camera, Shemp announces, "I'm Shemp!" The announcer continues, "Looney and lunatic!" Up pops the last Stooge: "I'm Larry!" This acts as a cue for the notes

of the show's theme song, "Crazy People," to ascend while the camera pulls back to a three-shot of the Stooges in painters' overalls. The announcer continues his spiel: "Yes, The Three Stooges are versatile gentlemen! When it comes to any kind of business, they're as spry as monkeys. Let us look at their spry monkey business now."

The pilot finds the boys at work as painters and wallpaper hangers, whom Mr. Pennyfeather (Emil Sitka) visits in hopes of redecorating his opulent mansion. A typical gag results after Pennyfeather makes his entrance into the Stooges' office and asks, "Pardon me, gentlemen. Are you painters and paperhangers?" Larry begins to talk in circles: "Are we painters and paperhangers?" Then Moe chimes in: "Are we painters and paperhangers?" A puzzled Shemp queries, "Are we?" Moe stomps on his foot, causing Shemp to smack the top of a desk with his hand, sweeping off a bottle of ink onto Pennyfeather's three-piece suit. Livid, Pennyfeather eyes his soiled clothing and then glares at Shemp. Moe, apologetic, tries wiping off the ink stains, but instead spreads them all over the suit's expensive-looking jacket. Larry, trying to help out, runs over, picks up a gallon can of ink remover, and pours the entire contents onto Pennyfeather's suit. The potent liquid removes more than ink, as it burns away portions of the jacket as well.

Pennyfeather's temper rises as he takes out his vengeance on Shemp, pouncing on him. His assault is stopped in its tracks as Moe steps in to reprise one of his favorite routines, "Insulting the State of Texas." Strutting up to Pennyfeather, Moe spouts, "Just a minute! Do you realize that you have just struck one of the toughest men from the state of—" (all three clap their hands) "—Texas! Go ahead, tell him, Tex!" Shemp sidles over to Pennyfeather and manages to squeal, "Yeah, I'm . . ." Pennyfeather hauls off and wallops him again. Moe steps back in front of Pennyfeather in the same fashion as before. "Sir, you have again sullied the fair name of the great, sovereign state of—" (the usual claps) "—Texas!" Motioning to Shemp, Moe says, "Order him off the premises!" The boys proceed to throw Pennyfeather out the door, paint remover can and all.

The phone rings and it's Mrs. Pennyfeather, calling the Stooges to come over to paint her house. The boys agree, not realizing they just brutalized her husband. Enthused over the chance to prove their worth as interior decorators, Larry dashes to the three-drawer file cabinet to find their book of color samples.

Moe spots Larry struggling to open the middle drawer of the file cabinet. Infuriated, Larry bangs the top drawer with his fists, which sends the bottom drawer flying out, cracking him on the shins. While Larry hops about in pain, Moe remarks, "How did you ever get so stupid?" Larry snaps back, "I gotta charge account—what's your excuse?" Shoving Larry aside, Moe shouts, "Remind me to lower your salary and raise your forehead. Out of the way!"

Of course, Moe quickly proves he's as brainless as the rest of the Stooges. He tugs fruitlessly at the middle drawer—it won't budge. Furious, he kicks the bottom drawer closed. *Whap!* The top one flies out, smashing him in the face.

And now it's Shemp's turn. "Step aside, boys. Let an intelligent man show you how." Moe is angry now and shouts, "Intelligent? What makes you so smart?" Shemp remarks, "I graduated from college—Swedish Massage College." Moe queries, "Then why didn't you go into the business?" Shemp chuckles stupidly, "I couldn't find any Swedes to massage!"

Following a series of comedy miscues, Shemp gets the file drawer open and mistakes a folder plainly marked "Culinary Art Book" for the book of wallpaper and color samples. He drags it along as the Stooges go to the Pennyfeathers' house. Mrs. P. knows she's in big trouble when Shemp, reading from his cookbook, suggests tomato red as the color for the living room.

In addition to the customary slapstick tomfoolery, Moe, Shemp, and Larry recreate another famous routine from the Stooges' 1938 comedy *Tassels in the Air*. The boys are asked to refinish an expensive antique table but instead ruin it.

The show's ending comes as no surprise, reminiscent as it is of their films on high society. Mr. Pennyfeather finally returns to find the Stooges destroying his house. He gets back at them for creating the mess by dumping paint over their heads and physically assaulting them.

This scene segues to the weary Stooges leaving their office—all three in a sorry state. Moe has a bandage on his head, Larry has his arm in a sling, and Shemp is walking with a crutch and has bandages on his face. Suddenly, we are interrupted by the announcer, who says, "And so ends the episode in which our Three Stooges tried their luck as interior decorators but met

with misfortune. However, will they be cowards and never try it again? Are they spineless jellyfish? Quitters?" The boys quickly turn to camera and snap back an answer: "Ya betcha life we are!"

Although the Stooges' performances were adequate, many of their antics were missing. The direction was extremely poor, and the show lacked the spontaneity of their shorts. In addition, the writers crammed too many routines into one episode, which actually bogged it down.

The pilot was never aired. B. B. Kahane, Columbia Pictures' vice president of business affairs, stopped the show from being broadcast. Kahane warned the Stooges that their contract with Columbia prohibited them from performing in a TV series that might compete with their two-reel comedies. Columbia further threatened to cancel the boys' contract and take them to court if they tried to sell the series. To avert a legal hassle, they shelved the pilot and abandoned the project.

Although the Stooges were contractually forbidden from doing their own TV series, personal appearances were permitted, and they appeared in a guest shot on CBS's *Camel Comedy Caravan*, sponsored by Camel cigarettes and starring Ed Wynn. Also known as *The Ed Wynn Show*, it was the first live Los Angeles–based variety show. In this particular episode, broadcast on March 11, 1950, the Stooges play CBS executives (Moe as Mr. C, Larry as Mr. B, and Shemp as Mr. S) who order Wynn to overhaul his entire program, from its comedy material to its studio sets. In the show's opening scene, Moe introduces Larry to Wynn, informing him that Larry is vice president in charge of network soap operas. Larry proves it by blowing a stream of bubbles from his mouth. Later, the Stooges mess up a dramatic sketch, and Wynn attempts to rid himself of the trio by standing them below sandbags hanging high overhead, perfectly positioned to clobber them. Helen Forrest, a popular singer of the day, also guest-starred, along with William Frawley. The Stooges were a tremendous hit with the studio audience.

Following the Wynn show, the Stooges were invited to appear on NBC's *Damon Runyon Memorial Fund* telethon to benefit the American Cancer Society. The show, which aired April 29, 1950, was hosted by Milton Berle. Afterward, Berle asked them to appear again on *Texaco Star Theater*, which was broadcast on NBC every Tuesday from 8 to 9 PM. The trio's second appearance aired May 2, 1950, and they shared the spotlight with the Lee Sheldon Dancers, Victoria Troupe, Rose Marie, Robert Alda, Sid Stone, and Morton Downey (who earlier had taken the Stooges on an extended nationwide tour).

The Stooges' return appearance on *Texaco Star Theater* features many of their tried-and-true routines. In the middle of their opening sketch, Shemp interrupts Berle, advising him that they are running out of time. Here, Shemp cleverly slips in a comedy bit the Stooges had been using since their days with Ted Healy, "Telling Time." Berle notices that Shemp is wearing three watches on his wrist and asks him why he's wearing them. Shemp explains, "Oh, I use those to tell time. Ya see, this one is twenty minutes slow, and this one is ten minutes fast, and this one

Larry (far right) makes the most of his appearance on Ed Wynn's *Camel Comedy Caravan* in 1950, as Moe and Shemp look on.
*Courtesy of Jeff and Greg Lenburg Collection*

is stopped at two o'clock." Alarmed, Berle inquires, "Then . . . how do you tell the time?" Shemp says, smirking, "Well, I subtract the ten on this watch from the twenty on this watch, then I add them all together and divide by two—" Berle interrupts: "Oh yeah! Well then, what time is it?" Shemp yanks out a fourth watch from his coat pocket, checks the time, and retorts, "Eight twenty!" After finishing the bit, Moe, Larry, and Shemp convince Berle to let them sing "Swanee River."

A couple of acts later, the Stooges return in a Foreign Legion sketch that features Robert Alda as their com-

manding officer. Only Moe and Shemp have lines of dialogue, while Larry remains mute. Alda gets into the act by asking Shemp, "Have you been in the Foreign Legion before Pearl Harbor?" Shemp cracks, "I've been in the Foreign Legion before Pearl White!" (White was a famous actress from the early days of film.) Shemp snickers at his own remark as Moe shouts, "Put out your hand!" He smacks Shemp's hand, which swings around and clobbers Shemp's skull.

Berle was so pleased with the trio that he called them back for a third guest shot on October 10, 1950. The episode's other guest stars included Bert Gordon, The Weavers, Alice Pearce, Yogi Berra, Evelyn Knight, Sid Stone, Walter Winchell, and George Price. Moe, Larry, and Shemp performed another stock routine for the first time on television: their famous "The Maharaja" sketch. While Curly had been superb as the nearsighted Maharaja in *Three Little Pirates* (1946), Shemp's performance was just as convincing, and the time-tested sketch had the audience howling.

To kick off the riotous lunacy, Shemp enters as the Maharaja, wearing a turban, a garish "Indian" costume, and glasses with thick, beveled lenses that give him the appearance of a startled owl. As one would lead a blind man, Moe guides the Maharaja out onto the stage. Shemp comically bumps into tables and chairs during his absurd entrance. Shemp finally stops, his back to the audience, and bows as Moe spins him around to face the throng, pushing him into a chair. Then Moe inquires, "Like to talk to people?" Shemp chuckles, mutters, "Razbanyas yatee benee-futch ah skidoo kiddo." In the midst of Moe's questions, Shemp gets up from his seat and begins to wander. Moe orders him to sit down. Shemp reacts to his command, searches aimlessly for the chair, sits, misses the seat, and falls flat on his duff.

Moe keeps the act moving as he continues his spiel to the audience, "The Rajah never on any occasion uses any helper, assistant, or confederate, but for this particular group of tricks, he'd like to have a young—" Before Moe finishes, Larry dashes up onstage from the audience shouting, "Here I am!" Berle enters the scene as Larry asks, "What does the Maharaja do?" "Yeah, what does he do?" shouts Berle. "We shall see!" Moe chimes in.

Seating himself next to Shemp, Moe shouts, "Maha!" Shemp looks dazedly in several directions, finally spots Moe, and stammers, "Ah-ha!" Moe answers with his patented double-talk, "Razbanyas yata benee futch ah timiney herongha dot pickle-head askee taskee wateecha fertziek you goddit?" (Translation: Moe wants to know what trick Shemp will perform.) Shemp replies, "Nyothing!" Flabbergasted, Moe remarks, "Nyothing?" Moe regains his composure, grabs Larry by the hair, and shouts that the Maharaja is an expert sharpshooter and for his first trick will shoot a raisin from the top of this gentleman's head. Given his trusty rifle, half-blind Shemp points it directly at the audience, who scream in panic. Moe twirls him around, helps him aim toward Larry. Kablam! He impresses all, shooting the raisin cleanly off Larry's head.

Larry's cowardice and the Maharaja's blindness are put to the test again in a wild knife-throwing demonstration. Shemp blindly throws knives, which miss the target completely and send Larry into a trembling panic. Finally, Moe shouts to the audience, "The Rajah says the next blade will come within one-eighth of an inch of the victim's brain." The victim, being Larry, quips, "What brain?" A squeamish Berle runs offstage to escape from the firing line. Shemp then throws his last knife, which sails offstage in Berle's direction. A beat and Berle emerges screaming, with the trick knife piercing his head.

Berle was a long-time admirer of The Three Stooges and their comedy. His own rapid-fire delivery was akin to Bud Abbott's—and Ted Healy's. Larry recalled that "Berle was kind of like Healy. He was fast with the jokes and would slap us around. We got into all kinds of messes, of course. And Milton liked having us on the show."

Television producers often used the Stooges as comic relief in musical-variety shows such as *Texaco Star Theater*. Ted Collins, Kate Smith's personal agent, signed the trio for NBC's *The Kate Smith Hour*. The series was a live weekly show that featured Broadway and Hollywood stars in music numbers and comedy sketches, so the Stooges fit quite well into her format. The team appeared on the October 13, 1950, broadcast. Then, on May 18, 1951, they guest starred on the CBS variety program *Star of the Family*, hosted by Morton Downey.

The same year, the boys appeared on NBC's *The Colgate Comedy Hour*, making their debut on Sunday, December 16, 1951, at the El Capitan Theatre in Hollywood. Other performers who headlined the series at one time or another were such top-name comedians as Abbott and Costello, Fred Allen, Martin and Lewis, and Ed Wynn. For the Stooges' episode, Carmen Miranda, Alan Young (who played Wilbur Post on *Mister Ed*), and Roy Rogers were hired to guest alongside them. Kingman Moore directed and Jack Paar hosted.

In many respects, *The Colgate Comedy Hour* surpassed the trio's previous television performances, since most of their material for the show was new. Their first sketch casts Larry as the manager of Fay's Department Store. As he prepares for a big Christmas sale, a crush of customers appears outside, anxiously waiting to get into the store. Larry forces his way through the mob, unlocks the doors, and is trampled by a stampede of patrons trying to get in. (Jerry Lewis later reworked this same gag in the film *Who's Minding the Store?*)

The camera cuts to Larry, flattened on the ground. Moe, a floorwalker, shouts, "Five minutes after nine and he's sleeping already. Come on, Sleeping Beauty, get up!" Moe grabs a handful of Larry's hair and pulls him to his feet. Then, pointing to a table full of miscellaneous goods, he shouts, "Here's a bunch of junk we haven't been able to sell all year. You are going to sell it!" Larry whimpers, "But where are we going to find someone *stupid* enough to buy this stuff?"

On cue, Shemp enters as a customer garbed in an ill-fitting suit and sporting thick-lensed eyeglasses. Moe and Larry believe they've found the perfect sucker to take their useless junk. But Shemp isn't interested. All he wants is a full refund on the faulty fountain pen he bought. Inspecting the pen carefully, Moe asks, "What seems to be wrong with the article?" As Shemp pulls open the pen's lever filler and says, "When I do this . . ." Zap! Moe gets a faceful of ink. Shemp continues, ". . . it squirts all over." Moe responds angrily, burning as he wipes the ink off his face, "So it does." He belts Shemp with his inky hand.

Moe and Larry refuse to refund Shemp in cash and instead offer their worn-out merchandise in exchange. Shemp remains adamant; he wants a cash refund. The word "refund" ignites Moe's violent temper, and he begins to punch Shemp around uncontrollably, trying to change his mind. But Shemp won't concede—he wants his money back. In the same vein as "Niagara Falls," another reaction-on-word sketch, Moe reacts violently each time he hears the word "refund." He wallops Shemp so hard that he is nearly out cold on his feet. As he staggers around comically, about to fall, Moe catches him, holds him upright, and in the process feels for Shemp's wallet. He yanks it out and removes a sheaf of bills, moves them close to his ear, and riffles them. Moe counts out ninety-eight dollars and pockets it as payment in full for the worthless sale items. Moe and Larry then stuff the junk merchandise and the dazed Shemp into a crate. The camera zooms in on the words "Do Not Open Until Christmas!"

In their second sketch, Roy Rogers introduces the Stooges as renowned chefs and explains that they are preparing delicacies for a lavish party. Typical bits of business include Shemp stuffing a turkey by throwing in eggs and oysters—shells and all—and canned items still in the can. Meanwhile, Larry cleans lettuce in dirty dishwater and hangs the leaves to dry on a clothesline. To make things worse, all three Stooges accidentally spike the punch with Tabasco sauce. Of course, their cooking erupts into an outrageously wild melee that not even the show's announcer can bring under control.

As a result of their successes on *Texaco Star Theater* and *The Colgate Comedy Hour*, the Stooges' services were in constant demand. One of their finest achievements was their work on *The Frank Sinatra Show*, a one-hour weekly series for CBS. Sponsored by Ekco ("the Greatest Names in Housewares"), the series was telecast live from Hollywood and featured celebrated guest stars and plenty of singing by Ol' Blue Eyes. Such noted luminaries as Louis Armstrong, CBS president William Paley, George DeWitt, and Yvonne De Carlo were cast opposite the Stooges in the January 1, 1952, episode.

Larry, Moe, and Shemp appear as servants at Sinatra's New Year's Eve party. The Stooges brighten up the sketch in their patented slapstick manner, messing up the simple task of taking coats from partygoers. They toss the guests' clothing about, until Shemp finally flings everything out the window. Sinatra keeps the show moving at a fast clip, hosting and singing songs to the delight of the audience.

Coming off the Sinatra show, the Stooges received an offer to star in a weekly series of their own. Two friends of Shemp's—Al Winston and Edwin Gale—conceived *We Wuz There* (with the alternate title *Where Were You?*), a spoof of the title of Walter Cronkite's famous CBS series *You Are There*. The main setting was to be a schoolroom, with the Stooges as students

recounting historical events to their teacher. In the midst of the Stooges' storytelling, the show would flash back to the actual event, with the Stooges in the lead roles. The series never materialized—it got no further than the treatment stage—and one wonders if the previous contract threats from Columbia had something to do with it.

Moe, Larry, and Shemp made three additional television appearances in 1952. On June 22, they joined the star-studded *Olympic Fund Telethon*, broadcast live on CBS and NBC from Hollywood's El Capitan Theatre, to benefit the financially strapped US Olympic Committee, and cohosted by Bob Hope and Bing Crosby. Next they appeared on the live July 29 telecast of the popular NBC daytime variety/talk program *The Johnny Dugan Show*. The boys performed one of their classic Stooge routines and were also presented with a plaque from *Motion Picture Exhibitor* magazine for being the top headliners in two-reel comedies in 1951. Rounding out the year, on Saturday, December 27, 1952, the trio appeared on NBC's *All Star Revue*. The hour-long variety show, hosted by Walter O'Keefe (who filled in for the regular host, comedian George Jessel, who fell ill), aired live in Eastern and Central time zones; a kinescope of the show was broadcast on January 3, 1953, on the West Coast. Other guests included comedian Buster Keaton and his wife Elea-

Larry, Moe, and Shemp with Bob Hope and Bing Crosby during the live telecast of the *Olympic Fund Telethon* in 1952. *Courtesy of Academy of Motion Picture Arts and Sciences, Margaret Herrick Library Collection*

nor, singers Frankie Laine and Dorothy Shay, and a comedian by the name of Johnny Carson (later the longtime host of NBC's *Tonight Show*).

In 1953, as part of a family vacation to Mexico City and Acapulco City with his wife, Helen, and son, Paul, Moe appeared on the Mexican version of the popular American game show *What's My Line?* The program emanated from Churubusco Studios, a Columbia studio affiliate, in Mexico City. The set was pretty stark and simple: one TV camera and a boom mike. Contestants wore black masks over their eyes as Moe, flashing a mischievous grin, was introduced to the live studio audience by a sign on an easel that read "Uno del 'Los Tres Chilflados' Comico." As Paul Howard later remembered, "The funny part is Dad didn't speak a word of Spanish."

A year later, in 1954, Moe made his second known solo television appearance, this time with comedian Danny Thomas on the May 18 broadcast of the popular television game show *Strike It Rich*, a program that assisted people in unfortunate circumstances. The comics helped two contestants, real-life couple Mom and Pop Cooprider, win $500 for their Hillside House in Santa Barbara, California, which aided children suffering from polio.

Moe guest starring on the *Strike It Rich* game show in 1954 with comedian Danny Thomas (far left). *Courtesy of Jeff Lenburg Collection*

Moe appearing on a 1953 Mexican TV show version of *What's My Line? Courtesy of Moe Howard Collection*

The Stooges' next joint TV appearance was on April 29, 1955, as guests on *The Eddie Cantor Comedy Theatre* in an episode titled "What Do You Want in a Show?" (Cantor frequently admitted that he was a Stooges fan and was delighted at the opportunity to finally work with them.) At first, the story takes off like the old Mickey Rooney–Judy Garland MGM musicals, in which Rooney dreams up all kinds of grandiose moneymaking ideas with Garland. Cantor employs similar tactics, coming up with the idea of producing a stage revue to save his theater from bankruptcy. The Stooges star as crooks, Butch, Lefty, and Spike, in a production titled "A Night at the U.S. Mint." The show within a show is a financial triumph and lifts Cantor's theater out of debt. This was the Stooges' last TV appearance with Shemp, who died of a heart attack seven months later.

The Three Stooges appear with Eddie Cantor and Pat Dennie on Cantor's TV show *The Eddie Cantor Comedy Theatre*. It was Shemp's last TV appearance with the team. *Courtesy of Jeff and Greg Lenburg Collection*

Following Shemp's death, Joe Besser took over the role of third Stooge on January 1, 1956. Besser came close to making a new series of television shows with the Stooges when Moe seriously considered abandoning their two-reel deal with Columbia to do a weekly television comedy-news program. On August 14, 1957, *Daily Variety* reported that Moe Howard had taken this proposal to Columbia Pictures executives only to be met with instant rejection, since the shorts were still turning out profits for Columbia. (Moe was slightly ahead of his time: the nightly news programs were spoofed twenty years later with the creation of the "Weekend Update" segments on NBC's *Saturday Night Live*.)

In late 1958, after Columbia released the Stooges' shorts to TV and they enjoyed a sudden resurgence in popularity, producers began vying for the trio's services. Norman Maurer began discussions with the major networks to star the Stooges in a new series. He planned for it to use his patented animation process, Artiscope, which he had coinvented with his brother Leonard.

When the Maurers began to develop this new animation method in 1954, they'd been financed first by Moe and subsequently by the Wall Street firm of Mabon and Company. Artiscope was a revolutionary automated system that took live-action footage of actors and utilized an optical-chemical process to transform each frame of the film into line drawings that looked like they were hand drawn. The result was a high-fidelity animated cartoon, literally drawn by machine, with no artists needed except for minor touch-ups. In 1955, the Maurers had started their own company, Illustrated Films Inc., for the purpose of producing television commercials, industrial films, television adventure series, and religious, scientific, and theatrical films using this innovative technique. In 1958, Norman had ongoing discussions with the networks to produce other half-hour television series, as well as discussions with Walt Disney Studios, Harold Cohen of Ashley-Steiner (for the latter to produce new *Popeye* cartoons), and Bob Clampett Productions about licensing their Artiscope process for new productions.

Norman's plan for the Stooges was to create a weekly TV series titled *Stooge Time*, which would feature them in both live-action segments and Artiscope cartoons. The series would have a unique format, with each show opening with a snappy Three Stooges theme song over titles that were a combination of cartoon and live Stooges. This was to segue into a seven-minute, live-action, slapstick-comedy Stooges film, followed by a thirty-second routine of them squirting each other with seltzer bottles. The bottles' spray would magically transform them into Artiscope animated characters to introduce "Cartoon Time," and the episode's first seven-minute Stooges cartoon.

Norman Maurer's 1958 concept for *Stooge Time*, a live-action/animated series using his Artiscope process.
© *Normandy Productions, courtesy of Norman Maurer Collection*

Two cartoons were to be included in each half-hour show, along with a healthy amount of new live footage of the Stooges. Twenty-six half-hours, containing a combination of seventy-eight live and animated films, were proposed. Norman planned to have Edward Bernds direct the live segments, and Academy Award–winning cartoon director Friz Freleng helm the Artiscope cartoons. Moe Howard and Felix Adler were set as story writers, with Maurer producing. Unfortunately, Norman's original concept didn't sell; network executives refused to believe that the revolutionary Artiscope process could actually produce thousands of drawings without artists.

(Incidentally, when Norman first coinvented the Artiscope concept back in 1954, he filmed a test reel starring Moe Howard and Don Lamond titled *Captain Lafitte.* The test was photographed in Moe's garage, with Moe and Don clashing swords as two swashbuckling pirates. Lamond later narrated and appeared in the team's feature films of the 1960s.)

Although Norman's pioneering live-cartoon show didn't sell, other television producers deemed the Stooges surefire entertainment for existing series. Comedian Steve Allen was one of them. Moe, Larry, and Curly-Joe appeared in three highly publicized guest spots on *The Steve Allen Show,* originating from the Colonial Theatre in New York and broadcast by NBC. On January 11, 1959, they performed a hysterical "Hospital Operation" skit, which would later be reprised on *The Ed Sullivan Show.*

After the Steve Allen show, Moe, Larry, and Curly-Joe appeared on the television panel quiz show

An Artiscope-animated Moe as a pirate from the 1954 test reel *Captain Lafitte*. © *Illustrated Films, courtesy of Norman Maurer Collection*

*Masquerade Party*, hosted by Bert Parks. Internationally known celebrities were disguised in elaborate costumes and contestants were asked to identify them. The Stooges dressed as the Gabors—Jolie, Eva, and Zsa Zsa—and fooled the experienced panelists (Faye Emerson, Sam Levenson, Audrey Meadows, and Lee Bowman). The show was broadcast on CBS on January 15, 1959.

Following this quiz show, the Stooges began rehearsals on their second Steve Allen appearance, which would air February 22, 1959, doing their "The Stand-In" skit. Moe's wife Helen accompanied the team and recalled how Moe came down with pneumonia hours before he was to appear on the show. "Moe had rehearsed all day for the Allen show and returned to the hotel to go to bed. There he was with no voice and a high fever and dictating the entire 'Stand-In' routine to a script girl. I remember his adding that hysterical bit where they attach candles to each side of the camera and every time the director shouted, 'Cut!' Moe would shout, 'Save the

lights!' And the crew would rush in to blow out the candles. Moe's voice cracked and squeaked throughout the show. And those who loved him—and there were untold numbers—suffered with him."

The Stooges had first performed the sketch "The Stand-In" during the Broadway stage run of *George White's Scandals of 1939*, featuring a young newcomer, dancer Ann Miller. Matty Brooks and Eddie Davis, who occasionally supplied material for the Stooges, wrote the original sketch. Brooks granted permission for the Stooges to reuse it on Allen's show. (Brooks wrote another sketch, called "Happy Holiday." Presumably it was for the Stooges' later appearances on *The Ed Sullivan Show*, but it appears the sketch was never used.)

In the *Steve Allen Show* version of "The Stand-In," Moe plays the director of a feature movie, Larry is the film's star, and Curly-Joe is Larry's stand-in. Each time Larry is about to get involved in a wild action scene, Moe yells, "Cut!" Curly-Joe then takes Larry's place and gets clobbered. Similar slapstick action continues as Curly-Joe takes the brunt of everything from saloon fights to pies in the face, while spotless Larry gets all the credit for the terrific scenes. Curly-Joe burns.

In the finish, Larry is to be buried alive in a big box by the villains. Just as he is about to be shoved

The Stooges reprise the sketch "The Stand-In" on *The Steve Allen Show*. *Courtesy of Moe Howard Collection*

inside the box, Moe yells, "Cut!" Curly-Joe is shoved inside and the box is nailed shut. At this moment a lunch whistle blows and Moe calls out, "OK! Lunch, everybody!" As the crew leaves, one of them points to the box and asks, "How about the stand-in?" Moe snaps his fingers, "Holy smoke, I almost forgot about him!" He runs up to the box, raps on it a couple of times, and shouts, "Hey! Take an hour for lunch!"

Moe's spirits and health improved after the success of the Allen show, and an offer to reappear prompted him to dictate material for the trio's third Allen show appearance, which aired April 5, 1959. To the delight of millions, the Stooges reprised their world-famous "The Maharaja" sketch, performing it with Curly-Joe for the first time on live television.

Suddenly one of the hottest television acts, the Stooges became the topic of conversation in all circles of show business, including the April 7, 1959, telecast of the prestigious Academy Awards show. During the conclusion of the show, master of ceremonies Jerry Lewis quipped, "Now nobody leave yet! The management told me that they're going to show a Three Stooges comedy for the losers!"

Riding the wave of their newfound popularity, during one of their visits to New York in 1959, the Stooges reportedly made their first guest appearance on NBC's *Today Show* (details of their appearance are unknown). From that year through the mid-1960s, they made numerous appearances as well on many locally hosted children's programs across the country that aired the team's old Columbia Pictures two-reel comedies. After the box-office success of *Have Rocket--Will Travel* in the summer of 1959, Moe, Larry, and Curly-Joe made the first of many appearances on WPIX-TV's daily kids' show, *The Three Stooges Funhouse*, hosted by Officer Joe Bolton. WPIX was the first New York–based station to broadcast the shorts. (After *Funhouse* went off the air in September 1961, the Stooges' films were broadcast on other WPIX-hosted programs, including Todd Russell's *The Three Stooges Firehouse*, Chuck McCann's *Let's Have Fun*, and others.) The Stooges appeared on Bill Camfield's *Slam-Bang The-*

*atre* on KFJZ-TV, Fort Worth, Texas; Hal Fryar's *The Three Stooges Show* and others on WFBM-TV, Indianapolis; Wayne Mack's show on WDSU-TV, New Orleans; Paul Shannon's *Adventure Time* on WTAE-TV, Pittsburgh; Sally Starr's program on WFIL-TV, Philadelphia; and *Billy Barty's Big Show* on KTTV Channel 11, Los Angeles. All the hosts except Barty later appeared as the West's most wanted outlaws in the Stooges last feature film, *The Outlaws IS Coming!* (1965).

By the fall of 1959, Moe, Larry, and Curly-Joe were planning to star in two one-hour television "spectaculars" on ABC. In February of that year, Moe mentioned plans for the programs—most likely spe-

Moe sports his famous scowl during an appearance on Officer Joe Bolton's *The Three Stooges Funhouse* on WPIX-TV, the first New York station to begin airing the Stooges' old comedy shorts in 1958. *Courtesy of Moe Howard Collection*

cials—in an interview with a reporter. Unfortunately, for whatever reason, they never materialized.

With the Stooges' popularity becoming so mercurial, the William Morris Agency urged them to produce a pilot for a weekly half-hour color television series. Norman Maurer and the Stooges pooled their resources and, in a joint venture with Norman Maurer Productions and the trio's own company, Comedy III Productions, started developing a new series of thirty-nine episodes in which they would star, which would combine live segments with animated cartoons, to be called *Three Stooges Scrapbook*. (It is believed that as early as February 1959, Maurer may have proposed the series to Screen Gems, which was actively producing comedy and dramatic series for television. Moe noted in a newspaper interview then that talks with Screen Gems were underway to produce "a series of 39 original half-hours for TV.")

A year later, on February 1, 1960, Maurer formally announced a deal for the series. TV Spots Inc.—makers of the *Crusader Rabbit* cartoons—agreed to animate seventy-eight five-minute cartoons, with the deal calling for Maurer to deliver thirteen scripts at a time. Filming of the live-action sequences for the pilot commenced on March 7, 1960. Two animated segments were planned for each episode: one with the Stooges and slippery con man Benedict Bogus, who had previously been a steady character in the Three Stooges comic books, and the second starring the Li'l Stooges and Muff, an ensemble of juvenile Stooges and their kooky dog. The premise of the originally announced live-action segments called for the Stooges to get into "all kinds of jams that prevent them from getting to the studio on time."

As the concept for the series evolved, the Stooges cartoons, as described by Moe in numerous newspaper interviews, were to feature their interpretation of incidents based on historical events. As Moe recalled, "We'll show how these happenings succeeded in *spite* of the Stooges. And there'll be some cute bits of business as well. For instance, Larry will loan Washington a half a buck to throw across the Potomac, and Moe will loan his cigarette lighter to the guy who lit the signal lantern for Paul Revere."

Hollywood trade paper reports indicated that the show's volume of violence and deliberate head-banging was to be reduced. In an interview, Moe echoed these same sentiments. "In the live portions of these films, we will cut out the deliberate physical horseplay and substitute unintentional violence—if you have to call it violence. In other words, I won't purposely clunk Larry or Curly-Joe, but if I'm carrying a ladder, let's say, and I make a quick turn, it could accidentally clip Curly on the bean. The deliberate stuff will only be seen in the cartoon segments. That will make everybody happy." Moe was obviously directing his closing remark at network censors and parental action groups, who often criticized the boys' films as being "too violent."

In accordance with network censorship codes of the day, cartoons were allowed greater freedom when it came to violent slapstick humor. Cartoon

producers and animators were able to get away with intentional violence—à la the Road Runner cartoons—while live performers were condemned for the same actions. The idea of casting the Stooges in a format combining live wraparounds and cartoons alleviated two problems: the trio would be able to star in parent-approved weekly live segments while also exhibiting their two-fisted humor in cartoons.

The formula for *Three Stooges Scrapbook* seemed to have all the earmarks of a winner. In a July 1960 interview, Moe noted that NBC had the "inside track" to pick up the series, because they were equipped with the facilities to broadcast the program in color (the pilot, which Maurer and the Stooges financed, was the first time the Stooges had appeared on film in color since *Nertsery Rhymes* in 1933). But, he added, all three networks were showing interest. Yet television sponsors interested in the series were unable to acquire the proper time slots from networks to broadcast the show. Three times *Scrapbook* was sold,

The Stooges mugging broadly, displaying their oversized scrapbook, from *Three Stooges Scrapbook*. © *Norman Maurer Productions, courtesy of Moe Howard Collection*

but all three times, the only available time slot was after 10 PM. A late-night slot was unacceptable to the sponsors, since the Stooges' audience was composed mainly of children. Subsequently, the sponsors withdrew their bids, and a short time later *Scrapbook* was shelved permanently.

Television viewers and Stooge fans alike missed out on what might have been a hit series. The pilot of *Three Stooges Scrapbook* was a combination of many elements that made it shine as a topflight production. The live-

A full-page April 20, 1960, *Variety* ad saluting the cast and crew of *Three Stooges Scrapbook*.

*Courtesy of Moe Howard Collection*

action sequences generate their share of laughs, as the Stooges take up residence in an old haunted mansion. The cartoon, in which the animated Stooges contribute to Christopher Columbus's discovering that the world is round, is the show's one dull spot.

A surprise addition was the title song, "I Wanna Be a Stooge," written by Academy Award winner George Duning with Stanley Styne. As the opening credits roll, a symphony of sproing-ing springs and hollow clunks can be heard over the following lyrics:

> Larry, Moe, Curly-Joe
> They're the funniest guys I know.
> Golly gee, that's for me,
> I wanna be a Stooge.
>
> Well, you can be, like those three
> If you don't use common sense.
> Yes indeed, all you need
> Is a high intelligence.
> Yes, siree, they're the Three
> Musketeers of comedy.
> They have fun,
> We have fun,
> I wanna be a Stooge.

Following this hilarious animated title sequence, the camera fades in on "Hollywood, glamour capital of the world, where Valentino and Pickford wrote the first pages of movie history. But changing times have resulted in the formation of a new medium: television. And bringing their brand of humor to it . . . The Three Stooges."

With an audience laugh track added throughout, the pilot, titled "Home Cooking," opens on the boys rehearsing for their weekly television show. Much of the same live footage would be reprinted in black-and-white and used in the 1962 feature *The Three Stooges in Orbit*. Inside their apartment, where no cooking is allowed on the premises, Curly-Joe is preparing lunch while the other two Stooges go over their lines. Despite their attempts to disguise the smell of their cooking, the landlady, Mrs. McGinnis (Marjorie Eaton), manages to sniff them out and evicts them.

The story is the same as in *Orbit*, with the boys finding residence at Creepy Manor in Lompoc, California. Here, Professor Doyle (Emil Sitka) has devised a newfangled, multipurpose war machine—a combina-

tion tank/helicopter/submarine that Norman Maurer designed and for which he drew the actual blueprints that appeared in the scene. (In the TV pilot, Sitka's character, though scripted as Doyle, is referred to as "Dolottle," a play on the popular children's character, Dr. Dolittle; but in *Orbit* he is known as Danforth). A monster with a lobster-like claw haunts the mansion in an attempt to steal the plans. Naturally, after several wild, spooky sequences, the Stooges foil his efforts and expose him. You guessed it—he's the butler!

Moe, Curly-Joe, and Larry try amusing an eccentric professor (Emil Sitka) in a scene from *Three Stooges Scrapbook*.
© *Norman Maurer Productions, courtesy of Norman Maurer Collection*

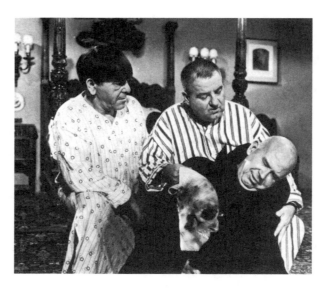

Moe and Curly-Joe, in *Three Stooges Scrapbook*, capture the butler, disguised as a haunted-house monster. © *Norman Maurer Productions, courtesy of Norman Maurer Collection*

Finally, after escaping from Creepy Manor, the Stooges make it to the studio for their TV show and relate their experiences to their viewers. Then they proceed to pull out an oversized scrapbook, turning to a page containing one of their favorite stories and recalling the time they set sail with Columbus in 1492. This segues into a live introduction in which the boys, dressed as sailors, argue over whether the world is round or flat. Curly-Joe adds further confusion to the scene by clutching a cube-shaped desk globe.

Suddenly, an animated parrot named Feathers flies into the scene to address this flat-versus-round debate. He lands on Joe's shoulder and whispers in his ear. The parrot informs the trio that Columbus needs three sailors to help him on a historic expedition, and that Mr. C. promises to pay them union scale and a thousand Blue Chip stamps to make the journey. It's an offer the Stooges can't refuse.

Thus begins a segment titled "The Spain Mutiny," in which the trio sets sail—in cartoon form—to prove that the world is round. Moe had stated in his interview that the cartoons would have a good deal of violence throughout—and he was right. In one example, Moe uses the ship's anchor to clobber Larry. In another violent scene, Moe grabs Larry and Joe off the ground and crushes their heads together.

The Stooges must have realized their cartoon debut was a bust. In one scene, Moe becomes tired

Scene from the animated cartoon "The Spain Mutiny," in *Three Stooges Scrapbook*. © Norman Maurer Productions, courtesy of Jeff and Greg Lenburg Collection

of the sailor's life and remarks, "Wait a minute! You guys havin' fun?" Larry chimes in: "No, I'm not havin' fun!" Quips Joe, "This isn't fun!" Nor would the cartoon have been fun for viewers, since its production values are poor and the animation is flat and grotesque. The Stooges' facial expressions are distorted beyond recognition, with the only recognizable features being their trademark haircuts. The movement of the animated characters is rickety, and the end result seems lifeless. This bottom-of-the-barrel animation makes the Stooges' later Cambria-produced cartoon series look like an award winner.

As the episode winds down, Feathers takes over the expedition and gains the support of a local Indian tribe in his quest to learn the world's real shape. The Stooges, however, abandon all hope of immortalizing themselves as ship's mates and dive overboard. They take to swimming across the high seas, bound for safer waters. But to their surprise, their watery journey comes to an abrupt halt as the ocean suddenly drops off vertically, proving that the world is square after all.

Once the cartoon fades out, the live Stooges reappear and Moe and Larry express their disbelief at the idea of anyone believing the world is square. "You mean it ain't?" Curly-Joe remarks innocently. Moe yanks

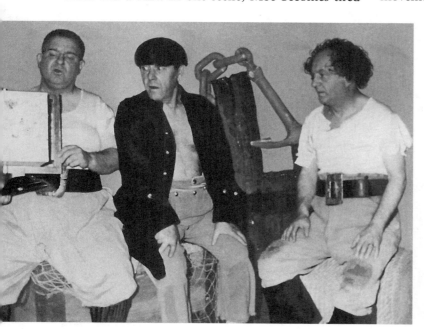

Curly-Joe, Moe, and Larry as confused sailors in a scene from *Three Stooges Scrapbook*. © Norman Maurer Productions, courtesy of Norman Maurer Collection

a round globe from behind his back and smashes it over Curly-Joe's head. The globe now looks like a crumpled paper bag. They stare at it in disbelief. It's not round or square!

The end credits roll and the march song returns once again, only this time with slightly different lyrics:

> Larry, Moe, Curly-Joe
> They're the funniest guys I know.
> Golly, gee, that's for me,
> I wanna be a Stooge.
> Larry clowns, Moe he frowns,
> Joe makes all of those crazy sounds.
> What a scream,
> What a team,
> I wanna be a Stooge.

Although the pilot never sold, in September 1963 Normandy Productions and Columbia would codistribute *Three Stooges Scrapbook* to theaters as two short subjects: a fourteen-minute short utilizing the first two-thirds of the film, and a ten-minute short with the final third, including the cartoon "The Spain Mutiny."

By 1960, sponsors were also clamoring for the team to endorse their products. The trio's first TV commercial was for Hot Shot insecticide, a product of the Amsco Chemical Company; it was broadcast from March 1 to September 30, 1960. It was quickly followed by a fondly remembered commercial for Chunky Chocolates. That same year, the Stooges also filmed a one-minute black-and-white public service announcement for The Arthritis Foundation, with Moe and Larry playing a pair of con men trying to sell bogus arthritis cures to Curly-Joe.

But the commercial that rises above them all is for Simoniz Car Wax. This sixty-second spot, filmed between February 25 and March 5 of 1960, contains some bright moments. It opens with the Stooges as scientists experimenting in a research laboratory. Moe is mixing chemicals when Larry and Curly-Joe announce that they have developed a new product to wax cars. "Moe," Larry enthuses, "we got it. We got it." An agitated Moe asks,

"What?" Curly-Joe gushes, "We've found a way to put Simoniz Car Wax—" Larry, beaming with pride, interrupts: ". . . and Simoniz Car Kleener all into one can." Moe grumpily asks Larry, "And just how does it work, Professor Nitwit?" Larry and Curly-Joe remark in unison, "Come on, we'll show you," as they drag Moe to an automobile, squirt liquid from a can onto the hood, watch as it powders, and then wipe it off. The car sparkles as a whistling Curly-Joe enthuses, "Look at that shine!" "We'll be famous. We'll make a fortune," Larry excitedly exclaims. Thinking he has a clever name for the product, he adds, "We'll call it Instant Simoniz."

"Instant Simoniz? You lamebrain." Moe, scowling, smacks Larry and whips out a can of the company's product. "You can already buy Instant Simoniz everywhere!" Disappointed, Larry retorts, "Instant Simoniz? They thought of it, too." Moe concludes, "Simoniz thinks of everything!" On his words the commercial freeze-frames on the product.

The Stooges were paid $8,500 for this commercial, which aired nationally from March 15 to September 15, 1960. The brief segment caught the attention of filmmaker Frank Tashlin, who was writing and directing "The Frances Langford Show" for *Sunday Showcase* on NBC. *Showcase* featured different forms of enter-

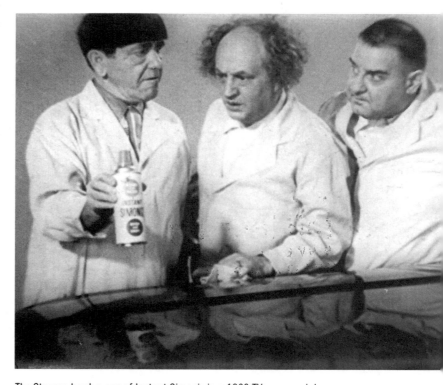

The Stooges hawk a can of Instant Simoniz in a 1960 TV commercial.
*Courtesy of Moe Howard Collection*

tainment weekly, including variety, drama, and comedy formats. For Langford's installment, which was telecast on May 1, 1960, she was teamed with Don Ameche, her former costar in radio's *The Bickersons*, and the Stooges added their special style of slapstick in several segments. The program saluted the mothers of famous motion picture personalities, with Langford's troupe of stars making a trip to Hollywood to stage an honorary show for the "Hollywood Motion Picture Mothers." In one sentimental sequence, the Stooges prepare for bed while Larry cries pitifully, emitting a cascade of tears as he recounts how they never had a mother. Curly-Joe tries to comfort him with words of encouragement but fails. Then Moe steps in and places a handkerchief over Larry's eyes to contain the torrent of tears. But the hanky does little to alleviate the situation as the tears literally explode out of Larry's ears. Curly-Joe tries to stop the flow by covering Larry's ears with his hands, but another leak breaks out from the top of his head. Joe cracks, "Hey, Moe, maybe we can charge admission and call him Old Faithful!"

In another segment, Mary Costa comes on and sings her rendition of the Dave Rose recording "Holiday for Strings." During the last eight bars of the tune, the Stooges disrupt this serious melody by prancing onstage in their cockamamie version of ballet costumes. They break up not only the song's dramatic tempo but Costa and the audience as well. Charles Wick, who also produced *Snow White and the Three Stooges*, produced both this hour-long special and a promotional soundtrack album, which featured such top stars as Bob Cummings, Johnny Mathis, and Hermione Gingold.

A month earlier, on April 15, 1960, the Stooges had turned up on *On the Go*, a half-hour morning series broadcast from Los Angeles and hosted by Jack Linkletter. During an interview filmed on location at a family picnic, they talk about their real-life personalities, the origin of their famous haircuts, and their prolific careers. In May, the boys also appeared on the Chicago-based panel discussion program *The Fran Allison Show*, on WGN-TV hosted by actress Fran Allison of Kukla, Fran, and Ollie fame.

Still to come was "a really big shew!"—their first appearance on *The Ed Sullivan Show*, broadcast by

Larry, Curly-Joe, and Moe clown around backstage with Frances Langford on the set of "The Frances Langford Show" for NBC's *Sunday Showcase*. *Courtesy of Moe Howard Collection*

CBS on May 14, 1961. Due to their heightened popularity, the Stooges received $8,500 and three airfares for their guest appearance, which was good money for its day.

Sullivan made a classic goof when he introduced the Stooges as the Three Ritz Brothers, later adding,

The Stooges as cockamamie ballet dancers, with a hysterical guest, Mary Costa, on "The Frances Langford Show." *Courtesy of Moe Howard Collection*

Larry, Moe, and Curly-Joe from their appearance on *The Fran Allison Show* in 1960. *Courtesy of WGN Television*

"who look more like The Three Stooges to me." The boys' performance didn't disappoint anyone, including Sullivan. He certainly had no problems remembering their name after the show.

In answer to many requests, the Stooges reprised the highly renowned "The Stand-In" sketch—which they had previously performed on Steve Allen's TV

show—to gales of audience laughter. In the wake of this newest triumph, George White, the producer of the stage show in which the Stooges had originated the sketch in 1939, *George White's Scandals*, filed a lawsuit against the Stooges, claiming he owned all rights to it. Rather than enter into a drawn-out court battle, White agreed to settle out of court for a marginal fee.

Undaunted by this legal action, the Stooges took their treasure chest of comedy material over to NBC. There they were signed for a July 27, 1961, guest appearance on the celebrity interview show *Here's Hollywood*, cohosted by Dean Miller and JoAnn Jordan. Three additional appearances followed. On January 14, 1962, Moe, Larry, and Curly-Joe appeared on the popular game show *Play Your Hunch*, hosted by Merv Griffin. Afterward, they did guest shots on NBC's *Today Show* (their second) and *The Tonight Show*, hosted by Jimmy Dean, which aired on January 26, 1962, and July 10, 1962, respectively.

As he had done previously, in 1962 Moe appeared sans his famous partners on two other programs. In February, he costarred on MetroMedia's (also often known as Metromedia) nightly syndicated interview show hosted by Mike Wallace and Joyce Davidson, *PM East*. Then, in July, he performed a five-minute bit in a pilot for a projected series that never sold, *Strictly for Laffs*. Hosted by comedian Dave Barry, the half-hour program featured television's top actors and comics, including Alan Reed, Sid Melton, Paul Gilbert, Ken Murray, Rose Marie, Buddy Lester, Mel Blanc, Jesse White, and Tommy Noonan, sharing jokes and funny stories.

In the early 1960s, Moe, Larry, and Curly-Joe also played multiple roles in a series of three funny and fast-paced one-minute commercials for Aqua Net hair products. In one of the spots, filmed in 1963, the Stooges appear in multiple roles, as pharmacists, warehousemen, truckers, and three gentlemen with flowers in tow for their "hot dates" who are waiting for delivery of Aqua Net Hair Spray.

Almost two years after their last visit, the Stooges made their second guest appearance on *The Ed Sullivan Show*. The February 20, 1963, telecast also featured comedian Bill Dana as Jose Jimenez, comedian Dave Madden, The Bob De Voye Trio, and ventriloquists Fred and Angela Roby. The Stooges performed their classic "Hospital Operation" sketch. This sce-

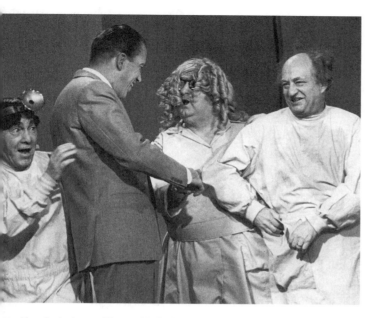

Moe, Curly-Joe, and Larry with Ed Sullivan after performing their famous "Hospital Operation" sketch on their February 10, 1963, appearance on Sullivan's show. *Courtesy of Moe Howard Collection*

you doing here?" Larry protests, "I don't know from nothing—I came to deliver a telegram." The scene fades out as chaos prevails inside the operating room.

The Stooges appeared a third time on Sullivan's program, this time in clip form. A segment of them performing their "The Stand-In" sketch from their May 14, 1961, appearance was featured as part of a ninety-minute compilation tribute of past shows to celebrate Sullivan's fifteenth year on CBS. *The Ed Sullivan Show 15th Anniversary Special* was broadcast on June 23, 1963.

The Stooges' fourth appearance on the Sullivan show was on October 6, 1963. They took this opportunity to perform their classic "The Maharaja" routine. With this appearance, their salary climbed to $10,000 for a single television guest shot. The boys

nario lampoons the finest in TV medical shows of the time—*Ben Casey*, *The Nurses*, and *Dr. Kildare*—with Moe as Dr. Ben Crazy and Curly-Joe dressed as his near-sighted nurse. Moe requests a patient, and Larry is hastily brought in. As he is prepped for surgery, Moe asks Larry, "Now, my good man, what kind of operation would you like?" Larry asks for the day's specials. "I don't know. What kind have you got?" Curly-Joe hands a menu to Moe, which he holds up for the camera: "$60.00 . . . $65.00 . . . $70.00. Liver 75 With Onions $1.00." Larry wants a bargain and says to Moe, "Okay, Doctor. I'll take the works." Moe barks to Curly-Joe, "Nurse, give him the anesthetic." Curly-Joe shoves him down and starts applying the anesthesia. He begins with ether, which doesn't work, followed by a mallet to Larry's head, which does. The operation proceeds smoothly until the actual removal of Larry's heart. At this point, Moe shoves his hands under the sheet and comes out with a rubber heart, which he holds up as the other two Stooges join him in a chorus of "Heart of My Heart."

After a commercial, Moe returns to the business at hand. He continues with the operation until he's suddenly interrupted by a patient who asks him, "Are you Ben Crazy?" Moe replies, "Why, yes, I am!" The patient grumbles, "You were to operate on me two hours ago!" Fuming, Moe shouts at Larry, "You impostor, what are

Curly-Joe, Moe, and Larry, along with bandleader Skitch Henderson, reprising the routine "The Maharaja" on their fourth appearance on *The Ed Sullivan Show* in 1963. *Courtesy of Moe Howard Collection*

graced the Sullivan stage a fifth and final time on May 9, 1965, opposite guest stars Della Reese, Richard Pryor, Juliet Prowse, and others to perform the hilarious comedy routine "Niagara Falls," in which a man searches for his estranged wife.

The year before, in September 1964, Moe, Larry, and Curly-Joe had made their only appearance together on the syndicated daytime talk show *The Mike Douglas Show*, along with guest cohosts Phil Ford and Mimi Hines and guests Ed McMahon and Richard Gehman. Despite their advanced ages, Moe, Larry, and Curly-Joe were still performing admirably, still comedians of the highest caliber.

National Association of Broadcasters (NAB) trade show ad for *The New 3 Stooges* cartoons. *Courtesy of Moe Howard Collection*

Opening credits (top) and scene (below) from *The New 3 Stooges*. © *Normandy Productions, courtesy of Moe Howard Collection*

People have always maintained that watching the Stooges is like watching an animated cartoon. Thus it came as no surprise when the attempts to create a cartoon version of the trio finally came to fruition. On April 5, 1965, Normandy Productions entered into an agreement with Heritage Productions and Cambria Studios (producers of three popular limited-animation Syncro-Vox cartoon series, *Clutch Cargo*, *Space Angel*, and *Captain Fathom*) to work on a series of 156 five-and-a-half-minute color cartoons called *The New 3*

*Stooges*. Cambria president Dick Brown spearheaded the project and completed all the necessary arrangements to animate the films. The series' budget was set at $1.5 million, and the Stooges and Norman Maurer received $163,000 in advance of their efforts.

The pilot cartoon, "That Little Old Bomb Maker" (originally titled "The First World War"), was a freelance animation job. When the series sold, Cambria took over the animation and the style changed radically. The pilot's style of animation was much like that of Jay Ward's Rocky and Bullwinkle characters, in that it was more comically exaggerated.

Forty-one live-action wraparounds would be used to open and close each cartoon. These segments, some of which were filmed at the Balboa Bay Club in Balboa, California, contained many of the Stooges' traditional routines. The Stooges began filming on July 13, 1965, averaging four live shows per day and completed filming all forty-one segments in six and a half weeks, an incredible job. Out of the forty-one wraparounds, forty of them were used for many different cartoons, with one of them, titled "Soldiers," appearing only once in the series.

Curly-Joe DeRita remarked that this repetition presented some problems. "There were 156 cartoons, and we made only forty live-action segments. So after they ran the whole forty, they'd just start over by using these same introductions on *new* cartoons. This turned out to be misleading because the viewers would say, 'Oh, I've seen this one before,' and they'd turn off the television. They didn't know it was a new cartoon."

Lion hunters Moe, Larry, and Curly-Joe survey the premises in a live-action scene from their TV cartoon series.
© Normandy Productions, courtesy of Moe Howard Collection

Director Ed Bernds (foreground), Norman Maurer, and Dick Brown watch the Stooges rehearse for their cartoon show.
© Normandy Productions, courtesy of Moe Howard Collection

With the Stooges in these live segments was a small group of character actors. Emil Sitka appeared in most of the live sequences, in a variety of roles. Norman Maurer's son Jeff, and Dick Brown's wife, Peggy (formerly Margaret Kerry, famous for her role as Charles Ruggles's TV daughter on *The Ruggles* and as the model for Tinkerbell in Disney's animated film *Peter Pan*) and children—Cary, Tina, and Eileen— also appeared in various episodes.

Norman Maurer was executive producer of the live-action segments, and Edward Bernds directed them; Bernds also wrote many of the stories. Animator Dave Detiege, from Warner Bros., served as animation director, while Lee Orgel secured distribution of the cartoons to over forty-five television stations. The films were syndicated nationally by Heritage Productions, starting in October 1965.

The Stooges introduce their next cartoon as golfers during a live-action segue from their TV cartoon series. © *Normandy Productions, courtesy of Moe Howard Collection*

The Stooges, dressed as pilots, ride off on motorbikes in a scene from *The New 3 Stooges*.
© *Normandy Productions, courtesy of Moe Howard Collection*

Moe and Larry's advanced ages start to show during the making of the *New 3 Stooges* color cartoon series; pictured is a scene from their live-action wraparound, in which they play waiters. *© Normandy Productions, courtesy of Moe Howard Collection*

Curly-Joe, Larry, and Moe play around with an innocent beachgoer during filming of their TV cartoon show. *© Normandy Productions, courtesy of Moe Howard Collection*

In accordance with their contract, Cambria's distributor was supposed to forward quarterly statements to the Stooges reporting the series' profits. Maurer recalled receiving only one or two statements over a period of five years. Consequently, the series became grounds for a lawsuit filed by the Stooges—which they lost. It was a bad break for the Stooges, as the presiding judge knew absolutely nothing about the film business and ruled in favor of the distributor. In 1975, the Stooges would appeal to a higher court and win. Despite this belated victory, nothing would change with regard to the distributor's failure to provide statements.

(In 1987, Muller Media would acquire the North American distribution rights to *The New 3 Stooges* and begin airing it in syndication in some markets. Five years later, DIC Enterprises Inc. secured the international broadcasting rights to fifty episodes of the series, with Bohbot Distribution handling the syndication of the series. DIC added new main titles to the package and digitally remastered the audio and video tracks. On September 7, 1992, *The New 3 Stooges* began airing weekdays from 4:00 to 4:30 PM on Chicago superstation WGN, where it remained until the mid-1990s. It then occasionally aired on Boomerang and Cartoon Network.)

About a month after *The New 3 Stooges* originally premiered on television stations throughout the country, Danny Thomas invited the Stooges to appear on his NBC comedy-variety special *Danny Thomas Meets the Comics*, which aired on November 8, 1965. This hour-long program was originally titled *What Makes People Laugh?*, and it showcased the Stooges rather prominently. As a critic for *Daily Variety* wrote, "The Stooges do what comes naturally and this only compounds the insanities." The insanities arise in the form of three sketches. The first one finds the trio attempting to perform Shakespeare but getting derailed because of interruptions from passersby. Then the Stooges wander out into the audience and attempt to drive three members of the audience from their seats, resorting to pie throwing as a means of persuasion. In the last sketch, Moe, Larry, and Curly-Joe meet their match in Martha Raye. The all-star lineup of guests also included the Spike Jones' Band (formed by Spike Jones Jr., sixteen-year-old son of the bandleader), Tim Conway, and Bill Cosby. Critics lauded the special as "wild and orgiastic" and delightfully entertaining.

A pie-besmirched Danny Thomas with the Stooges on his 1965 NBC variety special. *Courtesy of Moe Howard Collection*

Toward the end of the 1960s, the Stooges' popularity began to fade. Fewer offers crossed the desks of their agent, the William Morris Agency, and their producer-manager, Norman Maurer. Maurer attributed the decline in popularity to several factors: their vast army of young fans had grown up, rising production costs had rendered children's films economically impossible, and the Stooges were getting on in years. Many producers, on hearing they were available, envisioned them as old men no longer capable of performing their wild slapstick antics.

During these slow periods, Moe kept Norman busy contacting producers on whose programs the Stooges wanted to appear. Sometimes the trio would catch a particular program and remark, "Hey, why don't we get on that show!" Moe would then call Norman, who would pursue these different avenues. The Stooges were strongly considered for such hit programs as NBC's *Rowan and Martin's Laugh-In*, CBS's *The Red Skelton Show*, NBC's *The Dean Martin Show*, and ABC's *The Hollywood Palace*, hosted by Milton Berle. Berle expressed interest to Maurer in using the Stooges on one episode of *Hollywood Palace*, either doing a six- or seven-minute sketch with him as their straight man, or spotting them throughout the show. None of these potential appearances ever materialized. Maurer also spoke with Columbia Pictures about producing a ninety-minute TV special with film clips and interviews called *They Stooged to Conquer*, but it, too, failed to happen.

Since the Stooges weren't receiving many new offers, Norman tried creating two series for the team himself. He approached Metromedia's Los Angeles station KTTV with two unique game show formats, *Obstacle Course* and *The Three Stooges' Junior Olympics*. The idea was to produce these shows in Hollywood and distribute them nationally through Metromedia's syndication division.

*Obstacle Course* was the first proposal. Three young contestants would be chosen from the audience and brought up onstage, where they would battle their way through a life-sized game board of oddly constructed obstacles. The object was to pass through the hazardous maze to the finish line in order to win top prizes. Obstacles were to include a rickety bridge over a shallow tank of muddy water, an automatic pie-throwing machine, and a tightrope over a vat of gooey strawberry jam. The Stooges would act as hosts and accompany the contestants on their way down the zigzag path to victory or defeat.

*Junior Olympics,* created fresh on the heels of the country's full-scale physical fitness craze, was just as wild and inventive. The Stooges would introduce young contestants from all over the country who would participate in various sporting events. Each week would be like a World Series of junior athletic competition. The half-hour shows would include elimination tournaments in such sporting events as bowling and soap box derbies. Comedy would result from the Stooges showing off their brand of sports expertise before each segment.

A pilot segment for *Junior Olympics* would feature the Stooges giving instructions in bowling. The trio would come out in ill-fitting jerseys and throw balls down the lane, where they would suddenly ricochet off the pins and begin racing back toward the Stooges. The boys would turn to run for their lives but the balls would connect and bowl them over. This hilarious sequence would segue into a bowling tournament featuring young bowlers from all over the United States who would compete for the special jackpot of prizes.

Both of these concepts would have been fantastic vehicles for the Stooges, but unfortunately Metromedia didn't see the full market potential for these concepts and turned them down.

In 1967, Continental Baking Company, one of the largest manufacturers of bread products, hired the Stooges to promote its Astro Snacks. As part of an extensive campaign, their advertising firm of Ketchum, MacLeod and Grove signed the Stooges for a sixty-second commercial titled "Wonderful World of Magic." The commercial featured, as agency vice president Charles W. Llewellyn later recalled, footage of the Stooges performing a live stage show with a magician in a large auditorium in Washington, DC. Admission to the show was several proofs of purchase from Astro Snacks wrappers. Contracts indicate that the commercial was to start airing on April 1, 1967, and that the Stooges received $3,000 plus three all-expense-paid round-trip airfares from Los Angeles to Washington, DC, for their performance.

Television roles remained few and far between, but the Stooges did show up for a guest shot on ABC's *Off to See the Wizard* on October 13, 1967. Produced by MGM, this hour-long weekly prime-time series, which aired opposite CBS's *Wild Wild West* and NBC's *Tarzan* series, was an anthology of films geared to children, most taken from the studio's own feature library. The movies were introduced in wraparound segments featuring animated versions of characters from the MGM classic *The Wizard of Oz* (1939). In October 1966, the Stooges had agreed to terms to make a cameo in an original episode (titled in correspondence as "'Mother Goose' Special"), with rehearsals to commence on or about October 18 and taping to be completed on October 24. In the finished, Emmy-nominated episode, titled "Who's Afraid of Mother Goose?," the trio appeared as Three Men in a Tub. The episode also starred Maureen O'Hara as Mother Goose, Dick Shawn as Old King Cole, and Nancy Sinatra and Frankie Avalon as Jack and Jill. Originally it was understood that the show would be telecast on any date between March 15 and April 30, 1967, but it aired that fall instead.

The Stooges were paid $10,000 for the show's two network runs, but their names were pulled from newspaper and television advertisements. ABC made no mention of the team in a half-page announcement or in listings in *TV Guide* and the *Los Angeles Times* television section. The Stooges were, needless to say, furious over the situation. This was just another example of television executives treating the Stooges as a classless act of has-beens and bowing to the PTA and other pressure groups.

On February 12, 1968, the Stooges signed a deal to appear in a sixty-second spot for Metropolitan Life

Insurance—the television commercial that Stooges fans remember most. The boys were paid $5,000 for the spot, which Larry Fine once recalled was filmed in San Francisco and shot entirely in long shots. Entitled "The Door," the ad has the Stooges promoting the insurance company's Security Family Plan. What is remembered goes down as classic comedy at its zenith. A narrator gives his spiel: ". . . be protected from fire, flood, and other calamities and—"

Curly-Joe, Moe, and Larry in their appearance on ABC's *Off to See the Wizard. Courtesy of Moe Howard Collection*

The narrator is suddenly cut off as the Stooges enter on cue, driving a beat-up, loaded-down truck, and demonstrate just what kind of calamities the narrator is talking about.

Moe pulls up before a house and the Stooges begin unloading axes and mallets. The boys then charge up to the house with tools at the ready and start smashing open the front door. A beat, and the door falls to pieces, followed by the entire house, which comes crashing to the ground like a house of cards. This scene-destroying episode prompts the narrator to conclude his spiel on protection from disasters with ". . . even The Three Stooges."

Comedian Joey Bishop soon learned how this destructive trio wreaked havoc wherever they went. He invited the Stooges onto several installments of his popular late-night ABC variety-talk show, *The Joey Bishop Show*, and each time he was assaulted by the Stooges. In one of their appearances, the Stooges once again performed their sketch "The Maharaja"

for television audiences. Moe introduced the routine this way: "*The Joey Bishop Show* has spared no expense in bring the next novelty to this program. With his mental agility, muscular control, and keenness of eye, this man is the sensation of two continents. He speaks very little of our language and I was asked to act as his interpreter. I take great pleasure in presenting for your approval His Royal Highness, the Maharaja of Blintz."

Turkish music swells offstage as as Curly-Joe, wearing the Maharaja's Coke-bottle eyeglasses and garish turban and outer garments, enters from stage left and walks into a small table, knocking it over, along with the pizza platter and air rifle that were on it. Moe helps the Maharaja straighten up the table and proceeds into the usual nonsensical patter for which this sketch is famous.

The Stooges' most memorable *Joey Bishop* appearance—which possibly aired sometime in April 1968—features the Stooges reprising their "Hospital Operation" sketch under the name "Hectic Medic." Later they illustrate the art of pie making. The pies find other uses than as dessert, of course. Bishop is clobbered when a large-scale pie battle breaks out onstage, with pie crust and gooey meringue splattering him and everything in sight, including an expensive gown worn by a fellow guest, actress Jane Kean (Trixie Norton of *The Jackie Gleason Show* fame), seated quietly in the guest chair. The stage became a mishmash of meringue that took hours to clean up.

The team's last television commercial, first broadcast on March 31, 1969, was for Williamson-Dickie

Larry, Curly-Joe, and Moe on ABC's *The Joey Bishop Show. Courtesy of Moe Howard Collection*

The Stooges demonstrate the art of pie making on *The Joey Bishop Show. Courtesy of Moe Howard Collection*

Mfg. Co. During this sixty-second production, the Stooges demonstrate the durability of Dickie work clothes and the good sportsmanship of announcer Russell Arms. The boys get buried in a shower of bricks, swim in wet cement, and otherwise demolish one another. "But don't worry," Arms says, stepping into the scene of destruction. "They're wearing Dickie work clothes."

Arms then describes the features that enable Dickies to snap back after rough treatment and shows the Stooges in their tailored, dirt-free Dickies. "If Dickies can make The Three Stooges look good, imagine how great you'll look," Arms concludes. The Stooges then show a token of their appreciation, smacking Arms in the face with a pie.

The commercial was filmed in Los Angeles by Elektra Films, and aired on ABC's *Wide World of Sports* through both the spring and fall of 1969. Newspaper ads were also published simultaneously.

The Three Stooges wreak havoc testing out a new line of work clothes in a Dickies Slacks TV commercial from 1969.
*Courtesy of Moe Howard Collection*

The Stooges next started production on a comedy-travel series for television, produced by Normandy Productions, called *Kook's Tour* (1970). The basic formula was for the Stooges to travel across the United States and later Europe, Japan, and Australia.

The project had been in the works for years. On October 10, 1958, six days before the Stooges' first professional nightclub engagement with Curly-Joe in Bakersfield, California, which ran for two weeks, producer/director Norman Maurer first announced plans in the Hollywood trades to produce a pilot for an untitled "projected comedy-travel vidseries" to star The Three Stooges. Moe spoke publicly about the idea for the first time in September 1961 when the Stooges visited Mitchell, South Dakota, to perform at the Corn Palace; after starring in three more features for Columbia Pictures, they were to star in twenty-six color comedy travelogues. As he told a reporter for the *Daily Republic* newspaper, "We feel these comedy travelogues will be very educational, acceptable and probably more interesting than the regularly cut and dried travelogues."

In November 1965, when the trio was promoting their appearance on *Danny Thomas Meets the Comics*, Moe again discussed the concept for the series, which continued to evolve. "Listen to this," he enthused. "We go to France and visit the wine country. The narrator plays it straight as the camera roams over the vineyards, and then moves into a close-up on the workers. That's us. We carry the grapes into the winery, take off our shoes, and hop about on the grapes. This leads to a wild fight and we get tossed out. The next week we visit a ceramic factory and soon all dickens breaks loose."

Moe was persistent in his enthusiasm for the travelogue series. In April 1966, during a trip to Hong Kong, he claimed to a reporter that he was there on a resting and working vacation and was shooting his own location shots for a forthcoming comedy travelogue starring the trio.

In 1968, ten years after his original announcement, producer/director Norman Maurer announced plans to film thirty-nine half-hour travelogues for television, instead of twenty-six. After several changes in the format, Maurer and the team finally started production on the pilot the following year. According to Joe DeRita, the Stooges and Maurer pooled their resources and financed the pilot themselves.

In September 1969, the Stooges and the Normandy film unit traveled to Idaho and Wyoming and commenced production. Scenes were filmed amid the majestic splendor of the area's lakes. Once location shooting was completed, the cast and crew returned to Los Angeles with three-fourths of the film finished. Maurer planned on lensing close-ups on several integral segments in the Angeles National Forest and at Lake Piru.

The Stooges try their hand at camping during filming of their comedy travelogue pilot, *Kook's Tour* (1970). *Photo by Norman Maurer, © Normandy Productions*

Larry watches out for Norman Maurer's Labrador retriever Moose while fishing in a scene from *Kook's Tour*. *Photo by Norman Maurer, © Normandy Productions*

Series of still photographs illustrating a deleted pie-fight scene, one of many omitted from the never-released *Kooks Tour*, in which the Stooges comically celebrate Moe's birthday. *Photos by Norman Maurer,* © Normandy Productions

"The boys didn't want to travel outside the country at this point in their lives," recalled Maurer in an interview. "They were older now than when we first planned the series; they wanted to stay close to home." The Stooges also rejected the notion of slapping each other around, because of their advanced ages (Moe was seventy-one and Larry sixty-seven). For this reason the film is not as zany as their old classic comedies. Instead, the team created a more relaxed atmosphere in *Kook's Tour* by portraying themselves as retired Stooges. Moe and Larry even wore their hair out of character.

On October 27, 1969, between lensing scenes for *Kook's Tour*, Moe, Larry, and Curly-Joe taped their last television appearance together on the long-running syndicated game show *Truth or Consequences*. Hosted by Ralph Edwards, the program aired in most markets in January 1970.

That same month, on the night of January 9, 1970, as Maurer was preparing to film vital close-ups to complete *Kook's Tour*, Larry Fine suffered a paralyzing stroke in his apartment, which affected the left side of his body and confined him to a wheelchair. Later, he was able to walk with the aid of a cane, but paralysis remained. Obviously, with vital sequences unfinished, all plans for a weekly half-hour television series had to be canceled.

Nevertheless, "they hoped I would get well enough so they could complete the film by shooting scenes with me from the waist up," Larry once said.

In the tradition of "the show must go on," Maurer screened every salvageable inch of film and then edited it together into a one-hour show. He was able to stretch the film's length to sixty minutes by adding extra footage of Idaho's scenic beauty. He tried selling it to the networks—NBC expressed some interest—but the buying season had passed by then. He considered releasing the film as a feature and, in the early 1980s, editing it back down to its original half-hour format and syndicating it to independent TV stations, but such plans never materialized. As a result, the project was never released to movie theaters or television.

Even though The Three Stooges were no longer working together as a team, in 1973 Moe Howard and Larry Fine started to appear separately in personal appearances and on television talk shows. Moe's television performances stand out most clearly, however. He made frequent appearances on *The Mike*

*Douglas Show*, re-creating such fondly remembered routines as "The Maharaja" and "Niagara Falls." Moe definitely knew the old routines inside and out and could have done all three Stooges parts if he had wanted to (in fact, in college appearances he did just that). His agility was remarkable for his age, and his reactions were incredible. Moe participated in the Douglas show sketches with renewed energy and enthusiasm, perhaps because he dreaded retirement and felt he would like to embark on a solo career.

Moe's first guest shot on the Douglas show was on June 6, 1973, with Ted Knight and Soupy Sales rounding out the cast. During the show, Moe instructs Douglas and the audience in the technique of pie-throwing. When Soupy Sales demands one of the creamy desserts, a pie fight ensues, and Moe blasts the entire cast with pies.

But fans consider Moe's third appearance on the program, which aired on November 29, 1973, to be his most notable. During an interview with Douglas, Moe talks about his charming wife, Helen. Douglas then urges Howard to introduce her to the audience. Moe obligingly steps down from the stage to get Helen, his wife of fifty years. When he reaches her, Helen smashes a pie right into his face!

Helen once recalled that when the show's producer asked her to do the scene, she conceded after some hesitation. "In all our years together, I had never done anything physical to hurt Moe. I was afraid I'd cut him with the pie tin, so I put my hand between the tin and the pie and threw chunks of pie in his face," she said.

Douglas said it was a pleasure to work with Moe, and he appreciated the fact that Howard brought his own material. The popular talk show host was also amazed at Howard's ability to undertake such vigorous routines as "Niagara Falls" despite his age, and he admired Moe's seasoned professionalism. "My recollection of Moe Howard, from the times he appeared on our show, was that you were immediately aware that he was a man totally dedicated to his profession. He was wonderful . . . possessing a great sense of comedic timing and an inspiration to many young performers."

At the same time, Larry appeared on quite a number of television talk shows in the Los Angeles area. One of them, a local magazine interview program called *The Sunday Show*, was hosted by KNBC news anchorman Tom Snyder, who went on to national fame as the host of NBC's *Tomorrow with Tom Sny-*

Larry in a Los Angeles television appearance with Tom Snyder on KNBC's *The Sunday Show* in March 1973. *Photo by Jeff and Greg Lenburg, © Jeff and Greg Lenburg, all rights reserved*

*der* (1973–82). On March 4, 1973, Snyder's crew went out to the Motion Picture Country House and Hospital in Woodland Hills and interviewed resident celebrities, including Larry Fine. Larry discussed his love for painting, showing Snyder his finished works—one of them a pencil sketch of Peter Falk—and mentioned his will to live. Snyder introduced the comedian with a clip from the Stooges short *Men in Black* (1934).

Fine next appeared in an episode of PBS station KCET's *City Watchers*, which also highlighted the Motion Picture Country House and the various celebrities who were residents. Finally, on November 17, 1974, Sandy Hill, who later found fame on ABC's *Good Morning America*, interviewed Larry when she hosted a program for CBS affiliate KNXT called *Follow-Up*, in what was the comedian's last TV appearance.

Moe Howard's final television appearance came after his death, in a segment on the *NBC Nightly News* for April 23, 1976. Reporter Jack Perkins had taped an interview with Howard several weeks before his passing in May 1975; the interview was a discussion of the Stooges' sudden resurgence in popularity. The ten-minute report also featured Perkins's interview with Joe Besser and showcased the talent of young fans who impersonated Curly and the other Stooges.

Even though fans saw the Stooges finish their television careers as separate entities, The Three Stooges, as a team, have never left television. Over four hundred of their films—including their 190 two-reel

Columbia Pictures comedy shorts, numerous feature films (since their first with Ted Healy in 1930), and 156-episode animated cartoon series—still run on cable networks and television stations around the world, continuing to prove the team's worth as one of television's most enduring commodities. To quote Mike Douglas, "It was great that The Three Stooges left their legacy of these wonderful films so that future generations will be able to enjoy their zany antics and learn to love them as we did."

Moe Howard during his final days of life in an *NBC Nightly News* interview, which aired April 1976. *Photo by Greg Lenburg,*

# Chapter 5

The Stooges recording songs for their Coral Records album.
© Norman Maurer Productions, courtesy of Moe Howard Collection

# The Three Stooges on Record

The Three Stooges continued to grow as superstars in television and movies—and soon climbed the charts as recording artists. In 1959, when the Stooges' popularity was rising ever higher, record industry executives awoke to the fact that the Stooges were one of TV's hottest children's commodities, equaling and often rating higher than *Captain Kangaroo, Popeye,* and *Yogi Bear.* And so the trio's long but rocky recording career was launched.

On March 27, 1959, the Stooges inked a record contract with Coral Records, and later that same month they signed with Golden Records, a subsidiary of A.A. Records Inc., to do children's records for them as well. (A.A. Records also produced Little Golden Records, and Disneyland Records for

Walt Disney Studios' record division) On April 28, Moe, Larry, and Curly-Joe began rehearsing songs for their first Coral album in Chicago. Then, on Sunday, May 3, they cut four songs for the album. They finished the record in Los Angeles.

At the same time that they were wrapping work for Coral Records, they also began recording songs for Golden Records. On June 10, 1959, the Stooges entered into a joint venture with A.A. Records Inc. and Bell Records Inc. to produce Stooges recordings for plastic phonograph records for Golden. Under this arrangement, the trio would record a series of songs and song skits to be issued individually and/or collectively and on their first Golden album, originally to be called *The Three Stooges Madcap, Musical, Mayhem at Your House.*

The week of June 14, 1959, Moe, Larry, and Curly-Joe recorded seventeen songs altogether, including cuts for their first Golden album and tracks for a series of Christmas-themed records: "All I Want for Christmas Is My Two Front Teeth," "I Gotta Cold for Christmas," "I Want a Hippopotamus for Christmas," "Down Through the Housetop," "Wreck the Halls with Boughs of Holly," and "Jingle Bells Drag." They also recorded the theme song to their upcoming feature *Have Rocket--Will Travel* (1959) for Columbia Pictures' Colpix Records.

The Stooges display their singing prowess on the cover of their first Coral Records album, *The Three Stooges Nonsense Songbook: Music to Have Fun By!* (1959), which is still popular with fans today.

*Courtesy of Moe Howard Collection*

On July 25, 1959, Coral Records released the Stooges' first album, *The Three Stooges Nonsense Songbook: Music to Have Fun By!* (Coral Records CRL57289), which is still popular with fans today. Of all their recordings, this LP has the best orchestration and song selection; Lew Douglas backs the Stooges with his fine orchestra, and the boys perform a wide variety of material, some dating back to the 1900s.

The Coral album was surefire entertainment from the first groove to the last, beginning with a revival of "Swingin' the Alphabet," which was first popularized in the 1938 Stooge short *Violent Is the Word for Curly.* Retitled "The Alphabet Song," it has as much flair as the original, as Moe leads his partners through a singsong sequence of consonants against vowels: "B-A, Bay. B-E, Be. B-I, Bicky-Bi. B-O, Bo. Bicky-Bi-Bo. B-U, Bu. Bicky-Bi-Bo-Bu." The song becomes progressively sillier as the Stooges swing through the alphabet.

A lyric from the big band era surfaces in "Three Little Fishies," written by a member of Hal Kemp's Orchestra, Saxie Dowell. With their next entry, "The Aba Daba Honeymoon," a 1914 hit by Arthur Fields and Walter Donovan, it becomes apparent that the Stooges are focusing less on slapstick and more on singing—a welcome change that doesn't hurt their performance, or the album. In fact, it proves that their comedy was equally effective minus the roughhouse.

The next theme, "The Merry-Go-Round Broke Down," was first introduced in the 1930s; a speeded-up version was used as the opening music for Warner Bros. cartoons. Big band sounds return with "Two Little Birdies," a popular tune composed by Dolly Dawn and Her Dawn Patrol. The Stooges wind down side A with "The Children's Marching Song/Nick Nack Paddy Wack."

Side B becomes even more of a nostalgic throwback as the Stooges revive sounds from the early 1900s, starting with the novelty song "Peggy O'Neil," which features a multiword patter chorus. Their nonsensical fun reaches its zenith in "Chickery Chick," and they revive Irving Berlin's 1915 classic "Play a Simple Melody." Then it's back to a popular children's song with "Old MacDonald Had a Farm," followed by a silly rendition of "Mairzy Doats."

The human side of the Stooges surfaces in "Thanks." For a brief moment, we envision three slapstick heroes without makeup, impressing listeners with a side of their personalities never seen before. Their fragility and humility shine through as they sing:

The Stooges, in Pittsburgh to perform at Holiday House, present their first Coral LP to local station WTAE-TV hosts Paul Shannon and Rickie Wertz. *Courtesy of Moe Howard Collection*

Give thanks for the wonderful sunshine
that helps you smile when you're blue
Give thanks for the birds in the springtime
singing a song to cheer you along
The raindrops bring happy hours
God's teardrops bless the flowers
Give thanks everyday when you kneel and pray
and give thanks for your blessings each day.

Although an Associated Press reviewer noted, "Despite the inane nature of the material, the album should prove popular with children," this album's appeal actually lay beyond the children's market. This was due perhaps to the number of old songs it contained, songs that only adults could remember and appreciate. In addition, the record's price of $4.98 was steep for that era, more affordable for adults than children. The album was not financially successful, but it is undoubtedly the Stooges' best. We witness them not just as comedians but as true recording artists with an extraordinary range.

Though some believe Coral spared no expense in acquiring the Stooges and making their record, reports show just the opposite. The Stooges were paid a smaller advance than they received from Golden Records, a paltry $1,000, and never one penny after the album's release. It was the first and last record deal made by their longtime manager Harry Romm. Soon thereafter, the William Morris Agency became their agent, and Norman Maurer took over as their personal manager and worked out the deal with Golden.

Also in 1959, using slightly different artwork of the Stooges than was featured on the LP, Coral issued

a rare 45 rpm entitled *The Three Stooges Crazy-Sing-A-Long* (CX-10554). The two-sided disc featured cuts from the *Nonsense Songbook* LP, including (on side A) "The Merry Go Round Broke Down" and "Old Mac-Donald Had a Farm," as well as (on side B) "Mairzy Doats" and "The Children's Marching Song/Nick Nack Paddy Wack" (also spelled "Whack" on reissues).

In 1959, Coral also issued this hard-to-find 45 rpm record featuring cuts from *The Nonsense Songbook* LP, entitled *The Three Stooges Crazy-Sing-A-Long*. © *Norman Maurer Productions, courtesy of Jeff Lenburg Collection*

(In 1967, Vocalion Records, by letter of permission from the Stooges, reissued *The Three Stooges Nonsense Songbook*, with a made-over cover, under the new title *The Three Stooges Sing for Kids* [Vocalion 73823]. This version contained ten cuts instead of twelve; the two deleted selections were "Two Little Birdies" and "Peggy O'Neil." Customers found the disc mainly on budget racks or in discount department stores, where it did striking business. In 1984, MCA Records issued *The Nonsense Songbook* as a traditional album, using its original 1959 Coral cover. *The Three Stooges Sing for Kids* was similarly reissued on MCA Records [COPS4620], manufactured and distributed by Australian-owned independent label Astor Records—which, coincidentally, was the record label for the American rock band The Stooges, later known as Iggy and the Stooges. In 1992, MCA Records produced an audiocassette version of *The Nonsense Songbook: Music to Have Fun By!*, followed by a compact disc edition three years later.)

In August 1959, Colpix Records was the next to capitalize on the trio's popularity, with the release of the 45 rpm *The Three Stooges Sing Have Rocket, Will Travel* (Colpix CP120). On the two-sided disc (the sides were simply titled "Have Rocket Will Travel, Part I" and "Have Rocket Will Travel, Part II"), the trio sings the title song, written by George Duning with lyrics by Stanley Styne, from their first starring Columbia Pictures feature. This ditty revolves around the Stooges entering the race for outer space. The record (which was originally called *Race for the Moon*, as was the feature) has good tonal quality and glorifies the trio as singers. But Columbia made no hoopla over the record's release; instead, they just quietly shipped it to record stores shortly after the film's theatrical release. Despite this fact, it sold exceptionally well, though it didn't make the Top 40.

most of the Stooges' audience, the Stooges were just right for Golden Records and its company of juvenile superstars.

In October 1959, Golden released *The 3 Stooges Madcap Musical Nonsense at Your House* (Golden Records GLP43), a $2.98 twelve-inch album containing a dozen songs, complete with a color photograph of the Stooges as band members on the cover. The Music Wreckers supplied the tender musical accompaniment (they would also be featured on subsequent 45s and 78s). Madcap lyrics were written by producers Bill Buchanan and Dick Cella, who did a commendable job of adapting children's songs to the team's two-fisted humor. The album was an instant hit with children.

The Stooges' third record release, a 45 rpm record of *Have Rocket--Will Travel*, from 1959. *Courtesy of Moe Howard Collection*

The Stooges' popular first LP for Golden Records, *The 3 Stooges Madcap Musical Nonsense at Your House* (1959).
*Courtesy of Moe Howard Collection*

Golden Records cashed in next by releasing an album and three singles derived from the Stooges' recordings from earlier in the year. Golden specialized in children's songs and had a gallery of juvenile favorites already available, such as *Ruff n' Reddy* (Hanna-Barbera cartoon stars), *The Lone Ranger*, *Smokey the Bear*, *Captain Kangaroo*, and, most popular of all, *Santa Claus*. Since crowds of small fries composed

*Madcap Musical Nonsense* consists of a rich selection of parodies and satirical humor that would appeal to new audiences even today. Side A leads off with "We're Coming to Your House," in which Moe, Larry, and Curly-Joe constantly refer to their small-fry followers and adult listeners as "nice people." This was obviously a vain attempt to clean up their poor image with adults who were upset over the television rebroadcasts of their violent two-reel comedies.

Nevertheless, the lyrics are catchy when all three sing, "We're coming to your house / To have a good time. To bring you some laughter, and happiness, too." Then Larry ruins the tempo, demonstrating his ability to count ("three-four-five-six-seven"), resulting in some wild knocks on the head by Moe. Another hilarious moment follows after they harmonize, "Though Mommy won't like us / And neither will Dad / We're coming to your house." Troublemaker Larry interjects in a gruff gangster voice, ". . . to break up the joint!"

This segues to the second cut, "The Concert." Here, the Stooges flex their muscles—not on each other but on musical instruments. Of course, the instruments serve as a perfect foundation for a series of comedy vignettes. One in particular has Moe thinking he is playing a banjo, prompting him to ask if he's playing it correctly. Larry surprises Moe with, "You're playing a trombone, not a banjo." Moe gushes, "Oh boy, I can play a trombone, too!" The record is full of these sorts of hokey gags and even contains a few moments of audience participation, when the boys invite listeners to pick up their own instruments and join in.

More fun ensues with "At a Baseball Game," sung to the tune of "Skip to My Lou." The Stooges have

Curly-Joe, Larry, and Moe show their displeasure after recording a number for their album *The 3 Stooges Madcap Musical Nonsense at Your House.* Courtesy of Moe Howard Collection

tickets to a crosstown ball game, which they attend despite Curly-Joe's remarks that he doesn't like the sport. Inside the ballpark, Curly-Joe voices his displeasure, and Moe tells him to pipe down or he'll quell him with a baseball bat to the head. Insulted, Curly-Joe goes away to get some popcorn and doesn't return for hours. When he does, he comes back as a vendor and tries to sell some popcorn to Moe and Larry. It appears to Moe that Curly-Joe has been taking in more food than profits. So Moe shuts Curly-Joe up and prevails on him to sit down and enjoy the game. Tired of Moe's demands, Curly-Joe races onto the field, kicks out the umpire (voiced by Moe), and smacks a home run to win the game.

Next on the trio's hit parade is "Click Dart's Bandstand," a spoof of Dick Clark's *American Bandstand*, in which the Stooges receive an invitation to perform on Click Dart's musical variety program. Curly-Joe asks Moe, "What are we gonna do there? We can't sing!" Moe sardonically replies, "Neither can his other guests!" The Stooges poke fun at Dick Clark's reputation at the time as TV's "youngster on the block," telling Dart, upon meeting him, "Take a walk, sonny boy!" Finally, convinced he is the *real* Dart, the boys take over the program and belt out their own songs!

Side A's fifth selection is "The Three Chipped Munks," a parody of David Seville's popular children's stars Alvin and the Chipmunks. Out for a walk, the Stooges notice that a new theater program has come to town, *White Snow and the Seven Dwarfs*, featuring a personal stage appearance by the Three Chipped Munks. Mistaken for the singing chipmunks, Larry and Curly-Joe serenade the audience with "A-Tisket, A-Tasket" and "Ten Little Indians." Punctuating the satire, the trio finishes with impersonations of the Chipmunks.

An age-old folk song rounds off side A. "Go Tell Aunt Rhody," which has been retitled "Go Tell Aunt Mary," takes place at a recording studio where Moe, Larry, and Curly-Joe want to learn how a record is produced. Curiosity overcomes Curly-Joe so much that he gets caught in a record machine and stuck in the actual grooves of the Stooges' album. Helplessly trapped, he screams, "Boys and girls, maybe if you turn the record over you can get me out!" Suddenly, as if his prayers have been answered, the music stops. Then, addressing the listeners who must now turn over the record, Larry adds, "Careful! That's it! Don't hurt him with the needle!"

The Stooges' comedy exploits pick up speed on side B with the two-part "At the Circus," in which they win jobs as circus clowns. Curly-Joe becomes less interested in clowning and more enthused about climbing a rope ladder. While he's in the process, a tiger breaks loose from its cage and rampages through the audience. Curly-Joe loses his balance, falls, knocks the tiger unconscious, and becomes the hero of the day.

The previous cut blends nicely with a similar childhood tale, another two-parter, "At the Toy Store." Here, Curly-Joe clashes with a polite toy store manager. Moe apologizes for his fat partner, who seems to be in another one of his sarcastic moods (a trait of DeRita's that permeates most cuts on the album). Salvation is near, however, as the Stooges prevent a spineless criminal from robbing the store's cash register. A grateful store manager rewards the trio, telling them to take all the toys they want. Since they have a large following of fans, the Stooges back up a truck and haul away the store's entire inventory.

The Stooges' second album ends on a sad note, with them singing their own rendition of "Auld Lang Syne," retitled "Goodbye, Auld Lang Syne." Unlike "Thanks," the touching and uplifting final song on their Coral album, this cut fails to hit its mark. Perhaps they hoped to tug on the heartstrings of millions of fans left wanting more. But a somewhat more upbeat ending might have been more appropriate. Fans were not accustomed to these zany comedians turning dramatic and would

likely have preferred a more comedic ending. Despite this flaw, the record stands up as top-notch entertainment and showcases the trio's full range of talents.

(In 1983, Rhino Records repackaged and reissued *The 3 Stooges Madcap Musical Nonsense at Your House* as a picture disc LP titled *The 3 Stooges Madcap Musical Nonsense* [Rhino RNLP 808]. A year later, they also distributed *Madcap Musical Nonsense* as both a regular album and an audiocassette, featuring a new cover with a color pose of Curly-Joe and Moe tightening a vise on Larry's head.)

Still in 1959, two selections from *The 3 Stooges Madcap Musical Nonsense at Your House*, "We're Coming to Your House" and "We're Cutting a Record," were transformed into a twenty-nine-cent 78 rpm record called *The 3 Stooges Come to Your House and Make a Record* (Golden Records 586).

In time for Christmas that year, Golden released three perfect stocking stuffers starring the Stooges: two 45s—one a special extra-long-playing (EP) edition—and the team's second 78, all featuring the Christmas songs the Stooges had recorded the previous June. The 45 rpm EP, *The 3 Stooges Sing 6 Happy Yuletide Songs* (Golden Records EP561), was the first release of the three. Once again, the Music Wreckers add their special style of music to the arrangements. The EP begins on a glorious note with "All I Want for Christmas Is My Two Front Teeth," followed by the hilarious novelty song "I Want a Hippopotamus for Christmas," and concluding with "I Gotta Cold for Christmas."

The Stooges' second and third records for Golden Records, *The 3 Stooges Come to Your House and Make a Record* (1959) and *The 3 Stooges Sing 6 Happy Yuletide Songs* (1959). *Courtesy of Moe Howard Collection*

In 1959, Golden Records also issued recordings from *The 3 Stooges Sing 6 Happy Yuletide Songs* as 45 and 78 rpm records, including *The 3 Stooges Sing All I Want for Christmas Is My Two Front Teeth*. *Courtesy of Jeff Lenburg Collection*

On side B, decorating a tree turns into havoc with "Wreck the Halls with Boughs of Holly." More comedy ensues in "Jingle Bells Drag," wherein the Stooges attempt to ride an ancient sleigh, complete with an old, broken-down horse who, Moe quips, "is older than the sleigh!" In "Down Through the Housetop," they explore another yuletide tale: how Santa Claus comes down the chimney.

Recordings from *The 3 Stooges Sing 6 Happy Yuletide Songs* were also released that same year as 45 and 78 rpm discs with identical ID numbers, entitled *The 3 Stooges Sing All I Want for Christmas Is My Two Front Teeth* (Golden Records 559); "I Gotta Cold for Christmas" was on side B. (In 1983, Rhino Records rereleased the full album on audiocassette and as an extended-play LP, retitled *Christmas with The Three Stooges* [RNEP606] with a new cover.)

All five original 1959 Golden Records—the album and singles—combined to bring the Stooges royalties of $15,000. The advance on these records was $5,000, and the income was derived from gross sales of all releases. Perhaps these records did so well because of the rare and unusual content, and the fact they were sung by the comedians themselves. Who would have ever dreamed of the Stooges heralding themselves as Santa Clauses—or as recording artists, for that matter?

The next year, Golden Records combined six cuts from the Stooges' *Madcap Musical Nonsense at Your House* album into a new 45, *The 3 Stooges Give a Concert, Go to a Circus, Baseball Game and Toy Store*. On side A were "We're Coming to Your House," "The 3 Stooges Give a Concert," and "At a Baseball Game"; on side B, "At the Circus," "At the Toy Store," and "Auld Lang Syne." In time for Christmas, Golden similarly repackaged and reissued the Stooges' previously released yuletide recordings of "I Want a

In 1960, Golden Records reissued the Stooges' previously released Christmas songs as a new extra-long-playing 45 called *The 3 Stooges Sing Happy Yuletide Songs*. *Courtesy of Moe Howard Collection*

Hippopotamus for Christmas," "I Gotta Cold for Christmas," "Wreck the Halls with Boughs of Holly," "Jingle Bells," and "Down Through the Housetop" as a 45 EP called *The 3 Stooges Sing Happy Yuletide Songs* (Golden Records EP623). In addition, Golden Records released the trio's versions of "Wreck the Halls with Boughs of Holly" and "Jingle Bells" as *The 3 Stooges Sing Wreck the Halls with Boughs of Holly* (Golden Records 622), in 45 and 78 rpm editions.

Also in 1960, England's Grizzly Grouch Records issued *The Three Stooges Greatest Hits* (Grouch KC76103), the first 33⅓ rpm version of their Golden Records recordings released in the United Kingdom. The seven-inch disc featured (on side A) "We're Cutting a Record," "Go Tell Aunt Mary," and "At the Ball Park," and (on side B) "We're Coming to Your House."

In addition, Moe, Larry, and Curly-Joe were featured that year on a cast and crew soundtrack, not distributed commercially, of their 1960 appearance on "The Frances Langford Show," from NBC's *Sunday Showcase*. The boys can be heard on two cuts: (side 1) "Rockin' Chair," with Bob Cummings, Hermione Gingold, Don Ameche, and Langford herself, and (side 2) "Holiday for Strings," with songstress Mary Costa.

The Stooges' lackluster seller, *The Three Stooges Happy Birthday Record* (1961), which required them to record 283 individual children's names. *Courtesy of Jeff Lenburg Collection*

Like all recording stars, the Stooges were bound to have their share of both hits and misses. In 1961, their string of hits ebbed with the release of a true record oddity, *The Three Stooges Happy Birthday Record* (RCA Records X4LM-8766). This seven-inch vinyl disc was recorded in November, pressed for Ardee Records, and distributed through RCA Victor Records. It focuses on the story of the Stooges performing at a birthday party, singing "Old MacDonald Had a Farm" and "Goldilocks and the Three Bears" before serenading a lucky youngster with "Happy Birthday."

Some old gags (written by Elwood Ullman) surface early on, when the Stooges want to hail a taxi to get to the party. "Call me a taxi!" Moe shouts to Larry and Curly-Joe. "You're a taxi!" Larry and Joe shout back. Kids likely got a kick out of these vintage wheezes, while most adults probably held their noses.

The twelve minutes of nonstop song and jokes sold for $1 in department stores and for $1.25 through a special mail order firm, Hargo Company. The marketing twist was that each record was personalized, with The Three Stooges singing to the birthday boy or girl by name. In fact, the Stooges had to record 238 individual names. Their manager, Norman Maurer, had advised them against the idea, since dealers could not stock all 238 versions and thus sales could be poor. Despite this advice, the Stooges went ahead with the deal, because of their friendship with Harry Harris, the record's producer. Upon its initial release, RCA Records reported the disc was selling poorly, just as Maurer had anticipated. Larry stated later, "They just didn't go. We didn't make a dime off them.

Columbia Records' soundtrack album of *Snow White and the Three Stooges* (1961). *Courtesy of Jeff Lenburg Collection*

It would have worked if they hadn't personalized each one and had produced just a general happy birthday record." Incidentally, on April 10, 1961, the same day the Stooges agreed to record the *Happy Birthday Record*, Harry Harris also contracted the Stooges to record another comedy single, featuring the sketches "The Milk" and "Hot Dog" (the latter also written by Elwood Ullman), but due to the *Birthday* disc's lethargic sales, the team nixed the agreement.

Their next release that year, a stereophonic soundtrack of the feature film *Snow White and the Three Stooges* (Columbia Records CS8450; also released in a mono version), fared no better. Although the film was released through 20th Century-Fox, which lost its shirt on the overbudgeted, underperforming production, the soundtrack was distributed on the Columbia Records label.

The soundtrack leaves a much more favorable impression than the feature itself. In fact, it actually makes the picture sound like a winner. Copies of this disc are rare, and they usually sell for as much as twenty dollars. The album is ideal for collectors interested in a well-produced audio version of the film that spares them the tedium of watching it.

The Stooges can be heard in several dialogue scenes from the film and in a happy-go-lucky song, "Looking for People, Looking for Fun." Originally, this upbeat melody was planned for a film sequence in which the Stooges are medicine-show peddlers. However, at the last minute, Fox cut the scene, perhaps hoping to cut down the film's length. As a result, they may have trimmed out the best sequence featuring the Stooges. On the album, musical instruments embellish the lickety-split timing of the Stooges singing the upbeat lyrics. Dialogue scenes command a good deal of side A, which serves as a great reference for buffs wanting scene dialogue but is less impressive for music enthusiasts wanting a collection of songs.

Unknown to record dealers and collectors, Columbia Records was considering the release of "Looking for People, Looking for Fun" as a 45 rpm single. Research indicates that Columbia Records made a special recording of the song on a ten-inch acetate that only took up seven inches of space to record (the normal size for a 45 and 78). The disc itself was to be titled simply *The Three Stooges* (with "Stooges" misspelled). However, a single was never produced, and the song's only distribution was within the album's soundtrack. For reasons unknown, what could have been another historical Stooge novelty became a shelved artifact.

(In 1965, a full soundtrack of *Snow White and the Three Stooges* was produced on 33⅓ rpm acetate to be played simultaneously with a silent home movie version of the movie released by Americom. Twenty years later, CBS Records reissued the *Snow White and the Three Stooges* soundtrack, using the original cover.)

By 1963, the Stooges' volume of record releases began to taper off. Even so, their talents were put to good use that year on a new children's LP from Peter Pan Records, *The Three Stooges: A Rocket Ship Ride Through Time & Space to Storyland* (Peter Pan 8019). Here, by means of a typically zany rocket ship journey through time and space, the Stooges encounter a host of storybook characters and situations. Segments were written by Ronald Singer, who provides a mini-

mum of humor and a maximum of serious drama. The story opens with the trio launching themselves back into history in "The 3 Stooges and the Time Rocket." We discover where their expedition has taken them in "The Crash," in which they wind up in Storyland and match wits with Cinderella. On side B, additional storybook characters appear in "The 3 Stooges Meet the Ugly Duckling," "The 3 Stooges Meet the Princess and the Pea," and "The 3 Stooges and the Magic Lamp."

In 1963 and 1964, Golden and Peter Pan issued two tracks from the album as separate 45 and 78 rpm discs, titled *The Three Stooges: The Story of the Magic*

In 1963, Moe, Larry, and Curly-Joe recorded a new children's album—and their first release for Peter Pan Records—*The Three Stooges: A Rocket Ship Ride Through Time & Space to Storyland*. *Courtesy of Randy Skretvedt Collection*

In 1964, Peter Pan reissued tracks from the *Storyland* album, in both 45 and 78 rpm versions, under the title *The 3 Stooges in The Princess and the Pea*. *Courtesy of Randy Skretvedt Collection*

*Lamp* and *The Three Stooges in The Princess and the Pea*. (In 1973, Peter Pan rebranded and remarketed the trio's *Storyland* LP, with a new cover using a different illustration of the team, as *The Three Stooges and Six Funny Bone Stories* [Peter Pan 8098]. It also released *The 3 Stooges Meet Cinderella* [Peter Pan 2322], a seven-inch, 33⅓ rpm "Little LP," as it was called, of material originally recorded for the *Storyland* album, with new artwork.)

In April 1966, the boys agreed on terms to record what would be the final Stooges LP, Hanna-Barbera Records' *Yogi Bear and The Three Stooges Meet the Mad, Mad, Mad Dr. NO-NO* (HLP2050). Charles Show wrote and directed, with Dan Finnerty doing a competent job of editing. Richard Olsen and Bill Getty combined their expertise as recording engineers. And H. C. Pennington offered his sharp art direction. The stock background music from the Hanna-Barbera library, so common in hundreds of Hanna-Barbera shows, is here as well—as is some good comedy spoofing of the James Bond film *Dr. No*.

A caucus of forest rangers is held at Jellystone National Park. President Lyndon Johnson has ordered them to protect Yogi Bear, since he is important to Jellystone's tourism. The rangers vote to call on the services of The Three Stooges, who are appointed Yogi's round-the-clock guardians. Nothing must happen to him or the boys will be sawing trees in Alcatraz rather than caring for them in the confines of Jellystone.

"Don't worry, we'll keep seven eyes on him." Curly-Joe reassures his fellow ranger. "How do you get seven?" Moe demands. "Everybody knows that two times three equals seven!" Joe proclaims. This, of course, induces a slap in the face from Moe, who screams in dead seriousness, "Don't you know two times three equals *eight*!"

Though the story is rather conventional, the Stooges' humor is first rate. Yogi doesn't stay under the Stooges' careful watch for long. He escapes, dressed like a sweet, innocent old lady. Noticing he's missing, the boys, on Moe's orders, scour the grounds for footprints, which provokes Curly-Joe to quip, "Yogi doesn't wear any shoes—he goes *bear* footed!"

During their comical search to find Yogi, a storm breaks out and complicates their hunt. Meanwhile, Yogi finds his way to a mysterious old mansion, high atop a hill, where Dr. NO-NO and his not-so-bright assistant, Fang, have been experimenting with

a kooky new invention, a Molecule Mixing Machine that has the ability to rearrange the molecules of a human body into those of an animal. Dr. NO-NO has already successfully experimented with animals but yearns for a human guinea pig. Instead, he must settle for Yogi, whom Fang invites in from the cold. The evil NO-NO prepares to turn him into a chicken as Fang squeals, "I hope it works. We haven't had eggs in days!" NO-NO succeeds, and the Stooges arrive to discover that Yogi has been transformed into a candidate for Colonel Sanders's Kentucky fryers.

Dr. NO-NO is elated at the sight of the Stooges, realizing that he finally has three humans for his next experiment. He asks for volunteers. Larry and Curly-Joe instantly suggest Moe, who volunteers because

The Stooges' final LP, *Yogi Bear and The Three Stooges Meet the Mad, Mad, Mad Dr. NO-NO* (1966). *Courtesy of Randy Skretvedt Collection*

he doesn't believe the crazy machine works. NO-NO asks them for suggestions as to what he should turn Moe into. Larry cracks, "Turn him into a monkey!"

Larry's suggestion becomes hard fact as Moe emerges from the machine as a full-sized gorilla. Taking advantage of Moe's new physique and Herculean strength, Larry and Curly-Joe come up with a brilliant scheme to save Yogi. They lure Dr. NO-NO right into the clutches of Gorilla Moe, who threatens to clobber him if he doesn't return Yogi and himself to normal (which is quite a challenge if you consider neither of them *is* normal). Dr. NO-NO, panicked, surrenders to Moe's demand but later becomes a victim of his own invention when the Stooges turn him into a duck. Back at Jellystone Park, the park ranger inquires about who was

Curly-Joe, Moe, and Larry trying out as a new rock group. *Photo by Norman Maurer, © Norman Maurer*

standard Stooges comedy routines. Later, they experimented with a variety of formats and selections, both comedic and dramatic. Their most successful were the Golden Records releases, which devoted more time to their singing. The Yogi LP was a departure from their Coral and Golden Records releases and wins on its own merits as a cartoon story with plenty of action and situations that complemented the Stooges' patented brand of humor and allowed them to wind up their recording careers with a well-deserved success.

Since their original release, the popularity of the Stooges' recordings has not dimmed with time. Besides several reissues previously noted, over the years many of the songs from their albums have appeared on various compilations: "Swingin' the Alphabet" on *Dr. Demento's Delights* (Warner Bros. Records #BS2855); "Wreck the Halls" on *The World's Worst Records* (Rhino Records, #RNLP-809) and *Dr. Demento's Greatest Novelty Hits of All Time, Vol. 6* (Rhino Records #RNLP825); and the Stooges' theme, "Three Blind Mice," on *Television's Greatest Hits, Volume II* (Tee Vee Toons Records #TVT1200).

In retrospect, Larry, Moe, and Curly-Joe were impressive as slapstick comedians turned recording artists. Despite the army of critics who felt their brand of wild comedy wasn't adaptable to record albums, the Stooges were not fazed by the challenge and proved that their totally visual, insane comedy style could be successfully transformed into aural form.

involved in Yogi's disappearance. The Stooges remark, "Why Doctor NO-NO." In disbelief, the ranger says, "Well, OK, let's see this Dr. NO-NO." As they drag in Dr. NO-NO Duck, Curly-Joe quips, "Whatta ya know—a quacked doctor!"

This record has all the surefire material that became Hanna-Barbera's trademark, like the corny but funny ending, typical in all of their cartoon shows. As a result, the Stooges are funnier—since they thrive more on old puns and jokes and stock-in-trade material than in any of their previous recordings. It is too bad, however, that the producers didn't consider making this into an hour-long Yogi Bear television special. No doubt, combining Yogi and The Three Stooges— with the James Bond satire to boot—would have drawn high ratings in prime time.

The Stooges' recording careers ended with the Yogi Bear album. With it, they had come full circle by returning to the slapstick comedy material they had used so successfully in their early records. Their initial albums wisely used

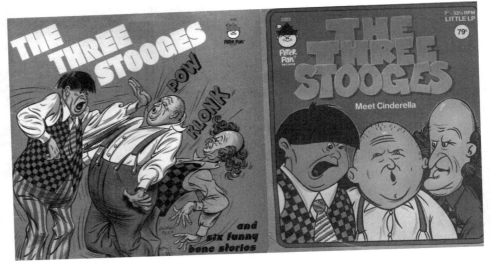

In 1973, Peter Pan reissued the Stooges' *Storyland* LP—as an album and as seven-inch, 33 rpm "Little LP"—retitled *The Three Stooges and Six Funny Bone Stories* and *The Three Stooges Meet Cinderella*, respectively. *Courtesy of Jeff Lenburg Collection*

# Chapter 6

As The Gentle Maniacs, comedians Sammy Wolfe, Paul "Mousie" Garner, and Dick Hakins made a career out of impersonating the Stooges. *Courtesy of Jeff and Greg Lenburg Collection*

# Three Stooges Impersonators

**W**hoever coined the phrase "Imitation is the sincerest form of flattery" knew what he was talking about. It certainly applies to The Three Stooges, who were flattered enormously throughout—and beyond—their monumental career by a parade of imitators.

The Stooges have been "cloned" in a variety of forms, including animated cartoons, newspaper comic strips, and television shows, and they have even influenced other comedians to imitate their look and style. Some impersonators have clearly done this *not* to cash in on their popularity but to salute the Stooges as the unsung heroes of the comedy world. Several comedians even attempted to establish themselves as members of the Three Stooges team.

Specifically, comedians Paul "Mousie" Garner and Sammy Wolfe used their past performances with Ted Healy to suggest that they were part of the original Three Stooges; but their claims were more fiction than fact: Healy's performers never bore the name "The Three Stooges," which was first used by Larry, Moe, and Curly, after they left Healy and started making their own films for Columbia.

Before elaborating further, it should be noted that the word "stooge" had been a part of the theater vernacular since the 1920s and had held a specific connotation. Ken Murray had his stooges, meaning actors who would run up and down theater aisles or act as hecklers in box seats. Phil Baker used to bill himself as "King of the Stooges," with Sid Silvers as his stooge. In 1925 comedian-turned-producer Joe Rock pioneered the "three comedian" format in silent movies with The Three Fatties, Hilliard "Fat" Karr, Kewpie Ross, and Frank "Fatty" Alexander—although they weren't stooges per se—in his studio's A Ton of Fun slapstick comedy shorts series, which ran for two years, "starring the three fattest men on the screen."

Under Ted Healy the idea of the stooge evolved. Healy was the first vaudeville star to feature stooges as broad physical performers. His original Stooges—including Shemp and Moe Howard—weren't just assistants or actors but also comedians in their own right, who took some pretty rough punishment for their comic mistakes. In doing so, they created the concept of the stooge as we know it today and set themselves above any other performers who would attempt to lay claim to the Three Stooges title. Subsequent stooges were just comic imitators who merely copied the slapstick humor the originals had pioneered in Healy's act.

The earliest and first impersonators came in 1930, when Moe, Larry, and Shemp left Ted Healy to form their own act, eventually billed as "Three Lost Souls." Healy quickly assembled a motley trio as replacements: Eddie Moran (soon replaced by Dick Hakins), Jack Wolf, and Paul "Mousie" Garner.

Garner later remembered how his team joined Healy. "Jack Wolf, Dick Hakins, and I found out that Healy had to replace the Stooges. We went down to the Imperial Theatre where he was holding auditions. There must have been a hundred guys there. What do you think my audition was? Healy smacked me in the head and I jumped on him and bit his ear and grabbed his nose. He said, 'You're great. Get in the corner, you're hired.'"

The new act was a copy of the original Stooges, with Healy cracking them over the head and employing other stock physical gags. But there were still some significant differences. Garner explained: "What they did with the smacking, the poking in the eyes, we did with instruments, breaking fiddles across heads, squirting seltzer bottles." Hakins, Wolf, and Garner went on to star in two Broadway shows with Healy, *The Gang's All Here* and *Crazy Quilt*.

Little did Garner and his fellow stooges realize that their career as Stooge replacements would be short lived, since Moe, Larry, and Shemp would rejoin Ted Healy in 1932. Years later, however, Garner would continue to entertain theatergoers with partners Hakins and Wolf—and later Hakins and Sammy Wolfe—as The Gentle Maniacs.

Another trio of imitators toured the vaudeville circuit in the 1930s, led by Jack Pepper, Ginger Rogers's first husband. His entourage included Sam Pokrass, a bushy-haired, wild-looking, Russian-born pianist whom Pepper would bang over the head every time he sat down to play. Occasionally, he let Pokrass get through a beautifully executed tune on the piano, but not before smashing a pie in his face. (Pokrass would pass away in 1939.)

Imitators sprung up overseas as well. On the variety circuit in Britain, comedian Douglas Wakefield became known for doing knockabout sketches accompanied by his own team of stooges—Chuck O'Neil, Jack Butler, and Billy Nelson. Their appearances included a Royal Command Performance at the London Palladium in 1931. In May 1933, American producer Hal Roach, admittedly partial to British comedians, brought Wakefield and Nelson over from Europe to cast them as a new comedy team in films, pairing them in the comedy short *Crook's Tour* (1933). Roach also attempted to form his own slapstick comedy trio, teaming Wakefield, Nelson, and Don Barclay as his All-Star Trio, in a new short-subject series of the same name that featured them in a couple of rather un-stooge-like slapstick comedies, *Twin Screws* (1933) and *Mixed Nuts* (1933). In 1935, after costarring for Roach in the Thelma Todd–Patsy Kelly comedy *I'll Be Suing You* (1934), Wakefield and Nelson returned to England and went back to performing on the British variety circuit.

The next trio of Three Stooges imitators included none other than Curly Howard. While making films at MGM with Moe, Larry, and Ted Healy, he was cast opposite two other comedians—George Givot and Bobby Callahan—in a Technicolor short, *Roast-Beef and Movies* (1934). The film was a blatant attempt on the part of MGM to spawn another team of Stooges. It contains a mélange of bizarre routines and equally strange dialogue, written by Richy Craig Jr., a former vaudeville comedian who was considered the Bob Hope of his day.

In the film, Givot plays Gus Parkyurkarkus, who, with his two comic contemporaries, invades the Masterpiece Film Corporation in the hope of breaking into filmmaking. Listening at an open transom, they hear the studio president (Frank O'Connor) say that he will pay $100,000 for a good, quality film production. They immediately rush out to produce four films within the film—including two segments featuring The Albertina Rasch Dancers—which are screened for the potential buyers. Some pretty inane sequences result; in "Prepare to Die," for instance, a Mae West lookalike makes love to a house detective.

Givot also narrates the films, in his thick European accent, which makes some important dialogue unintelligible. Nevertheless, he is able to deliver the necessary comic punch, including occasionally knocking sense (with Stooge-like sound effects added) into his two dim-witted accomplices, Howard and Callahan. Givot's comedy is interspersed with Busby Berkeley–type musical numbers to bring the film to length, but it loses no spontaneity despite the interruptions. (Incidentally, Givot's previous film experience included appearances in Vitaphone comedies. Callahan went on to make his living in such films as Laurel and Hardy's *Helpmates* [1932], and *Men in Black* [1934] with The Three Stooges. Moe Howard once recalled, after viewing *Men in Black*, that "Callahan made a career out of playing Western Union delivery boys in our pictures and others.")

Extremely fascinated by the characters' films, the studio president in *Roast-Beef* acclaims them—fittingly, we might add—as "masterpieces" and offers $100,000 for distribution rights. First, however, he must consult with the studio's board of directors to approve the deal. But the board members turn out to be escapees from a local mental institution. Punctuating this funny scene is a shot of the board members

MGM's version of the Stooges—George Givot, Curly Howard, and Bobby Callahan—from *Roast-Beef and Movies* (1934).
© *Metro-Goldwyn-Mayer, courtesy of Moe Howard Collection*

making deranged faces and playing with children's toys. Later, a sanitarium attendant orders the supposed studio executives back into the wagon with the rest of the patients, dragging along the producer and the three filmmakers.

It is interesting to see a young Curly Howard in this experimental Technicolor short, sans his usual Stooges ensemble. He and Callahan prove to be an awkward pair, as the latter tries to upstage him. Basically, Curly's involvement is limited to harassing Callahan and introducing Givot's next film. Despite the bright moments with Givot scattered throughout, the awkward new trio offered no great threat to the real Stooges ensemble. MGM gave up any attempt to regroup them.

In March 1934, after The Three Stooges left Ted Healy and signed with Columbia Pictures, Healy yearned once more for a group of stooges to menace. A short time later, he took a new trio of comedians under his wing—Jimmy Brewster, Sammy Wolfe (whose real name was Sammy Glasser), and John "Red" Pearson—and toured the nightclub circuit. Many critics contended that Healy's new act offered nothing original and that they seemed out of place. In 1936, they would return to Hollywood for bit parts with Healy in MGM's *San Francisco*, starring Clark Gable, Jeanette MacDonald, and Spencer Tracy. They

Ted Healy and new stooges Jimmy Brewster, Sammy Glasser (a.k.a. Sammy Wolfe), and John "Red" Pearson, in their first appearance together in the MGM feature *San Francisco* (1936).
© *Metro-Goldwyn-Mayer, courtesy of Jeff and Greg Lenburg Collection*

were cast in the film as bartenders in a big stage revue, but their footage was cut from the final release.

Back in 1934, even Shemp Howard got into the Stooges impersonation act. He starred in two comedy shorts produced by the Van Beuren studio and released by RKO Radio Pictures. In these films, *The Knife of the Party* and *Everybody Likes Music*, his act was billed as Shemp Howard and His Stooges. *Knife of the Party* was a musical-comedy revue starring Jack Good and Lillian Miles as singers attempting to pull a hotel out of debt. A critic for *Motion Picture Herald* called it "fair," but thought "a good portion of the comedy" was provided by Shemp Howard and His Stooges. Howard's roughhouse humor reminded audiences of The Three Stooges, but it lacked the spontaneity of the original Stooges comedies.

That same year, impostors were also used when Universal was unable to hire the original Three

Stooges for its production *Gift of Gab*. This musical-comedy feature was originally planned with the trio in cameo roles. Lew Breslow, who directed the Stooges in *Punch Drunks* (1934), wrote the film's original screenplay. Producer Ryan James's efforts to secure the Stooges failed, however, when Harry Cohn of Columbia nixed the deal. Instead, James threw together three comedians named Sid Walker, Skins Miller, and Jack Harling and billed them as "The Three Stooges."

Producers of cartoons also decided to jump on the Three Stooges bandwagon, creating caricatures of Larry, Moe, and Curly to be used in many animated films. At Warner Bros., Friz Freleng, an avid fan of the Stooges, became the first cartoon director to animate the trio. His *The Miller's Daughter*, the second-to-last Merrie Melodies cartoon to be released in October 1934, is a bright, cheerful adventure in which the Stooges appear as "see no evil, hear no evil, speak no evil" statues in a gallery of figurines that come to life. In May 1935, Warner Bros. director Jack King included cartoon versions of the Stooges as cannibals opposite the studio's short-lived star Buddy in the Looney Tunes cartoon *Buddy's Lost World*.

Also in 1935, writer/director Ben Harrison was working on a cartoon in the Color Rhapsody series released through Columbia Pictures. Naturally, working in close proximity to the Stooges at Columbia, Harrison had been inspired by their antics, and he inserted them into the installment, *Bon Bon Parade*, as Valentine's candy cupids. The Stooges appeared subsequently in more Color Rhapsody releases, such as *The Novelty Shop* (1936), *The Merry Mutineers* (1936), *Hollywood Picnic* (1937), *Happy Tots* (1939), and *A Hollywood Detour* (1942).

Bob Clampett was another Warner Bros. director who loved entertaining the viewers of his cartoons with a sprinkling of animated "cameos" by radio and film personalities. In *Porky's Hero Agency*, a December 1937 Looney Tunes installment, the Stooges are among the many victims affected by the evil magic of Gorgon. The sorcerer turns the boys into the Wise Monkeys of Japan—in other words, another "see no evil, hear no evil, speak no evil" statue.

*Wholly Smoke* (1938) was another Looney Tunes cartoon featuring Porky and the Stooges. Directed by Frank Tashlin, it concerns Porky's many sleepless nights; among his dreams are hallucinations of the

Warner Bros. cartoon version of the Stooges from *Porky's Hero Agency* (1937). © *Warner Bros, courtesy of Bob Clampett*

Stooges as cigars (called "Pittsburg Stooges") who poke him in the eyes.

Meanwhile, legendary cartoon producer/director Walter Lantz produced a new cartoon series, "Meany, Miny and Moe," featuring of a trio of mischievous monkeys. He first introduced them in November 1935 as costars in the Oswald the Lucky Rabbit cartoon *Monkey Wretches*. Lantz has admitted that The Three Stooges influenced the characters' creation. In an interview, he recalled, "They were more like the Three Stooges, where their actions were very physical and broad. They didn't have to speak, because they were doing the kind of pantomime that Charlie Chaplin and Harry Langdon did." (Prior to this series, Lantz had also attempted to animate the Stooges in a Cartune Classic he directed, *Candyland* [1935].)

Lantz produced thirteen Meany, Miny and Moe cartoons between 1936 and 1937 and released

Renowned producer/director Walter Lantz's own version of the Stooges—three chimpanzees, Meany, Miny, and Moe, who starred in their own theatrical cartoon series. © *Walter Lantz Productions, courtesy of Walter Lantz*

them through United Artists. Their stories struck a familiar chord, reminiscent of the world-renowned Stooges comedies with Curly. In *The Golfers* (1936), for example, the three monkeys make a go of playing golf, with disastrous results. They not only have a rough time on the green but also wreck the golf cart, the golf clubs, and the golf course. Only the golf balls come out of this nightmare unscathed. In many respects, this cartoon resembles an earlier Stooges comedy, *Three Little Beers* (1935), in which the boys tear up a municipal golf course— sand trap and all.

Back at Warner Bros., in September 1938, Bob Clampett returned with our three heroes in a brand-new Looney Tunes cartoon, *Porky in Wackyland*. The Stooges were naturals for Bob's crazy, anything-for-a-laugh style of humor. This time around, Porky visits Wackyland, where all creatures are . . . well, wacky! He even meets a three-headed goon whose heads argue among themselves and slap each other violently. It's the Stooges, of course.

Lavish Hollywood parties and film premieres proved even better backdrops for the Stooges' antics

The Stooges as a three-headed monster in a scene from the Warner Bros. cartoon *Porky in Wackyland* (1938). © *Warner Bros., courtesy of Bob Clampett*

in their next Warner Bros. cartoon appearance: Tex Avery's *Hollywood Steps Out* (1941), in which a number of stars make their way to a big Hollywood bash. Seen in cartoon form for the very first time are Bing Crosby, Cary Grant, Peter Lorre, James Cagney, Mickey Rooney, and Joan Crawford. But what would

The Stooges demonstrate their slapstick style on each other in Tex Avery's Warner Bros. cartoon *Hollywood Steps Out* (1941). *© Warner Bros., courtesy of Jeff Lenburg Collection*

a party be like without the Stooges banging, socking, and crushing each other to conga rhythm? This scene would be used again in a 1975 documentary feature, *Brother Can You Spare a Dime?*, and in a compilation feature entitled *Bugs Bunny, Superstar*.

The Stooges' last Warner Bros. cartoon appearance was in *Dough for Do-Do* (1949), directed by Friz Freleng. In this remake of *Porky in Wackyland*, Freleng used the same footage of the trio as a three-headed monster. This time, however, the cartoon is in Technicolor, and Moe's hair has been painted white!

Warner Bros. animators also replicated the antics of future third Stooge Joe Besser, then a comedian in his own right, in three cartoons: as a dog in *Hollywood Canine Canteen* (1946); as a Keystone Kop–like studio guard in *Hollywood Daffy* (1946), with Daffy Duck; and as a prissy elephant ("If you do, I'll give you such a pinch!") in *Rabbit Fire* (1951), starring Bugs Bunny, Daffy Duck, and Elmer Fudd. Vocal virtuoso Mel Blanc provided the voices for all the characters, including Besser's. Besser's childlike characterization would also be mined in two later cartoons: as Huckleberry Hound's horse in the 1959 television episode "Pony Boy Huck" of Hanna-Barbera's *The Huckleberry Hound Show* and as a delivery stork in the 1960 Paramount Famous Studios cartoon *Monkey Doodles*.

Live performers continued to imitate the Stooges as well. In England, a trio of comedians gained permission from Moe Howard to bill themselves as The Three Stooges and reenact the same kind of violent

slapstick. This British ensemble played at the Trocadero Theatre in England for six days, beginning July 4, 1938, opposite Archie McKay (who was their straight man). Their use of the Three Stooges name was restricted to within the boundaries of the United Kingdom, since billing themselves as another Three Stooges team in America would have been illegal.

Joe Besser recalled that this British trio never impersonated the same act twice. Whoever caught their fancy would become their next impersonation subject. "After I finished playing the Palladium," Besser remembered, "they came up to me and said, 'Do you mind if we do you?' What could I say? I figured even if I said no, they'd probably do *me* anyway."

Around this same time, in October 1938, Mousie Garner, Dick Hakins, and Sammy Wolfe began booking themselves at vaudeville theaters as "Ted Healy's Original Stooges." This alarmed Moe, Larry, and Curly so much that they filed a legal action to stop the new act from using the word "original" in the billing. The dispute was settled out of court, with the American Guild of Variety Artists (AGVA) ruling in favor of The Three Stooges. Joe Smith (of Smith and Dale fame) was a member of AGVA's board of arbitration. Years later, he recalled in a letter to Moe Howard that everyone on the board knew Moe and company were Ted Healy's original Stooges and that the trio had the unanimous support of the guild's board.

By the 1940s, the Stooges had reached their first peak in popularity and showed no signs of taper-

Shemp Howard, Billy Gilbert, and Maxie Rosenbloom mugging as stooges in Monogram's low-budget comedy feature *Crazy Knights* (1944). *Courtesy of Jeff and Greg Lenburg Collection*

member Gabriel Dell actually calls Hall "lamebrain!" Shemp Howard worked with the gang in three films, and Hall later cited Shemp as having a tremendous influence on his comedic style. In addition, several of Hall's Bowery Boys comedies (with Leo Gorcey) were directed and written by Stooges/Columbia alumni Edward Bernds and Elwood Ullman.

Universal Pictures, in their musical whodunit *Murder in the Blue Room* (1944), decided to cross The Three Stooges and The Andrews Sisters to create

ing off; naturally, it was a good time to imitate the trio. Shemp Howard started to reestablish himself in Stoogedom in several film productions of his own. As a Monogram contract player, he starred in three features opposite veteran comics Billy Gilbert and Maxie Rosenbloom. The trio took on Stooge-like roles, and they did not bill themselves under character names but rather as themselves. The first film, *Three of a Kind* (1944)—spelled *3 of Kind* on exhibitors' materials—mustered up some pretty good box office and was reissued through Astor Pictures as *Cooking Up Trouble*. It was followed by *Crazy Knights* (retitled for television as *Ghost Crazy*) in 1944 and *Trouble Chasers* in 1945. Critics for the *Motion Picture Herald* gave all three of these films a "fair" rating. Because of Shemp's vast background as a former Stooge, his impersonations of the Stooges were more acceptable than those of other imitators.

Film historian Brent Walker has cited several other films that utilized some form of Stooges material. A trace of their influence can be detected in the films of Universal's Little Tough Guys, an early-1940s spinoff of the Dead End Kids that was substantially less entertaining than the Dead End Kids–related pictures made by Warner Bros. and Monogram. The Little Tough Guys were led by Billy Halop, whose communications with buddy Huntz Hall (a close friend of Shemp's) were in the form of Moe Howard–type slaps and pokes (though without Moe's flair). In one series entry, *Tough as They Come* (1942),

The Three Jazzybelles—half Andrews Sisters and half Three Stooges—as they appeared in Universal's *Murder in the Blue Room* (1944). © *Universal Pictures, courtesy of Jeff Lenburg Collection*

Larry Fine, Moe Howard, and Joe Besser (center) with six Stooge impersonators on the set of *A Merry Mix-Up* (1957). *© Columbia Pictures, courtesy of Moe Howard Collection*

Three young fan impersonators at a 1950s masquerade party.
*Courtesy of Moe Howard Collection*

The presidential team of the people—Richard "Larry" Nixon, John "Moe" Kennedy, and Lyndon "Curly" Johnson.
© Norman Maurer, courtesy of Norman Maurer Collection

The Three Jazzybelles, a female vaudeville team who find themselves in an old mansion that houses a mysterious room. Grace McDonald is the leader, with Betty Kean in what might be termed the Curly role and June Preisser rounding out the threesome. They eventually spend the night in the eerie Blue Room, where they have to share a king-size bed. Naturally, a hand reaches through a hole in the wall and slaps them each on the head, causing them to blame each other for the deed in typical Stooges fashion.

The Stooges' own films dating back to the mid-1930s featured impostors in the form of stunt doubles, some more obvious to the naked eye than others. There are far too many double appearances to discuss, but two of the most glaring examples are stunt man Joe Palma filling in as Fake Shemp in four comedies after Shemp Howard's death in 1955, and the 1957 Three Stooges comedy with Joe Besser *A Merry Mix-Up*. In the latter film, the Stooges play three sets of identical triplets. In the scene in which all nine are "reunited," it is rather obvious that the other six brothers, despite wearing identical wardrobes and hairdos, are nothing more than fakes.

In the 1960s, split-second appearances of Stooge impostors were likewise evident in the Stooges' feature films, with stuntmen wearing studio-created latex masks in the spitting images of Moe, Larry, and Curly-Joe. In *Snow White and the Three Stooges* (1961), for example, those aren't the real Stooges doing their own skating in the extravagant musical number with Carol Heiss. Nor is it Curly-Joe driving a Land Rover with Moe and Larry as passengers at the airport or crashing it in scenes from *The Three Stooges Go Around the World in a Daze*. (Pause these scenes and then play them back at the slowest possible speed and you'll see the evidence for yourself.) The Stooges even employed a Japanese look-alike trio who slap, bonk, and eye-poke (after the last, Moe interjects, "We don't do that anymore!") in *The Three Stooges Go Around the World in a Daze* (1963). Moe's hairdo is also satirized when he meets another Japanese counterpart in their last feature film, *The Outlaws IS Coming!* (1965).

Outside of the Stooges' own films, interest in "Stooge impostors" had started to slacken by the 1950s. It was not until the early 1960s, following the Stooges' resurgence on children's television, that impersonators began to resurface.

Producers Jay Ward and Bill Scott got everything rolling again in the July 7, 1962, broadcast of Ward's popular NBC television cartoon series *The Bullwinkle Show*. An episode ("The Fox and the Minks") of the recurring Aesop and Son segment featured three minks, loosely based on the Stooges, who slap and bonk each other and even laugh, "N'yuk-n'yuk-n'yuk!"

Bob Clampett got back into the act as well, this time with his popular half-hour cartoon series *Beany and Cecil* (originally titled *Matty's Funnies with Beany and Cecil*). He featured the Stooges as a three-headed monster, the Threep, in an episode titled "The Capture of the Dreaded Three-Headed Threep," broadcast

**JACKIE-OF-ALL-TRADES DEPT.**

If you've been watching the covers of Movie Magazines on the newsstands lately, you're probably aware that they all look something like this...

When you get right down to it, all Movie Magazine covers are composed of two basic ingredients: (1) Wild and sensational story-titles, most of which are misleading and/or phony; and (2) Come-on articles and photos dealing with—of all people—JACKIE KENNEDY! Apparently, in the eyes of Movie Magazine editors, Jackie hasn't suffered enough in her life time. Now she is forced to undergo the indignity of seeing photos and idiotically-contrived stories about her in every Film Fan Publication in the country. Which got us to thinking: Since Movie Mags have found the magic success formula, isn't it a matter of time before all the other magazines latch on to the same formula? Here, then, is what we can expect...

# IF OTHER PUBLICATIONS USED THOSE SENSATIONAL MOVIE MAG COVER GIMMICKS
## (INCLUDING THE SHAMELESS EXPLOITATION OF JACKIE KENNEDY)

Cartoon satire of the Stooges from an early-1960s edition of *MAD* magazine. *Courtesy of Moe Howard Collection*

in October 1962. The Stooges are drawn in a manner similar to Clampett's original three-headed monster in *Porky in Wackyland*. In this episode, however, Captain Huffenpuff, Beany, and Cecil set sail to bring back the Threep to star in its own weekly television series. Clampett does a good job of building suspense as to what his Threep/Stooges look like: Beany blows his beany top when Cecil gets three coconuts stuck on his head and the coconuts cast a gigantic shadow of The Three Stooges' heads on the ground. Finally, Beany ventures into an out-of-the-way cavern, where the Threep/Stooges invite Cecil and him for dinner. Afterward, the Threep agrees to return with them and do the television series.

Cartoon producers William Hanna and Joseph Barbera had come close to matching the Stooges' violent humor with their award-winning MGM cartoon series *Tom and Jerry*. While producing TV's *The Flintstones*, they decided that the Stooges' ancient style of humor would enhance their Stone Age series. So Joe and Bill included caricatures of the Stooges in "The Most Beautiful Baby in Bedrock," broadcast April 17, 1964. In this episode, Fred and Barney are appealing for votes from the local citizenry for a "most beautiful baby" contest, in which their children, Pebbles and Bamm-Bamm, are competing. It is during their tour from neighborhood to neighborhood that they meet three familiar characters, The Three Stooges, going by the names of Manny, Moe, and Jack. Fred and Barney show the trio photographs of their children and

The Stooges are once more a three-headed monster, this time in Bob Clampett's *Beany and Cecil* cartoon "The Capture of the Dreaded Three-Headed Threep," in 1962. © *Bob Clampett Productions, courtesy of Bob Clampett*

Three Stooges doubles stand offstage (top) in a scene from *Three Stooges Scrapbook* (1960) and masquerade as ice-skating Stooges (center, with latex masks) in *Snow White and the Three Stooges* (1961) and high-flying Stooges (bottom) in a scene from *The Three Stooges in Orbit* (1962). © *Normandy Productions,* © *20th Century Fox, and* © *Normandy Productions Courtesy, respectively, all courtesy of Moe Howard Collection*

ask them which one is the most beautiful. Unable to agree, the trio begin thwacking and bopping one another around; Fred and Barney make a quick exit.

In 1965, Edward Bernds and Elwood Ullman were contracted to script *Tickle Me*, a vehicle for Elvis Presley, and they wound up utilizing many gags they had used in their Stooge days. The finale takes place in a "haunted house" (Ullman's favorite comedy setting) and features closeted spooks, doors that open to bottomless depths, and lots of hallway chases. At one point, a villain throws a knife at Elvis. The King ducks and then reaches back for the handle and makes threats with it, not realizing the blade is still stuck in the wall—another old Stooges gag. Elvis continued his Stooges associations with *Spinout* (1966), in which his lead guitarist and bass player are named Larry and Curly. Does this, by chance, mean Elvis is Moe?

Greater noise and media hoopla were made over the fact that The Beatles—Paul McCartney, Ringo Starr, George Harrison, and John Lennon—sported, as some writers called them, "Moe haircuts." Full-page accounts were published in newspapers and magazines on this Liverpool group copying Howard's world-famous bowl cut. *MAD* magazine got into the act as well, running an imaginary letter from Moe Howard addressed to The Beatles. This bizarre publicity did the Stooges no harm; it served to add to their recognition.

The Beatles, in turn, inspired the hit US rock 'n' roll group The Monkees, consisting of Michael

Moe meets his Japanese counterpart in *The Outlaws IS Coming!* (1965). © *Normandy Productions, courtesy of Moe Howard Collection*

Nesmith, Davy Jones, Mickey Dolenz, and Peter Tork. Their television series, also called *The Monkees* (1966), featured some of the same wild, nonsensical situations the Stooges first made famous during the 1930s and 1940s. Stories lacked the Stooges' knockabout gags but featured slapstick romps embellished by fast-motion photography. Interestingly, these color, half-hour shows were filmed on the Columbia

Larry, Moe, and Curly-Joe mugging with a set of Japanese Stooge impersonators (left) who replicate their slapstick humor (right) in *The Three Stooges Go Around the World in a Daze* (1963). © *Normandy Productions, courtesy of Moe Howard Collection*

Four Moe-haircut impersonators who made it as The Beatles.
*Courtesy of Mike Lefebvre/Pepperland*

identity crisis. While the authors were Xeroxing some photographs of the Stooges at a local copy center, a clerk noticed the pictures and wanted to demonstrate her incredible knowledge of The Three Stooges. She poked her head around the corner of the machine and blurted out, "Boy, those guys were funny. Good ole' Manny, Moe, and Jack."

In 1972 Hanna-Barbera premiered another highly rated cartoon series, *The New Scooby-Doo Movies*, which featured the Stooges in two episodes broadcast in September and November of that year, both written by Norman Maurer. Moe, Larry, and Curly-Joe were paid $2,000 apiece for the use of their names and likenesses in the shows, but they didn't provide the voices for their characters. Larry's speech was partially impaired, as a result of a stroke in 1970. After watching these shows, Fine remarked sadly, "I wish they had let us do the voices for the shows. If I was given the lines ahead of time, I could have rehearsed them and sounded pretty much like my old self." The first cartoon, "The Ghastly Ghost Town," casts them as proprietors of a run-down amusement park; in "The Ghost of the Red Baron," they are crop dusters teamed with Scooby and company to capture the Red Baron.

In the 1970s, The Three Stooges' fame and popularity continued to rise—thanks to an incredible nostalgia craze that was sweeping the country. Revival theaters held a series of Three Stooges Festivals, while television stations scheduled Stooges marathons. A Boston television station ran three hours of nonstop Stooges comedies every day for a solid month!

Pictures back lot, where many Three Stooges comedies had been produced.

But being impersonated had its share of drawbacks for the Stooges, too. For instance, a puzzling but hilarious identity crisis arose when a chain of automobile supply stores, The Pep Boys, expanded nationally. Emblazoned on the stores' facades were three toothy, grinning auto mechanics, posed like The Three Stooges with their names in bold letters underneath: Manny, Moe, and Jack. Customers—not true fans—would invariably point at these ugly dudes and shout, "There's The Three Stooges!" In fact, the authors of this book once experienced a humorous incident that points up the Pep Boys/Three Stooges

Moe, Larry, and Curly-Joe team up with Scooby and the gang in an episode of *The New Scooby-Doo Movies* in 1972. © *Hanna-Barbera Productions, courtesy of Jeff Lenburg Collection*

Colleges, high schools, and grade schools were filled with Three Stooges impersonators. Students became so enthralled with their screen idols that some staged pie fights at noontime rallies and reenacted such favorite Stooge routines as "The Maharaja." Moe enjoyed saving newspaper clippings, sent to him by fans, depicting student activities and fan impersonators. He once recalled three students in particular, at Loara High School in Anaheim, California, who did their impersonation of "Niagara Falls" in a variety show production. One student went so far as to cut his hair like Moe, while another tousled his curls like Larry. (The students looked oddly like authors Greg and Jeff Lenburg, respectively.) Understandably, the third student refused to shave his head; he wore a bald headpiece to make him look like Curly.

During this period of exploding interest in the Stooges, in August 1973, Norman Maurer held serious negotiations with 20th Century-Fox to reprise the trio in a new weekly series about the sons of The Three Stooges, tentatively titled *The Three Stooges, Jr.* or *The Little Stooges.* (Maurer was already writing a

Little Stooges comic book for Gold Key Comics; the series had debuted the previous year.) Maurer and producer Alan J. Factor were set to produce, through Fox's television division; their first task was casting the three lead roles. Maurer set up an office at Fox to hold auditions. Press releases were issued and local radio stations announced that three young actors were needed to play The Three Stooges in a new television series.

It seemed like it would be an easy job, but it wasn't. The producers couldn't find a teenager to play Curly—and he was supposed to have been the easiest to cast. "Even worse were the young adults we had coming in to play Moe and Larry," Maurer said. Consequently, Maurer and Factor disbanded the project.

The concept was briefly revived in another form when Hanna-Barbera Productions, the largest single producer of Saturday-morning cartoons, reviewed the possibility of producing an animated version of

Loara High School students Doug "Curly" Suppa, Greg "Moe" Lenburg, and Jeff "Larry" Lenburg reprise the routine "The Maharaja" during school spirit week. *© Jeff and Greg Lenburg, all rights reserved, courtesy of Jeff and Greg Lenburg Collection*

Norman Maurer's proposed *Little Stooges* TV cartoon series: the young characters with their dog Muff (top), and in a spoof set in King Arthur's court, "The Time Trespassers" (bottom). *Courtesy of Norman Maurer Collection*

Norman Maurer's TV cartoon concept of The Little Stooges as a teenage rock band. *Courtesy of Norman Maurer Collection*

The Little Stooges. Maurer adapted the idea from an earlier unsold concept, titled *The Li'l Stooges*, which had also featured three juvenile Stooges, as well as their mischievous companion Muff the dog. Unfortunately, as winsome as the premise was, it was never produced. He also pitched an altogether new concept of The Little Stooges as a teenage rock band, which also never sold.

Over the years, however, artists' renderings of the Stooges *have* appeared in political cartoons and daily comic strips. Satirists have used the Stooges' likenesses to make political points in one-column editorial cartoons, while strip cartoonists have periodically called on them to top off specific gags, or even to serve as featured characters. The Stooges have appeared in cartoon form in popular publications, from *MAD* magazine to the *Saturday Evening Post*, and in such widely read strips as *Momma*, the *Wizard of Id*, and many, many others. In the comic strip *B.C.*, the Three Stooges were used for two weeks straight following Larry Fine's death in 1975.

As for the Stooges themselves, one member attempted to carry on by forming perhaps the least-known trio

of Three Stooges impersonators. In 1974, Curly-Joe DeRita launched a nightclub act he called The New 3 Stooges—Moe gave him permission to use the Three Stooges name. Hired to complete the trio were Frank Mitchell and former Healy stooge Mousie Garner. DeRita adapted The Three Stooges' act, using a combination of music and comedy, with Garner doing his shtick behind the piano. The new threesome opened in Boston and played in several eastern cities. According to Curly-Joe, the team would have made better seltzer water, because it fizzled just as fast.

Carol Burnett was one of several comedians who impersonated the team on their weekly television series. She reprised the Stooges' antics in the February 24, 1973, broadcast of CBS's *The Carol Burnett Show*, costarring Harvey Korman and Ken Berry. In the sketch, Burnett and her comic associates are founders of The Three Stooges National Bank, and they can't decide who'll take over ownership. The usual slapstick abounds, with Korman impressive as Moe and Burnett convincing as Larry (frizzy-haired wig and all), but Berry's Curly is not up to par. They reenact some

The Stooges' classic humor has played out in countless editorial cartoons and daily cartoon strips, among them *Momma* and the *Wizard of Id*.
*Courtesy of Norman Maurer Collection*

traditional routines: Korman pokes Burnett, who raises her hand in front of her nose to stop the attacking fingers. In another good bit of business, Korman orders Berry to put his left fist out; Korman smacks it up, driving it into Berry's own forehead. The gags, including the sound effects, were typical of many scenes from the Stooges' two-reel comedies. In the final scene, an executive walks in and remarks to the Stooges, "Sorry, gentlemen, you're fired. We've hired someone more sophisticated to run the bank." Out of nowhere strut three Marx Brothers look-alikes.

Although they didn't physically resemble the Stooges, the American music group The Hudson

Carol Burnett, Harvey Korman, and Ken Berry imitating the Stooges on CBS's *The Carol Burnett Show.* © *CBS, courtesy of Moe Howard Collection/CBS*

Even though they don't look like them, Bill, Mark, and Brett—better known as The Hudson Brothers—also impersonated the Stooges on their ill-remembered summer replacement TV series *The Hudson Brothers Show. Courtesy of First Artists*

Brothers—Bill, Mark, and Brett—also mirrored the comedy styles of both the Stooges and the Marx Brothers. This was apparent in sketches they performed on their ill-fated summer replacement series for CBS, *The Hudson Brothers Show*, in 1974 and in a series of six short films they later produced for Showtime.

Rich Little—the man of a thousand impressions—also paid tribute to the team in four episodes of his 1976 comedy/variety series for NBC, *The Rich Little Show*. The best of the bunch was from its March 15 telecast. Guests Joe Baker and R. G. Brown essayed the roles of Curly and Larry, respectively, while Little did Moe, in "The Three Stooges Stop Smoking Clinic" and a courtroom sketch featuring Michael Landon.

Rich "Moe" Little yuks it up in a scene with Stooges partners R. G. "Larry" Brown and Joe "Curly" Baker and their victim Michael Landon in a sketch from *The Rich Little Show.* © *NBC, courtesy of Moe Howard Collection/NBC*

Little's effort to duplicate the Stooges was met with a strong complaint from the attorneys for Norman Maurer Productions objecting to the show's use of The Three Stooges' names and likenesses without permission. An out-of-court settlement was subsequently reached with NBC whereby the network agreed to cease using scenes with The Three Stooges, and all previously produced segments were struck from syndicated prints of *The Rich Little Show*.

The previous year, in February 1975, American moviegoers had been fooled by another set of impostors—until they got a closer look—when American International Pictures released a Technicolor widescreen cheapie from director Alfonso Brescia (proclaimed "Italy's director of cinematic trash"), *SuperStooges vs. the WonderWomen*. Doubled-billed with Vincent Price's *Madhouse*, the film was Brescia's so-called follow-up to his silly 1973 sword-and-sandal epic *Battle of the Amazons*. Dubbed and retitled in English (in its foreign release it was called *Amazons vs. Supermen*), it left audiences expecting to see Moe, Larry, and Curly-Joe, but they were instead treated to three greasy, muscle-bound, supernaturally powered men (one white, one black, one Asian). Aru (Nick Jordan), Moog (Marc Hannibal), and Chung (Hua Yueh) perform incredible feats as they try to prevent a

Three more-than-mere-mortal men take on powerful amazon women, Three Stooges–style, in *SuperStooges vs. the Wonder-Women* (1975). *Courtesy of Jeff Lenburg Collection*

bevy of beautiful and amazing white-bikini-clad amazon women from destroying inhabitants of a village—but the film justifies its use of the word "Stooges" in the title by having the mighty male warriors perform a great deal of Stooge-style slapstick as well. Panned by critics (how surprising!), fortunately *SuperStooges vs. the WonderWomen* left theaters as fast as it arrived.

Of all the impersonations on record, perhaps the greatest and clearest was in a 20th Century-Fox release from Mel Brooks, *Silent Movie* (1976). Brooks, Marty Feldman, and Dom DeLuise were more sophisticated in their Stooge impressions. Mel was apparently the overbearing boss of the trio. Feldman, replete with bulging eyes and a wild head of hair, was a carbon copy of Larry. And DeLuise didn't

have a moment in the film in which he was without a sandwich to eat—obviously portraying Curly.

Critics had high acclaim for *Silent Movie* and wrote that Brooks was bringing The Three Stooges' act "up-to-date." Indeed, Mel successfully adapted his own brash, nonsensical humor to the Stooge-like characters of the film. In one particularly funny segment, Brooks and his two comrades crash a convalescent home. Following a bizarre mishap, they end up in a chase scene, racing through the grounds in electric wheelchairs—an updated version of a similar scene in the 1937 Stooges comedy *Dizzy Doctors*.

Unlike other impersonation attempts that were blatant character rip-offs, Brooks did a commendable job in making his tribute to the Stooges honorable and memorable. Film historians have since called *Silent Movie* his best film.

Another performer, Frank Welker, sought to make his particular niche in Three Stooges history as a Curly Howard impersonator. Welker has joined the ranks of such prominent cartoon voice artists as Mel Blanc and Daws Butler. In 1976, he was asked to voice a lovable but stupid white shark in a *Jaws*-inspired Hanna-Barbera cartoon series, ABC's *Jabberjaw*. The sharp-toothed headliner, who had the brain of a sardine and the courage of a guppy, served as mascot for a rock group composed of four teenagers who lived in an underwater civilization. With the permission of Norman Maurer Productions, Welker shaped his character around Curly

Dom DeLuise, Marty Feldman, and Mel Brooks portray modern-day Stooges in Brooks's film *Silent Movie* (1976). *© Warner Bros., courtesy of Mel Brooks*

Howard, recreating the comedian's unusual mannerisms and falsetto voice in shark form. The sight of the obnoxious shark belting out "Wooo-wooo-wooo!" and "N'yuk-n'yuk-n'yuk!" can best be described as bizarre. Premiering on September 11, 1976, the Saturday-morning series ran for sixteen episodes.

At this time, Norman Maurer was writing scripts for several other Hanna-Barbera shows, most notably *Dynomutt, Dog Wonder*; and then, finally, he sold the company on a new cartoon series starring The Three Stooges. In *The Robonic Stooges*, Moe, Larry, and Curly are bionic, secret-agent superheroes who get into typical—and not-so-typical—Stooges jams to the dismay of their boss, Agent 000. Unlike the old trio, these new

the Pelican, Knock-Knock the Woodpecker, and Scat Cat—were nothing more than weak imitations of the studio's former live foursome The Banana Splits.

The Nielsen ratings indicated that the Stooges cartoons received more viewers than any other segment in the show. As a result, *Skatebirds* was canceled and CBS installed the trio in a half-hour show of their own, *The Three Robonic Stooges* (which also featured Woofer and Wimper). The series comprised a total of thirty-two five-minute Robonic Stooges cartoons with stories ranging from conventional situations to traditional myths; it aired from January 28, 1978, to December 30, 1979. Even after that, stations continued to broadcast these wacky animated romps in many parts of the world.

A scene from the Hanna-Barbera and Norman Maurer Productions cartoon series *The Robonic Stooges*. © Hanna-Barbera/Norman Maurer Productions, courtesy of Norman Maurer Collection

A previous unproduced animated cartoon satire, *Superstooges*. Courtesy of Norman Maurer Collection

models are capable of telescoping their limbs, heads, and torsos into goofy positions while on assignment. Supplying the voices for the Stooges were Paul Winchell as Moe, Joe Baker as Larry—and Frank Welker as Curly. Agent 000 was expertly voiced by the late Ross Martin of *Wild Wild West* television fame.

At first, Hanna-Barbera produced these five-minute cartoons as part of their live-action series *The Skatebirds*, which debuted on CBS on September 10, 1977. Two *Robonic Stooges* cartoons were shown every week, along with *Wonder Wheels*; *Woofer and Wimper, Dog Detectives*; *Mystery Island*, a live-action adventure; and segments featuring the Skatebirds themselves. The Skatebirds—Scooter the Penguin, Satchel

(Previously, another Stooges cartoon series had been proposed to Norman Maurer Productions. Fine Arts Productions submitted the concept titled *Superstooges*, which was ultimately turned down.)

Of all the Stooge impersonations of the late 1970s, the best and funniest were consistently on *Second City TV*, a spin-off of Chicago's Second City comedy troupe featuring an all-Canadian cast. Originally syndicated in the United States in 1977, NBC would add it to its late-night Saturday night lineup in 1981, expanding it to a ninety-minute format and renaming it *SCTV Network 90*. One of the show's earliest impersonations was in a May 1977 spoof of the movie *Ben-Hur* in which costar John Candy, as Judah Ben-Hur, "channels" Curly Howard for inspi-

Helene Curtis magazine ad featuring Stooge impersonators.
*Courtesy of Norman Maurer Collection*

ration. In December 1978, in a spoof of TV's *Alfred Hitchcock Presents*, Candy (as Hitchcock) again goes Curly Howard on the audience. This time, while describing the plots of the Hitchcock films *Psycho* and *The Birds*, Candy frantically drops to the floor and does a Curly-like spin.

Stooge impersonations continued to surface on many other top television shows. In March 1978 on CBS's *All in the Family*, Archie Bunker went Moe-stal on his Stooge-loathing son-in-law Mike in the episode "The Dinner Guest." After watching the fictitious film *The Three Stooges Meet Frankenstein* on TV, Archie performs the famous Moe Howard nostril pull on Mike, much to the younger man's chagrin.

Also on the list was *The Chevy Chase National Humor Test*, a one-hour NBC special that aired May 10, 1979. Chase was one of several young comedians influenced by an earlier generation's masters of comedy—including but not limited to The Three Stooges. He brought back the Buster Keaton form of pratfalls—notably through his mocking of President Gerald Ford—and other trademark shtick from the 1930s and 1940s.

For this impersonation, Chase's writers developed the kind of sketch in which viewers would least expect the Stooges: they lampoon the trials and tribulations of banking with The First National Funny Bank. Chase narrates the scene, explaining to viewers that perhaps the least humorous times of our lives are spent in an ordinary bank. But one particular branch wants to alleviate this humdrum atmosphere, since it can't compete with the giants in the industry who are offering the same old serious style of banking.

In an attempt to rectify the situation, bank president H. R. "Cuddles" McBride dreams up the idea of mixing "funny with money." Among the bank's many services are its personal checks. McBride takes great pride in being the only bank to have checks featuring a wide assortment of comedians—everybody from Jack Benny to Pinky Lee to The Three Stooges. Naturally, mentioning the Stooges creates the need for an impersonation.

Chase and McBride listen in as a teller (Debbie Harmon) watches her customer (Robert Morris) leaf through samples of the different checks the bank has to offer. When she comes to the Stooges she says, "Then we have The Three Stooges—Moe, Larry, and Shemp." (While pointing at the photographs, she confuses Moe for Shemp, and vice versa.) Morris appears totally confused. He says, "Where's Curly?" The teller explains, "I think he came later, it was Shemp first!" Morris, attempting to imitate Shemp, remarks, "Curly was the one who went 'Yeng-yeng-yeng!'" The teller corrects him: "No, that was Shemp." She proceeds to reprise Curly's famous catchphrase, followed by the familiar wave of the hand. "Curly was 'Wooo-wooo-wooo!'" The best part of this sketch was, naturally, this surprise inclusion of the Stooges, so often neglected in salutes to great comedians.

In 1981, a series of impersonations that belongs in the "poor taste" column appeared on ABC's *Fridays*, the network's take on NBC's *Saturday Night Live*. Three comedians—Bruce Mahler (Moe), Larry David (Larry), and John Roarke (Curly)—brought a different dimension to the team, imagining them as drug-culture comedians. They managed to include the customary slapstick but interwove it around sick drug-oriented jokes in three successive episodes, in sketches titled "The Numb Boys," "The Atomic Bong," and "Long-Lost Brothers."

One segment opens with the Stooges in bed, asleep and snoring (a traditional opening in several Stooges comedies). They awaken and perform what they believe are constructive duties around the house. Curly begins cleaning out a drug instrument of some kind, which accidentally squirts ink in Moe's face. This was one of the least offensive gags that appeared in the show. A more typical one was Curly smoking marijuana for the first time, getting high, and spinning on the floor like a top. In another scene a pusher tries selling the Stooges some drugs. The boys resist momentarily, and then Curly remarks, "I'll do it when I'm ready!" The pusher whips out a switchblade knife and cracks, "Are you ready?" A frightened Curly gasps, "Yeah, I'm ready!"

Slightly amusing was the third and final sketch ("Long-Lost Brothers"), in which George Hamilton plays the Ted Healy role, in a reunion with his three long-lost brothers (the Stooges). The trio's visit leaves Hamilton's mansion in a shambles, and in the end, Hamilton vents his anger by performing Moe's triple slap on the Stooges.

Actually, the *Fridays* impersonations could have stood up as timeless masterpieces if not for the constant drug references. Instead, they were distasteful tributes to three comedians who always had good, clean fun and never used foul language in their films. As with the Rich Little Stooge impersonations, Norman Maurer Productions' attorneys made a strong protest to ABC for this unlicensed use of the Stooges' name and likenesses, and an out-of-court settlement was reached.

Following *Fridays*' string of sketches, NBC's *SCTV Network 90* came up with a new hilarious satirical take on the 1980 movie *Melvin and Howard* entitled "Melvin and Howards." Like the movie, the sketch depicts the odd relationship between gas station attendant Melvin Dummar and billionaire Howard Hughes. Broadcast on May 29, 1981, this sketch was touted as a Movie of the Week promo and divided into three segments. In each one, Dummar (Rick Moranis) and Hughes (Joe Flaherty) are seen driving on a cross-country trip through the Arizona desert. At each turn, they pick up a passenger with the first or last name of Howard—first Howard Cosell (Eugene Levy) and then Senator Howard Baker (Dave Thomas). By now, television viewers realize that another person named Howard will be picked up. The question is who.

The final segment puts to rest all questions and surprises everyone. Hughes takes over the cross-country driving chores, and as he struggles to keep his eyes from closing, a hand comes in under them, wriggles back and forth, and thrusts downward, smacking Hughes in the face. The camera cuts to our new passenger, Curly Howard (John Candy), looking on innocently as Hughes barks, "Who the hell are you?"

Candy replies, "Curly . . . Curly Howard. N'yuk-n'yuk!"

Hughes quickly retorts, "Well, start singing, pea-brain!"

Curly first refuses, but Hughes changes his mind with a whack in the mouth. Curly then cries, "Oh, Elaine, won't you come out tonight . . . at least until the morning's bright. Oh, Cedric's here, your darling Cedric's here . . ." At this point, Dummar raises his hand to lead the group as they finish this happy-go-lucky tune together, and the sketch as well.

Candy's performance as Curly was not only well rehearsed but the best on record. He had every mannerism and nuance down to perfection, even Curly's famous "n'yuk-n'yuk" catchphrase.

John Candy as Curly, Joe Flaherty as Larry, and Eugene Levy as Moe, in an episode of NBC's *SCTV*. © *NBC, courtesy of John Candy/NBC*

The *SCTV Network 90* cast took two more stabs as Stooge impostors. In the November 1982 sketch "Curly Howard Sings," a bogus commercial has Candy reprising his role as Curly, touting the new record *Curly Howard Sings the Great Movie Love Themes*. Then, in a March 1983 skit, "Give 'Em Hell Larry," Joe Flaherty plays as a porcupine-haired Larry Fine, lampooning James Whitmore's one-man stage show on the life of President Harry Truman, *Give 'Em Hell Harry*—even subjecting himself to some self-inflicted eye pokes.

Another impersonation of the Stooges team worth noting was broadcast in an episode of CBS's *Jessica Novak* titled "Kenny," broadcast November 26, 1981. In this story, written by Ira Behr, a young Stooges fan named Moe Tannenbaum solicits over two thousand signatures, including those of Merv Griffin, Danny Thomas, Joey Bishop, and Steve Allen, for a petition to secure The Three Stooges their star on the Hollywood Walk of Fame. Tannenbaum meets up with TV news reporter Jessica Novak in the lobby of a local movie theater and appeals to her for support, to help inform TV viewers through her broadcast that the Stooges are not represented on the Walk of Fame. When Novak is unable to help, the ardent Stooges fan corners Jessica's cameraman and his assistant and

convinces them to let him and his friends Ricky and Bonelli into the newsroom.

The three friends descend upon the newsroom to reenact some traditional Stooges antics. Ricky and Bonelli play Larry and Curly, while Moe is of course Moe. They hope to convince the producer of the show to give them airtime in order to promote their cause. But their comic antics, though hilarious and well timed, fail to impress the producer. Resigned, the mock Stooges exit scene, with impostor Curly wooo-wooo-ing as the scene fades out. Curly, Larry, and Moe were expertly played by Barry Pearl, Danny Goldman, and Mike Tucci, respectively.

Throughout the 1970s, 1980s, and beyond, additional homages have included subtle throwaway scenes created by television and film writers who also happened to be Three Stooges buffs. For instance, in a January 1, 1975, telecast of his top-rated sitcom *The Bob Newhart Show* on CBS, Bob Newhart offered a hilarious tribute. While watching a celebrity soccer match on television with wife Emily (Suzanne Pleshette), Newhart quips, "I never knew The Three Stooges were that coordinated. Nice kick, Moe!"

CBS's long-running television series *M*A*S*H* used the Stooges' names as part of their comic patter on more than one occasion. In the 1982 episode, "Pressure Points," for example, when Colonel Potter asks army psychiatrist Major Sidney Freedman, "Bump into anybody else yet?" he replies, "Just Larry, Moe, and Curly over in the swamp."

Those working behind the scenes of TV's *Nurse* (1981–82), starring Michael Learned, took a line of dialogue straight from *Men in Black* (1934). In that short, a hospital loudspeaker would page Curly, Larry, and Moe as "Dr. Howard, Dr. Fine, Dr. Howard!" Those exact words also graced hospital loudspeakers in one episode of *Nurse*. And in an episode of the 1987 television series *Spies*, starring Ian Stone and Ben Smythe, Stone exclaims, while guarding a man

Actors Barry Pearl, Danny Goldman, and Mike Tucci impersonating the Stooges in an episode of CBS's *Jessica Novak.* © *CBS, courtesy of Norman Maurer Collection/CBS*

Stooges director Edward Bernds, producer/director Norman Maurer, and writer Elwood Ullman as The Three Stooges that could have been, in an unpublished photo mocking impersonators, created by Norman Maurer. © Norman Maurer, courtesy of Norman Maurer Collection

from terrorists, "Isn't this how Moe, Larry, and Curly got started?"

A feature-film example was the low-budget comedy *Gas*, released to theaters for one week in 1981. Featured in this piecemeal cheapie was Steve Furst, who had made his film debut in such comedies as *Animal House* and *Meatballs*. Here, as a gas station attendant, he stole scenes, notably one in which he eyes the attractive figure of a buxom female customer. He reacts deliriously, flapping his hand up and down on top of his head and shouting, "Wooo-wooo-wooo-wooo!"

The Fat Boys (Kool Rock, Markie, and Buffy) as a trio of totally inept Three Stooges–like orderlies who come to the aid of an ailing millionaire (Ralph Bellamy) in a scene from their ill-fated 1987 comedy feature *Disorderlies*. © Warner Bros., courtesy of Jeff Lenburg Collection

Several more sustained Three Stooges homages fell short, unfortunately. One example was filmmaker Chuck Workman's 1985 feature *Stoogemania*. It starred Josh Mostel as a young man named Howard F. Howard, whose life is falling apart due to his obsession with the famed comic trio. Intercut throughout—à la Steve Martin's film noir comedy *Dead Men Don't Wear Plaid*—are many clips of Moe, Larry, Curly, and Shemp from colorized public domain shorts with newly shot footage of Mostel presented in black and white to match the original Stooges work. *Variety* called Workman's effort an "embarrassingly inept homage" and added, "Mostel tries hard but his slapstick routines aren't funny." Another homage that failed to impress the critics was hip-hop trio The Fat Boys' attempt to mime the Stooges' slapstick humor in their 1987 comedy film *Disorderlies*. As a writer for *The Miami Herald* opined, "There's no hint of comic timing or any of the slapstick that was implied by the TV commercials comparing them to the Three Stooges. If the Fat Boys had an iota of the Stooges' technique, at least 'Disorderlies' would have been bearable."

Robot Number 5 (shown here with costar Ally Sheedy) adopts Curly Howard's personality, including mimicking his famous "n'yuk-n'yuk-n'yuk" laugh, after watching Three Stooges films on television in the hit sci-fi comedy *Short Circuit* (1986). © *Columbia Pictures, courtesy of Jeff Lenburg Collection/Norman Maurer Productions*

The best overall cinematic lunacy inspired by the Stooges was doled out in five films made in the mid-to-late 1980s, each a classic in its own right. In Tri-Star Pictures' sci-fi comedy *Short Circuit* (1986), military scientist Steve Guttenberg's robot-on-the-loose, "Number 5," adopts Curly Howard's personality after watching footage of the Stooges' comedies on television, even mimicking Howard's famous "n'yuk-n'yuk-n'yuk" laugh. As suicidal loose cannon Sergeant Martin Riggs in Warner Bros.' *Lethal Weapon* (1987), Mel Gibson (an avowed Stooges fan) delivers a standout impersonation of Curly, not to mention two well-placed pokes in the eyes, when confronting two drug dealers. In the 1989 sequel *Lethal Weapon 2*, Gibson turns Stooge again. Holding a diplomat and smuggler at gunpoint, he maniacally recites, "Eeney, meeney, miney . . ." Then, after a high-pitched Curly-like "Hey, Moe!" he opens fire on the diplomat's prized aquarium, shattering it to pieces.

That same year, in a scene in *Good Morning, Vietnam*, zany Robin Williams eats some really hot Vietnamese food and turns into all three Stooges at once, saying to the lady who cooked it, "Maybe you like this too [he pokes himself in the eyes], or maybe you like this [he starts slapping himself around]." In the 1988 David Zucker–Jim Abrahams–Jerry Zucker Paramount Pictures comedy *The Naked Gun* (based on the television series *Police Squad!*) actor Leslie Nielsen, as bumbling Police Lt. Frank Drebin, does his Moe-like best, poking a look-alike of Ayatollah Khomeini in the eyes.

In 1993, actor Bruce Campbell, a rabid Stooges fan and future costar of USA Network's *Burn Notice*, put his best Stooge forward in Dino DeLaurentis's *Army of Darkness*. In this third entry in Sam Raimi's Evil Dead series, Campbell and Raimi (also a longtime fan of the Stooges) included several Stooge-style slaps, eye pokes, and head bonks—even adding Stooge-like sound effects—during fight scenes between Campbell and his undead adversaries.

As always, not every effort to clone the Stooges materialized. In 1984, Norman Maurer developed an idea and conceptual artwork for a brand-new Three Stooges feature he hoped to get off the ground called *OhOh3 Stooges*. In this spoof of the James Bond 007 spy movies, the fate of mankind would rest in the hands of the Stooges—and the new actors playing them. It was one of the last projects Maurer developed before his death in 1986.

The Stooges continued to show up in other kinds of media as well. In 1986, Tru Studios of Chicago launched a new comic book series called *Trolloids*, featuring three alien-like creatures, Harry, Larry, and Jerry, who talk and act like the Stooges. In his 1986

Incompetent Police Lt. Frank Drebin (Leslie Nielsen), known for his Stooge-like shtick in the television series *Police Squad!* and the *Naked Gun* films, tries to foil an attempt to assassinate Queen Elizabeth II with hilarious results in the 1988 feature *The Naked Gun: From the Files of Police Squad!* © *Paramount Pictures, courtesy of Jeff Lenburg Collection*

novel *IT*, bestselling novelist Stephen King likewise named three scarecrows Larry, Moe, and Curly. And in 1988's second issue of the *Sledge Hammer* comic book, the Stooges appear as Christmas tree salesmen—called The Tree Stooges (Moebius, Curly-ius, Shempius, and Larry)—who try to force people to buy trees from them. These appearances represent only the tip of the iceberg; the Stooges have been referenced countless other times in comic books and popular literature.

By the mid-1980s, however, it was the medium of television that would be dishing out some of the most outrageous excuses to Stooge on many popular shows. In a 1986 episode of ABC's *Mr. Belvedere*, after daughter Marsha tells her father George Owens (Bob Uecker) and two brothers, Kevin and Wesley, to turn off the Stooges on television because her boyfriend is coming over, they respond by breaking into a medley of wooo-wooo-wooos and n'yuk-n'yuk-n'yuks. In an episode of ABC's *Perfect Strangers*, Larry (Mark Linn-Baker) tries teaching his distant Eastern European cousin Balki (Bronson Pinchot) how to get a date. "First you need eye contact," he suggests, but the advice gets lost in the translation. Balki retorts, "Oh, eye contact, like The Three Stooges." He then promptly pokes Larry in the eyes.

In an episode from the 1988 season of ABC's *Full House* ("It's Not My Job"), the family heads to a Halloween party with the guys dressing up as the Stooges: Jesse as Moe, Danny as Larry, and Joey as Curly. Later, NBC's hit sitcom *Cheers* replicated the Stooges slapstick humor in the 1989 episode "What's Up, Doc?," featuring bartender Sam Malone (Ted Danson) and bar manager Rebecca Howe (Kirstie Alley). Depressed over the fact that his life seems empty, revolving only around women and sex, Sam suddenly realizes his life has meaning after Rebecca reminds him of his love for the Stooges by tweaking his nose à la Moe and doing a few Curly-like n'yuk-n'yuk-n'yuks.

In a 1990 broadcast of the ABC comedy *Roseanne*, Roseanne Barr's TV husband, Dan (John Goodman), wears a three-headed Three Stooges costume to the annual Halloween party and, in the show's closing credits, impersonates Curly in a haunted house. FOX's short-lived Sunday-night comedy/variety show *The Sunday Comics* also feted the Stooges in a Sep-

Peter Jurasik as an alien sporting an extreme Larry Fine–like do in the popular television series *Babylon 5* (1993). *Courtesy of PTEN*

tember 1991 telecast featuring comediennes Cathy Ladman as Moereen, Judy Toll as Larrietta, and Judy Nazemetz as Curly Anne in two comedy shorts, one called "Café Calamities." Similarly, in a 1992 episode of FOX's comedy sketch show *The Edge*, cast members Tom Kenny (Moe), Paul Feig (Larry), and Wayne Knight (Curly) star as The Three Exorcists in a spoof of the cult horror film *The Exorcist*.

Beginning in 1993, actor Peter Jurasik took Larry Fine's frizzy Einstein-like hairdo to extremes as the alien Londo Mollari in the popular syndicated sci-fi series *Babylon 5*. In October of that year, on ABC's *Home Improvement*, the sons of Tim "The Tool Man" Taylor (Tim Allen) and wife Jill (Patricia Richardson) turn up at a Halloween party—all dressed as Moe. In December 1994, comedian Adam Sandler paid tribute to the Stooges and their Jewish heritage in the lyrics of "The Hanukkah Song" on NBC's *Saturday Night Live*.

One of the funniest tributes to the Stooges was in a February 1996 sketch on FOX's *MADtv* that lampoons the Stooges as Da Trey Stoogez in the off-the-wall "Menace II High Society," with Phil LaMarr as Cool Moe, Debra Wilson as Larry Larr, and Orlando Jones as Curly Dog. The trio plays exterminators hired as hit men to take down high-society competitor Rupert (played by guest host David Faustino). Another standout effort was on FOX's *That '70s Show* in February 2004. It featured members of the cast as Moe (Topher Grace), Larry (Danny Masterson), and Curly (Ashton Kutcher) in a fantasy Stooge short called *The Pie Guys*.

As in the past, the Stooges would also appear in animated form on popular children's and prime-time shows. A 1987 episode of PBS's *Square One Television* features a slightly different take from the usual: Larry, Curly, and Mo-reen (a woman) are put in charge of arranging seating for a royal banquet. In a September 1989 broadcast of Film Roman's *Garfield and Friends* on CBS, Moe, Larry, and Curly appear as three saber-toothed cats inhabiting an island in "The Legend of the Lake."

The Stooges, in one form or another, showed up several times on Matt Groening's *The Simpsons* for FOX. One early example is the third episode of the show's fourth season, broadcast in early October 1992: in "Homer the Heretic," Homer watches a fictional Stooges short on television ("You must be the three chiropractors I sent for . . .") and notes sagely, "Moe is their leader." In the February 1995 episode "Bart's

Comet," the Stooges appear in the night sky as the constellation The Three Wise Men. In the January 2001 episode "The Mansion Family," they lend their names to a new affliction, Three Stooges Syndrome, which a doctor demonstrates by attempting to shove some diseased puppets through a door unsuccessfully, as they mimic the sounds of Moe, Larry, and Curly. And the February 2010 episode "Boy Meets Curl" juxtaposes the US Olympic Team's National Curling Trials with the National Curly Trials, which attracts a crowd of Curly impersonators.

In 1997 and 1998, the Stooges went over to the dark side, turning evil in two episodes of The WB television network's *The New Adventures of Batman* ("The Holiday Knights" and "Beware of the Creeper") in recurring roles as the Joker's henchmen Cur, Lar, and Mo. More far-fetched was the Stooges (in Claymation form) taking on The Three Tenors (Placido Domingo, Jose Carreras, and Luciano Pavarotti) in the ring in the July 15, 1999, episode of MTV's extremely surreal series *MTV Celebrity Deathmatch*. Larry accidentally kills Moe with a plunger. Then, in an attempt to become a younger, stronger fighter, he sends himself back in time—but he goes too far and becomes a sperm. In the end, Curly is victorious.

Not far behind in terms of over-the-top outrageousness was the use of the Stooges in a 2010 episode of FOX's *Family Guy*, "Partial Terms of Endearment," which deals with the sensitive issue of abortion. In it, Peter unsuccessfully tries to force his wife Lois to "lose" a baby, until an activist shows him a video of people never born because of abortion, including a man who would have become the fourth member of The Four Stooges. Due to the dark subject matter, FOX never aired the episode in the United States.

Although numerous television commercials have aired over the years incorporating clips of the real Stooges at their slapstick best, only rarely have commercial impersonators captured the true essence of their personalities and their unique humor. In 1987, two such efforts emerged, as actors successfully embodied the trio in commercials for *The Three Stooges: The VCR Game* by Pressman Toy Corporation and the RCA Programmable Remote (the latter ad was produced by Leo Burnett, a leading Chicago advertising agency). In the spring of 1989, the Stooges turned up again, this time in "The Nut," a commercial for Dole pistachios. As the commercial opens, the camera pans through a

Three Stooges look-alikes promoting a Michigan lottery. *Courtesy of Jeff and Greg Collection/Michigan State Lottery*

gallery of bronzed nut trophies and freezes on one with the heads of Moe, Larry, and Curly.

In 1991, outspoken artist Mark Heckman, known for creating billboards addressing contemporary issues, unveiled his latest billboard targeting the irreversible loss of tropical forests. Featuring The Tree Stooges, it targeted the irreversible loss of tropical rainforests each year by featuring a bumbling trio of lumberjacks. Each "Stooge" represented a different nationality to illustrate his point that people all around the globe are responsible for the problem. After a brief showing in Los Angeles, the billboards appeared mostly in the Chicago area.

Even advertising campaigns for state lotteries have featured Stooge impostors. But the one advertisement that will go down as a classic in Stoogedom is a July 2001 television commercial for Verizon Super-

Pages titled "Family Counseling." In the midst of a crisis, the Stooges use Verizon's online SuperPages to locate a family counselor to help them overcome their "anger" issues. Bob Caso is Larry and Patrick Thomas is Curly— and the actor playing Moe is none other than Moe's real-life grandson Jeffrey Scott.

It was not the first time Scott walked in his famous grandfather's shoes. In 1993, he cowrote, executive produced, and performed in a live Three Stooges stage show with Caso and Thomas at the MGM Grand Hotel in Las Vegas, which was highly successful. It was an experience he would never forget as he slapped and shticked before packed houses, doing comedy routines with two performers whom he immediately came to love, much as Moe loved his "boys."

Since then, other larger-scale efforts to mimic the Stooges' bigger-than-life personalities and wacky brand of humor have materialized. Mel Gibson produced a full TV-movie biography of the team, *The Three Stooges*, which aired on ABC on April 24, 2000. Actors personifying the Stooges were Paul Ben-Victor (Moe), Evan Handler (Larry), John Kassir (Shemp), Michael Chiklis (Curly), Laurence Boy (Joe Besser), and Peter Callan (Joe DeRita). The movie overdramatized events and was rife with inaccuracies, but it was still a tremendous success, with more than 16.5 million households watching.

Then came the most anticipated homage of them all: *The Three Stooges* (originally announced as *The Three Stooges: The Movie*), produced and directed by the famous sibling duo Peter and Bobby Farrelly, of *Dumb and Dumber* and *There's Something About Mary* fame. After many years of development, false starts, and failed casting attempts (Benicio Del Toro, Sean Penn, and Jim Carrey were among the most notable targets), principal photography finally began in April 2010 at an old plantation in Cartersville, Georgia. The site would serve as a mock orphanage in the new feature-length comedy, which would be released to theaters in April 2012 by 20th Century Fox (the same studio for which the Stooges, with Ted Healy, starred in their first film). The film follows the famed comedy trio—Chris Diamantopoulos as Moe, Sean Hayes as Larry, and Will Sasso as Curly—in a series of original adventures. *The Three Stooges* is set in the modern day, but in the end the boys are what they have always been . . . stooges.

Impersonators have likewise turned out in droves to participate in Stooge look-alike contests at college campuses and other popular establishments in different regions of the country. Curly and his famous catchphrases are among the most frequently imitated.

Indeed, the Stooges have been imitated in just about every form known to man. It truly boggles the mind to realize that the Stooges have been impersonated so extensively—perhaps more than any other comedy team Hollywood has ever known. Despite fan allegations that the team has been constantly neglected, it is clear that The Three Stooges have been greatly appreciated as the grand masters of comedy.

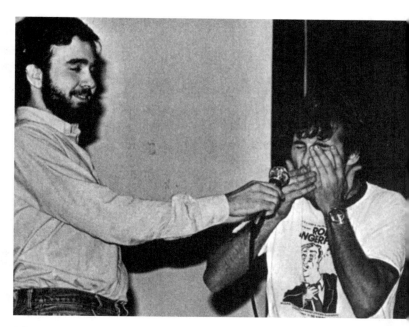

A fan covering his version of "Wooo-wooo-wooo!" as a contestant during a Stooge look-alike festival. *Courtesy of Jeff and Greg Lenburg Collection*

# Chapter 7

Newspaper ad for one of many film festivals held at theaters throughout the country featuring Stooges films with Curly, shown on the big screen, complete and uncut.

# A Growing Cult

*I*t can safely be said that a show business performer can only achieve prominence with the support of devoted fans. This certainly is true of The Three Stooges. Since the trio's formation as a movie comedy team in the 1930s, their legions of fans have been responsible for many record-setting events, including their enormous television popularity starting in the late 1950s, and a resurgence in the 1970s and 1980s, fueled by baby boomers weaned on old reruns of their films since childhood. Since then, it has largely been up to the fans to carry on the Stooge legacy, and they have certainly been up to the challenge. Despite the fact that the Stooges' films have been televised for more than five decades, the team's popularity has never waned.

In 1981, Columbia Pictures' merchandising director, Glenn Dyckoff, reported that nearly ninety domestic television markets carried the Screen Gems' syndicated package of 190 Three Stooges comedies. The group's antics were broadcast Monday through Friday in many major cities, including New York, Chicago, San Francisco, San Diego, Philadelphia, Atlanta, Portland, Minneapolis, St. Louis, and Dallas.

Various television stations in such prime areas as Chicago (WFLD Channel 12) and New York (WPIX Channel 11) aired the Stooge comedies during adult viewing hours (as early as 10 PM and as late as midnight in half-hour and hour time slots). In the past, station program directors had shied away from scheduling these films in nighttime slots, since they were primarily thought to be for the children's market. But stations were discovering that the avid Stooges fans of the 1950s and 1960s, who were now adults, wanted to experience the team's antics all over again. A station manager for KVZK-TV in Pago Pago in American Samoa took a survey of programming and found that The Three Stooges ranked number one against such competition as *The Wonderful World of Disney*, *Hawaii Five-O*, and first-run network movies. Besides domestic runs, Stooges comedies were available dubbed into Japanese, Spanish, Portuguese, and Italian. (The year 1981 marked the first time that Three Stooges films were shown over Italian airwaves.)

The incredible phenomenon of the Stooges' resurgence encompassed more than scheduled broadcasts of their two-reelers. On January 25, 1981, KTLA-TV Channel 5 in Los Angeles broadcast two Three Stooges features back to back— *The Three Stooges in Orbit* and *The Three Stooges Go Around the World in a Daze*—in a four-hour time slot opposite the Super Bowl. Norman Maurer appeared on the program and recalled many intimate stories about the team. The next day, program host Tom Hatten advised Maurer that KTLA's screening of the Stooges features was the highest-rated Los Angeles program next to the Super Bowl itself, beating out all other competition. The films were part of the station's *Family Film Festival*, a program that, according to Hatten, drew primarily adult viewers and movie buffs.

The team's shorts were also being played on numerous cable and pay-TV outlets nationwide. In February 1979, Los Angeles–based SelecTV, one of the largest subscription television services in the country, had started showing Stooges films ten times monthly after 8:30 PM. According to Bill Mechanic, then program director for SelecTV, the trio's two-reel comedies had a loyal adult following, continued to outdraw many top feature films, and had about a 12 percent viewership rating (which was higher than any other nonfeature selection broadcast on the service). Realizing the potential adult Stooges market, SelecTV double-billed *Miss Sadie Thompson* (1953), starring Rita Hayworth, with *Spooks!*, a 1953 3-D short featuring The Three Stooges. Mechanic maintained that *Spooks!* drew 30.6 percent of SelecTV's seventy-five thousand subscribers and was the first 3-D film ever telecast. Subscribers were sent 3-D glasses with their monthly film guide.

Ted Turner's Superstation WTBS, based in Atlanta, Georgia, and broadcasting twenty-four hours a day, rated the Stooges comedies as the station's number-one nostalgic installment, attracting nearly 60 percent of its audience. And speaking of hits, Petry Television Inc., a firm representing a num-

Fan letter sent to Columbia Pictures in 1936, complete with cutouts of the Stooges.
© *Columbia Pictures, courtesy of Moe Howard Collection*

ber of leading independent stations, came up with some interesting data. In a television survey, they listed the following titles as the most-watched black-and-white programs at the time: *I Love Lucy*, *You Bet Your Life* (with Groucho Marx), *Leave it to Beaver*, and The Three Stooges.

Stoogemania triumphed on the big screen as well. Mann and United Artists theater chains started things off by booking the 1974 film *The 3 Stooges Follies*, which packed them in at every show. Noting the team's remarkable commercial value, revival theaters began scheduling Three Stooges festivals. Fans were willing to shell out the three- to five-dollar admission prices—despite the fact that many stations broadcast these same films for free. The idea of viewing them complete and uncut, in a large theatrical venue, piqued the interest of many fans. The greatest advantage was the clarity of the 35 mm prints, as opposed to the scratched, edited TV prints of the era.

One of the most memorable festivals was held on January 26, 1981, at the Tiffany Theatre on Hollywood's Sunset Strip. "The Best of the Three Stooges" featured a one-night, four-hour program of twelve Stooges shorts with Curly. Both shows were sellouts. Lines started stretching around the block several hours before the first show. At an admission price of

$3.50, the three-hundred-seat theater was filled to capacity—not with children, but with adults. The Tiffany's ticket seller estimated that more than 150 potential customers had to be turned away, and others were undoubtedly scared away by the sight of a line three blocks long. Because of the festival's success, Tiffany management wound up extending the engagement, which was unheard of even with such classic films as *Dr. Zhivago* and *Singin' in the Rain*.

The Tiffany's Three Stooges festival realized such tremendous box office, in fact, that additional events were arranged, including one featuring comedies with Ted Healy and His Stooges. MGM hadn't issued these musical comedies to theaters since their original release dates in 1933 and 1934. As it turned out, MGM would have been wiser to have kept them under lock and key, since fans reacted violently to them. A chorus of boos erupted at one showing as a result of too much Healy and not enough Stooges in the films. Understandably, a sizeable part of the audience went home disgruntled, commenting, "I wanted to see more of Curly!" Curly had joined the ranks of superstar comedians in an age when superstar comedians were scarce.

The Stooges' popularity was on display at another 1981 festival that took place over the July Fourth

A wrought-iron weather vane, designed by Helen Howard for the bathhouse of the Howards' valley home as a surprise for Moe. It now rests on the cupola of Joan Maurer's garage. *Courtesy of Moe Howard Collection*

Samples of fans' letters of adulation to the Stooges. *Courtesy of Moe Howard Collection*

weekend. The Balboa Theatre, located in Balboa, California, sponsored a Three Stooges festival similar to the first one held at the Tiffany Theatre. This show was also a sellout. In the tradition of previous festivals, fans couldn't wait for the program to start and went berserk when it did. Cheers went up as each film appeared on the screen, and the audience turned extremely boisterous—jeering, hollering, screaming with laughter, and going totally bonkers. When a coming-attractions trailer interrupted the program at its midpoint, chants echoed throughout the theater: "We want the Stooges!" and "Stooges! Stooges! Stooges!" The shouting became so alarming that the screening of the trailer was quickly aborted.

But bedlam was reigning in revival theaters all over the country. Dan Weiss, manager of Take One Cinema in Coral Gables, Florida, could attest to it. In 1980, a local radio station, Love 94 FM, sponsored a Three Stooges Festival at Take One. Weiss's bill usually consisted of MGM musicals, not comedies. The result of this sudden change in programming: not one empty seat!

The Three Stooges renaissance had also overwhelmed theater owners in Pittsburgh, New Jersey, Philadelphia, Indiana, Boston, Illinois, and New York. Crowds were just as phenomenal, selling out at every program. A chain of several dozen theaters in New York ran a successful combination of Three Stooges and Little Rascals comedies. The turnout was so tremendous that theaters held the program over for two weeks.

On April 20, 1983, United Artists Classics released a compilation celebrating the Stooges' work at MGM with Ted Healy. It was called *The MGM Three Stooges Festival*, even though they did not become known by their rightful name until joining Columbia Pictures in 1934. The compilation, which premiered in New York at the St. Marks Theater, was well attended. It covered nearly every one of the group's short films for the studio (with the exception of *Hello Pop!*), including *Nertsery Rhymes*, *Beer and Pretzels*, and *Plane Nuts* from 1933 and *The Big Idea* from 1934, as well as Curly Howard's solo venture *Roast-Beef and Movies* (1934). United Artists minted four 35 mm prints of the ninety-five-minute feature for repertory theater use.

Revival theaters weren't the only ones keen on booking Stooges festivals. Universities and colleges continued to program similar festivals, securing the films through local rental houses. The University of Michigan, for example, had made it a tradition, since 1966, to schedule an annual Three Stooges Festival. The parade of Stooges enthusiasts had also invaded church groups. One in West Chester, Pennsylvania, strung together Three Stooges comedies with an original organized sporting event, The Three Stooges Olympics. Youths in grades nine through twelve participated in soccer with an oversized ball, a well-organized game called bedlam, and something known as flamingo football.

As a salute to Curly and his appetite for sandwiches, a restaurateur in the town of Hammond, Louisiana, erected The Three Stooges Deli, which served sandwiches named after the Stooges. A fantastic array of Three Stooges photographs adorned the walls behind the sales counter, and at times the owner offered glossy reproductions for sale. T-shirts, baseball caps, and drink holders were also available, with the deli's insignia printed on each. In addition

Menu and bumper sticker for the former Three Stooges Deli in Hammond, Louisiana. *Courtesy of Three Stooges Deli*

Series of charming cartoons drawn by Stooges fan Joanne Alcalde. *Courtesy of Joanne Alcalde*

to these novelties, customer giveaways included deli menus, bumper stickers, and for a few cents, Three Stooges Deli matches. Some of the deli's more notable dishes included Larry's Log, Moe's Muffalotta, Stooges' BBQ, Curley's Combo, and the Stooges Sub.

The Three Stooges Deli is no more, but another fan institution, The Three Stooges Fan Club Inc., remains in operation to this day. The club was established in 1974 by Ralph Schiller, with the endorsements of Moe Howard and Larry Fine, because of the increasing demand for information about the team. Schiller's successor as president was Morris Feinberg, Larry Fine's brother, and the club was headquartered in his hometown of Philadelphia until his death in 1985. The club is now headed by Gary Lassin and located in Ambler, Pennsylvania. It keeps fans abreast of the latest in Three Stooges happenings through a quarterly journal, which features articles on the team and special reports by correspondents from around the globe. It remains the oldest and largest Stooges fan club, with more than two thousand members worldwide. (The club can be contacted at P.O. Box 747, Gwynedd Valley, PA 19437.)

Another Stooges fan club, The Official Three Stooges Fan Club, was licensed by Columbia Pictures and Norman Maurer Productions in October 1981 and was an instant success. Ira Friedman, who formed the Official Star Wars Club, organized this second Stooges society. It was set up primarily to promote Three Stooges posters and novelty items and to inform and entertain fans through a monthly newsletter, with articles written by coworkers and friends of the Stooges. This club has since discontinued its operation.

The outpouring of interest in Stooges swelled throughout the 1980s, with many manufacturers and advertisers jumping on board to capitalize on their popularity. In 1987, for example, Moe was featured in a major print ad campaign for Nikon's new N4004 camera. The two-page spread used photos of Moe (from 1945's *If a Body Meets a Body*) and Albert Einstein both wearing Nikon's newest cameras around their necks under the headline "Nikon introduces the perfect camera for both." The ad appeared in *Time*, *Newsweek*, *Sports Illustrated*, *Rolling Stone*, *Gentleman's Quarterly*, *Smithsonian*, *Travel & Leisure*, and other publications and was named "Best Ad of the Month" by *The Gallagher Report* in 1988. From February to December 1987, Delta Dental Plan of New Jersey built its latest print ad campaign around a large photo of Moe yanking on Curly's tooth with a pair of pliers while Larry holds Curly's head still; underneath was the caption "Give Your Employees More Than a Do-

From 1987, a major print ad campaign for Nikon's N4004 camera featuring Moe Howard and Albert Einstein.
*Courtesy of Norman Maurer Collection/Nikon*

It-Yourself Dental Plan!" It appeared in such publications as *Time*, *Newsweek*, and *Sports Illustrated*.

Likewise, Moe, Larry, and Curly's iconic likenesses were utilized in numerous print ad campaigns and premium promotions for Fiberglas Pink Home Insulation, Anheuser-Busch Natural Light beer, Barrel O' Fun snacks, The Phoenix Mutual Life Insurance Co., and Superior Brands Inc.'s line of new Bacon Krisps crackers. Via film clips, they appeared in television commercials for Burger King, McDonald's, Gillette Foamy Sensitive Shaving Cream, Chex Party Mix, and Hershey's chocolate bars. In November 1987, Coors featured the Stooges in a new beer campaign, "The American Original," which incorporated film clips of celebrities who also included boxer Sugar Ray Leonard and Marilyn Monroe.

That same year, Moe's daughter, Joan Maurer, launched a nationwide effort to have the US Postal Service honor the Stooges with a stamp to commemorate the sixtieth anniversary of their film debut in the Fox feature *Soup to Nuts* (1930). (The committee reviews stamp proposals three years prior to the suggested date of issuance.) Unfortunately, her proposal was denied. Oddly, in 1991 the Postal Service issued a series of stamps featuring Al Hirschfeld caricatures of other famous comedians: Abbott and Costello, Laurel and Hardy, Edgar Bergen and Charlie McCarthy, Fanny Brice, and Jack Benny.

Instead, the boys were granted a different honor: as had been the case in the past, many of the biggest names in the entertainment industry lauded the Stooges for their importance to the world of comedy and their influence on American culture and their personal lives. During his acceptance speech at the 1987 Emmy Awards, Bruce Willis, a self-proclaimed rabid Stooges fan, thanked the people responsible for his success, adding that "three of them you already know: Moe, Larry, and Curly." (Willis, during an interview that year, added that he would love to play Larry—with John Candy as Curly—in a new Stooges movie.)

Comedian Mel Brooks, also a devout fan of the trio's work, noted, "They were so good. You believed that Moe was sticking his fingers in Curly's eye sockets, and the sound effects made it utterly convincing." As famed director Quentin Tarantino (*Pulp Fiction*, *Jackie Brown*, *Kill Bill*) explained, "I think that, to me and my friends, and people of my generation, the Stooges sound effects have become the sound track of

our lives. The woop-woops, nyuk, nyuks—they're in our psyche, we've been marinated in it."

Oscar-winning director Robert Zemeckis counted himself among those who had seen "every single episode, watched them as I grew up in Chicago where they played every afternoon, and have most of the dialogue memorized." And writer/director Steve Oedekerk (*Ace Ventura: When Nature Calls* and the 1996 remake of *The Nutty Professor*) added, "With the Stooges, you felt like they were a family, hung out together all the time. . . . You got the sense they never did anything alone, ever, like they were one guy."

Among the many other self-professed admirers was the late "King of Pop," Michael Jackson. The soft-spoken native of Gary, Indiana, became a huge fan of them while watching reruns of their comedies on television with his brothers growing up. "Curly was definitely my favorite," he said. "He was unquestionably a comic genius who understood ad-libbing better than anyone. I loved the Stooges' slapstick action and especially Curly's funny noises and his silly, child-like mannerisms and attitudes."

Comedian Whoopi Goldberg was just as forthcoming in her praise. Sometime in 1987, she gushed, "What wonderful memories I have of the Stooges. When I was growing up I remember coming home and turning on Channel 11 with Officer Joe Bolton. Man! The whole evening for me was set on the Stooges. My older brother and I watched, as did my mother. . . . To me, and to millions of others who grew up weaned on their comedies, the Stooges were something special. Today, as a professional, I marvel at what they achieved in their lengthy, fifty-year careers."

And Penn Jillette, one-half of the comedy team Penn & Teller, proclaimed in an interview, "The Three Stooges taught me the most important lesson a kid could learn, which is the difference between fantasy and reality. They taught me about a kind of friendship that lived outside of society, and that you could do wonderful violence in art, without having it spill into life at all."

This admiration for the Stooges and their humor is shared by super Stooge fan Michael Stich, noted television director. For him, every Friday is "Stooge Friday": ensconced in his director's chair at CBS studios in Hollywood, he plays Stooge comedies on twenty-one of the studio's monitors while allocating the remaining

Joan Maurer (fourth from left) with *The Bold and the Beautiful* crew (front row) Steven Wacker, Clyde Kaplan, her cousin Bonnie Reich, Rhonda Friedman, Chuck Guzzi, and (back row) director Michael Stich on Stage 31, on "Stooge Friday" at the CBS studios in Hollywood in 2001. *Courtesy of Joan Maurer*

half-dozen screens to his and his crew's work directing and editing the latest episode of the popular daytime soap opera *The Bold and the Beautiful.*

Various musical artists, rock groups, and songwriters—too numerous to list—have similarly exalted the Stooges in their music. On their fourth album, 1983's *Soak It Up*, Barnes & Barnes, consisting of Robert Haimer and Bill Mumy (the same Bill Mumy who played child prodigy Will Robinson on TV's *Lost in Space*), impersonated Curly's "Hi ya, toots!" on the song "Objectivity," and on the album's jacket dedicated the LP to the world-famous third Stooge. Longtime Stooges fan Russ Dwarf of Toronto-based Killer Dwarfs wore a Three Stooges T-shirt in the group's first music video, *Heavy Mental Breakdown*. In one of its late 1980s albums, Cheap Trick included samples of some famous Stooges sounds (n'yuk-n'yuk-n'yuks, face slapping, wooo-wooo-wooos, etc.), while members of the group Black Oak Arkansas spouted Stooge sayings—"Hey, Moe! Hey, Larry! Soitenly! Hey, Moe! Wooo-wooo-wooo-wooo-wooo!"—on their album *Ready as Hell*. In the song "Hairstyles and Attitudes," Timbuk 3 sang, "Scientists put us into three categories, according to which one of the Three Stooges we resemble the most." And the group Interlewd performed a Curly impersonation for the song "Taxidermy."

The biggest-selling musical homage to the Stooges was the 1983 novelty song "The Curly Shuffle," recorded on the ACME Records independent label by the Jump 'N the Saddle Band. With the band's lead vocalist, Peter Quinn, mimicking many of Curly Howard's catchphrases, the song rocketed up to number 15 on Billboard's Hot 100 in early 1984.

Later, in 1990, Alan Lieberman wrote and recorded a hilarious new song honoring the late, great Larry Fine, called "Along Came Larry," which aired on Dr. Demento's syndicated radio program. The song features comical lyrics about the Stooges sung to the tune of the mid-1960s hit "Along Came Mary" by The Association.

Meanwhile, a growing army of late-night comics, comedians, and famous television personalities were also paying tribute to the Stooges, frequently making them the topic of their timely jokes. For instance, in a spring 1988 broadcast of NBC's *Tonight Show*, Johnny Carson incorporated a reference into his nightly monologue: in talking about Gary Hart's reentry into the presidential race that year, he quipped that "Jesse Jackson must feel like Shemp of The Three Stooges felt when Curly returned to the act." In a December 1988 broadcast of NBC's *Late Night with David Letterman*, Letterman gave his list of "The Top Ten Things Overheard at the General Electric Christmas Party"; number 8 was "No, no, first it was Curly, then Shemp, then Joe." In the January 1989 premiere of his new television talk show, Pat Sajak of *Wheel of Fortune* fame held a small rubber reflex hammer up to the camera and said, "It's sad. This is all that's left of the Moe Howard estate." And on a later broadcast

of *Saturday Night Live*, comedian Dennis Miller, as the host of the popular "Weekend Update" segment, displayed a picture of Moe, Larry, and Curly-Joe riding a rocket ship (from *Have Rocket--Will Travel*) and announced, "The Pentagon this week unveiled its newest weapon, the Stooge missile, which can be computer programmed to hit a target in *both* eyes at a range of over ten thousand miles!"

On August 24, 1988, in honor of their contributions to motion picture comedy, the famous tourist attraction the Movieland Wax Museum in Buena Park, California, added wax statues of The Three Stooges (Moe, Larry, and Curly) to its collection. During a special ceremony hosted by well-known radio and TV personality Gary Owens, Moe's daughter, Joan, and grandson, Jeffrey Scott, unveiled the life-sized wax and fiberglass statues sculpted by artist David Cellitti. Comparing the statues to the works of French impressionist Monet, Owens joked, "As the Stooges so often pointed out, a fool and his Monet are soon parted." The museum closed in 2005, but

Joan Maurer and son Jeffrey Scott join master of ceremonies Gary Owens at the 1987 unveiling of the Stooges wax figures at the Movieland Wax Museum in Buena Park, California. *Courtesy of Joan Maurer Collection*

in San Antonio, Texas, wax figures of the Stooges are among more than two hundred lifelike statues of famous figures on display at the Louis Tussaud's Waxworks museum.

The Stooges also continued to be held in high esteem internationally, where translated versions of their film comedies aired on television after being shown in theaters. In China, they would become famous as *Sānge Chòu Píjiàng* ("Three Smelly Shoe-makers"), in Japan as *San Baka Taishō* ("Three Idiot Generals"), in Spain as *Los Tres Chiflados* ("The Three Crackpots"), and in Brazil as *Os Três Patetas* ("The Three Goofies"). Not until 1990 were the Stooges finally broadcast on New Zealand television when their later features with Curly-Joe DeRita, *Have Rocket--Will Travel*, *The Three Stooges in Orbit*, *The Three Stooges Meet Hercules*, and *The Three Stooges Go Around the World in a Daze* aired on the Sky Channel; fans awaiting that day, who had previously had to find other ways to see the Stooges' films, were elated.

The previous year, the most outrageous alleged example of the Stooges' international appeal was widely reported. On the March 31 broadcast of the television investigative news program *Inside Edition*, then-host Bill O'Reilly listed the "Top Five Tabloid Newspaper Headlines" of the week; at number one was the *National Examiner* story "Three Stooges Worshipped by Weird Savages." The tabloid claimed that a leading anthropologist had discovered a strange island where tribesmen revered the Stooges, wearing their hair like Moe, throwing their food, and slapping each other.

It was not the only time the Stooges were the subject of bizarre stories in supermarket tabloids. In 1988, the *Weekly World News* featured them in a story about Libyan leader Moammar Gadhafi titled "Has Madman Moammar Lost His Marbles—His Heroes Are the 3 Stooges!" In May 1990, the paper profiled a woman seeking a divorce from her husband of four years in the story "The Year's WACKIEST Divorce— My Hubby Thinks He's One of the 3 Stooges!" Not to be outdone, that same year the *National Enquirer* published several questionable stories of its own. The first was entitled "3 Stooges Make Queen Bust a Gut," about Queen Elizabeth II reportedly mimicking the trio after watching their films, with some aides calling Buckingham Palace "Yuk-ingham Palace" because of her outrageous antics.

In the 1990s, Columbia and the successor to its television division, Sony Pictures Television, began the practice of licensing the Stooges shorts to cable networks and precluding them from being broadcast on local television stations. Only a few major mar-ket stations currently air the Stooges shorts, thanks to the long-term syndication contracts they'd pre-viously signed with Columbia Pictures Television: WSBK-TV, Boston, where the films have been broadcast since the 1960s (the station resumed air-ing them in September 1997 after a two-year hiatus), and WMEU-CA, Chicago, which airs the films on its *Stooge-a-Palooza* block, hosted by Rich Koz. After dropping the package in 1994, KTLA-TV in Los Angeles began airing the films again in 2007 as part of the station's sixtieth anniversary celebration and occasionally broadcasts its original 16 mm prints as holiday marathons.

Although the new licensing tactics largely removed the Stooges from local broadcast television, the Stooges' popularity thrived in the 1990s thanks to rebroadcasts and tributes on cable stations and network television. On Friday, October 22, 1993, the ninetieth anniversary of Curly Howard's birth, TBS held a Curly All Nighter! marathon, airing thirty different Stooges shorts with Curly, plus videos of Curly impersonators sent in by viewers. Earlier in the month, the superstation had aired several Stooge specials: an all-night showing of the six feature films with Curly-Joe DeRita and an eleven-hour marathon titled All the World's a Stooge. In December 1995, the A&E cable network aired a new hour-long doc-umentary of the team as part of its highly watched *Biography* series.

Then, from February 19, 1996, to January 2, 1998, The Family Channel ran the Stooges shorts as part of its *Stooge TV* block. The network officially launched the series with a seven-hour marathon of twenty-one shorts (fourteen with Curly, seven with Shemp), and subsequently aired the series as part of its late-night lineup, from 11 PM to midnight EST. After the showings produced high ratings, more were added, weekdays from 6 to 7 PM.

But the Stooges received their biggest exposure in years on network television. On May 15, 1997, ABC aired a prime-time Three Stooges special, *The Three Stooges Greatest Hits*. Hosted by Martin Short, the one-hour tribute featured Little Richard singing

"The Curly Shuffle" and Barry Williams—Greg on TV's *The Brady Bunch*—singing "The Three Stooges Three," to the tune of *The Brady Bunch*'s famous theme. Intercut throughout the program were many film clips of the Stooges.

By 1998, Columbia Pictures had given the Stooges shorts' syndication package a fresh new look by digitally remastering the team's 190 comedies and incorporating them into half-hour segments. Each segment featured one unedited short with trivia and background on the making of the films. Cable network American Movie Classics (AMC) bought the rights to the digitally enhanced, uncut films and originally aired them in two-hour blocks on Saturday and Sunday mornings, under the name *Stooges Playhouse*. In 1999, AMC repackaged the films as part of a new series called *N.Y.U.K.* (New Yuk University of Knuckleheads), featuring Leslie Nielsen as a host/professor of Stoogeology. In this form, the Stooges aired nightly (three shorts per hour) until 2002. AMC continued to broadcast the films until 2004, when Spike TV picked up the package and aired it as the *Stooges Slap-Happy Hour* until 2007. Periodic showings followed until Spike TV canceled the Stooges in late April 2008. On December 31, 2009, AMC resumed broadcasting the Stooges films with a New Year's Eve marathon called *Countdown with the Stooges*.

It was not only on television that Three Stooges shorts continued to make a splash. Since 1998, the historic Alex Theatre in Glendale, California, has maintained a post-Thanksgiving tradition—an annual Three Stooges Big Screen Event, showing many classic Three Stooges comedies with Curly and Shemp on the silver screen.

The Stooges remained an attractive property for advertisers as well. From May 1 through August 31, 1997, Stroh Brewery Co. used Moe, Larry, and Curly in a major Stooge-themed promotion—part of its recurring "Stroh-a-Party" campaign—giving consumers the opportunity to win one of one thousand free rounds of golf for finding Curly's face on multi-packs of Stroh's or Stroh's Light. In 1999, the boys turned up the laughs when California-based fast-food chain Carl's Jr. featured the trio, in film-clip form, in a series of four nationally broadcast ads. A year later, the Dairy Council, as part of its ongoing national "Got Milk?" ad campaign, spotlighted Curly Howard in a new ad; he was pictured with a bent piece of metal over his head and the caption, "Want Strong Bones?"

The 1990s also saw the Stooges expand their reach to a new medium: the Internet. In 1995, the first Usenet group dedicated to the group (alt .comedy-slapstick.3-stooges) debuted. In the years since then, many sites have sprouted up on the World Wide Web. Launched by fans and devotees, these sites cover all aspects of the Stooges' careers, their films, and their humor, and they have become places for Stooges fans to interact and display their appreciation of these great comedy masters. Popular sites include C3 Entertainment's official Three Stooges website, www.threestooges.com; www.stoogeworld.com; and www.threestooges.net, the most comprehensive Three Stooges site on the Internet.

In 1999, a major newspaper survey gave further evidence of the Stooges' enduring name recognition and likeability. The survey, published around the country, showed that 59 percent of teenagers polled said they could name The Three Stooges, while only 41 percent could name the three branches of the federal government.

Interest in the Stooges skyrocketed in 2003, as fans marked the team's seventy-fifth anniversary. During the yearlong celebration, C3 Entertainment released new officially licensed products, and on April 1, NBC produced and aired an original prime-time special to fete the famed comedy trio. The hour-long program, *The Three Stooges 75th Anniversary Special*, was hosted by former *Cheers* star Woody Harrelson.

In 2005, Philadelphia's homegrown Stooge, Larry Fine, was honored with a new larger-than-life mural at the corner of Third and South Streets downtown. After a previous mural, erected in 2000, deteriorated and had to be removed, artist David McShane created a new design to replace it, featuring Larry playing a violin over a bull's-eye background.

The previous year, nearby Ambler, Pennsylvania, was the site of an even greater tribute to all the Stooges. There, in 2004, The Stoogeum was opened. It is the world's first and only museum dedicated to the longest-running comedy act in the history of show business. Located in a ten-thousand-square-foot, three-story former bank building (also the headquarters of Gary Lassin's The Three Stooges Fan Club), The Stoogeum exhibits nearly ten thousand pieces of Three Stooges memorabilia and artifacts cel-

An interactive display and visual history of the Stooges as presented at the Stoogeum, the only museum dedicated to the wacky comedy trio, in Pennsylvania. *Courtesy of the Stoogeum*

ebrating the trio's legacy, from 1918 to the present. It also features a research library, 16 mm film storage vault, and eighty-five-seat theater for film screenings and special presentations.

"What is so compelling about The Three Stooges, and why have they endured?" asked comedy writer and *Mystery Science Theater 3000* star Michael J. Nelson in an article in *TV Guide*. His answer: "It's the universal nature of their predicaments, their struggles." Susan Wloszczyna of *USA Today* put it another way: "Here it is, the dawn of an era exploding with technically sophisticated entertainment and the most primitive purveyors of lowbrow comedy the show biz gods ever blessed are about to become top bananas again." And media psychologist Stuart Fischoff explained, "The longevity of the funnymen [the Stooges] who originally took a licking on the vaudeville stage, just like *South Park*, there is an irreverent hostility but it's *safe hostility*. There's great appeal to youth, not just nostalgia buffs."

Jack Kerouac, that unique voice in American literature, wrote a book in 1952 called *Visions of Cody*, in which he sought to understand America and looked with compassion toward its bygone days. It's amazing to find that in doing so, Kerouac chose to write about The Three Stooges.

In one passage, Kerouac's stand-in, Jack Duluoz, discusses the Stooges with his idol, Cody. He describes

Moe: "Moe the leader, mopish, mowbry, mope-mouthed, mealy, mad, hanking, making others quake; whacking Curly on the iron pate, backhanding Larry (who wonders); picking up a sledgehammer, honk and ramming it down nozzle first on the flatpan of Curly's skull, boing."

Then he goes on to characterize Curly and Larry. "All big dumb convict Curly does is muckle and yukkle and squeal, pressing his lips, shaking his old butt like jelly knotting his Jell-o fists, eyeing Moe, who looks back and at him with that lowered and surly, 'Well what are you gonna do about it?' under the thunderstorm eyebrows like the eyebrows of Beethoven, completely ironbound in his surls, Larry in his angelic or rather he really looks like he conned the other two to let him join the group, so they had to pay him all these years a regular share of the salary to them who work so hard with the props."

After this . . . how can anyone say the Stooges are second rate? They've withstood the test of time handsomely. As *Chicago Sun-Times* critic Gary Deeb wrote, "It looks more like Curly Howard, Larry Fine and Moe Howard may have been the cleverest practitioners of farce comedy ever to ply their trade in this country."

It's no wonder—The Three Stooges were really funny.

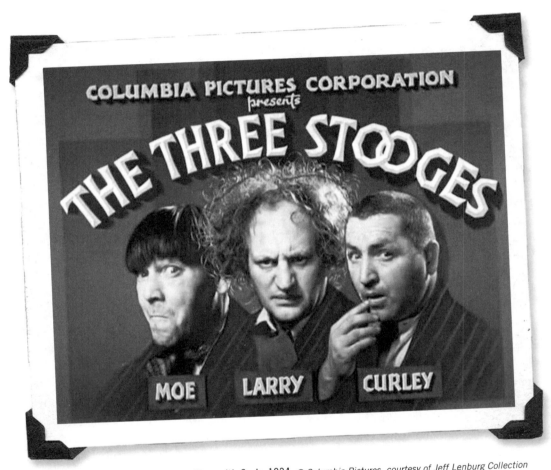

Opening title for the Stooges films with Curly, 1934. © *Columbia Pictures, courtesy of Jeff Lenburg Collection*

# Filmography

In 1982, when *The Three Stooges Scrapbook* was first published, the authors strove to present not only the first Three Stooges filmography ever but the most complete one possible. However, some of the films the authors identified through their original research could not be verified, and without proof of their existence, those movies could not be included. Thirty years have passed since then. During these three decades, dedicated Three Stooges fans and historians around the world have confirmed the existence of these and other film appearances by the Stooges, as a team and as individuals. As a result, this revised filmography contains many new entries. In addition, it contains expanded cast listings and other information that was unavailable when *Scrapbook* was first published.

Each Three Stooges film includes an entertainment rating of ☆ to ☆☆☆☆; the release date, production number, and running time; production credits, a cast listing, and a synopsis; and, where available, working titles, shooting dates, and production footnotes. From June 1959 to June 1968, Columbia Pictures rereleased earlier Three Stooges comedies starring Shemp, Joe, and Curly—and, surprisingly, only four Curly shorts in all—to theaters. Reissued dates, compiled by the authors from previous research and from Richard Finegan's article on the subject in *The Three Stooges Journal* 71 (Fall 1994), are likewise listed.

Each solo film appearance includes the release date, running time, director/writer credits, partial cast listing, and, where available, role portrayed.

Additional information about the listed films may be found at ThreeStooges.net.

Key to Filmography

| | | |
|---|---|---|
| a | = | Art director |
| ad | = | Assistant director |
| AKA | = | Also known as |
| ap | = | Associate producer |
| Br. | = | Broadcast date |
| c | = | Cast |
| d | = | Director |
| ds | = | Dance sequences by |
| e | = | Film editor |
| EPS | = | Episode title(s) |
| exp | = | Executive producer |
| FN | = | Production footnote(s) |
| l | = | Lyrics by |
| m | = | Minutes (running time) |
| md | = | Musical director |
| mu | = | Music by |
| p | = | Producer |
| ph | = | Director of photography |
| Prod. no. | = | Production number |
| PS | = | Production sidelight(s) |
| re. | = | Reissue date |
| Rl. | = | Release date |
| s | = | Sound |
| scr | = | Screenplay by |
| SD | = | Shooting dates |
| sd | = | Set decorator |
| st | = | Story by |
| Synd. | = | Syndication date |
| SYN | = | Synopsis |
| WT | = | Working title(s) |

## TED HEALY AND HIS STOOGES (Larry, Moe, and Shemp)

*Fox Feature*

### 1930

1. SOUP TO NUTS ☆☆ • Rl. Sept. 28 • Prod. no. 331 • 71m • *ap* A. L. Rockett • *d* Benjamin Stoloff • *st* Rube Goldberg • *scr* Rube Goldberg and Howard J. Green • *ph* Joseph Valentine • *e* Clyde Carruth • *s* Al Bruzlin • *c:* Frances McCoy (Queenie), Stanley Smith (Carlson), Lucile Browne (Louise), Charles Winninger (Schmidt), Hallam Cooley (Throckmorton), George Bickel (Klein), and William H. Tooker (Ferguson) • SYN: In this smorgasbord of comedy, Mr. Schmidt's (Charles Winninger's) costume store is bankrupt because he spends his time on Rube Goldberg–style inventions; the creditors send a young manager who falls for Schmidt's niece Louise (Lucile Browne), but she'll have none of him. Schmidt's friends Ted (Ted Healy), Queenie (Francis McCoy), and some goofy part-time firemen (the Stooges and Freddie Sanborn) try to help out; things come to a slapstick head when Louise needs rescuing from a fire. • FN: The Stooges' wives in this film are played by actresses, even though the boys call them by the names of their real-life wives. . . . Presumed lost, *Soup to Nuts* was rediscovered in 1976 by Leonard Maltin in the UCLA Film & Television Archive. With the assistance of The Three Stooges Fan Club Inc., it was restored in the 1990s. On April 26, 2005, it was released on DVD by 20th Century Fox.

## TED HEALY AND HIS STOOGES (Larry, Moe, and Curly)

*MGM Shorts*

### 1933

1. NERTSERY RHYMES ☆☆☆ • Rl. July 6 • Prod. no. 685 • Technicolor • 20m • *d* Jack Cummings • *c:* Ted Healy (Father) and Bonnie Bonnell (Fairy Princess) • SYN: As children, the Stooges are unable to sleep in their oversized crib and ask their father, Ted Healy, to tell them a bed-time story. In order to appease them, Healy croons a comedic rendition of "The Midnight Ride of Paul Revere." When his comical tale fails to put them into slumber, Healy produces a Fairy Princess out of the boys' bedroom closet to put them to sleep with her own fairytale. Her storytelling is a success, and Ted and the Fairy Princess try tiptoeing out of the trio's room to have a night on the town. Curly wakes up, however, spots the couple together, and wakes up Moe and Larry, screaming at Ted to tell them another bed-time story. Enraged, Ted brandishes a mallet and wallops his Stooges unconscious as the film fades out. • WT: *Nursery Rhymes* • FN: Originally Edward Sedgwick, an MGM director, was reported to have directed the film, but instead he supervised its making. Jack Cummings assumed directorial duties, replacing director/screenwriter Nick Grinde, best known for helming an MGM Pete Smith comedy short and cowriting the Laurel and Hardy feature *Babes in Toyland* (1934). . . . Ted Healy, Moe Howard, and Matty Brooks collaborated on the original eight-page script, as well as on scripts in the entire series. . . . Act is billed on-screen as Ted Healy, Howard, Fine and Howard, and Bonny. . . . *Nertsery Rhymes* was the team's first musical-comedy revue (billed as Colortone Musical Revues) and the first of two experimental two-strip Technicolor shorts for MGM.

2. BEER AND PRETZELS ☆☆ • Rl. Aug. 26 • Prod. no. 690 • 20m • *d* Jack Cummings • *mu* Al Goodhart • *l* Gus Kahn • *c:* Bonnie Bonnell (Nightclub Singer) and Ed Brophy (Happy Hour Theatre Manager) • SYN: This brassy comedy is based on Ted Healy's controversial offstage life. Healy and his Stooges are thrown off the bill at the Happy Hour Theatre, since Ted is more interested in women then he is in performing. He promises to give up women but soon spots a statuesque blonde (Bonnie Bonnell) bending over to pick up a handkerchief. Bonnie brushes off Ted, and the Stooges insist that they better find jobs if they are going to eat. When they win jobs as head waiter and three assistants at a local nightclub, Bonnie turns up again as the nightclub's singer and belts out a medley of songs, while Larry and Curly wreak havoc in the swank restaurant. With the club left like a battlefield, our story comes full circle when the manager fires Ted and his Stooges for demolishing the restaurant. This time Ted swears off women for good. But his promise is short-lived, as he eyes a beauteous woman leaning over and turning up her stockings. When Healy puts on the charm, however, the lady turns out to be an undercover policeman. • WT: *Beer Gardens* • FN: Act is billed on-screen as Ted Healy, Howard, Fine and Howard, and Bonny.

3. HELLO POP! ☆☆☆ • Rl. Sept. 16 • Technicolor • Prod. no. 696 • 17m • *d* Jack Cummings • *song* "I'm Sailing on a Sunbeam" by Irving Berlin • *c:* Bonnie Bonnell (Bonnie), Henry Armetta (Italian Musician), The Albertina Rasch Girls (Dancers), Edward Brophy (Brophy), and Tiny Sandford (Strongman) • SYN: While putting on a costume show, Ted is beset by producer problems and aggravated by the undependability of his "pals," the Stooges. The climax comes when the Stooges slip onto the stage underneath the enormous hoopskirt of the featured vocalist, ruining the scene and the show. • WT: *Back Stage, New Musical Short by Suber,* and *Ted Healy Short* • FN: Act is billed on-screen as Ted Healy, Howard, Fine and Howard, and Bonny. . . . Since MGM no longer has prints available of this film, the rating and synopsis are derived from Hollywood trade paper reviews.

4. PLANE NUTS ☆☆½ • Rl. Oct. 14 • Prod. no. 680 • 20m • *d* Jack Cummings • *c:* Bonnie Bonnell (Bonnie). • SYN: In their fourth musical-comedy revue, the third in black-and-white, Ted Healy and his Stooges rehash their old vaudeville act intact; the film also features sev-

eral other acts as well. Three-fourths of the production, however, is strewn with musical numbers taken from MGM musicals, or Ted Healy singing his favorite love song, "The Dance Until the Dawn." The comedy usually hits a feverish pitch when the Stooges interrupt Healy during his singing segments. One sketch that appears in the film—Healy taking a mental test—was later incorporated in several of the Stooges' Columbia comedies. The film dissolves into several army musical numbers near the film's closing. The last dance number features The Albertina Rasch Girls dressed as fighter airplanes! • WT: *Aviation Short* and *Around the World Backwards* • FN: Deleted is a segment in which Ted and the Stooges board a plane and embark on a trip around the world—only backward. Photos of this missing sequence may be found on pages 57 and 58 of *Moe Howard & the 3 Stooges.* . . . Act billed on-screen as Ted Healy, Howard, Fine and Howard, and Bonny.

**1934**

5. THE BIG IDEA ☆ • Rl. May 12 • Prod. no. 628 • 20m • *d* William Crowley • *ds* Sammy Lee • *c:* Bonnie Bonnell (Cleaning Lady), Muriel Evans (Ted's Girlfriend), Tut Mace (Dancer), The Three Radio Rogues (Themselves), and the MGM Dancing Girls (Themselves) • SYN: Ted Healy is a frustrated scriptwriter in search of that "big idea." He is working late in the office to finish and deliver one of his new screenplays when a building matron breaks into his office, spilling garbage on the floor and combining it with the rubbish found in Healy's office. Her constant interruptions ruin Ted's intense concentration, but the main series of noisy interruptions occurs when the Stooges enter Healy's office sounding trumpets, then squirting water in Ted's face. This turns into a running gag throughout the film, with the Stooges returning each time with a different instrument, only to douse Healy with water again and again. • FN: When *The Big Idea* was

later reissued, new title cards were inserted in the existing preprint material in order for MGM to cash in on the Stooges' newfound popularity at Columbia, minus Ted Healy. Hence, the billing was changed from "Ted Healy, with Howard, Fine and Howard" to "Ted Healy . . . With His Three Stooges (Howard, Fine and Howard)." Gee, those studio people were sure clever. . . . Film clip used in *Hollywood: The Gift of Laughter* (ABC-TV, 5/16/82).

Ted Healy and His Stooges also appeared in the following newsreels: Columbia's *Screen Snapshots Series 13 #5* (2/18/34) and Paramount's *Hollywood on Parade No. B-9* (3/30/34).

## Feature Films
All were released by MGM unless otherwise noted.

**1933**

1. MEET THE BARON ☆☆½ • Rl. Oct. 20 • Prod. no. 710 • 68m •

One-sheet for the Ted Healy and His Stooges short *Plane Nuts* (1933).
© Metro-Goldwyn-Mayer, courtesy of Jeff Lenburg Collection

*p* David O. Selznick • *d* Walter Lang • *st* Herman Mankiewicz and Norman Krasna • *scr* Allen Rivkin and P. J. Wolfson • *ph* Al Siegler • *e* James E. Newcom • *c:* Jack Pearl (Baron Impersonator), Jimmy Durante (Joe McGoo), Zasu Pitts (Zasu), Edna May Oliver (Dean Primrose), Ben Bard (Charley), Henry Kolker (Real Baron), and William B. Davidson (Radio Interviewer) • SYN: In this film, Jack Pearl is a pants presser who assumes the identity of Baron Munchausen. Ted Healy is the campus janitor of Cuddles College, who calls on three plumbers, played by the Stooges, to mend a leak. "Ted Healy and His Stooges nearly steal the picture" (*Times-Mirror*).

One-sheet for Ted Healy and His Stooges' first feature film, *Meet the Baron* (1933).

© Metro-Goldwyn-Mayer, courtesy of Jeff Lenburg Collection

2. DANCING LADY ☆☆½ • Rl. Nov. 24 • Prod. no. 694 • 94m • *exp* David O. Selznick • *ap* John W. Considine • *d* Robert Z. Leonard • *scr* Allen Rivkin and P. J. Wolfson,

from the novel by James W. Bellah • *ph* Oliver T. Marsh • *ds* Sammy Lee and Eddie Prinz • *songs* Burton Lane and Harold Adamson, Richard Rodgers and Lorenz Hart, and Jimmy McHugh, Dorothy Fields, and Arthur Freed • *e* Margaret Booth • *c:* Joan Crawford (Janie Barlow), Clark Gable (Patch Gallagher), Franchot Tone (Tod Newton), Ted Healy (Steve), Moe Howard, Larry Fine, and Jerry Howard (Stage Hands), Winnie Lightner (La Rue), Fred Astaire (Himself), Robert Benchley (Ward King), Gloria Foy (Vivian Warner), Art Jarrett and Nelson Eddy (Themselves), Grant Mitchell (Bradley Sr.), Maynard Holmes (Bradley Jr.), May Robson, and Sterling Holloway • SYN: A musical-comedy extravaganza centering on the romances of singer-dancer Janie Barlow with Patch Gallagher and playboy Tod Newton. In several sequences, Healy and His Stooges, as stage manager and stage assistants, are seen with Joan Crawford.

3. MYRT AND MARGE ☆☆ • Rl. Dec. 4 by Universal • Prod. no. F8 • 65m • *d* Al Boasberg • *st* Beatrice Banyard • *scr* Al Boasberg • *ph* J. A. Valentine • *songs* M. K. Jerome • *ds* Jack Haskell • *c:* Myrtle Vail (Myrt), Donna Damerel (Marge), Ted Healy (Mullins), Moe Howard, Larry Fine, and Jerry Howard (Mullins's Helpers), Bonnie Bonnell (Suzannah), Eddie Foy Jr. (Eddie Hanley), Grace Hayes (Grace), Trixie Friganza (Mrs. Minter), Thomas Jackson (Jackson), Ray Hedges (Clarence), J. Farrell MacDonald (Grady) and The Colenette Ballet (Dancers), Jimmy Conlin (Comedian in Show), Peter Lind Hayes (Young Man at Radio Station), and Bo-Ching and Bo-Ling (Themselves) • SYN: A meagerly bankrolled musical-comedy troupe is en route to New York where Myrt hopes to discover a savior in the form of a rich financial backer. Stagehands Ted Healy and His Stooges, who hope to join the show, encounter a backstage crasher, played by Bonnie Bonnell. "Ted Healy and his Stooges,

by sticking to their own vaudeville technique, and probably undirected except for Healy, come through with a minimum of stilted moments" (*Variety*). FN: Reports that Healy, Howard, Fine, and Howard did not appear in *Myrt and Marge* are erroneous. (See *Moe Howard & the 3 Stooges*, page 58. Bottom photo is from *Myrt and Marge*, not *Dancing Lady*.)

**1934**

4. FUGITIVE LOVERS ☆☆½ • Rl. Jan. 5 • Prod. no. 716 • 84m • *ap* Lucien Hubbard • *d* Richard Boleslavsky • *st* Ferdinand Reyher and Frank Read • *scr* Albert Hackett, Frances Goodrich, and George B. Seitz • *a* Arnold Gillespie • *ph* Ted Tetzlaff • *e* William S. Gray • *c:* Robert Montgomery (Porter), Madge Evans (Letty), Ted Healy (Withington Jr.), Nat Pendleton (Legs), C. Henry Gordon (Daly), Ruth Selwyn (Babe), and Moe Howard, Larry Fine, and Jerry Howard (The Three Julians) • SYN: A chorus girl (Madge Evans) takes a bus trip west in hope of becoming a star. Her unwelcome suitor (Nat Pendleton) keeps following her from bus station to bus station, determined to win her love. A comic drunk (Ted Healy) and three assistant drunks (the Stooges) are also passengers. • WT: *Overland Bus* and *Transcontinental Bus*

5. HOLLYWOOD PARTY ☆☆½ • Rl. June 1 • Prod. no. 695 • 70m • *d* Edmund Goulding, Russell Mack, Richard Boleslavsky (musical sequences), George Stevens (comedy sequences), Sam Wood (one skit), Allan Dwan (added scenes), Charles Reisner (remaining scenes), and Roy Rowland, all uncredited • *scr* Howard Dietz and Arthur Kober • *mu* Richard Rodgers and Lorenz Hart, Walter Donaldson and Gus Kahn, Nacio Herb Brown and Arthur Freed • *ds* Seymour Felix, George Hale, and David Gould • Animated cartoon sequences courtesy of Walt Disney Productions • Color sequence photographed by Technicolor • *ph* James

Wong Howe • *e* George Boemler • *c:* Jimmy Durante (Himself/Schnarzan), Jack Pearl (Baron Munchausen), Charles Butterworth (Harvey Clemp), Polly Moran (Henrietta), Eddie Quillan (Bob), June Clyde (Linda), George Givot (Liondora), Ted Healy (Ted), Moe Howard (Moe), Larry Fine (Larry), and Jerry Howard (Curly), Stan Laurel and Oliver Hardy (Themselves), Richard Carle (Knapp), Ben Bard (Charley), Frances Williams (Herself), Robert Young, Arthur Treacher, Tom Kennedy, Walt Disney (Voice of Mickey Mouse), Lupe Velez • SYN: Jimmy Durante throws an elegant Hollywood party, inviting affluent professional people. At the same time, however, Durante tries increasing his collection of animal artifacts by influencing Baron Munchausen (Jack Pearl) to sell him his menagerie. Outside Durante's party, Ted Healy and His Stooges, posing as a reporter and photographers, try to crash this swank affair. A group of professors mistake the Stooges for prime examples of Cro-Magnon man! • WT: *Broadway to Hollywood* • FN: None of the above-mentioned directors received screen credit. Their names were expertly compiled by author Randy Skretvedt.

**1964**

6. MGM'S THE BIG PARADE OF COMEDY • ☆☆½ • Rl. Sept. 23 • 110m • *ap* Alfred Dahlem • *d p scr l* Robert Youngson • *mu* Bernard Green • *c:* Les Tremayne (Narrator), Stan Laurel and Oliver Hardy, Bud Abbott (Doc) and Lou Costello (Wishy), the Marx Brothers, W. C. Fields, Lucille Ball, Wallace Beery, Robert Benchley, Joan Crawford, Jimmy Durante, James Finlayson, Clark Gable, Buster Keaton, Bert Lahr, Myrna Loy, Nat Pendleton, Zasu Pitts, William Powell, Spencer Tracy, Franchot Tone, Lupe Velez, Lee Tracy, Polly Moran, John Gilbert, Harry Gribbon, Leo Carrillo, Clarence H. Wilson, Frank Austin, Richard Cramer, Jean Harlow, Robert Taylor, George Tobias, Brian Don-

levy, Barnett Parker, Marion Davies, Carole Lombard, Elisha Cook Jr., Charlie Chaplin, Marie Dressler, Owen Moore, John Carroll, Lionel Barrymore, Cary Grant, Lew Cody, Freddie Bartholemew, Melvyn Douglas, Anita Page, Greta Garbo, Red Skelton, Katharine Hepburn, Gail Patrick, Lewis Stone, Chester Morris, Karl Dane, George K. Arthur, Dave O'Brien, Monta Bell, Tod Browning, Josephine Crowell, Marceline Day, William Haines, John Ireland, and Diana Lewis • SYN: A compilation of scenes from classic MGM comedies from the silent era to the late 1940s. Ted Healy and His Stooges are included in a scene from *Hollywood Party* (6/1/34).

**1983**

7. THE MGM THREE STOOGES FESTIVAL • ☆☆☆½ • Rl. Apr. 20 by United Artists Classics • 100m • *d* Jack Cummings and William Beaudine • *st* Ted Healy • *st scr* Matty Brooks • *l* Gus Kahn • *mu* Al Goodhart • SYN: Ted Healy and His Stooges short subjects *Nertsery Rhymes*, *Beer and Pretzels*, *Plane Nuts*, and *The Big Idea*, as well as Curly Howard's solo short *Roast-Beef and Movies*, were featured in this theatrical presentation.

In her March 8, 1934, "Hollywood in Person" syndicated column, industry insider Molly Merrick reported that Ted Healy and His Stooges were costarring together in the MGM feature *Operator 13*. As Merrick wrote, "Ted Healy and His Stooges are running about in M.G.M. in confederate uniforms" in their latest MGM feature. However, only Ted Healy and Curly Howard appeared in the final released print of the film.

**MOE, LARRY, AND CURLY**
*Feature*
**1933**

1. TURN BACK THE CLOCK ☆☆ • Rl. Aug. 25 by MGM • Prod. no. 689 • 80m • *ap* Harry Rapf • *d* Edgar Selwyn • *st scr* Edgar Selwyn and Ben Hecht • *ph* Harold Rosson • *e* Frank Sullivan • *a* Stanwood Rogers

• *sd* Edwin B. Willis • *mu* Herbert Stothart • *ad* Fred M. Wilcox • *s* Fred Morgan • *c:* Lee Tracy (Joe), Mae Clarke (Mary), Otto Kruger (Ted), George Barbier (Evans), Peggy Shannon (Elvina), C. Henry Gordon (Holmes), and Clara Blandick (Joe's Mother) • SYN: Joe Gimlet is paid a visit at the tobacco store he runs with his wife Mary, by his old friend Ted Wright and his wife Elvina. It seems Ted has done really well for himself. He married the local rich girl, Elvina, whom Joe could have wed. Compared to Ted, Joe is just getting by and wishes he had done things differently. Following a fight with Mary, he is struck by a car. When he wakes up, it is twenty years earlier. Trying to live his life over again, he marries Elvina and becomes wealthy. But, eventually his former life catches up with his new life. And he realizes that is where true happiness lies. The Stooges make a brief appearance as singing guests at Joe and Elvina's wedding reception.

According to ThreeStooges.net, the discovery of promotional *Movietone News* footage and production stills indicate Moe, Larry, and Curly participated in the filming of *The Prizefighter and the Lady* released by MGM on May 27, 1933. However, the footage was cut from the final print of the film.

**THE THREE STOOGES**
**(Moe, Larry, and Curly)**
*Columbia Shorts*
**1934**

1. WOMAN HATERS ☆☆½ • A Musical Novelty • Rl. May 5 • 21m • Prod. no. 112 • *d* Archie Gottler • *st* Jerome S. Gottler • *ph* Joseph August • *e* James Sweeney • *s* Edward Bernds • *c:* Marjorie White (Mary, Larry's Wife), Monty Collins (Mr. Zero, Member), Bud Jamison (Club Chairman), Fred "Snowflake" Toones (Porter), Jack Norton (Justice of the Peace), Tiny Sandford (Mary's Brother, Cop), Walter Brennan (Train Conductor), A. R. Haysel (Mary's Father), Dorothy Vernon (Mary's Mother), June Gittelson (Mary's Sister), Don Roberts (Wed-

ding Guest), Leslie Goodwin, Charles Richman and Gilbert C. Emery, and George Gray • SYN: Larry (Jim) reneges on the Woman Haters Club's oath when he secretly marries a girl named Mary. Moe (Tom) and Curly (Jack) learn of the marriage during Mary and Larry's honeymoon train trip west. While inside Moe and Curly's train berth, Mary informs them that Larry is her husband and that their earlier no-women agreement is no longer binding. To prove her point, she pushes them out the train's window. • SD: four (Tu 3/27–F 3/30/34) • FN: When the film was originally released, Marjorie White received top billing over the Three Stooges, who were credited as "Jerry Howard, Larry Fine, and Moe Howard." White was killed in an automobile accident shortly after the production. (See *Moe Howard & the 3 Stooges,* page 78.)

2. PUNCH DRUNKS ☆☆☆ • Rl. July 13 • Prod. no. 116 • 17m • *d* Lou Breslow • *scr* Jack Cluett • *st* Jerry Howard, Larry Fine, and Moe Howard • *ph* Henry Freulich • *e* Robert Carlisle • *c:* Dorothy Granger (Girlfriend), Casey Columbo (Mr. McGurn), Al Hill (Killer Kilduff, the Champ), Billy Bletcher (Fight Announcer), Arthur Houseman (Fight Timekeeper), Larry McCrath (Referee), and William Irving (Kilduff's Manager) • SYN: Moe, a boxing manager, and Larry, a violinist, discover that when Larry plays "Pop Goes the Weasel," Curly explodes and starts punching any available target. Consequently, Moe offers to manage Curly as the ring's newest boxing sensation and hires Larry to play "Weasel" at ringside, enabling Curly to win each fight. During the championship bout, Larry's violin gets broken and he returns with a campaign bandwagon, blaring the "Weasel" song, which revives Curly, who wins the fight. • WT: *Symphony of Punches* and *A Symphony of Punches* • SD: four (W 5/2–Sa 5/5/34) • FN: *Punch Drunks* is the only Stooges film to credit the

Stooges as writers. In the original treatment, Curly turns boxer and wins every fight when Fuzzy (Larry) plays "Stars and Stripes Forever." . . . Curly becoming fighting mad upon hearing "Weasel" was redone in *The Three Stooges Go Around the World in a Daze* (8/21/63). Remade as *A Hit With a Miss* (12/13/45) with Shemp Howard. (See *Moe Howard & the 3 Stooges,* pages 74–75 and 78.) • PS: According to director Lou Breslow, the song was changed from "Stars and Stripes" to "Weasel" because the latter was public domain and "the only song that was half-funny."

3. MEN IN BLACK ☆☆☆½ • Rl. Sept. 28 • Prod. no. 152 • 19m • Stooges No. 1 • *d* Raymond McCarey • *st scr* Felix Adler • *ph* Benjamin Kline • *e* James Sweeney • *c:* Dell Henderson (Dr. Graves), Jeanie Roberts (Hiccupping Nurse), Billy Gilbert (D. T. Patient), Ruth Hiatt (Whispering Nurse), Bud Jamison (Doctor), Little Billy Rhodes (Midget Patient), Hank Mann (Window Glass Installer), Bobby Callahan (Telegram Messenger), Phyllis Crane (Anna Conda), Arthur "Pat" West and Joe Mills (Bit Men), Irene Coleman, Carmen Andre, Helen Splane, Kay Hughes, Eve Reynolds, Eve Kimberly, Lucile Watson, Billie Stockton and Betty Andre (Nurses), Arthur Rankin, Neal Burns, Joe Fine and Charles Dorety (Attendants), and Charles King (Anesthesiologist) • SYN: At the Los Arms Hospital, three brainless interns—Doctors Howard, Fine, and Howard—promise Dr. Graves, the hospital superintendent, that they will devote the rest of their lives to the glorious cause of "duty and humanity." The first official Three Stooges comedy and first (and only) Stooges film nominated for an Academy Award. • SD: four (W 8/29–Sa 9/1/34) • FN: On August 8, 1934, Columbia moved its comedy department from Gower Street to the California Studio on Beechwood Drive. . . . In *Men in Black*, the Stooges ad-libbed the bizarre medical terminology for their surgical instru-

ments, and several scenes were also cut from Felix Adler's script, including an alternate ending in which the Stooges meet Nell, "their" girl. She turns out to be Siamese triplets!

4. THREE LITTLE PIGSKINS ☆☆☆ • Rl. Dec. 8 • Prod. no. 156 • 20m • *d* Raymond McCarey • *st scr* Felix Adler and Griffin Jay • *ph* Henry Freulich • *e* James Sweeney • *c:* Lucille Ball (Daisy Simms), Gertie Green (Lulu Banks), Phyllis Crane (Molly Gray), Walter Long (Joe Stacks), Joseph Young (Pete, Joe's Henchman), Milton Douglas (Henchman), Lynton Brent (Man Panhandled by Moe), Johnny Kascier (Man Panhandled by Curly), Bobby Burns (Man Panhandled by Larry), Al Thompson (Man with Honest Work), William J. Irving and Charles Dorety (Photographers), Harry Bowen (Man Who Pays Stooges to Carry Signs), Jimmie Phillips, Joe Levine (Little Larry, scenes deleted), Alex Hirschfield (Little Moe, scenes deleted) and Billy Wolfstone (Little Curly, scenes deleted) • SYN: Larry, Moe, and Curly are mistaken for the Three Horsemen, Boulder Dam University's top football players. Joe Stacks, a two-bit gangster, wagers his money on these "athletes" to win the big football matchup of the week. But he soon learns that the boys' knowledge of football is very limited when the Stooges lose the game. Upset over this defeat, Stacks empties his gun into the derrieres of the fleeing Stooges. • SD: four (Th 10/25–F 10/26, M 10/29–Tu 10/30/34) • FN: Loyola University's football team appears in the game-action scenes photographed at Gilmore Stadium in Los Angeles. . . . On many occasions, Moe Howard reported that *Three Little Pigskins* ends with the Stooges relating the climax of the story to their three children. According to an earlier draft script, the scene was planned as an "alternate ending." Stills reprinted in *Moe Howard & the 3 Stooges,* pages 6, 7, and 68, suggest that the segment was indeed filmed, but evi-

dently, the ending was cut from the final release print. • PS: Larry Fine once recalled that numerous injuries were sustained during production of the film. Curly broke his leg after riding down the dumbwaiter, and Larry lost a tooth when Joseph Young, actor Robert Young's brother, socked him in the jaw. (See *Moe Howard & the 3 Stooges,* pages 79 and 81.)

In a deleted scene, Billy Wolfstone, "Little Curly," asks his screen father, "Big Curly," to explain the climax of the story in *Three Little Pigskins* (1934). © *Columbia Pictures, courtesy of Moe Howard Collection*

## 1935

5. HORSES' COLLARS ☆☆☆ • Rl. Jan 10 • Prod. no. 159 • 17m • *d* Clyde Bruckman • *st scr* Felix Adler • *ph* John Boyle • *e* James Sweeney • *c:* Dorothy Kent (Nell), Fred Kohler (Double Deal Decker), Fred Kelsey (Detective Hyden Zeke), Leo Willis (Lobo), Sam Lufkin (Cowboy Shot by Decker), Slim Whittaker (Cowboy), Nelson McDowell (Bartender), Milton Douglas (Waiter), Bobby Callahan (Drunk), June Gittleson (Larry's Dance Partner), Alice Dahl and Nancy Caswell (Dancers), Johnny Kascier (Moe's Double), Bert Young (Curly's Double), Ed Brandenberg (Larry's Double), and Allyn Drake. •

SYN: Double Deal Decker has just robbed poor, sweet Nell of her deed to the ranch, and she hires detective Hyden Zeke to send her three of his *best* men. Who else comes to her aide but The Three Stooges? The boys find Decker at a local saloon, where it is disclosed that Curly goes bonkers every time he sees a mouse. When the Stooges attempt to regain the deed, Curly becomes delirious upon spotting a squiggly mouse and clobbers the villains before Moe and Larry can calm him down. • SD: four (F 11/23–Sa 11/24, M 11/26–Tu 11/27/34) • FN: Painted-on eyelids gag was later reenacted in *Slaphappy Sleuths* (11/9/50).

6. RESTLESS KNIGHTS ☆☆☆½ • Rl. Feb. 20 • Prod. no. 160 • 16½m • *d* Charles Lamont • *st scr* Felix Adler • *ph* Benjamin Kline • *e* William A. Lyon • *c:* Geneva Mitchell (Queen), Walter Brennan (Father), George Baxter (Prince Boris), Chris Franke (Crier), James Howard and Bud O'Neill (Wrestlers), Stanley Blystone (Captain of the Guard), Ernie Young (Henchman), Billy Franey (Toothless Attendant), Jack Duffy, Lynton Brent, Bob Burns, and William Irving (Guards), Al Thompson and Bert Young (Prison Guards), Joe Perry, Dutch Hendrian, Marie Wells, Eadie Adams, Corinne Williams, Dorothy King, and Patty Price • SYN: The Stooges are appointed the queen's royal bodyguards but wind up before a firing squad when she is kidnapped. Their deaths, however, are avoided when the soldiers are distracted by a pretty girl undressing near her window. The Stooges quickly escape as the guards enjoy their peep show, and track down the queen, who is tied up in a wine cellar not far from her captors. Curly leads the kidnappers, one by one, past Moe and Larry, who clobber them unconscious with their clubs. While all of this continues, the queen breaks loose of her bonds and strides past Moe and Larry, getting smashed on the head with their clubs by mistake. • SD: four (W 12/19–Sa 12/22/34) • PS: Charles Lamont, who started directing in 1918 and later piloted many Abbott and Costello features, had his own technique for handling the Stooges: "I made them follow the script. If there was anything I didn't like, I'd cut it out. I was never a great admirer of ad-libs."

7. POP GOES THE EASEL ☆☆☆
• Rl. Mar. 29 • Prod. no. 163 • 20m
• *d* Del Lord • *st scr* Felix Adler • *ph* Henry Freulich • *e* James Sweeney • *c:* Bobby Burns (Professor Fuller), Jack Duffy (Bearded Man), Elinor Vanderveer (Dignified Woman), Phyllis Fine and Joan Howard (Girls Playing Hopscotch), Phyllis Crane (Model in Tights), William Irving (Man Curly Panhandles for Meal), Leo White (French Artist), and Al Thompson (Man in Car) • SYN: Jobless, the Stooges decide that the only way to find employment is to create work. So they grab three brooms in front of a nearby novelty store and begin cleaning up the sidewalks. The store's owner, however, views this act of kindness as an act of robbery and screams for the police, who chase the Stooges into Kraft's College of Arts. There, they ruin the studio with a clay-throwing free-for-all. • FN: Moe's daughter, Joan, and Larry's daughter, Phyllis, appear together in the hopscotch sequence. It was the only time the two girls appeared with their fathers in a Stooges comedy. Jules White's final shooting script included an alternate version of the clay fight scene that was either unfilmed or edited.

8. UNCIVIL WARRIORS
☆☆☆☆½ • Rl. Apr. 26 • Prod. no. 165 • 20m • *d* Del Lord • *st scr* Felix Adler • *ph* John Stumar • *e* Charles Hochberg • *c:* Ted Lorch (Colonel Filbert), Lew Davis, Marvin Loback, Billy Engle, Ford West, and Si Jenks (Officers), Bud Jamison (Butts), Phyllis Crane (Judith), Celeste Edwards (Clementine), Lou Archer (Charlie, Soldier with Limp), James C. Morton (Union General), Charles Dorety, Heinie Conklin, Jack Kenney, Hubert Diltz, Charles Cross, George Gray, Jack Rand, and Harry Keaton (Soldiers), and Wes Warner (Stunt Man) • SYN: During the Civil War, a Northern general summons three undercover agents, Operators 12 (Larry), 14 (Moe), and 15 (Curly), to pose as Southern officers, Lieutenant Duck, Captain Dodge, and Major Hyde. Their mission is to recover enemy secrets from Colonel Butts's mansion. Later that evening, as part of their plan, the Stooges socialize with the Colonel's daughter, Judith, and Curly offers to help frost a layer cake. He pays more attention to Judith, however, and accidentally frosts a quilted potholder; as a result, everyone who eats the "cake" ends

up coughing feathers. Later, to avoid discovery, Larry and Curly leave the room at separate moments to return disguised as Moe's father and mother, Mr. and Mrs. Dodge. Their masquerade is successful until they are asked the whereabouts of the Dodge's baby. Curly's delirious reaction prompts Moe to dash outside and steal any baby that resembles the real one. Moe finds one all right—only this baby turns out to be black. • SD: four (W 3/13–F 3/15, M 3/18/35). • FN: Initially, the characters of Duck, Dodge, and Hyde were supposed to be called Greps, Burp, and Belch. . . . The coughing up feathers gag was redone in *Three Hams on Rye* (9/7/50). The "Charlie, the Guy with the Goofy Limp" bit was revived in *From Nurse to Worse* (8/23/40) and *Hold That Lion!* (7/17/47).

9. PARDON MY SCOTCH ☆☆☆
• Rl. Aug 1 • Prod. no. 168 • 19m
• *d* Del Lord • *st scr* Andrew Bennison • *ph* George Meehan • *e* James Sweeney • *c:* Nat Carr (Bootlegger), James C. Morton (J. T. Walton), Billy Gilbert (Signor Louis Balero Cantino), Grace Goodall (Mrs. Walton), Barlowe Borland and Scotty Dunsmuir (Scotchmen), Gladys Gale (Mrs. Martin), Wilson Benge (Butler), Alec Craig (Bagpiper), Al Thompson (Jones), Symona Boniface and Pauline High (Party Guests), Nena Campana (Piano Player), and Johnny Kascier (Moe's Stand-In) • SYN: The Stooges are hired as handymen at Jones's Drugstore to wait on their boss's customers during his short absence. A local bootlegger enters the store and asks the trio for a pick-me-up. The boys rush to the pharmacy department and mix every conceivable liquid into an old boot, which the bootlegger guzzles down later. Impressed with the brew, he offers the Stooges a chance to make thousands of dollars. All they have to do is masquerade as the McSnort brothers, three Scottish distillers, and crash a party at J. T. Walton's house to sell their "Breath of Heather" to his distinguished guests. At the

Lobby card for *Pop Goes the Easel* (1935). © Columbia Pictures, courtesy of Moe Howard Collection

party, the bootlegger suggests that the Stooges haul in a keg of their home-made Scotch for everyone to taste. All is well until the trio has trouble driving a spigot into the huge barrel. Impatient, Moe raises his mallet and smacks the cask a tremendous blow, causing the keg to explode into a fountain of foam, dousing the party guests. • SD: four (Th 4/11–Sa 4/13, M 4/15/35) • FN: The "Point to the Right" routine was reused many times by the team. Mixing of liquids in a worn-out boot can also be seen in *Out West* (4/24/47), *All Gummed Up* (12/18/47), *Bubble Trouble* (10/8/53), and *Pals and Gals* (6/3/54). Likewise, the segment involving flipping grapes into an opera singer's mouth appears (with cherries instead of grapes) in *Micro-Phonies* (11/15/45). The roll on the fork gag was lifted from Chaplin's *The Gold Rush* (1925).

10. HOI POLLOI ☆☆☆☆ • Rl. Aug. 29 • Prod. no. 207 • 19m • *d* Del Lord • *st scr* Felix Adler • *ph* Benjamin Kline • *e* John Rawlins • *c:* Harry Holman (Professor Richmond), Robert Graves (Professor Nichols), Bud Jamison (Butler), Grace Goodall (Mrs. Richmond), Betty McMahon (Nichols's Daughter), Phyllis Crane (Nichols's Daughter), Geneva Mitchell (Dance Instructor), Kathryn "Kitty" McHugh (Duchess, Curly's Ugly Dance Partner), Blanche Payson (Brunette Dance Partner), James C. Morton (Party Guest with Toupee), William J. Irving (Man Who Dances with Larry), Arthur Rankin, Robert McKenzie, Celeste Edwards, Harriett DeBussman, Mary Dees, George B. French, Gail Arnold, Don Roberts, and Billy Mann. • SYN: In a café, two educators are seen discussing what factors influence the development of human personality. Professor Richmond believes "environment is the keynote to social distinction," while Professor Nichols argues that "heredity is the backbone of all social life." Nichols then wagers $10,000 that he can produce—through exposure to the proper environment—a regular

"social lion" from the lowest strata of life. He picks three rubbish workers, the Stooges, for his experiment. Following months of tutoring, Nichols unleashes the boys at a swank party, but the Stooges' old habits resurface and become contagious with the party-goers, causing a full-scale war. Having had enough of such vulgar behavior, the Stooges leave Professor Nichols's mansion in tuxedos and top hats. • SD: four (Th 5/2–Sa 5/4, M 5/6/35) • FN: Reworked as *Half-Wits Holiday* (1/9/47) and *Pies and Guys* (6/12/58). Stock footage used in *In the Sweet Pie and Pie* (10/16/41). The spring on the trousers gag was also seen in *Asleep at the Switch* (1923) with Ben Turpin, and in the Stooges' *An Ache in Every Stake* (8/22/41) and *Have Rocket--Will Travel* (1959). . . . Holland's film censorship board in The Hague blocked both *Hoi Polloi* and *Half Shot Shooters* from being shown in that country.

11. THREE LITTLE BEERS ☆☆☆½ • Rl. Nov. 28 • Prod. no. 210 • 17m • *p* Jules White • *d* Del Lord • *st scr* Clyde Bruckman • *ph* Benjamin Kline • *e* William Lyon • *c:* Bud Jamison (A. Panther), Nanette Crawford and Eve Reynolds (Girls on Golf Course), Frank Terry (Golfer), Harry Semels (Groundskeeper), Jack "Tiny" Lipson (Foreman), Eddie Laughton (Relief Desk Clerk), George Gray (Caddy), Frank Mills (Golfer), and Harry Semels (Gardener) • SYN: The Panther Brewery Co. is sponsoring a big golf tournament and three of its employees, the Stooges, enter the competition even though they have never played the game before! The golf course, however, never looks the same after the Stooges are through practicing. Curly's ball gets stuck in a tree, and he chops down the tree in order to retrieve the ball. Larry, meanwhile, gets distracted by a small root sticking out of the ground, and starts tugging on it. He keeps yanking on the root until, finally, the course looks like a disjointed jigsaw puzzle. It comes as no surprise when the Stooges are chased off the

golf course. • SD: four (W 10/9–Sa 10/12/35) • FN: The Rancho Golf Course on Pico Boulevard in Beverly Hills, located across the street from the 20th Century-Fox Studios, was the golf course used in the making of this film. . . . The "Press, Press, Pull" gag later appeared in *Even As I O U* (9/28/42). Beer trucks and rolling barrels also can be seen in *What No Beer?* (1933) with Buster Keaton.

## 1936

12. ANTS IN THE PANTRY ☆☆☆ • Rl. Feb. 6 • Prod. no. 218 • 17½m • *ap* Jules White • *d* Preston Black • *st scr* Al Giebler • *ph* Benjamin Kline • *e* William Lyon • *c:* Clara Kimball Young (Mrs. Burlap), Harrison Greene (A. Mouser), Bud Jamison (Professor Repulso), Isabelle LaMal (Clara), Vesey O'Davoren (Gawkins, the Butler), Douglas Gerrard (Lord Stoke Pogis), Anne O'Neal (Matron), Phyllis Crane (Debutante), Al Thompson (Dignified Man), Helen Martinez (Maid), Hilda Title (Mouser's Secretary), Bobby Burns (Guest Who Gets Mouse Down His Back), Lynton Brent, James C. Morton, Arthur Rowlands, Bert Young, Lew Davis, Ron Wilson, Lynton Brent, Arthur Thalasso, Charles Dorety, Elaine Waters, Althea Henley, Idalyn Dupre, Stella LeSaint, Flo Promise, Gay Waters, and Eddie Laughton (Party Guests) • SYN: The Stooges are pest exterminators for the Lightning Pest Control Co., and their boss, A. Mouser, orders them to start stirring up some business if they plan on keeping their jobs. The Stooges select a swank mansion as their first target in which to drum up some new business. As part of their plan, the trio bugs the house—literally—with ants, mice, and termites and then rushes in to ward off the pests when the owner, Mrs. Burlap, screams for help. But, as expected, the Stooges are no help at all. Later, however, Moe, Larry, and Curly make up for their blunders when they enter Burlap's fox hunt. Curly, suffering from a terrible head cold, temporarily becomes the hero when

his sinuses clear upon smelling what he thinks is a fox—but is actually a skunk! • WT: *Pardon My Ants* • SD: four (W 12/11–Sa 12/14/35) • FN: Partially remade as *Pest Man Wins* (12/6/51). (See *Moe Howard & the 3 Stooges*, page 81.)

13. MOVIE MANIACS ☆☆☆ • Rl. Feb. 20 • Prod. no. 213 • 18m • *p* Jules White • *d* Del Lord • *st scr* Felix Adler • *ph* Benjamin Kline • *e* William Lyon • *c:* Bud Jamison (Fuller Rath), Lois Lindsay and Althea Henley (Sound Stage Girls), Kenneth Harlan (Leading Man), Mildred Harris (Leading Lady), Harry Semels (Cecil Z. Sweinhardt, Director), Antrim Short (Cameraman), Jack Kenney, Charles Dorety and Elaine Waters (Studio Employees), Bert Young (Assistant Cameraman), Hilda Title (Script Girl) and Eddie Laughton (Grip) • SYN: With aspirations of becoming movie stars, the Stooges sneak into the Carnation Pictures Studio and, mistaken for the new management team from the East, gain complete control of the lot from the general manager, Fuller Rath. Showing off their new authority, the Stooges invade a movie sound stage and force director Cecil Z. Sweinhardt and his cast to quit. Moe becomes the new director, and Curly and Larry fill in as Carnation's romantic screen couple. When Rath learns that the Stooges are impostors, however, he chases them off the set with the help of two studio guards, right into the lion's den. After a narrow escape, Moe, Larry, and Curly race out of the studio in a limousine, with the lion inside, for parts unknown. • WT: *G-A-G Men* • SD: four (F 10/25–Sa 10/26, M 10/28–Tu 10/29/35) • FN: Deleted was an alternate film ending in which the Stooges accidentally burn down the studio.

14. HALF SHOT SHOOTERS ☆☆☆ Rl. Apr. 30 • Prod. no. 225 • 19m • *ap* Jules White • *d* Preston Black • *st scr* Clyde Bruckman • *ph* Benjamin Kline • *e* Charles Hochberg • *c:* Stanley Blystone (Sergeant MacGillicuddy), Vernon Dent (Man in Restaurant, Dent), Edward LeSaint (Examining Officer),

Harry Semels (Officer Hit by Tomato), Heinie Conklin (Man Exiting Recruiting Office), Bert Young (Messenger Officer), Eddie Laughton (Induction Office Civilian), Lew Davis (Recruiting Officer), and Johnny Kascier (Soldier Hit When Curly Salutes) • SYN: With World War I over, Sergeant MacGillicuddy wakes the Stooges and beats them up for sleeping through the entire war; they receive medals of valor for their wounds. Years later and unemployed, the Stooges accidentally sign up again with the army and meet up with their old comrade, Sergeant MacGillicuddy, who's assigned to their regiment. The Stooges' first duty is to retrieve ammunition for target practice. During their absence, however, target practice is postponed because the admiral's flagship is late in arriving. Unaware of the news, the Stooges fire the cannon and blow up the admiral's flagship. • SD: four (W 3/18–Sa 3/21/36) • FN: Holland's film censorship board in The Hague blocked both *Half Shot Shooters* and *Hoi Polloi* from being shown in that country.

15. DISORDER IN THE COURT ☆☆☆½ • Rl. May 30 • Prod. no. 217 • 16½m • *ap* Jules White • *d* Preston Black • *st scr* Felix Adler • *ph* Benjamin Kline • *e* William Lyon • *c:* Suzanne Kaaren (Gail Tempest), Bud Jamison (Defense Attorney), Harry

Semels (District Attorney), Edward LeSaint (Judge), James C. Morton (Bailiff), Dan Brady and Bill O'Brien (Jurors), Hank Bell (Court Clerk), Nick Baskovitch, Arthur Thalasso, and Ed Mull (Men in Hallway), Al Thompson (Bailiff), Eddie Laughton (Co-Counsel), Solomon Horwitz (Spectator in Courtroom), and Tiny Jones • SYN: Kirk Robbin is found dead at the Black Bottom Cafe, with club dancer Gail Tempest holding a gun and standing over his body. Did she kill him? To find the answer, Larry, Moe, and Curly are called to appear as star witnesses in the murder trial. Throughout their testimony, a trained parrot and witness keeps repeating, "Find the letter." The Stooges break the case wide open when they recover the letter, which is attached to the parrot's claw and proves the dancer's innocence. • WT: *Disorder in the Courtroom* • SD: four (W 4/1–F 4/3, M 4/6/36) • FN: When Moe demonstrates on Curly how Buck Wing shoved Kirk Robbin's skull into a letter press, a rubber head was used to give the effect of Curly's noggin being twisted out of shape. . . . Curly's courtroom testimony is borrowed from *Sidewalks of New York* (1931) with Buster Keaton, directed by Jules White and Zion Myers. . . . Look for the mustachioed Solomon Horwitz, father of Moe,

Lobby card for *Disorder in the Court* (1936). © *Columbia Pictures, courtesy of Jeff Lenburg Collection*

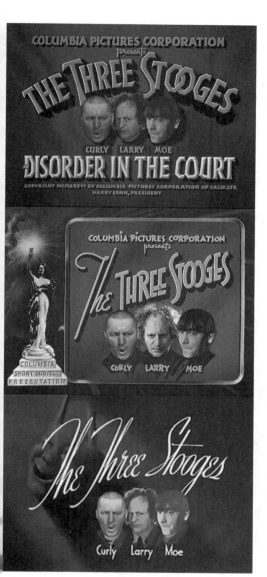

Three other title openings from the Three Stooges shorts starring Curly: (from top to bottom) *Disorder in the Court* (1936), *You Nazty Spy!* (1940), and *Idiots Deluxe* (1945).
© *Columbia Pictures, courtesy Greg Lenburg Collection*

Curly, and Shemp, in the front row of the courtroom audience, second from right.

### 16. A PAIN IN THE PULLMAN

☆☆½ • Rl. June 27 • Prod. no. 223 • 18m • *ap* Jules White • *d st scr* Preston Black • *ph* Benjamin Kline • *e* William Lyon • *c:* Bud Jamison (Johnson), James C. Morton (Paul Pain), Eddie Laughton (Train Conductor), Loretta Andrews, Ethelreda Leopold, Gale Arnold (Showgirls), Ray Turner (Porter), Mary Lou Dix (Karen), Hilda Title (Herself, Shorty), Joe the Mon-

key (Himself), Phyllis Crane (Girl Curly Kisses), Eddie Laughton (Train Conductor), Bobby Burns (Himself/ Man in Berth), and Anne O'Neal (Landlady) • SYN: The Stooges are an unemployed vaudeville act living in a boardinghouse and are behind on their rent. When they get the chance to be in a show, Moe, Larry, and Curly, with their pet monkey, Joe, sneak out of the boarding house and rush to catch a train containing the rest of the show's cast, including Paul Pain, the leading man (who wears a toupee). On board, Joe and the Stooges prove to be nothing but a *pain* for Pain! Joe complicates matters when he wreaks havoc with the sleeping passengers by pulling the emergency cord to stop the train. • SD: four (W 4/29–F 5/1, M 5/4/36) • FN: A remake of *Show Business* (8/20/32) with Thelma Todd and ZaSu Pitts, directed by Jules White. The ending was reused in *A Ducking They Did Go* (4/7/39). (See *Moe Howard & the 3 Stooges*, pages 81–82.) The film was also remade as *Training for Trouble* (1947) with Schilling and Lane.

### 17. FALSE ALARMS ☆☆½ • Rl. Aug. 16 • Prod. No 224 • 18m • *ap* Jules White • *d* Del Lord • *st scr* John Grey • *ph* Benjamin Kline • *e* Charles Hochberg • *c:* Stanley Blystone (Captain), June Gittelson (Minnie), Johnny Grey (Fireman), Bert Young (Car Deliveryman), and Eddie Laughton (Passerby) • SYN: Larry, Moe, and Curly are inept firemen, taking showers when the fire alarm sounds, almost losing their jobs as a result. Despite this near catastrophe, Curly is invited to a party by his girlfriend, where two other girls insist that Curly call Moe and Larry to join them. Rather than telephone them, Curly steps outside and triggers the city's fire alarm system, which rings not only at the Stooges' firehouse but at every other station in the county. Moe and Larry make it to the girls' house by borrowing the chief's brand-new automobile, arriving minutes before the other fire departments respond to the alarm. Disaster strikes,

however, when the Stooges and the girls take a pleasure jaunt in the chief's car, totaling it in an accident. • SD: four (Tu 5/19–F 5/22/36) • FN: ThreeStooges.net, the home of the Three Stooges Online Filmography, reports that Solomon Horwitz, father of Moe, Curly, and Shemp, is seen as a passerby in two scenes: after Moe and Larry arrive at the false alarm called in by Curly (Solomon is wearing a white hat) and after the car crashes into a streetlamp pole.

### 18. WHOOPS, I'M AN INDIAN!

☆☆☆ • Rl. Sept. 11 • Prod. no. 226 • 17m • *ap* Jules White • *d* Del Lord • *st* Searle Kramer and Herman Boxer • *scr* Clyde Bruckman • *ph* Benjamin Kline • *e* Charles Hochberg • *c:* Bud Jamison (Pierre), Elaine Waters and Beatrice Blinn (Saloon Girls), Robert McKenzie (Sheriff), William J. Irving (Bartender), Eddie Laughton (Sidekick), Al Thompson (Deputy Sheriff), Lew Davis, and Blackie Whiteford • SYN: Moe, Larry, and Curly escape a "hanging jury" following some sleight-of-hand tricks during a poker game between them and French Canadian trooper Pierre. Back at his cabin, Pierre learns that his wife has left him for an Indian chief, and he vows to kill all Indians. Sometime later at another saloon, Pierre again meets up with the Stooges, only this time they are garbed as Indians. Although he hasn't forgotten his pledge, Pierre soon weakens at the sight of Curly dressed like an Indian squaw and marries "her." When Pierre realizes Curly is an impostor, however, a chase ensues, with the Stooges taking refuge in the city's jail. • WT: *Frontier Daze* • SD: four (W 6/3–Sa 6/6/36)

### 19. SLIPPERY SILKS ☆☆½ • Rl. Dec. 27 • Prod. no. 221 • 17½m • *ap* Jules White • *d* Preston Black • *st scr* Ewart Adamson • *ph* Benjamin Kline • *e* William Lyon • *c:* Vernon Dent (Mr. Morgan Morgan), Symona Boniface (Mrs. Morgan Morgan), June Gittelson (Mrs. Morgan Morgan's Friend), Elaine Waters, Beatrice

Blinn, Martha Tibbetts, and Beatrice Curtis (Fashion Show Women), Mary Lou Dix, Gale Arnold, and Loretta Andrews (Fashion Show Models), Gertrude Messenger and Hilda Title (Models' Assistants), Eddie Laughton (Manager), William J. Irving (Mr. Romani), Jack Lipson (Bureau Officer), Bert Young (Arresting Officer), Blackie Whiteford (Police Escort), and Elinor Vanderveer (Dress Customer on Turntable) • SYN: Carpenters Larry, Moe, and Curly find working in an antique shop difficult, as they break a valuable Ming vase belonging to Mr. Morgan, the irate owner. Later, they inherit their uncle's ultrasmart Fifth Avenue Dress Salon and stage their first fashion show, during which they meet up again with the angry vase owner, causing a massive cream-puff melee. • SD: four (W 6/10–F 6/12, M 6/15/36) (See *Moe Howard & the 3 Stooges,* pages 88 and 95.)

## 1937

20. GRIPS, GRUNTS AND GROANS ☆☆☆ • Rl. Jan. 15 • Prod. no. 259 • 19m • *ap* Jules White • *d* Preston Black • *st* Searle Kramer and Herman Boxer • *scr* Clyde Bruckman • *ph* Benjamin Kline • *e* Charles Nelson • *c:* Harrison Greene (Ivan Bustoff), Casey Columbo (Tony, Bustoff's Manager), Herb Stagman (Kid Pinkie), Cy Schindell and William J. Irving (Waiters), Blackie Whiteford (Tony's Assistant), Elaine Waters (Tony's Girl), Tony Chavex (Ironhead), Lew Davis (Tony's Gambling Coach), Eva McKenzie (Woman on Street), Budd Fine and Sam Lufkin, Harry Wilson, Chuck Callahan, and Everett Sullivan • SYN: Moe, Larry, and Curly win jobs as trainers and sparring partner, respectively, to the world champion wrestler Ivan Bustoff. The night before the big match, Bustoff gets drunk and Curly has a bout with a woman's bottle of Wild Hyacinth (a perfume that drives Curly wild). Before Bustoff's championship bout, Moe learns that Tony, the fight promoter, has wagered a huge bankroll

on Bustoff to win. But when Curly and Larry accidentally drop dumbbells on Bustoff's head, the champ is unable to answer the bell, and Moe makes Curly take his place, disguised as Bustoff. During the match, however, Curly does miserably until Moe grabs a lady spectator's bottle of Wild Hyacinth. The scent of the perfume enables Curly not only to win the fight but also to knock out everyone else in sight! • SD: four (M 1/12–Tu 1/15/36)

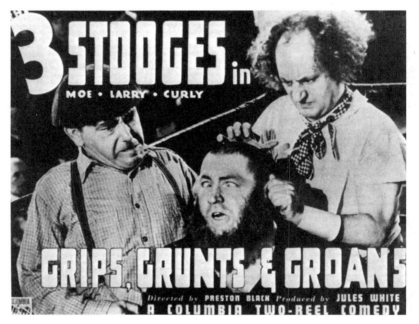

Lobby card for *Grips, Grunts and Groans* (1937). © *Columbia Pictures, courtesy of Moe Howard Collection*

21. DIZZY DOCTORS ☆☆☆ • Rl. Mar. 19 • Prod. no. 263 • 17½m • *ap* Jules White • *d* Del Lord • *scr* Al Ray • *st* Charles Nelson • *ph* Benjamin Kline • *e* Charles Nelson • *c:* June Gittelson (Moe's Wife), Eva Murray (Larry's Wife), Ione Leslie (Curly's Wife), Vernon Dent (Dr. Harry Arms), Frank Mills (Dr. Bright), Louise Carver (Ugly Lady by Car), Ella McKenzie and Harlene Wood (Nurses), Bud Jamison (Cop), Cy Schindell (Orderly), Wilfred Lucas and Eric Bunn (Bit Men), A. R. Haysel (Dandruff Patient), Jack Lipson (Shoe Shine Customer), Lew Davis (Man in Small Car), William J. Irving and Al Thompson (Surgeons), Bert Young (Traffic Cop), and Betty

McMahon • SYN: With their wives upset at them for not working, the Stooges land jobs selling Dr. Brighto's Brighto, a cure-all medicine which the boys use for every *other* conceivable household task. Brighto is the miracle medicine that removes the finish clean off automobiles and burns through the shoulder of a policeman's uniform, as the Stooges find out. Naturally, sales increase when the Stooges realize that Brighto is actually a medicine. They invade the Los Arms Hospital and peddle the stuff to everyone, including Dr. Harry Arms (who lost his hair buying a bottle from the Stooges earlier). He chases them out of the hospital and back home to their wives, where they belong. • SD: four (W 12/9–Sa 12/12/36) • FN: In the closing street scene, Solomon Horwitz, father of Moe, Curly, and Shemp, appears behind the cop, according to ThreeStooges.net.

22. 3 DUMB CLUCKS ☆☆☆ • Rl. Apr. 17 • Prod. no. 266 • 17m • *ap* Jules White • *d* Del Lord • *st scr* Clyde Bruckman • *ph* Andre Barlatier • *e* Charles Nelson • *c:* Lynton Brent (Salesman), Frank Austin (Prison

Guard), Lucille Lund (Daisy), Eddie Laughton (Daisy's Boyfriend), Frank Mills (Henchman), Lynton Brent (Men's Store Clerk), Al Thompson (Pop Howard's Butler), Cy Schindell and Charles Dorety (Wedding Guests) • SYN: The Stooges break out of jail to prevent their pa from marrying a curvaceous blonde named Daisy, who's linked to two gangsters, Butch and Chopper, who plan to kill Pa and collect his money. Curly, who resembles his father (he plays dual roles), doubles for Pa at the wedding in Daisy's penthouse. Complications arise, however, when the *real* Pa arrives during the wedding. As a result, the two crooks chase the Stooges up a flagpole, break the pole, and watch the trio fall two stories below on top of Pa, who just happens to be in front of the hotel. • SD: four (M 2/1–Th 2/4/37) • FN: Remade, with stock footage, as *Up in Daisy's Penthouse* (2/5/53). The hat routine was also in *Steamboat Bill, Jr.* (1928) with Buster Keaton. . . . On the last day of shooting, Curly fell down an elevator shaft and suffered a severe head wound. (See *Moe Howard & the 3 Stooges,* page 101.)

### 23. BACK TO THE WOODS ☆☆½

• Rl. May 14 • Prod. no. 268 • 19½m • *ap* Jules White • *d* Preston Black • *st* Searle Kramer • *scr* Andrew Bennison • *ph* George Meehan • *e* Charles Nelson • *c:* Bud Jamison (Prosecutor), Vernon Dent (Governor), Ted Lorch (Chief Rain in the Puss), Bert Young (Indian) • SYN: Larry, Moe, and Curly are convicted of battling with His Majesty's Guard in colonial times and are sentenced to defend the colonists from the Indians. While the Stooges are protecting their fellow man, however, Larry is captured by savages, prompting a rescue from Moe and Curly. Making their escape, the Stooges hop into a canoe and, with one paddle stroke, cross the lake. • SD: four (W 3/3–Sa 3/6/37) • FN: The ending is stock footage from *Whoops, I'm an Indian!* (9/11/36), making *Back to the Woods* the first Stooges short to contain footage from a previous short.

### 24. GOOFS AND SADDLES ☆☆½

• Rl. July 2 • Prod. no. 274 • 17m • *ap* Jules White • *d* Del Lord • *st scr* Felix Adler • *ph* Benjamin Kline • *e* Charles Nelson • *c:* Ted Lorch (General Muster), Hank Mann (Lem), Stanley Blystone (Longhorn Pete), Sam Lufkin (Colonel), Joe Palma (Man Carrying Stretcher), Eddie Laughton (Bartender), Lew Davis (Gambler), Hank Bell, George Gray, and Ethan Laidlaw • SYN: With cattle rustlers becoming a scourge, General Muster sends for his three best undercover agents to wipe these varmints out: Wild Bill Hiccup (Moe), Buffalo Bilious (Curly), and Just-Plain Bill (Larry). Their target: Longhorn Pete, the leading cattle thief in the country. Disguised as gamblers, the boys play a wild (and dishonest) game of poker with Longhorn Pete, who eventually sees through their cheating ways and threatens to kill them. The Stooges make their exit in a covered wagon, with Pete and his gang in hot pursuit. Upon arriving at an abandoned cabin, Curly accidentally dumps a box of bullets into a meat grinder, creating a terrific machine gun that blasts the outlaws, causing them to surrender. • SD: four (W 4/14–F 4/16, M 4/19/37) • FN: Footage was reused in *Pals and Gals* (6/3/54, covered wagon escape and ending) and *Stop! Look! and Laugh!* (7/1/60). Exchanging cards under the table is also seen in *Out West* (4/24/47) and *Pals and Gals* (6/3/54). The homing pigeon to headquarters gag was milked in *The Private Eyes* (1981) with Don Knotts and Tim Conway.

### 25. CASH AND CARRY ☆☆

• Rl. Sept 3 • Prod. no. 400 • 20m • *ap* Jules White • *d* Del Lord • *st* Clyde Bruckman • *scr* Clyde Bruckman and Elwood Ullman • *ph* Lucien Ballard • *e* Charles Nelson • *c:* Sonny Bupp (Jimmy, the Crippled Boy), Harlene Wood (Jimmy's Sister), Lew Davis and Nick Copeland (Con Men), Eddie Laughton (Bank Teller), Cy Schindell (Vault Guard), John Ince (Captain of the Guard), Lester Dorr (President's Secretary), and Al Richardson (President Roosevelt) • SYN: The Stooges discover that their city dump shack has been taken over by Jimmy, a crippled boy, and his sister. Jimmy needs a leg operation but doesn't have the money. The Stooges take the boy's small life savings and try opening a bank account, thinking it will grow because of interest. Two con men overhear the Stooges and swindle them out of Jimmy's money by selling them a map to Captain Kidd's buried treasure, located in an old mansion. The Stooges dynamite their way into the building, which turns out to be the United States Sub-Treasury. The Stooges are pardoned after explaining their innocence before President Roosevelt, and arrangements are made for Jimmy's leg operation. • WT: *Golddigging in the Treasury* • SD: four (W 5/5–Sa 5/8/37) • FN: Remade as *A Miner Affair* (11/1/45) and *Two April Fools* (6/17/54), both with Andy Clyde.

### 26. PLAYING THE PONIES ☆

• Rl. Oct. 15 • Prod. no. 401 • 17m • *ap* Jules White • *d* Charles Lamont • *st* Will Harr and Irving Frisch • *scr* Al Giebler, Elwood Ullman, and Charley Nelson • *ph* Allen G. Siegler • *e* Charles Hochberg • *c:* William J. Irving (Customers with Dog's Plate), Jack "Tiny" Lipson (Food-Stained-Tie Customer), Billy Bletcher (Track Announcer), Charles Dorety (Pepperino-Eating Customer), and Lew Davis (Con Man) • SYN: Restaurant owners Moe, Larry, and Curly swap the ownership of their restaurant with two city slickers for the con men's alleged prize horse, Thunderbolt. The Stooges soon learn, however, that the thoroughbred is nothing more than a broken-down, half-starved filly. Curly saves the deal when he accidentally feeds Thunderbolt chili pepperinos (thinking they're peanuts), causing the horse to race around the track at blazing speed. With this surefire ingredient, the Stooges enter Thunderbolt in a big sweepstakes race. Jockey Larry energizes Thunderbolt with a handful of the peppers, while Moe and Larry aid the cause, racing in front of the horse with a bucket of water, thus powering her to victory. Afterward, the Stooges wine and dine in their new mansion. • SD: (W 5/12–F 5/14, M 5/17/37) • FN: The gag of chasing a dog past a customer ordering franks and beans was later used in *Malice in the Palace* (9/1/49) and *Rumpus in the Harem* (6/21/56).

27. THE SITTER DOWNERS ☆☆☆ • Rl. Nov. 26 • Prod. no. 402 • 17m • *ap* Jules White • *d* Del Lord • *st scr* Ewart Adamson • *ph* George Meehan • *e* Charles Nelson • *c:* Marcia Healy, June Gittelson, and Betty Mack (Flora Belle, Cora Belle, and Dora Belle), James C. Morton (Mr. Belle), Robert McKenzie (Justice of the Peace), and Bert Young (Truck Driver) • SYN: Mr. Belle refuses to allow the Stooges to marry his daughters, Dora Belle, Flora Belle, and Cora Belle, causing the boys to stage a sit-down strike. Their strike gains national exposure and fame for the trio, including several complimentary gifts, the best being a house on a lot. As a result of their new fame, Mr. Belle gives his blessing, and the Stooges take their brides to their new home, which turns out to be a prefabricated house they have to assemble. When the boys refuse to build the house, the wives stage their own sit-down strike, "No House, No Honeymoon!" Eventually the Stooges weaken and construct the house, which crashes to the ground when Cora Belle carelessly removes one wooden post. • SD: four (F 5/28, M 5/31–W 6/2/37) • FN: Premise was reworked from Buster Keaton's *One Week* (1920). Clyde Bruckman also utilized this same idea in "Honeymoon House," the forty-eighth TV episode of *The Abbott and Costello Show* (1953–4). . . . Marcia Healy, who is featured in this short, is Ted Healy's sister.

**1938**
28. TERMITES OF 1938 ☆☆☆ • Rl. Jan. 7 • Prod. no. 416 • 16½m • *ap*

Charley Chase and Hugh McCollum • *d* Del Lord • *st scr* Elwood Ullman • *ph* Andre Barlatier • *e* Arthur Seid • *c:* Dorothy Granger (Mrs. Sturgeon), Bud Jamison (Lord Wafflebottom), Bess Flowers (Mrs. Muriel Van Twitchett), Symona Boniface, Beatrice Blinn, and Lew Davis (Party Guests), and John Ince • SYN: Mrs. Van Twitchett is in an unenviable predicament. She's throwing a party for some society matron friends and has no escorts. So Van Twitchett misdials the telephone number for Acme Escorts, winding up with the Acme Exterminators, also known as Moe, Larry, and Curly. The Stooges are more than happy to help and end up dining with some most distinguished people, teaching them an entirely different set of table manners, which the guests soon imitate. Later, the Stooges stage a musical act for the guests and then get to work on exterminating the house • SD: four (Tu 10/19–F 10/23/37) • FN: Remade as *Society Mugs* (9/19/46) with Shemp Howard and Tom Kennedy. The gag of playing musical instruments with the aid of a record player was reworked by Abbott and Costello as the famous "All Right!" sketch.

29. WEE WEE MONSIEUR ☆☆½ • Rl. Feb. 18 • Prod. no. 404 • 17m • *ap* Jules White • *d* Del Lord • *st scr* Searle Kramer • *ph* Andre Barlatier • *e* Charles Nelson • *c:* Bud Jamison (Legionnaire Sergeant), Vernon Dent (Tsimmis), John Lester Johnson (Guard), Harry Semels (Landlord), William J. Irving (Captain), and Ethelreda Leopold (Harem Girl from Brooklyn) • SYN: "Paris. Somewhere in France." The landlord is tired of harboring three bogus artists, Moe, Larry, and Curly, who owe him many months back rent. When the landlord threatens to kill the boys, they escape and accidentally sign up for the Foreign Legion. When their commanding officer, the General, is captured, the Stooges rescue him, disguised as Santa Clauses. • WT: *The Foreign Legioneers* and *We We Monsieur* • SD: four (F

11/12, M 11/15–W 11/17/37) • FN: Stock footage and new scenes of the Stooges as Santas were used in *Malice in the Palace* (9/1/49) and in its remake, *Rumpus in the Harem* (6/21/56), including some footage from *Wee Wee Monsieur* (2/18/38).

30. TASSELS IN THE AIR ☆☆☆½ • Rl. Apr. 1 • Prod. no. 420 • 18m • *ap* Charley Chase and Hugh McCollum • *d* Charley Chase • *st scr* Al Giebler and Elwood Ullman • *ph* Allen G. Siegler • *e* Arthur Seid • *c:* Bess Flowers (Maggie Smirch), Vernon Dent (Building Superintendent), Bud Jamison (Thaddeus Smirch), and Victor Travers (Man Leaving Elevator) • SYN: When janitors Moe, Larry, and Curly paint occupation stencils on the wrong office doors, Mrs. Smirch accidentally mistakes Moe for Omay, the famous interior decorator. The real Omay also works in the same office building, but the stencil on his door reads "Maintenance Room." The sight of Mrs. Smirch's tassels makes Curly react violently, but Moe calms him down, taking a paint brush to his chin. In the meantime, the Stooges agree to redecorate Mrs. Smirch's house during her bridge game, and the three ruin her antique table and everything else in the house. Later, when the real Omay drops in, Mrs. Smirch kicks the trio out, since, as Moe says, "Our genius isn't appreciated." • FN: A partial reworking of *Luncheon at Twelve* (1933) with Charley Chase. The gag of painting a cuckoo clock and revarnishing an antique table was later used in *A Snitch in Time* (12/7/50).

31. HEALTHY, WEALTHY AND DUMB ☆☆☆ • Rl. May 20 • Prod. no. 422 • 16m • *ap* Jules White • *d* Del Lord • *st scr* Searle Kramer • *ph* Allen G. Siegler • *e* Charles Nelson • *c:* Lucille Lund (Daisy), Jean Carmen (Marge), Earlene Heath (Lil), James C. Morton (Hotel Manager), Bud Jamison (House Detective), and Bobby Burns (Waiter). • SYN: Curly wins a $50,000 radio jackpot, and the Stooges celebrate lavishly, renting

an elegant suite at the Hotel Costa Plente (and it does). In a matter of hours, three luscious gold diggers try spooning off the boys' earnings. Then, after the hotel manager delivers the Stooges their whopping bill, Curly receives a telegram informing him that, after tax deductions, only $4.85 remains out of his winnings! • WT: *Cuckoo Over Contests* • FN: Remade as *A Missed Fortune* (1/3/52).

32. VIOLENT IS THE WORD FOR CURLY ☆☆☆½ • Rl. July 2 • Prod. no. 423 18m • *ap* Charley Chase and Hugh McCollum • *d* Charley Chase • *st scr* Al Giebler and Elwood Ullman • *ph* Lucien Ballard • *e* Arthur Seid • *c:* Gladys Gale (Mrs. Catsby), Marjorie Deanne (Catsby's Daughter), Bud Jamison (Gas Station Manager), Al Thompson (Professor), Pat Gleason, Eddie Fetherstone, and John T. Murray. • SYN: Gas station attendants Moe, Larry, and Curly blow up an automobile carrying three foreign professors, whom the Stooges replace as guest instructors at Mildew's Girl College. In class, the Stooges teach the girls how to sing "Swingin' the Alphabet," and instruct them on the finer points of playing football. But since the college doesn't have an athletic budget, the boys borrow a basketball (loaded with the three professors' nitroglycerin). • SD: four (M 3/14–Th 3/17/38) • FN: The song known to Stooges fans as "Swingin' the Alphabet" was composed by Septimus Winner in 1875 as "The Spelling Bee." Director Charley Chase, whose family's maid had taught the song to his children, was responsible for bringing it to the Stooges.

33. THREE MISSING LINKS ☆☆☆ • Rl. July 29 (also given as Sept 2) • Prod. no. 426 • 18m • *ap* Jules White • *d* Jules White • *st scr* Searle Kramer • *ph* Henry Freulich • *e* Charles Nelson • *c:* Monty Collins (Director Herbert Herringbone), Jane Hamilton (Mirabel Mirabel), James C. Morton (B. O. Botswaddle), John Lester Johnson (Dr. Ba Loni Sulami) • SYN:

Studio president B. O. Botswaddle is conferring with film director Herbert Herringbone over his trouble in locating a leading man to portray a gorilla, opposite Mirabel Mirabel, in *Darkest Africa*. Who could they find to play the missing link? Following their meeting, Botswaddle and Herringbone stumble across three studio janitors (the Stooges) rehearsing Shakespeare in the broom closet. Herringbone looks no further, hiring Curly as the lead gorilla and Moe and Larry as his assistants. The following day, the entire cast and crew shift production to Africa, where the Stooges meet Dr. Ba Loni Sulami, a

witch doctor, who sells "love candy" (which produces instant passion when consumed). Curly is sold on this taffy-like substance, buying some for his leading lady, Mirabel. While filming a scene, however, Curly (in an ape costume), has a face-to-face confrontation with a *real* female gorilla. She chases Curly through the jungle and back to the witch doctor's hut. Curly offers the gorilla love candy, but the animal doesn't accept his peace offering. Curly then swallows the potent stuff himself and, like a shot from Cupid's bow, springs after his new sweetheart, the gorilla • SD: four (Th 4/7–F 4/8, M 4/11–T 4/12/38).

One-sheet for *Violent Is the Word for Curly* (1938). © *Columbia Pictures, courtesy of Jeff Lenburg Collection*

**34. MUTTS TO YOU** ☆☆☆ • Rl. Oct. 14 • Prod. no. 427 • 18m • *ap* Charley Chase and Hugh McCollum • *d* Charley Chase • *st scr* Al Giebler and Elwood Ullman • *ph* Allen G. Siegler • *e* Arthur Seid • *c:* Bess Flowers (Mrs. Manning), Lane Chandler (Doug Manning), Vernon Dent (Mr. Stutz, the Landlord), Bud Jamison (O'Halloran, Irish Cop), and Cy Schindell (Cop) • SYN: The Stooges, after a blistering day's work, find an infant left by its mother on the doorstep of their K-9 Laundry store. Thinking the child is abandoned, the Stooges decide to take the baby home. When the newspapers carry screaming banner headlines that the baby was kidnapped, the boys panic. In an attempt to return the tot unobserved, Moe and Larry disguise Curly as the infant's Irish mother. Curly's costume, however, doesn't fool an Irish cop on the beat, Officer O'Halloran, who chases them directly into a nearby Chinese laundry where, minutes later, the baby is reunited with its parents • WT: *Muts to You* • SD: four (W 3/30–Sa 4/2/38)

**35. FLAT FOOT STOOGES** ☆☆½ • Rl. Dec. 5 (Also given as May 13 and Nov. 25) • Prod. no. 439 • 15½m • *ap* Charley Chase and Hugh McCollum • *st scr d* Charley Chase • *ph* Lucien Ballard • *e* Arthur Seid • *c:* Chester Conklin (Fire Chief Kelly), Dick Curtis (Fred Reardon, Salesman), Lola Jensen (Miss Kelly, Chief's Daughter), Heinie Conklin (Traffic Cop), and Al Thompson (Holding Net) • SYN: A salesman, Fred Reardon, unsuccessfully tries to sell Fire Chief Kelly new motor-driven fire engines, replacing the station's old, inefficient horse-drawn ones. In an attempt to punish Kelly's stubbornness, Reardon sneaks into the department's garage and plants a keg of TNT in the stack of an old fire engine. When the chief's daughter tries to stop Reardon, they struggle, knocking each other out. Meanwhile, a duck starts consuming the trail of spilled gun powder, later laying an explosive egg that sets the firehouse on fire. When the fire alarm sounds, Chief Kelly and the Stooges dash off for another location, not realizing that their own firehouse is ablaze. Fortunately, the Stooges notice that their station is burning down and arrive in time to douse the fire, saving Reardon and the fire chief's daughter from any harm. • SD: four (M 10/25–Th 10/28/37)

## 1939

**36. THREE LITTLE SEW AND SEWS** ☆☆½ • Rl. Jan. 6 • Prod. no. 419 • 16m • *ap* Jules White • *d* Del Lord • *st scr* Ewart Adamson • *ph* Lucien Ballard • *e* Charles Nelson • *c:* Harry Semels (Count Alfred Gehrol), Phyllis Barry (Olga), James C. Morton (Admiral H. S. Taylor), Bud Jamison (Cop), Vernon Dent (Party Guest), Cy Schindell (Guard), Ned Glass (Sailor), and John Tyrrell • SYN: The Stooges are three sailors who press naval uniforms, including Admiral Taylor's. Curly poses as Admiral Taylor, and Larry and Moe impersonate ship lieutenants. Count Gehrol, a German spy, invites the trio to his home for a special get-together. The count makes them steal submarine plans unknowingly so he can sink the navy's latest sub. The count takes the Stooges on his mission, with Curly signaling the navy flagship to rescue them. Curly himself saves the day, however, knocking the German spies unconscious with a lead pipe. When Admiral Taylor arrives on board the sub, Curly illustrates how he single-handedly wiped out the Germans. He repeats his killer swing by clobbering an aerial bomb with the pipe, causing it to explode. As the smoke clears, the Stooges are seen dressed as angels. Curly glances back, remarking "Step on it. Look who's following us!" The Stooges turn around and see the admiral (also in wings) flying away into the heavens. • WT: *Three Goofy Gobs* and *Submarine Behave!* • SD: four (Tu 3/22–F 3/25/38) • FN: Stock shot of the submarine landing on the ocean floor comes from *Playground* (1937, Columbia).

**37. WE WANT OUR MUMMY** ☆☆☆ • Rl. Feb. 24 • Prod. no. 443 • 17m • *ap* Jules White • *d* Del Lord • *st scr* Searle Kramer and Elwood Ullman • *ph* No credit • *e* No credit • *c:* Bud Jamison (Dr. Powell), James C. Morton (Professor Wilson, Curator), Dick Curtis (Jackson, the Crook), Eddie Laughton (Taxi Driver), Ted Lorch (Thug in Mummy Suit), and John Tyrrell (Thug in Egyptian Garb) • SYN: Professor Tuttle has disappeared. He is the only man in the world who knows the exact location of the King Rutentuten mummy. To solve this mystery, Professor Wilson summons the Stooges. Once in Egypt, the boys search aimlessly through an underground tomb, finding that a gang of desperadoes are holding Professor Tuttle in another cavern. The crooks' main interest is to unearth precious jewels hidden in the Rutentuten mummy. In order to circumvent this plot, Moe applies his previous experience as a tailor, dressing Curly up as a makeshift King Rutentuten. When the gang's leader searches through Curly's mummy attire for the diamonds, he finds an old newspaper and reads it aloud: "Yanks Win World Series! Can you beat that!" Blowing his disguise, Curly says, "Ya. And I won five bucks!" A short chase ensues, with Jackson and his gang falling into an open pit that the Stooges covered earlier with an Egyptian rug. With the case now solved, Professor Tuttle reveals that the mummy they found wasn't Rutentuten, but rather his wife, Queen Hotsitotsie. It turns out that the real king is a midget! • SD: four (Tu 11/1–F 11/4/38) • FN: The "Yanks Win World Series" gag and Curly's brief scene with a mummy alligator were not in the film's final draft screenplay. . . . "Rutentuten" is the spelling in the film's script. . . . That's Moe providing the voice of the radio announcer.

**38. A DUCKING THEY DID GO** ☆☆☆ • Rl. Apr. 7 • Prod. no. 444 • 16½m • *ap* Jules White • *d* Del Lord • *st scr* Andrew Bennison • *ph* Lucien Ballard • *e* Charles Nelson • *c:* Lynton Brent (Blackie), Vernon Dent (Vegetarian in Hallway), Bud Jamison (Police Chief), Victor Travers (Club Member), and Cy Schindell (Fruit Vendor) • SYN: Hungry and unemployed, the Stooges steal a watermelon from a fruit vendor and conclude their getaway in the Canvas Back Duck Club, where they win jobs as sales promoters. The Stooges quickly amaze the two crooked bosses by selling memberships to the police chief and the mayor, with the governor next on their list! The day of the club's duck hunt, the police chief warns the Stooges that they better produce ducks or they'll wind up in jail. Decoy ducks seem to hold the guest hunters until the Stooges devise another solution: Curly arrives (à la the Pied Piper) followed by a huge flock of domestic ducks. The hunting goes full blast until an irate farmer arrives, claiming payment for his prize ducks. The police chief and his men start shooting three other ducks, the Stooges, who dive behind a row of bushes and ride off on the backs of three bulls. • SD: four (Tu 11/15–F 11/18/38) • FN: Ending footage was reused from *A Pain in the Pullman* (6/27/36).

**39. YES, WE HAVE NO BONANZA** ☆☆☆ • Rl. May 19 • Prod. no. 438 • 16m • *ap* Jules White • *d* Del Lord • *st scr* Elwood Ullman and Searle Kramer • *ph* Lucien Ballard • *e* Charles Nelson • *c:* Dick Curtis (Boss), Lynton Brent (Pete), Vernon Dent (Sheriff), Suzanne Kaaren, Jean Carmen, and Lola Jensen (Girl-friends) • SYN: As singing waiters at a saloon, the Three Stooges learn that three chorus girls are indebted to their boss. If the girls don't work for him, their boss will throw their father in jail. Into the saloon staggers the boss's henchman. He pays for a drink with a twenty-dollar gold piece, whereupon the Stooges quit their jobs to become gold prospectors in order to get the girls out of debt. During their search the boys unearth a gold filling missing from their boss' mouth. As the Stooges shovel deeper, they uncover a satchel full of gold, money, and bonds. Believing that they are millionaires, the Stooges return to the saloon, decked out in fancy western attire, and ask the girls to quit their jobs and marry them. However, the boss recognizes the satchel as his own buried loot. In the ensuing chase, the boss and his henchman crash their automobile right into the sheriff's office and are captured. • WT: *Yes, We Have No Bonanzas* • SD: four (M 11/28–Th 12/1/38) • FN: On Columbia's Stage 6, a lake set was built for *A Ducking They Did Go* (4/7/39). This same structure was used in *Yes, We Have No Bonanza.* . . . The complete two-reeler was reused in *The 3 Stooges Follies* (11/74). . . . The taglines accompanying Curly's remark "Yes, we have no bonanza" were ad-libbed.

**40. SAVED BY THE BELLE** ☆☆½ • Rl. June 30 • Prod. No, 430 • 17m • *ap* Charley Chase and Hugh McCollum • *d* Charley Chase • *st* Elwood Ullman and Searle Kramer • *scr* Charley Chase • *ph* Allen G. Siegler • *e* Arthur Seid • *c:* Carmen Laroux (Rita), LeRoy Mason (Joe), Gino Corrado (General), Vernon Dent (Mike), and Al Thompson (Wagon Driver) • SYN: Moe, Larry, and Curly are traveling salesmen for a winter clothing manufacturer, marketing their wares in Valeska, an earthquake region of the tropical isles. As guests at a hotel, the boys are mistaken for the masterminds of an uprising against President Ward Robey. Arrested on suspicion of being spies, the Stooges are escorted to the general's office, where they meet Señorita Rita, who believes the boys are innocent. The general orders the Stooges thrown in a dungeon to be executed the next day, despite Rita's pleas. On the day of the execution, however, Rita rescues the boys, and they help her recover a battle map from the general's headquarters for her leader, Joe, the hotel owner. When the boys deliver the chart, however, it turns out to be a rolled-up calendar they picked up by mistake. The Stooges are spared execution again when Rita comes to their rescue with the right map. • SD: four (M 12/12–Th 12/15/38)

**41. CALLING ALL CURS** ☆☆☆ • Rl. Aug. 25 • Prod. no. 445 • 17½m • *ap d* Jules White • *at* Thea Goodan • *scr* Elwood Ullman and Searle Kramer • *ph* No credit • *e* Charles Nelson • *c:* Lynton Brent (Duke), Cy Schindell (Tony), Beatrice Blinn (Nurse Thomas), Dorothy Moore, Robin Raymond, and Ethelreda Leopold (Nurses) • SYN: The Stooges run a stylish dog hospital, and one of their patients is Garcon, a prize pooch that is to be entered in a dog show by its owner, Mrs. Bedford. Two crooks, Tony and Duke, posing as newspaper reporters, come to the hospital and steal the Bedford dog. Unable to recover the canine in time for delivery to Mrs. Bedford, the Stooges disguise another dog with black mattress stuffing to resemble the real Garcon. At the Bedford home, when the boys introduce their Garcon look-alike, the maid accidentally vacuums off the pup's disguise. The Stooges then frantically enlist the aid of a hunting dog to sniff out the missing pooch. Successful, the Stooges track down the crook's hideout, overpower Duke and Tony, and locate Garcon, only to discover that she has given birth to puppies. • WT: *Dog Hospital* • SD: four (Tu 12/27–F 12/30/38)

**42. OILY TO BED, OILY TO RISE** ☆☆☆ • Rl. Oct. 6 • Prod. no. 449 • 18½m • *ap d* Jules White • *st scr* Andrew Bennison and Mauri Grashin • *ph* Henry Freulich • *e* Charles Nelson • *c:* Dick Curtis (Clipper), Richard Fiske (Farmer), Eddie Laughton (Crook), Eva McKenzie

One-sheet for *Calling All Curs* (1939). © *Columbia Pictures, courtesy of Jeff Lenburg Collection*

(Mrs. Jenkins), Victor Travers (Justice of the Peace), Lorna Gray (May), Dorothy Moore (June), and Linda Winters (April) • SYN: The widow Jenkins has just sold her farmhouse to three con men. Meanwhile, Curly has the unusual gift of making any wish come true. His latest wish produces an abandoned automobile, which transports the Stooges to Mrs. Jenkins house in time for roast chicken, dumplings, and apple pie (another one of Curly's wishes). In return for the meal, the Stooges work for their keep and, in so doing,

uncover an oil well on the widow's property. When the Stooges inform Mrs. Jenkins of their discovery, Moe realizes that she has been defrauded by land swindlers and heads up the search for the three hoodlums. During their trip back to town, the boys come across three hitchhiking crooks (the owners of the abandoned car and the land swindlers) and recover the deed after a rip-roaring chase back to Jenkins's farm. Now heroes, Curly makes one last wish: that the Stooges get married. As if by magic, the widow's daughters—April, May,

and June—enter and the Stooges get hitched. • SD: four (Th 3/16–Sa 3/18, M 3/20/39) • FN: Remade as *Oil's Well That Ends Well* (12/4/58). (See *Moe Howard & the 3 Stooges,* pages 95 and 101.)

43. THREE SAPPY PEOPLE ☆☆☆ • Rl. Dec. 1 • Prod. no. 451 • 18m • *ap d* Jules White • *st scr* Clyde Bruckman • *ph* George Meehan • *e* Charles Nelson • *c:* Lorna Gray (Sherri Rumsford), Don Beddoe (J. Rumsford Rumsford), Bud Jamison (Williams the Butler), Ann Doran (Countess), Eddie Laughton (Painter/Party Guest), Victor Travers, Beatrice Blinn, and Richard Fiske (Party Guests) • SYN: Sherry Rumsford is a thrill addict, and her millionaire husband is tired of her stunts. Seeking professional help, he calls the office of psychiatrists Ziller, Zeller, and Zoller, accidentally reaching the Three Stooges, who are telephone repairmen working on the office's switchboard. Smelling a fast buck, the Stooges fill in for the vacationing pyschiatrists, reporting immediately to the Rumsford mansion in time for Sherry's birthday party. Naturally, the Stooges' table manners don't win any contests—they start a pie-throwing battle, much to the amusement of Mrs. Rumsford. • WT: *3 Sloppy People* • SD: four (Th 4/6–Sa 4/8, M 4/10/39)

## 1940

44. YOU NAZTY SPY! ☆☆☆☆ • Rl. Jan. 19 • Prod. no. 472 • 18m • *p d* Jules White • *st scr* Clyde Bruckman and Felix Adler • *ph* Harry Davis • *e* Arthur Seid • *c:* Dick Curtis (Onay), Don Beddoe (Amscray), Richard Fiske (Ixnay/Second Delegate), Florine Dickson (Miss Pfiffernuss), Little Billy Rhodes (Midget Gestapo), John Tyrrell (Minister of Oomphola), Joe Murphy (Peasant), Lorna Gray (Mattie Herring), Eddie Laughton (Delegate Vance Rippemup), Bert Young (Storm Trooper), and Al Thompson • SYN: The kingdom of Moronica is in financial trouble. The king wants peace, but the only way the country

YOUR FAVORITE SCREWBALLS—NUTSY BUT NICE!

Lobby card for *You Nazty Spy!* (1940). © *Columbia Pictures, courtesy of Jeff Lenburg Collection*

can thrive economically is to go to war. Three cabinet members decide to oust the king, replacing him with a dictator stupid enough to follow their every command. In another room are three brainless paperhangers: Hailstone (Moe), Pebble (Larry), and Gallstone (Curly). Mr. Amscray, one of the cabinet advisors, appoints Moe as dictator, Larry as minister of propaganda, and Curly as field marshal. What follows is the burning of "bookmakers," the march on Bolognia, the conquest of Starvania, and the famous Peace Conference of Oomphola, where Moe argues for a corridor through Double Crossia. The Stooges capably display their talent for satire in this film. • WT: *Oh, You Nazty Spy!* • SD: four (W 12/6–Sa 12/9/39) • FN: Both Moe Howard's and Jules White's favorite two-reeler, as well as one of Larry Fine's.

**45. ROCKIN' THRU THE ROCK-IES** ☆☆½ • Rl. Mar. 8 • Prod. no. 461 • 17m • *p d* Jules White • *st scr* Clyde Bruckman • *ph* Henry Freulich • *e* Arthur Seid • *c:* Linda Winters (Daisy), Dorothy Appleby (Tessie), Lorna Gray (Flossie), Kathryn Sheldon (Nell), Dick Curtis (Indian Chief), and Bert Young (Indian) • SYN: The Stooges are hired as guides by Nell and her three chorus girls, who are crossing the plains for an engagement in San Francisco. At one of their overnight campsites, wild bears steal their food, and an Indian chief and his braves surround Nell's wagon, kidnapping Daisy, Tessie, and Flossie and prompting the Stooges to come to the rescue. • WT: *Nell's Belles* • SD: four (W 11/8–Sa 11/11/39) • FN: Linda Winters changed her name to Dorothy Comingore in later film productions and went on to play the prestigious role of one of the wives of *Citizen Kane* (1941).

**46. A PLUMBING WE WILL GO** ☆☆☆☆ • Rl. Apr. 19 • Prod. no. 462 • 18m • *p* Del Lord and Hugh McCollum • *d* Del Lord • *st scr* Elwood Ullman • *ph* Benjamin Kline • *e* Arthur Seid • *c:* Symona Boniface (Party Guest), Bud Jamison (Officer Kelly), John Tyrrell (Judge Hadley), Bess Flowers (Mrs. Hadley), Eddie Laughton (Prosecuting Attorney), Monty Collins (Professor Bilbo), Dudley Dickerson (Cook), and Al Thompson (Owner) • SYN: In order to keep out of jail, the Stooges pose as plumbers trying to fix leaky pipes in Mrs. Hadley's mansion during a swank party. While Larry searches vainly for a water shutoff valve, Moe and Curly get busy in the basement, where Curly deduces that the pipes are clogged with electrical wiring! Consequently, Moe and Curly remove the wiring from the pipes, hooking them up to the house's water pipes. The house becomes so bugged as a result that household appliances shower blasts of water rather than volts of electricity. When Mrs. Hadley calls the police, the Stooges take flight; meanwhile a traveling magician, Professor Bilbo, is outside entertaining Hadley's guests. In an attempt to make his female assistant disappear, Bilbo shuts and then reopens the door, producing a rushing stream of girls, the Stooges, six policemen, and a squad of motorcycle cops! • SD: four (W 12/13–F 12/15, M 12/18/39) • FN: Curly Howard's favorite film. . . . Reworked with stock footage as *Vagabond Loafers* (10/6/49), *Scheming Schemers* (10/4/56), and *Pick a Peck of Plumbers* (7/23/44), an El Brendel–Shemp Howard comedy. (See *Moe Howard & the 3 Stooges,* page 107.) . . . ThreeStooges.net reports that Jules White provided the voice of the TV announcer.

**47. NUTTY BUT NICE** ☆☆☆ • Rl. June 14 • Prod. no. 465 • 18m • *p d* Jules White • *st scr* Clyde Bruckman and Felix Adler • *ph* John Stumar • *e* Mel Thorsen • *c:* Vernon Dent (Doctor), Ned Glass (Mr. Williams, the Girl's Father), John Tyrrell (Dr. Lyman), Cy Schindell (Crook/ Pedestrian), Evelyn Young (Nurse), Ethelreda Leopold (Hostess), Lew Davis (Pedestrian), Charles Dorety (Hot Foot Victim), Bert Young (Police Detective), Johnny Kascier (Man with Beer), Lynton Brent (Spike), and Eddie Garcia. • SYN: As singing waiters, the Stooges overhear two doctors reviewing the fate of a little girl who cries pitiably for her missing father. Moe, Larry, and Curly rush to the hospital to make the child laugh. All that can save her, the doctors say, is the return of her daddy. The Stooges obtain a description of the man (he's five-ten, bald, and likes to yodel) and begin their search. While investigating through the city, the Stooges suddenly hear someone yodeling from an apartment building; they race inside to rescue the girl's father from his kidnappers. • FN: The yodeling song, "I'm a Cowboy from the Western Plains," was an original composition by Jules White, and was reused in *From Nurse to Worse* (8/23/40).

48. HOW HIGH IS UP? ☆☆☆ • Rl. July 26 • Prod. no. 458 • 16m • *p* Del Lord and Hugh McCollum • *d* Del Lord • *st scr* Elwood Ullman • *ph* Allen G. Siegler • *e* Arthur Seid • *c:* Bruce Bennett, Edmund Cobb, and Bert Young (Workmen), Vernon Dent (Blake, the Building's Owner), and Cy Schindell (Blake's Assistant) • SYN: The Stooges are Minute Menders who travel from city to city performing all kinds of odd jobs. While passing a construction site, however, the boys try drumming up business by punching holes in the workmen's lunch pails, taking flight when the workers detect the leaks in their food boxes. In their haste to escape, the Stooges take refuge in a line of workers seeking employment, and are accidentally hired as riveters to work on the new steel building's ninety-seventh floor. When the building owner notices the wild mess the boys are creating on the structure, the Stooges jump off the building, land safely in a truck below, and roar off to safety. • FN: Footage reused in *Stop! Look! and Laugh!* (7/1/60).

49. FROM NURSE TO WORSE ☆☆☆☆ • Rl. Aug. 23 • Prod. no. 468 • *p d* Jules White • *st* Charles L. Kimball • *scr* Clyde Bruckman • *ph* Benjamin Kline • *e* Mel Thorsen • *c:* Vernon Dent (Dr. D. Lerious), Dorothy Appleby (Receptionist), Marjorie Kane (Woman in Office), Cy Schindell (Cop), Blanche Payson (Tall Nurse), Johnny Kascier (Attendant), Dudley Dickerson (Orderly), Ned Glass (Dog Catcher), Al Thompson (Orderly), Bert Young (Photographer), John Tyrrell, Joe Palma, Charlie Phillips, and Poppy Wilde • SYN: The Stooges are paperhangers refurbishing the house of their friend, Jerry, who convinces them to act mentally ill in order to collect health insurance. Following his advice, Moe and Larry put Curly on a leash and take him to see Dr. D. Lerious, the company physician. Curly imitates a dog so ferociously that the doctor declares that only a brain operation can save him. The Stooges refuse the idea of Curly getting this cheap haircut and escape momentarily. Later, they are recaptured by Dr. D. Lerious, who prepares to operate on Curly. In the excitement that follows, the ether cone is applied to the wrong nose during Curly's operation, making the unconscious patient the doctor instead of Curly. The trio escapes on a hospital gurney by making a sail. They speed out of the hospital and knock an innocent bicycle rider into a tub of cement. As the man starts emerging from the gooey mess, the boys recognize that he is Jerry and shove him back into the cement. • FN: A stock shot of the paperhanging routine comes from *You Nazty Spy!* (1/19/40). The "Charlie, the Man with the Goofy Limp" gag was borrowed from *Uncivil Warriors* (4/26/35) and later used in *Hold That Lion!* (7/17/47). . . . The song "I'm a Cowboy from the Western Plains" is an original composition by Jules White. It was first used in *Nutty but Nice* (6/14/40). . . . Yes, that's Moe providing the voice of the radio announcer.

50. NO CENSUS, NO FEELING ☆☆☆ • Rl. Oct. 4 • Prod. no. 474 • *p* Del Lord and Hugh McCollum •

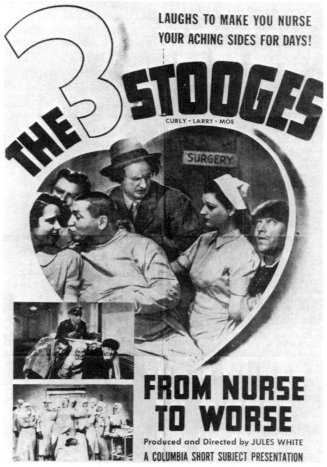

One-sheet for *From Nurse to Worse* (1940). © *Columbia Pictures, courtesy of Jeff Lenburg Collection*

*d* Del Lord • *st scr* Harry Edwards and Elwood Ullman • *ph* Lucien Ballard • *e* Arthur Seid • *c:* Symona Boniface (Hostess), Elinor Vanderveer (Bridge Player), Vernon Dent (Party Guest), Bruce Bennett (Football Player), Max Davidson (Storekeeper), Bert Young (Referee), Marjorie Kane, and John Tyrrell • SYN: Census takers Moe, Larry, and Curly crash an affluent women's bridge party, with Moe and Larry joining the group of players. In the meantime, Curly is mixing punch in the kitchen, adding alum instead of sugar by mistake. The Stooges are shown the door when the women, with their alum-puckered lips, are humiliated since they can't speak. In search of new customers, the Stooges, disguised as football players, start taking the census of a crowd at a local football game. The Stooges' plan backfires, however, when Curly steals an ice cream wagon. That forces the boys to flee from an angry mob of football players • FN: The Stooges are also census takers in *Don't Throw That Knife* (5/3/51). . . . Football sequences were filmed at the University of Southern California, located in the heart of Los Angeles.

**51. COOKOO CAVALIERS** ☆☆½ • Rl. Nov. 15 • Prod. no. 455 • 17m • *p d* Jules White • *st scr* Ewart Adamson • *ph* Henry Freulich • *e* Arthur Seid • *c:* Dorothy Appleby (Rosita), Lynton Brent (Pedro Ruiz), Bob O'Connor (Manuel), Blanche Payson (Fish Customer), and Anita Garvin • SYN: In an opening segment similar to Laurel and Hardy's *Towed in a Hole*, the Stooges are fish vendors working out of San Diego. When their business begins floundering, a Mexican real estate agent sells them a beauty salon—when they think they're buying a beer saloon—south of the border. Although the mix-up disappoints them, the Stooges cheer up when they realize that all of their customers will be women! Their first customers are four pretty ladies who need their hair dyed for a new stage revue that is playing in town. Larry, Moe, and Curly find the

job is a cinch . . . well, almost. The girls emerge hairless, nailless, and eyebrowless; another woman's face is encased in cement instead of a mud pack! • WT: *Beauty a la Mud* • FN: This short's title is indeed *Cookoo*—not *Cuckoo—Cavaliers*. . . . Curly's wiggling ears were achieved through invisible threads (a gag Stan Laurel used many times). . . . Several publications have erroneously attributed photographs of the three bald-headed women in this film to a scene from *Loco Boy Makes Good.*

**52. BOOBS IN ARMS** ☆☆☆½ • Rl. Dec. 27 • Prod. no. 486 • 18m • *p d* Jules White • *st scr* Felix Adler • *ph* John Stumar • *e* Mel Thorsen • *c:* Richard Fiske (Dare), Evelyn Young (Mrs. Dare), Lynton Brent (Pedestrian), Eddie Laughton (Apartment Door Man), Charles Dorety (Trainee/Guard), John Tyrrell (Enemy Officer), Cy Schindell (Enemy Soldier), and Johnny Kascier (Guard) • SYN: The Stooges are door-to-door greeting-card salesmen who, escaping from a jealous husband, wind up in what appears to be a breadline. Instead, the boys end up enlisting in the army, and the jealous husband, Mr. Dare, turns up as their sergeant. Dare presses the Stooges into service on a real battlefront, ordering them to fire a new type of shell at the enemy: laughing gas. Curly fires the shell, all right, exploding it right in front of the Stooges, who laugh uncontrollably as the enemy captures them. This culminates in a wild melee breaking loose, and Moe, Larry, and Curly render the enemy unconscious. The celebration of their heroics, however, ends with them riding a speeding artillery shell out into the heavens beyond. • WT: *All This and Bullets Too* • FN: The film's original working title parodied the Warner Bros. film *All This and Heaven Too.* . . . The storyline was a partial reworking of Laurel and Hardy's *The Fixer Uppers.* Footage from this film was used in *Dizzy Pilots* (9/24/43). . . . Columbia's costume department was given strict orders

to design army uniforms that only somewhat resembled the regulation style, rather than producing exact replicas. . . . The Columbia Ranch in Burbank, California, was the location used for much of this film.

**1941**

**53. SO LONG MR. CHUMPS** ☆☆☆ • Rl. Feb. 7 • Prod. no. 484 • 17m • *p d* Jules White • *st scr* Clyde Bruckman and Felix Adler • *ph* Barney McGill • *e* Mel Thorsen • *c:* Vernon Dent (Desk Sergeant), John Tyrrell (B. O. Davis), Dorothy Appleby (Pomeroy's Girlfriend), Eddie Laughton (Pomeroy), Bruce Bennett (Rockpile Prison Guard), Bert Young (Cop), and Lew Davis (Pedestrian Laughing at Cop) • SYN: Street cleaners Larry, Moe, and Curly find some bonds belonging to B. O. Davis, an ailing millionaire. When they return the bonds, Davis offers the boys $5,000 in return for tracking down an honest man with executive ability to take over his position. Eventually their search leads to a sobbing young woman who claims that her sweetheart, Percy Pomeroy, is an honest man who is in prison by mistake. In order to release Pomeroy, the Stooges force the police to arrest them for robbing a bank, which, coincidentally, was just robbed. Sent to prison, the trio meet Pomeroy (Number 41144), their honest man, who is freed when police detectives round up the real criminal, Lone Wolf Louie. The Stooges, however, continue serving their sentence on the rock pile. • FN: Footage from this short was used in *Beer Barrel Polecats* (1/10/46). The idea of getting arrested purposefully was also used in *Three Smart Saps* (7/30/42) and in *The Noose Hangs High*, a 1948 feature with Abbott and Costello. . . . Omitted from the final script was one scene in which a street policeman notices the Stooges and Pomeroy's girl crying. A double-talk routine develops concerning why each person is crying.

**54. DUTIFUL BUT DUMB** ☆☆½ • Rl. Mar. 21 • Prod. no. 485 • 17m • *p* Del Lord and Hugh McCollum

• *d* Del Lord • *st scr* Elwood Ullman • *ph* Benjamin Kline • *e* Arthur Seid • *c:* Vernon Dent (Editor of *Whack* Magazine), Bud Jamison (Vulgarian Sergeant), Bruce Bennett (Vulgarian Messenger), Chester Conklin (Waiter), Fred Kelsey (Vulgarian Colonel), Stanley Brown (Percival DePuyster), Marjorie Deanne (Mrs. DePuyster), Eddie Laughton (Officer), Harry Semels (Citizen), and Bert Young (Sentry) • SYN: Moe, Larry, and Curly—photographers Click, Clack, and Cluck for *Whack* magazine ("If It's a Good Picture, It's Out of Whack!")—are sent to Vulgaria to snap pictures of an invisible ray machine, the country's top-secret invention. Inside Vulgaria, however, where cameras are forbidden under the penalty of death, police arrest the Stooges and line them up for execution. But before meeting their maker, the trio makes one last request: a final smoke. Their request granted, Curly produces a jumbo-size cigar that takes several days to finish. While the soldiers are sleeping, the Stooges escape and break into the colonel's office, mistaking the invisible ray machine for a new camera. Then, disguised as Vulgarian soldiers, the Stooges take refuge in the local commissary, where Curly pits his wits against a bowl of live oyster stew. • FN: Many comedians have performed the oyster gag: The gag received one of its first showings in the Billy Bevan comedy *Wandering Willies* (1926), directed by Del Lord. Lou Costello performed it in *Keep 'Em Flying* (1941) and *The Wistful Widow of Wagon Gap* (1948), both features, and in the fourteenth episode (entitled "Hungry") of Abbott and Costello's TV series. The Stooges themselves repeated the gag in *Income Tax Sappy* (2/4/54), *Shivering Sherlocks* (1/8/48), and *Of Cash and Hash* (2/3/55), using clams in the last two.

## 55. ALL THE WORLD'S A STOOGE

☆☆☆½ • Rl. May 16 • Prod. no. 487 • 16m • *p* Del Lord and Hugh McCollum • *d* Del Lord • *st scr* John Grey • *ph* Benjamin Kline • *e* Arthur Seid • *c:* Lelah Tyler (Lotta Bullion), Emory Parnell (Ajax Bullion), Bud Jamison (Cop), Olaf Hytten (Butler), Richard Fiske (Dr. I. Yankum, Dentist), Johnny Tyrrell (Building Superintendent), Symona Boniface, Gwen Seager, Poppy Wilde, and Ethelreda Leopold (Party Guests) • SYN: Following a zany escapade as window washers turned dentists, the Stooges are abducted by millionaire Ajax Bullion, who dresses them as children and presents them to his wife as three refugees: Johnnie (Moe), Frankie (Curly), and Mabel (Larry). The next day, Mrs. Bullion throws an expensive party to introduce her newly adopted offspring to her many upper-class friends. Curly makes a big impression when he enters the party smelling like a brick of Limburger cheese (he rubbed some on his chest to clear up his cold). In fact, the Stooges are so cute that their cuteness even irritates Mr. Bullion, who chases them out of the house, wielding an axe. • FN: The storyline of a millionaire wanting three children was later reprised in *Quiz Whizz* (2/13/58). . . . Mabel was Larry's wife's first name.

## 56. I'LL NEVER HEIL AGAIN

☆☆☆½ • Rl. July 11 • Prod. no. 500 • 18m • *p d* Jules White • *st scr* Felix Adler and Clyde Bruckman • *ph* L.W. O'Connell • *e* Jerome Thoms • *c:* Mary Ainslee (Gilda), Lynton Brent (Amscray), Vernon Dent (Ixnay), Bud Jamison (Umpchay), Don Barclay (Russian Representative), Jack Lipson (Bay of Rum), Cy Schindell (Chizzilini), Johnny Kascier (Napoleon in Picture Frame), Bert Young (Guard), Bobby Burns (Attendant), and Al Thompson (Valet) • SYN: Amscray, Ixnay, and Umpchay regret their appointment of Hailstone (Moe) as dictator of Moronica and pledge to put King Herman 6⅞ back in power. They hire Gilda, the king's daughter, to spy on Hailstone and plant an eight ball loaded with gunpowder on the dictator's pool table. Successful in her mission, Gilda convinces Hailstone, Pebble (Larry), and Gallstone (Curly) that their Axis partners are plotting to overthrow them. The Stooges call for an important meeting with the Axis Powers, and the conference turns out to be an earthshaking experience: The ministers and the Stooges play catch around the room with a model globe, arguing over who gets ownership. In the midst of this unfriendly game, Curly picks up the loaded eight ball and throws it at one of his henchmen, blowing up the conference room. When the smoke clears, Gilda is seen reporting her victory to the king, while the Stooges' heads are seen mounted as trophies on a wall. • FN: A sequel to *You Nazty Spy!* (1/19/40).

## 57. AN ACHE IN EVERY STAKE

☆☆☆☆ • Rl. Aug. 22 • Prod. no. 488 • 18m • *p* Del Lord and Hugh McCollum • *d* Del Lord • *st scr* Lloyd A. French • *ph* Philip Tannura • *e* Burton Kramer • *c:* Vernon Dent (Poindexter Lawrence), Bess Flowers (Mrs. Lawrence), Bud Jamison (Baker), Gino Corrado (Chef), Blanche Payson (Chef's Assistant), Symona Boniface (Party Guest), and Victor Travers (Ice Customer) • SYN: The Stooges' exploits as three clumsy ice deliverymen cause Mrs. Lawrence's cook and maid to quit prior to Mr. Lawrence's big birthday party. The Stooges, however, help Mrs. Lawrence prepare for her husband's party, not realizing that Mr. Lawrence was the same man they injured earlier while delivering ice. While in the process of cooking the main entreé, Larry pulls a cake out of the oven and deflates it with a pin. In order to rectify his blunder, he reinflates the cake with a gas hose from the oven. When Mr. Lawrence blows out the candles, the cake explodes, plastering his face with frosting. • FN: Reminiscent of Laurel and Hardy's *The Music Box*. Partially reworked later as *Listen, Judge* (3/6/52). Curly's spring-pants gag was also reprised in *Have Rocket--Will Travel* (1959) and was done earlier in *Hoi Polloi* (8/29/35). The sequence

One-sheet for *I'll Never Heil Again* (1941). © Columbia Pictures, courtesy of Jeff Lenburg Collection

of carrying ice upstairs and tangling with a man was also in *Ice Cold Cocos* (1926), with Billy Bevan, as directed by Del Lord. Seven years earlier, Shemp Howard performed the turkey-stuffing gags in his Vitaphone short *A Peach of a Pair* (12/29/34). Interestingly, the director of that film was Lloyd French, the screenwriter of *An Ache in Every Stake*.

### 58. IN THE SWEET PIE AND PIE
☆☆☆ • Rl. Oct. 16 • Prod. no. 482 • 17m • *p d* Jules White • *st* Ewart Adamson • *scr* Clyde Bruckman • *ph* George Meehan • *e* Jerome Thoms • *c:* Dorothy Appleby (Tiska), Mary Ainslee (Taska), Ethelreda Leopold (Baska), John Tyrrell (Butler), Symona Boniface (Party Guest), Vernon Dent (Senator), Eddie Laughton (Hunter at Party), Bert Young (Guard), Richard Fiske (Diggins), Lynton Brent (Vendor), Al Thompson (Warden), Geneva Mitchell (Dance Instructor, stock footage), Victor Travers (Justice of the Peace), and Lew Davis (Convict in Bleachers) • SYN: Tiska, Taska, and Baska, three beautiful sisters, must be married by midnight to collect a legacy. At the advice of their attorney, the girls marry Larry, Moe, and Curly, three convicts facing a public hanging for murders they didn't commit. The ladies can collect, however, only after the boys are executed. When the real killer confesses to the murders, the Stooges are freed from prison and find that their aristocratic wives are not too pleased. The Stooges try to become gentlemen by taking up dancing lessons. Then, at one of the great social digs of the year, the Stooges' wives conclude, after a pie-throwing melee, that their attorney is the cause of all their troubles, and they decide to remain married. • WT: *Well, I'll Be Hanged* • FN: Footage from this short was reused in *Beer Barrel Polecats* (1/10/46). The dance-lesson sequence was pulled from *Hoi Polloi* (8/29/35). The gag of Larry shaving while the society matron is applying her makeup was adapted from *Hoi Polloi* as well. • PS: Larry Fine once recalled that the most grueling scenes in this film as well as others were those involving pies. "Sometimes we would run out of pies, so the prop man would sweep up the pie goop off of the floor, including nails, splinters, and tacks. Another problem was pretending you didn't know a pie was coming your way. To solve this, Jules would tell me, 'Now Larry, Moe's going to smack you with a pie on the count of three.' Then Jules would tell Moe, 'Hit Larry on the count of two!' So when it came time to counting, I never got to three, because Moe crowned me with a pie!" (See *Moe Howard & the 3 Stooges*, page 82, last paragraph.)

### 59. SOME MORE OF SAMOA
☆☆½ • Rl. Dec. 4 • Prod. no. 511 • 17m • *p* Del Lord and Hugh McCollum • *d* Del Lord • *st scr* Harry Edwards and Elwood Ullman • *ph* L. W. O'Connell • *e* Burton Kramer • *c:* Louise Carver (King's Sister), Mary Ainslee (Nurse), Symona Boniface (Mrs. Winthrop), John Tyrrell (Gardener), Tiny Ward (The King),

and Duke York (Kingfisher) • SYN: An ailing millionaire, Mr. Winthrop (played by an unknown actor), hires tree surgeons Howard, Fine, and Howard to track down a mate for his persimmon tree so it will be able to bear fruit. The millionaire sends the Stooges to the Isle of Rhum Boogie to complete their quest. But Curly is appointed the island cannibals' new chief. The old chief offers the Stooges a persimmon tree and their freedom, providing one of them will marry his sister. Uninterested in the chief's ugly sister, the Stooges take flight with the tree, paddling off in their sinking canoe. • FN: This short's idol gag was later reused in *Hula-La-La* (11/1/51). . . . In the Stooges' office, Curly's sudden growth (caused by an injection of vitamin PDQ) was accomplished by dressing him in longer trousers and raising him on a jack through the floor.

## 1942

**60. LOCO BOY MAKES GOOD** ☆☆☆☆½ • Rl. Jan. 8 • Prod. no. 510 • 17m • *p d* Jules White • *st scr* Felix Adler and Clyde Bruckman • *ph* John Stumar • *e* Jerome Thoms • *c:* Dorothy Appleby (Twitchell's Date), Vernon Dent (Balbo the Magician), Bud Jamison (Happy Haven Landlord), Eddie Laughton (Drunk), John Tyrrell (Waldo Twitchell), Symona Boniface (Dancer with Mouse Down Dress), Al Thompson (Nightclub Patron with Seltzer Bottle), Lynton Brent (Bearded Man), Victor Travers (Bald Man), Elinor Vanderveer (Woman in Twitchell's Party), Bobby Burns and Heinie Conklin (Dancers), and George Gray (Nightclub Patron) • SYN: The Stooges help the widow owner of the Happy Haven Hotel raise money to pay off her note by remodeling the hotel into the Kokonutz Grove, a ritzy nightclub. On opening night, the boys provide the entertainment as "Nil, Null and Void, Three Hams Who Lay Their Own Eggs," singing "She Was Bread in Old Kentucky but She's Just a Crumb Up Here." In attendance is a well-known columnist, whose rave

review of the Stooges' show saves the hotel from debt. • WT: *Poor but Dishonest* • FN: The segment of Curly unrolling linoleum (instead of carpeting or wallpaper) is an old standard. The "Driving Nails" routine was later redone in *The Three Stooges in Orbit* (1962). . . . The song "She Was Bread in Old Kentucky" does not appear in the final draft script. Instead, Curly was supposed to mime playing "Yankee Doodle" on several harmonicas like a seal. . . . On March 7, 1946, comedian Harold Lloyd sued writers Clyde Bruckman and Felix Adler, director Jules White, and Columbia Pictures for Bruckman's use of Lloyd's magician's coat sequence from *Movie Crazy* (1932) in *Loco Boy Makes Good*. Lloyd sought $500,000 in damages.

**61. CACTUS MAKES PERFECT** ☆☆☆☆½ • Rl. Feb. 26 • Prod. No. 513 • 17m • *p* Del Lord and Hugh McCollum • *d* Del Lord • *st scr* Elwood Ullman and Monty Collins • *ph* Benjamin Kline • *e* Burton Kramer • *c:* Monty Collins (Mother), Vernon Dent and Ernie Adams (Prospectors), and Eddie Laughton (Con Man) • SYN: Curly receives a letter from the Inventors' Association saying that his gold-collar-button retriever (a weird-looking bow-and-arrow combination) "is incomprehensible and utterly impractical." The Stooges misinterpret the letter to imply that they're a success, and head west to use Curly's invention to prospect for gold. The trio buys a phony deed to the Lost Mine, which supposedly contains 187,000 tons of gold worth thirty-five dollars an ounce. Two down-on-their-luck prospectors try swindling the Stooges out of their claim, but the trio wins out.

**62. WHAT'S THE MATADOR?** ☆☆☆½ • Rl. Apr. 23 • Prod. no. 519 • 16½m • *p d* Jules White • *st* Jack White • *scr* Jack White and Saul Ward • *ph* L. W. O'Connell • *e* Jerome Thoms • *c:* Suzanne Kaaren (Dolores), Harry Burns (Jose), John Tyrrell (Shamus O'Brien), Dorothy Appleby (O'Brien's Receptionist), Don Zelaya

(Mexican Who Is Asked for Directions), Paul Ellis (Pedro Alverez), Eddie Laughton (Telegram Clerk), Cy Schindell and Eddie Laughton (Bullring Attendants) • SYN: A jealous husband, Jose, gets even with the Stooges for allegedly having a love affair with his wife, Dolores. While the Stooges are performing their comedy bullfight act at a local bullfight arena, Jose arranges a real bull to be substituted for the fake one containing Moe and Larry. When matador Curly notices the real bull, he takes evasive action and runs head first into the animal, knocking it unconscious, much to the delight of the crowd, who chant "Ole Americano!" Curly is crowned the matador of the century! • WT: *Run, Bull, Run!* FN: Remade, with stock footage, as *Sappy Bullfighters* (6/4/59). Scenes from this film were also used in *Stop! Look! and Laugh!* (7/1/60). . . . Originally, when the bull spotted the Stooges bowing to the crowd, he was supposed to zero in on their derrieres, uttering, "Eenie, Meenie, Minie, Moe!"

**63. MATRI-PHONY** ☆☆½ • Rl. July 2 • Prod. no. 527 • 17m • *p* Del Lord and Hugh McCollum • *d* Harry Edwards • *st scr* Elwood Ullman and Monty Collins • *ph* George Meehan • *e* Paul Borofsky • *c:* Vernon Dent (Emperor Octopus Grabus), Marjorie Deanne (Diana), Monty Collins (Grabus's Assistant), Eddy Chandler (Pottery Shop Guard), and Cy Schindell (Guard) • SYN: Mohicus, Larrycus, and Curlycue are potters in ancient Erysipelas during the reign of the rash emperor Octopus Grabus. When Grabus, seeking a bride, orders all beautiful redheads to report to the palace immediately, one of them, Diana, takes refuge with the Stooges. It is Diana whom Grabus is intent on marrying. When Octopus calls on Diana, Curly disguises himself as the luscious redhead, wooing Octopus. The near-sighted emperor warms up to Curly, chasing him around the room and, finally, catching and unmasking him • FN: The gag of acting as a puppeteer from behind a curtain for an unconscious victim was reused with Shemp in two Stooge comedies, *Fright Night* (3/6/47) and its remake, *Fling in the Ring* (1/6/55). . . . In an earlier version of the *Matri-Phony* screenplay, Diana and the Stooges made their final escape up a snake charmer's rope. Also in an earlier draft, Larry was to take Diana's place instead of Curly.

**64. THREE SMART SAPS** ☆☆☆ • Rl. July 30 • Prod. no. 532 • 16½m • *p d* Jules White • *st scr* Clyde Bruckman • *ph* Benjamin Kline • *e* Jerome Thoms • *c:* Julie Gibson, Ruth Skinner, and Julie Duncan (Stella, Mella, and Bella), John Tyrrell (Their Father), Bud Jamison (Moe's First Rumba Partner), Sally Cairns (Moe's Dancing Partner), Eddie Laughton (Guard), Victor Travers (Justice of the Peace), Frank Coleman (Cop), Frank Terry (Man on Street), Vernon Dent (Man with Tailor), Johnny Kascier (Party Doorman), Barbara Slater (Curly's Rumba Partner), Lew Davis (Card Player), and Dorothy Vernon • SYN: It's The Three Stooges' wedding day! Their fiancées, Stella, Mella, and Bella, refuse to commence with the ceremony because their father, the warden of the city jail, is a prisoner in one of his own cells. The Stooges promise the girls they'll save their father so that the marriage can go as planned. A short time later, at the county jail, the Stooges uncover their future father-in-law and learn that the new warden is a crook who is operating the jail as a members-only casino (the members are gangsters). In order to free the new warden, the Stooges sneak into the casino and take candid pictures as evidence. Since formal attire is required, Moe clobbers a guest and steals his suit, while Curly finds and dons a suit with loose stitching. The stitching falls apart when Curly takes to dancing with one of the female casino members. In the middle of several dance numbers, Curly sidles over to a curtain for repairs (Larry is behind the drape with a sewing kit). Curly's last pass before the curtain becomes painful when Larry pokes

him with a sewing needle, right in the trousers! On the floor in pain, Curly is helped up by his dance partner, who accidentally rips off his suit. With the necessary pictorial evidence in hand, Moe and Larry escort Curly (in his underwear) out of the party. Their future father-in-law is released when the Stooges' photographic evidence undermines the members-only club. • WT: *Father's in Jail Again* • FN: The premise of getting pinched to help someone else also appears in *The Noose Hangs High* (1948) with Abbott and Costello, and in *So Long Mr. Chumps* (2/7/41), starring the Stooges. The "Are You Dancing?" gag originally appeared in *Hoi Polloi* (8/29/35). Curly's struggle with loosely hemmed trousers was borrowed from Harold Lloyd's *The Freshman* (1925). • PS: *Three Smart Saps* marked screen actress Julie Gibson's first film with the Stooges. She related her impressions of working with Curly: "I don't think we exchanged *one* word. He was just absolutely quiet. Moe and Larry were a lot of fun, more than Curly. Larry would do a soft-shoe and tell funny stories. Moe was smart and cute, kind of a smart-ass, but fun. I was afraid to even say 'hello' to Curly. He was fine when he was with Moe and Larry, but

seemed deathly afraid of women. The scene I hated the most was when I had to kiss him. I think I closed my eyes because he was like a piece of wood."

**65. EVEN AS I O U** ☆☆½ • Rl. Sept. 18 • Prod. no. 507 • 15½m • *p* Del Lord and Hugh McCollum • *d* Del Lord • *st scr* Felix Adler • *ph* L. W. O'Connell • *e* Paul Borofsky • *c:* Ruth Skinner (Evicted Mother), Stanley Blystone (Joe, the Ventriloquist), Wheaton Chambers (Con Man), Vernon Dent (Driver), Bud Jamison (Cop), Billy Bletcher (Seabascuit's Voice), Heinie Conklin (Turnstile Guard), Lew Davis (Race Announcer Voice), Bert Young (Betting Window Winnings Clerk), and Jack Gardner • SYN: Bookmakers Moe, Larry, and Curly try raising the necessary money to pull an evicted woman and her child out of debt by betting the girl's piggy bank money on a winning filly. Two racetrack con artists, however, fast-talk the Stooges out of their winnings, trading the cash in for a broken-down mare named Seabascuit (the horse talks because one of the thugs is a ventriloquist). To remedy the horse's poor physical condition, Curly grabs a pipe and tries blowing a vitamin

Lobby card for *Three Smart Saps* (1942). © *Columbia Pictures, courtesy of Moe Howard Collection*

down the thoroughbred's throat, but the Stooge accidentally swallows the pill himself. Within seconds, Curly starts acting and sounding like a horse, and when his condition worsens, Moe and Larry rush him to the hospital where he gives birth to a colt that really talks! • FN: The "Press, Press, Pull" routine first appeared in *Three Little Beers* (11/28/35), while Curly's bit involving blowing a vitamin through a pipe was reprised in *Scrambled Brains* (7/7/51) and *Hoofs and Goofs* (1/31/57). Selling old dope sheets is reused in "Las Vegas," episode twenty-two of *The Abbott and Costello Show* (1952–53).

66. SOCK-A-BYE BABY ☆☆½ • Rl. Nov. 13 • Prod. no. 539 • 18m • *p d* Jules White • *st scr* Clyde Bruckman • *ph* Benjamin Kline • *e* Jerome Thoms • *c:* Julie Gibson (Mrs. Collins), Clarence Straight (Mr. Collins), Bud Jamison (Motorcycle Cop), Baby Joyce Gardner (Jimmy), and Dudley Dickerson (Worker) • SYN: The Stooges find a baby on their doorstep left by a policeman's wife. Delighted Moe, Larry, and Curly set out to fix breakfast for the child but later read in the newspaper that police are looking for the kidnapped infant. Thus, when two officers and the child's mother come knocking at the door, the Stooges take the baby and flee in their station wagon. The police pursue on motorcycles and, following a whirlwind chase, recover the baby, while the cop and his wife patch up their differences. Meanwhile, the Stooges get away disguised as bushes. • WT: *Their First Baby* • FN: Footage from this short was revived in *Stop! Look! and Laugh!* (7/1/60).

## 1943

67. THEY STOOGE TO CONGA ☆½ • Rl. Jan. 1 • Prod. no. 533 • 15½m • *p* Del Lord and Hugh McCollum • *d* Del Lord • *st scr* Elwood Ullman and Monty Collins • *ph* George Meehan • *e* Paul Borofsky • *a* Carl Anderson • *c:* Vernon Dent (Hans), Dudley Dickerson (Chef), Lloyd Bridges, John Tyrrell, and Julie

Duncan (Telephone Callers), Eddie Laughton (Radio Quiz Announcer), and Stanley Brown (Pilot) • SYN: The Stooges are repairmen fixing a doorbell in a house where top Nazi and Japanese conspirators are planning to conquer the world with their new high-powered submarine. While searching for the house's electrical wiring system, the boys overhear the spies' plan to operate the submarine via remote control. Moe and Larry then disguise themselves as Hitler and Tojo, overtake the conspirators, man the controls, and blow up the submarine • PS: *They Stooge to Conga* is one of the most violent Three Stooges comedies, featuring a spike gag that makes even ardent fans cringe. Moe's eyes and ears are on the receiving end of a spike from Curly's shoe while Curly is scaling a telephone pole. Just who is responsible for the crudeness of its presentation—the writer, the producer, or the director? Screenwriter Elwood Ullman is innocent. In the script, Ullman calls for Curly's spike to dig *once* into Moe's ear and never into his eye. In an interview session, Norman Maurer and Edward Bernds discussed the spike gag. As Maurer said, "In the scene you're talking about, that is strictly cutting. And there's only one man who's going

to cut that scene, and that's the producer." Edward Bernds added, "You can't blame the producer for a scene that the director directed, but you can blame him for the way he cuts it." In the case of the scene in question, however, it is believed that both the director and producer were responsible: the director for going farther with the gag than the script intended, and the producer for not having the taste to cut it out.

68. DIZZY DETECTIVES ☆☆☆☆ • Rl. Feb. 5; re. Sept. 1965, Aug. 1966 • Prod. no. 529 • 18½m • *p d* Jules White • *st scr* Felix Adler • *ph* Benjamin Kline • *e* Jerome Thoms • *a* Carl Anderson • *c:* John Tyrrell (Mr. Dill), Bud Jamison (I. Doolittle), Dick Jensen (Crook), and Lynton Brent (Ape's Handler) • SYN: The Ape Man strikes again in the latest of a string of mysterious burglaries. Joe Dill, the head of the Citizens' League, demands that the police inspector, I. Doolittle, track down the gorilla or he'll ask for his resignation. Doolittle has no other choice than to hire three new detectives, the Stooges, to solve the case. Hot on the trail, the boys come upon the animal in a curio shop and have a series of freak adventures. In the course of the spooky

The crew reassures Curly as he hangs twenty feet in the air during production of *They Stooge to Conga* (1943). © *Columbia Pictures, courtesy of Moe Howard Collection*

night, they capture three crooks who own the trained ape; one of them is Joe Dill. • WT: *Idiots DeLuxe* • FN: The carpenter routine was used previously in *Pardon My Scotch* (8/1/35). This short was remade with Joe Besser and Jim Hawthorne as *Fraidy Cat* (12/13/51), and later as *Hook a Crook* (11/24/55), also with Besser.

69. SPOOK LOUDER ☆☆☆ • Rl. Apr. 2 • Prod. no. 549 • 16m • *p* Del Lord and Hugh McCollum • *d* Del Lord • *st scr* Clyde Bruckman • *ph* John Stumar • *e* Paul Borofsky • *a* Carl Anderson • *c:* Stanley Blystone (Spy Leader/Undertaker), Lew Kelly (Special Investigator), Symona Boniface (Wet Customer), Ted Lorch (Mr. Graves, Inventor), and Charles Middleton (Butler) • SYN: A newspaper reporter calls upon a special investigator to sniff out the inside story behind the breaking up of a great spy ring. As the investigator tells the story, the Stooges are seen in flashback as salesmen peddling the Miracle Reducing Machine. Two unsuccessful sales later, Moe, Larry, and Curly pay a visit to the house of an eccentric scientist, who mistakes them for caretakers. When the scientist is called to Washington to demonstrate his new death ray machine, however, he asks the Stooges to stay overnight so spies won't break in to steal his invention. That night, in the climax to a series of eerie events, conspirators invade the premises and pies mysteriously explode out of nowhere, plastering the Stooges. Still in pursuit of the spies, however, Curly finally scares them away when he whips out a bomb. But the spirit of another being remains in the house and throws another round of lemon meringue pies at the Stooges. Out of flashback, the question remains, "Who threw those pies?" The investigator turns to the screen and answers, "Oh, *I* threw the pies!" Chuckling devilishly, he gets clobbered with a pie himself • SD: four (F 7/17–Sa 7/18, M 7/20– Tu 7/21/42) • FN: A remake of Mack Sennett's *The Great Pie Mystery*, also directed by Del Lord.

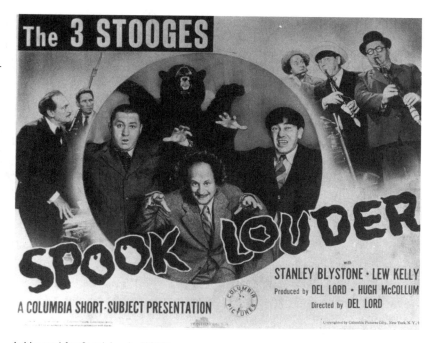

Lobby card for *Spook Louder* (1943). © *Columbia Pictures, courtesy of Jeff Lenburg Collection*

70. BACK FROM THE FRONT ☆☆☆½ • Rl. May 28 • Prod. no. 522 • 19m • *p d* Jules White • *st scr* Jack White and Ewart Adamson • *ph* John Stumar • *e* Edwin Bryant • *a* Carl Anderson • *c:* Vernon Dent (Lieutenant Dungen), Bud Jamison (German Officer), Stanley Blystone (German Captain), Tiny Lipson (Heavy German Sailor), Harry Semels (German Sailor Guard), Heinie Conklin and George Gray (German Sailors), Johnny Kascier (Wrestling German Sailor), and Al Thompson (Wrestling German Sailor/German Officer) • SYN: Moe, Larry, and Curly are Merchant Mariners serving their country. The boys' first mission is cut short when their ship is torpedoed, leaving the Stooges stranded on a raft at sea until they climb aboard a passing German cruiser. Immediately disguising themselves as German soldiers, the Stooges learn that their old commanding officer, Lieutenant Dungen, has been supplying top secret information to the Germans. The trio knocks out every crew member and poses as Hitler, Goering, and Goebbels before capturing the vessel's commanding officers and Dungen. • WT: *A Sailor's Mess* • FN: The seasick gag was reused as stock footage in both

*Dunked in the Deep* (11/3/49) and *Commotion on the Ocean* (11/8/56).

71. THREE LITTLE TWIRPS ☆☆☆ • Rl. July 9 • Prod. no. 551 • 15½m • *p* Del Lord and Hugh McCollum • *d* Harry Edwards • *st scr* Monty Collins and Elwood Ullman • *ph* John Stumar • *e* Paul Borofsky • *a* Carl Anderson • *c:* Chester Conklin (Circus Worker), Heinie Conklin (Louie), Stanley Blystone (Herman), Bud Jamison (Detective), Duke York (Sultan of Abadaba), Al Thompson (Ticket Salesman), and Hank Bell (Effie the Bearded Lady) • SYN: The Stooges wreak havoc at a local circus, with Curly hiding in a dressing room only to be mistaken by Effie the Bearded Lady as her blind date. He shaves the girl's beard off, causing her to faint. So when Herman, the circus owner, calls on Effie to come out and perform inside the big top, Curly disguises himself as the Bearded Lady, but his bonnet gets knocked off, revealing his true identity, and the chase begins. He meets up with Moe and Larry (wearing a horse costume), and they take refuge among some real mares. The Stooges' disguise soon fails when Joe, the circus attendant, tries serving them as

a lion's next meal. Later, the Stooges are arrested, but Herman gives them one last break; the Sultan needs three volunteers as human targets for his spear-throwing act • FN: Moe and Larry in a horse costume was reprised in *Horsing Around* (9/12/57).

**72. HIGHER THAN A KITE** ☆☆☆☆ • Rl. July 30 • Prod. no. 568 • 17m • *p* Del Lord and Hugh McCollum • *d* Del Lord • *st scr* Elwood Ullman and Monty Collins • *ph* Benjamin Kline • *e* Paul Borofsky • *a* Victor Greene • *c:* Duke York (Kelly), Vernon Dent (Boring), and Dick Curtis (Bommel) • SYN: Larry, Moe, and Curly travel to England with intentions of joining the Royal Air Force as pilots, but they wind up as garage mechanics. Of course, the Stooges prove they know very little about cars by ruining the colonel's automobile (it only had a *little* squeak). When the colonel threatens to kill them, the trio takes refuge in what appears to be a sewer pipe—but turns out to be a blockbuster bomb heading for Germany. But the Stooges end up getting a free ride when the bomb is dropped on Nazi Bommel's headquarters. Uninjured by the explosion, Larry hides in the wine cellar, while Moe and Curly disguise themselves as German officers. When Boring arrives to review Nazi war plans, he requests a bottle of wine, and Larry (dressed like a German fräulein) is discovered. Bommel falls for Larry, and the boys steal the war plans.

**73. I CAN HARDLY WAIT** ☆☆ • Rl. Aug. 13 • Prod. no. 570 • 16½m • *p d* Jules White • *st scr* Clyde Bruckman • *ph* John Stumar • *e* Charles Hochberg • *a* Victor Greene • *c:* Bud Jamison (Dr. A. Yank, Dentist), Lew Davis (Dr. Tug, Dentist) Adele Mara (Receptionist), and Al Thompson (Patient) • SYN: While consuming a ham bone, Curly develops a terrible toothache, and the pain eventually becomes so intense that he can't sleep. But when he does fall into slumber, he dreams that Moe and Larry rush him to the dentist. Moe shows him

there is nothing to be frightened of as he sits in the dentist's chair. The dentist enters and pulls Moe's tooth by accident. Hence, Curly's dream turns into a nightmare; he tosses and turns in his sleep, causing his upper bunk to crash down on the two lower bunks containing Moe and Larry. Tired of this ordeal, Moe socks Curly in the jaw, popping out his tooth. • WT: *Nothing but the Tooth* • FN: The collapsing-bed sequence is from *In the Sweet Pie and Pie* (10/16/41). The pulling teeth gag is also in *Leave 'Em Laughing* (1928), with Laurel and Hardy.

**74. DIZZY PILOTS** ☆☆½ • Rl. Sept. 24 • Prod. no. 555 • 17m • *p d* Jules White • *st scr* Clyde Bruckman • *ph* Benjamin Kline • *e* Charles Hochberg • *a* Victor Greene • *c:* Richard Fiske (Drill Sergeant, stock footage), Harry Semels and Al Thompson (Aircraft Company Reps), Charles Dorety (Soldier, stock footage), and Sethma Williams (Girl in Hangar) • SYN: The Stooges, as the Wrong brothers, have thirty days to prove to the army that their new airplane, *The Buzzard*, can revolutionize flying. At last, when the boys are ready to test this newfangled flying machine, Moe discovers one more snag: the plane is too wide to move out of the hangar. This problem is quickly solved when the Stooges cut a larger opening. The trio encounter two additional setbacks: their test flight fails, and they are drafted into the army. For their sergeant's benefit, the Stooges perform a peculiar marching sequence, disrupt the works, and make a menace of their commanding officer. • WT: *Pest Pilots* • FN: The army drill scenes are from *Boobs in Arms* (12/7/40). The gag of an oversized aircraft in a small hangar was later revived in *The Three Stooges in Orbit* (1962).

**75. PHONY EXPRESS** ☆☆ • Rl. Nov. 18 • Prod. no. 569 • 17m • *p* Del Lord and Hugh McCollum • *d* Del Lord • *st scr* Elwood Ullman and Monty Collins • *ph* John

Stumar • *e* Paul Borofsky • *a* Victor Greene • *c:* Shirley Patterson (Lola), Chester Conklin (Bartender), Snub Pollard (Sheriff), Bud Jamison (Red Morgan), Sally Cleaves and Gwen Seager (Dancing Partners), John Merton (Morgan's Assistant), Blackie Whiteford (Henchman), Joel Friedkin (Dr. Abdul), and Victor Travers (Newspaper Editor) • SYN: In pursuit of a mine payroll, Red Morgan and his gang invade the town of Peaceful Gulch. The city's newspaper editor publishes a photograph of the Stooges, wanted for vagrancy, claiming they are really three famous marshals coming to town. In the meantime, Larry, Moe, and Curly are across the border selling patent medicine for their boss, Abdul. When the team's patent medicine sales backfire, it's off to the Peaceful Gulch Saloon, where Red Morgan mistakes them for the marshals. Unfortunately, Morgan soon learns from the saloon's waiter that the Stooges are actually wanted for vagrancy. In the ensuing chase, the boys accidentally render Morgan unconscious, and later they are deputized to guard the bank from Morgan's gang of bank robbers. Naturally, Red and his mob rob the bank, with the Stooges recovering the loot to save the day. • FN: Remade, with stock footage, as *Merry Mavericks* (9/6/51).

**76. A GEM OF A JAM** ☆☆☆ • Rl. Dec. 30 • Prod. 575 • 16½m • *p* Hugh McCollum • *d* Del Lord • *st scr* Del Lord • *ph* John Stumar • *e* Paul Borofsky • *a* Victor Greene • *c:* Fred Kelsey and Al Thompson (Cops), Frank O'Connor (Cop in Alley), John Tyrrell (Joe, Wounded Crook), Al Hill (Crook), and Dudley Dickerson (Watchman) • SYN: Janitors Moe, Larry, and Curly are mistaken for three doctors when three bank robbers suddenly rush in to the doctor's office they are in and order them to remove a bullet from one of the wounded robbers. With no time to explain, the Stooges start operating and accidentally lose their patient: he slides off the operating table and right out the window into a waiting police car. When the remaining two crooks find a skeleton instead of their partner on the operating table, they chase the Stooges into a room of mannequins and wax models. During the commotion, Curly trips into a tray of plaster and arises as a ghost, scaring everyone except the police, who arrest the crooks • FN: Curly was seriously injured in a scene in which he had to slide out the window; his head hit the ledge, requiring fourteen stitches.

## 1944

**77. CRASH GOES THE HASH**
☆☆☆½ • Rl. Feb. 5 • Prod. no. 4010 • 17m • *p d* Jules White • *st scr* Felix Adler • *ph* George Meehan • *e* Charles Hochberg • *a* Charles Clague • *c:* Vernon Dent (Fuller Bull), Bud Jamison (Flint, the Head Butler), Dick Curtis (Prince Shaam), Symona Boniface (Mrs. Van Bustle), Wally Rose, Johnny Kascier (Reporter with Broken Foot), John Tyrrell (Bruised Reporter), Judy Malcolm (Bull's Secretary), Beatrice Blinn, Ida Mae Johnson, Victor Travers, and Elise Grover (Party Guests) • SYN: The Stooges, working as deliverymen for the Star Pressing Company, are accidentally hired as reporters for the *Daily News* and sent to cover the wedding of social beauty Mrs. Van Bustle and her fiancé Prince Shaam. In order to gain entry into the wedding, the Stooges pose as footmen and butlers, serving the guests a wild array of entrées, including their own bizarre version of canapés (dog biscuits smothered in peas) and a walking turkey (brought to life by a parrot inside). Following dinner, however, the trio snaps a picture of the prince, showing him in the act of robbing Mrs. Van Bustle's safe. For solving the case, the Stooges' boss gives them a bonus, and Curly receives an added prize—the hand of Mrs. Van Bustle • FN: The parrot in the turkey gag was reprised in *G.I. Wanna Home* (9/5/46), *Three Dark Horses* (10/16/52), and *Listen, Judge* (3/6/52).

Lobby card for *Crash Goes the Hash* (1944). © *Columbia Pictures, courtesy of Jeff Lenburg Collection*

**78. BUSY BUDDIES** ☆☆½ • Rl. Mar 18 • Prod. no. 4001 • 16½m • *p* Hugh McCollum • *d* Del Lord • *st scr* Del Lord and Elwood Ullman • *ph* George Meehan • *e* Henry Batista • *a* Charles Clague • *c:* Vernon Dent (Hotcakes Customer), Victor Travers (Soup Customer), Fred Kelsey (Pie Vendor), Eddie Laughton (Sellwell Rep), John Tyrrell (Referee), Eddie Gribbon (Milking Champ), and Johnny Kascier (Champ's Cornerman) • SYN: In order to pay off a pastry bill as operators of a cheap beanery, Moe and Larry enter Curly as one of the contestants in the county fair's cow-milking contest, with the top prize being $1,000. When Curly experiences difficulty milking a real cow, Moe dons a cow costume featuring a giant milk bottle covered with a glove. His substitution plan works successfully until Curly yanks the glove off the bottle, causing the milk to gush out rapidly, disqualifying the Stooges. • FN: See *Hoofs and Goofs* (1/31/57).

**79. THE YOKE'S ON ME** ☆ • Rl. May 26 • Prod. no. 571 • 16½m • *p d* Jules White • *st scr* Clyde Bruckman • *ph* Glen Gano • *e* Charles Hochberg • *a* Charles Clague • *c:* Eva McKenzie (Ma), Robert McKenzie (Pa), Emmett Lynn (Smithers), Al Thompson (Sheriff), and Victor Travers (Deputy Sheriff) • SYN: The Stooges decide to become farmers as a last resort when every branch of the armed service turns them down as physical liabilities. So the boys buy a dilapidated farmhouse and survey the grounds to find that no livestock exists, except for an ostrich. Later, the Stooges encounter three Japanese soldiers who have escaped from a local relocation center. The soldiers' flight is cut short, however, when the Stooges' ostrich consumes some gun powder, laying an explosive egg. • WT: *Fowled by a Fowl*

**80. IDLE ROOMERS** ☆☆½ • Rl. July 16 • Prod. no. 4013 • 16½m • *p* Hugh McCollum • *d* Del Lord • *st scr* Del Lord and Elwood Ullman • *ph* Glen Gano • *e* Henry Batista • *a* Charles Clague • *c:* Christine McIntyre (Mrs. Leander), Duke York (Lupe, the Wolf Man), Vernon Dent (Mr. Leander), Joanne Frank (Hazel), Esther Howard (Hazel's Roommate), and Eddie Laughton (Hotel Clerk) • SYN: The Stooges are working as bellboys at a hotel when two vaudeville performers arrive with a trunk containing a wolf man who goes wild whenever he hears music. Curly unloads the trunk and turns on the radio, causing the wolf man to escape, running into rooms occupied by other guests. When petrified guests report seeing a hairy burglar in the hotel, the manager orders the Stooges to find him. Their frantic search ends in the elevator, which is occupied by—who else?—the wolf man.

### 81. GENTS WITHOUT CENTS
☆☆☆ • Rl. Sept. 22 • Prod. no. 4020 • 19m • *p d* Jules White • *st s cr* Felix Adler • *ph* Benjamin Kline • *e* Charles Hochberg • *a* Charles Clague • *c:* Lindsay Bourquin, Laverne Thompson, and Betty Phares (Flo, Mary, or Shirley), Johnny Tyrrell (Manny Weeks), Judy Malcolm (Weeks's Secretary), Bob Burns and Eddie Borden (Men in Audience), and Lynton Brent (Lieutenant in Sketch) • SYN: Following an audition for talent scout Manny Weeks, the Stooges and a trio of dancing girls are hired to replace a shipyard act, the Castor and Earle Revue. The Stooges perform "Niagara Falls" and an army routine, "At the Front," while the girls provide the dancing. The show closes a triumphant success, and the Stooges marry the girls, embarking on a honeymoon in—of course—Niagara Falls! • WT: *Tenderized Hams* • FN: The "Niagara Falls" sequence was originally filmed for Columbia's 1943 feature *Good Luck, Mr. Yates,* but was cut out of the final release print.

### 82. NO DOUGH BOYS ☆☆☆ • Rl. Nov. 24 • Prod. no. 564 • 16½m • *p d* Jules White • *st scr* Felix Adler • *ph* George Meehan • *e* Charles Hochberg • *a* Charles Clague • *c:* Vernon Dent (Hugo), Christine McIntyre (Delia), Brian O'Hara (Waiter), Kelly Flint (Amelia), Judy Malcolm (Celia), and John Tyrrell (Director) • SYN: The Stooges are modeling as Japanese soldiers for a photographer. When their shutterbug boss is called away, the trio grabs lunch at a res-

taurant, still in costume. The waiter mistakes them for three real escaped Japanese soldiers and summons the police. Before the police can arrest them, however, the Stooges flee and take refuge in a room full of Nazi spies awaiting the arrival of three jujitsu experts. The Stooges pose as the jujitsu men until the real guys show up. • WT: *The New World Odor* • FN: The smoking an imaginary pipe gag was also used in *Way Out West* (1937), with Laurel and Hardy.

## 1945

### 83. THREE PESTS IN A MESS
☆☆☆ • Rl. Jan. 19 • Prod. no. 4022 • 15m • *p* Hugh McCollum • *d st scr* Del Lord • *ph* Benjamin Kline • *e* Henry Batista • *a* Charles Clague • *c:* Vernon Dent (Philip Black), Victor Travers (Patent Office Man), Snub Pollard (Watchman), Christine McIntyre (Secretary/Con Woman), Brian O'Hara (I. Cheatam), and Heinie Conklin (Devil) • SYN: When Larry, Moe, and Curly try selling a Patent Office clerk on their fly-catching device, a con woman from the Cheatam Investment Company mistakes the Stooges for winners of a big sweepstakes ticket. Once she discovers she's goofed, however, her two crooked associates return and chase the Stooges into a sporting goods shop, where a rifle falls on Curly's head. He takes the weapon and accidentally fires it. The gunfire hits a mannequin, and Curly thinks he's killed a real man. The trio stuffs the mannequin into a trash bag and tries to bury the evidence at Ever Rest Pet Cemetery. A night watchman hears them digging, however, and calls the cemetery owner, Mr. Black, who leaves a costume party, bringing along his two partners who are dressed as a devil and a skeleton. Naturally, Black and his men scare the Stooges out of their shoes and out of the cemetery! • FN: To achieve the gag of Larry sliding underneath the door, the prop man dug a hole and covered it with rubber, then pulled Larry below in a speed shot. . . . The gag of disposing of a mock dead body

was also in *Habeas Corpus* (1928), with Laurel and Hardy.

### 84. BOOBY DUPES ☆☆½ • Rl. Mar. 17 • Prod. no. 4006 • 17m • *p* Hugh McCollum • *d st scr* Del Lord • *ph* Glen Gano • *e* Henry Batista • *a* Charles Clague • *c:* Vernon Dent (Captain), Rebel Randall (Captain's Girlfriend), Dorothy Vernon (Customer), Johnny Tyrrell (Boat Man), Snub Pollard (Ice Cream Vendor), Wanda Perry, Gene Courtney, and Lola Gogan (Bathing Beauties) • SYN: Fish salesmen Moe, Larry, and Curly set sail on their first fishing expedition and sink the boat when Curly goes after a fish with an axe. Fortunately, the Stooges yank out a spare boat but find that it has no motor. At this same moment, the boys hear a squadron of airplanes passing overhead. Moe quickly manufacturers a flag (a white sheet with a red-stained circle in the center) on a pole and begins waving it wildly. One of the pilots, however, mistakes his distress signal for a Japanese flag and starts bombing the Stooges' boat. • FN: A partial reworking of Laurel and Hardy's *Towed in a Hole* (12/31/32).

### 85. IDIOTS DELUXE ☆☆☆ • Rl. July 20; re. Sept. 1965, Oct. 1966 • Prod. no. 4030 • 17½m • *p d* Jules White • *st scr* Elwood Ullman • *ph* Glen Gano • *e* Charles Hochberg • *a* Hilyard Brown • *c:* Vernon Dent (Judge), Paul Kruger (Cop), and Al Thompson (Courtroom Spectator) • SYN: The scene is a courtroom. Moe is accused of assaulting his two brothers-in-law, Larry and Curly, with an axe while on a hunting trip searching for peace and quiet. A zany escapade with a ferocious bear in the wilderness is responsible for triggering the altercation. In the courtroom, Moe mumbles that the trip cost him $300, ruined his car (the bear crashed it into a tree), and gave him a complete nervous breakdown. Sympathetic, the judge finds Moe not guilty and allows him to keep his axe. Thanking the judge, Moe wields the sharp tool at

Larry and Curly and chases them out of the courtroom • WT: *The Malady Lingers On* • FN: Remade, with stock footage, as *Guns A Poppin!* (6/13/57).

**86. IF A BODY MEETS A BODY** ☆☆½ • Rl. Aug. 30 • Prod. no. 4033 • 18m • *p d* Jules White • *st* Gilbert Pratt • *scr* Jack White • *ph* Benjamin Kline • *e* Charles Hochberg • *a* Charles Clague • *c:* Ted Lorch (Jerkington), Fred Kelsey (Detective Clancy), Joe Palma (Housekeeper), Al Thompson (Uncle Bob O. Link), John Tyrrell (Lawyer), and Victor Travers (Link Family Member) • SYN: Moe and Larry read in the newspaper that the relatives of the late Professor Robert O. Link are searching for Curly Q. Link, the heir to his big estate. When Curly informs Moe and Larry that Link was his uncle, the Stooges leave immediately for the reading of the will at a spooky old mansion. But the will gets stolen. At the mansion, meanwhile, there have been reports of murders and other weird happenings. In their room, the Stooges witness so many strange goings-on themselves that they flee downstairs, knocking over the maid, who turns out to be a man and the thief who stole the Link will. Curly grabs the document, anxious to know his inheritance, and learns that his uncle has bequeathed him the sum of sixty-seven cents! • WT: *Nearly in the Dough* • FN: A remake of *Laurel and Hardy Murder Case* (1930). The parrot in the skull gag was also used in *The Hot Scots* (7/8/48) and in *Scotched in Scotland* (11/4/54). . . . Curly's health problems begin to affect his timing and voice.

**87. MICRO-PHONIES** ☆☆☆ • Rl. Nov. 15 • Prod. no. 4044 • 17m • *p* Hugh McCollum • *d st scr* Edward Bernds • *ph* Glen Gano • *e* Henry Batista • *a* Charles Clague • *c:* Christine McIntyre (Alice Andrews, a.k.a. Alice Van Doren), Gino Corrado (Signor Spumoni), Symona Boniface (Mrs. Bixby), Sam Flint (Alice's Father), Fred Kelsey (Mr. Dugan),

Chester Conklin (Drunk Party Pianist), Bess Flowers (Party Guest), Lynton Brent (Mr. Allen), Ted Lorch (Masters), John Tyrrell (Recording Engineer), Heinie Conklin (Radio Station Pianist), and Judy Malcolm (Receptionist) • SYN: When Curly mimes a girl's recording of "Voices of Spring" at a local radio station, Mrs. Bixby, a wealthy dowager, observes his antics and signs Moe, Larry, and Curly up to perform on her Krispy Krunchies radio program. Mrs. Bixby is unaware that the person singing on the demonstration record is actually

her own daughter, Alice Van Doren, who records under the name Alice Andrews. The woman also asks the Stooges to sing at her musical party. That evening the boys are reunited at the party with Signor Spumoni, whom the Stooges antagonized earlier at the radio station. The Stooges are also spotted by Alice, the real singer of "Voices of Spring." When Moe accidentally smashes the demo recording, Alice offers to sing for the boys behind a curtain. At the conclusion of their song, however, Spumoni exposes their fake setup as the

One-sheet for *Micro-Phonies* (1945). Note that Harry Edwards is incorrectly billed as writer and director. © *Columbia Pictures, courtesy of Jeff Lenburg Collection*

Stooges make a hasty exit, and Alice is asked to appear on her mother's show instead. • FN: Edward Bernds commenced scripting the short on February 27, 1945, after producer Hugh McCollum told him he wanted their next short to be a Stooge operetta. . . . Footage was reused in *Stop! Look! and Laugh!* (7/1/60). The gag in which the Stooges flip cherries into an opera singer's mouth was also used in *Pardon My Scotch* (8/1/35), though they used grapes instead. The *Micro-Phonies* plot was also used in *Hot Sports* (1929), with Monty Collins, which was directed by Jules White.

## 1946

### 88. BEER BARREL POLECATS ☆☆
• Rl. Jan. 10 • Prod. no. 4045 • 17m • *p d* Jules White • *st scr* Gilbert W. Pratt • *ph* George Kelley • *e* Charles Hochberg • *a* Charles Clague • *c:* Vernon Dent (Warden), Robert Williams (Guard), Eddie Laughton (Convict 41144, stock footage), Al Thompson (Photographer), Bruce Bennett (Guard, stock footage), and Joe Palma and Blackie Whiteford (Convicts) • SYN: It's Prohibition, and Curly suggests the Stooges produce their own beer rather than search for it. Their first customer is a police officer, who throws them in jail. Curly refuses to be deprived of his beer, however, smuggling in a keg under his coat. While he is posing for a prison photograph, the hot lights cause his barrel to explode, sending a torrent of suds in all directions. Now in prison for their misdeed, the Stooges plan their escape (stock footage from *In the Sweet Pie and Pie* [10/16/41]). Later, in the prison recreation room, the boys have a run-in with the warden and are sent to the rock pile. His orders are postponed temporarily, however, when a guard orders them to repaint the prison walls (old footage from *So Long Mr. Chumps* [2/7/41]). Instead, the boys paint their prison clothes into guard uniforms and dash for the front gate, only to be captured (new footage). Finally, the Stooges wind up on the rock pile, making little ones of big

ones (again stock footage from *So Long Mr. Chumps*). Then, almost half a century later, the Stooges, sporting long, gray beards, are released from prison. Curly's first request: a nice cold bottle of beer! • WT: *Three Duds in the Suds* • FN: The extensive amount of stock footage was used because Curly's failing health did not permit him to work a normal three-to-four-day shooting schedule.

### 89. A BIRD IN THE HEAD ☆☆
• Rl. Feb. 28 • Prod. no. 4043 • 17m • *p* Hugh McCollum • *d st scr* Edward Bernds • *ph* Burnett Guffey • *e* Henry Batista • *a* Charles Clague • *c:* Vernon Dent (Professor Panzer), Robert Williams (Mr. Beedle), Frank Lackteen (Nikko), and Art Miles (Igor, the Gorilla) • SYN: Paperhangers Moe, Larry, and Curly wreck Mr. Beedle's apartment and lose their jobs. They find work at the home of Professor Panzer, an eccentric scientist. Soon, however, the Stooges learn that the scientist is actually eager to have them around as possible material for a daring experiment. It seems he is trying to transfer the brain of a man to his pet ape, Igor, and naturally Curly's brain is just the right size: tiny. Realizing the professor's plan, the three fight their way out, aided by a machine gun and the ape, which has, understandably, developed a strong affinity for Curly. • SD: five (M 4/9–F 4/13/45); filmed on Stage 19 • FN: Until the script was completed and ready to be mimeographed, it was simply known as "The Ape" script. • PS: For the most part, Stooges two-reelers took three to four days to film. But *A Bird in the Head* went a fifth day because of the death of President Roosevelt, director Edward Bernds said. (It was Bernds's second time a the helm of a Stooges short.)

### 90. UNCIVIL WAR BIRDS ☆☆☆
• Rl. Mar. 29 • Prod. no. 4050 • 17m • *p d* Jules White • *st* Clyde Bruckman • *scr* Jules White • *ph* Philip Tannura • *e* Charles Hochberg • *a* Charles Clague • *c:* Faye Williams

(Mary Belle), Eleanor Counts (Ringa Belle), Marilyn Johnson (Lulu Belle), Robert Williams (Union Lieutenant), Ted Lorch (Union Colonel), Maury Dexter, Al Rosen, and Blackie Whiteford (Union Officers), Joe Palma and Cy Schindell (Union Soldiers), John Tyrrell (Union Sergeant/Union Officer), Brian Lew Davis (Confederate Soldier), and Victor Travers (Justice of the Peace) • SYN: The Stooges' plans to marry their three Southern belles, Lulu, Mary, and Ringa, are disrupted by the Civil War. Moe and Larry join the Union army, while Curly becomes a Confederate soldier. The mix-up results in Moe and Larry posing as Curly's prisoners and vice versa. • WT: *Three Southern Dumbbells* • FN: A scene-for-scene remake of Buster Keaton's *Mooching Through Georgia* (8/11/39), including stock footage from that film. . . . A new rendition of "Dixie" replaced "Three Blind Mice" as the Stooges standard theme song over the opening titles.

### 91. THE THREE TROUBLEDOERS ☆☆☆
• Rl. Apr. 25 • Prod. no. 4046 • 17m • *p* Hugh McCollum • *d* Edward Bernds • *st scr* Jack White • *ph* George Kelley • *e* Henry Batista • *a* Charles Clague • *c:* Christine McIntyre (Nell), Dick Curtis (Badlands Blackie), Ethan Laidlaw and Blackie Whiteford (Blackie's Gang Members), Hank Bell (Mustached Town Elder), Steve Clarke and Budd Fine (Townsmen), Joe Garcia (Waiter), and Victor Travers (Justice of the Peace) • SYN: The boys enter Dead Man's Gulch to learn that the last six sheriffs were killed by Badlands Blackie and his gang. Soon the Stooges meet a young girl named Nell at a local blacksmith shop. She tells them her father is being held captive and won't be released unless she marries Blackie. So Curly becomes sheriff and rescues Nell's father. • SD: four (known dates F 5/11–Sa 5/12/45); shot at Providencia Ranch and Stage 10 on Columbia Ranch • PS: *The Three Troubledoers* was previewed in Compton, Califor-

nia, on January 11, 1946. Director Edward Bernds recalled that the audience response was only fair and that it was poorest of his previews. Bernds also related that Stooges comedies were usually previewed at one of three theaters: The Alexander in Glendale (now the Mann Alexander), The Tower in Compton, and the California Theater in Huntington Park.

## 92. MONKEY BUSINESSMEN

☆☆☆ • Rl. June 20 • Prod. no. 4058 • 17½m • p Hugh McCollum • d st scr Edward Bernds • ph Philip Tannura • e Paul Borofsky • a Charles Clague • c: Kenneth MacDonald (Dr. Mallard), Fred Kelsey (Smiling Sam McGann), Snub Pollard (Mr. Grimble), Jean Donahue Willes (Nurse Shapely), Cy Schindell and Rocky Woods (Nurses), and Wade Crosby (George) • SYN: The Stooges are electricians who manage to wreck the first place in which they work. Fired, Curly suggests they go somewhere else for a nice, long rest, and they check into Dr. Mallard's Rest Home and Clinic (where the owner is soaking his patients for every nickel). When the Stooges discover that the clinic is operated by gangsters, they take flight, colliding with Mr. Grimble, a man in a wheelchair, landing on his bandaged foot. Suddenly, the man pronounces his foot cured and begins speeding after Moe, Larry, and Curly, later paying them $1,000 for fixing his bad foot. Elated, the Stooges begin planning how to spend it. Curly has one suggestion: taking a vacation for a nice, long rest! • SD: four (W 1/30–Sa 2/2/46) • WT: *Sanitarium Stooge* • FN: Two special effects in the film were achieved as follows: a smoke tube was hidden in Larry's hand when he feels Curly's burning forehead, and compressed air pipes were used to blow Moe's hair upwards. Unlike the finished film, in the first draft script of *Monkey Businessmen*, the Stooges are janitors who end up repairing the electricity at a gymnasium called Simone's Body Beautiful, where their motto is "Trade in Your Old Curves

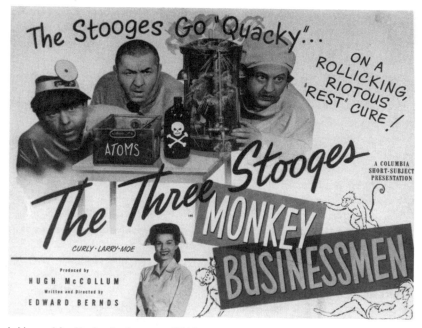

Lobby card for *Monkey Businessmen* (1946). © *Columbia Pictures, courtesy of Jeff Lenburg Collection*

for New Ones, Whistles Guaranteed or Your Money Back." . . . A remake of *Mutiny on the Body* (1938), with Smith and Dale.

## 93. THREE LOAN WOLVES ☆☆ •

Rl. July 4 • Prod. no. 4053 • 16½m • p d Jules White • st scr Felix Adler • ad Tommy Flood • ph George Kelley • e Edwin Bryant • a Charles Clague • c: Beverly Warren (Molly), Harold Brauer (Butch McGee), Wally Rose and Joe Palma (Henchmen), Jackie Jackson (Boy), Danny Craig (Curly's Stand-In), Eli Schmuckler (Larry's Stand-In), and Dave Levitt (Moe's Stand-In) • SYN: The boys are pawnbrokers whose first customers are Butch McGee and his girlfriend, Molly. When the gang skips town, Molly leaves her sister's baby and a phony diamond with Larry at the hock shop. Moe and Curly return from lunch to help Larry entertain the infant. • WT: *In Hock*

## 94. G.I. WANNA HOME ☆☆☆½ • Rl.

Sept. 5 • Prod. no. 4063 • 15½m • p d Jules White • st scr Felix Adler • ph George Kelley • e Edwin Bryant • a Charles Clague • c: Judy Malcolm (Jessie), Ethelreda Leopold (Tessie),

Doris Houck (Bessie), Symona Boniface (Landlady), and Al Thompson (Hobo) • SYN: The Stooges are now ex-GI's confronted with all the trials and tribulations of discharged veterans. Their biggest problem is finding a home for their three love mates, Jessie, Tessie, and Bessie, who have been dispossessed. The Stooges and their future wives finally make their new home in a vacant lot, until a tractor comes along to plow it under. Then they convert a one-room apartment into a midget-sized bungalow where the six retire after being married. • FN: The film title has been mistakenly listed as *G.I. Wanna Go Home*. . . . The parrot in the turkey gag also appears in *Crash Goes the Hash* (2/5/44), *Three Dark Horses* (10/16/52), and *Listen, Judge* (3/6/52).

## 95. RHYTHM AND WEEP ☆☆½ •

Rl. Oct. 3 • Prod. no. 4057 • 17½m • p d Jules White • st scr Felix Adler • ph Philip Tannura • e Edwin Bryant • a Charles Clague • c: Jack Norton (Escaped Lunatic), Gloria Patrice (Wilda), Ruth Godfrey (Tilda), Nita Bieber (Hilda), and Robert Stevens (Theater Manager) • SYN: The

Stooges, having lost numerous acting jobs, decide to end it all by jumping from the roof of a skyscraper, along with three young actresses in the same sad predicament. At the last moment, however, the Stooges and the girls hear some wonderful piano music and discover an eccentric millionaire who's casting a new Broadway musical. He offers the boys and girls parts in his new show, which they accept. The Stooges begin rehearsing an army medical exam sketch, and the millionaire is so impressed that he prepares to double their salaries and give them star billing. His generous offer is cut short, however, when two attendants drive up and haul him, an escaped patient, back to Dr. Dippy's Retreat Home. • WT: *Acting Up* • FN: The rooftop sequence was filmed at the Monogram Studios on Sunset Boulevard, a few blocks east of Columbia, according to ThreeStooges.net. . . . An originally scripted scene featuring actresses Gloria Patrice, Nita Bieber, and Ruth Godfrey dressed as Curly, Moe, and Larry was deleted from the production.

96. THREE LITTLE PIRATES ☆☆☆
• Rl. Dec. 5 • Prod. no. 4067 • 17½m
• *p* Hugh McCollum • *d* Edward Bernds • *st scr* Clyde Bruckman • *ph* Philip Tannura • *e* Paul Borofsky • *a* Charles Clague • *c:* Christine McIntyre (Rita Yolanda), Vernon Dent (Governor), Dorothy DeHaven (Chiquita), Jack Parker and Larry McGrath (Soldiers), Robert Stevens (Black Louie), Ethan Laidlaw and Joe Palma (Henchman), Al Thompson and Cy Schindell (Pirates) • SYN: Three sailors working on a New York City garbage barge become shipwrecked on an island and are sent to jail by the governor, who orders their execution. However, Rita, the governor's beauteous captive and his unwilling bride-to-be, helps the Stooges escape and tags along. The Stooges appease the governor, reprising their roles in the routine "The Maharaja." Afterward, the Stooges escape to Black Louie's Pirate Den, hoping for safer quarters, while Chiquita, a palace beauty, informs the governor of the Stooges' masquerade. A zany

knife-throwing contest ensues between the Stooges and Black Louie, with one knife going haywire and cutting through a chandelier, which crashes down on the pirate and his men. • SD: four (M 4/15–Th 4/18/46) • FN: The routine "The Maharaja" was first enacted in the Columbia feature *Time Out for Rhythm* (6/5/41) and later appeared in *The Three Stooges Go Around the World in a Daze* (8/21/63). The Stooges also performed it on television on the *Texaco Star Theatre*, *The Steve Allen Show*, and *The Ed Sullivan Show*. The knife-throwing act was also repeated in *Around the World*. • PS: According to director Edward Bernds, Moe dictated the entire "The Maharaja" routine to writer Clyde Bruckman, "crazy syllable for crazy syllable," in a writer's conference on April 2, 1946. According to Bruckman's script, the correct spelling of the words as dictated by Moe are "Razbanyas yatee benee futch ah tinney herongha . . ."

**1947**

97. HALF-WITS HOLIDAY ☆☆☆
• Rl. Jan. 9 • Prod. no. 4056 • 17½m
• *p d* Jules White • *st scr* Zion Myers
• *ph* George Kelley • *e* Edwin Bryant
• *a* Charles Clague • *c:* Vernon Dent (Professor Quackenbush), Barbara Slater (Lulu), Ted Lorch (Professor Sedletz), Emil Sitka (Sappington), Symona Boniface (Mrs. Smythe Smythe), Helen Dickson (Mrs. Gotrocks), Victor Travers (Sleeping Party Guest), Johnny Kascier (Party Guest), and Al Thompson (First Party-Guest Pie Victim) • SYN: The Stooges are plumbers who crash a psychologist's home and find themselves the subjects of a bet. Professor Quackenbush wagers he can turn them into polished gentlemen in sixty days. With the aid of his daughter, Lulu, the professor attempts to teach the boys proper table manners. Following weeks of hard training, the night finally arrives when the Stooges are unleashed on society. All goes well—until the Stooges commence with a pie-throwing melee. • WT: *No Gents—No Cents* • SD: four (Th 5/2– Sa 5/4, M 5/6/46) • FN: A reworking

of *Hoi Polloi* (8/29/35). The pie-fight footage was reused in *Pest Man Wins* (12/6/51) and *Scheming Schemers* (10/4/56), in yet another remake, *Pies and Guys* (6/12/58), and in *Stop! Look! and Laugh!* (7/1/60). . . . Moe's wife, Helen, who inspired the original premise for *Hoi Polloi*, also created the memorable scene in *Half-Wits Holiday* in which Moe eludes a pie hanging from the ceiling as Mrs. Smythe Smythe approaches. (See *Moe Howard & the 3 Stooges*, pages 145 and 147 for details.) . . . Sadly, during the making of this film, Curly suffered a stroke and had to retire from the act. • PS: *Half-Wits Holiday* was actor Emil Sitka's first film with the team. Sitka recalled, "When I met Curly, I said, 'My name is Emil Sitka and I'm playing the butler in this picture.' Curly stood up, politely shook my hand, then said seriously, 'Yes, sir. I see.' Then, he sat back down. Now, I don't know if he called me sir because I was dressed like a butler, or if he was trying to be dignified."

Moe, Larry, and Curly also appeared in the following newsreels: *Movietone News* (1934), *Screen Snapshots Series 14 #2* (10/26/34), *Screen Snapshots Series 14 #6* (2/22/35), *Screen Snapshots Series 15 #7* (2/28/36), *Screen Snapshots Series 18 #9* (5/12/39), *Screen Snapshots Series 19 #5* (2/23/40), *Screen Snapshots Series 19 #6* (3/29/40), *Screen Snapshots Series 20 #3* (11/22/40), *Screen Snapshots Series 21 #3* (11/7/41), *Screen Snapshots Series 22 #8* (3/31/43), *Screen Snapshots* (1945; exact release number and date not yet determined)

## Feature Films

All Columbia releases unless otherwise noted.

**1934**

1. THE CAPTAIN HATES THE SEA ☆☆ • Rl. Oct. 22 • Prod. no. 16 • 92m • *d* Lewis Milestone • *scr* Wallace Smith • *e* Gene Milford
• *c:* Victor McLaglen (Schulte), Wynne Gibson (Jeddock), Alison Skipworth (Mrs. McGruder), John Gilbert (Steve), Helen Vinson (Janet

Grayson), Fred Keating (Danny), Walter Connolly (Captain), Tala Birell (Gerta Klargi), Leon Errol (Layton), Jack Wray (Mr. Jeddock), Walter Catlett (Joe Silvers, Bartender), Claude Gillingwater (Judge Griswold), Emily Fitzroy (Mrs. Griswold), Donald Meek (Josephus Bushmills), Geneva Mitchell (Miss Hockson), Luis Alberni (Juan Gilboa), Akim Tamiroff (Salazaro), Arthur Treacher (Major Warringforth), and Inez Courtney (Flo) • SYN: In this *Grand Hotel*–style movie featuring a series of intertwining stories about passengers on a cruise ship, the Stooges appear as a crazy group of musicians in the background, in less than a half dozen scenes.

## 1938

2. START CHEERING ☆☆☆ • Rl. Mar. 3 • Prod. no. 8 • 79m • *ap* Nat Perrin • *d* Albert S. Rogell • *st* Corey Ford • *scr* Eugene Solow, Richard E. Wormser, and Phillip Rapp • *ph* Joseph Walker • *e* Gene Havlick • *mu* Johnny Green • *md* Morris Stoloff • *c:* Jimmy Durante (Willie Gumbatz), Walter Connolly (Sam Lewis), Joan Perry (Jean Worthington), Craig E. Earle (Professor Quiz), Gertrude Niesen (Sarah), Raymond Walburn (Dean Worthington), Ernest Truex (Blodgett), Hal LeRoy (Tarzan Biddle), Charles Starrett (Ted Crosley), Virginia Dale (Mabel), Chaz Chase (Shorty), Broderick Crawford (Biff Gordon), Louis Prima and His Orchestra (Themselves), and Johnny Green and His Orchestra (Themselves) • SYN: Fed up with Hollywood, film star Ted Crosley (Charles Starrett) quits the movies and enrolls at Midland College under a phony name. But Ted's managers (Walter Connolly and Jimmy Durante) have another idea. They try to have him expelled from the college so he can resume his Hollywood film career. The Stooges are campus firemen at the college. • WT: *College Hero* and *College Follies of 1938*

## 1941

3. TIME OUT FOR RHYTHM ☆☆½ • Rl. June 5 • Prod. no. 90

Lobby card for The Three Stooges' first Columbia Pictures feature in a supporting role, *Start Cheering* (1938). © Columbia Pictures, courtesy of Jeff Lenburg Collection

• 75m • *p* Irving Starr • *d* Sidney Salkow • *st* Bert Granet • *scr* Edmund L. Hartmann and Bert Lawrence • *ph* Franz F. Planer • *e* Arthur Seid • *md* Morris Stoloff • *c:* Rudy Vallee (Daniel Collins), Ann Miller (Kitty Brown), Rosemary Lane (Frances Lewis), Allen Jenkins (Off-Beat Davis), Joan Merrill (Herself), Richard Lane (Mike Armstrong), Stanley Andrews (James Anderson), Brenda and Cobina and Six Hits and a Miss (Themselves), and Glen Gray and His Casa Loma Band • SYN: In this musical extravaganza, the Stooges play unemployed actors who find work after using Danny's and Mike's Agency. What follows is classic Stooges. Appearing throughout the film, the boys perform two memorable routines, "The Maharaja" and "Melodrama." But the climax is the trio performing a rhumba dance number with costars Brenda and Cobina and Curly dressed as a Carmen Miranda! • WT: *Show Business*

## 1942

4. MY SISTER EILEEN ☆☆ • Rl. Sept. 24 • Prod. no. 161 • 96m • *p* Max Gordon • *d* Alexander Hall • *st* Ruth McKenney • *scr* Joseph Fields

and Jerome Chodorov • *ph* Joseph Walker • *e* Viola Lawrence • *md* Morris Stoloff • *c:* Rosalind Russell (Ruth Sherwood), Brian Aherne (Baker), Janet Blair (Eileen Sherwood), George Tobias (Appopolous), Allyn Joslyn (Chic Clark), Elizabeth Patterson (Grandma Sherwood), Grant Mitchell (Walter Sherwood), Richard Quine (Frank Lippincott), June Havoc (Effie Shelton), Donald MacBride (Officer Lonigan), Gordon Jones (Wreck Loomis), Jeff Donnell (Helen Loomis), Frank Sully (Jenson), and Clyde Fillmore (Ralph Craven) • SYN: Rosalind Russell and Janet Blair star as sisters who move from Ohio to New York City to succeed as a writer and stage actress, respectively, coming across a succession of wacky characters in the process. They include the Stooges, subway workers, who dynamite their way up into Russell's apartment at the end of the film, solving the mystery of who is responsible for the series of dynamite blasts that have been rocking her dwelling • FN: The Stooges were not listed on the original cast call sheet.

## 1945

5. ROCKIN' IN THE ROCKIES ☆☆½ • Rl. Apr. 17 • Prod. no. 3017

• 67m • *p* Colbert Clark • *d* Vernon Keays • *st* Louise Rousseau and Gail Davenport • *scr* J. Benton Cheney and John Grey • *ph* Glen Gano • *e* Paul Borofsky • *c:* Mary Beth Hughes (June McGuire), Jay Kirby (Rusty), Gladys Blake (Betty), Moe Howard (Shorty), Jerry Howard (Curly), Larry Fine (Larry), Jack Clifford (Sheriff Zeke), Forrest Taylor (Sam Clemens), Vernon Dent (Stanton), Tim Ryan, the Hoosier Hotshots, the Cappy Barra Boys, and Spade Cooley and His Orchestra (Themselves), and Lew Davis (Roulette Wheel Operator) • SYN: Moe plays the straight man while Curly and Larry play aspiring Broadway actors who work as bumbling ranch hands in this musical western. • FN: Larry and Curly are teamed as a comedy duo. Larry assumes most of the comedic work, due to the start of Curly's physical deterioriation, which clearly shows.

## 1946

6. SWING PARADE OF 1946 ☆☆☆ • Rl. Mar. 16 by Monogram • Prod. no. 4517 • 74m • *p* Lindsley Parsons and Harry A. Romm • *d* Phil Karlson • *st* Edmund Kelso • *scr* Tim Ryan • *ph* Harry Neumann • *e* Richard Currier • *a* Ernest R. Hickson • *md* Edward Kay • *c:* Gale Storm (Carol), Phil Regan (Danny), Connee Boswell (Herself), Edward Brophy (Moose), Mary Treen (Marie), John Eldredge (Bascomb), Russell Hicks (Daniel Warren Sr.), Windy Cook, Jack Boyle, Will Osborne and His Orchestra, and Louis Jordan and His Tympany Five (Themselves), and Leon Belasco (Pete Welsh) • SYN: Waiters Moe, Larry, and Curly and their boss (Edward Brophy) aid an aspiring singer (Gale Storm) in saving a posh nightclub from being closed • FN: The plumbing scenes were adapted from *Meet the Baron* (10/20/33), and some waiter gags were borrowed from *Beer and Pretzels* (8/26/33).

## 1960

7. STOP! LOOK! AND LAUGH! ☆☆ • Rl. June 26 (premiered in select theaters), July 1 (nationally) •

78m • *p* Harry A. Romm • *d* Don Appell, Lou Brandt, and Jules White • *scr* Sid Kuller • *c:* Paul Winchell (Himself), Jerry Mahoney (Voice of Paul Winchell), Knucklehead Smiff (Voice of Paul Winchell), Officer Joe Bolton (Joe Bolton), and The Marquis Chimps (Themselves) • SYN: A compilation of Moe, Larry, and Curly in clips from eleven of their shorts intermixed with new segments featuring ventriloquist Paul Winchell, his dummies Jerry Mahoney and Knucklehead Smiff, and The Marquis Chimps. Includes clips from *Oily to Bed, Oily to Rise* (10/6/39), *How High Is Up?* (7/26/40), *Violent Is the Word for Curly* (7/2/38), *Sock-a-Bye Baby* (11/13/42), *Higher Than a Kite,* (7/30/43) *What's the Matador?,* (4/23/42) *Goofs and Saddles,* (7/2/37) *Calling All Curs,* (8/25/39) *Micro-Phonies,* (11/15/45) *A Plumbing We Will Go* (4/19/40), and *Half-Wits Holiday* (1/9/47). • FN: This compilation feature premiered in select theaters on June 26, 1960. Producer Harry Romm attended the eastern premieres at the Hi-Way and Beverly theaters in Bridgeport, Connecticut.

## 1974

8. THE 3 STOOGES FOLLIES • ☆☆☆ • Rl. Nov. • 106m • *c:*

Theatrical poster for *Stop! Look! and Laugh!* (1960), producer Harry Romm's compilation feature with new footage of Paul Winchell and his dummies and the famous Marquis Chimps. © *Columbia Pictures, courtesy of Jeff Lenburg Collection*

Buster Keaton, Vera Vague, and Kate Smith • SYN: A collection of vintage Columbia short subjects. Featured three Stooges' shorts, *Violent Is the Word for Curly* (7/2/38), *Yes, We Have No Bonanza* (5/19/39), and *You Nazty Spy!* (1/19/40). Also featured were *Nothing But Pleasure* (1940) with Buster Keaton, the serial *Batman: Chapter 1—The Electrical Brain* (1943), Vera Vague's *Strife of the Party* (1944), and *America Sings with Kate Smith* (1942), a one-reel short. • FN: Promotional materials included a clever radio spot with audio clips from the some of the shorts featured.

Ad for Columbia Pictures film *The 3 Stooges Follies* (1974), featuring complete shorts of the Stooges and other studio short-subject stars. © *Columbia Pictures, courtesy of Jeff Lenburg Collection*

Larry, Moe, and Curly also appeared in Ken Murray's *Hollywood My Home Town* (1/1/65) and *Ken Murray Shooting Stars* (7/79), both with a home-movie clip of the Stooges shot by Murray from *Screen Snapshots* (1945).

## THE THREE STOOGES (Larry, Moe, and Shemp)

### Columbia Shorts
**1947**

98. FRIGHT NIGHT ☆☆☆ • Rl. Mar. 6 • Prod. no. 4071 • 17m • *p* Hugh McCollum • *d* Edward Bernds

The Three Stooges opening with Shemp, 1947. © *Columbia Pictures, courtesy of Jeff and Greg Lenburg Collection*

• *st scr* Clyde Bruckman • *ph* Philip Tannura • *e* Paul Borofsky • *a* Charles Clague • *c:* Harold Brauer (Big Mike), Dick Wessel (Chopper Kane), Cy Schindell (Moose), Claire Carleton (Kitty), Sammy Stein (Gorilla Watson), Heinie Conklin (Gorilla's Trainer), Tommy Kingston (Chuck), and Dave Harper and Stanley Blystone (Cops) • SYN: Larry, Moe, and Shemp are Chopper Kane's managers and receive warning from Big Mike, a gangster, that their boxer better lose or else! To decondition Chopper, the boys overfeed him on cream puffs and make him spend time with Kitty, his girlfriend. The night of the match, Chopper learns that Kitty has dumped him for Gorilla Watson and that his opponent has a broken fist, thus making him unable to fight. The Stooges think this puts them in the clear when all the bets are called off. But an irate Big Mike decides to

take them for a ride to a warehouse. • FN: Shemp's first Stooge short and his personal favorite. . . . Remade as *Fling in the Ring* (1/6/55). The gag of acting as a puppeteer for an unconscious victim was also staged in *Matri-Phony* (7/2/42) and *Fling in the Ring* (1/6/55). . . . The first draft screenplay for *Fright Night* was completed by Clyde Bruckman on May 24, 1946, featuring Curly, even though he had suffered a stroke eighteen days earlier.

99. OUT WEST ☆☆☆ • Rl. Apr. 24 • Prod. no. 4077 • 17½m • *p* Hugh McCollum • *d* Edward Bernds • *st scr* Clyde Bruckman • *ph* George Kelley • *e* Paul Borofsky • *a* Charles Clague • *c:* Jack Norman (Doc Barker), Jock Mahoney (Johnny, the Arizona Kid), Christine McIntyre (Nell), Vernon Dent (Doctor), Stanley Blystone (Colonel), George Chesebro (Quirt), Frank Ellis (Jake), Heinie Conklin (Bartender), and Blackie Whiteford (Cowboy) • SYN: Shemp has an infected vein in his leg, so his doctor orders him to go west, where the Stooges take refuge in a local saloon. Here, a pretty girl named Nell informs them that the notorious Doc Barker has murdered her father, locked up the Arizona Kid downstairs in a cell, and taken over ownership of the saloon. The boys succeed in releasing the Arizona Kid and summoning the US

Lobby card for *Fright Night* (1947), in which Shemp receives top billing in his first short with the Stooges. © *Columbia Pictures, courtesy of Jeff Lenburg Collection*

cavalry, which arrives late, after the Stooges' have nabbed the Barker gang themselves. • FN: The "mixing liquids in an old boot" gag was also used in *Pardon My Scotch* (8/1/35), *All Gummed Up* (12/18/47), *Bubble Trouble* (10/8/53), and *Pals and Gals* (6/3/54), a remake of *Out West*. The gag of fighting in the dark was reworked in *Who Done It?* (3/3/49), in its remake, *For Crimin' Out Loud* (5/3/56), and in *The Three Stooges Go Around the World in a Daze* (8/21/63). The US cavalry riding in late for the rescue was reprised later in *The Outlaws IS Coming!* (1/1/65). The "exchanging cards under the table" gag was also used in *Goofs and Saddles* (7/2/37) and in *Pals and Gals* (6/3/54).

## 100. HOLD THAT LION! ☆☆☆
• Rl. July 17 • Prod. no. 4087 • *p d* Jules White • *st scr* Felix Adler • *ph* George Kelley • *e* Edwin Bryant • *a* Charles Clague • *c:* Kenneth Mac-Donald (Icabod Slipp), Emil Sitka (Attorney), Dudley Dickerson (Porter), Jerry Howard (Sleeping Train Passenger, with Derby Over His Face), Heinie Conklin (Train Conductor), and Victor Travers (Bearded Man on Train) • SYN: While celebrating their girls' birthdays, the Stooges receive news that the estate of their uncle, Ambrose Rose, deceased millionaire junk dealer, is now being held by its executor, Mr. Icabod Slipp. Slipp turns out to be con artist, however, giving the Stooges—what else?—the slip. The boys catch up with Slipp on a train that is also carrying a ferocious lion. (Curly Howard is the passenger with the derby and clothespin on his nose.) Justice prevails when the Stooges outwit Slipp, cornering him in a baggage car and recovering their inheritance. • WT: *The Lion and the Louse* • SD: four (Tu 1/28–F 1/31/47) • FN: *Hold That Lion!* marked the only time the three Howard brothers appeared in a short together. However, Curly's cameo was later reused in a remake entitled *Booty and the Beast* (3/5/53), which used stock footage from the original. Footage from this short is also used in *Loose Loot* (4/2/53) and *Tricky Dicks* (5/7/53). The gag with the file cabinet is also in *Go West* (1940) with the Marx Brothers. The "Charlie, the Man with the Goofy Limp" gag is also featured in *Uncivil Warriors* (4/26/35) and in *From Nurse to Worse* (8/23/40). . . . Shemp's fear of working in the scenes with a real lion resulted in the prop men inserting a pane of glass between the Stooges and the lion in the box they shared so no harm would come to the boys. . . . Curly's cameo was not scripted, and it was filmed without the rest of the cast on the set.

## 101. BRIDELESS GROOM ☆☆☆½
• Rl. Sept. 11 • Prod. no. 4095 • 16½m • *p* Hugh McCollum • *d* Edward Bernds • *st scr* Clyde Bruckman • *ad* Carter DeHaven Jr. • *ph* Vincent Farrar • *e* Henry DeMond • *a* Charles Clague • *c:* Dee Green (Fanny), Christine McIntyre (Lulu Hopkins), Emil Sitka (Benton, Justice of the Peace), Nancy Saunders (Ex-Girlfriend), Doris Houck (Aggressive Ex-Girlfriend), Johnny Kascier (Bellboy), B. Edney (Moe's Stand-In), Harold Breen (Shemp's Stand-In), and J. Murphy (Larry's Stand-In). • SYN: Shemp is a vocal instructor who receives word that he will inherit half a million dollars if he marries within forty-eight hours after the reading of his deceased uncle's will. With only seven hours left in which to locate a suitable mate, Shemp tries calling a few former girlfriends and is met with instant rejection. Desperate, Shemp proposes to Fanny, one of his adoring pupils, who accepts his offer of marriage immediately. Moe and Larry rush him to the justice of the peace, where Shemp gets involved in a melee with all of his old girlfriends (they've just learned of his inheritance). Following this elaborate slugfest, however, Shemp gets married right on time and receives his legacy. • WT: *Love and Learn* • FN: In the justice of the peace segment, rubber hands were substituted for piano wires, and Moe and Larry wore shin guards under their trousers during the brawl with Shemp's old girlfriends. . . . Footage from this short also appeared in *Husbands Beware* (1/5/56). The film's plot was derived from *Seven Chances* (1925), with Buster Keaton, cowritten by Clyde Bruckman.

## 102. SING A SONG OF SIX PANTS
☆☆☆ • Rl. Oct. 30 • Prod. no. 4088 • 16½m • *p d* Jules White • *st scr*

Felix Adler • *ph* Henry Freulich • *e* Edwin Bryant • *a* Charles Clague • *c:* Harold Brauer (Terry Hargen), Virginia Hunter (Flossie), Vernon Dent (Officer), Phil Arnold (Customer with Shredded Jacket), and Cy Schindell (Torpedo) • SYN: The Stooges are in the tailoring and cleaning business, hard pressed to pay for their equipment, which is about to be repossessed by a finance company. Over the radio, the boys hear that a large reward is being offered for the capture of Terry Hargen, a notorious bank robber. Hargen himself slips into their shop and masquerades as a mannequin to elude the police. When the Stooges try interesting a customer in a pair of pants, they remove the trousers from the nearby "mannequin" and find a bank safe combination in a pocket. Embarrassed, the pantsless Hargen slips out of the store and later returns with his henchman to recover the combination. The Stooges save the day, however, securing Hargen in their pressing machine until the police arrive. • WT: *Where the Vest Begins* • FN: Remade as *Rip, Sew and Stitch* (9/3/53), with stock footage. . . . ThreeStooges.net credits Jules White as the radio announcer.

103. ALL GUMMED UP ☆☆ • Rl. Dec. 18 • Prod. no. 4104 • 18m • *p d* Jules White • *st scr* Felix Adler • *ph* Allen Siegler • *e* Edwin Bryant • *a* Charles Clague • *c:* Christine McIntyre (Cerina Flint), Emil Sitka (Amos Flint), Al Thompson (Pen Customer), Symona Boniface (Woman Who Loses Skirt), Cy Schindell (Prescription Customer), and Victor Travers (Bubblegum Customer) • SYN: Under the threat of losing their lease to operate their drug store, the Stooges produce a serum that makes old people young again, trying it first on Cerina, the landlord's wife. Within minutes she changes into a sprightly, beautiful young blonde. When Amos Flint, her husband, returns to the store, he flips over his wife's new shapely figure, offering the Stooges ownership of the store in exchange for making him young too. The serum, however, transforms him into an infant by mistake. • WT: *Sweet Vita-Mine* • FN: Remade as *Bubble Trouble* (10/8/53), with stock footage. The gag of mixing liquids in on old boot can also be seen in *Pardon My Scotch* (8/1/35), *Out West* (4/24/47), *Bubble Trouble* (10/8/53), and *Pals and Gals* (6/3/54).

## 1948

104. SHIVERING SHERLOCKS ☆☆☆ • Rl. Jan. 8 • Prod. no. 4103 • 17m • *p* Hugh McCollum • *d* Del Lord • *st scr* Del Lord and Elwood Ullman • *ad* Bill O'Connor • *ph* Allen Siegler • *e* Henry DeMond • *a* Charles Clague • *c:* Christine McIntyre (Gladys Harmon), Kenneth MacDonald (Lefty Loomis), Frank Lackteen (Red Watkins), Duke York (Angel), Vernon Dent (Police Captain Mullins), Stanley Blystone (Customer), Cy Schindell (Cop), Harold Breen (Moe's Stand-In), Joe Murphy (Shemp's Stand-In), and B. Edney (Larry's Stand-In) • SYN: Larry, Moe, and Shemp are mistaken for three armored car robbers. Captain Mullins gives the boys a lie detector test but finds no reason to hold them. He releases them, under protective custody, to Gladys Harmon, owner of a small café where the Stooges work. When Gladys is informed that she inherited some money and a spooky old mansion, the Stooges escort her to check out the property, where the real armored car bandits and their hideous hatchet man, Angel, are hiding. When the mob abducts Gladys, the Stooges come to the rescue with style. • SD: (known dates Tu 3/25–W 3/26/47); shot at the Columbia Ranch on Stage 10 • FN: The only Stooges short with Shemp directed by Del Lord. . . . Remade as *Of Cash and Hash* (2/3/55), with stock footage. The restaurant gags with preparing chicken soup were borrowed from *Playing the Ponies* (10/15/37). The clam soup gag is a revision of the timeworn oyster stew gag. Plot and other similar gags are found in *Taxi Spooks* (1928) with Jack Cooper, directed by Del Lord and written by Lord and Ewart Adamson.

105. PARDON MY CLUTCH ☆☆½ • Rl. Feb. 26 • Prod. no. 4093 • 15m • *p* Hugh McCollum • *d* Edward Bernds • *st scr* Clyde Bruckman • *ph* Allen Siegler • *e* Henry DeMond • *a* Charles Clague • *c:* Matt McHugh

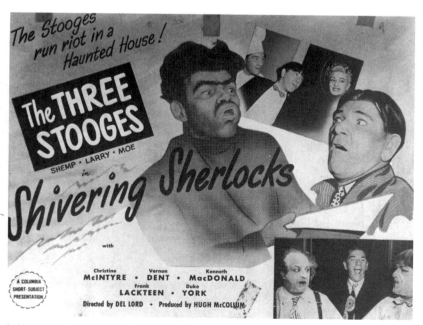

Lobby card for *Shivering Sherlocks* (1948). © Columbia Pictures, courtesy of Jeff Lenburg Collection

(Claude), Emil Sitka (Escaped Lunatic), Alyn Lockwood (Petunia), Doria Revier (Marigold), Wanda Perry (Narcissus), Stanley Blystone (Dippy, the Attendant), and George Lloyd (Gas Station Attendant) • SYN: Shemp's nerves are frazzled, so the Stooges' friend Claude sells them his old car and recommends that Shemp go camping. The Stooges, however, never get started, because Claude's automobile breaks down. An eccentric old man offers the Stooges $1,000 for the car so he can use it in a movie he's producing—but the glamour of the event sours when two attendants arrive to haul the gentlemen back to the local asylum! • FN: Remade as *Wham-Bam-Slam!* (9/1/55), with stock footage. The changing the flat tire gag and the premise for a delayed departure were borrowed from Laurel and Hardy's *Perfect Day* (1929).

**106. SQUAREHEADS OF THE ROUND TABLE** ☆☆☆½ • Rl. Mar. 4 • Prod. no. 4082 • 18m • *p* Hugh McCollum • *d* Edward Bernds • *st scr* Edward Bernds • *ph* Allen Siegler • *e* Henry DeMond • *a* Harold MacArthur • *c:* Phil Van Zandt (Black Prince), Vernon Dent (King Arthur), Jock Mahoney (Cedric), Christine McIntyre (Elaine), Harold Brauer (Sir Satchel), Robert Stevens and Joe Palma (Guards), Douglas Coppin (Soldier), and Joe Garcia (Executioner/Trumpeter) • SYN: Shemp, Larry, and Moe are troubadours in the days of King Arthur and the Round Table. The boys aid in the elopement of the king's daughter, Elaine, with Cedric the Blacksmith. But the Black Prince (the Stooges and Cedric's main nemesis) plans to murder the king and marry Elaine. Moe, Larry, and Shemp prevail, however, exposing the Black Prince and convincing the king to give Cedric permission to marry Elaine • FN: Remade as *Knutzy Knights* (9/2/54), with stock footage.

**107. FIDDLERS THREE** ☆☆☆ • Rl. May 6 • Prod. no. 4070 • 17m • *p d* Jules White • *st scr* Felix Adler •

*ad* Jack Corrick • *ph* Allen Siegler • *e* Edwin Bryant • *a* Charles Clague • *c:* Vernon Dent (King Cole), Phil Van Zandt (Mergatroyd the Magician), Virginia Hunter (Princess Alicia), Sherry O'Neil (Girl in Magician's Box), Al Thompson (Cup Bearer), Joe Palma and Cy Schindell (Guards), Harold Breen (Shemp's Stand-In), Johnny Kascier (Moe's Stand-In), and Joe Murphy (Larry's Stand-In) • SYN: In the kingdom of Coleslawvania, the Stooges, as King Cole's fiddlers, ask for permission to marry Princess Alicia's three handmaidens. Their request is granted under the condition that Alicia wed the prince first. But Mergatroyd the Magician gets wind of Alicia's wedding plans and tries overthrowing the king so he can marry the princess himself (sound familiar?). Mergatroyd then kidnaps Alicia and promises the king he'll make her reappear in his magician's box in exchange for the princess's hand in marriage. When Alicia escapes, however, the Stooges take her place in the box, exposing Mergatroyd and seizing him. • FN: Remade as *Musty Musketeers* (5/13/54), with stock footage.

**108. THE HOT SCOTS** ☆☆☆½ • Rl. July 8 • Prod. no. 4094 • 17m

• *p* Hugh McCollum • *d* Edward Bernds • *st scr* Elwood Ullman • *ph* Allen Siegler • *e* Henry DeMond • *a* Harold MacArthur • *c:* Herbert Evans (The Earl), Christine McIntyre (Lorna Doone), Ted Lorch (MacPherson), and Charles Knight (Angus) • SYN: The Stooges are aspiring detectives who travel to Scotland Yard, answering advertisements for "yard men," only to find out that yard men are the headquarters' gardeners. When the boys are mistaken for real detectives, however, they call on the earl of Glenheather Castle, staying overnight to protect his valuables while he's away. The Stooges thwart two servants, Angus and MacPherson, who plan to steal the earl's heirlooms. Later, the earl and the Stooges celebrate over a glass of his "Breath O'Heather." • WT: *Scotland Yardbirds* • FN: Remade as *Scotched in Scotland* (11/4/54), with stock footage. Scotland Yard scenes were reused in *Hot Ice* (10/6/55). The parrot in the skull gag was also used in *If a Body Meets a Body* (8/30/45) and in *Scotched in Scotland* (11/4/54). The moving beds gag was also in *Cursed by His Beauty*, a 1914 Keystone Comedy.

**109. HEAVENLY DAZE** ☆☆☆ • Rl. Sept. 2 • Prod. no. 4090 • 16½m • *p d* Jules White • *st scr* Zion Myers •

Lobby card for *Fiddlers Three* (1948). © Columbia Pictures, courtesy of Jeff Lenburg Collection

*ph* Allen Siegler • *e* Edwin Bryant • *a* Charles Clague • *c:* Vernon Dent (I. Fleecem), Sam McDaniel (Spiff-ingham), Victor Travers (Mr. De Peyster), Symona Boniface (Mrs. De Peyster), Moe Howard (Moe/Uncle Mortimer), and Marti Shelton (Miss Jones, the Blonde Angel) • SYN: Shemp dies and is told by an angel that in order to enter heaven he must go back to earth and reform Moe and Larry. His spirit returns to old terra firma, punishing the boys for trying to sell a businessman a fountain pen that can write under whipped cream. • WT: *Heaven's Above* • FN: ThreeStooges.net credits Jules White as the voice of the train announcer in heaven. . . . Remade as *Bedlam in Paradise* (4/14/55), with stock foot-age. • PS: Larry Fine once recalled that when the pen sprung out of the mixer, it actually jabbed into his forehead. Evidently Moe chased director Jules White off the set because he had promised the gag was harmless.

### 110. I'M A MONKEY'S UNCLE

⭐⭐⭐½ • Rl. Oct. 7 • Prod. no. 4091 • 15½m • *p d* Jules White • *st scr* Zion Myers • *ph* George Kelley • *e* Edwin Bryant • *a* Charles Clague • *c:* Dee Green (Baggie), Virginia Hunter (Aggie), Nancy Saunders (Maggie), Cy Schindell and Joe Palma (Cavemen), and Heinie Conklin (Milkman) • SYN: Shemp, Larry, and Moe are three Stone Age cavemen who meet three Stone Age women; Aggie, Maggie, and Baggie. All goes smoothly until the girls' old boyfriends show up in a blast of dinosaur eggs and lava rocks • FN: Remade as *Stone Age Romeos* (6/2/55), with stock footage.

### 111. MUMMY'S DUMMIES ⭐⭐⭐

• Rl. Nov. 4; re. June 1968 • Prod. no. 4105 • 15½m • *p* Hugh McCollum • *d* Edward Bernds • *st scr* Elwood Ullman • *ph* Allen Siegler • *e* Henry DeMond • *a* Charles Clague • *c:* Dee Green (Princess), Phil Van Zandt (Tutamon), Ralph Dunn (Rhadames), Vernon Dent (King Rootentootin), Suzanne Ridgeway and Virginia Ellsworth (Attendants), and Wanda Perry (Fatima) • SYN: The Stooges are chariot dealers in ancient Egypt who unload a real clunker on King Rootentootin's chief of the palace guards. He seizes the boys and brings them before the king, who spares the Stooges' lives when they cure his bad toothache. Then, when the boys thwart the prime minister's plot to steal all of the taxpayers' money, the king offers the Stooges the hand of one of his daughters in marriage. She turns out to be an ugly old dame, and Moe and Larry elect Shemp the unlucky groom. • FN: The spelling of "King Rootentootin" is per the film's script.

### 112. CRIME ON THEIR HANDS

⭐⭐⭐ • Rl. Dec. 9; re. Mar. 1968 • Prod. no. 4111 • 17½m • *p* Hugh McCollum • *d* Edward Bernds • *st scr* Elwood Ullman • *ph* Henry Freulich • *e* Henry DeMond • *a* Clarles Clague • *c:* Kenneth MacDonald (Dapper), Christine McIntyre (Bee), Charles C. Wilson (J. L. Cameron), Lester Allen (Runty), Cy Schindell (Muscles), George Lloyd (McGuffey), Heinie Conklin (Bartender), Budd Fine and Blackie Whiteford (Thugs), Ray Corrigan (Gorilla), and Frank O'Connor (Cop) • SYN: Dapper and his gang have stolen the priceless Punjab Diamond. Runty, one of Dapper's henchmen, defects when Dapper decides to peddle the jewel, and he blows the news of Dapper's plan to

The Hays Office, a movie censorship board, ordered that this musical Ten Commandments scene with Shemp and Moe be struck from the final print of the film *Heavenly Daze* (1948).

the *Daily Gazette*'s janitors, Moe, Larry, and Shemp, mistaking them for reporters. A short time later, the Stooges start investigating the matter further and wind up in the thick of trouble. When the Stooges search the room where Dapper's girlfriend, Bee, is, Shemp accidentally swallows the diamond (it was placed in a bowl of candy, from which Shemp is eating). Dapper and his men return and try operating on Shemp, but the Stooges' pet gorilla intercedes and blows the case wide open. • FN: Remade as *Hot Ice* (10/6/55), with stock footage. Newspaper office footage reused in *Commotion on the Ocean* (11/8/56).

**1949**

**113. THE GHOST TALKS** ☆☆ • Rl. Feb. 3; re. Feb. 1968 • Prod. no. 4108 • 18m • *p d* Jules White • *st scr*

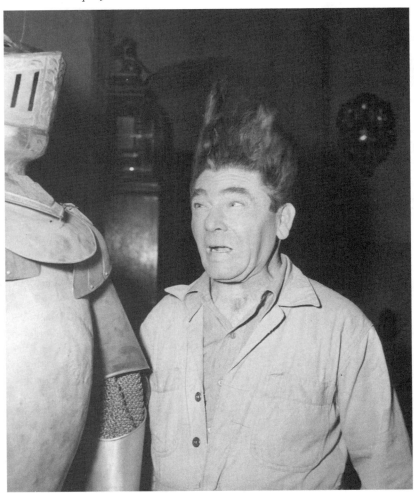

An air compressor makes Moe's hair stand on end in *The Ghost Talks* (1949).

© *Columbia Pictures, courtesy of Moe Howard Collection*

Felix Adler • *ph* M. A. Anderson • *e* Edwin Bryant • *a* Charles Clague • *c:* Phil Arnold (Voice of Peeping Tom) and Nancy Saunders (Lady Godiva) • SYN: Shemp, Larry, and Moe are hired to move furniture out of an ancient castle. While they are lifting a suit of armor, the crumpled old suit comes to life, asking the Stooges to leave him alone. It seems he is the ghost of Sir Tom, a man beheaded for peeping at Lady Godiva. Now, after one thousand years of imprisonment, Tom will meet the spirit of Lady Godiva, and they will drift off happily ever after. • WT: *That's the Spirit* • FN: Remade as *Creeps* (2/2/56), with stock footage. . . . ThreeStooges.net credits Jules White as the voice of Red Skeleton.

**114. WHO DONE IT?** ☆☆☆☆ • Rl. Mar. 3; re. Dec. 1967 • Prod. no.

4112 • 16m • *p* Hugh McCollum • *d* Edward Bernds • *st scr* Edward Bernds • *ph* Ira H. Morgan • *e* Henry DeMond • *a* Charles Clague • *c:* Christine McIntyre (Niece), Emil Sitka (John Goodrich), Dudley Dickerson (Janitor), Duke York (Nikko, the Goon), Ralph Dunn (Henchman), and Charles Knight (Butler) • SYN: Detectives Moe, Larry, and Shemp (of the Alert Detective Agency) foil the murder plot directed at old man Goodrich, leading them into a zany chase with a gang of crooks and a born-again monster, The Goon. A hilarious in-the-dark fight sequence ensues, and the Stooges emerge victorious, producing out of a trapdoor a very-much-alive old man Goodrich. Shemp becomes the hero by crowning the crooks with his "trusty little shovel." • SD: four (Tu 12/9–F 12/12/47) • FN: There's a reason why Emil Sitka has a hole in his right shoe in the closing scene. Actors had to provide their own footwear (Columbia provided the costumes), and Sitka couldn't afford to have his shoes resoled! . . . A reworking of Schilling and Lane's *Pardon My Terror* (9/12/46), originally intended for the Stooges. Remade as *For Crimin' Out Loud* (5/3/56), with stock footage. The fight in the dark also appeared in *Out West* (4/24/47), *For Crimin' Out Loud* (5/3/56), and *The Three Stooges Go Around the World in a Daze* (8/21/63).

**115. HOKUS POKUS** ☆☆☆½ • Rl. May 5; re. Nov. 1965, Nov. 1967 • Prod. no. 4116 • 16½m • *p d* Jules White • *st scr* Felix Adler • *ph* Vincent Farrar • *e* Edwin Bryant • *a* Robert Peterson • *c:* Mary Ainslee (Mary), Vernon Dent (Insurance Adjustor), Jimmy Lloyd (Cliff), David Bond (Svengarlic), and Ned Glass (Svengarlic's Agent) • SYN: As part of a publicity stunt, the Great Svengarlic ("He'll Steal Your Breath Away") hypnotizes the Stooges to walk on a horizontal flagpole high above the ground. When a bicyclist knocks the hypnotist unconscious, however, the Stooges break out of their spell and grab onto the pole for dear life. Suddenly, when the pole breaks, the Stooges crash into an insurance office, startling their invalid friend, Mary, who is receiving a $25,000 check for her injury. The Stooges fall makes Mary jump out of her wheelchair, thus blowing her claim that she is crippled. • WT: *Three Blind Mice* • FN: Reworked as *Flagpole Jitters* (4/5/56), with stock footage. Stock shot of the flagpole cracking comes from *The Taming of the Snood* (6/28/40), with Buster Keaton.

116. FUELIN' AROUND ☆☆☆ • Rl. July 7; re. Oct. 1967 • Prod. no. 4114 • 16½m • *p* Hugh McCollum • *d* Edward Bernds • *st scr* Elwood Ullman • *ph* Vincent Farrar • *e* Henry Batista • *a* Robert Peterson • *c:* Jock Mahoney (Cell Guard), Christine McIntyre (Snead's Daughter), Emil Sitka (Professor Snead), Vernon Dent (General), Phil Van Zandt (Captain Rork), Harold Brauer (Leon), and Andre Pola (Colonel) • SYN: The Stooges are hired to recarpet the home of Professor Snead, a world-famous scientist who has invented a secret super-rocket fuel. While the Stooges are working, three spies from the State of Anemia crash into the premises and kidnap the Stooges, mistaking Larry for Professor Snead. The boys are held captive until the

Lobby card for *Fuelin' Around* (1949). © *Columbia Pictures, courtesy of Jeff Lenburg Collection*

real professor and his daughter are kidnapped, too. Snead, his daughter, and the Stooges manage to escape with the help of a girl-shy guard. • FN: Remade as *Hot Stuff* (9/6/56), with stock footage.

117. MALICE IN THE PALACE ☆☆☆ • Rl. Sept. 1; re. Nov. 1966 • Prod. no. 4119 • 16½m • *p d* Jules White • *st scr* Felix Adler • *ph* Vincent Farrar • *e* Edwin Bryant • *a* Charles Clague • *c:* George Lewis (Ghinna Rumma), Frank Lackteen (Haffa Dalla), and Vernon Dent (Hassan Ben Sober) • SYN: Two customers of a café ask waiters Moe, Larry, and Shemp to recover the Ruttin' Tuttin diamond from the Emir of Shmow. The Stooges, disguised as Santa Clauses, invade the Shmow's palace and make off with the gem. • WT: *Here We Go Shmow* • FN: Remade as *Rumpus in the Harem* (6/21/56), with stock footage. The gag of chasing a dog past a customer waiting for franks and beans was also used in *Playing the Ponies* (10/15/37). The Stooges' Santa Claus disguise was lifted (using some old footage) from *Wee Wee Monsieur* (2/18/38). . . . "Ruttin' Tuttin" is the spelling in the film's script. . . . Curly Howard filmed a cameo appearance as a restaurant cook, but the scene was deleted from the final print. ThreeStooges.net reports that dialogue for the deleted scene was uncovered in Jules White's script. All that remains from the scene is a production still showing the actor waving a hatchet and pulling Larry's hair while Moe and Shemp cower. The still was also used on the film's one-sheet and lobby title card.

118. VAGABOND LOAFERS ☆☆☆ • Rl. Oct. 6; re. Dec. 1966 • Prod. no. 4140 • 16m • *p* Hugh McCollum • *d* Edward Bernds • *st scr* Elwood Ullman • *ad* F. Briskin • *ph* Vincent Farrar • *e* Henry DeMond • *a* Charles Clague • *c:* Christine McIntyre (Ethel Allen), Kenneth MacDonald (Mr. Allen), Symona Boniface (Mrs. Norfleet), Emil Sitka (Mr. Walter

Norfleet), Dudley Dickerson (Chef), Herbert Evans (Wilks, the Butler), Johnny Kascier (Moe's Stand-In), Harold Breen (Larry's Stand-In), Charlie Cross (Shemp's Stand-In), and Boyd Stockman (Kenneth MacDonald's Stunt Double) • SYN: Norfleet Mansion is seriously plagued with leaky pipes. So the butler summons Moe, Larry, and Shemp—the Day and Nite Plumbers. The Stooges reroute the plumbing and recover Mrs. Norfleet's priceless Van Brocklin painting, stolen by a pair of crooks. • SD: (known dates W 1/26–Th 1/27/49); shot at the Darmour Studios • FN: A reworking of *A Plumbing We Will Go* (4/19/40). Remade as *Scheming Schemers* (10/4/56), with stock footage.

119. DUNKED IN THE DEEP ☆☆ • Rl. Nov. 3; re. Jan. 1967 • Prod. no. 4137 • 17m • *p d* Jules White • *st scr* Felix Adler • *ph* Vincent Farrar • *e* Edwin Bryant • *a* Charles Clague • *c:* Gene Roth (Bortch) and Moe Howard (Radio Announcer Voice) • SYN: Bortch, a seedy-looking foreign spy, must return to his native land and invites his neighbors, the Stooges,

One-sheet for *Malice in the Palace* (1949) with the deleted cameo of Curly at the bottom. © *Columbia Pictures, courtesy of Jeff and Greg Lenburg Collection*

to accompany him. On board a ship heading for Bortch's homeland, the Stooges discover their friend has a watermelon that is loaded with microfilm of government documents. The Stooges then proceed to overthrow Bortch and turn him over to the authorities. • FN: Remade as *Commotion on the Ocean* (11/8/56), with stock footage. The seasick gag is also seen in *Back from the Front* (5/28/43) and in *Commotion on the Ocean* (11/8/56).

### 1950

**120. PUNCHY COWPUNCHERS** ☆☆☆☆ • Rl. Jan. 5; re. Feb. 1967 • Prod. no. 4142 • 17m • *p* Hugh McCollum • *d st scr* Edward Bernds • *ad* Sam Nelson • *ph* Vincent Farrar • *e* Henry DeMond • *a* Charles Clague • *c:* Kenneth MacDonald (Dillon), George Chesebro (Jeff), John L. Cason (Black Jeff), Ted Mapes (Red), Stanley Price (Lefty), Jock Mahoney (Elmer), Christine McIntyre (Nell), Dick Wessel (Sergeant Mullins), Vernon Dent (Colonel), Emil Sitka (Captain Daley), Heinie Conklin (Bartender), Johnny Kascier (Moe's Stand-In), Charlie Cross (Larry's Stand-In), and Harold Breen (Shemp's Stand-In). • SYN: The Killer Dillons are in town, this time to steal the gold from a nearby saloon. Wise to their plan, Nell, a pretty saloon girl, sends the Arizona Kid to Fort Scott to alert the US cavalry. There, the Kid asks Sergeant Mullins to volunteer three men for a dangerous mission. The Stooges, disguised as desperadoes, are sent to foil the Dillon Gang, which they fail to do until Nell comes to their aid. • SD: (known dates Tu 2/8–W 2/9/49); shot on the Columbia Ranch and on Stage 10.

**121. HUGS AND MUGS** ☆☆ • Rl. Feb. 2; re. Mar. 1967 • Prod. no. 4115 • 16m • *p d* Jules White • *st scr* Clyde Bruckman • *ad* Gilbert Kay • *ph* Vincent Farrar • *e* Edwin Bryant • *a* Charles Clague • *c:* Christine McIntyre (Lily), Nanette Bordeaux (Fifi), Kathleen O'Malley (Ella), Joe Palma (Mugsy), Pat Moran (Chuck),

Emil Sitka (Clerk), Wally Rose (Bill), Johnny Kascier (Moe's Stand-In), Charlie Cross (Larry's Stand-In), and Harold Breen (Shemp's Stand-In) • SYN: Three girls—Lily, Fifi, and Ella—are released from jail after serving time for shoplifting a pearl necklace that the police never found. Now, one year later, the girls return to the warehouse where they hid the item to learn that the parcel containing it has been sold to the Stooges, who are working as furniture repairmen. Shemp finds the necklace and

keeps it. Lilly, Fifi, and Ella—along with a gangster and his henchmen, who are likewise interested in the jewelry—pay the Stooges a visit at their upholstery shop, hoping to retrieve the necklace. The result is slapstick mayhem, Stooges style. • SD: three (Tu 2/15–Th 2/17/49); shot at the Darmour Studios.

**122. DOPEY DICKS** ☆☆☆ • Rl. Mar. 2; re. July 1967 • Prod. no. 4131 • 15½m • *p* Hugh McCollum • *d st scr* Edward Bernds • *ph* Vincent

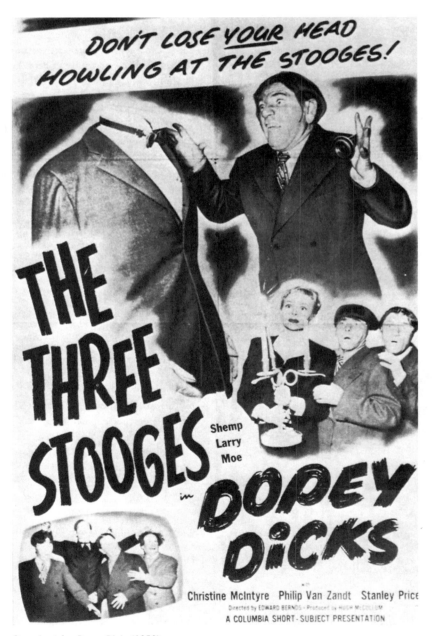

One-sheet for *Dopey Dicks* (1950). © *Columbia Pictures, courtesy of Jeff Lenburg Collection*

Farrar • *e* Henry DeMond • *a* Charles Clague • *c:* Phil Van Zandt (Professor Potter), Christine McIntyre and Stanley Price (Potter's Assistants) • SYN: While painting the office of a famous private investigator, Shemp, Larry, and Moe discover a note leading them to a woman who is being held captive at a scientist's mansion. The Stooges confront the mad scientist, who needs a human brain for his headless mechanical man. His choice: one of the Stooges. Fortunately, the Stooges manage to escape, along with the girl, hitching a ride in a car driven by the headless monster.

**123. LOVE AT FIRST BITE** ☆☆½ • Rl. May 4; re. June 1967 • Prod. no. 4129 • 16m • *p d* Jules White • *st scr* Felix Adler • *ph* Rex Wimpy • *e* Edwin Bryant • *a* Charles Clague • *c:* Christine McIntyre (Katrina), Yvette Reynard (Fifi), Marie Monteil (Maria), and Al Thompson (Father) • SYN: In a few hours, the Stooges will be reunited with their fiancées, who are arriving in town on an ocean cruiser. In celebration, the Stooges start drinking toasts to their brides-to-be and wind up drunk. After Shemp gets his feet stuck in cement, Moe and Larry dynamite him out, blasting the three of them to a nearby dock, where their sweethearts await. • WT: *New Grooms Sweep Clean* • FN: Reworked as *Fifi Blows Her Top* (4/10/58), with stock footage.

**124. SELF MADE MAIDS** ☆☆½ • Rl. July 6; re. Aug. 1967 • Prod. no. 4141 • 16m • *p d* Jules White • *st scr* Felix Adler • *ph* Vincent Farrar • *e* Edwin Bryant • *a* Charles Clague • *c:* Shemp Howard (Shemp/Shempetta/Infant), Moe Howard (Moella/Moe/Father/Infant), and Larry Fine (Larry/Larraine/Infant) • SYN: As artists, the Stooges commence painting portraits of three beautiful sisters: Moella, Larraine, and Shempetta. The boys fall in love with the girls and ask for their hands in marriage, pending approval of the girls' father. Their father resists but changes his mind when the Stooges

tickle his feet. A year after their marriages, the Stooges' wives give birth to three baby sons. • FN: All roles were portrayed by the Three Stooges themselves. Moe was also the girl's father. During filming, Moe, wearing high heels as Moella, accidentally injured himself when he twisted his ankle, fell, and hit his head on a bedpost.

**125. THREE HAMS ON RYE** ☆☆☆ • Rl. Sept. 7 • Prod. no. 4107 • 15½m • *p d* Jules White • *st scr* Clyde Bruckman • *ph* Al Zeigler • *e* Edwin Bryant • *a* Charles Clague • *c:* Nanette Bordeaux (Lulabelle), Emil Sitka (B. K. Doaks), Christine McIntyre (Janiebelle), Mildred Olsen and Judy Malcolm (Showgirls), Brian O'Hara and Danny Lewis (Tall and Short Actors), Ned Glass (Nick Barker), and Blackie Whiteford (Stagehand) • SYN: Barker, a difficult theater critic, has panned producer B. K. Doaks's last *ten* shows, and Doaks is annoyed. So he asks the Stooges, his three prop men (and part-time bit players), to disguise themselves and stop Barker from sneaking backstage before the premiere performance of a big play. A hilarious segment results when the Stooges and cast start coughing up feathers during the show, as a result of eating a cake Moe accidentally infested with a torn potholder. After the show, Barker rushes backstage and commends Doaks for producing a terrifically funny satire. • WT: *How Hammy Was My Hamlet* • FN: The Stooges wrote "Jane," the serenade tune they sang in this short. It was later reprised in *Gold Raiders* (9/14/51) and retooled as "Nora" in *Scrambled Brains* (7/7/51). The lettuce-washing/clothesline gag was reworked using money in Allied Artists' *Jail Busters* (1955), featuring the Bowery Boys, and later in a 1965 live-action wraparound sequence of *The New 3 Stooges* color cartoon series. The coughing up feathers gag was also used in *Uncivil Warriors* (4/26/35).

**126. STUDIO STOOPS** ☆☆☆ • Rl. Oct. 5; re. Dec. 1965 • Prod. no.

4143 • 16m • *p* Hugh McCollum • *d* Edward Bernds • *st scr* Elwood Ullman • *ad* Gilbert Kay • *ph* Vincent Farrar • *e* Henry DeMond • *a* Charles Clague • *c:* Kenneth MacDonald (Dandy Dawson), Charles Jordan (Tiny), Christine McIntyre (Dolly DeVore), Vernon Dent (Captain Casey), Joe Palma (Louie), Stanley Price (Brown), Johnny Kascier (Moe's Stand-In), Harold Breen (Larry's Stand-In), and Charlie Cross (Shemp's Stand-In) • SYN: At B.O. Pictures, termite exterminators, Moe, Larry, and Shemp turn amateur publicity agents, suggesting to a studio executive that they can make starlet Dolly DeVore famous overnight by faking a kidnapping. The kidnapping becomes real, however, when two crooks overhear the plan and abduct DeVore. The Stooges make a successful rescue, without Shemp, who gets caught on the building's tenth floor ledge trapped in a garment bag. • FN: The gag of hanging out a window on an accordion telephone was also used in *The Lion's Whiskers* (1926), with Billy Bevan, directed by Del Lord.

**127. SLAPHAPPY SLEUTHS** ☆☆½ • Rl. Nov. 9; re. Oct. 1965 • Prod. no. 4139 • 16m • *p d* Jules White • *st scr* Felix Adler • *ph* Vincent Farrar • *e* Edwin Bryant • *a* Charles Clague • *c:* Gene Roth (Fuller Grime), Emil Sitka (Customer), Nanette Bordeaux (Louise), Stanley Blystone (Head Crook), Joe Palma and Blackie Whiteford (Crooks) • SYN: The Onion Oil Company is in deep financial trouble. Many of their gasoline stations have been held up by a gang of organized mobsters. To solve the case, the company utilizes three brainy but stupid-looking private detectives posing as gas station attendants. Who else? The Three Stooges. • FN: The painted-on eyelids gag was originally used in *Restless Knights* (2/20/35).

**128. A SNITCH IN TIME** ☆☆½ • Rl. Dec. 7 • Prod. no. 4154 • 16½m • *p* Hugh McCollum • *d* Edward

Bernds • *st scr* Elwood Ullman •
*ph* No credit • *e* Henry DeMond
• *a* Charles Clague • *c:* Jean Willes
(Gladys Scudder), Henry Kulky
(Steve), John Merton (Cook), and
John L. Cason (Louie) • SYN:
Furniture shop owners Moe, Larry,
and Shemp deliver new furniture
to Miss Scudder's boarding house.
There, they discover the new boarders are crooks. Following a chase, the
Stooges save the day, defeating the
crooks. • FN: Gags involving painting a cuckoo clock and revarnishing
an antique table were also used in
*Tassels in the* Air (4/1/38).

## 1951

### 129. THREE ARABIAN NUTS
☆☆☆ • Rl. Jan. 4 • Prod. no.
4156 • 16m • *p* Hugh McCollum
• *d* Edward Bernds • *st scr* Elwood
Ullman • *ph* No credit • *e* Henry
DeMond • *a* Charles Clague • *c:* Vernon Dent (Bradley), Phil Van Zandt
(Ahmed), Dick Curtis (Hassan), and
Wesley Bly (Genius of the Lamp) •
SYN: Shemp takes possession of a
valuable Aladdin's lamp at a storage
company where the Stooges work
after a businessman junks the item.
The lamp produces a real live genie
who grants the Stooges three wishes.
But the genie causes more trouble
than he's worth when two Arabian
spies try to recover the lamp. The
Stooges succeed, however, in main-
taining ownership of the lamp, with
their last wish producing a harem of
girls and many treasures. • WT: *Genii
with the Light Brown Hair* • SD: four
(M 1/9–Th 1/12/50)

### 130. BABY SITTERS JITTERS
☆☆½ • Rl. Feb. 1 • Prod. no. 4155
• 16m • *p d* Jules White • *st scr* Felix
Adler • *ph* No credit • *e* Edwin Bryant • *a* Charles Clague • *c:* Lynn
Davis (Joan Lloyd), David Windsor
(Junior), Margie Liszt (Mrs. Crump),
and Myron Healey (George Lloyd)
• SYN: Behind on their rent, the
Stooges turn to babysitting for a
child named Junior to earn some
money to pay off their debt. Junior's
mother leaves the Stooges in charge

while she slips away for the evening.
Early the next morning, however,
she returns to find Shemp, Larry,
and Moe sleeping in Junior's crib.
But where's Junior? Evidently, the
woman's ex-husband kidnapped the
baby. So the Stooges take matters
into their own hands, attempting to
recover the baby from Mr. Lloyd.
He refuses and a fight ensues, which
is quickly resolved when the young
couple decide to give their marriage
one more try.

### 131. DON'T THROW THAT KNIFE
☆☆☆ • Rl. May 3 • Prod. no.
4158 • 16m • *p d* Jules White • *st
scr* Felix Adler • *ph* Fayte Browne •
*e* Edwin Bryant • *a* Charles Clague
• *c:* Dick Curtis (Mr. Wycoff), Jean
Willes (Lucy Wycoff, His Wife),
Johnny Kascier (Moe's Stand-In),
Harold Breen (Shemp's Stand-In),
and Charlie Cross (Larry's Stand-
In) • SYN: The boys are loco census
takers who pay a visit to Mrs. Lucy
Wycoff. She answers the Stooges'
questions, until her insanely jealous
husband, a magician, returns home.
Time for the Stooges to hide! When
the magician elects to take a nap,
he quickly discovers his wife *isn't* his
wife (it's Shemp)—and that there
are two more men in the house. He
chases the Stooges from room to
room until Mr. Wycoff rehearses his
knife-throwing act and hauls out his
egg-throwing machine, using the
boys as human targets. • WT: *Non-
census Takers* • SD: (known date Th
6/22/50); shot at Columbia Studios
on Stage 10 • FN: The gag of a wife
faking a headache to fool her jealous
husband was reused in *Sappy Bullfighters* (6/4/59). The Stooges are also
census takers in *No Census, No Feeling* (10/4/40).

### 132. SCRAMBLED BRAINS
☆☆☆☆ • Rl. July 7 • Prod. no.
4157 • *p d* Jules White • *st scr* Felix
Adler • *ph* Henry Freulich • *e* Edwin
Bryant • *a* Charles Clague • *c:* Babe
London (Nora), Vernon Dent (Nora's
Father), Royce Milne (Marybelle),
Emil Sitka (Dr. Gseundheitt), B.

Edney (Shemp's Stand-In), Johnny
Kascier (Moe's Stand-In), and Joe
Murphy (Larry's Stand-In) • SYN:
Shemp continues to suffer from hallucinations after being released from
the sanitarium. His most constant
hallucination is imagining that the
hospital's nurse, Nora, is a slim, viva-
cious blonde instead of fat and ugly.
What makes matters worse is that
Shemp is engaged to marry her! In
the process of returning Shemp to
the sanitarium for a second time,
Moe and Larry confront a fat man
in the telephone booth, causing the
booth to fall over. Enraged, the man
promises to tear Moe and Larry apart
if he ever sees them again. Next, Moe
and Larry join Shemp and his bride,
Nora, on their wedding day. Shemp
and Nora get married, even though
her father turns out to be the man
in the phone booth. He beats up on
Moe and Larry, as promised. • WT:
*Impatient Patient* • SD: (known dates
W 3/22–Th 3/23/50); shot on Stage
10 • FN: The serenade tune "Jane,"
sung and written by the Stooges for
*Three Hams on Rye* (9/7/50), returns
in this film, retooled as "Nora."
Blowing a pill through a pipe is a
gag that also appears in *Even As I O
U* (9/18/42) and in *Hoofs and Goofs*
(1/31/57). • PS: Although Larry Fine
(like Moe Howard) had an affinity for *You Nazty Spy!*, Larry later
admitted that his real favorite was
*Scrambled Brains*. It was also one of
the few films Larry had in his personal collection.

### 133. MERRY MAVERICKS ☆☆½ •
Rl. Sept. 6 • Prod. no. 4161 • 16m •
*p* Hugh McCollum • *d* Edward
Bernds • *st scr* Edward Bernds • *ph*
Allen Siegler • *e* Edwin Bryant • *a*
Charles Clague • *c:* Don Harvey (Red
Morgan), Marion Martin (Gladys),
Paul Campbell (Pete), Emil Sitka
(Sheriff), Blackie Whiteford (Al), Al
Thompson (Bartender), and Victor
Travers (Newspaper Editor, stock
footage) • SYN: In Peaceful Gulch,
Red Morgan and his outlaw hom-
bres are back, and they've just run
the sheriff out of town. The Stooges

are mistaken for three famous marshals and are asked to stop Morgan from stealing money buried in an old house haunted by the ghost of a headless Indian chief. Shemp, Larry, and Moe soon find out that the Indian chief, in reality, is one of Morgan's henchmen. Shemp dons the chief's costume and knocks out the crooks to save the day. • SD: (Tu 6/13–F 6/16/50) • FN: A reworking of *Phony Express* (11/18/43), with stock footage. The scene in which the Stooges find handbills showing they're "Wanted for Vagrancy" was photographed during the production of their next film, *The Tooth Will Out*, and was included in that picture's budget. See *The Tooth Will Out* (10/4/51).

134. THE TOOTH WILL OUT ☆☆½ • Rl. Oct. 4 • Prod. no. 4162 • 16m • *p* Hugh McCollum • *d st scr* Edward Bernds • *ad* Gilbert Kay • *ph* Fayte Browne • *e* Edwin Bryant • *a* Charles Clague • *c:* Margie Liszt (Miss Beebe), Vernon Dent (Doc Keefer), Emil Sitka (Chef), Slim Gaut and Dick Curtis (Patients), Johnny Kascier (Moe's Stand-In), Harold Breen (Shemp's Stand-In), and Charlie Cross (Larry's Stand-In) • SYN: The Stooges emerge as graduates from dental school and move out west to open their first dental office, where they take care of their first patient: an old man. His appointment is cut short when a western outlaw, evidently in pain, kicks the old man out and asks the Stooges to pull his tooth. The Stooges stall for time as Shemp consults a carpenter's handbook for another opinion. In the end, Shemp pulls the wrong tooth. • WT: *A Yank at the Dentist* • SD: two (M 2/19–T 2/20/50); shot on Stage 10 at the Columbia Ranch • FN: Moe, Larry, and Shemp wrote the song "My Lucky Strike." . . . Dentist office gags in the film are similar to those in W. C. Fields's *The Dentist*. • PS: The origin of the dental office scenes themselves is unique. Director Edward Bernds explained: "The dentist office sequences were

originally filmed for *Merry Mavericks*. The scene ran so long that Mac [Hugh McCollum] was unwilling to cut it. Then he came up with the idea that we had nearly enough footage for another picture. So we took the sequence out of *Merry Mavericks*, shot two extra days, and *The Tooth Will Out* was born."

135. HULA-LA-LA ☆☆½ • Rl, Nov. 1; re. Sept. 1965 • Prod. no. 4179 • 16m • *p d* Hugh McCollum • *st scr*

Edward Bernds • *ph* Henry Freulich *e* Edwin Bryant • *a* Charles Clague • *c:* Jean Willes (King's Daughter, Luana), Kenneth MacDonald (Vananu), Emil Sitka (Mr. Baines), Maxine Doviat (Kawana), and Lei Aloha (Armed Idol) • SYN: B.O. Pictures is in deep trouble. Its next film—a South Pacific musical—is being postponed until the natives on the island where this epic is being produced learn how to dance. Studio president Mr. Baines asks for the studio's finest dance

One-sheet for *Hula-La-La* (1951). © Columbia Pictures, courtesy of Greg Lenburg Collection

instructors, Moe, Larry, and Shemp, to solve this predicament by teaching the natives how to dance. When the boys arrive on the island, however, they meet a witch doctor who wants their heads for his collection and native girl Luana for his bride. The Stooges thwart both plans. • FN: The many-armed idol gag was first used in *Some More of Samoa* (12/4/41). *Hula-La-La* marked the directorial debut of Hugh McCollum and was his only film as a director with the Stooges. McCollum replaced director Edward Bernds, who was directing a B feature for Columbia.

136. PEST MAN WINS ☆☆☆☆ Rl. Dec. 6; re. Sept. 1963 • Prod. no. 4163 • 16m • *p d* Jules White • *st scr* Felix Adler • *ph* Fayte Browne • *e* Edwin Bryant • *a* Charles Clague • *c:* Margie Liszt (Mrs. Castor), Nanette Bordeaux (Fifi), Emil Sitka (Meadows), Vernon Dent (Mr. Philander), Eddie Laughton (Party Guest Who Tells Hunting Story, stock footage), Victor Travers (Sleeping Party Guest), Helen Dickson (Party Guest), Al Thompson, Heinie Conklin, Ethelreda Leopold, and Symona Boniface (Party Guests, stock footage), Johnny Kascier (Moe's Stand-In), Charlie Cross (Larry's Stand-In), and Harold Breen (Shemp's Stand-In) • SYN: Shemp, Larry, and Moe work for the Lightning Pest Control Company. They are called to a society matron's home for an extermination job—but ruin her lavish party instead. • WT: *Mousers in the Trousers* • SD: (known dates 2/12–Tu 2/13/51); shot at Columbia on Stage 10 • FN: A remake of *Ants in the Pantry* (2/6/36), with stock footage. The pie-fight stock footage comes from *In the Sweet Pie and Pie* (10/16/41) and *Half-Wits Holiday* (1/9/47).

**1952**

137. A MISSED FORTUNE ☆☆½ • Rl. Jan. 3; re. Oct. 1963 • Prod. no. 4159 • 16½m • *p d* Jules White • *st* Searle Kramer • *scr* Jack White • *ph* Fayte Browne • *e* Henry DeMond • *a* Charles Clague • *c:* Nanette Bordeaux (Fifi), Suzanne Ridgeway and Vivian Mason (Golddiggers), Vernon Dent (Hotel Manager), and Stanley Blystone (House Detective) • SYN: The Three Stooges come into big money when Shemp hits the $50,000 radio quiz show jackpot. Before the check arrives, the boys spend their earnings at a swank hotel and order a case of champagne to celebrate. A trio of gold diggers are staying in the next room, and these ladies do everything possible to milk the Stooges out of their winnings. But, as it turns out, the Stooges didn't need the ladies' help, since the government's tax deductions leave Shemp with only $4.85. • FN: A remake of *Healthy, Wealthy and Dumb* (5/20/38), with stock footage.

138. LISTEN, JUDGE ☆☆☆ • Rl. Mar. 6; re. Nov. 1963 • Prod. no. 4180 • 17m • *p* Hugh McCollum • *d* Edward Bernds • *st scr* Elwood Ullman • *ad* C. Hiecke • *ph* Ellis W. Carter • *e* Edwin Bryant • *a* Charles Clague • *c:* Kathryn "Kitty" McHugh (Mrs. Henderson), Vernon Dent (Judge Henderson), John Hamilton (Mr. George Morton), Mary Emory (Mrs. Lydia Morton), Gil Perkins (Officer Ryan), Chick Collins (Officer Casey), Emil Sitka (Chef), Johnny Kascier (Moe's Stand-In), Harold Breen (Shemp's Stand-In/ Stunt Double), Charlie Cross (Larry's Stand-In), and Teddy Mangean (Larry's Stunt Double) • SYN: The Stooges are repairmen who wind up in court on a vagrancy charge but are released for lack of evidence. The boys are next hired to fix a lady's doorbell, and their unorthodox work habits annoy the chef, butler, and waiter, causing them to quit. With the woman empty-handed for her husband's birthday party, the Stooges prepare all the food and an explosive birthday cake. The lady's husband gets plastered by the cake after he blows out the candles. He also recognizes the Stooges, since he was the judge who tried them. • SD: four (Tu 1/16–F 1/19/51); shot on Stage 10 • FN: A reworking of *An Ache in*

*Every Stake* (8/22/41) and *They Stooge to Conga* (1/1/43). The parrot in the turkey gag is also seen in *Crash Goes the Hash* (2/5/44), in *G.I. Wanna Home* (9/5/46), and in *Three Dark Horses* (10/16/52). The film borrows other story devices from three previous Stooges comedies with Curly: the chicken stealing in the courtroom scene from *A Plumbing We Will Go* (4/19/40); the food preparation scene and exploding cake gag from *An Ache in Every Stake* (8/22/41); and the doorbell repair bit from *They Stooge to Conga* (1/1/43).

139. CORNY CASANOVAS ☆☆☆☆☆ • Rl. May 1; re. Jan 1964 • Prod. no. 4178 • 16½m • *p d* Jules White • *st scr* Felix Adler • *ph* Henry Freulich • *e* Aaron Stell • *a* Charles Clague • *c:* Connie Cezan (Mabel) • SYN: Moe, Larry, and Shemp try proposing to the same girl, Mabel. Each one makes a separate visit, without the others knowing it. When one Stooge arrives, Mabel escorts her recent caller into another room and then greets her next lover. Soon Moe and Larry are disposed of, each of them in different bedrooms. But they eventually get curious and peep out of their rooms only to bump into each other. Shemp, meanwhile, is also proposing to Mabel. The three soon find that each Stooge has been double-crossing the others, and a fight ensues, while Mabel escapes. • WT: *One Won* • FN: Remade as *Rusty Romeos* (10/17/57), with stock footage.

140. HE COOKED HIS GOOSE ☆☆ Rl. July 3; re. Feb. 1964 • Prod. no. 4181 • 16m • *p d* Jules White • *st scr* Felix Adler • *ad* Earl Bellamy • *ph* Fayte Browne • *e* Aaron Stell • *a* Charles Clague • *c:* Mary Ainslee (Belle), Angela Stevens (Millie), Diana Darrin (Miss Lapdale, Secretary), Johnny Kascier (Stunt Waiter/Moe's Stand-In), Harold Breen (Shemp's Stand-In), and Charlie Cross (Larry's Stand-In) • SYN: Larry owns a pet shop and the only pets he wants are Moe's wife, Belle, and Shemp's fiancée,

Millie. • WT: *Clam Up* • SD: three (M 1/7–W 1/9/52); shot on Stage 10 • FN: Remade as *Triple Crossed* (2/2/59), with stock footage.

## 141. GENTS IN A JAM ☆☆☆☆ •
Rl. July 4 • Prod. no. 4183 • 16½m • *p* Hugh McCollum • *d st scr* Edward Bernds • *ph* Fayte Browne • *e* Edwin Bryant • *a* Charles Clague • *c:* Emil Sitka (Uncle Phineas Bowman), Kathryn "Kitty" McHugh (Mrs. Magruder, the Landlady), Mickey Simpson (Rocky Dugan, the Wrestler), and Dani Sue Nolan (Mrs. Dugan) • SYN: Shemp's rich uncle Phineas Bowman is coming to stay with the Stooges for two weeks. The Stooges promise the landlady that with their uncle in town they'll be able to pay their back rent. The Stooges get in trouble, however, when Mrs. Dugan, the wife of a champion wrestler, borrows sugar from the trio. When Shemp escorts her to the door after filling her request, he accidentally trips and falls, tearing off her dress. Enter Mr. Dugan. He tears telephone books in half for a living, and spotting his wife with a torn dress, Dugan starts tearing the Stooges apart, all at the same time. When Uncle Phineas tries to break up the fight, he gets pummeled as well until Mrs. Magruder, the landlady, knocks out Dugan with a vicious left hook. Uncle Phineas rekindles his romance with Mrs. Magruder, an old sweetheart, and marries her. • FN: The "hiding the lady in a trunk" gag is also used in *Fifi Blows Her Top* (4/10/58) and Laurel and Hardy's *Block-Heads* (1938). . . . The last short directed by Edward Bernds.

## 142. THREE DARK HORSES
☆☆☆☆ • Rl. Oct. 16; re. May 1964 • Prod. no. 4200 • 16m • *p d* Jules White • *st scr* Felix Adler • *ad* James Nicholson • *ph* Henry Freulich • *e* Edwin Bryant • *a* Cary Odell • *c:* Kenneth MacDonald (William "Bill" Wick), Ben Welden (Wick's Assistant), Johnny Kascier (Shemp's Stand-In), Harold Breen (Moe's Stand-In), and D. White (Larry's Stand-In) • SYN: If Hammond Egger is elected president, he'll be able to pull off the biggest "oil grab" of the century. To assure his victory, Egger's campaign managers hire three stupid janitors, Shemp, Larry, and Moe, as convention delegates. At the convention, however, the boys learn that their man is a crook and throw their support for the other leading candidate, Abel Lamb Stewer. Stewer wins. • WT: *Small Delegates at Large* • SD: four (Tu 8/26–F 8/29/52); shot on Stage 10 • FN: The parrot in the turkey gag is also seen in *Crash Goes the Hash* (2/5/44), *G.I. Wanna Home* (9/5/46), and *Listen, Judge* (3/6/52).

## 143. CUCKOO ON A CHOO CHOO
zero stars • Rl. Dec. 4; re. July 1964

Bud Jamison's face appears on the Hammond Egger poster (here, behind Larry) in *Three Dark Horses* (1952), as a tribute to the longtime character actor, who died suddenly on September 30, 1944. © *Columbia Pictures, courtesy of Moe Howard Collection*

• Prod. no. 4194 • 15½m • *p d* Jules White • *st scr* Felix Adler • *ph* Henry Freulich • *e* Edwin Bryant • *a* Charles Clague • *c:* Patricia Wright and Victoria Horne (Roberta and Lenore), Reggie Dvorak (Carrie the Canary), and Moe Howard (Radio Announcer) • SYN: Larry, Shemp, and two girls, Roberta and Lenore, steal a railroad car named *Schmow* but are discovered by Moe, an ace detective for the Transylvania Railroad Company. As luck would have it, Moe discovers that Roberta is the same woman he once dated, and he is still so crazy about her that he tries to rekindle their relationship. However, it becomes a cuckoo time on the choo choo as Larry proposes to marry Lenore but she won't until Shemp ties the knot with Roberta first. Shemp wins the hearts of both women, but in the end he's so drunk he prefers his imaginary giant canary, Carrie. Without a doubt, this is the worst Stooge comedy ever made. • WT: *A Train Called Schmow* • FN: A parody of Marlon Brando's *A Streetcar Named Desire* (1951) and Jimmy Stewart's *Harvey* (1950). • PS: Larry Fine liked this film because of his Marlon Brando–type role. When he lived at the Motion Picture Country House and Hospital, Larry sometimes screened his own print of this film for friends. During one such showing, Larry fell asleep as the film progressed. (Larry wasn't the only one!)

## 1953
## 144. UP IN DAISY'S PENTHOUSE
☆☆☆ • Rl. Feb. 5; re. Sept. 8, 1959 • Prod. no. 4182 • 16½m • *p d* Jules White • *st* Clyde Bruckman • *scr* Jack White • *ph* Henry Freulich

• *e* Edwin Bryant • *a* Charles Clague • *c:* Shemp Howard (Pop Howard), Connie Cezan (Daisy Flowers), John Merton (Butch), Jack Kenney (Chopper), Blackie Whiteford, and Suzanne Ridgeway • SYN: Now that the Stooges' mother is getting old, their father is divorcing her and marrying a young blonde moll, Daisy. Mother Stooge asks the boys to stop the marriage. • FN: A remake of *3 Dumb Clucks* (4/17/37), with stock footage.

**145. BOOTY AND THE BEAST**
☆☆☆ • Rl. Mar. 5; re. Oct. 15, 1959 • Prod. no. 4196 • 16½m • *p d* Jules White • *st* Felix Adler • *scr* Jack White • *ad* Carter DeHaven • *ph* Fayte Browne • *e* Edwin Bryant • *a* Walter Holscher • *c:* Kenneth MacDonald (Icabod Slipp), Vernon Dent (Security Guard), Jerry Howard (Sleeping Train Passenger, stock footage), Dudley Dickerson (Porter, stock footage), Heinie Conklin (Train Conductor, stock footage), Victor Travers (Man with Beard, stock footage), and Blackie Whiteford (Train Passenger, stock footage) • SYN: The Stooges' automobile runs out of gasoline in front of an imposing mansion. The boys notice the owner, Icabod Slipp, trying to budge open the front door and politely offer to help him. The Stooges not only help him break into the house but also assist him in blowing open a wall safe. The explosion renders the Stooges unconscious, and Slipp, actually a burglar, flees with the bag of loot. When the night watchman catches the Stooges in front of the empty safe, the boys escape and take after Slipp, who is on a train bound for Las Vegas. On board the train, the Stooges succeed in recovering the loot. • WT: *Fun for the Money* • SD: one (M 5/19/52); shot on Stage 10 • FN: This partial remake of *Hold That Lion!* (7/17/47) uses stock footage for the train scenes, including Curly's cameo and a lion in a baggage car.

**146. LOOSE LOOT** ☆☆☆½ • Rl. Apr. 2; re. Nov. 19, 1959 • Prod. no. 4197 • 16m • *p d* Jules White •

*st* Felix Adler • *scr* Jack White • *ad* Carter DeHaven • *ph* Fayte Browne • *e* Edwin Bryant • *a* Walter Holscher • *c:* Kenneth MacDonald (Icabod Slipp), Tom Kennedy (Joe), Emil Sitka (Attorney Poole, stock footage), Suzanne Ridgeway and Nanette Bordeaux (Showgirls), Johnny Kascier (Napoleon/Moe's Stand-In), Harold Breen (Shemp's Stand-In), and D. White (Larry's Stand-In) • SYN: In order to collect their late uncle's inheritance, Shemp, Larry, and Moe are advised to subpoena Icabod Slipp, the executor of the estate. He, of course, gives them the slip! The Stooges corner this con man at the Circle Follies Theatre, assaulting Slipp and his assistants with an arsenal of fruit. They wind up with their inheritance. • WT: *Filthy Lucre* • SD: two (Tu 5/20–W 5/21/52); shot on Stage 10 • FN: Scenes with the Stooges' attorney and inside Slipp's office are stock footage from *Hold That Lion!* (7/17/47).

**147. TRICKY DICKS** ☆☆☆☆ • Rl. May 7; re. Jan. 7, 1960 • Prod. no. 4199 • 16m • *p d* Jules White • *st scr* Felix Adler • *ad* Paul Donnelly • *ph* William E. Whitley • *e* Edwin Bryant • *a* George Brooks • *c:* Benny Rubin (Antonio Zuchini Salami Gorgonzola de Pizza), Connie Cezan (Chick), Ferris Taylor (Police Chief B. A. Copper), Phil Arnold (Chopper), Suzanne Ridgeway (Policewoman), Murray Alper (Magirk), Johnny Kascier (Moe's Stand-In), and Cy Malis (Shemp's Stand-In) • SYN: Police Chief B. A. Copper gives detectives Moe, Larry, and Shemp just twenty-four hours to catch the killer of Slug McGurk. The Stooges promptly start screening two prime suspects: an Italian organ grinder with a fake accent and Gilbraith Q. Tiddlewadder, a frustrated actor. Tiddlewadder (Chopper for short) begins to confess—and then the real killer enters, admitting to the crime. • WT: *Cop and Bull Story* • SD: three (M 7/14–W 7/16/52); shot on Stage 10 • FN: The filing cabinet sequence is stock footage from *Hold That Lion!* (7/17/47).

**148. SPOOKS!** ☆☆☆ • Rl. June 15 (2-D version rl. Apr. 15); re. July 21, 1960 • Prod. no. 4210 • 16m • *pd* Jules White • *st scr* Felix Adler • *ad* Eddie Saeta • *ph* Lester H. White • *e* Edwin Bryant • *a* Carl Anderson • *c:* Phil Van Zandt (Dr. Jeckyl), Tom Kennedy (Mr. Hyde), Norma Randall (Bea Bopper), Frank Mitchell (Mr. Bopper), Shemp Howard (Bat), Johnny Kascier (Moe's Stand-In), B. Rose (Shemp's Stand-In), and B. Edney (Larry's Stand-In) • SYN: When George Bopper's daughter, Bea, disappears, Bopper hires the Super Sleuth Detective Agency— Moe, Larry and Shemp—to find her. Disguised as pie salesmen, the Stooges stumble eventually upon a spooky old mansion where Bea is being held captive by Dr. Jeckyl, a mad scientist, Mr. Hyde, his burly assistant, and a rather large gorilla. In one of the best scenes, the Stooges dodge a low-flying bat whose face resembles Shemp's. • SD: four (M 5/11–Th 5/14/53); shot at Columbia Sunset Studios, Stage 18 • FN: Filmed and released in 3-D. . . . The script cover was ghost white.

**149. PARDON MY BACKFIRE** ☆☆☆½ • Rl. Aug. 15; re. Oct. 13, 1960 • Prod. no. 4212 • 16m • *p d* Jules White • *st scr* Felix Adler • *ad* Milton Feldman • *ph* Henry Freulich • *e* Edwin Bryant • *a* Walter Holscher • *c:* Benny Rubin (Gang Leader), Frank Sully (Gang Member), Phil Arnold (Knife Thrower), Fred Kelsey (Girl's Father), Ruth Godfrey (Nettie), Angela Stevens (Hettie), Diana Darrin (Bettie), and Barbara Bartay (Moll) • SYN: Garage mechanics Moe, Larry, and Shemp will lose their brides-to-be, Nettie, Hettie, and Bettie, to three plumbers if they don't make good soon. Well, the boys succeed beyond their dreams when they apprehend three dangerous criminals at their automobile garage. For their efforts, the Stooges receive a reward, and they use the money to marry their sweethearts. • FN: Contrary to previously published reports, *Pardon My Backfire* was also filmed and released in 3-D. . . . ThreeStooges.net credits Jules White as the voice of the radio announcer.

**150. RIP, SEW AND STITCH** ☆☆½ • Rl. Sept. 3; re. Feb. 4, 1960 • Prod. no. 4201 • 17m • *p d* Jules White • *st* Felix Adler • *scr* Jack White • *ad* James Nicholson • *ph* Ray Cory • *e* Edwin Bryant • *a* Cary Odell • *c:* Vernon Dent (Sharp), Phil Arnold (Customer in Shredded Coat), and Harold Brauer (Hargen) • SYN: Moe, Larry, and Shemp have just twenty-four hours to make overdue payments on their tailor shop equipment or lose it. Enter bank bandit Terry "Slippery Fingers" Hargen, who leaves his coat in their tailor shop along with the combination to a safe. Hargen and his henchmen return to the shop to get his coat and the combination. A fight ensues, leading to the defeat of the crooks and the Stooges' receiving a reward for Hargen's capture. • WT: *A Pressing Affair* • SD: one (date not known) • FN: A remake of *Sing a Song of Six Pants* (10/30/47), with stock footage. . . . ThreeStooges.net credits Jules White as the voice of the radio announcer.

**151. BUBBLE TROUBLE** ☆☆ • Rl. Oct. 8; re. Apr. 14, 1960 • Prod. no. 4202 • *p d* Jules White • *st* Felix Adler • *scr* Jack White • *ad* James Nicholson • *ph* Ray Cory • *e* Edwin Bryant • *a* Cary Odell • *c:* Emil Sitka (Amos Flint/Gorilla) and Christine McIntyre (Cerina Flint) • SYN: Unless the Stooges pay back rent, their landlord, Amos Flint, will evict them from their drug store. The trio convinces Flint to let them stay when Shemp, Moe, and Larry concoct a fountain-of-youth elixir that changes Flint's middle-aged wife back into a voluptuous blonde. But when the landlord consumes the serum, he turns into the world's only talking gorilla. • WT: *Drugstore Dubs* • SD: one (M 10/13/52); shot on Stage 10 • FN: A reworking of *All Gummed Up* (12/18/47), with stock footage. A double for Christine McIntyre is

seen in one shot. The gag of mixing liquids in an old boot was used also in *Pardon My Scotch* (8/1/35), *Out West* (4/24/47), *All Gummed Up* (12/18/47), and *Pals and Gals* (6/3/54).

**152. GOOF ON THE ROOF** ☆☆☆ • Rl. Dec. 3; re. May 19, 1960 • Prod. no. 4203 • 16½m • *p d* Jules White • *st scr* Clyde Bruckman • *ad* James Nicholson • *ph* Sam Leavitt • *e* Edwin Bryant • *a* George Brooks • *c:* Frank Mitchell (Bill) and Maxine Gates (Bill's Wife) • SYN: The Stooges receive news from their pal Bill that they'll have to move out of his house since he'll be returning with his new bride. Before his homecoming, the boys install Bill's new TV antenna, with disastrous results. • FN: In 1974, Frank Mitchell teamed up with Paul "Mousie" Garner and Curly-Joe DeRita to form the short-lived group The New 3 Stooges.

## 1954

**153. INCOME TAX SAPPY** ☆☆ • Rl. Feb. 4; re. Sept. 15, 1960 • Prod. no. 4208 • 16½m • *p d* Jules White • *st scr* Felix Adler • *ad* Abner Singer • *ph* Ray Cory • *e* Edwin Bryant • *a* George Brooks • *c:* Joe Palma and

Vernon Dent (IRS Agents), Benny Rubin (Mr. Cash), Margie Liszt (Sis), and Nanette Bordeaux (Mrs. Cash) • SYN: Moe's wife wants a home so badly that she demands her husband start cheating on his income taxes to save money. Her brainstorm works, and the Stooges become professional tax advisors (they help their clients cheat, too). In celebration of their rise to success, the boys stage a lavish dinner party where one of the guests is an FBI agent! • WT: *Tax Saps* • FN: Larry reprises the time-worn oyster stew gag used in *Dutiful but Dumb* (3/21/41) and in other Stooges comedies.

**154. MUSTY MUSKETEERS** ☆☆½ • Rl. May 13; re. Nov. 17, 1960 • Prod. no. 4209 • 16m • *p d* Jules White • *st* Felix Adler • *scr* Jack White • *ad* Irving Moore • *ph* Gert Andersen • *e* Edwin Bryant • *a* Ross Bellah • *c:* Vernon Dent (King Cole), Phil Van Zandt (Mergatroyd the Magician), Virginia Hunter (Princess Alicia, stock footage), Wanda Perry (Princess Alicia, new footage), Sherry O'Neil (Girl in Magician's Box, stock footage), Joe Palma (Guard), Heinie Conklin (Guard), Diana Darrin (Tillie), Norma Randall (Millie),

Wanda Perry doubling for Virginia Hunter in the role of Princess Alicia in new footage for *Musty Musketeers* (1954), flanked by Phil Van Zandt and Joe Palma (the latter of whom also played the so-called Fake Shemp in films made after Shemp's death in 1955). © Columbia Pictures, courtesy of Moe Howard Collection

Longtime Stooge supporting player Vernon Dent (center) as King Cole in *Musty Musketeers* (1954). © *Columbia Pictures, courtesy of Moe Howard Collection*

and Ruth Godfrey (Lillie) • SYN: King Cole grants permission to three troubadour Stooges to marry their girlfriends after his daughter, Princess Alicia, ties the knot with Prince Galiant in the spring. Mergatroyd overhears the request and has another idea. He captures the princess to marry her himself. But it's the Stooges to the rescue! They free the princess and expose Mergatroyd. • SD: one (date not known) • FN: A remake of *Fiddlers Three* (5/6/48), with stock footage. New scenes include the Stooges riding into Coleslawvania, visiting their girlfriends, entangling with Mergatroyd in a sword fight, and reuniting at the conclusion with Tillieth, Millieth, and Lillieth.

155. PALS AND GALS ☆☆½ • Rl. June 3; re. Jan. 1961 • Prod. no. 4211 • 17m • *p d* Jules White • *st* Clyde Bruckman • *scr* Jack White • *ad* Irving Moore • *ph* Gert Andersen • *e* Edwin Bryant • *a* Ross Bellah • *c:* Christine McIntyre (Nell), George Chesebro (Quirt), Heinie Conklin (Bartender, stock footage), Vernon Dent (Doctor, stock footage), Stanley Blystone (Colonel, new and stock footage), Frank Ellis (Jake, stock

footage), Ruth Godfrey (Belle), Norma Randall (Zelle), Norman Willis (Doc Barker, stock footage), and Blackie Whiteford (Cowboy) • SYN: The Stooges go west, but it's not because they have gold fever— it's for health reasons. Shemp has a swollen vein in his leg and he needs rest. Soon, they befriend Nell, a bar singer, who informs them that Doc Barker (the local bad guy) is holding her two sisters hostage in an effort to make Nell marry him. (So much for Shemp's rest!) The Stooges, of course, defeat Barker and save Nell and her sisters. • WT: *Cuckoo Westerners* • SD: one (date not known) • FN: Remake of *Out West* (4/24/47). Features stock footage from *Goofs and Saddles* (7/2/37). The gag of mixing liquids in an old boot reappears again. Also making an appearance is the "exchanging cards under the table" routine, which was staged in *Goofs and Saddles* (7/2/37) and *Out West* (4/24/47).

156. KNUTZY KNIGHTS ☆☆☆ • Rl. Sept. 2; re. Feb. 16, 1961 • Prod. no. 4217 • 17½m • *p d* Jules White • *st* Edward Bernds • *scr* Felix Adler • *ad* Irving Moore • *ph* Ray Cory • *e* Edwin Bryant • *a* Carl

Anderson • *c:* Jock Mahoney (Cedric), Christine McIntyre (Elaine), Phil Van Zandt (Black Prince), Vernon Dent (King Arthur), Ruth Godfrey (Handmaiden), and Joe Palma (Sir Satchel, new footage; Soldier, stock footage), and Harold Brauer (Sir Satchel, stock footage) • SYN: The Stooges foil the Black Prince's plot to marry Princess Elaine, kill her father, the king, and assume control of the kingdom. Their actions enable the princess to marry Cedric the Blacksmith, whom she really loves. • SD: two (dates not known) • FN: This remake of *Squareheads of the Round Table* (3/4/48) includes a high volume of stock footage.

157. SHOT IN THE FRONTIER ☆☆☆½ • Rl. Oct. 7; re. Apr. 13, 1961 • Prod. no. 4216 • 16m • *p d* Jules White • *st scr* Felix Adler • *ad* Abner Singer • *ph* Ray Cory • *e* Edwin Bryant • *a* George Brooks • *c:* Emil Sitka (Sheriff), Ruth Godfrey White (Stella), Diana Darrin (Bella), Vivian Mason (Ella), Kenneth MacDonald (Bill Noonan), Joe Palma (Jack Noonan), Emmett Lynn (Lem), and Babe London (Mandy) • SYN: The Stooges become shooting targets for the Noonan brothers, following the trio's wedding to three voluptuous ladies: Stella, Bella, and Ella. A noontime shootout between the Noonans and the Stooges ensues (satirizing *High Noon*), complete with an old cowpoke singing and strumming his guitar off key. • WT: *Low Afternoon* • SD: (10/53) • FN: The film's original working title, *Low Afternoon*, was a parody of the classic 1952 western *High Noon*, starring Gary Cooper.

158. SCOTCHED IN SCOTLAND ☆☆☆ • Rl. Nov. 4; re. May 18, 1961 • Prod. no. 4218 • 15½m • *p d* Jules White • *st* Elwood Ullman • *scr* Jack White • *ad* Irving Moore • *ph* Ray Cory • *e* Robert B. Hoover • *a* Carl Anderson • *c:* Phil Van Zandt (O. U. Conga, Dean), Christine McIntyre (Lorna), Charles Knight (Angus, stock footage), Ted Lorch (MacPherson, stock footage), George Pembroke

(MacPherson), Herbert Evans (The Earl, stock footage) • SYN: The Stooges graduate as detectives from the Wide Awake Detective School, with the lowest possible honors. Dean O. U. Conga arranges for the boys' first case: guarding priceless heirlooms for an earl, the owner of Glenheather Castle in Scotland. • WT: *Hassle in the Castle* • SD: two (dates not known) • FN: A remake of *The Hot Scots* (7/8/48), with stock footage. A double was used for MacPherson in new castle scenes. The parrot-skull gag was also in *If a Body Meets a Body* (8/30/45) and in *The Hot Scots* (7/8/48). . . . ThreeStooges.net credits Jules White as the voice of the skeleton.

## 1955

### 159. FLING IN THE RING ☆☆☆
• Rl. Jan. 6; re. July 13, 1961 • Prod. no. 4223 • 16m • *p d* Jules White • *st* Clyde Bruckman • *scr* Jack White • *ad* Eddie Saeta • *ph* Ray Cory • *e* Robert B. Hoover • *a* Edward Ilou • *c*: Dick Wessel (Chopper Kane, stock footage), Claire Carleton (Kitty Davis, stock footage), Frank Sully (Big Mike), Harold Brauer (Big Mike, stock footage), Cy Schindell (Moose, stock footage), Joe Palma (Chuck), Tommy Kingston (Chuck, stock footage), Heinie Conklin (Gorilla's Trainer, stock footage), Johnny Kascier (Moe's Stand-In), Charlie Cross (Larry's Stand-In), and Hurley Breen (Shemp's Stand-In) • SYN: Moe, Larry, and Shemp handle Chopper Kane, a heavyweight boxer. Their boss, Big Mike, has bet a big bankroll on Chopper to lose his next fight to his opponent, Gorilla Watson—and he expects the Stooges to make sure it happens. • SD: one (T 3/27/54) • FN: A remake of *Fright Night* (3/6/47), with a high volume of stock footage. New scenes include a meeting with the new Big Mike (Frank Sully). Watch for the old Big Mike (Harold Brauer) from *Fright Night* in stock footage. The gag of acting as a puppeteer for an unconscious victim also appears in *Matri-Phony* (7/2/42) and in *Fright Night* (3/6/47). . . . Originally, Jack White's

screenplay ended with Moe and Larry speeding off for China in a motorcycle, with Shemp in a sidecar.

### 160. OF CASH AND HASH ☆☆☆
• Rl. Feb. 3 • Prod. no. 4225 • 16m • *p d* Jules White • *st* Del Lord • *scr* Jack White • *ad* Eddie Saeta • *ph* Ray Cory • *e* Robert B. Hoover • *a* Edward Ilou • *c*: Kenneth MacDonald (Lefty Loomis), Christine McIntyre (Gladys), Frank Lackteen (Red Watkins), Vernon Dent (Captain Mullins, stock footage), Duke York (Angel, stock footage), Cy Schindell (Cop, stock footage), and Stanley Blystone (Customer) • SYN: The Stooges are mistaken for three armored car robbers but prove their innocence by capturing the real crooks in an old spooky mansion. • WT: *Crook Crackers* • SD: one (date not known) • FN: A remake of *Shivering Sherlocks* (1/8/48), with stock footage. Doubles were cast in new scenes as Angel and Lefty. The clam soup gag is also used in *Shivering Sherlocks*.

### 161. GYPPED IN THE PENTHOUSE ☆☆☆
• Rl. Mar. 10 • Prod. no. 4224 • 16m • *p d* Jules White • *st scr* Felix Adler • *ad* Abner E. Singer • *ph* Ray Cory • *e* Henry Batista • *a* Carl Anderson • *c*: Jean Willes (Jane), Emil Sitka (Charlie), and Al Thompson (Club Member) • SYN: Larry and Shemp meet inside a woman-haters club to discuss their bygone romances with Jane, an attractive gold digger. After a series of flashbacks, Shemp and Larry are also reunited with Jane's vengeful husband, Moe • WT: *Blundering Bachelors* • SD: three (M 7/19–W 7/21/54); shot on Stage 9 at Columbia Studios • FN: Jules White is credited with writing the lyrics to the song "Home on the Farm."

### 162. BEDLAM IN PARADISE
☆☆☆ • Rl. Apr. 14 • Prod. no. 4228 • 16m • *p d* Jules White • *st* Zion Myers • *scr* Felix Adler • *ph* Ray Cory • *e* Paul Borofsky • *a* Carl Anderson • *ad* Jerrold Bernstein • *c*: Moe Howard (Moe/Uncle Mortimer), Marti Shelton (Miss Jones,

Blonde Angel, stock footage), Phil Van Zandt (The Devil/Mr. Heller), Sylvia Lewis (Helen Blazes), Vernon Dent (I. Fleecem), Symona Boniface (Mrs. De Peyster, stock footage), Judy Malcolm (Heavenly Switchboard Operator), and Victor Travers (Mr. De Peyster, stock footage) • SYN: When Shemp dies and goes to heaven, Uncle Mortimer, the keeper of the Pearly Gates, refuses him entrance into the divine kingdom. The deal: Shemp must reform his partners Moe and Larry, who are involved in a shady deal with the devil • WT: *Gruesome Threesome* • SD: one (F 7/9/54) • FN: A remake of *Heavenly Daze* (9/2/48), with stock footage. New scenes include Moe and Larry nursing Shemp before he dies; Shemp's encounter with the devil; the devil's meeting on earth with Moe and Larry; and the ending with Shemp in bed (it was all a dream). . . . An October 1954 press announcement originally listed actress Sally Jane Bruce among the film's supporting cast.

### 163. STONE AGE ROMEOS ☆☆☆
• Rl. June 2 • Prod. no. 4229 • 16m • *p d* Jules White • *st* Zion Myers • *scr* Felix Adler • *ad* Jerrold Bernstein • *ph* Ira Morgan • *e* Paul Borofsky • *a* Carl Anderson • *c*: Emil Sitka (Mr. Bopper, Curator), Dee Green (Baggie, stock footage), Nancy Saunders (Maggie, stock footage), Virginia Hunter (Aggie, stock footage), Joe Palma, Cy Schindell and Bill Wallace (Cavemen, stock footage), and Barbara Bartay (Secretary) • SYN: A museum curator will pay the Stooges $25,000 if they return from a scientific expedition with film footage showing that cavemen still exist. Later, the Stooges screen for the curator film footage of cavemen—who are actually the Stooges in disguise. • WT: *Caved in Cavemen* • SD: one (Th 8/26/54) • FN: A remake of *I'm a Monkey's Uncle* (10/7/48), with stock footage.

### 164. WHAM-BAM-SLAM! ☆☆½
• Rl. Sept. 1 • Prod. no. 4232 • 16m • *p d* Jules White • *st* Clyde Bruckman • *scr* Felix Adler • *ad* Willard

Sheldon • *ph* Fred Jackman • *e* Paul Borofsky • *a* Cary Odell • *c*: Matt McHugh (Claude, stock footage), Alyn Lockwood (Petunia), Doris Revier (Marigold, stock footage), and Wanda Perry (Narcissus, stock footage) • SYN: Shemp's nerves are shot, so Moe and Larry turn to their friend Claude, a self-educated health adviser, for help. When homemade remedies don't work, Claude recommends the Stooges buy his car and take a trip. The car turns out to be a lemon and won't start. But, that's OK; all of the excitement cures Shemp anyway. • WT: *Enjoying Poor Health* • SD: one (Tu 1/18/55) • FN: A remake of *Pardon My Clutch* (2/26/48), with stock footage. New segments: the Stooges eating hotcakes (consuming powder puffs by mistake), a lobster in Shemp's footbath, and the ending with Shemp being cured by all the excitement.

165. HOT ICE ☆☆☆½ • Rl. Oct. 6; re. Jan. 1966 • Prod. no. 4233 • 16½m • *p d* Jules White • *st* Elwood Ullman • *scr* Jack White • *ad* Willard Sheldon • *ph* Fred Jackman • *e* Tony DiMarco • *a* Cary Odell • *c*: Kenneth MacDonald (Dapper Malone), Christine McIntyre (Bee, stock footage), Lester Allen (Runty), Barbara Bartay (Woman in Café), Budd Fine (Thug), and Cy Schindell (Muscles, stock footage) • SYN: While cleaning up the grounds of Scotland Yard, gardeners Moe, Larry, and Shemp see a memo that fell from a window about the theft of the Punjab diamond. Deciding it's their chance to prove themselves as detectives, the boys investigate. • FN: A remake of *Crime on Their Hands* (12/9/48), with stock footage. Stock footage from *The Hot Scots* (7/8/48) is used in the opening Scotland Yard scenes. In new scenes, director Jules White cast a double for "Muscles." The Stooges' search through the dresser drawers is a revision of their file cabinet gag.

166. BLUNDER BOYS ☆☆☆ • Rl. Nov. 3 • Prod. no. 4222 • 16m • *p d* Jules White • *st scr* Felix Adler •

*ad* Willard Sheldon • *ph* Ray Cory • *e* Tony DiMarco • *a* Cary Odell • *c*: Benny Rubin (The Eel), Angela Stevens (Alma Matter), Kenneth MacDonald (Captain F. B. Eye), Barbara Bartay (Beautician), Bonnie Henjum, Barbara Donaldson, Marjorie Jackson, and June Lebow (Turkish Bathers) • SYN: Spoofing TV's *Dragnet*, the Stooges are Halliday (Moe), Tarraday (Larry), and St. Patrick's Day (Shemp). They've just graduated from criminology school and are now full-fledged detectives. Captain F. B. Eye assigns the boys to their first case: tracking down the Eel, a robber who masquerades as a woman. In a wild escapade at the Biltless Hotel, the Eel manages to slip through the Stooges' grasp; as a result, the three lose their jobs and become ditchdiggers instead. • WT: *Cuckoo Cops* • FN: Scenes of Larry on a building ledge were budgeted under *Wham-Bam-Slam!* (9/1/55). The last Stooges short with Shemp that features all new footage.

## 1956
167. HUSBANDS BEWARE ☆☆☆☆½ • Rl. Jan. 5; re. Sept. 1962 • Prod. no. 4236 • 16m • *p d* Jules White • *st* Clyde Bruckman • *scr* Felix Adler • *ad* Eddie Saeta • *ph* Henry Freulich • *e* Tony DiMarco • *a* Ross Bellah • *c*: Emil Sitka (Justice of the Peace), Christine McIntyre (Lulu Hopkins, stock footage), Maxine Gates (Flora), Lu Leonard (Dora), Dee Green (Fanny, stock footage), Nancy Saunders and Doris Colleen (Ex-Girlfriends, stock footage), Johnny Kascier (Moe's Stand-In), Hurley Breen (Shemp's Stand-In), and Charlie Cross (Larry's Stand-In) • SYN: It's revenge time for Moe and Larry after they marry Shemp's weight-challenged sisters, whom he introduced to them. They make up a story that Shemp has to marry a woman within seven hours to collect a $500,000 inheritance from his deceased uncle's estate. • WT: *Eat, Drink and Be Married* • SD: one (Tu 5/17/55); shot on Stage 2 at Columbia. • FN: A remake of

*Brideless Groom* (9/11/47), with stock footage. The Stooges' encounters with Shemp's sisters are new footage. In the wedding sequence, a double was used for the Fanny role.

168. CREEPS ☆☆½ • Rl. Feb. 2; re. Oct. 1962 • Prod. no. 4237 • 16m • *p d* Jules White • *st* Felix Adler • *scr* Jack White • *ad* Eddie Saeta • *ph* Henry Freulich • *e* Harold White • *a* Ross Bellah • *c*: Phil Arnold (Voice of Sir Tom) and Jules White (Voice of Red Skeleton) • SYN: The Stooges tell their sons (also the Stooges) a spooky bedtime story about "knights, ghosts, and murders" in a haunted castle, where the boys meet some lively, antiquated ghosts. • WT: *Three Brave Cowards* • FN: The haunted castle footage comes from *The Ghost Talks* (2/3/49), except for the Torture Room scenes.

169. FLAGPOLE JITTERS ☆☆½ • Rl. Apr. 5; re. Nov. 1962 • Prod. no. 4238 • 16m • *p d* Jules White • *st* Felix Adler • *scr* Jack White • *ad* Willard Sheldon • *ph* Irving Lippman • *e* Harold White • *a* Cary Odell • *c*: Vernon Dent (Insurance Adjustor, stock footage), Mary Ainslee (Mary, stock footage), David Bond (Svengarlic), Ned Glass (Svengarlic's Agent, stock footage), Barbara Bartay (Chorus Girl Hit by Ice Cream), Beverly Thomas and Bonnie Henjum (Chorus Girls), Don Harvey (Jack), Frank Sully (Jim), Richard Alexander (Cop), and Johnny Kascier (Delivery Boy on Bike, stock footage) • SYN: The Stooges try raising money for an operation that will make their invalid neighbor Mary walk again. Moe, Larry, and Shemp take on jobs pasting up posters at the Garden Theatre, where they are enlisted as volunteers in a hypnotist's flagpole stunt. The stunt is being staged so Svengarlic's accomplices can rob the Gottrocks Jewelry Company. The Stooges' weight, however, causes the flagpole to snap, and they crash down into the jewelry store, foiling the robbery attempt. • SD: two (Th 6/30–F 7/1/55); shot on Stage 3 at Colum-

bia • FN: A remake of *Hokus Pokus* (5/5/49), with stock footage. New scenes include establishing Svengarlic's crooked motives and the Stooges' encountering three chorus girls. Doubles fill in as Mary and Dick in new footage.

## 170. FOR CRIMIN' OUT LOUD
☆☆☆☆ • Rl. May 3; re. Jan. 1963 • Prod. no. 4239 • 16m • *p d* Jules White • *st* Edward Bernds • *scr* Felix Adler • *ad* Willard Sheldon • *ph* Irving Lippman • *e* Harold White • *a* Cary Odell • *c:* Barbara Bartay (Newsgirl), Emil Sitka (Goodrich), Christine McIntyre (Goodrich's Niece, stock footage), Duke York (Nikko, stock footage), Charles Knight (Butler, stock footage), and Ralph Dunn (Niece's Husband, stock footage) • SYN: The Stooges work for the Miracle Detective Agency ("If We Solve Your Crime, It's A Miracle!") and answer a middle-aged councilman's call to track down some racketeers who have threatened his life. • WT: *Nutty Newshounds* • FN: A remake of *Who Done It?* (3/3/49), with stock footage. The Stooges appear in some new scenes, the most notable being the scene at their detec-tive agency. The fighting in the dark gag is also used in *Out West* (4/24/47) and *Who Done It?* (3/3/49) and later in *The Three Stooges Go Around the World in a Daze* (8/21/63). This was the last Stooge short containing new footage of Shemp.

## 171. RUMPUS IN THE HAREM
☆☆½ • Rl. June 21; re. Feb. 1963 • Prod. no. 4244 • 16m • *p d* Jules White • *st* Felix Adler • *scr* Jack White • *ad* Willard Sheldon • *ph* Ray Cory • *e* Harold White • *a* Ross Bellah • *c:* Vernon Dent (Hassen Ben Sober, stock footage), George Lewis (Ghinna Rumma, stock footage), Harriette Tarler and Suzanne Ridgeway (Harem Girls), Diana Darrin, Helen Jay, Ruth Godfrey White (Stooges' Girlfriends), Frank Lackteen (Haffa Dalla, stock footage), and Joe Palma (Fake Shemp) • SYN: The Stooges' girls have a few days to pay the taxes they owe or they will be sold into slavery. To raise the money, Moe, Larry, and Shemp, waiters at the Cafe Casbahbah, promise two customers to recover the King Rootin' Tootin' diamond from the Emir of Shmow. They'll be handsomely compensated with reward money to pay off their sweethearts' taxes. Disguised as Santa Clauses, the Stooges get the job done. • WT: *Diamond Daffy* (scripted Dec. 12, 1955) • FN: A reworking of *Malice in the Palace* (9/1/49), with stock footage. The first of four films made after Shemp's death, with Joe Palma doubling as Shemp in new footage. New scenes: the Stooges' girls report their bad news to Moe and Larry (Shemp is conveniently missing, having left a note informing the boys that he couldn't sleep because of their snoring and had gone to open the restaurant early); Moe, Larry, and Fake Shemp reunite for their traditional football huddle in the restaurant; and the Stooges flee from a Nubian guard (not the same actor as in the stock footage)—right into a harem. The gag of disguising themselves as Santa Clauses also appeared in *Wee Wee Monsieur* (2/18/38) and in *Mal-*

Original Belgium theatrical poster for The Three Stooges comedies featuring Shemp.
*© Columbia Pictures, courtesy of Jeff Lenburg Collection*

*ice in the Palace* (9/1/49). The waiter chasing a dog past a customer waiting for franks and beans is also used in *Playing the Ponies* (10/15/37) and in *Malice in the Palace* (9/1/49). . . . The diamond is spelled "Rootin' Tootin" in film's script.

**172. HOT STUFF** ☆☆☆ • Rl. Sept. 6; re. Apr. 1963 • Prod. no. 4245 • 16m • *p d* Jules White • *st* Elwood Ullman • *scr* Felix Adler • *ad* Willard Sheldon • *ph* Irving Lippman • *e* Harold White • *a* Ross Bellah • *c:* Jock Mahoney (Cell Guard, stock footage), Emil Sitka (Professor Snead), Christine McIntyre (Snead's Daughter, stock footage), Evelyn Lovequist (Uranian Secretary), Connie Cezan (Uranian Officer), Andre Pola (Clutz), Vernon Dent (General, stock footage), Harold Brauer (Leon, stock footage), Phil Van Zandt (Captain Rork), Gene Roth (His Excellency of Anemia), and Joe Palma (Fake Shemp) • SYN: The boys are undercover agents enlisted to protect a professor whom foreign agents would like to kidnap to obtain his secret rocket fuel formula. It works until foreign agents kidnap the Stooges, including Larry, whom they mistake for the professor. Just when they succeed in making some kind of rocket fuel, the real professor and his daughter are brought in, and they are all put behind bars. But don't worry, they escape. • WT: *They Gassed Wrong* (scripted on December 12, 1955) • FN: A remake of *Fuelin' Around* (7/7/49), with stock footage. New scenes, filmed after Shemp's death: The Stooges, wearing beards, enter the Uranian Department of the Inferior. A pretty girl passes by, so Moe orders "Shemp"—Joe Palma— to "follow her, she may be a spy!" Palma utters, "Right," and skips off after her while Moe and Larry engage in a separate scene with two female Uranian officers. Later, in the laboratory, Palma tries to imitate Shemp's famous tagline: "Heep-heep-heep!"

**173. SCHEMING SCHEMERS** ☆☆☆ • Rl. Oct. 4; re. May 1963

• Prod. no. 4246 • 16m • *p d* Jules White • *st* Elwood Ullman • *scr* Jack White • *ad* Willard Sheldon • *ph* Ray Cory • *e* Harold White • *a* Ross Bellah • *c:* Christine McIntyre (Mrs. Allen, stock footage), Kenneth MacDonald (Mr. Allen), Symona Boniface (Mrs. Norfleet, stock footage), Emil Sitka (Walter Norfleet), Dudley Dickerson (Chef, stock footage), Herbert Evans (Butler, stock footage), Victor Travers (Sleeping Party Guest, stock footage), Helen Dickson and Al Thompson (Party Guests, stock footage), and Joe Palma (Fake Shemp) • SYN: As plumbers, the Stooges are summoned to the Norfleet mansion to recover a valuable diamond ring that slipped down a washbasin. Instead, the Stooges wreak havoc and start a pie fight. • WT: *Pixilated Plumbers* (scripted Dec. 29, 1955) • SD: one (M 1/16/56) • FN: A remake, with stock footage, of *Vagabond Loafers* (10/6/49), which is in turn a reworking of *A Plumbing We Will Go* (4/19/40). The film also incorporates stock footage from *A Plumbing We Will Go* (4/19/40) and some pie-fight footage from *Half-Wits Holiday* (1/9/47). New segments: Moe and Larry search for the missing ring in a sink and throw pies at Allen (Kenneth MacDonald). Joe Palma doubles for Shemp in one shot, honking the horn in the trio's jeep. Christine McIntyre is likewise doubled in some scenes. . . . ThreeStooges.net gives this short the Insensitivity Award: "Whoever thought it would be funny to close out the short with Moe asking 'Hey, where is that puddinhead Shemp?' And then Moe and Larry look upward [to the 2nd floor, where Shemp was trapped in a maze of stock footage]. One can only guess what was going through Moe's thoughts when he was directed to perform that short sequence."

**174. COMMOTION ON THE OCEAN** ☆☆½ • Rl. Nov. 8; re. July 1963 • Prod. no. 4247 • 17m • *p d* Jules White • *st scr* Felix Adler • *ad* Willard Sheldon • *ph* Ray Cory • *e* Harold White • *a* Ross Bellah •

*c:* Charles Wilson (J. L. Cameron, stock footage), Gene Roth (Bortch, stock footage), Emil Sitka (Smitty), Harriette Tarler (Emma Blake), and Joe Palma (Fake Shemp) • SYN: When the Stooges learn in a newspaper editor's office that some secret atomic documents have been stolen, they decide to pose as reporters and investigate the matter. It turns out that their neighbor, Bortch, a seedy-looking foreign spy, has swiped the documents and is planning to return by boat to his native land. The Stooges accompany him and thwart his plan. WT: *Salt Water Daffy* (scripted December 30, 1955) • SD: one (Tu 1/17/56) • FN: A remake of *Dunked in the Deep* (11/3/49), with stock footage. Newspaper office sequence, except for a few shots, is stock footage from *Crime on Their Hands* (12/9/48). The seasick gag was reprised from *Back from the Front* (5/28/43) and *Dunked in the Deep* (11/3/49). New footage includes the Stooges' seizure of Bortch, the foreign spy, as well as Moe and Larry's search for food (they mistakenly eat a wooden fish, then spew out sawdust à la their coughing up feathers gag, which was first staged *in Uncivil Warriors* [4/26/35]). . . . Joe Palma, doubling as Shemp, is featured briefly in the scene in which Bortch is captured. It would be his last appearance as the so-called Fake Shemp.

## Feature Films
### 1951

**1. GOLD RAIDERS** ☆☆ • Rl. Sept. 14 by United Artists • Prod. no. 524 • 56m • *p* Bernard Glasser • *d* Edward Bernds • *st scr* Elwood Ullman and William Lively • *ph* Paul Ivano • *e* Fred Allen • *m* Alexandre Starr • *c:* George O'Brien (George), Sheila Ryan (Laura Mason), Clem Bevans (Doc Mason), Monte Blue (John Sawyer), Lyle Talbot (Taggert), John Merton (Clete), Andre Adore (Bartender), Remy Pequet (Singer), Hugh Hooker (Sandy), Fuzzy Knight (Sheriff), Bill Ward (Red), and Roy Canada (Slim) • SYN: The Stooges help George O'Brien, an insurance agent, outwit a gang of desperadoes who are after a valuable gold-mine shipment • AKA: *The Stooges Go West* • SD: five (Tu 12/26–Sa 12/30/50) • FN: The Stooges reprise their serenade song, "Jane," which they wrote. The song was first used in *Three Hams on Rye* (9/7/50) and then retooled as "Nora" in *Scrambled Brains* (7/7/51). . . . In 1958, the film was reissued to theaters as *The Stooges Go West*, and television distributor Associated Artists Productions (a.a.p.) issued two 8 mm home-movie abridgements of the film in the 1960s. On November 21, 2006, Warner Home Video released on DVD a rare treat for Stooge fans: a double feature of *Gold Raiders* and *Meet the Baron* (10/20/33) with Ted Healy and His Stooges.• PS: *Gold Raiders* was not exactly director Edward Bernds' favorite, as he explained: "I should have never made that picture. It was an ultra-quickie shot in five days at the unbelievable cost of $50,000, which, even then, was ridiculously low. I'm afraid the picture shows it!"

**1956**

2. LAFF HOUR (Unrated) • Rl. Jan. by Columbia • 90m • *c:* Andy Clyde, Hugh Herbert, Buster Keaton, Tom Kennedy, Billy Gilbert, Leon Errol, and more • SYN: *Laff Hour* consisted of comedies hand picked by theaters from Columbia's 1932–56 short-subjects library. Each theater's program differed. Three Stooges shorts with Curly and Shemp were among those available for theaters to select.

In 2006, the discovery was reported of a script for a never-produced Stooges feature with Moe, Larry, and Shemp. Entitled *Where There's a Will*, the feature was written by veteran Stooge writer Elwood Ullman. The script, dated August 12, 1948, is on display at The Stoogeum in Ambler, Pennsylvania, the world's first and only museum dedicated to The Three Stooges. The storyline is somewhat familiar: The Stooges, city laborers, learn they are heirs to a family fortune in Dixie. The fortune

they find, however, is a broken-down family homestead, and there's a plot afoot by others to rob the Stooges and the residents.

## THE THREE STOOGES (Larry, Moe, and Joe Besser)

### Columbia Shorts
**1957**

175. HOOFS AND GOOFS ☆☆☆ • Rl. Jan. 31; re. Oct. 1964 • Prod. no. 4251 • 15½m • *p d* Jules White • *st scr* Jack White • *ph* Gert Andersen • *e* Harold White • *ad* Willard Sheldon • *a* Paul Palmentola • *c:* Benny Rubin (Mr. Dinklespiel), Harriette

The Three Stooges opening with Joe Besser, 1957. *© Columbia Pictures, courtesy of Moe Howard Collection*

Tarler (Dinklespiel's Daughter), Moe Howard (Moe/Birdie, the Stooges' Sister), and Tony the Wonder Horse (Birdie the Horse) • SYN: The Stooges' sister, Birdie, has been reincarnated as a horse and is about to give birth to a beautiful colt! The scene changes to Joe, sound asleep, mumbling, "I'm an uncle! I'm an uncle!" Moe and Larry wake up Joe (he dreamed the whole story), as Birdie, alive and well, comes from the kitchen carrying a casserole. Joe tells her he just dreamed that she was a horse. Far from flattered, Birdie crowns Joe with her casserole. • WT: *Galloping Bride* (scripted March 30, 1956) • SD: three (dates not known) • FN: In the final draft screenplay of *Hoofs and Goofs*, writer Jack White calls for Birdie to whack Joe over the

head with a breakaway rolling pin instead of a casserole. . . . The gag of tying a heavy object to an animal's tail is also enacted in *Busy Buddies* (3/18/44) and Abbott and Costello's *Ride 'Em Cowboy* (1943). Blowing a pill through a pipe is a gag borrowed from *Even As I O U* (9/18/42) and *Scrambled Brains* (7/7/51). . . . Technically, Joe Besser's first Stooges' short was an award winner of sorts. In 1958, the Patsy Awards presented their Award of Excellence to Tony the Wonder Horse for his work in this film. • PS: It has been said that the worst subjects to direct are children and animals. But according to Joe Besser, Tony the Wonder Horse was no problem: "That horse was wonderful. When Moe, Larry, and I were on the set, we fed him carrots."

176. MUSCLE UP A LITTLE CLOSER ☆☆½ • Rl. Feb. 28; re. Oct. 1964 • Prod. no. 4250 • 17m • *p d* Jules White • *st scr* Felix Adler • *ad* Mitchell Gamson • *ph* Irving Lippman • *e* Harold White • *a* Cary Odell • *sd* Robert Priestley • *c:* Maxine Gates (Tiny), Ruth Godfrey White (May), Harriette Tarler (Mary), and Matt Murphy (Elmo Drake) • SYN: Tiny, Joe's girlfriend, is upset. Her five-karat diamond engagement ring has been stolen! Moe has a hunch that Elmo Drake, the trucking foreman at the plant

where the Stooges and their girls work, stole the ring, since he has a pass key to all the employees' lockers. At work, the Stooges and Tiny confront Elmo in the gymnasium and, after some fancy wrestling, recover the ring so Joe and Tiny can get married. • WT: *Builder Uppers* • SD: three (W 6/27–F 6/29/56); shot on Stage 3 at Columbia Studios • FN: Deleted are some scenes at the Seabiscuit Food Corporation: Joe plays detective, but Moe searches him and finds a concealed weapon—a salami; and Joe answers a telephone call, unaware that a wad of gum he discarded is stuck to the earpiece. . . . This is the first short in which Moe and Larry adopt normal haircuts.

177. A MERRY MIX-UP ☆☆☆ • Rl. Mar. 28; re. Dec. 1964 • Prod. no. 4252 • 16m • *p d* Jules White • *st scr* Felix Adler • *ad* Irving Moore • *ph* Irving Lippman • *e* Harold White • *a* Paul Palmentola • *sd* Dave Montrose • *c:* Moe Howard (Moe/Max/Morris), Larry Fine (Larry/Louie/Luke), Joe Besser (Joe/Jack/Jeff), Suzanne Ridgeway (Jill, Louie's Wife), Harriette Tarler (Letty, Max's Wife), Nanette Bordeaux (May, Jack's Wife), Ruth Godfrey White (Leona, Luke's Fiancée), Jeanne Carmen (Mary, Jeff's Fiancée), Diana Darrin (Jane, Morris' Fiancée), and Frank Sully (Waiter) • SYN: This is the story of nine brothers, three sets of identical triplets born one year apart, who have lost track of each other since the war. The mix-up starts when Moe, Larry, and Joe meet the wives of their brothers, Louis, Max, and Jack, in a nightclub, much to the consternation of a very confused waiter. The Stooges play all three sets of triplets. • WT: *A Merry Marriage Mix-Up* • SD: three (dates not known) • FN: A reworking of *Our Relations* (1936) with Laurel and Hardy. For the ending, screenwriter Felix Adler suggested that the waiter hit himself over the head with a champagne bottle instead of a meat cleaver. • PS: The second-to-last shot in *A Merry Mix-Up* was carefully exposed three different times

to achieve the effect of Moe, Larry, and Joe as the three sets of triplets standing side by side. For each section of film exposed, each Stooge had his own marker on the floor to stand behind. A *real* merry mix-up developed when Jules White believed Larry was standing behind the wrong marker as compared to the previous exposure. Larry insisted that Jules was wrong and that he was standing in the right spot. Fortunately, Jules listened to Larry, who proved to be right. If Jules hadn't listened, the stu-

dio would have had to spend thousands of dollars for a retake.

178. SPACE SHIP SAPPY ☆☆ • Rl. Apr. 18; re. Jan. 1965 • Prod. no. 4253 • 16m • *p d* Jules White • *st scr* Jack White • *ad* Donald Gold • *ph* Henry Freulich • *e* Saul A. Goodkind • *a* William Flannery • *sd* Frank A. Tuttle • *c:* Benny Rubin (Professor A. K. Rimple), Doreen Woodbury (Lisa Rimple), Lorraine Crawford (Flora), Harriette Tarler (Fauna), Marilyn Hanold (Amazon), and Emil Sitka

Columbia Pictures goofed when they inadvertently billed Moe as Shemp on this one-sheet for *A Merry Mix-Up* (1957). *© Columbia Pictures, courtesy of Jeff Lenburg Collection*

(Liar's Club Emcee) • SYN: Professor Rimple takes three sailors (the Stooges) and his daughter Lisa on an adventurous cruise on a spaceship bound for the planet Sunev (that's Venus spelled backward). Here, the boys flee from three cannibalistic amazon women who want to devour them! As they reach the door to the spaceship, it bursts open, knocking the professor and Lisa out cold. But there is no cause for alarm. Moe believes he can operate the spaceship. He does until Joe grabs hold of the control lever and breaks it off! As the spaceship takes a nose dive, the scene dissolves to the Liars Club 27th Annual Convention, where an emcee awards the Stooges first prize for being the biggest liars in the world! • WT: *Rocket and Roll It* • SD: three (M 8/27–W 8/29/56) • FN: Screenwriter Jack White originally planned for the Stooges to go into their "Viva! Viva!" routine after receiving their award.

### 179. GUNS A POPPIN! ☆☆☆ • Rl. June 13; re. Feb. 1965 • Prod. no. 1902 • 16½m • *p d* Jules White • *st* Jack White and Elwood Ullman • *scr* Jack White • *ad* Herb Wallerstein • *ph* Henry Freulich • *e* Saul A. Goodkind • *a* Cary Odell • *sd* Kay Bobcock • *c:* Frank Sully (Sheriff), Joe Palma (Mad Bill Hookup), and Vernon Dent (Judge, stock footage) • SYN: Moe is accused of assaulting his two brothers-in-law, Larry and Joe, with intent to commit mayhem. But the incident would never have happened if Larry and Joe hadn't taken Moe on a hunting trip to quiet his nerves • WT: *Nerveless Wreck* • SD: one (W 11/28/56); shot on Stage 34 at the Columbia Ranch • FN: A remake of *Idiots DeLuxe* (7/20/45), with some stock footage. In the new subplot, the Stooges' cabin becomes the site of a standoff between the sheriff and an escaped bandit, Mad Bill Hookup. The boys eventually capture the crook and a grateful sheriff reveals that they'll receive a $10,000 reward (the same amount Moe owes his creditors!). The news delights the boys so much that they give the Sheriff a big hug while Mad

Bill escapes! The cabin set was reused in *Horsing Around* (9/12/57) and *Oil's Well That Ends Well* (12/4/58).

### 180. HORSING AROUND ☆☆ • Rl. Sept. 12; re. Apr. 1965 • Prod. no. 1901 • 15½m • *p d* Jules White • *st scr* Felix Adler • *ad* Herb Wallerstein • *ph* Ray Cory • *e* William Lyon • *a* Cary Odell • *sd* Fay Babcock • *c:* Emil Sitka (Schnapp's Owner), Harriette Tarler (Attendant's Daughter), and Tony the Wonder Horse (Birdie) • SYN: Joe learns that the famous circus horse, Schnapps, who is the mate of their reincarnated sister Birdie, is about to be destroyed. The Stooges and Birdie ride to the fairgrounds and save him. • WT: *Just Horsing Around* and *Just Fooling Around* • SD: three (M 11/19–W 11/21/56); shot on Western and Rock Streets at Columbia Ranch • FN: This sequel to *Hoofs and Goofs* (1/31/57) includes a cow milking sequence that was reused in *Oil's Well That Ends Well* (12/4/58). Moe and Larry in a horse costume was a gag first seen in *Three Little Twirps* (7/9/43). . . . ThreeStooges.net credits Jules White as the voice on the street and the voice of the radio announcer.

### 181. RUSTY ROMEOS ☆☆☆½ • Rl. Oct. 17 • Prod. no. 1904 • 16½m • *p d* Jules White • *st* Felix Adler • *scr* Jack White • *ad* Sam Nelson • *ph* Henry Freulich • *e* Saul A. Goodkind • *a* Cary Odell • *sd* Tom Oliphant • *c:* Connie Cezan (Mary/Mabel/Sally) • SYN: The Stooges are about to propose marriage to the same girl but don't know it. • WT: *Sappy Lovers* • SD: two (Tu 2/12–W 2/13/57); shot on Stage 9 at Columbia Studios • FN: A remake of *Corny Casanovas* (5/1/52), with stock footage. New scenes: the Stooges have pancakes ("Flipper's Fluffy Fablongent Flapjacks") for breakfast, and when Mabel prepares to walk out on the boys, Joe suddenly returns with an automatic BB gun loaded with tacks and uses Mabel's derriere for target practice! . . . Watch for Shemp's portrait in the stock footage of the girlfriend's apartment.

### 182. OUTER SPACE JITTERS ☆☆ • Rl. Dec. 5; re. May 1965 • Prod. no. 1909 • 16½m • *p d* Jules White • *st scr* Jack White • *ad* Max Stein • *ph* William Bradford • *e* Harold White • *a* Walter Holscher • *sd* Sidney Clifford • *c:* Moe Howard (Moe/Little Moe), Larry Fine (Larry/Little Larry), Joe Besser (Joe/Little Joe), Emil Sitka (Professor Jones), Gene Roth (Grand Zilch of Zunev), Phil Van Zandt (High Mucky Muck), Joe Palma (Captain Tsimmes), Don Blocker (The Goon), Harriette Tarler, Diana Darrin, and Arline Hunter (Zunevian Women) • SYN: The Stooges and Professor Jones are sent to the planet Zunev to learn about its lifestyle; they find it inhabited by three beautiful girls charged with high voltage (they love to eat empty clam shells and drink battery acid!) and a brawny-looking zombie called The Goon. When the Stooges discover they're next in line to become zombies, they grab the professor and escape. The last scene dissolves to the Stooges in their apartment finishing this spooky bedtime story for their children (also played by the Stooges), before going out for dinner. But instead of leaving through the front door, the boys jump out the window; the babysitter's a vampire! • WT: *Outer Space Daze* • SD: two (dates not known) • FN: "Don Blocker" who played The Goon, is actually Dan Blocker, who later become famous for the role of Hoss on TV's long-running western series *Bonanza*.

## 1958

### 183. QUIZ WHIZZ ☆☆½ • Rl. Feb. 13; re. Sept. 1961, July 1965 • Prod. no. 1907 • 15½m • *p d* Jules White • *st scr* Searle Kramer • *ad* Jerrold Bernstein • *ph* Irving Lippman • *e* William Lyon • *a* John McCormack • *sd* Sidney Clifford • *c:* Milton Frome (G. Y. Prince), Harold Brauer (R. O. Broad), Gene Roth (Montgomery M. Montgomery), Greta Thyssen (Montgomery's Secretary), and Emil Sitka (J. J. Figbee) • SYN: Joe wins a big TV jackpot but then allows two swindlers, G. Y. Prince and R.

O. Broad, to invest his earnings in a losing proposition: Consolidated Fujiama California Smog Bags, filled with smog! When the Stooges confront the crooks in their office, they find themselves adopted by a lonesome old eccentric millionaire and his female accomplice, who just happen to be "hit men" for Prince and Broad! Fortunately, the Stooges manage to battle off all parties involved, recover the check for Joe's TV winnings, and divvy up the money, tearing the check into thirds! • SD: two (Th 5/2–F 5/3/57); shot on Stage 7 at Columbia Studios

### 184. FIFI BLOWS HER TOP ☆☆½ •
Rl. Apr. 10; re. Oct. 1961 • Prod. no. 1903 • 16½m • *p d* Jules White • *st scr* Felix Adler • *ad* Sam Nelson • *ph* Henry Freulich • *e* Saul A. Goodkind • *a* Cary Odell • *sd* Tom Oliphant • *c:* Vanda Dupre (Fifi), Christine McIntyre (Katrina, stock footage), Yvette Reynard (Maria, stock footage), Harriette Tarler (Waitress), Suzanne Ridgeway (Girl in Restaurant), Phil Van Zandt (Mort, Fifi's Husband), Al Thompson (Maria's Father, stock footage), Joe Palma (Military Policeman), Heinie Conklin (Bartender), and Wanda D'Ottoni (Girl in Restaurant) • SYN: Joe is depressed. Today is the anniversary of the day he met his former girlfriend Fifi, but Moe and Larry tell him to forget her. Later, however, the boys take turns reminiscing how they each met their sweethearts overseas. Then, with storytime over, a knock comes at the door and in enters Joe's darling Fifi, who now lives across the hall with Mort, her husband. Soon the husband pays the Stooges a visit, and they hide Fifi in a trunk while Mort tells them he has another girl lined up and plans to divorce his wife. Furious, Fifi emerges from the trunk, bashes a chair over Mort's head, and reunites with Joe. • WT: *Rancid Romance* • SD: two (Tu 2/12–W 2/13/57) • FN: A reworking of *Love at First Bite* (5/4/50), with stock footage. The gag of hiding a lady in a trunk is also used in *Gents in a Jam* (7/4/52) and Laurel and Hardy's *Block-Heads* (1938).

### 185. PIES AND GUYS ☆☆☆ • Rl.
June 12; re. Nov. 1961 • Prod. no. 1908 • 16½m • *p d* Jules White • *st* Zion Myers • *scr* Jack White • *ad* Jerrold Bernstein • *ph* Irving Lippman • *e* Harold White • *a* John McCormack • *sd* Sidney Clifford • *c:* Gene Roth (Professor Sedletz), Milton Frome (Professor Quackenbush), Greta Thyssen (Miss Lulu), Helen Dickson (Mrs. Gotrocks), Harriette Tarler (Countess), Symona Boniface, Barbara Slater and Al Thompson (Party Guests, stock footage), and Emil Sitka (Sappington the Butler) • SYN: Professor Quackenbush wagers a bet that he can turn three plumbers, Moe, Larry, and Joe, into polished gentlemen. With the aid of Lulu, the professor attempts the impossible: to teach the boys the proper way of eating. After weeks of hard effort, the night finally arrives when the Stooges are presented to society. Old habits soon emerge, however, when the boys commence with a pie-throwing melee. • WT: *Easy Come, Easy Go* • SD: two (M 5/6–Tu 5/7/57); shot on Stage 7 at Columbia Studios • FN: A scene-for-scene remake of *Half-Wits Holiday* (1/9/47), with some stock footage from the original.

### 186. SWEET AND HOT ☆☆☆ •
Rl. Sept. 4; re. Mar. 1960 • Prod. no. 1910 • 17m • *p d* Jules White • *st* Jerome S. Gottler • *scr* Jerome S. Gottler and Jack White • *ad* Mitchell Gamson • *ph* Irving Lippman • *e* Edwin Bryant • *a* Adam Gosse • *sd* Sidney Clifford • *c:* Larry Fine (Larry/Uncle Louie), Joe Besser (Joe/Uncle Joe), Moe Howard (Dr. Hugo Gansamacher/Tiny's Father), and Muriel Landers (Tiny) • SYN: Joe's sister, Tiny, has an extreme case of "ochlophobia" (she's afraid to sing in front of people), so Larry and Joe take her to see Dr. Hugo Gansamacher (Moe), a German psychiatrist. Gansamacher—or Doc, for short—puts Tiny under hypnosis, and she recalls that when she was a child, her father (again Moe) pressured her into singing for her two uncles, Louie (Larry) and Joe (Joe). Once Tiny's cured, her wish to become a singer is realized when she performs in a nightclub act with Joe and Larry. • SD: two (Th 8/22–F 8/23/57) • FN: Muriel Landers singing "The Heat Is On" (until the chorus) is stock footage from *Tricky Chicks* (10/57), her own two-reel comedy for Columbia. . . . The story and screenplay were written by Jerome S. Gottler. Gottler also wrote the story and screenplay for the Stooges' first short, *Woman Haters*, a musical (5/5/34).

### 187. FLYING SAUCER DAFFY
☆☆☆ • Rl. Oct. 9; re. Mar. 1960 • Prod. no. 1906 • 17m • *p d* Jules White • *st* Warren Wilson • *scr* Jack White • *ad* Jerrold Bernstein • *ph* Fred Jackman • *e* Saul A. Goodkind • *a* Cary Odell • *sd* Milton Stumph • *c:* Gail Bonny (Auntie/Mother), Emil Sitka (Mr. Barton), Harriette Tarler (Girl at Party), Joe Palma (Government Official), Bek Nelson (Tyrin), and Diana Darrin (Elektra) • SYN: Joe takes a photograph on a camping trip. Cousins Moe and Larry think it's a photo of a flying saucer and submit it to *Facts and Figures* magazine, winning a big cash prize. With their prize money, Moe and Larry stage a lavish party. Their party is disrupted by Mr. Barton, the magazine's president, who storms in and informs them that their photo turned out to be of a dirty paper plate with a gob of potato salad and jelly stains on it. Moe and Larry are hauled off to jail, and Joe is thrown out of the house by his auntie. While camping in the forest, Joe meets two real Martian women, who let him take a picture of their spaceship. Jubilant, Joe returns home and offers Moe and Larry, who are out on bail, his new photograph in order to prove their innocence. The boys refuse his offer, so Joe submits the picture himself and wins a big photographic contest, becoming a hero. While he receives a ticker-tape parade for his efforts, Moe and Larry, in straitjackets, serve time in prison! • WT: *Pardon My Flying Saucer*

• SD: two (Th 12/19–F 12/20/57) • FN: Joe Besser named this his favorite film. . . . . The last Stooges short with all-new footage of the boys. The shot of dirty dishes in the sink is from *He Flew the Shrew* (1/11/51), a Wally Vernon–Eddie Quillan comedy. Footage of "real" flying saucer lifted from *Earth vs. the Flying Saucers* (1956).

**188. OIL'S WELL THAT ENDS WELL** ☆☆☆ • Rl. Dec. 4; re. Mar. 1960 • Prod. no. 1911 • 16m • *p d* Jules White • *st scr* Felix Adler • *ad* Mitchell Gamson • *ph* Irving Lippman • *e* Edwin Bryant • *a* Adam Gosse • *sd* Sidney Clifford • *c:* No supporting cast • SYN: The Stooges leave for the country in search of uranium, in order to pay for their father's operation, and find an oil gusher instead. • SD: two (M 8/26–Tu 8/27/57); shot on Stage 3 at Columbia Studios and on the Rock and Water Pump Sets at Columbia Ranch • FN: A reworking of *Oily to Bed, Oily to Rise* (10/6/39), with some stock footage. . . . The film was tentatively titled *Oil's Well That Ends Well* and, according to the final shooting script, was planned to be retitled before its release, but it never was.

**1959**
189. TRIPLE CROSSED ☆☆ • Rl. Feb. 2; re. Sept. 1960, May 1962 • Prod. no. 1913 • 16m • *p d* Jules White • *st scr* Warren Wilson • *ad* Jerrold Bernstein • *ph* Fred Jackman • *e*

The girl to Joe Besser's left, Connie Cezan, doubled for Mary Ainslee in new footage for *Triple Crossed* (1959). Angela Stevens stands at Joe's right. *© Columbia Pictures, courtesy of Moe Howard Collection*

Saul A. Goodkind • *a* Cary Odell • *sd* Milton Stumph • *c:* Diana Darrin (Miss Lapdale, stock footage), Angela Stevens (Millie, Joe's Girl), Mary Ainslee (Belle, Moe's Wife, stock footage), Connie Cezan (Belle's Double, new footage), and Johnny Kascier (Waiter, stock footage) • SYN: Larry owns a pet shop, and the only two "pets" he really wants are Moe's wife, Belle, and Joe's fiancée, Millie. • WT: *Chiseling Chiseler* • SD: one (W 12/18/57) • FN: A remake of *He Cooked His Goose* (7/3/52), with stock footage. . . . When Moe fires his gun up the chimney, listen for Shemp's yell!

190. SAPPY BULLFIGHTERS ☆☆ • Rl. June 4; re. Sept. 1960 • Prod. no. 1912 • 15½m • *p d* Jules White • *st scr* Jack White • *ad* Max Stein • *ph* Irving Lippman • *e* Harold White • *a* Walter Holscher • *sd* Sidney Clifford • *c:* Greta Thyssen (Greta), George Lewis (Jose), Joe Palma, Cy Schindell, and Eddie Laughton (Bull Ring Attendants, stock footage) • SYN: Moe, Larry, and Joe perform their comedy bullfight act while stranded in Mexico and run afoul of a beautiful blonde's jealous husband. • WT: *That's Bully* • SD: two (July 1957) • FN: A remake of *What's the Matador?* (4/23/42), with stock footage. The bit with the wife faking a headache is also staged in *Don't Throw That Knife* (5/3/51).

*Feature Films*
**1959**
1. THREE STOOGES FUN-O-RAMA (Unrated) • Rl. Sept. by Columbia • 90m • *p d* Jules White • SYN: A collection of Three Stooges shorts starring Moe, Larry, and Joe Besser. Ten of sixteen shorts with Joe were offered to movie theaters. Theaters selected four to six shorts to create their own programs. The ten shorts offered were *Triple Crossed* (2/2/59), *Fifi Blows Her Top* (4/10/58), *Oil's Well That Ends Well* (12/4/58), *Quiz Whizz* (2/13/58), *Flying Saucer Daffy* (10/9/58), *Horsing Around* (9/12/57), *Sweet and Hot* (9/4/58), *Rusty Romeos* (10/17/57),

*Pies and Guys* (6/12/58), and *Outer Space Jitters* (12/5/57).

**THE THREE STOOGES (Larry, Moe, and Joe DeRita)**

*Miscellaneous Shorts*
**1963**
1. THREE STOOGES SCRAPBOOK ☆½ • Rl. Sept. by Columbia • Color • Prod. no. 4651 • 10m and 14m • *p* Norman Maurer • *d* Sidney Miller • *st scr* Elwood Ullman • *ad* Harry Slott • *ph* Hal McAlpin • *e* Chuck Gladden • *sd* Frank Lombardo • *s* Glen Glenn • *mu* Paul Dunlap and George Duning • *l* Stanley Styne • *c (live-action):* Marjorie Eaton (Mrs. McGinnis), Emil Sitka (Professor), Don Lamond (Announcer), Norman Maurer (TV Cameraman), Edward Innes (Landlord), and Nick Grazier (But-

One-sheet for *Three Stooges Fun-O-Rama* (1959). *© Columbia Pictures, courtesy of Jeff Lenburg Collection*

ler) • SYN: A color version of The Stooges' unsold 1960 color TV pilot was released to theaters in two short subjects: a fourteen-minute two-reel version featuring the live-action scenes, and a ten-minute one-reel version featuring the cartoon "The

Part of a 1963 Columbia Pictures trade ad offering the unsold TV pilot *Three Stooges Scrapbook* as the first of two short-subject specials released to theaters. *Courtesy of Jeff Lenburg Collection*

Spain Mutiny." • FN: Much of the pilot's live-action footage was used in the feature *The Three Stooges in Orbit* (7/4/62). . . . Photographs printed in *Moe Howard & the 3 Stooges* on pages 176 and 185 (top) are erroneously marked. They are actually from *Scrapbook*.

**1968**

2. STAR SPANGLED SALESMAN ☆☆½ • Rl. Feb. 9 by the United States Treasury Department (US Sav-

ings Bond Division) • Color • 17m • *p d* Norman Maurer • *st scr* Bruce Howard • *ad* Wingate Smith • *ph* Emil Oster • *e* Harold F. Kress and Tom Patchett • *song* "Follow the Eagle" by John J. Coyle • *c:* Howard Morris and Carl Reiner (Themselves), Carol Burnett (Miss Grebs), Milton Berle (Studio President), John Banner (Chef), Werner Klemperer (Head Chef), Rafer Johnson, Tim Conway (Telephone Repairman), Harry Morgan (TV Cop), and Jack Webb (Security Man)

• SYN: Milton Berle hires Howard Morris to conduct a payroll savings plan drive at Columbia Studios. Morris's second customers are three lighting technicians, the Stooges, on their lunch break. • FN: The Stooges scenes were filmed on the patio set of the *I Dream of Jeannie* TV series.

Moe, Larry, and Joe DeRita also appeared in the following newsreels: MGM's *News of the Day—Days Are Flying 'Til Christmas* (12/1/59) and *Fox Movietone News* (5/2/61).

*Feature Films*

Unless otherwise indicated, films were released by Columbia Pictures.

**1959**

1. HAVE ROCKET--WILL TRAVEL ☆☆ • Rl. Aug. 1 • Prod. no. 8556 • 76m • *p* Harry Romm • *d* David Lowell Rich • *st scr* Raphael Hayes • *ph* Ray Cory • *e* Danny B. Landres • *a* John T. McCormack • *sd* Darrell Silvera • *mu* Mischa Bakaleinikoff • *title song* George Duning and Stanley Styne • *s* Harold Lewis • *c:* Jerome Cowan (J. P. Morse), Anna-Lisa (Dr. Ingrid Naarveg), Robert Colbert (Dr. Ted Benson), Marjorie Bennett (Mrs. Huntingford), Don Lamond (Reporter/Narrator), Nadine Ducas (French Dancer), and Dal McKennon (Voice of the Unicorn) • SYN: The Stooges, handymen in a space laboratory, accidentally launch themselves in a rocket while trying to help Dr. Ingrid Naarveg, a beautiful scientist. On the planet Venus, they encounter a fiery monster, a talking unicorn, a Thinking Machine, and robots made in the Stooges' own images. Right there and then, the boys decide it's time to return home! Back on earth, they're hailed as heroes—the first men to traverse space. • WT: *Race for the Moon* • FN: The spring on the trousers gag was also used in *Hoi Polloi* (8/29/35), *An Ache in Every Stake* (8/22/41), and Ben Turpin's *Asleep at the Switch* (1923). In addition, Joe DeRita follows in the footsteps of his third Stooge predecessors, Curly and Shemp, by getting trapped in

One-sheet for *Have Rocket--Will Travel* (1959). © *Columbia Pictures, courtesy of Jeff Lenburg Collection*

In the Stooges' first full-length feature with Joe DeRita, *Have Rocket--Will Travel*, the new third Stooge (right) re-creates Curly Howard's famous plumbing gag (left) from *A Plumbing We Will Go* (1940), which Shemp (center) also redid in *Vagabond Loafers* (1949). © *Columbia Pictures, courtesy of Moe Howard Collection*

a maze of pipe à la *A Plumbing We Will Go* (4/19/40), *Vagabond Loafers* (10/6/49), and *Scheming Schemers* (10/4/56). . . . In the opening credits, unlike all movie posters and exhibitor materials released with DeRita's first feature, the title is spelled without a comma: *Have Rocket--Will Travel*.

**1961**

2. SNOW WHITE AND THE THREE STOOGES ☆☆½ • Rl. July 1 by 20th Century-Fox • DeLuxe Color and CinemaScope • Prod. no. 887 • 107m • *p* Charles Wick • *d* Walter Lang • *scr* Charles Wick (*st*) and Elwood Ullman • *ph* Leon Shamroy • *e* Jack W. Holmes • *a* Jack Martin Smith • *sd* Walter M. Scott and Paul S. Fox • *mu* Lynn Murray • *ad* Eli Dunn • *s* Arthur Kirbach and Frank W. Moran • *c:* Carol Heiss (Snow White), Edson Stroll (Quatro/Prince Charming), Patricia Medina (Queen/Witch), Guy Rolfe (Oga), Michael David (Rolf), Buddy Baer (Hordred), Edgar Barrier (King Augustus), Peter Coe (Captain), Lisa Mitchell (Linda), Chuck Lacey (Frederick), Owen McGivney (Physician), Gloria Doggett and Leon McNabb (Skater), Blossom Rock (Servant), Leslie Farrell (Snow White, Age Four), Craig Cooke (Young Prince Charming), Burt Mustin (Farmer), Richard Collier (Turnkey), Herbie Faye (Head Cook), and Edward Innes (Second Cook) • SYN: The queen of Fortunia, fearful that her stepdaughter will someday become queen, orders her to be slain, along with the prince of neighboring Bravuria, to whom Snow White was betrothed when a child. Her orders, however, are not carried out. Instead, the prince is adopted and raised by the Stooges, strolling minstrels, and Snow White is spared through an act of kindness. The Stooges are not aware that their ward is a prince until they are called upon to entertain at the palace after a chance meeting in the house of the Seven Dwarfs, where Snow White has taken refuge. When the queen learns that Snow White is not dead and that the prince is also

alive, she orders them seized, which sets off a fast and furious chase, with duels and fights, until the queen is vanquished and the lovers reunited. • SD: ten weeks (length of principal photography per Stooges contract; filming commenced 12/60; day-to-day breakdown not available) • FN: As reported by *Variety* columnist Army Archerd on November 3, 1960, when Stage 15 on the 20th Century-Fox lot was used for the skating scenes in *Snow White and the Three Stooges*, it was frozen for the first time since 1943, when it had been made into a rink for petite Norwegian skating star Sonja Henie for her feature *Wintertime* (1943). . . . Actor Edson Stroll, who played Prince Charming,

previously played the title role of Investigator Thompson in the 1959 first-run syndicated television series *Congressional Investigator*.

### 1962

3. THE THREE STOOGES MEET HERCULES ☆☆☆½ • Rl. Jan. 26 (New York premiere), Feb. 15 (nationally) • Prod. no. 8617 • 89m • *p* Norman Maurer • *d* Edward Bernds • *st* Norman Maurer • *scr* Elwood Ullman • *ad* Herb Waller-stein • *ph* Charles S. Welborn • *e* Edwin Bryant • *a* Don Ament • *sd* William Calvert • *mu* Paul Dunlap • *s* James Flaster • *c:* Vicki Trickett (Diane Quigley), Quinn Redeker (Schuyler Davis), George N. Neise

(Mr. Dimsel/King Odius), Samson Burke (Hercules), Mike McKeever (Ajax, the Siamese Cyclops), Mar-lin McKeever (Argo, the Siamese Cyclops), Emil Sitka (Shepherd/Ice Cream Salesman), Hal Smith (King Theses), John Cliff (Ulysses), Lewis Charles (Achilles), Barbara Hines (Anita), Terry Huntingdon (Hecuba), Diana Piper (Helen), Gregg Martell (Simon), Gene Roth (Rhodes Harbor Captain), Edward Foster (Freddie the Fence), Cecil Elliott (Matron), Rusty Wescoatt (Philo), and Don Lamond (Narrator) • SYN: Larry, Moe, and Curly-Joe are friends of Schuyler Davis, a young scientist, and his girlfriend Diane. They help Schuyler make a time machine, which carries them all back to ancient Ithaca, ruled over by King Odius. The king promptly takes a liking to Diane and ships Schuyler and the Stooges off to the galleys to get them out of the way. In the galleys, Schuyler works so hard he soon becomes a muscle man. When he and his pals escape, the Stooges begin promoting him as Hercules in local gladiatorial com-bats. Then the *real* Hercules appears, and things look bad for the Stooges. But finally they persuade Hercules to help them in a palace coup against Odius. Diane is rescued, and all hap-pily return to the twentieth century. • WT: *Hercules and The Three Stooges* • SD: thirteen (Tu 6/6–F 6/9, M 6/12–F 6/16, Tu 6/20–Th 6/22, M 6/19–Th 6/22/61); filmed on Stages 15 and 18 at Columbia Sun-set Studios and at Columbia Ranch (Rock Set, Carmen Street, Skid Row Street, and Tank Set) • FN: The film was first announced in *Variety* in December 1960 as *Hercules and the Three Stooges*. . . . This was Larry Fine's favorite Stooge feature. . . . *The Three Stooges Meets Hercules* (the concept for which Maurer actually created in 1959) was nearly made for another studio. After Columbia refused to improve the terms of the Stooges' contract to star in a quick, inexpensive follow-up to *Have Rocket--Will Travel*, the studio hired Stooges manager Harry Romm as the

One-sheet for *Snow White and the Three Stooges* (1961). © *20th Century Fox, courtesy of Moe Howard Collection*

One-sheet for *The Three Stooges Meet Hercules* (1962). © *Normandy Productions, courtesy of Moe Howard Collection*

producer of a new Stooges feature assembled from clips of their old shorts, titled *Stop! Look! and Laugh!* (7/1/60). Furious, the Stooges fired Romm as their manager (replacing him with Maurer), sued Columbia over its "paste job" unauthorized feature, and took the Hercules concept to American International Pictures (AIP), the same studio responsible for releasing the 1959 blockbuster *Hercules*. AIP jumped at the opportunity to produce the Stooges mythical send-up under one condition: they wanted it ready for an Easter 1961 release. With the Stooges already in the middle of filming the 20th Century-Fox feature *Snow White and the Three Stooges* for worldwide release in the summer of 1961, they considered it unethical to make *Hercules* ahead of Fox's release and thus turned down AIP's offer. When Columbia settled with the Stooges over their *Stop! Look! and Laugh!* lawsuit, the terms included, among other things,

Columbia taking on *Hercules* with Maurer as its producer. . . . *Hercules* contains an interesting blend of stock shots: a fireworks sequence and crowd reactions from *You Can't Take It With You* (1938, Columbia); a battle between armies, an eclipse and a den of lions from *Slaves of Babylon* (1953, Columbia); heralds trumpeting atop a stone parapet, galley scenes and galley slaves rowing, waterfront footage of a small seaport, and townspeople storming palace gates from *Salome* (1953, Columbia); a charging bull from *What's the Matador?* (4/23/42); and a tall chimney exploding from *Half Shot Shooters* (4/30/36). The gag of knocking a cell bar upward is reprised from *Out West* (4/24/47). . . . *The Three Stooges Meet Hercules* premiered in New York on the same bill with Chubby Checker's *Twist Around the Clock*; when the film was released nationally in February, it was booked with Columbia Pictures' "atomic-proof" adventure *The Underwater City*. . . . Produced on a budget of $420,000, *Hercules* would become the Stooges' top moneymaker of all time and the most successful of all of their films, including their 190 comedy shorts for Columbia. Worldwide gross: $2 million. • PS: One scene in *Hercules* depicts the Stooges running and then jumping into a moving chariot. It was during this scene, on the first take, that Larry Fine lost his grip and fell out, taking Curly-Joe with him. Joe landed on top of Larry, knocking him unconscious. Larry was rushed to the hospital, where a series of tests revealed that he had diabetes, a disease he would deal with for the rest of his life. . . . Director Edward Bernds revealed that actor Samson Burke, who played Hercules, unlike most men of his stature, was a little uncomfortable with his role: "He was a thorough amateur! Scene after scene, his eyes would seek me out for direction! Eventually, it got so bad that I had to hide from his view. Samson was a bit on the timid side. I would say Moe was braver in doing all the physical stuff than this mighty mass of muscle."

Storyboard of cyclops sequence from *The Three Stooges Meet Hercules* (1962). © *Normandy Productions, courtesy of Norman Maurer Collection*

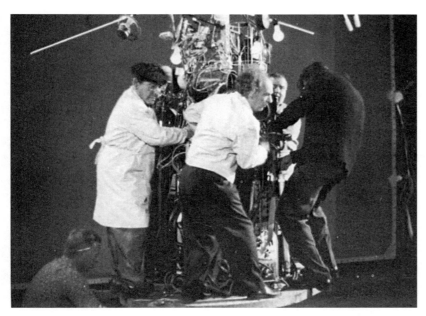

The Stooges prepare for a process shot in their time machine, from *The Three Stooges Meet Hercules* (1962). *Photo by Norman Maurer, © Normandy Productions*

Miniature Moe doll used in the cyclops scenes of *The Three Stooges Meet Hercules* (1962). *Photo by Greg Lenburg, courtesy of Moe Howard Collection*

4. THE THREE STOOGES IN ORBIT ☆☆½ • Rl. July 4 • Prod. no. 8666 • 87m • *p* Norman Maurer • *d* Edward Bernds • *st* Norman Maurer • *scr* Elwood Ullman • *ad* Eddie Saeta • *ph* William E. Whitley • *e* Edwin Bryant • *a* Don Ament • *sd* Richard Mansfield • *mu* Paul Dunlap • *s* William Bernds • *c:* Carol Christensen (Carol), Edson Stroll (Captain Tom Andrews), Emil Sitka (Professor Danforth), George N. Neise (Ogg/Airline Pilot), Rayford Barnes (Zogg/Airline Co-Pilot), Norman Leavitt (Williams the Butler), Nestor Paiva (Martin Chairman), Peter Dawson (General Bixby), Peter Brocco (Dr. Appleby), Don Lamond (Colonel Smithers/Announcer), Thomas Glynn (George Galveston), Marjorie Eaton (Mrs. McGinnis, the Landlady), Maurice Manson (Mr. Lansing), Jean Charney (WAF Sergeant), Duane Ament (Personnel Clerk), Bill Dyer (Colonel Lane), Roy Engel (Agent Welby), Jane Wald (Bathing Girl), Cheerio Meredith (Woman in Toothpaste TV Commercial), and Rusty Wescoatt (Cook) • SYN: The Three Stooges rent a room in a gloomy old castle owned by eccentric Professor Danforth (Emil Sitka) and his lovely daughter Carol (Carol Christensen). A Martian spy, posing as a servant, is interested in the Professor's newly invented combination submarine/helicopter/tank. Tom Andrews (Edson Stroll), an air force captain who arrives to test the machine, is more interested in Carol than in the invention. The Stooges soon turn the whole demonstration into a complete shambles. Later, Martian spies capture the machine and go winging through space—with Moe, Larry, and Joe clinging to its side. Our three heroes finally manage to destroy the all-purpose military weapon and its out-of-space passengers before making their own hilarious escape. • WT: *The Three Stooges Meet the Martians* • SD: eleven (F 4/6–F 4/27/62; day-to-day breakdown not available) • FN: The following scenes from *In Orbit* are composed of stock footage from

*Scrapbook*: apartment eviction for home cooking; searching for a new residence; retiring for the night in Danforth's mansion and then meeting a Martian spy (the butler); and a montage of the Stooges, in pajamas, thumbing a ride, traveling in a boat, taking off in a helicopter, and parachuting into the studio in time for their TV show. Segments depicting the Martians' reign of terror (buildings exploding, people fleeing) are lifted from *Earth vs. the Flying Saucers* (1956). . . . Worldwide gross: $1.5 million. • PS: *In Orbit* was born out of *Three Stooges Scrapbook*, an unsold TV pilot, as producer Norman Maurer recalled: "I approached the Columbia executives with the half-hour *Scrapbook* film (a $30,000

Ogg and Zogg meet see and saw on the set of *The Three Stooges in Orbit* (1962). © Normandy Productions, courtesy of Moe Howard Collection

investment), and an expanded story outline, and they bought it." Needless to say, the studio saved some production costs on the deal.

### 1963

5. THE THREE STOOGES GO AROUND THE WORLD IN A DAZE ☆☆½ • Rl. Aug. 21 • Prod. no. 8705 • 94m • *p d st* Norman Maurer • *scr* Elwood Ullman • *ad* Eddie Saeta • *ph* Irving Lippman • *e* Edwin Bryant • *a* Don Ament • *sd* James M. Grove • *m* Paul Dunlap • *s* William Bernds • *c:* Jay Sheffield (Phileas Fogg III), Joan Freeman (Amelia), Walter Burke (Filch), Peter Forster (Vickers Cavendish), Maurice Dallimore (Inspector Crotchet), Richard Devon (Maharajah), Anthony Eustrel (Kandu), Iau Kea (Itchy Kitchi), Phil Arnold (Wrestling Referee), Robert Kino (Charlie Okuma), Murray Alper (Gus, Truck Driver), Jack Greening (McPherson), Don Lamond (Bill, Truck Driver), Emil Sitka (Reformers Club Butler), Jeffrey Maurer (Timmy, Boy Who Takes Flute), Audrey Betz (Timothy's Mother), Ramsay Hill (Gatesby), Colin Campbell (Willoughby), Michael St. Clair (First Mate), Ron Whelan (Harry), Kei Thin Chung (Chinese Guard), Mark Harris (Tremble), Aki Aleong (Chinese Solider), Tom Symonds (Bowers), Ger-

THOSE BRAINLESS ASTRO-NUTS MEET THE MARTIANS!

WHOOSH!

THE THREE STOOGES IN ORBIT

WITH CAROL CHRISTENSEN • EDSON STROLL

SCREENPLAY BY ELWOOD ULLMAN • BASED ON A STORY BY NORMAN MAURER
PRODUCED BY NORMAN MAURER • DIRECTED BY EDWARD BERNDS
A NORMANDY PRODUCTION • A COLUMBIA PICTURES RELEASE

THEIR NEWEST SCREWIEST ESCAPADE EVER!

‌eet for *The Three Stooges in Orbit* (1962). © Normandy Productions, courtesy of Moe
‌lection

ald Jann (Chinese General), Laurie Main (Carruthers), Magda Harout (Handmaiden), Joe Wong (Chinese "Curly-Joe"), Harold Fong (Chinese "Larry"), and Guy Lee (Chinese "Moe") • SYN: To win a bet with scoundrel Vickers Cavendish (Peter Forster), Phileas Fogg III (Jay Sheffield) attempts to duplicate his great-grandfather's famous trip around the world in eighty days, with the added proviso that he will neither pay for, nor work for, his transportation. His three servants, Larry, Moe, and Curly-Joe, go along as accomplished chiselers. Cavendish, meanwhile, loots the Regent Street Bank with the help of his own henchmen and then sets out to throw the blame on Fogg, thus ensuring Fogg's defeat. Fogg and the Stooges stow away on a freighter bound for Calcutta, where they rescue Amelia Carter (Joan Freeman) from a pair of thugs. They continue their journey through India to China, Tokyo, and San Francisco, circumventing Cavendish and Scotland Yard. Their adventures in Asia and America are hectic and hilarious, but they continue to abide by the terms of the bet. Returning to London with but thirty seconds to spare, Phileas wins the bet and the lovely Amelia, while Cavendish and

Norman Maurer's original concept art and title for *The Three Stooges Go Around the World in a Daze* (1963). © *Normandy Productions, courtesy of Norman Maurer Collection*

Original American and Belgian one-sheets for *The Three Stooges Go Around the World in a Daze* (1963). © *Normandy Productions, courtesy of Moe Howard and Jeff Lenburg Collections*

his henchmen are arrested with the help of the Stooges. • WT: *The Three Stooges Go Around the World on 80 Cents, The Three Stooges Go 'Round the Globe on 80 Cents, The Three Stooges Circle the World on 80 Cents, The Three Stooges Circle the Globe on 80 Cents, Around the World on 80 Cents, The Three Stooges Circle the World on 99 Cents, The Three Stooges Go Around the World on 79 Cents, The Three Stooges Go Around the World on $1.98, The Three Stooges Meet Phileas Fogg,* and *Merry Go Round the World* • SD: thirteen (Th 5/9–F 5/10, M 5/13–F 5/17, M 5/20–F 5/24, M 5/27/63); shot on Stages 12, 12A, and 14 at Columbia Studios and on Columbia Ranch (Stages 30, 33, and 34, Large Tank, Water Tank, Carmen Street, and Firehouse) • FN:

Wonder why this Stooge picture had so many working titles? Well, there's a simple explanation: United Artists, producers of the 1956 film classic *Around the World in Eighty Days*, objected to Normandy Productions' original title, even though the Jules Verne story on which it was based was in the public domain. Eventually, after many title changes, both parties agreed upon *The Three Stooges Go Around the World in a Daze*. . . . The routine "The Maharaja" was enacted by the Stooges first in *Time Out for Rhythm* (6/5/41) and later in *Three Little Pirates* (12/5/46). The gag of fighting in the dark is reprised from *Out West* (4/24/47) and also appears in *Who Done It?* (3/3/49) and its remake, *For Crimin' Out Loud* (5/3/56). Curly-Joe becoming fighting mad when he hears "Pop Goes the Weasel" is reworked from *Punch Drunks* (7/13/34). . . . Joe DeRita's favorite Stooges film. . . . Worldwide gross: $1 million.

6. IT'S A MAD, MAD, MAD, MAD WORLD ☆☆ • Rl. Nov. by United Artists Color • Prod. no. 113 • 162m (originally 195m of "laffs," as promoted by the studio) • *p d* Stanley Kramer • *st scr* William and Tania Rose • *ph* Ernest Laszlo • *e* Fred Knudtson • *mu* Ernest Gold • *s* John Keene • *c:* Spencer Tracy (Captain Culpepper), Jimmy Durante (Smiler Grogan), Jonathan Winters (Pike), Sid Caesar (Melville Crump), Edie Adams (Monica Crump), Milton Berle (J. Russell Finch), Dorothy Provine (Emeline Finch), Ethel Merman (Mrs. Marcus), Mickey Rooney ("Dingy" Bell), Buddy Hackett (Benji Benjamin), Phil Silvers (Otto Meyer), Terry-Thomas (Algernon Hawthorne), Dick Shawn (Sylvester Marcus), Eddie "Rochester" Anderson (First Cab Driver), Peter Falk (Second Cab Driver), Selma Diamond (Voice of Culpepper's Wife), Louise Glenn (Voice of Billie Sue Culpepper), Norman Fell and Nicholas Georgiade (Police at Crash ), Jim Backus (Tyler Fitzgerald), Stang (Ray), Marvin Kaplan

(Irwin), William Demarest (Police Chief Aloysius), Lloyd Corrigan (Mayor), Charles McGraw (Lieutenant Mathews), Andy Devine (Sheriff), Stan Freberg (Deputy Sheriff), Ben Blue (Airplane Pilot), Bobo Lewis (Pilot's Wife), Barrie Chase (Sylvester's Girlfriend), Paul Ford (Colonel Wilberforce), Carl Reiner (Tower Director), Jesse White (Radio Tower Operator), Eddie Ryder (Air Traffic Controller), Howard Da Silva (Airport Officer), Charles Lane (Airport Manager), Jack Benny (Driver in Desert), Don Knotts (Nervous Driver), Buster Keaton (Jimmy), Nick Stewart (Truck Driver), Edward Everett Horton (Hardware Store Owner), Doodles Weaver (Hardware Store Clerk), Jerry Lewis (Driver Who Runs Over Hat), Mike Mazurki (Hitchhiker), Bob Mazurki (Eddie), Zasu Pitts (Gertie, Switchboard Operator), Madlyn Rhue (Police Secretary), Joe E. Brown (Rally Speaker), Sterling Holloway (Fireman), Alan Carney (Police Sergeant), Tom Kennedy (Traffic Cop), Leo Gorcey (Taxi Cab Driver), Ben Lessy (George), Sammee Tong (Chinese Laundryman), and more • SYN: Hollywood's greatest comedians of the period come together in this blockbuster comedy in which eight vacation-bound motorists speed off in search of a stolen fortune divulged to them by a mysterious stranger dying in the desert. The film features scores of cameo appearances, including a five-second appearance by the Stooges (a pan shot from left to right) as firemen. • SD: one (9/17/62) for Stooges scene • FN: The Stooges were contracted on September 14, 1962, by Casey Productions, the producers of the film, to appear in their one scene, which took one day to film, at a salary of $3,000 for their services. . . . Joe Besser was first offered the role of Irwin, the garage mechanic, but he was unable to accept because he could not get time off from his costarring role in TV's *The Joey Bishop Show*. • PS: Larry Fine told authors Jeff and Greg Len-

burg in an interview that he handled all the negotiations for this film himself and arranged a much higher fee—a claim their manager Norman Maurer later refuted. But as Larry recalled it, "Moe was in Las Vegas and Curly-Joe was in Palm Springs at the time. I received a phone call one day, and the man on the other end said, 'This is Stanley Kramer and we're making a film called *It's a Mad, Mad, Mad, Mad World*.' He said they wanted us in the picture. I negotiated the deal. I told him we'd take color TVs for four rooms in each house. He said they couldn't make that sort of deal—it had to be cash. He asked how much we'd do it for. I told him twenty thousand dollars [split three ways]. There was a long pause on the phone, and than he said, 'Okay.' I called Moe and DeRita and told them I made the deal. We were to report for filming the next day. So they took planes and flew out here. We arrived on the set on time, dressed in firemen uniforms. We stood there and they said, 'That's it!' That's it? We wondered if they wanted us to do a routine, but that was it. A three-second shot at $20,000. Moe thought he [Kramer] was crazy, but they made that and more at the box office."

7. 4 FOR TEXAS ☆☆½ • Rl. Dec. 23 by Warner Bros. • Technicolor • Prod. no. 470 • 124m (also given as 115m) • *exp* Howard W. Koch • *ap* Walter Blake • *p d* Robert Aldrich • *st scr* Teddi Sherman and Robert Aldrich • *ad* Tom Connors and Dave Salven • *ph* Ernest Laszlo • *e* Michael Luciano • *a* William Glasgow • *sd* Raphael Bretton • *mu* Nelson Riddle • *s* Jack Solomon • *c:* Dean Martin (Joe Jarrett), Frank Sinatra (Zach Thomas), Ursula Andress (Maxine Richter), Anita Ekberg (Elya Carlson), Charles Bronson (Matson), Victor Buono (Harvey Burden), Edric Connor (Prince George), Mike Mazurki (Chad), Nick Dennis (Angel), Richard Jaeckel (Mancini), Wesley Addy (Winthrop Trowbridge), Percy Helton (Ansel), Marjorie Ben-

nett (Miss Emmaline), Ellen Corby and Jesslyn Fax (Widows), Jack Elam (Dobie), Fritz Feld (Maître d'), Bob Steele (Bank Board Member), Jack Lambert (Monk), Paul Langton (Beauregard), Teddy Buckner and His All Stars (Themselves), Jonathan Hole (Reneé), Joe Gray (Cowboy), Jack Perkins and Marvin Willens (Stunts), Virginia Christine, Abraham Sofaer, Dave Willock, Ralph Volkie, William Washington, Max Wagner, Maidie Norman, Michele Montau, Mario Siletti, Eva Six, and Michael St. Angel • SYN: Zach Tomas (Frank Sinatra) plays a tough guy who hooks up with Joe Jarrett (fellow Rat Packer Dean Martin) to open a casino in nineteenth-century Galveston, Texas. In a guest star appearance, the Stooges are cast as inept deliverymen whose job is to deliver a nude painting to a riverboat casino. On the way, they encounter two elderly women (Ellen Corby and Jesslyn Fax) who are strongly against the delivery of the painting. As part of their guest appearance, the Stooges perform their "Point to the Right" and "Insulting the State of Texas" routines. • WT: *Two for Texas* • SD: one (7/22/63) for Stooges scene

## 1965

8. THE OUTLAWS IS COMING! ☆☆☆ • Rl. Jan. 13 (world premiere, San Antonio, TX), Jan. 14 (nationally) • Prod. no. 8731 • 89m • *p d st* Norman Maurer • *scr* Elwood Ullman • *ph* Irving Lippman • *e* Aaron Nibley • *a* Robert Peterson • *sd* James W. Crowe • *ad* Donald Gold • *mu* Paul Dunlap • *s* James Z. Flaster • *c:* Adam West (Kenneth Cabot), Nancy Kovack (Annie Oakley), Mort Mills (Trigger Mortis), Don Lamond (Rance Roden), Rex Holman (Sunstroke Kid), Emil Sitka (Abernathy/Medicine Man/Colonel), Henry Gibson (Charlie Horse), Murray Alper (Chief Crazy Horse), Harold Brauer (Bartender), Sidney Marion (Hammond), Jeffrey Alan (Maurer) (Young Boy), Marilyn Fox (First Girl), Audrey Betz (Fat Squaw), Lloyd Kino (Japanese "Beatle"), Paul Frees (Narrator), and Special Guests: Joe Bolton

(Rob Dalton), Bill Camfield (Wyatt Earp), Hal Fryar (Johnny Ringo), Johnny Ginger (Billy the Kid), Wayne Mack (Jesse James), Ed T. McDonnell (Bat Materson), Bruce Sedley (Cole Younger), Paul Shannon (Wild Bill Hickok), and Sally Starr (Belle Starr) • SYN: When he sends his editor, Kenneth Cabot, out into the Great Plains of the West to stop the slaughter of American buffalo, a Boston newspaper publisher uses the occasion to get three troublesome printers, the Stooges, out of his hair. In no time at all, the editor and his pals are targets of every gunslinger west of the Mississippi,

but aided by the celebrated trick-shot artiste Annie Oakley, they expose the schemes of a dastardly frontier gang boss and persuade the notorious gunslingers to mend their ways • WT: *The Three Stooges Meet the Gunslingers* • SD: eleven (W 5/6–F 5/8, M 5/11–F 5/15, M 5/18–F 5/22, M 5/25/64); filmed on the Columbia Ranch (Stages 30, 32, and 33, Glenmoore Cattle Ranch, Western Street, and Boston Street) and on the sixty-six-thousand acre B-Bar-B Buffalo Ranch near Gillette, Wyoming • FN: Moe Howard's and Norman Maurer's favorite Stooges feature. . . . The film's title was inspired

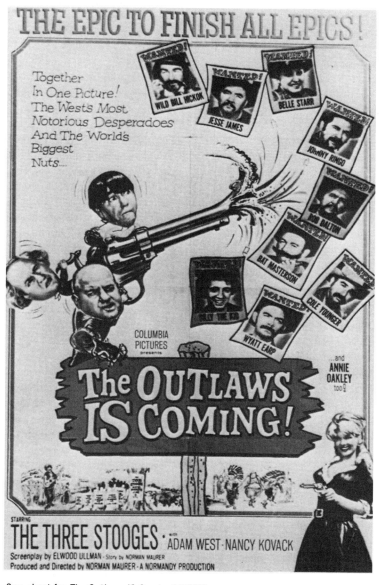

One-sheet for *The Outlaws IS Coming!* (1965). © *Normandy Productions, courtesy of Jeff Lenburg Collection*

by Universal's promotion campaign for Hitchcock's *The Birds*: "The Birds *Is* Coming!" . . . On February 28, 1964, Maurer completed the final revised shooting script, three months before commencing filming. . . . The US cavalry riding in late for the rescue was revived from *Out West* (4/24/47). . . . The special guest stars who portray the gunslingers were hosts of children's TV programs from across the country that aired the Stooges' shorts. . . . On January 13, 1965, *The Outlaws IS Coming!* made its world premiere with the Stooges on hand at the Texas Theater in San Antonio, Texas, for San Antonio–area dignitaries. Elaborate nighttime festivities including a barbecue and parade were held in the Stooges' honor. The film opened for the public nationwide the next day. Original accounts that *The Outlaws IS Coming!* was released nationally on January 1, 1965, are erroneous; that instead marks the date the film was originally copyrighted. . . . By February 25, 1965, the film was playing in Texas City, Texas, on a double bill with the 1964 20th Century-Fox feature *Fate Is the Hunter*, costarring Glenn Ford and Nancy Kwan. . . . Worldwide gross: $1 million. • PS: Writer-producer-director Norman Maurer remembered that selling the script for this project was the easiet transaction he ever made: "I was riding an elevator in Columbia's New York office when Leo Jaffe, the company's chairman of the board, saw the cover artwork on my script outline for *Three Stooges Meet the Gunslingers (The Outlaws IS Corning!)*. He looked at it and said, 'That's funny! Let's make the picture.'"

## Television Films
### 1960
1. THREE STOOGES SCRAPBOOK ☆☆½ • Never br. • Color • 30m • *p* Norman Maurer • *d* Sidney Miller • *st scr* Elwood Ullman • *ad* Harry Slott • *ph* Hal McAlpin • *e* Chuck Gladden • *sd* Frank Lombardo • *s* Glen Glenn • *mu* Paul Dunlap and George Duning • *l* Stanley Styne • *c (live-action):* Marjorie Eaton (Mrs. McGinnis), Emil Sitka (Professor),

Don Lamond (Announcer), Norman Maurer (TV Cameraman), Edward Innes (Landlord), and Nick Grazier (Butler) • SYN: The Stooges are hosts of their own weekly live-action and animated TV series. They introduce themselves in a cartoon, "The Spain Mutiny." • EPS: "Home Cooking" • FN: Much of this unsold pilot's live-action footage was used in the feature *The Three Stooges in Orbit* (7/4/62). A color version of the pilot was released to theaters as two short subjects in September 1963: a fourteen-minute two-reel version featuring the live-action scenes, and a ten-minute one-reel version featuring the cartoon "The Spain Mutiny."

### 1965
2. THE NEW 3 STOOGES • Synd. in Oct. by Heritage • Color • 30m • *exp* Norman Maurer (live-action) and Dick Brown (animation) • *ap* David Detiege • *d* Edward Bernds (live-action), Eddie Rehberg, Sam Cornell, and Dave Detiege (animation) • *st* Edward Bernds (live-action), Jack Miller, Sam Cornell, Art Diamond, Warren Tufts, Cecil Beard, Barbara Chain, Jack Kinney, Nick George, Pat Kearin, Homer Brightman, Lee Orgel, and Dave Detiege (animation) • *ph* Jerry Smith and Ed Gillette • *e* William J. Faris • *mu* Paul Horn • *c:* varies (see below) • SYN: When the Three Stooges cartoon series debuted, it was syndicated as thirty-nine half-hour episodes consisting of four five-minute cartoons with live-action wraparounds. Forty-one wraparounds were filmed, and forty were reused several times with different cartoons throughout the series; the first wraparound, "Soldiers," appeared only once. In addition to appearing in the wraparounds, the Stooges supplied their voices for all 156 color cartoons. • LIVE-ACTION WRAP-AROUNDS: #1 "Soldiers." The Stooges celebrate the anniversary of their induction into the army with their old sergeant (Harold Brauer). This live segment is used in cartoon #1 only. . . . #2 "Lost." Larry, Moe, and Joe believe they're lost in the

woods until they spot a group of teenagers whom they mistake for cannibals. . . . #3 "Campers." The Stooges embark on a carefully planned camping trip and forget one thing: a horse. . . . #4 "Bakers." The boys work in a bakery for Mr. Hossenfefler (Emil Sitka) and wind up in a pie fight. . . . #5 "Orangutan." Moe orders Joe to feed an orangutan and later returns to find both Joe *and* Larry in the animal's cage. . . . #6 "Flat Tire." The Stooges repair a flat tire only to learn that Joe forgot to buy gasoline. . . . #7 "Fan Belt." Curly-Joe's suspenders come in handy when the fan belt on the Stooges' car breaks. . . . #8 "Fishermen." Moe asks Joe to fetch the fishing gear on the pier, and Joe returns with a large gear from the boys' boat instead. . . . #9 "Dentists." Larry is the unwilling patient, Moe is the dentist, and Joe is the nurse. . . . #10 "Janitors." The Stooges attempt to clean a deserted mansion inhabited by a ghostly knight. . . . #11 "Artists." Larry, Moe, and Joe create three paintings only an escaped lunatic (Emil Sitka) would buy. . . . #12 "Decorators." When a wealthy homeowner (Peggy Brown, a.k.a. Margaret Kerry) hires the Stooges to redecorate her house, Moe promises her that when she returns she won't recognize the place. . . . #13 "Golfers." The Stooges invade the golf course, much to the dismay of its owner (Emil Sitka). Gags revived from *Three Little Beers* (11/28/35). . . . #14 "Hunters." Moe lectures the boys on the fine art of hunting while a real-live lion lurks behind him. . . . #15 "Weighing In." The boys encounter a fortune-telling weight machine that predicts their futures. . . . #16 "Telegram." Curly-Joe receives a telegram, intended for Curly *John*, proclaiming him sole heir to his Uncle Dudley's estate. . . . #17 "Buried Treasure." The Stooges dig up a chest without treasure and find oil instead. . . . #18 "Outdoor Breakfast." Moe is unable to speak after he consumes a mouthful of pancakes smothered in glue as prepared by chefs Joe and Larry. . . . #19 "Setting

Up Camp." Larry and Joe learn that erecting a tent is not that easy. . . . #20 "Rare Bird." The Stooges want to snap a picture of a rare bird, but Joe forgets to remove the lens cap. . . . #21 "Caretakers." Larry and Joe clean out the elephant cage while Moe plays checkers with a chimpanzee. . . . #22 "Seasick Joe." The wild surf becomes too much for Joe's stomach, and the Stooges' boat hasn't even left the pier. Emil Sitka costars as the Ship Captain. . . . #23 "Electricians." The Stooges are electricians from the Live Wire Company called to fix a buzzer in a secretary's office. Gags borrowed from *They Stooge to Conga* (1/1/43) and *Monkey Businessmen* (6/20/46). . . . #24 "Salesmen." Selling ice cream proves successful until Joe begins devouring the profits. With Jeff Maurer and the Brown children (Cary, Tina, and Eileen). #25 "Barbers." An overprotective mother (Peggy Brown) asks the Stooges to be careful when cutting her little boy's *long* hair. Her request, however, develops split ends when a representative of the Barber's Union (Emil Sitka) challenges the trio's license. . . . #26 "Prospectors." The boys search for uranium and instead find an old prospector (Emil Sitka) who tells them a story: "The Gunfight at the K.O. Corral." . . . #27 "Sweepstakes Ticket." The Stooges possess the winning sweepstakes ticket until, in all the excitement, Moe accidentally tosses the ticket stub out the window. . . . #28 "Sunbathers." The Stooges offer a female beachgoer (Peggy Brown) their suntan lotion ("Liquid Cement") and soon find a lifeguard (Emil Sitka) chasing after them. . . . #29 "Inheritance." Joe inherits a house from his grandfather that is occupied by a headless ghost. . . . #30 "Melodrama." The boys stage an old-fashioned melodrama, with Moe as the villain, for a group of youngsters (Jeff Maurer and the Brown children). . . . #31 "Waiters." Larry, Moe, and Joe are waiters who give their customers, especially a businessman and his wife (Emil Sitka and Peggy

Brown), "super service!" Reprised is the Stooges' "Insulting the State of Texas" routine. . . . #32 "Athletes." The Stooges take instructions on physical fitness from a record album. With Jeff Maurer. . . . #33 "Doctors." Surgeons Howard, Fine, and DeRita encounter two patients (both Emil Sitka), one of whom has a broken leg in traction. . . . #34 "Shipmates." The boys decide to rent their boat out to customers, and Mr. Guffy (Emil Sitka) is the first to get hooked. . . . #35 "High Voltage." The Stooges' TV set is on the blink, so Larry tries to fix it and gets the shock of his life. . . . #36 "Pilots." An escaped lunatic (Emil Sitka) asks Larry, Moe, and Joe to let him ride on one of their motorbikes. They do and he does—right into the ocean. . . . #37 "Turkey Stuffers." Larry, Moe, and Joe take a hand at stuffing a turkey in an unconventional way. With Emil Sitka. . . . #38 "Piemakers." A fly disrupts the Stooges' piemaking efforts, causing Moe to lose his temper. . . . #39 "The Sharpshooter." Joe, as "Eagle-Eye, the Sharpshooter" takes dead aim at a raisin on the forehead of Larry, "Fearless Frizzle-Top." With Jeff Maurer and the Brown children. . . . #40 "Magicians." The Stooges stage all sorts of magic tricks for youngsters, including making themselves disappear. With Jeff Maurer and the Brown children. . . . #41 "Sunken Treasure." The Stooges man the motorboat in search of sunken treasure. Unfortunately they forget to untie it, and it is torn apart. • CARTOONS: (four per show; titles of live-action wraparounds for each cartoon follow in parentheses) #1 "That Little Old Bomb Maker" ("Soldiers"), #2 "Woodsman Bear That Tree" ("Lost"), #3 "Let's Shoot the Player Piano Player" ("Campers"), #4 "Dentist the Menace" ("Bakers"), #5 "Safari So Good" ("Orangutan"), #6 "Think or Thwim" ("Flat Tire"), #7 "There Auto Be a Law" ("Fan Belt"), #8 "That Old Shell Game" ("Fishermen"), #9 "Hold That Line" ("Dentists"), #10 "Flycycle Built for Two" ("Janitors"), #11 "Dizzy Doodlers"

("Artists"), #12 "The Classical Clinker" ("Decorators"), #13 "Movie Scars" ("Golfers"), #14 "A Bull for Andamo" ("Hunters"), #15 "The Tree Nuts" ("Weighing In"), #16 "Tin Horn Dude" ("Telegram"), #17 "Thru Rain, Sleet, and Snow" ("Sunken Treasure"), #18 "Goldriggers of '49" ("Outdoor Breakfast"), #19 "Ready, Jet Set, Go" ("Setting Up Camp"), #20 "Behind the 8 Ball Express" ("Rare Bird"), #21 "Stop Dragon Around" ("Caretakers"), #22 "To Kill a Clockingbird" ("Golfers"), #23 "Who's Lion" ("Flat Tire"), #24 "Fowl Weather Friend" ("Caretakers"), #25 "Wash My Line" ("Seasick Joe"), #26 "Little Cheese Chaser" ("Fan Belt"), #27 "Big Wind Bag" ("Weighing In"), #28 "Baby Sitters" ("Magicians"), #29 "Clarence of Arabia" ("Electricians"), #30 "Three Jacks and a Beanstalk" ("Salesmen"), #31 "That Was the Wreck That Was" ("Barbers"), #32 "The Three Astronutz" ("Prospectors"), #33 "Peter Panic" ("Sweepstakes Ticket"), #34 "When You Wish upon a Fish" ("Janitors"), #35 "A Little Past Noon" ("Sunbathers"), #36 "Hair of a Bear" ("Doctors"), #37 "3 Lumps and a Lamp" ("Buried Treasure"), #38 "Who's for Dessert?" ("Waiters"), #39 "Watts My Lion" ("Athletes"), #40 "Which Is Witch?" ("Buried Treasure"), #41 "Suture Self" ("Doctors"), #42 "The Yolks on You" ("Artists"), #43 "Tally Moe with Larry and Joe" ("Inheritance"), #44 "The 1ST in Lion" ("Melodrama"), #45 "The Transylvania Railroad" ("Shipmates"), #46 "What's Mew Pussycat?" ("High Voltage"), #47 "It's a Bad, Bad, Bad, Bad Word" ("Pilots"), #48 "Bridge on the River Cry" ("Decorators"), #49 "Hot Shots" ("Janitors"), #50 "Mel's Angels" ("The Sharpshooter"), #51 "Bee My Honey" ("Barbers"), #52 "That Dirty Bird" ("Rare Bird"), #53 "Stone Age Stooges" ("Orangutan"), #54 "Smoke Gets in Your Skies" ("Piemakers"), #55 "Queen Quong" ("Lost"), #56 "Campsite Fright" ("Sunken Treasure"), #57 "Goldibear and the 3 Stooges" ("High Voltage"),

#58 "The Lyin' Tamer" ("Golfers"), #59 "The Pen Game" ("The Sharpshooter"), #60 "It's a Small World" ("Piemakers"), #61 "Late for Launch" ("Doctors"), #62 "Focus in Space" ("Buried Treasure"), #63 "The Noisy Silent Movie" ("Pilots"), #64 "Get Out of Town By Sundown Brown" ("Salesmen"), # 65 "Table Tennis Tussle" ("Athletes"), #66 "Phony Express" ("Prospectors"), #67 "Best Test Pilots" ("Pilots"), #68 "Litter Bear" ("Hunters"), #69 "A Fishy Tale" ("Turkey Stuffers"), #70 "The Unhaunted House" ("Sunbathers"), #71 "Aloha Ha Ha" ("Hunters"), #72 "Rise and the Fall of the Roman Umpire" ("Piemakers"), #73 "Deadbeat Street" ("Dentists"), #74 "Cotton Pickin' Chicken" ("Sweepstakes Ticket"), #75 "Larry and the Pirates" ("Shipmates"), #76 "Tree Is a Crowd" ("Outdoor Breakfast"), #77 "Feud for Thought" ("Electricians"), #78 "Bat and Brawl" ("Bakers"), #79 "Knight Without End" ("Telegram"), #80 "Up a Tree" ("Campers"), #81 "Turnabout Is Bearplay" ("Magicians"), #82 "Pow Wow Row" ("Lost"), #83 "Flat Heads" ("Sunbathers"), #84 "No News Is Good News" ("High Voltage"), #85 "Bully For You, Curly" ("Turkey Stuffers"), #86 "Tee for Three" ("Bakers"), #87 "Goofy Gondoliers" ("Fishermen"), #88 "Bearfoot Fishermen" ("High Voltage"), #89 "Washout Below" ("Waiters"), #90 "The 3 Marketeers" ("Decorators"), #91 "Follo the White Lion" ("Orangutan"), #92 "One Good Burn Deserves Another" ("Fishermen"), #93 "Curly's Bear" ("Turkey Stuffers"), #94 "Land Ho, Ho, Ho" ("Seasick Joe"), #95 "Surfs You Right" ("The Sharpshooter"), #96 "7 Faces of Timbear" ("Melodrama"), #97 "Bearfoot Bandit" ("Flat Tire"), #98 "None Butt the Brave" ("Prospectors"), #99 "Three Good Knights" ("Janitors"), #100 "Call of the Wile" ("Setting Up Camp"), #101 "Snowbrawl" ("Caretakers"), #102 "Rob N. Good" ("Shipmates"), #103 "There's No Mule Like an Old Mule" ("Fan Belt"), #104 "Squawk Valley" ("Weighing In"), #105 "Mummies Boys" ("Sunken Treasure"), #106 "The Plumber's Friend" ("Electricians"), #107 "Rub-A-Dub-Tub" ("Fishermen"), #108 "Under the Bad-Bad Tree" ("Inheritance"), #109 "Hairbrained Barbers" ("Barbers"), #110 "Waiter Minute" ("Pilots"), #111 "Souperman" ("Pilots"), #112 "Abominable Showman" ("Rare Bird"), #113 "Curly in Wonderland" ("Weighing In"), #114 "Boobs in the Woods" ("Sweepstakes Ticket"), #115 "Chimney Sweeps" ("Turkey Stuffers"), #116 "The Mad Mail Mission" ("Janitors"), #117 "Out of Space" ("Seasick Joe"), #118 "Three Wizards of Odds" ("Magicians"), #119 "Three for the Road" ("Telegram"), #120 "Feudin', Fuss'n Hillbully" ("Rare Bird"), #121 "Don't Misbehave Indian Brave" ("Campers"), #122 "You Ain't Lion" ("Orangutan"). #123 "Muscle on the Mind" ("Artists"), #124 "Badmen of the Briny" ("Shipmates"), #125 "Furry Fugitive" ("Golfers"), #126 "How the West Was Once" ("Prospectors"), #127 "Bowling Pinheads" ("The Sharpshooter"), #128 "The Mountain Ear" ("Dentists"), #129 "Norse West Passage" ("Sunken Treasure"), #130 "Lastest Gun in the West" ("Dentists"), # 131 "Toys Will Be Toys" ("Outdoor Breakfast"), #132 "First Glass Service" ("Flat Tire"), #133 "Strictly for the Birds" ("Telegram"), #134 "Lé Stoogenaires" ("Athletes"), #135 "The Bear Who Came in Out of the Cold" ("Artists"), #136 "The Bigger They Are, The Harder They Hit" ("Salesmen"), #137 "Little Red Riding Wolf" ("Artists"), #138 "Bell Hop Flops" ("Waiters"), #139 "Dig That Gopher" ("Piemakers"), #140 "Gagster Dragster" ("Fan Belt"), #141 "Just Plane Crazy" ("High Voltage"), #142 "From Bad to Verse" ("Campers"), #143 "Droll Weevil" ("Caretakers"), #144 "The Littlest Martian" ("Melodrama"), #145 "The Bear Showoff" ("Setting Up Camp"), #146 "No Money, No Honey" ("Outdoor Breakfast"), #147 "Get That Snack Shack Off the Track" ("Buried Treasure"), #148 "Curly's Birthday-A-Go-Go" ("Bakers"), #149 "The Men From U.C.L.A." ("Magicians"), #150 "Super Everybody" ("Inheritance"), #151 "Kangaroo Catchers" ("Electricians"), #152 "No Smoking Aloud" ("Shipmates"), #153 "The Chicken Delivery Boys" ("Decorators"), #154 "Sno Ball" ("Sunken Treasure"), #155 "Rug-A-Bye, Baby" ("Doctors"), and #156 "Dinopoodi" ("Turkey Stuffers") • FN: "That Little Old Bomb Maker" (#1) and "Curly in Wonderland" (#113) are the best cartoons in the series.

## 1970

3. KOOK'S TOUR ☆☆ • Never br. • Color • Prod. no. 1191 • 60m • *p d st scr* Norman Maurer • *ph* James T. Flocker and Michael Maurer • *e* Pat Somerset • *s* Audio Effects • *c:* Moe Howard (Moe/Narrator), Larry Fine (Larry), Joe DeRita (Curly-Joe), Moose the Dog (Himself), Norman Maurer (Moe Double/Larry Stand-In), Lois Goleman (Littering Woman), and Emil Sitka (stock footage) • SYN: Whack! The Stooges are socked in the jaws, thus leading off a black-and-white montage of slapstick clips from *The Three Stooges Meet Hercules* to *The Outlaws IS Coming!* Then the boys, now well-groomed, enter in *color*, explaining that although they've entertained audiences for fifty years, they've never seen anything except the inside of their dressing rooms. So they decide to retire from show business, purchase a self-contained camper and a trailer boat, and take off on their first camping trip. But, as the title implies, no matter how hard the Stooges try acting *normal*, their journey will always prove to be a *kook's* tour . . . especially for Larry! The poor guy just can't catch a fish! "If you don't hook 'em, you don't eat 'em!" Moe tells Larry. Thus, fishing trip after fishing trip, Larry comes up empty handed, and on one occasion must settle for a gourmet dinner of cornflakes and milk! As the days wear on, however, Moe and Joe begin feeling sorry for their pal and decide to accompany him to Lake Pend

Oreille, the best site for trout fishing in all of Idaho. But their kind gesture backfires when the day comes to a close and poor Larry has struck out again! Frustrated, Larry tosses his hat decorated with lures into the lake, and ironically, his hat proves to be a better fisherman than he is: it hooks enough trout for Moe, Joe, and Moose the Dog! • SD: twenty-five (M 9/8–Su 9/14, M 9/15–W 9/17, F 9/19–F 9/26, Su 11/30–F 12/5, Su 12/7/69), additional footage without Larry Fine shot in 1970; Snake River, Jackson Lake and Lodge, Old Faithful Geyser and Inn, Castle and Sawmill Geysers, Yellowstone National Park and Lake, Bridge Bay Marina, Grand Canyon, Jack Lott's Ranch, Henry's Lake, Stanley Springs Lodge, Fishing Bridge at Big Springs, Massacre Rocks at Snake River outside American Falls, Redfish Lake and Marina, Lowman Highway on Idaho State 21 before Lowman, Idaho, Lucky Peak near Boise, Lake Pend Oreille and Priest Lake in Idaho, Angeles National Forest, Charlton Flats Picnic Area on Angeles Crest Highway, Lake Piru, Moe Howard's home, and Los Angeles International Airport • FN: In 1969, as the Stooges began lensing their comedy travelogue feature, comedian Jerry Lewis was wrapping up production of his latest comedy feature for Columbia Pictures, then tentatively titled *Kook's Tour*. From April 1 to June 20, 1968, he filmed the comedy after buying the script of the same name for $2,500, but he didn't like the title so he changed it to *Hook, Line & Sinker*. Lewis is on record as saying that he agreed to give the rights to the title *Kook's Tour* to the Stooges for their film, providing he could still use the words in advertisements for his film, something Maurer himself refuted. Consequently, posters for Lewis's film featured the tagline "Columbia Pictures presents Jerry Lewis on a 'Kook's Tour' in his new comedy riot 'Hook, Line & Sinker.'" . . . Larry's picture-taking contraption, à la Rube Goldberg, was designed and assembled by Jeff Maurer (also

known as Jeffrey Scott). . . . Neither Joan Howard Maurer nor Don Lamond appear in this film as some filmographies have reported. Emil Sitka appears in archive footage from *The Three Stooges Go Around the World in a Daze* (8/21/63). . . . Lois Goleman, who portrays the Littering Woman, was Norman Maurer's former secretary at Columbia. . . . Moose was actually producer Norman Maurer's Labrador retriever and a former character in the *Little Stooges* comic book series. Moose died in 1980. . . . Norman Maurer omitted numerous scenes he'd either shot or planned to shoot from the final version of *Kook's Tour*. One was a filmed pie-fight scene in which Larry and Curly-Joe clobber Moe with pies on the Stooges' houseboat; another was a campground cooking routine with Moe, in a cook's hat and apron, frying up fresh trout their dog, Moose, caught and serving it to him on a huge silver platter for being a better fisherman than Larry (who is stuck eating "dehydrated" food). Others deleted scenes included a gas station sequence in which the Stooges try to cash a check; a bit in which Curly-Joe tosses an inflatable kayak into the water to be "alone," only to have Moose steal it from him and float away; and a "hair growing routine" for Curly-Joe, who puts on a funny wig to avoid autograph seekers when tourists come along in a rowboat with an outboard motor. Also omitted was a flat-tire bit in which Curly-Joe accidentally drops the tire iron on Moe's foot, the tire rolls off into the lake and sinks, and, finally, a tow-truck driver comes and tows them off into the sunset. . . . Maurer also doubled for Moe in the long shots of him steering the Stooges' boat and also filled in for Larry, after his stroke, in a close-up of his hands crumbling corn flakes into a bowl that was shot in 1970. The scene in which Moe tries to help Curly-Joe into his upper berth and orders Larry to finish the dishes was also shot after Larry's stroke, in 1970. . . . Although *Kook's Tour* was never released to

television, it was first distributed in 1973 on Sears Cartvision videocassette. In 1975 the film was then released on Super 8 color-sound film by Niles Film Products Inc. In 1999, a copy of the Niles Super 8 color-sound film was used as source material for a video release in VHS format. In 2002, it was included in the DVD *The Three Stooges: All Time Favorites*.

Larry, Moe, and Joe DeRita were also seen in commercials for The Arthritis Foundation, Hot Shot insecticide, Chunky Chocolates, and Simoniz Car Wax (all 1960), Aqua Net Hair Spray (1963), Astro Snacks (1967), Metropolitan Life (1967, color), Dickie Slacks (1969, color), and Coca-Cola (1976, color, in a film clip from 1962's *The Three Stooges in Orbit*).

## TED HEALY AND THE STOOGES ALONE

The following is a listing of the solo film achievements of Ted Healy, Moe, Curly, and Shemp Howard, Larry Fine, Joe Besser, and Joe DeRita. Except where noted, all films are black-and-white, and the comic's role in the film, where available, follows the cast list.

### TED HEALY

*Miscellaneous Shorts*

**1926**

1. WISE GUYS PREFER BRUNETTES • Rl. Oct. 3 by Hal Roach • *d* Stan Laurel • *scr* H. M. Walker, James Parrott, and Carl Harbaugh • *c:* Helen Chadwick and James Finlayson • "Napolean Fizz"

**1935**

2. LA FIESTA DE SANTA BARBARA • MGM Musical Revue • Rl. Dec. 7 • *d* Louis Lewyn • Tehnicolor • *p* Pete Smith • *c:* Pete Smith (Narrator), Chester Conklin, Mary Carlisle, Cecilia Parker, Shirley Ross, Rosalind Keith, Ida Lupino, Toby Wing, Edmund Lowe, Gilbert Roland, Binnie Barnes, Robert Taylor, Harpo Marx, Andy Devine, Buster Keaton, Irvin S. Cobb, Joe Morrison, Maria Gambarelli, Gary Cooper, James Brewster, Leo Carrillo, Adrienne

Ames, Stefi Duna, Paul Procasi, and the Garland Sisters • "Himself" (with James Brewster, a later stooge in his act, performing a routine)

Ted Healy also appeared in the MGM musical short *Stop, Sadie, Stop*, produced in 1933 and costarring Cliff Edwards (originally titled *Singing in the Rain*, with Edwards as the character Sadie and Healy as Reverend Dawson), but the film was never released. In addition, he appeared in *Hearst Metrotone News Vol. 3 #220* (12/5/31), the 20th Century-Fox promotion reel *Fall 1936 Exhibitor's Reel* (8/1/36) and Columbia's *Screen Snapshots Series 21 #2* (9/12/41) on Hollywood stars who died too young.

### Feature Films
Unless otherwise noted, films were released by Metro-Goldwyn-Mayer.

### 1933
1. STAGE MOTHER • Rl Sept. 29 • Prod. no. 702 • 87m • *d* Charles R. Brabin • *scr* John Meehan and Bradford Ropes • *c:* Alice Brady, Maureen O'Sullivan, and Franchot Tone • "Ralph Martin"

2. BOMBSHELL • Rl Oct. 13 • Prod. no. 706 • 97m • *d* Victor Fleming • *scr* John Lee Mahin and Jules Furthman • *c:* Jean Harlow, Franchot Tone, and Pat O'Brien • "Junior Burns," the lamebrain brother • AKA: *Blonde Bombshell*

### 1934
3. LAZY RIVER • Rl. Mar. 16 • Prod. no. 684 • 77m • *d* George B. Seitz • *scr* Lucien Hubbard • *c:* Jean Parker and Robert Young • "Gabby," one of Bill's (Robert Young's) stooges

4. OPERATOR 13 • Rl. June 15 • 86m • *d* Richard Boleslavsky • *st* Robert W. Chambers • *scr* Harvey Thew, Zelda Sears, and Eva Greene • *c:* Gary Cooper and Marion Davies • "Captain Hitchcock"

5. PARIS INTERLUDE • Rl. July 27 • Prod. no. 774 • 73m • *d* Edwin L.

Marin • *scr* Wells Root • *c:* Madge Evans and Robert Young • "Jimmy," the bartender's helper

6. DEATH ON THE DIAMOND • Rl. Sept. 14 • Prod. no. 783 • 72m • *d* Edward Sedgwick • *st* Cortland Fitzsimmons • *scr* Harvey Thew, Joseph Sherman, and Ralph Spence • *c:* Robert Young, Madge Evans, and Nat Pendleton • "Terry Crawfish O'Toole" • FN: Healy's role in *Death on the Diamond* garnered him many impressive reviews, including this one from *Daily Variety:* "With Ted Healy and Nat Pendleton, as an umpire and a catcher respectively, they stage a baseball Flagg-Quirt affair, battling all through the film and constantly getting laughs. The picture's strength is practically confined to them. Towards the finish, Healy, never anything but a comic, gets a chance to spread out with a high pressure 'He wuz my pal' cry-

ing scene when Pendleton dies. And Healy makes good."

7. THE BAND PLAYS ON • Rl. Dec. 21 • Prod. no. 804 • 88m • *d* Russell Mack • *scr* Bernard Schubert, Ralph Spence, and Harvey Gates • *c:* Robert Young, Betty Furness, Leo Carrillo, and Stuart Erwin • "Joe," a side-street mug • WT: *Backfield*

### 1935
8. THE WINNING TICKET • Rl. Feb. 8 • Prod. no. 809 • 70m • *d* Charles F. Riesner • *st* Robert Pirosh and George Seaton • *scr* Ralph Spence and Richard Slayer • *c:* Leo Carrillo and Louise Fazenda • "Eddie," Joe Tomasello's ne'er-do-well hick brother-in-law

9. THE CASINO MURDER CASE • Rl. Mar. 13 • Prod. no. 790 • 85m • *d* Edwin L. Marin • *scr* Florence Ryerson and Edgar Allan Woolf • *c:*

Ted Healy, as Gabby Stone, demonstrates an eye poke on a Chinaman in a publicity photo for the 1934 MGM feature *Lazy River*. © Metro-Goldwyn-Mayer, courtesy of Jeff Lenburg Collection/MGM

Paul Lukas, Rosalind Russell, and Alison Skipworth • "Sergeant Heath" • FN: The film was the seventh book-to-screen adaptation in the Philo Vance feature film series, based on the popular crime novels written by written by S. S. Van Dine in the 1920s and 1930s.

10. RECKLESS • Rl. Apr. 19 • Prod. no. 807 • 99m • *d* Victor Fleming • *st* Oliver Jeffries • *scr* P. J. Wolfson • *c:* Jean Harlow and William Powell • "Smiley"

11. MURDER IN THE FLEET • Rl. May 24 • 70m • *d scr* Edward Sedgwick • *c:* Robert Taylor and Jean Parker • "Gabby Mac O'Neill"

12. MAD LOVE • Rl. July 12 • Prod. no. 842 • 83m • *d* Karl Freund • *scr* Guy Endore, P. J. Wolfson, and John L. Balderston • *c:* Peter Lorre, Frances Drake, and Colin Clive • "Reagan"

13. HERE COMES THE BAND • Rl. Aug. 30 • Prod. no. 860 • 85m • *d* Paul Sloane • *st scr* Paul Sloane, Ralph Spence, and Victor Mansfield • *c:* Ted Lewis and Virginia Bruce • "Happy," a member of an army band • FN: Former Healy stooge Fred Sanborn is cast in a bit role as a comedian.

14. IT'S IN THE AIR • Rl. Oct. 11 • Prod. no. 864 • 82m • *d* Charles F. Riesner • *st scr* Bryon Morgan and Lew Lipton • *c:* Jack Benny, Una Merkel, and Nat Pendleton • "'Clip' McGurk" • WT: *Let Freedom Ring* • FN: Stooge impersonator Skins Miller from Universal's *Gift of Gab* also appears in a bit role.

**1936**
15. SPEED • Rl. May 8 • Prod. no. 894 • 72m • *d* Edwin L. Marin • *st* Milton Krims and Larry Bachman • *scr* Michael Fessier • *c:* James Stewart and Wendy Barrie • "Gadget"

16. SAN FRANCISCO • Rl. June 26 • Prod. no. 870 • 117m • *d* W. S. Van Dyke • *st* Robert Hopkins • *scr* Anita Loos • *c:* Clark Gable, Jeanette

MacDonald, and Spencer Tracy • "Mat" • FN: Healy's stooge replacements Jimmy Brewster, Sammy Wolfe, and Red Pearson were cast to appear as Mat's stooges, but their footage was cut from the final release print. . . . Stooge impersonator Skins Miller is seen as "Man on a Stretcher."

17. SING, BABY, SING • Rl. Aug. 21 by 20th Century-Fox • 87m • *d* Sidney Lanfield • *scr* Milton Sperling (*st*), Jack Yellen, and Harry Tugend • *c:* Alice Faye, Adolphe Menjou, Patsy Kelly, and the Ritz Brothers • "Al Craven," an agent's assistant

18. THE LONGEST NIGHT • Rl. Oct. 2 • Prod. no. 942 • 51m • *d* Errol Taggart • *st* Cortland Fitzsimmons • *scr* Robert Andrews • *c:* Robert Young and Florence Rice • "Sergeant Magee"

19. MAD HOLIDAY • Rl. Nov. 13 • Prod. no. 954 • 71m • *d* George B. Seitz • *st* Joseph Stanley • *scr* Florence Ryerson and Edgar Allan Woolf • *c:* Edmund Lowe and Zasu Pitts • "Mert Morgan" • WT: *The Cock-Eyed Cruise, The White Dragon,* and *Murder in the Chinese Theater*

**1937**
20. MAN OF THE PEOPLE • Rl. Jan. 29 • Prod. no. 979 • 81m • *d* Edwin L. Marin • *st scr* Frank Dolan • *c:* Joseph Calleia and Florence Rice • "Joe 'The Glut' Dwire"

21. GOOD OLD SOAK • Rl. Apr. 23 • Prod. no. 998 • 67m • *d* J. Walter Ruben • *st* Don Marquis • *scr* A. E. Thomas • *c:* Wallace Beery and Una Merkel • "Al Simmons," a bootlegger • WT: *The Old Soak*

22. VARSITY SHOW • Rl. Sept. 4 by Warner Bros. • 80m • *d* William Keighley • *st* Warren Duff and Sig Herzig • *scr* Jerry Wald, Richard Macauley, Dick Whiting, and Johnny Mercer • *c:* Dick Powell, Rosemary and Priscilla Lane • "Willy Williams," a hard-boiled stage manager

**1938**
23. LOVE IS A HEADACHE • Rl. Jan. 14 • Prod. no. 1034 • 73m • *d* Richard Thorpe • *scr* Marion Parsonnet, Harry Ruskin, William R. Lippman, Lou Heifetz, and Herbert Klein • *c:* Gladys George, Franchot Tone, and Mickey Rooney • "Jimmy Slattery," a publicity promoter

24. HOLLYWOOD HOTEL • Rl. Jan. 15 by Warner Bros. • 109m • *d* Busby Berkeley • *scr* Jerry Wald (*st*), Maurice Leo (*st*), and Richard Macauley • *c:* Dick Powell, Rosemary and Lola Lane, Hugh Herbert, and Glenda Farrell • "Fuzzy"

Healy was reportedly scheduled to make another feature for MGM, *Of Human Hearts,* but he died in late 1937, and the film was completed without him.

## MOE HOWARD

As a child actor, Moe Howard, using the name Harry Moses Horwitz, made his screen debut in *We Must Do Our Best* (1909). Soon thereafter, he costarred in countless other Vitagraph films, also possibly *Fish Hookey* (1910), before joining Captain Billy Bryant's stock company in 1914. Unfortunately, no more information is available about Moe's early screen roles prior to those listed below.

### *Shorts*
**1909**
1. WE MUST DO OUR BEST • Rl. by Vitagraph • 10m • *d* Van Dyke Brooke • *c:* Kenneth Casey • "Bully" • FN: Additional information about this is film is unavailable because neither the film nor the studio records exist. The information listed is here is from Moe's personal recollection.

**1934**
1. JAIL BIRDS OF PARADISE • MGM Musical Revue Series • Rl. Mar. 10 • Prod. no. 728 • Technicolor • 18m • *d st scr* Al Boasberg • *c:* Dorothy Appleby, Shirley Ross, The Dodge Twins, Jerry Howard, and

Moe Howard in an early solo appearance with costar Lou White from *Jail Birds of Paradise* (1934). © *Metro-Goldwyn-Mayer, courtesy of Moe Howard Collection*

the MGM Dancing Girls • "Escaped Convict" • WT: *Stars and Stripes, Reformers,* and *Reformania* • SD: three (TH 12/28–Sa 12/30/33)

Moe Howard also appeared with Shemp in the *Fox Movietone Newsreel* (1929) and by himself in a MGM public service announcement with Jimmy Durante, *Give a Man a Job* (9/9/33).

## Feature Films
### 1933
1. BROADWAY TO HOLLYWOOD • Rl. Sept. 15 by MGM • Prod. no. 462 • 85m • *d* Willard Mack • *scr* Willard Mack and Edgar Allan Woolf • *c:* Frankie Morgan, Alice Brady, Jackie Cooper, Madge Evans, Mickey Rooney, et al. • "Dutch Clown #1"

### 1958
2. SPACE MASTER X-7 • Rl. June 1 by 20th Century-Fox • 71m • *d* Edward Bernds • *scr* George Worthing Yates and Daniel Mainwaring • *c:* Bill Williams and Lyn Thomas

• "Cab Driver" who endeavors to describe a fugitive woman to police

### 1966
3. DON'T WORRY, WE'LL THINK OF A TITLE • Rl. May by United

Artists • 83m • *d* Harmon Jones • *scr* John Hart and Morey Amsterdam • *c:* Morey Amsterdam, Rose Marie, Richard Deacon, and many familiar TV faces • "Mr. Raines"

### 1973
4. DOCTOR DEATH: SEEKER OF SOULS • Rl. Oct. by Cinerama • 93m • *d* Eddie Saeta • *scr* Sal Ponti • *c:* John Considine, Barry Coe, Cheryl Miller, and Leon Askin • "Volunteer in the Audience"

## Feature Film, Offscreen Role
Moe Howard served as associate producer on the following feature.

### 1959
1. SENIOR PROM • Rl. Dec. 31 by Columbia • 82m • *d* David Lowell Rich • *scr* Hal Hackady • *c:* Jill Corey, Paul Hampton, Jimmie Komack, Louis Prima, Ed Sullivan, Mitch Miller, Freddy Martin, and others.

## LARRY FINE
## Feature Film
### 1933
1. STAGE MOTHER • Rl. Sept. 29 by MGM • 87m • *d* Charles Brabin • *scr* John Meehan • *c:* Alice Brady, Maureen O'Sullivan, and Ted Healy • "Music Store Customer"

Moe making an appearance as a cab driver (in an effort to lure dramatic roles, as Columbia Pictures did not renew The Three Stooges' contract) in the sci-fi feature—which son-in-law Norman Maurer associate produced—*Space Master X-7* (1958). © *20th Century Fox, courtesy of Moe Howard Collection.*

**JEROME "CURLY" HOWARD**

*MGM Shorts*

**1934**

1. ROAST-BEEF AND MOVIES • MGM Revue Series • Rl. Feb. 10 • Prod. 701 • Technicolor • 17m • *d* Samuel Baerwitz • *st* Richy Craig Jr. • *c:* George Givot, Bobby Callahan, and The Albertina Rasch Dancers • "One of Three Bogus Movie Producers" • WT: *Wax Museum, Let Us Spray,* and *Movie Bugs*

2. JAIL BIRDS OF PARADISE • MGM Musical Revue Series • Rl. Mar. 10 • Prod. no. 728 • Technicolor • 18m • *d st scr* Al Boasberg • *c:* Dorothy Appleby, Moe Howard, Shirley Ross, The Dodge Twins, and the MGM Dancing Girls • "Escaped Convict" • WT: *Stars and Stripes, Reformers,* and *Reformania* • SD: three (Th 12/28–Sa 12/30/33)

*Feature Films*

**1933**

1. BROADWAY TO HOLLYWOOD • Rl. Sept. 15 by MGM • Prod. no. 462 • 85m • *d* Willard Mack • *scr* Willard Mack and Edgar Allan Woolf • *c:* Frankie Morgan, Alice Brady, Jackie Cooper, Madge Evans, Mickey Rooney, et al. • "Dutch Clown #2"

2. OPERATOR 13 • Rl. June 15 by MGM • Prod. no. 738 • 86m • *d* Richard Boleslavsky • *scr* Harvey Thew, Eve Greene, and Zelda Sears • "Confederate Soldier"

**SHEMP HOWARD**

*Vitaphone Shorts*

**1933**

1. SALT WATER DAFFY • Jack Haley Series • Rl. Sept. 16 • 21m • *d* Ray McCarey • *st* Jack Henley and Glen Lambert • *c:* Jack Haley, Charles Judels, and Lionel Stander • "Wilbur"

2. IN THE DOUGH • Fatty Arbuckle Series • Rl. Sept. 25 • 22m • *d* Ray McCarey • *st* Jack Henley • *c:* Roscoe "Fatty" Arbuckle, Lionel Stander, Marc Marion, Fred Harper, and Dan Coleman • "Bug"

3. CLOSE RELATIONS • Fatty Arbuckle Series • Rl. Sept. 30 • 20m • *d* Ray McCarey • *st* Glen Lambert and Jack Henley • *c:* Roscoe "Fatty" Arbuckle, Charles Judels, Mildred Van Dorn, Harry Shannon, and Hugh O'Connell • "Cousin Mole"

4. PAUL REVERE JR. • Rl. Oct. 7 • 21m • *d* Roy Mack • *c:* Gus Shy, Kathleen Lockhart, Gene Lockhart, Janet Reade, Bobby Watson, and Almira Sessions • role not available

5. HERE COMES FLOSSIE • Ben Blue Series • Rl. Dec. 9 • 18m • *d* Ray McCarey • *st* Glen Lambert and Jack Henley • *c:* Ben Blue, Paul Everton, J. Cherry, and Jack Barne • "Ezry"

**1934**

6. HOW'D YA LIKE THAT? • George Givot Series • Rl. Jan. 13 • 18m • *d* Ray McCarey • *st* Jack Henley and Glen Lambert • *c:* George Givot, Charles Judels, and Lionel Stander • "Sailor"

7. THE WRONG, WRONG TRAIL • Rl. Feb. 10 • 10m • *d* Joseph Henabery • *c:* Jesse Block, Eve Sully, and Donald MacBride • "Patient"

8. MUSHROOMS • Harry Gribbon Series • Rl. Feb. 14 • 20m • *d* Ralph Staub • *st* Dolph Singer and Jack Henley • *c:* Harry Gribbon, Loretta Sayres, Cora Witherspoon, and Lionel Stander • "Thorndike"

9. PUGS AND KISSES • Charles Judels and Lionel Stander Series • Rl. Feb. 17 • 21m • *d* Ray McCarey • *st* Glen Lambert and Jack Henley • *c:* Charles Judels, Lionel Stander, Greta Grandstedt, and Tony Hughes • role not available.

10. VERY CLOSE VEINS • Ben Blue Series • Rl. Apr. 14 • 20m • *d* Ralph Staub • *st* Jack Henley and Dolph Singer • *c:* Ben Blue, Doro-

thy Dare, Robert Glecker, and Harry T. Morey • "Frostbitten Drunk"

11. PURE FEUD • Rl. Apr. 21 • 10m • *d* Joseph Henabery • *scr* Jack Henley, Dolph Singer, and Edwin B. DuPar • *c:* Edgar Bergen, Charlie McCarthy, and Vicki Cummings • "Clem McCarthy"

12. CORN ON THE COP • Harry Gribbon and Shemp Howard Series • Rl. Apr. 28 • 20m • *d* Ralph Staub • *st* Jack Henley and Dolph Singer • *c:* Harry Gribbon, Mary Doran, and Boyd Davis • "Reginald, a Hobo"

13. RAMBLIN' ROUND RADIO ROW #7 (Series 2 #1) • Rl. May 19 • 11m • *c:* George Jessel, Pat C. Flick, Bonnie Poe, Vera Van, and Ramon and Rosita • "Songwriters' Representative" • FN: Some sources have misspelled the film's title *Rambling 'Round Radio Row*

14. I SCREAM • Gus Shy Series • Rl. May 19 • 20m • *d* Ray McCarey • *st* Jack Henley and Eddie Moran • *c:* Gus Shy, Lionel Stander, and Curtis Karpe • "Moran's Henchman"

15. ART TROUBLE • Harry Gribbon and Shemp Howard Series • Rl. June 23 • 20m • *d* Ralph Staub • *st* Jack

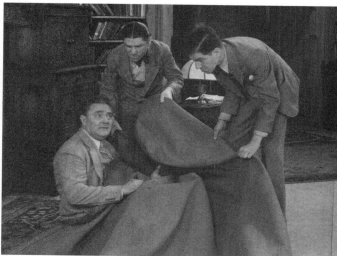

Shemp with Harry Gribbon (seated) and costar Lionel Stander in Gribbon's short-subject series comedy *Mushrooms* (1934) for Vitaphone. © Warner Bros., courtesy of Jeff Lenburg Collection

Henley and Dolph Singer • *c:* Harry Gribbon, Beatrice Blinn, and Leni Stengel • "Shemp"

16. MY MUMMY'S ARMS • Harry Gribbon and Shemp Howard Series • Rl. June 28 • 19m • *d* Ralph Staub • *st* Jack Henley and Justin Herman • *c:* Harry Gribbon, Sheldon Leonard, Russell Hicks, and Louise Latimer • "Kenneth"

17. DAREDEVIL O'DARE • Ben Blue Series • Rl. Aug. 11 • 19m • *d* Ralph Staub • *st* Dolph Singer and Jack Henley • *c:* Ben Blue, Vicki Cummings, Joe Vitale, and Owen Martin • "Circus Barker"

18. SMOKED HAMS • Daphne Pollard and Shemp Howard Series • Rl. Oct. 19 • 18m • *d* Lloyd French • *st* Jack Henley and Dolph Singer • *c:* Daphne Pollard • "Henry Howard"

19. SO YOU WON'T T-T-T-TALK • Rl. Nov. 1 • 20m • *d* Lloyd French • *scr* Dolph Singer, Royal King Cole, and Edwin B. DuPar • *c:* Roscoe Ates, Billie Leonard, Ruth Gilette, Donald MacBride, and Jackie Kelk • "Henry"

20. DIZZY AND DAFFY • Dizzy and Daffy Dean Series • Rl. Dec. 15 • 19m • *d* Lloyd French • *st* Dolph Singer and Jack Henley • *c:* Jerome and Paul Dean • "Nearsighted Baseball Pitcher"

21. A PEACH OF A PAIR • Daphne Pollard and Shemp Howard Series • Rl. Dec. 29 • 20m • *d* Lloyd French • *st* Dolph Singer and Jack Henley • *c:* Daphne Pollard • "Shemp Butler"

**1935**

22. HIS FIRST FLAME • Daphne Pollard and Shemp Howard Series • Rl. Mar. 9 • 19m • *d* Lloyd French • *st* Jack Henley and Dolph Singer • *c:* Daphne Pollard, John Sheehan, Fred Harper, and Don McBride • "Smokey Moe" • WT: *The Fireman's Bride*

23. WHY PAY RENT? • Roscoe Ates and Shemp Howard Series • Rl. May 4 • 22m • *d* Lloyd French • *st* Dolph Singer and Jack Henley • *c:* Roscoe Ates, Billie Leonard, Ethel Sykes, and Ray LeMay • "Henry" • FN: A reworking of Keaton's *One Week* (9/7/20).

24. SERVES YOU RIGHT • Shemp Howard Series • Rl. June 15 • 21m • *d* Lloyd French • *st* Jack Henley and Bob McGowan • *c:* Nell O'Day, Don McBride, Eddie Hall, Connie Almy, and Fred Harper • "Johnny Spivens"

25. ON THE WAGON • Roscoe Ates and Shemp Howard Series • Rl. Aug. 24 • 21m • *d* Lloyd French • *st* Jack Henley and Burnet Hershey • *c:* Roscoe Ates, Gertrude Mudge, Dorothy Brown, Lillian Pertka, and Billie Leonard • "Henry"

26. THE OFFICER'S MESS • Shemp Howard Series • Rl. Oct. 19 • 22m • *d* Lloyd French • *st* Burnet Hershey and Jack Henley • *c:* Charles Kemper, Detmar Poppen, and Louise Swuires • "Gus Doaks"

**1936**

27. WHILE THE CAT'S AWAY • Shemp Howard Series • Rl. Jan. 4 • 20m • *d* Lloyd French • *st* Jack Henley and Burnet Hershey • *c:* Johnny Berkes, Anita Garvin, and Jean Cleveland • "Henry"

28. FOR THE LOVE OF PETE • Joe Palooka Series • Rl. Mar. 14 • 21m • *d* Lloyd French • *st* Jack Henley and Burnet Hershey • *c:* Robert Norton, Lucy Parker, Johnny Berkes, Richard Lane, Michael Dennis, Charlie Althoss, Buddy Bueler, and Rex • "Knobby Walsh," Joe Palooka's manager

29. ABSORBING JUNIOR • Shemp Howard Series • Rl. May 9 • 21m • *d* Lloyd French • *st* Jack Henley and Burnet Hershey • *c:* Johnny Berkes, Gertrude Mudge, Gerrie Worthing, Kenneth Lundy, and Arthur and Morton Havel • "Henry"

30. HERE'S HOWE • Joe Palooka Series • Rl. June 6 • 21m • *d* Lloyd French • *st* Jack Henley, Burnet Hershey, and Robert Mako • *c:* Robert Norton, Leo Webberman, and Beverly Phalon • "Knobby Walsh," Joe Palooka's manager

31. PUNCH AND BEAUTY • Joe Palooka Series • Rl. Aug. 15 • 20m • *d* Lloyd French • *st* Jack Henley, Burnet Hershey, and Eddie Forman • *c:* Robert Norton, Beverly Phalon, and Johnny Berkes • "Knobby Walsh," Joe Palooka's manager

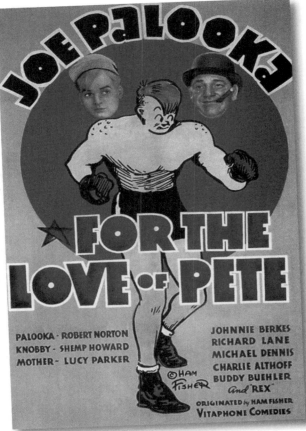

One-sheet for the Vitaphone Joe Palooka series short *For the Love of Pete*, costarring Shemp Howard as Palooka's boxing manager Knobby Walsh. *© Warner Bros., courtesy of Jeff Lenburg Collection*

32. THE CHOKE'S ON YOU • Joe Palooka Series • Rl. Sept. 12 • 21m • *d* Lloyd French • *st* Jack Henley, Burnet Hershey, and Eddie Forman • *c:* Robert Norton, Beverly Phalon, and Johnny Berkes • "Knobby Walsh," Joe Palooka's manager

33. THE BLONDE BOMBER • Joe Palooka Series • Rl. Nov. 28 • 20m • *d* Lloyd French • *st* Jack Henley, A. Dorian Otvos, and Eddie Forman • *c:* Robert Norton, Lee Weber, Harry Gribbon, Johnny Berkes, and Mary Doran • "Knobby Walsh," Joe Palooka's manager

### 1937

34. KICK ME AGAIN • Joe Palooka Series • Rl. Feb. 6 • 21m • *d* Lloyd French • *st* Jack Henley and Eddie Forman • *c:* Robert Norton, Beverly Phalon, and Lee Weber • "Knobby Walsh," Joe Palooka's manager

35. TAKING THE COUNT • Joe Palooka Series • Rl. Apr. 24 • 21m • *d* Lloyd French • *st* Jack Henley and Eddie Forman • *c:* Robert Norton, Beverly Phalon, Charles Kemper, Johnny Berkes, Regina Wallace, John Vosbough, and Jack Shutta • "Knobby Walsh," Joe Palooka's manager

## Van Beuren/RKO Radio Shorts

### 1934

1. HENRY THE ACHE • Bert Lahr Series • Rl. Jan. 26 • 19m • *d* Ray McCarey • *st* Burnet Hershey and Bert Granet • *c:* Bert Lahr and Janet Reade • "Artie, King's Lackey"

2. THE KNIFE OF THE PARTY • Shemp Howard and His Stooges • Rl. Feb. 16 • 20m • *d* Leigh Jason • *st* H. O. Kusell and Art Jarrett Sr. • *c:* Jack Good and Lillian Miles • "Shemp Howard"

3. EVERYBODY LIKES MUSIC • Rl. Mar. 9 • 19½m • *d* Leigh Jason • *scr* Arthur Jarrett and H. O. Kusell • *c:* Donald Novis, Irene Taylor, Mrs. Pennyfeather, Merry Davis and His Orchestra • "Shemp Howard and His Stooges"

## Columbia Shorts

### 1938

1. NOT GUILTY ENOUGH • Andy Clyde Series • Rl. July 30 • 16m • *d* Del Lord • *c:* Andy Clyde, Bud Jamison, and John Tyrrell. • role not available

2. HOME ON THE RAGE • Andy Clyde Series • Rl. Dec. 9 • 17m • *d* Del Lord • *st scr* James W. Horne • *c:* Andy Clyde, Lela Bliss, Gene Morgan, and Vernon Dent • "Andy Clyde's Brother-in-Law"

### 1939

3. THE GLOVE SLINGERS • The Glove Slingers Series • Rl. Nov. 24 • 18m • *d* Jules White • *st scr* L. A. Sarecky • *c:* Noah Beery Jr., Paul Hurst, Dorothy Vaughn, Betty Campbell, Dick Curtis, Cy Seymour, Elaine Waters, Julieta Naldi, Bob Ryan, and John Kascier • "Uncle Pat Patrick"

### 1940

4. MONEY SQUAWKS • Andy Clyde Series • Rl. Apr. 5 • 16m • *d* Jules White • *st scr* Ewart Adamson • *c:* Andy Clyde • "Shemp"

5. BOOBS IN THE WOODS • Andy Clyde Series • Rl. May 31 • 16m • *d* Del Lord • *scr* Harry Edwards (*st*) and Elwood Ullman • *c:* Andy Clyde, Esther Howard, Bud Jamison, and Jack Lipson • "Gus"

6. PLEASED TO MITT YOU • The Glove Slingers Series • Rl. Sept. 6 • 18m • *d* Jules White • *st scr* Ewart Adamson and Clyde Bruckman • *c:* not available • "Pat Patrick"

### 1943

7. FARMER FOR A DAY • Andy Clyde Series • Rl. Aug. 20 • 17½m • *d* Jules White • *st scr* Clyde Bruckman • *c:* Andy Clyde, Betty Blythe, Douglas Leavitt, Adele Mara, and Bud Jamison • "Andy Clyde's Brother-in-Law"

### 1944

8. PICK A PECK OF PLUMBERS • All-Star Comedy Series • Rl. July 23 • 17m • *d* Jules White • *st scr* Felix Adler • *c:* El Brendel, Al Thompson, Johnny Tyrrell, Kathryn Keyes, Willa Pearl Curtis, Frank "Billy" Mitchell, Bea Blinn, Jean Murray, Judy Mal-

Shemp appearing solo in the Van Beuren/RKO Radio comedy short *Everybody Likes Music* (1934). *Courtesy of Jeff Lenburg Collection*

colm, Brian O'Hara, and Joe Palma • "Elmer" • FN: A reworking, with some stock footage, of *A Plumbing We Will Go* (4/19/40), with the Three Stooges.

9. OPEN SEASON FOR SAPS • Shemp Howard Series • Rl. Oct. 27 • 18m • *d* Jules White • *st scr* Elwood Ullman • *c:* Christine McIntyre, George Lewis, Early Cantrell, Harry Barris, Jack Lipson, and Al Mortino • "Woodcock Q. Strinker" • FN: A remake of Charley Chase's *The Grand Hooter* (5/7/37).

**1945**

10. OFF AGAIN, ON AGAIN • Shemp Howard Series • Rl. Feb. 16 • 16m • *d* Jules White • *st* Searle Kramer (*scr*) and Victor Travers • *c:* Christine McIntyre, Russell Trent, Dick Curtis, Grace Lenard, Judy Malcolm, Charles Willey, Frances Haynes, Heinie Conklin, and Joe Palma • "Woodcock Q. Strinker"

11. WHERE THE PESTS BEGIN • Shemp Howard Series • Rl. Oct. 4 • 17m • *d* Edward Bernds • *st scr* Edward Bernds and Russell Malmgren • *c:* Rebel Randall, Tom Kennedy, Christine McIntyre, and Harry Tenbrook • "Shemp Howard"

12. A HIT WITH A MISS • Shemp Howard Series • Rl. Dec. 13 • 16m • *d* Jules White • *st* Jerry Howard, Larry Fine, and Moe Howard • *scr* Jack White • *c:* Bob Williams, Wally Rose, Joe Palma, Heinie Conklin, Marilyn Johnson, Charles Rogers, Blackie Whiteford, George Gray, and Johnny Tyrrell • "Rameses" • FN: A remake of the Three Stooges comedy *Punch Drunks* (7/13/34).

**1946**

13. MR. NOISY • Shemp Howard Series • Rl. Mar. 22 • 16½m • *d scr* Edward Bernds • *st* John Grey • *c:* Vernon Dent, Walter Soderling, Daniel Kerry, Wally Rose, John Ince, Claire James, Matt Willis, Marilyn Johnson, Don Gordon, Tom Coleman, Brian O'Hara, and Fran

O'Connor • "Noisy, Loudmouth Sports Fan" • FN: A remake, with some stock footage, of the Charley Chase film *The Heckler* (2/16/40).

14. JIGGERS, MY WIFE • Shemp Howard Series • Rl. Apr. 11 • 18m • *d* Jules White • *st scr* Zion Myers • *c:* Symona Boniface, Early Cantrell, Christine McIntyre, Tom Kennedy, and Cy Schindell • "Woodcock J. Strinker"

15. SOCIETY MUGS • Shemp Howard Series • Rl. Sept. 19 • 16m • *d*

Edward Bernds • *st scr* Al Giebler • *c:* Tom Kennedy, Etta McDaniel, Charles Williams, Christine McIntyre, Gene Roth, Rebel Randall, Vernon Dent, Bess Flowers, and Helen Benda • "Shemp" • FN: A remake of the Stooges' *Termites of 1938* (1/7/38).

**1947**

16. BRIDE AND GLOOM • Shemp Howard Series • Rl. Mar. 27 • 16m • *d scr* Edward Bernds • *st* John Grey • *c:* Dick Curtis, Jean Donahue [Willes], and Christine McIntyre

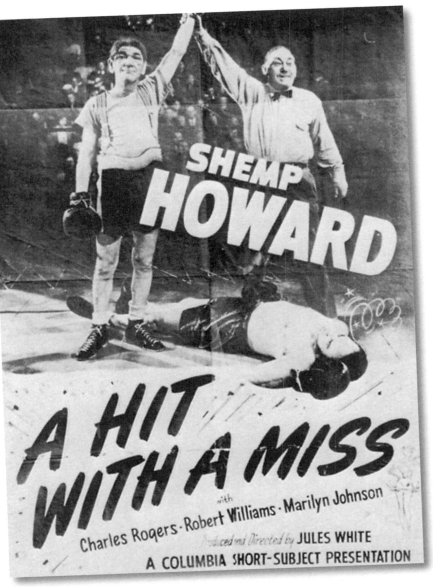

One-sheet for *A Hit with a Miss* (1945), a remake of *Punch Drunks*, a 1934 Stooges comedy. The man on the mat is Joe Palma. © *Columbia Pictures, courtesy of Greg Lenburg Collection*

• "Shemp" • SD: four (W 2/20–Sa 2/23/47)

Shemp also appeared with Moe Howard in a *Fox Movietone Newsreel* (1929) and by himself in a Hearst-Metrotone public service announcement featuring Abbott and Costello to promote buying US Defense Bonds.

## Feature Films

Unless otherwise noted, films were released by Universal Pictures.

### 1935

1. CONVENTION GIRL • Rl. Oct. 31 by First Division • 62m • *d* Luther Reed • *st scr* George Boyle • *c:* Rose Hobart and Herbert Rawlinson • "Dan Higgins"

### 1937

2. HOLLYWOOD ROUND-UP • Rl. Nov. 6 by Columbia • 63m • *d* Ewing Scott • *st scr* Joseph Hoffman and Monroe Shaff • *c:* Buck Jones, Helen Twelvetrees, and Grant Withers • "Oscar," an assistant movie director

3. HEADIN' EAST • Rl. Dec. 13 by Columbia • 63m • *d* Ewing Scott • *st* Joseph Hoffman and Monroe Shaff • *scr* Ethel LaBlanche • *c:* Buck Jones and Ruth Coleman • "Windy Wylie"

### 1939

4. BEHIND PRISON GATES • Rl. July 28 by Columbia • 63m • *d* Charles Barton • *scr* Arthur T. Horman and Leslie T. White • *c:* Brian Donlevy, Julie Bishop, Joseph Crehan, Jacqueline Wells, Paul Fix, George Lloyd, Dick Curtis, and Richard Fiske • "Mess Hall Trustee"

5. ANOTHER THIN MAN • Rl. Nov. 17 by MGM • 103m • *d* W. S. Van Dyke • *scr* Anita Loos, Albert Hackett, and Frances Goodrich • *c:* William Powell, Myrna Loy, Virginia Grey, Otto Kruger, Ruth Hussey, and Sheldon Leonard • "Wacky"

### 1940

6. MURDER OVER NEW YORK • Rl. Jan. 1 by 20th Century-Fox • 65m • *d* Harry Lachman • *scr* Lester Ziffen • *c:* Sidney Toler, Marjorie Weaver, Robert Lowery, Donald MacBride, and Victor Sen Yung • "Shorty McCoy, the Carnarsie Kid"

7. THE LONE WOLF MEETS THE LADY • Rl. May 30 by Columbia • 71m • *d* Sidney Salkow • *st scr* John Larkin • *c:* Warren William, Eric Blore, Jean Muir, and Victor Jory • "Joe"

8. MILLIONAIRES IN PRISON • Rl. July 12 by RKO • 63m • *d* Ray McCarey • *st* Martin Mooney • *scr* Lynn Root and Frank Fenton • *c:* Lee Tracy, Linda Hayes, and Raymond Walburn • "Professor"

9. THE LEATHERPUSHERS • Rl. Sept. 13 • Prod. no. 1086 • 64m • *d* John Rawlins • *scr* Larry Rhine, Ben Chapman, and Maxwell Shane • *c:* Richard Arlen and Andy Devine • "Sailor McNeill"

10. THE BANK DICK • Rl. Nov. 29 • Prod. no. 1100 • 74m • *d* Edward Cline • *st scr* Mahatma Kane Jeeves (W. C. Fields) • *c:* W. C. Fields • "Joe Guelpe," bartender at the Black Pussy Cat Cafe

11. GIVE US WINGS • Rl. Dec. 20 • Prod. no. 1095 • 62m • *d* Charles Lamont • *st* Eliot Gibbons • *scr* Arthur T. Horman and Robert Lee Johnson • *c:* Billy Halop, Huntz Hall, and the Dead End Kids • "Buzz"

12. THE INVISIBLE WOMAN • Rl. Dec. 27 • Prod. no. 1107 • 73m • *d* Eddie Sutherland • *scr* Gertrude Purcell, Frederic I. Rinaldo, and Robert Lees • *c:* Virginia Bruce, John Barrymore, Charlie Ruggles, and John Howard • "Hammerhead Frankie"

### 1941

13. LUCKY DEVILS • Rl. Jan. 3 • Prod. 1098 • 63m • *d* Lew Landers • *scr* Alex Gottlieb • *c:* Richard Arlen, Andy Devine, and Dorothy Lovett • "Pickpocket"

14. SIX LESSONS FROM MADAME LA ZONGA • Rl. Jan. 17 • Prod. no. 1116 • 62m • *d* John Rawlins • *scr* Stanley Crea Rubin, Marion Orth, Larry Rhine (*st*), and Ben Chapman (*st*) • *c:* Lupe Velez and Leon Errol • "Gabby," a member of a gangster's gang

15. BUCK PRIVATES • Rl. Jan. 31 • Prod. no. 1120 • 84m • *d* Arthur Lubin • *scr* Arthur T. Horman • *c:* Bud Abbott, Lou Costello, and The Andrews Sisters • "Mess Hall Cook"

16. MEET THE CHUMP • Rl. Feb. 14 • Prod. no. 1113 • 60m • *d* Edward F. Cline • *scr* Alex Gottlieb • *c:* Hugh Herbert • "Stinky Fink," a gangster • WT: *Who's Crazy Now?* and *Who's Wacky Now?*

17. ROAD SHOW • Rl. Feb. 18 by Hal Roach Studios • 87m • *d* Hal Roach • *scr* Mickell Novack, Harry Langdon, and Arnold Belgard • "Moe Parker"

18. MR. DYNAMITE • Rl. Mar. 7 • Prod. no. 1125 • 63m • *d* John Rawlins • *scr* Stanley Crea Rubin • *c:* Lloyd Nolan, Irene Harvey, and J. Carrol Naish • "Abdullah"

19. THE FLAME OF NEW ORLEANS • Rl. Apr. 25 • Prod. no. 1114 • 79m • *d* Rene Clair • *scr* Norman Krasna • *c:* Marlene Dietrich, Bruce Cabot, and Andy Devine • "Oyster Bed Café Waiter"

20. TOO MANY BLONDES • Rl. May 23 • Prod. no. 1145 • 60m • *d* Thornton Freeland • *scr* Maxwell Shane and Louis S. Kaye • *c:* Rudy Vallee, Helen Parrish, and Lou Chaney Jr. • "Ambrose Tripp"

21. IN THE NAVY • Rl. May 30 • Prod. no. 1144 • 85m • *d* Arthur Lubin • *scr* Arthur T. Horman (*st*) and John Grant • *c:* Bud Abbott, Lou Costello, Dick Powell, and The Andrews Sisters • "Dizzy," a not-too-bright sailor

22. TIGHT SHOES • Rl. June 13 • Prod. no. 1139 • 75m • *d* Albert S. Rogell • *at* Damon Runyan • *scr* Leonard Spigelgass and Art Arthur • *c:* John Howard, Binnie Barnes, Broderick Crawford, and Anne Gwynne • "Okay," Swifty's (Broderick Crawford's) confidante and bodyguard

23. SAN ANTONIO ROSE • Rl. June 20 • Prod. no. 1157 • 63m • *d* Charles Lamont • *st* Jack Lait Jr. • *scr* Hugh Wedlock Jr., Howard Snyder, and Paul Gerard Smith • *c:* Jane Frazee, Robert Paige, Eve Arden, and Lon Chaney Jr. • "Benny the Bounce," partner and shadow to Jigsaw (Lon Chaney Jr.)

24. HIT THE ROAD • Rl. June 27 • Prod. no. 1130 • 61m • *d* Joe May • *scr* Robert Lee Johnson (*st*) and Brenda Weisberg • *c:* Billy Halop, Huntz Hall, and the Dead End Kids • "Dingbat," Creeper's sidekick who hears and sees but never speaks

25. CRACKED NUTS • Rl. Aug. 1 • Prod. no. 1133 • 59m • *d* Edward F. Cline • *scr* Scott Darlin and Erna Lazarus • *c:* Stuart Irwin, Una Merkel, Mischa Auer, and William Frawley • "Eddie/Ivan"

26. HOLD THAT GHOST • Rl. Aug. 8 • Prod. no. 1118 • 86m • *d* Arthur Lubin • *scr* Robert Lees (*st*), Fred Rinaldo (*st*), and John Grant • *c:* Bud Abbott, Lou Costello, Richard Carlson, Evelyn Ankers, and Joan Davis • "Wisecracking Soda Jerk" • WT: *Oh, Charlie*

27. APPOINTMENT FOR LOVE • Rl. Oct. 31 • Prod. 1170 • 88m • *d* William A. Seiter • *scr* Felix Jackson and Bruce Manning • *c:* Charles

Shemp offers Abbott and Costello some doughnuts in a scene from *In the Navy* (1941).
© *Universal Pictures, courtesy of Jeff Lenburg Collection*

Boyer, Margaret Sullivan, Rita Johnson, Eugene Pallette, and Cecil Kellaway • "Man on the Street"

28. HELLZAPOPPIN' • Rl. Dec. 26 • Prod No. 1155 • 84m • *d* H. C. Potter • *scr* Nat Perrin (*st*) and Warren Wilson • *c:* Ole Olsen, Chic Johnson, Martha Raye, and an array of Universal contract players • "Louie," an awfully dumb movie projectionist • FN: Fred Sanborn appears in a bit role as a stooge.

**1942**

29. BUTCH MINDS THE BABY • Rl. Mar. 20 • Prod. no. 1217 • 75m • *d* Albert S. Rogell • *st* Damon Runyan • *scr* Leonard Spigelgass • *c:* Virginia Bruce, Broderick Crawford, and Dick Foran • "Squinty Sweeny," a near-sighted henchman

30. THE MISSISSIPPI GAMBLER • Rl. Apr. 17 • Prod. no. 1198 • 60m • *d* John Rawlins • *st* Al Martin and Marion Orth • *scr* Al Martin and Roy Chanslor • *c:* Kent Taylor and Frances Langford • "Milton Davis"

31. THE STRANGE CASE OF DR. RX • Rl. Apr. 17 • Prod. no. 1189 • 66m • *d* William Nigh • *scr* Clarence Upson Young • *c:* Lionel Atwill, Patric Knowles, and Anne Gwynne • "Detective Sergeant Sweeney," a police department stupor-sleuth • WT: *Dr. RX*

32. PRIVATE BUCKAROO • Rl. June 12 • Prod. no. 1228 • 68m • *d* Edward F. Cline • *st* Paul Gerard Smith • *scr* Edmund Kelso and Edward James • *c:* Dick Foran, The Andrews Sisters, Harry James, and Joe Lewis • "Sergeant Mugsy," a hard-boiled commanding officer • FN: Sidney Miller, director of *Three Stooges Scrapbook* (1960), appears briefly as the second Jeep driver.

33. STRICTLY IN THE GROOVE • Rl. Nov. 20 • Prod. no. 1225 • 60m • *d* Vernon Keays • *scr* Kenneth Higgens and Warren Wilson • *c:* Leon Errol, Franklin Pangborn, Mary Healy, Ozzie Nelson, and Richard Davies • "Pops," a campus character who becomes manager of the band

34. PITTSBURGH • Rl. Dec. 11 • Prod. no. 1270 • 98m • *d* Lewis Seiler • *st* George Owen • *c:* Marlene Dietrich, Randolph Scott, and John Wayne • "Shorty" • FN: Watch for Bess Flowers in a bit role.

**35. ARABIAN NIGHTS** • Rl. Dec. 25 • Prod. no. 1241 • Technicolor • 86m • *d* John Rawlins • *st scr* Michael Hogan • *c:* Sabu, Jon Hall, Maria Montez, Leif Erikson, and Billy Gilbert • "Sinbad," one of Scheherazade's associates in a traveling circus

### 1943

**36. HOW'S ABOUT IT?** • Rl. Feb. 5 • Prod. no. 1289 • 61m • *d* Erle C. Kenton • *scr* Mel Ronson • *c:* The Andrews Sisters, Grace McDonald, and Robert Paige • "Alf," a process server who romances Patty Andrews • WT: *Solid Senders*

**37. IT AIN'T HAY** • Rl. Mar. 19 • Prod. no. 1275 • 80m • *d* Erle C. Kenton • *st* Damon Runyan • *scr* Allen Boretz and John Grant • *c:* Bud Abbott, Lou Costello, and Grace McDonald • "Umbrella Sam" • WT: *Hold Your Horses* • FN: A remake of *Princess O'Hara* (1935).

**38. KEEP 'EM SLUGGING** • Rl. Apr. 2 • Prod. no. 1285 • 66m • *d* Christy Cabanne • *st* Edward Handler and Robert Gordon • *scr* Brenda Weisberg • *c:* Huntz Hall, Bobby Jordan, Gabe Dell, and the Dead End Kids • "Binky"

**39. CRAZY HOUSE** • Rl. Oct. 8 • Prod. no. 1320 • 80m • *d* Edward F. Cline • *scr* Robert Lees and Fred Rinaldo • *c:* Ole Olsen, Chic Johnson, Martha O'Driscoll, and Patric Knowles • "Mumbo," a wandering character • FN: Fred Sanborn plays Jumbo.

### 1944

**40. THREE OF A KIND** • Rl. July 22 by Monogram • 65m • *d* D. Ross Lederman • *scr* Earle Snell and Arthur Caesar • *c:* Billy Gilbert, Maxie Rosenbloom, Helen Gilbert, and June Lang • "Shemp Howard" • FN: The first of three films with Billy Gilbert, Shemp Howard, and Maxie Rosenbloom. . . . On US theatrical posters, the movie was titled *3 of a Kind*, and it was later renamed and reissued as *Cooking Up Trouble*.

**41. MOONLIGHT AND CACTUS** • Rl. Sept. 8 • Prod. no. 1341 • 60m • *d* Edward F. Cline • *scr* Eugene Conrad and Paul Gerard Smith • *c:* The Andrews Sisters and Leo Carrillo • "Punchy"

**42. STRANGE AFFAIR** • Rl. Oct. 5 by Columbia • 78m • *d* Alfred E. Green • *scr* Oscar Saul, Eve Greene, and Jerome Odium • *c:* Allyn Joslyn, Evelyn Keyes, Marguerite Chapman, Edgar Buchanan, and Nina Foch • "Laundry Man"

**43. CRAZY KNIGHTS** • Rl. Dec. 8 by Monogram • 63m • *d* William Beaudine • *scr* Tim Ryan • *c:* Billy Gilbert, Maxie Rosenbloom, Tim Ryan, and Jayne Hazard • "Shemp Howard" • WT: *Ghost Crazy and Ghost Knights* • AKA: *Murder in the Family* • FN: The second in a series of films starring Gilbert, Howard, and Rosenbloom.

### 1945

**44. TROUBLE CHASERS** • Rl. June 2 by Monogram • 62m • *d* Lew Landers • *scr* George Plympton and Ande Lamb • *c:* Billy Gilbert, Maxie Rosenbloom, and Patsy Moran • "Shemp" • WT: *Here Comes Trouble* • FN: The last film in the Gilbert, Howard, and Rosenbloom series.

### 1946

**45. THE GENTLEMAN MISBE-HAVES** • Rl. Feb. 28 by Columbia • 74m • *d* George Sherman • *st* Robert Wyler and John B. Clymer • *scr* Robert Wyler and Richard Weil • *c:* Robert Stanton, Osa Massen, Hillary Brooke, Frank Sully, and Sheldon Leonard • "Marty" • WT: *Lullaby of Broadway*

**46. ONE EXCITING WEEK** • Rl. June 8 by Republic • 69m • *d* William Beaudine • *st* Dennis Murray • *scr* Jack Townley and John K. Butler • *c:* Al Pearce, Pinky Lee, and Jerome Cowan • "Marvin Lewis" • FN: A reviewer for the *Independent Film Journal* cautioned exhibitors to "keep this one [film] in the sticks."

**47. DANGEROUS BUSINESS** • Rl. June 20 by Columbia • 59m • *d* D. Ross Lederman • *st* Harry J. Essex • *scr* Hal Smith • *c:* Forrest Tucker, Gerald Mohr, Lynn Merrick, Gus Schilling, and Frank Sully • "Monk"

**48. BLONDIE KNOWS BEST** • Rl. Oct. 17 by Columbia • 69m • *d* Abby Berlin • *scr* Edward Bernds • *c:* Penny Singleton, Arthur Lake, Larry Simms, and Marjorie Kent • "Jim Gray"

Lobby card for *Three of a Kind* (1944), spelled as *3 of a Kind* on theatrical exhibitors' materials. *Courtesy of Greg Lenburg Collection*

**1949**

49. AFRICA SCREAMS • Rl. May 27 by United Artists • 79m • *d* Charles Barton • *st scr* Earl Baldwin • *c:* Bud Abbott, Lou Costello, Hillary Brooke, Max Baer, Buddy Baer, Joe Besser, Clyde Beatty, Frank Buck, and Bobby Barber • "Gunner," a sharpshooter who can't see past his own nose

**1956**

50. LAFF HOUR • Rl. Jan. by Columbia • 90m • *c:* Andy Clyde, Hugh Herbert, Buster Keaton, Tom Kennedy, Billy Gilbert, Leon Errol, and more • SYN: *Laff Hour* consisted of comedies hand picked by theaters from Columbia's 1932–56 short-subjects library. Each theater's program differed. Shemp's solo shorts were among those available for theaters to select.

Shemp was either set to appear but did not, or his appearances were cut from the final release prints, of two other Universal features: *Badlands of Dakota* (1941), featuring Robert Stack, Ann Rutherford, and Richard Dix, and the Abbott and Costello comedy *Who Done It?* (1942). In a scene in the 1941 Universal comedy *Never Give a Sucker an Even Break*, starring W. C. Fields, Shemp appears by name only on a large billboard in the background along with other cast members' names promoting Fields's previous picture, *The Bank Dick*.

## JOE BESSER

### Columbia Shorts
**1938**

1. CUCKOORANCHO • All-Star Comedy Series • Rl. Mar. 25 • 16½m • *d* Ben K. Blake • *st* I. A. Jacoby • *c:* Lee Royce, Charles Master, and Lolita Cordoba • "Wanderer" mistaken by an impoverished hacienda owner for an American millionaire • FN: Filmed in New York.

**1949**

2. WAITING IN THE LURCH • All-Star Comedy Series • Rl. Sept. 8 • 16m • *d* Edward Bernds • *st scr* Elwood Ullman • *c:* Christine McIntyre, Vernon Dent, Rodney Bell, James Logan, Andre Pola, Charles Hamilton, and Joe Palma • "Eric Loudermilk Potts," a groom who almost misses his own wedding because he's addicted to chasing fire engines • WT: *Left in the Lurch*

**1950**

3. DIZZY YARDBIRD • Joe Besser Series • Rl. Mar. 9 • 17m • *d* Jules White • *st scr* Felix Adler • *c:* Dick Wessel, Brian O'Hara, Jessie Arnold, Bill Wallace, Jim Brown, Nick Arno, and Emil Sitka • "Private Rodney Marblehead"

**1951**

4. FRAIDY CAT • Joe Besser Series • Rl. Dec. 13 • 16m • *d scr* Jules White • *st* Felix Adler • *c:* Jim Hawthorne, Steve Calvert, Tom Kennedy, Joe Palma, and Eddie Baker • "Joe Besser" • WT: *Silly Sleuths* • SD: four (M 7/23–Th 7/26/51) • FN: A remake of the Stooges' *Dizzy Detectives* (2/5/43). . . . Joe Besser was paid $1,500 for four days' work.

**1952**

5. AIM, FIRE, SCOOT • Joe Besser Series • Rl. Mar. 13 • 16m • *d* Jules

One-sheet for the first Joe Besser series short for Columbia, *Dizzy Yardbird* (1950). © *Columbia Pictures, courtesy of Joe Besser*

Joe Besser in a scene from his first Columbia Pictures short subject, *Cuckoorancho*. © *Columbia Pictures, courtesy of Joe Besser*

White • *st scr* Felix Adler • *c:* Jim Hawthorne, Angela Stevens, Henry Kulky, and Heinie Conklin • "Private Joe Besser" • WT: *Daffy Draftees* • SD: three (M 10/22–W 10/24/51)

Jack White • *c:* Christine McIntyre, Vernon Dent, Rodney Bell, James Logan, Andre Pola, Charles Hamilton, and Joe Palma • 'Eric Loudermilk Potts,' a man whose fiancée

White • *c:* Jim Hawthorne, Steve Calvert, Tom Kennedy, Joe Palma, Eddie Baker, Dan Blocker, Lela Bliss, and Barbara Bartay • "Joe Besser" • WT: *Daffy Detectives* • FN: A reworking, with stock footage, of *Fraidy Cat* (12/13/51), which is a remake of the Stooges' *Dizzy Detectives* (2/5/43).

**1956**

11. ARMY DAZE • Joe Besser Series • Rl. Mar. 22 • 16½m • *d* Jules White • *st* Felix Adler • *scr* Jack White • *c:* Jim Hawthorne, Angela Stevens, Henry Kulky, and Heinie Conklin • "Private Joe Besser" • WT: *Army Days* and *Whacky in Khaki* • SD: one (Th 10/6/55) • FN: A reworking, with stock footage, of *Aim, Fire, Scoot* (3/13/52).

Joe puckers up to Angela Stevens as comic straight man Jim Hawthorne looks on in a scene from *Aim, Fire, Scoot* (1952). © Columbia Pictures, courtesy of Joe Besser

*Miscellaneous Shorts*
**1953**

1. A DAY IN THE COUNTRY • Lippert Pictures' 3-D Featurette Series • Rl. Mar. 13 • 3-D Anscocolor • 15m • *p* Jack Rieger • *c:* not available • SYN: Joe narrates the story of two young country boys' daily activities. • PS: In an interview, Joe Besser vividly remembered the closing shot in this unusual production: "They show a close-up of a cow's derriere (in 3-D) over which I say, 'Well, folks, this looks like 'The End!'"

6. CAUGHT ON THE BOUNCE • Joe Besser Series • Rl. Oct. 9 • 16m • *d* Jules White • *st scr* Felix Adler • *c:* Maxine Gates, Esther Howard, and Edward Coch Jr. • "Daddy" who needs $2,500 or the trailer home mortgage will be foreclosed • WT: *Gullible's Travels* • SD: three (M 4/28–W 4/30/52)

**1953**

7. SPIES AND GUYS • Joe Besser Series • Rl. Apr. 9 • 16½m • *d* Jules White • *st scr* Felix Adler • *c:* Angela Stevens and Emil Sitka (in two roles) • "Private Joe Besser" • SD: three (Tu 2/3–Th 2/5/53)

**1954**

8. THE FIRE CHASER • Joe Besser Series • Rl. Sept. 30 • 16m • *d* Jules White • *st* Elwood Ullman • *scr*

cancels their wedding plans because he has a habit of chasing fire engines • SD: one (Th 7/8/54) • FN: A reworking, with stock footage, of *Waiting in the Lurch* (9/8/49).

**1955**

9. G.I. DOOD IT • Joe Besser Series • Rl. Feb. 17 • 16m • *d* Jules White • *st* Felix Adler • *scr* Jack White • *c:* Dick Wessel, Emil Sitka, and Phil Van Zandt • "Private Rodney Marblehead," an army draftee who recovers some stolen documents and is promoted to sergeant • SD: one (W 8/25/54) • FN: A reworking, with stock footage, of *Dizzy Yardbird* (3/9/50).

10. HOOK A CROOK • Joe Besser Series • Rl. Nov. 24 • 18m • *d* Jules White • *st* Felix Adler • scr Jack

*Feature Films*
**1940**

1. HOT STEEL • Rl. May 24 by Universal • 64m • *d* Christy Cabanne • *scr* Clarence Upson Young and Maurice Tombragel (*st*) • *c:* Richard Arlen, Andy Devine, and Peggy Moran • "Siggie Landers"

**1944**

2. HEY, ROOKIE • Rl. Apr. 6 by Columbia • 74m • *d* Charles Barton • *scr* Henry Myers, Edward Eliscu, and Jay Gorney • *c:* Ann Miller, Larry Parks, and Jack Gilford • "Pudge Pfeiffer" • FN: Joe reenacts his famous "Army Drill" routine. . . . A critic for *Daily Variety* wrote, "Joe Besser's comic antics will keep audi-

ences titterpated." . . . Title is spelled without an exclamation mark in the film's opening credits.

Joe Besser mugs with costar Ann Miller in his first of three starring features for Columbia Pictures, *Hey, Rookie* (1944). © *Columbia Pictures, courtesy of Joe Besser*

### 1945

3. EADIE WAS A LADY • Rl. Jan. 23 by Columbia • 67m • *d* Arthur Dreifuss • *st scr* Monty Brice • *c:* Ann Miller, Jeff Donnell, and Jimmy Little • "Professor Dingle" • WT: *Lady Known as Lou*

### 1946

4. TALK ABOUT A LADY • Rl. Mar. 28 by Columbia • 71m • *d* George Sherman • *st* Robert D. Andrew and Barry Trivers • *scr* Richard Weil and Ted Thomas • *c:* Jinx Falkenburg, Forrest Tucker, Trudy Marshall, Richard Lane, and Jimmy Little • "Roly Q. Entwhistle," Falkenburg's guardian in her florist shop • WT: *Duchess of Broadway*

### 1948

5. FEUDIN,' FUSSIN,' AND A-FIGHTIN' • Rl. July by Universal • 78m • *d* George Sherman • *scr* D. D. Beauchamp • *c:* Donald O'Connor, Marjorie Main, and

Percy Kilbride • "Sharkey Dolan," sheriff of Rimrock • WT: *The Wonderful Race at Rimrock* • FN: Stooge character actors Kenneth MacDonald and Gene Roth are featured in supporting roles.

### 1949

6. AFRICA SCREAMS • Rl. May 27 by United Artists • 79m • *d* Charles Barton • *scr* Earl Baldwin • *c:* Bud Abbott, Lou Costello, Hillary Brooke, Max Baer, Buddy Baer, Shemp Howard, Clyde Beatty, Frank Buck, and Bobby Barber • "Harry the Butler"

### 1950

7. JOE PALOOKA MEETS HUMPHREY • Rl. Feb. by Monogram • 65m • *d* Jean Yarbrough • *scr* Henry Blanfort • *c:* Leon Errol, Joe Kirkwood, Jerome Cowan, and Pamela Blake • "Mr. Carlton the Hotel Manager" • WT: *Joe Palooka in Honeymoon for Five*

8. WOMAN IN HIDING • Rl. Jan. by Universal • 92m • *d* Michael Gordon • *scr* Oscar Saul • *c:* Ida Lupino, Howard Duff, and Stephen McNally • "Salesman with Drum" • WT: *Fugitive from Terror*

9. OUTSIDE THE WALL • Rl. Mar. by Universal • 80m • *d scr* Crane

Wilbur • *c:* Richard Basehart and Marilyn Maxwell • "Diner Owner," in a bit role

10. THE DESERT HAWK • Rl. Aug. by Universal • Technicolor • 77m • *d* Frederick De Cordova • *scr* Aubrey Weisberg, Jack Pollexfen, and Gerald Drayson Adams • *c:* Yvonne De Carlo, Richard Greene, George Macready, and Rock Hudson • "Sinbad," Aladdin's (Jackie Gleason's) sidekick • FN: According to the *Hollywood Citizen-News,* "Joe Besser and Jackie Gleason do beautifully as comic sidekicks."

### 1953

11. I, THE JURY • Rl. Aug. by United Artists • 3-D • 87m • *d scr* Harry Essex • *st* Mickey Spillane • *c:* Biff Elliott, Preston Foster, and Peggie Castle • "Elevator Operator"

12. SINS OF JEZEBEL • Rl. Sept. 4 by Lippert • Anscocolor • 74m • *d* Reginald LeBorg • *scr* Richard Landau • *c:* Paulette Goddard and George Nader • "Yonkel the Chariot Driver"

### 1955

13. ABBOTT AND COSTELLO MEET THE KEYSTONE KOPS • Rl. Feb. by Universal • 79m • *d* Charles Lamont • *at* Lee Loeb • *scr* John Grant • *c:* Bud Abbott, Lou Costello, Fred

Joe as a small-town sheriff with Donald O'Connor and company in the Universal Pictures comedy *Feudin', Fussin', and A-Fightin'* (1948). © *Universal Pictures, courtesy of Joe Besser*

Clark, Lyn Bari, and Mack Sennett • "Hunter," in a brief cameo

14. MAD AT THE WORLD • Rl. May 13 by United Artists • 76m • *d* Harry Essex • *scr* Harry Essex • *c:* Frank Lovejoy, Keefe Brasselle, and Cathy O'Donnell • "Gas Station Attendant" • FN: On July 30, 1954, *The Los Angeles Times* announced that the film was currently lensing and "that able comedian, Joe Besser, will provide light relief."

15. HEADLINE HUNTERS • Rl. July by Republic • 70m • *d* William Whitney • *scr* Frederic Louis Fox and John K. Butler • *c:* Rod Cameron and Ben Cooper • "The Coroner"

**1956**
16. LAFF HOUR • Rl. Jan. by Columbia • 90m • *c:* Andy Clyde, Hugh Herbert, Buster Keaton, Tom Kennedy, Billy Gilbert, Leon Errol, and more • SYN: *Laff Hour* consisted of comedies hand picked by theaters from Columbia's 1932–56 short-subjects library. Each theater's program differed. Joe Besser's solo shorts were among those available for theaters to select.

17. TWO-GUN LADY • Rl. Oct. 15 by Associated Film Releasing • 75m • *d st* Richard H. Bartlett • *scr* Norman Jolley • *c:* Peggie Castle, William Talman, and Marie Windsor • "Doc McGinnis" • FN: Star Peggie Castle was sometimes credited as "Peggy Castle."

**1957**
18. THE HELEN MORGAN STORY • Rl. Oct. 2 by Warner Bros. • 118m • *d* Michael Curtiz • *scr* Dean Reisner, Nelson Gidding, Oscar Saul, and Stephen Longstreet • "Speakeasy Bartender"

**1959**
19. PLUNDERERS OF PAINTED FLATS • Rl. Jan. 23 by Republic • Naturama • 70m • *d* Albert C. Gannaway • *scr* Shuken and John Green • *c:* Corinne Calvert, John Carroll, Skip Homeier, and George Macready • "Andy Heather," husband of Ella (Bea Benadaret) • WT: *Gun in the Dust*

20. SAY ONE FOR ME • Rl. June by 20th Century-Fox • DeLuxe Color and CinemaScope • 119m • *d* Frank Tashlin • *scr* Robert O'Brien • *c:* Bing Crosby, Debbie Reynolds, and Ray Walston • "Joe Greb," Robert Wagner's fourth-rate agent

Joe Besser in his first major dramatic role with young Robert Wagner (left) and Ray Walston (right) in *Say One for Me* (1959). © *20th Century Fox, courtesy of Joe Besser*

21. THE ROOKIE • Rl. Dec. by 20th Century-Fox • 84m • *d* George O'Hanlon • *scr* Tommy Noonan and George O'Hanlon • *c:* Tommy Noonan, Peter Marshall, and Julie Newmar • "Medic" • WT: *The Last Rookie* • FN: Joe Besser is the only saving grace in this wartime comedy starring the short-lived team of Noonan and Marshall.

**1960**
22. LET'S MAKE LOVE • Rl. Aug. by 20th Century-Fox • DeLuxe Color and CinemaScope • 118m • *d* George Cukor • *scr* Norman Krasna • *c:* Marilyn Monroe, Yves Montand, and Tony Randall • "Charlie Lamont," a heated joke writer • WT: *The Billionaire*

**1961**
23. THE ERRAND BOY • Rl. Dec. by Paramount • 95m • *d* Jerry Lewis • *scr* Jerry Lewis and Bill Richmond • *c:* Jerry Lewis, Brian Donlevy, and Kathleen Freeman • "Studio Projectionist"

**1962**
24. HAND OF DEATH • Rl. May by 20th Century-Fox • *d* Gene Nelson • *scr* Eugene Ling • *c:* John Agar and Paula Raymond • "Gas Station Attendant"

**1969**
25. SAVAGE INTRUDER • Rl. Jan. by Congdon Films • *d scr* Donald Wolfe • *c:* Miriam Hopkins, Gale Sondergaard, John Garfield Jr., and Minta Durfee Arbuckle • "Driver of a Sightseeing Bus" • WT: *The Comeback* • FN: Joe's role was filmed on 12/19/69.

**1970**
26. WHICH WAY TO THE FRONT? • Rl. July by Warner Bros. • Color • 90m • *d* Jerry Lewis • *scr* Gerald

Gardner and Dee Caruso • c: Jerry Lewis, Jan Murray, Kaye Ballard, Paul Winchell, and Sidney Miller • "CWO Blanchard," the chief warrant officer • FN: Joe performed his role for the cameras on 12/31/69.

## 1976

27. HEY ABBOTT! • Rl. June by ZIV International • Color • 90m • d Jim Gates • scr Stan Oliver • c: Milton Berle, Steve Allen, Phil Silvers, and in black-and-white clips, Bud Abbott, Lou Costello, Sidney Fields, Glenn Strange, and Hillary Brooke • Joe reveals the story behind the creation of his character "Stinky" for *The Abbott and Costello Show* in this semidocumentary on the famous comedy duo.

Joe Besser also costarred in an MGM feature (a horse story) as a "Dog Catcher," but the title of the film is still unknown. In addition, Joe made a one-reel color screen test in 1959 as "The Green Man," a live-action elf surrounded by animated characters, for *The Woodcutter's House*, a proposed Walt Disney feature à la *Darby O'Gill and the Little People*. The feature was never produced. The same year, Joe was cast as "Gallagher," owner and operator of Gallagher's Bar, in the 20th Century-Fox feature *The Story of Page One*, but his scenes were deleted from the final release print of the 123-minute film. Previously it was reported that he appeared as "Art" in the 1961 20th Century-Fox feature *Silent Call*, but another actor appears in that role and Joe does not. Lastly, in 1968, Joe was cast a "Chicken Deliveryman" in *With Six You Get Eggroll*. Records indicate he filmed his scenes, but the director recast the role with actor Vic Tayback (famous as Mel of the television show *Alice*) taking his place, and Joe's scenes were not used.

### Feature Film, Offscreen Role

Joe Besser served as an uncredited gag writer on the following feature.

## 1960

1. CINDERFELLA • Rl. Dec. by Paramount • Technicolor • 91m • d Frank Tashlin • c: Jerry Lewis, Ed Wynn, and Anna Maria Alberghetti

### Television Film
## 1969

1. THE MONK • Br. Oct. 21 on ABC in Color • 90m • d George McCowan • st Tony Barrett and characters created by Blake Edwards • c: George Maharis, Janet Leigh, Rick Jason, Carl Betz, and Jack Albertson • "Herbie" • EPS: "You Can't Judge a Book"

## JOE DeRITA

### Columbia Shorts
## 1946

1. SLAPPILY MARRIED • All-Star Comedy Series • Rl. Nov. 7 • 16½m • d scr Edward Bernds • st Elwood Ullman and Monty Collins • c: Dorothy Granger, Dick Wessel, Christine McIntyre, and Florence Auer • "Joe Bates," a dim-witted husband who is superstitious about Friday the Thirteenth

## 1947

2. THE GOOD BAD EGG • Joe DeRita Series • Rl. Mar. 20 • 17m • d scr Jules White • st Al Giebler and Elwood Ullman • c: Dorothy Granger, Norm Olestead, James C. Morton, Emil Sitka, Vernon Dent, and Symona Boniface • "Joe Priggle," an inventor who is unhappy about his bachelorhood • SD: four (Th 9/12–Sa 9/14, M 9/16/46) • FN: A remake of Andy Clyde's *Knee Action* (10/7/36), with one stock shot (of

Joe DeRita with costars Florence Auer and Christine McIntyre in a scene from the Columbia All-Star Comedy short *Slappily Married* (1946). © *Columbia Pictures, courtesy of Joe DeRita*

a book cover entitled *William Tell)* from the same film.

3. WEDLOCK DEADLOCK • Joe DeRita Series • Rl. Dec. 18 • 16m • *d* Edward Bernds • *st* Clyde Bruckman • *scr* Elwood Ullman • *c:* Christine McIntyre, Charles Williams, Dorothy Granger, Esther Howard, and William Newell • "Eddy," a man whose honeymoon is cut short when his relatives drop in

### 1948
4. JITTER BUGHOUSE • Joe DeRita Series • Rl. Apr. 29 • 18m • *d* Jules White • *st scr* Felix Adler • *c:* Christine McIntyre, Emil Sitka, Patsy Moran, and the Nov-Elites • "Joe"

## Feature Films
### 1944
1. THE DOUGHGIRLS • Rl. Nov. 25 by Warner Bros. • 102m • *d* James V. Kern • *st* Joseph A. Fields • *scr* James V. Kern and Sam Hellman • *c:* Ann Sheridan, Alexis Smith, Jack Carson, Jane Wyman, Charles Ruggles, and Eve Arden • "Wandering Stranger," a businessman who is in Washington, DC, for an appointment and wants nothing better than a peaceful night's sleep after losing his room reservation during a wartime housing shortage

### 1945
2. THE SAILOR TAKES A WIFE • Rl. Dec. 28 by MGM • 91m • *d* Richard Whorl • *scr* Chester Erskin (*st*), Anne Morrison Chapin, and Whitfield Cook • *c:* Robert Walker and June Allyson • "Waiter"

### 1946
3. PEOPLE ARE FUNNY • Rl. Jan. 1 by Paramount • 92m • *d* Sam White • *scr* Maxwell Shane and David Lang (*st*) • *c:* Rudy Vallee, Ozzie Nelson, Helen Walker, and Frances Langford • "Mr. Hinckley"

4. THE FRENCH KEY • Rl. May 18 by Republic Studios • 67m • *d* Walter Colmes • *scr* Frank Gruber • *c:* Albert Dekker, Evelyn Ankers, and Mike Mazurki • "Detective Fox"

5. HIGH SCHOOL HERO • Rl. Sept. 7 by Monogram Pictures • 69m • *d* Arthur Dreifuss • *scr* Hal Collins and Arthur Dreifuss • *c:* Noel Neill, June Preisser, and Freddie Stewart • "Tiny"

### 1948
6. CORONER CREEK • Rl. July by Columbia • Cinecolor • 93m • *d* Ray Enright • *scr* Kenneth Garnet • *c:* Randolph Scott, Marguerite Chapman, George Macready, Sally Eilers, and Edgar Buchanan • "Jack the Bartender" • WT: *Lawless*

### 1956
7. LAFF HOUR • Rl. Jan. by Columbia • 90m • *c:* Andy Clyde, Hugh Herbert, Buster Keaton, Tom Kennedy, Billy Gilbert, Leon Errol, and more • SYN: *Laff Hour* consisted of comedies hand picked by theaters from Columbia's 1932–56 short-subjects library. Each theater's program differed. Joe DeRita's solo shorts were among those available for theaters to select.

### 1958
8. THE BRAVADOS • Rl. July by 20th Century-Fox • DeLuxe Color and CinemaScope • 98m • *d* Henry King • *st* Frank O'Rourke • *scr* Phillip Yordan • *c:* Gregory Peck, Joan Collins, Stephen Boyd, and Henry Silva • "Mr. Simms," the hangman • FN: A critic for the *Los Angeles Examiner* wrote "on the brighter side—in casting—there is a character in the supporting cast, superbly played by Joe DeRita, who simply must give the first class creeps even the creeps!"

Joe DeRita was originally cast as a meek man in the 1943 Warner Bros. musical comedy *Thank Your Lucky Stars*, but his scenes were cut from the final release print.

# About the Authors

**Jeff Lenburg** is the author of more than thirty books and coauthor with his twin brother, Greg, of two books on famed comedy trio The Three Stooges: *The Three Stooges Scrapbook* (called "the ultimate Three Stooges fan bible" by *The Washington Post*) and *Once a Stooge, Always a Stooge*, the autobiography of third Stooge, Joe Besser. Both are foremost authorities on The Three Stooges and were longtime personal friends of Moe Howard, Larry Fine, Joe Besser, and Curly-Joe DeRita.

**Joan Howard Maurer**, the daughter of legendary comedian and Three Stooges founder Moe Howard, is coauthor of *The Three Stooges Scrapbook* and author of three other books: *The Three Stooges Book of Scripts*, *The Three Stooges Book of Scripts, Volume II*, and *Curly: An Illustrated Biography of the Superstooge*.

Besides being an expert on The Three Stooges, **Greg Lenburg** is a well-known Hollywood biographer. His books include a biography of Steve Martin and a line of movie trivia books, including his most recent, *Classic Comedy Teams: A Screenshots Book*.